CW00486392

TERMS OF SURVIVAL

The emergence of the Jewish State of Israel has fundamentally changed the conditions of Jewish existence. Yet the immense changes that have taken place since 1945 have rarely been comprehensively analysed. *Terms of Survival* sets out to fill this need, and to take stock of the Jewish world as it has emerged from the catastrophe of the Holocaust.

From a wide-ranging perspective, the book considers the demographic, occupational and behavioural transformations in Jewry. Contributors examine the new Jewish politics in Israel, the USA, Europe and the ex-USSR, changing religious patterns among Jews and new perceptions of them. Also considered are the ways in which some of the problems confronting contemporary Jews have found expression in literature. The book reflects the way in which post-war Jewry has become both more self-assertive in the defence of its interests, and more uncertain in the light of continuing anti-semitism.

Terms of Survival provides a vital aid to the process of reassessment and reflection on the terms of survival now confronting the Jewish people. It will be of great interest to students of history and Jewish studies, and to all those interested in current Jewish issues.

Robert S. Wistrich is the Professor of Jewish Studies at the University of London, and holds the Neuberger Chair of Modern European History at the Hebrew University of Jerusalem. He is the author of many books and articles, including *Anti-Semitism: The Longest Hatred* (1991) and *Between Redemption and Perdition* (1990).

TERMS OF SURVIVAL

The Jewish world since 1945

Edited by Robert S. Wistrich

London and New York

First published 1995
by Routledge
11 New Fetter Lane, London EC4P 4EE

Simultaneously published in the USA and Canada
by Routledge
29 West 35th Street, New York, NY 10001

Typeset in Garamond by
Florencetype Ltd, Stoodleigh, Devon

Printed and bound in Great Britain by
T.J. Press (Padstow) Ltd, Padstow, Cornwall

British Library Cataloguing in Publication Data

A catalogue record for this book is available from the British Library

Library of Congress Cataloging in Publication Data

Terms of Survival: the Jewish world since 1945 /
edited by Robert S. Wistrich.
p. cm.
Includes bibliographical references and index.
1. Jews—Politics and government—1948– 2. Jews—Social
conditions. 3. Jews—Identity. 4. Judaism—20th century.
I. Wistrich, Robert S., 1945– .
DS143. T425 1995
305.892'4–dc 20   94–22069

ISBN 0–415–10056–9

The publication of this volume was made possible by the generous donation of Mr Neftali Frankel, through the intermediary of the Mexican Friends of the Hebrew University

CONTENTS

Part III

Part IV

FIGURES AND TABLES

FIGURES

TABLES

ACKNOWLEDGEMENTS

The editor would like to thank the Institute of Contemporary Jewry at the Hebrew University of Jerusalem and its director, Professor Haim Avni, for their assistance in the realization of this project. It was the Institute which originated and organized the international conference on the post-war Jewish world, held in Jerusalem at the beginning of 1990, from which this book derives. Subsequently, the various contributions were updated or revised and new essays solicited to keep pace with the extraordinary fluidity and pace of events in the last few years that have affected the Jewish world. The aim of these essays extended, however, beyond more topicality, and it is hoped that the reader will obtain from them a new insight into the complexity of the structures, organizations, dilemmas and problems that shape the agenda of Jewish life, politics and culture in our time. Both the conference and the book have striven to achieve this objective by examining the continuity and changes in Jewish life since 1945 in a global perspective. Special thanks are due to Leah Cohen, who acted as coordinator for both the conference and the book, devoting all her consummate professionalism, knowledge, attention to detail and enthusiasm to the success of the project. Without her help at every stage, it would never have been completed.

Professor Robert Wistrich
Jerusalem/London
1993/1994

NOTES ON CONTRIBUTORS

Professor Geoffrey Alderman has held appointments at University College, London, the University College of Swansea and the University of Reading. He is currently Professor of Politics and Contemporary History at Royal Holloway and Bedford New College. He has published a number of books, including *The Federation of Synagogues* (1987); *London Jewry and London Politics* (1989); and *Modern British Jewry* (1992).

Professor Mordechai Altschuler received his PhD from the Hebrew University of Jerusalem. He is a professor at the Institute of Contemporary Jewry of the Hebrew University in Jerusalem. As well as several books, he has also published over a hundred scientific and academic papers on the social and political status of the Jews in the former Soviet Union, past and present.

Dr Yaakov Ariel received his PhD from the University of Chicago Divinity School. His book *On Behalf of Israel: American Fundamentalist Attitudes Toward the Jewish People, Judaism and Zionism* was published by Carlson Publishing Inc., New York. Dr Ariel is currently a researcher and teacher at the Institute of Contemporary Jewry, the Hebrew University of Jerusalem.

Professor Haim Avni PhD is professor of Contemporary Jewish History and Head of the Harman Institute of Contemporary Jewry at the Hebrew University in Jerusalem. He is the author of *Spain – the Jews and Franco* (1982); *Emancipation and Jewish Emigration* (1985, in Hebrew); and *Argentina and the Jews: History of Jewish Migration* (1991).

Professor Barry R. Chiswick is research professor and head of the Department of Economics at the University of Illinois at Chicago. He received his PhD in economics (1967) from Columbia University. He is an authority on both the economics of American Jewry and on the economics of immigration.

Professor Sergio DellaPergola is currently head of the Division of Jewish Demography and Statistics at the A. Harman Institute of Contemporary Jewry, the Hebrew University of Jerusalem. He has published widely in the field of Jewish demography in various parts of the world (including studies on Italy, France, the United States and Israel).

Dr Sidra DeKoven Ezrahi is a senior lecturer in Comparative Jewish Literature at the Hebrew University, Jerusalem. She has written extensively on Holocaust literature, and is completing a book *Exile and Homecoming in the Modern Jewish Imagination*.

Professor Calvin Goldscheider is professor of Judaic Studies and Sociology at Brown University and is a Faculty Associate of the Population Studies and Training Center. His major areas of research interest are the social scientific study of ethnicity and religion historically and comparatively, with a special emphasis on the United States and Israel. He has published extensively in these and related areas.

Professor Charles Liebman is a professor of Political Science and director of the Argov Center for the Study of Israel and the Jewish People at Bar-Ilan University. He is the author of books and articles on American Jewry, Israeli society and Israel–Diaspora relations. His most recent book, co-authored with Steven M. Cohen, is *Two Worlds of Judaism: The Israeli and American Experiences*.

Professor Seymour M. Lipset is the Hazel Professor of Public Policy at George Mason University and Senior Fellow of the Hoover Institution, Stanford University. His most recently completed book (with Earl Raab), which deals with the American Jewish community, will be published early in 1995 by Harvard University Press.

Professor Peter Y. Medding is a professor of Political Science and of Contemporary Jewry at the Hebrew University of Jerusalem, and heads the Jewish Sociology division of the Institute of Contemporary Jewry. He is an editor of the annual *Studies in Contemporary Jewry*, published by Oxford University Press (New York).

Dr Dalia Ofer is at the Abraham Harman Institute of Contemporary Jewry, Hebrew University, Jerusalem. Her fields of research are: history of the Holocaust, Zionism and Israel. She is the author of *Escaping the Holocaust: Illegal Immigration to the Land of Israel 1939–44* (Oxford University Press: New York) 1990 (Jewish Book Council Award 1991, Hebrew Edition, Ben Zvi Award, 1991).

Professor Uziel O. Schmelz, was born in 1918 in Vienna, Austria, and immigrated to Eretz Israel in 1939. His main fields of research are: comparative demography of the Jews and demography of Eretz Israel. He is the author of *Modern Jerusalem's Demographic Evolution* (1987); *Ethnic Differences Among Israeli Jews: A New Look* (1991) (together with S. DellaPergola and U. Avner).

Professor Dominique Schnapper is currently Director of Studies at the Ecole des Hautes Etudes Sociales, where she specializes in sociology. She has published a number of books, including *Juifs et Israélites* (1981), *La France de l'intégration: Sociologie de la nation en 1990* (1991) and *L'Europe des immigrés* (1992). **Sylvie Strudel** is co-author of the article on the Jewish vote in France and teaches at the University of Lille, II.

Gershon Shaked PhD has been Professor of Hebrew Literature at the Hebrew University of Jerusalem, since 1975. In 1986 he received the Bialik Literary Award and in 1993 the Israel Award for Literary Scholarship.

Dr David Singer is Director of Research for the American Jewish Committee and editor of the *American Jewish Year Book*.

Professor Steven L. Spiegel is professor of Political Science at UCLA, specializing in the analysis of world politics, American foreign policy and American foreign policy in the Middle East. His latest book, entitled *World Politics in a New Era*, will be published by Harcourt, Brace, Jovanovich in late 1994.

Benedict Thomas Viviano OP was ordained to the Roman Catholic priesthood in 1966 and received his PhD from Duke University in 1976, in New Testament studies. He has served as editor of the *Tergumic Newsletter*, as an associate editor of the *Catholic Biblical Quarterly* and is currently an associate editor of the *Revue Biblique*.

Professor Ruth Wisse is currently professor of Yiddish Literature at Harvard University and director of its Center for Jewish Studies. She is the author of *The Shlemiel as Modern Hero; A Little Love in Big Manhattan: Two Yiddish Poets in America; I. L. Peretz and the Mailing of Modern Yiddish Culture*; and a political study, *If I Am Not For Myself: The Liberal Betrayal of the Jews*.

Professor Robert Wistrich is professor of Modern Jewish History at the Hebrew University of Jerusalem and is the incumbent of the *Jewish Chronicle* chair in Jewish History at University College, London. He is the author of a number of distinguished books, including *The Jews of Vienna in the Age of Franz Joseph* (1989) and *Antisemitism: The Longest Hatred* (1991).

INTRODUCTION

The post-war Jewish world

Robert Wistrich

During the past fifty years the Jewish world has experienced some unprecedented, momentous changes which have transformed its structure, internal composition and future prospects. On the one hand, there has been the creation of an independent sovereign Jewish State in its ancient homeland, reconstituted for the first time in nearly 2,000 years. At the same time, the far-flung, extremely diverse Jewish Diaspora has enjoyed a sustained period of affluence, influence, empowerment and social acceptance in its Western branches, rare in the scarred, often tragic, annals of Jewish history. Tremendous shifts of population have also taken place with far-reaching consequences. In 1939, although the largest single Jewish community in the world already resided in the United States, the core of world Jewry (9.5 million or 57 per cent of the global Jewish population) still lived in Europe.

The great bulk of European Jewry was concentrated in the eastern half of the continent (Poland, the USSR, Romania, Hungary, Czechoslovakia, Austria, etc.) and they were to be dealt the most devastating blow by Hitler's premeditated, cold-blooded effort to mass murder the Jewish people. The British-mandated territory of Palestine, by contrast, represented no more than 3 per cent of the world Jewish population. The 445,000 Jews of Palestine (the Jewish population of what is now Israel has increased tenfold since then) were a drop in the ocean of what was still an overwhelmingly Diasporic nation. Today, there are nearly twice as many Jews in Israel as in the whole of the European continent.

The growth of the European Jewish population since the eighteenth century had been spectacular. In 1700 it was only 719,000, by 1800 it had risen to 2 million and by 1860 European Jews already represented around 90 per cent of world Jewry. Ever since the mid-seventeenth century the centre of gravity of the Jewish world had been steadily moving away from the Mediterranean to the area between the Baltic and the Black seas; from the Sephardim to the Ashkenazic Yiddish-speaking masses of central and east European Jewry. At the turn of the twentieth century there were already 8.7 million Jews in Europe – mainly concentrated in the Tsarist Russian empire (where they were deprived of all civil rights) and the multi-ethnic

Habsburg monarchy. But already in this period before the First World War, the foundations were being laid for the great American Jewish Diaspora, fuelled by a never-ending stream of immigrants fleeing from poverty and persecution in Russia and eastern Europe. A thin trickle of immigrants from the same regions were simultaneously establishing a foothold in the Ottoman Turkish backwater of Palestine, inspired by the age-old dream of a return to Zion mixed with visions of a modern Jewish national Risorgimento.

But in the period between the wars – especially in the 1930s under the impact of the Great Depression, the rise of Nazism and rapidly deteriorating conditions in eastern Europe – the core communities of world Jewry found themselves in an increasingly desperate situation. Even before the Holocaust Jews in Europe were increasingly seen as a superfluous people.

Feverish efforts were being made at the end of the 1930s by Jewish organizations and their leaders to find safe havens for impoverished Jewish refugees in an increasingly hostile world. The failure of the Evian Conference on refugees in 1938 was symptomatic of the growing atmosphere of panic and doom. The Night of the Broken Glass in Nazi Germany in November 1938 when all of the synagogues went up in flames was an ominous glimpse of the nightmare to come. The United States had since the early 1920s ceased to be a haven for the victims of such violent persecution and its gates were virtually sealed. Then, in 1939, the British White Paper on Palestine effectively closed the doors of the Jewish National Home. Nor were Jews welcome in the empty, wide open spaces of the British Dominions, let alone in a European continent already dominated by growing German power and ravaged by the inroads of anti-Semitism.

The Nazi terror that descended on Europe between 1939 and 1945 reduced the world Jewish population by almost 6 million or one-third of its total numbers. Ever since that time, Europe has ceased to be the centre of Jewish life and culture, which has virtually disappeared in countries like Germany, Austria, Czechoslovakia, Poland and Romania. Western Europe, it is true, has been less affected, despite the tragic losses sustained under Nazi rule. There are over a million Jews in the European Union today – mainly concentrated in France and Great Britain. In the East, figures are much more difficult to assess, with estimates for European Russia wildly fluctuating between a low of 400,000 and a high of 1.5 million. There is still a substantial Jewish community in the Ukraine and a smaller one in Hungary – 80–100,000 people.

But the global Jewish map has been simplified and is essentially split in bipolar fashion between North America (mainly the USA) which represents half of the 13 million Jews in today's world and Israel which already accounts for over 30 per cent of world Jewry. While the ex-USSR and Western Europe still exert some influence on the fate of Jewry, only the French Jewish community has actually increased in size and vitality since

1945. Outside of these areas the Jewish Diasporas of Africa, Asia, Latin America and Oceania are either static or dwindling, peripheral to the mainstream of contemporary Jewish history. Nevertheless, it is worth noting that the Jewries of Brazil and Australia *have* increased in size, belonging with Argentina, Canada and South Africa in the top ten ranking Jewish communities of today. In this context, the demographic decline of Anglo-Jewry from around 450,000 in 1939 to the present mark of 300,000 is something of an anomaly. Unlike European Jewish communities it did not suffer from German occupation nor has it been afflicted by post-war anti-Semitism in any significant measure. Nor did it endure the decolonizing pressures that drove 600,000 North African Jews to France and to Israel in the wake of Arab independence.

The post-war Jewish map is, then, a significantly changed one in terms of population. As the Israeli demographer Sergio DellaPergola points out, Jews are today concentrated in a smaller number of countries than before and they are a smaller part of an exploding world population (only 0.25 per cent) than they were in 1939. On the other hand, they have largely become a middle-class people inhabiting the core areas rather than the peripheral belts of the world economic and political system. In North and Latin America, Western Europe, South Africa and Australia, Jews enjoy, by and large, exceptional affluence. They are generally concentrated (to a much greater degree than in 1939) in advanced industrial countries that have high per capita incomes, health standards, literacy rates and cultural levels. No less importantly, they can reap the fruits of full civic liberties and a democratic way of life.

All these positive benefits also apply in Israel, despite the state of siege in which it has had to live and the difficulties encountered by the absorption of less favoured communities, who often arrived penniless – whether from Russia, Eastern Europe, the Middle East or Ethiopia. Israel, as a developed country with military and diplomatic influence in the world, provides more-over a shield of security for Jews world-wide, that manifestly did not exist before the Holocaust. When one adds to this the extraordinary economic and cultural influence of American Jewry and their intense involvement in the decision-making process in the world's most powerful country, then the contrast with the Jewish condition in 1945 is indeed remarkable.

Jews are no longer a people of homeless refugees, beggars vainly importuning the world's conscience or passive objects of international charity. They are, especially in Israel and the United States, independent actors in the historical dramas of the post-war world, whose influence on the events of our time has been far from negligible. This dramatic recovery from the nadir of the Holocaust and its devastation (even today world Jewry is still 3 million short of its numbers in 1939) is a stunning achievement and a genuine triumph over adversity. Moreover, the existence of Israel has served in the past forty-five years as a catalyst of Jewish identification and an undeniable core of Jewish identity, cohesion and continuity in the post-war world. It is the main *centripetal* force for Jewish unity in an increasingly centrifugal world, not only because of the security and freedom which it symbolizes, but also because it has developed a self-sustaining economy, culture and a collective Jewish identity of a new kind. In the contemporary Jewish world, Israel has effectively taken over the role once played by Eastern European Jewry as the main source of an independent, autonomous Jewish culture. As the old Diaspora Jewish languages (Yiddish, Ladino, Judaeo-Arab, etc.) wither, to be replaced by English as the dominant language of the world-wide Diaspora, it is the modernized Hebrew language of Israel which has become the main guardian of the continuity of a *distinctive* Jewish culture. Moreover, Israel on its own contains 40 per cent of the world Jewish population of school-age and about two-thirds of those enrolled in Jewish schools. Clearly, in the future, it will play the key role in the maintenance and transmission of a Jewish ethno-religious identity. This greatly strengthens its claims to be considered the core of Jewish peoplehood, especially when contrasted with the fissiparous, acculturated Jews of the Western Diaspora.

Nowhere is the contrast between Israel and the Diaspora clearer than in the area of intermarriage, the single most powerful centrifugal force in world Jewry today. Seventy years ago, in the United States, intermarriage was below 5 per cent but by 1970 it had leapt to 32 per cent and in 1990 it stood at an all-time high of 57 per cent. In pre-Holocaust Poland (then the largest Jewish community of Europe) intermarriage was still below 1 per cent and in nearly half of world Jewry it did not exceed 5 per cent before 1939. Only in highly assimilated Jewish communities like Germany, Austria, Italy, Holland or Australia did it remotely approach what it has commonly become in the contemporary Diaspora. But today, the American pattern is duplicated in France, Britain, Hungary, the former USSR and elsewhere – indeed in more than half of the Jewish Diaspora mixed marriages are currently running at around 50 per cent! Great Britain is a good illustration of this sobering trend. Between 1960 and 1990 the intermarriage rate rose almost tenfold. When one adds to this a high Jewish divorce rate (30 per cent), which is close to the current British levels, then it is clear that the Jewish family is beginning to fail and with it perhaps the most important vehicle for the transmission of a coherent Jewish identity. Thus a highly educated, successful, upwardly mobile Jewish community in Great Britain has found its numbers depleted by a third in the course of thirty years. When one puts together the trends of rampant intermarriage, high divorce figures, a low birthrate, an ageing population, lack of investment in Jewish education and general disaffiliation among the young, one can understand why British Chief Rabbi Jonathan Sacks has launched his 'Jewish Continuity' crusade. The problem is not however exclusively British or American, but a general Jewish Diasporic pattern in the open society. It is the downside of the affluence, the greater opportunities, the social mobility and cultural integration which post-war

4

modernity has offered to the Jewish Diaspora. Low intermarriage rates in pre-1939 Europe and America reflected societies which still discriminated against or even persecuted Jews; they echoed a more ethnically cohesive and separatist Jewish way of life; the greater influence of Orthodoxy on the Jewish masses and a deeper knowledge of Jewish history and culture. The Jewish family was more stable and the gulf between Jews and Gentiles was still considerable.

In contemporary society these factors no longer operate, except for the enclaves of Jewish Orthodoxy. There is far less opposition among Jews and non-Jews to intermarriage. Jewish distinctiveness has diminished and assimilation has increased, despite the experience of mass murder and the near extinction of the Jewish people only fifty years ago. Economic and political freedom, tolerance, pluralism and social acceptance paradoxically threaten to accomplish by peaceful, tranquil means what Nazi barbarism could not complete in the terror of the Holocaust – the gradual disappearance of the Jewish people! This is surely the greatest paradox of the post-war Jewish Diaspora. Never has it enjoyed such optimal conditions and never has it seemed more like an endangered species in the longer term. Its continuity and distinctiveness as an ethnic group, its religious practices and beliefs, its Jewish knowledge and literacy are seriously in doubt. As a recent advertisement in the London *Jewish Chronicle* put it (somewhat over-dramatically perhaps): 'Jews are not dying but Judaism and Jewish identity are'. This internal haemorraging of the Jewish body and spirit raises fundamental questions about the *raison d'être* of Diaspora Jewry. Can a people which miraculously recovered from the black hole of the Holocaust, which survived two millennia of exile, expulsions, pogroms and genocide, possibly reconcile itself to quietly fading from the scene? Can the continuity and survival of the Jewish people be assured in conditions of freedom and affluence? This is a 'Jewish question' in some ways more perplexing and difficult than the long shadow of anti-Semitism that has accompanied the Jews through their long march in exile.

Traditional and ultra-orthodox Jewry stands, at first sight, secure in splendid isolation amidst the confusing signals of modernity. Though almost decimated in its East European strongholds during the Nazi Holocaust, all the predictions of its demise – whether in Israel or the Diaspora – have proved to be premature. Far from being the fossils of history, the *Ḥaredim* (ultra-orthodox) are the fastest growing segment in contemporary Jewry. With their *rebbes* and *yeshivot*, their arranged marriages and extremely high birthrate, the *ḥaredi* communities have not only recovered, they are flourishing. Turning their backs on the secular world, they reject its culture, lifestyle, modes of dress and politics – except where it directly impinges on their way of life. In Israel (where they number about 350,000) they have made their influence felt in public life, eclipsing the traditional religious parties, despite their avowed anti-Zionism and reluctance to recognize the legitimacy of the State. In the Diaspora, where their numerical strength is similar, they have a growing impact on mainstream Orthodox institutions. One reason for this, sadly enough, is the lack of spiritual leadership coming from the Orthodox establishment in Israel and most of the Diaspora. But Jewish fundamentalism, despite its current revival, involves such a narrow-minded rejection of secular modernity and all its works, that it is difficult to imagine it achieving any major long-term impact on contemporary Jewry. Its importance is more as a symptom pointing to the problem rather than as a solution.

The majority of contemporary Jews, whether in Israel or in the Diaspora, remain – and are likely to remain – secularists. But they are secularists who know that the Jewish identity of their children and grandchildren can no longer be taken for granted. Nor can they assume that the collective survival of the Jewish people is assured, despite the existence of a Jewish State. True, Israel offers the model of a cohesive Jewish ethnicity, a bulwark against the forces of Jewish assimilation in the Diaspora and a haven of safety in times of persecution. In Israel there is no problem of intermarriage or of a low Jewish birthrate, no crisis of Jewish education or dilemma of transmitting Jewish values to the next generation. But Israel is also a distinct national entity with its own dynamics, interests and mental horizons, often different from those of the Diaspora. Moreover, despite the strength of the existing mutual ties and interdependence, Israel is founded on a Zionist outlook which ultimately denies the possibility of a long-term viable existence in *Galut* (the Hebrew term for exile). Diaspora can therefore only be a transitory condition in the Zionist perception, not the basis for a secure existence. This is possible only through a return to the sources of Jewish life, to the land of the ancestors, of Biblical heroes – kings, prophets, priests, psalmists – and to the old/new Hebrew language.

Diaspora Jews cannot compete with this territorial rootedness but they too have begun to put down different kinds of roots in the post-war world – especially in the enlightened, emancipated, secular West. Jews no longer appear quite so distinctive in the new multi-cultural, multi-ethnic mosaic of most Western democracies today. The tag of the perennial outsider, rootless nomad, wanderer between the worlds has shifted to others – blacks, Asians, Muslim Turks and Arabs, guest-workers, asylum-seekers, economic and political refugees, gypsies, gays and leftists. Against the background of ethnic minorities who currently bear the brunt of racism, xenophobia and intolerance in Europe and America, Jews often seem like insiders or even like well-integrated parts of the establishment. The Jewish 'otherness' is still there but it is less offensive to the Gentile eye and anti-Semitism since the Holocaust has been significantly muted both by its horrors and by other priorities.

Nevertheless, post-war anti-Semitism, while lacking the lethal vitality and murderousness of the Nazi paradigm, has still been a tenacious presence on the international scene since 1945. It acquired a new lease of life through the Cold War and the emergence of Israel, especially in the Soviet bloc and the Arab–Muslim world. In the form of anti-Zionism it proved to be one of the most persistent weapons in the hands of those seeking to delegitimize and put an end to the existence of an independent Jewish State in the Middle East. In Communist-controlled countries it was used for domestic and foreign policy purposes, thereby accentuating the emigration of Jews from post-war Eastern Europe and later from the Soviet Union. In conjunction with rising Arab nationalism and Muslim fundamentalism, it seriously infected the Arab world, helping to accelerate the departure of long-established Middle Eastern Jewish communities.

The bulk of this 'Oriental' Jewry ended up in Israel, thereby fortifying the Jewish State and helping to ensure its viability. Another paradoxical result of this migration has been the revival of Sephardic Jewry itself, today the majority segment in Israeli society. For the first time in over 300 years, the Sephardim, as a result of this migration, have become leading actors on the Jewish stage. Despite their initial deprivation and the discrimination they encountered in the new society fashioned by Ashkenazi settlers from Eastern Europe, they have now come into their own. Zionism, originally a European solution for the European 'Jewish Question', has acted as the modernizing vehicle for their own ascent and encounter with the West within a Jewish national framework. It was the demographic changes and 'ethnic' cleavages within Israel that made possible the political revolution that brought the Likud party to power in 1977. For fifteen years Israeli politics moved to the right partly as a result of the resentments of the Sephardim against Israel's mainly Ashkenazic Labour establishment. Many Sephardim were also deeply distrustful of Arab intentions and more traditionalist in outlook, factors that helped to fuel the dominant nationalist reflexes of Israel in the 1980s. This pattern has now begun to change again and it may well be that the Sephardim will help to ease Israel's future integration into the Middle East as an accepted and equal partner in the development of the region.

The mutual recognition of Israelis and Palestinians as well as the real possibility of a comprehensive settlement of the Arab–Israeli conflict have already begun to impact upon the future perspectives confronting the Jewish world. Peace in the Middle East would remove one of the darkest shadows over post-war Jewish existence – the physical danger to an Israel surrounded by bellicose enemies bent on its destruction. Israel's military prowess has successfully kept this threat at bay for the past forty-five years and in the process transformed the image of the Jew into that of an efficient warrior capable of heroically defending his homeland when so required. In turn this gave new confidence, backbone and pride to the Jewish Diaspora. It also helps to explain the intense politicization of Jewish life, the high-profile defence of Jewish interests and the new militancy in the face of threats, which has characterized much post-war Jewish behaviour, especially in Israel, the United States and other Diaspora communities. At the most basic level of physical survival, the lessons of the Holocaust have indeed been learnt and this has had a galvanizing effect on Jewish motivation. Particularly after the Six Day War of 1967, the Jewish world was seized by a fever of mobilization for the cause of Israel, in which accents of chauvinism were not always absent. At the same time, for communities like Soviet Jewry (termed 'the Jews of Silence' by Elie Wiesel only a few years earlier), the Israeli triumph provided a new lease of life and the courage to fight back against oppression. The struggle for Soviet Jewry – one of the great causes of the post-war Jewish world – helped salvage a community which had been cut off for decades from its brothers and sisters by Communist totalitarianism. The exodus of Soviet Jews to Israel and the West was one of the first breaches in the Communist fortress and it served to unify the Jewish world in a common fight for Jewish freedom, dignity and national identity.

The end of the Cold War and the demise of Communism, which reinforced this exodus, has in a sense vindicated the relevance of Zionism even fifty years after the Holocaust and the creation of Israel. The minimalist idea of the Jewish State as a Noah's ark in a cruel world where Jews may at any time find themselves victimized, was again shown to be an elemental necessity. Indeed, Zionism has always been vindicated during the past century whenever economic, political and international crises have threatened Jewish existence and exposed Jewish vulnerability as a beleaguered minority. Notwithstanding Jewish affluence, cultural achievements and political influence in the Western world, this still remains a basic truth. It was events like the Russian pogroms, the Dreyfus affair, the First World War, the anti-Semitic discrimination in Eastern Europe after 1918, the rise of Nazism and finally the Holocaust, which gave birth to and reinforced the message of Zionism. It has always been a doctrine of self-help and self-preservation, a secular survival kit for Jews living among the cannibals of the twentieth century. At its most primitive level that is also the meaning of Israel.

Even from the perspective of late twentieth-century Europe, this is a reality that only the most self-deluded utopians can afford to dismiss. The Western world, despite its underlying prosperity and stability, is mired in high unemployment, recession, racial problems and uncertainties about the future. Ethnic conflicts are rampant and have already produced a genocidal war in the former Yugoslavia, in the heart of Europe, which it has been unable or unwilling to stop. Fascism and neo-Nazism are on the rise and semi-respectable neo-populist parties spouting racist and anti-Semitic slogans are increasing their vote across Europe. Ironically, at the very time that Europe is seeking to draw closer together in economic and monetary union and to extend its membership to new entrants, the multi-cultural and multi-racial society is under increasing nationalist attack. Is the image of the new Europe to be found in Maastricht or in Sarajevo, in Brussels or in Northern Ireland?

Beyond the borders of the European Union there stands moreover the enigma of the former Soviet Union. Following the electoral results of December 1993 it would be a brave person who could guarantee the prospects of Russian Jewry to rebuild their communities, despite the new freedoms and opportunities. The future of President Yeltsin and his 'democratic' revolution appear extremely shaky, faced with a brown-red opposition of real strength, determined to check him. Anti-Semitism has played an important political role in cementing this opposition and in the rise of a neo-fascist movement whose chances increase as Russia's economic Chernobyl deepens. The prospect of Vladimir Zhirinovsky becoming the next president of Russia is frightening, not only to the West but to Russian Jews in particular.

Thus the politics of survival will continue to be relevant in the Jewish world of the 1990s and act as a cementing force across the fissures, the divisions and the centrifugal trends that will continue to afflict it. Jews, ever since the time of Abraham, have always been living at the crossroads of history and there is no reason to suppose that this will diminish in the near future. But mere survival has never been enough. The Jews are a people with an uncommon sense of vocation and purpose, a messianic belief in the validity of their own traditions and their monotheistic uniqueness. Living under siege is *not* the goal of their existence nor is a state of estrangement from the world ultimately conducive to the flourishing of their culture. It may well be that we are now moving into a new historical era when this will no longer be a dominant mode of Jewish existence for the majority of the Jewish people. An Israel at peace with its neighbours at the dawn of the twenty-first century would be a mighty step in this direction. The democratization of Russia and its integration into the world economy would be another. The strengthening of bonds in a prosperous, tolerant, pluralistic European Union and the maintenance of a powerful, democratic America would be further guarantees for the freedom and security of Jewish existence. But the survival of a meaningful Jewish identity in the Diaspora ultimately depends on the Jews themselves. Freedom, equality, wealth and empowerment cannot in themselves ensure the *content* of Jewish life, its quality and transmissibility to future generations. This in turn depends on Jewish education, Jewish commitment and preserving an ancient Jewish conviction – that the golden age of Judaism still lies in the future.

PART I

1

CHANGING CORES AND PERIPHERIES

Fifty years in socio-demographic perspective

Sergio DellaPergola

The socio-demographic changes undergone by world Jewry over the last fifty years are of such overwhelming magnitude and complexity that it seems justifiable, at least *prima facie*, to provide an unreservedly affirmative answer to the central theme of this volume: indeed, *a new Jewish world*.

Changing patterns of Jewish society in Israel and the Diaspora have been analysed in the light of different conceptual and thematic frames of reference. The main paradigms have included Jewish and Zionist history, the Middle East and its political and military conflicts, the absorption in Israel of large-scale heterogeneous Jewish immigration, and the responses of Jewish ethno-religious identity facing the challenges of modern socio-economic and cultural change. The changing reality of Israel's Jewish population has generally been referred to within one of two main alternative contexts to which it logically belongs – a (majority) segment of the larger society in a Middle Eastern country, or a (minority) segment of a globally dispersed Jewish people. The historical perspective underlying analyses of world Jewry has often focused on either or both of two major clusters of explanatory variables – general socio-economic and political factors shaping the Jewish experience from the outside, and distinctive Jewish socio-cultural and institutional forces shaping it from the inside (Bachi 1976; Baron 1952–83; Ben-Sasson 1976; DellaPergola 1983; Eisenstadt 1985; Mendelsohn 1987; Sharot 1976; Goldscheider and Zuckerman 1984).

This paper explores a number of demographic and identificational processes which affect over the last decades world Jewry and Israeli society at the crossroads of different and possibly conflicting relevant social contexts. Our study concerns, more particularly, the distribution of the Jewish population in Israel and the Diaspora *vis-à-vis* the unfolding of general political and socio-economic change in a broad view of world society and the emerging role of Israeli Jews in the light of recent demographic and cultural transformations among world Jewry. Understanding how Jewish society fares when assessed on two interdependent scales of general socio-economic

13

development and the maintenance of Jewish cultural identity may help to clarify basic questions of continuity and change in contemporary Jewry.

OVERVIEW OF MAJOR SOCIO-DEMOGRAPHIC CHANGES

Before different substantive processes are assessed, it should be noted that exacting methodological problems underlay the social–scientific evaluation of the trends themselves. First, the very definition of the Jews as individuals, and of Jewish communities as meaningful social aggregates, has become increasingly complex and controversial. Operative answers that can be provided to these definitional challenges involve the investment of growing time and resources, hindering research. By trying to provide quantitative estimates of major socio-demographic processes among Jews in given countries or world-wide, an investigator risks criticism for trying to measure what some deem to be unmeasurable (Schnapper 1987). This has to do both with the complex and multi-faceted character of Judaism which renders somewhat elusive its definition according to one or more simple parameters; and with the more generally widespread and increasing privatization and subjectivization of identificational patterns in contemporary societies (Petersen 1987; Waters 1990; Goldstein and Kosmin 1991).

In part connected with the above difficulties, availability of reliable data on Jewish populations is nowadays far less and of poorer quality than it was before the Second World War. While, at that time, about 90 per cent of world Jewry lived in countries providing official statistics on Jewish population characteristics, today this is true of only 25 per cent of Jews who live outside the State of Israel (Schmelz, Glikson and Gould 1983; Schmelz and DellaPergola 1991). Given the great geographical dispersion of the Jewish population, it is unlikely that definitive conclusions can be reached unless the local, national and international scope of the trends examined are articulated into one truly comprehensive research perspective. This, again, is almost unfeasible because of the limitations of available data. In spite of these shortcomings, reliance on the results of empirical research is indispensable if one wishes to seriously assess and grasp the meaning of at least some of the major aspects of continuity and change in the Jewish socio-demographic structure and dynamics.

A broad overview of the changes undergone by world Jewry over the last fifty years (late 1930s to late 1980s) reveals overwhelming socio-demographic transformations. The dramatic period of the *Shoah* (Holocaust) still dominates the demographic picture of world Jewry. The loss of 6 million lives caused the virtual disappearance or definitive erosion of the leading centres of Jewish life in Central and Eastern Europe, while longer-term demographic after-effects continue to influence current Jewish population trends (Schmelz 1991). But besides the *Shoah*, there were other major changes. Intercontinental migrations affecting over 3.5 million Jews led to a westward shift of the main centres of Jewish presence in the Diaspora, as well as to the rapid development of a new and independent pole of growth in Israel. Transformations affecting patterns of health and longevity, family formation, fertility and natality led to a drastic redirection in the main thrust of world Jewish population development, from the substantial natural increase still visible during the early 1930s, to zero population growth and prospective decline at the close of the 1980s. Of growing importance in this whole Jewish demographic equation was the role of identificational factors, operating through the chain of formal or informal accessions to, and secessions from, Jewish peoplehood. Demographic *and* cultural reproduction were increasingly becoming the inextricably tied motors of Jewish population trends (Bachi 1976; DellaPergola 1989a; Schmelz 1989).

Table 1.1 provides an illustration of the net balance of the numerical and geographical changes undergone by the Jewish population between 1939, on the eve of the Second World War, and 1988, before the recent revival of Jewish emigration from the Soviet Union. World Jewry is now smaller by more than one-fifth than it was in 1939: the losses of the *Shoah* have not been compensated since the Second World War by over forty years of moderate Jewish population increase. Israel's current Jewish population is eight times larger than former Palestine's Jewish *yishuv*, but the Diaspora is over 40 per cent smaller than it was in 1939. Drastic declines occurred in the Jewries of Eastern Europe and the Balkans, North Africa and Asia (outside of Israel). Smaller, yet significant declines occurred in Western Europe. Jewish population increased in North America, and in some smaller communities in the southern hemisphere. Little net population change occurred among Jews in Latin America.

Looking at the geographical distribution of world Jewry by individual countries (see Table 1.2), the list of ten largest communities changed quite substantially, yet six of the major ten in 1988 already made the list before the Second World War. The Jewish people was significantly more concentrated in 1988 than it was in 1939. The ten largest Jewish populations covered in 1988 an even larger share of world Jewry, 96 per cent as against 85 per cent in 1939. Much of this accrued concentration reflects the definitive rise of the United States as the largest Jewish population centre in any single country – not only today, but in the course of Jewish history as a whole. US Jewry already was the largest Jewish community on earth in 1939; during the intervening period, Israel has replaced Poland as the country with the second largest Jewish population in the world. Yet, beyond the two important exceptions of the United States and Israel, the sizes of the other largest Jewish populations are now significantly smaller than they were before the war. The critical mass of Jewish communities – an important background determinant of the prospects and quality of autonomous Jewish life – has generally declined. In a sense, these changes entail a simplification

Table 1.1 Estimated world Jewish population distribution, by continents and major geographical regions, 1939 and 1988

Region	1939		1988		Change 1939–88	
	N (000)	%	N (000)	%	N (000)	%
World	16,600	100.0	12,979	100.0	−3,621	−21.8
Diaspora	16,155	97.3	9,320	71.8	−6,835	−42.3
Israel	445	2.7	3,659	28.2	+3,214	+722.2
Europe	9,500	57.2	2,314	17.8	−7,186	−75.6
West	1,350[a]	8.1	1,053[a]	8.1	−297	−22
East, Balkans[b]	8,150	49.1	1,261	9.7	−6,889	−84.5
Asia	1,000	6.0	3,985	30.7	+2,985	+298.5
Palestine/Israel	445	2.7	3,659	28.2	+3,214	+722.2
Rest[b]	555	3.3	326	2.5	−229	−41.3
Africa	600	3.6	142	1.1	−458	−76.3
North	500	3.0	13	0.1	−487	−97.4
South, Central	100	0.6	129	1.0	+29	+29.0
America	5,472	33.0	6,448	49.7	+976	+17.8
North[c]	5,040	30.4	6,010	46.3	+970	+19.2
Latin	432	2.6	438	3.4	+6	+1.4
Oceania	28	0.2	90	0.7	+62	+221.4

a Including Jews in transit.
b Asian territories of USSR and Turkey are included in Asia.
c United States and Canada.

Sources: DellaPergola (1983); Schmelz and DellaPergola (1990).

of the Jewish geographic map at the world level. They also imply greater dependency of the present Jewish fate and future on the evolution of a relatively small number of countries.

In terms of the more recent dynamic processes involved, attention is called to the deep contrast between the emerging demography of Jews in Israel and in the Diaspora. On the Israeli side, large-scale and quite heterogeneous immigration radically transformed the size and structure of the Jewish population. Over the decades that followed, processes of immigrant absorption brought about steady levels of family formation and fertility and a comparatively young population structure which in turn produced a moderate but stable amount of Jewish population increase (Bachi 1977; Schmelz, DellaPergola and Avner 1991). This continued to be the case even during the years of scarce immigration which preceded the more recent revival of immigration from the Soviet Union. Throughout the Diaspora, on the other hand, diminishing Jewish nuptiality and fertility, a steady process of population ageing, along with an uncertain balance of (often informal) secessions and accessions among the younger adults have resulted

Table 1.2 Ten largest Jewish populations, 1939 and 1988

		1939				1988		
		Jewish population	Per cent of world Jewish population		Country	Jewish population	Per cent of world Jewish population	
Rank	Country	(000)	Simple	Cumulative		(000)	Simple	Cumulative
1	United States	4,870	29.3	29.3	United States	5,700	43.9	43.9
2	Poland	3,325	20.0	49.4	Israel	3,659	28.2	72.1
3	Soviet Union	3,020	18.2	67.6	Soviet Union	1,435	11.1	83.2
4	Romania	850	5.1	72.7	France	530	4.1	87.2
5	Palestine	445	2.7	75.4	United Kingdom	322	2.5	89.7
6	Hungary	404	2.4	77.8	Canada	310	2.4	92.1
7	Czechoslovakia	357	2.2	79.9	Argentina	220	1.7	93.8
8	United Kingdom	280	1.7	81.6	South Africa	114	0.9	94.7
9	France	280	1.7	83.3	Brazil	100	0.8	95.5
10	Argentina	254	1.5	84.8	Australia	85	0.6	96.1
Cumulative 1–10		14,065	84.8			12,475	96.1	
2–10		9,195	55.4			6,775	52.2	
11+		2,535	15.2			504	3.9	
World total		16,600	100.0			12,979	100.0	

Sources: DellaPergola (1983); Schmelz and DellaPergola (1990).

in a general pattern of Jewish population decline. Consequently, both the absolute and relative weight of the Israeli branch have grown significantly within world Jewry as a whole. International migrations between different Diaspora communities have also affected the respective growth or decline on the global Jewish scene.

One further important issue concerns Israel's position in the geographical region where it naturally belongs: the Mediterranean and the Middle East. Israel's position in this area has been deeply affected by the historical and sociological factors which led to its formation, and by the conditions of permanent political conflict that have accompanied the whole course of its existence. Considering the predominant migratory background of Israel's Jewish population, the question may be raised whether Jews in Israel, and Israeli society more generally, do not represent an artificial transplant in a strange area. The results of different multivariate analyses of the degree of similarity and dissimilarity existing between Israel and its regional neighbours provide quite contrasting answers to this question, according to the types of variables examined.

One perspective is provided by studying the network of international economic relations around the Mediterranean basin, which more generally illustrates the degree of economic integration and interdependence in the region. Examination of the matrix of commercial flows between each couple of Mediterranean countries shows that Israel is quite disconnected economically from its more specific region – the Eastern Mediterranean – with the recent exception of Egypt (Ricci 1990). The military and political conflicts that have long opposed Israel to several Arab countries explain the virtual lack of economic interchange with its neighbours. Israel's economic relations rather tend to be developed with countries on the western side of the Mediterranean, and more generally with the world at large, particularly Western Europe and the United States.

These findings stand in singular conflict with a similar attempt to assess Israel's position in the Mediterranean from the point of view of the physical–anthropological characteristics of the population. As already noted, the absolute majority of Israel's Jews are immigrants or the descendants of immigrants. It is therefore interesting to verify what kind of genetic pool characterizes these Israelis: do they fit or not their present regional context? Recent multivariate analyses of blood types and several other genetic markers for each national population around the Mediterranean show the genetics of Israeli Jews to be the more similar to that of other populations in the Eastern Mediterranean area to which Israel is geographically closer (Martuzzi-Veronesi, Pettener and Gueresi 1990). It thus appears that in spite of wide-ranging geographic dispersion over the centuries, and paying due attention to the very substantial in-group genetic heterogeneity that exists within the Jewish population, the Jews have maintained a measurable amount of genetic similarity – possibly thanks to the prevalence of endogamy in the past. Some of their early Middle-Eastern origins can still be recognized through scientific investigation of contemporary populations.

The vast majority of world Jewry live outside of Israel, but a network of family relations reaching back into the depths of history, and even more significantly, a complex of religious, cultural and ideal bonds tie together Israel and the Jewish Diaspora. Most of Israel's economic and political relations – in the absence of peace – connect the country to more distant parts of the world rather than to its immediate environment. These contrasting findings should underlay our understanding of the position of Jewish population and Israeli society in a broad description of social patterns of continuity and change at the world level.

CORE/PERIPHERY: SOME GENERAL CONCEPTS

While some of the processes mentioned above have been discussed in some detail elsewhere, the main purpose of this paper is to attempt a synthetic evaluation of the net consequences of such processes over the last fifty years. While the simple assumption of homogeneous and linear changes will be dismissed from the outset, an effort will be made to provide global generalizations about a variety of patterns whose ultimate significance is perceived at the level of specific local Jewish communities, or single Jewish individuals. Relying on a variety of quantitative indicators, we review what we consider to be the essential substance and implications of Jewish and Israeli societal change over the recent past, setting at the same time a frame of reference for an assessment of the types of change to be expected in the years ahead. The concepts of *core* and *periphery*, as defined and applied to the comparative socio-demographic study of Jewish populations, may usefully assist in this respect. We suggest that the extraordinary changes undergone by Jewish populations and societies over the last fifty years can be summarized by referring to shifts occurring within the framework of several different types of core/periphery systems.

In most general terms (Shils 1961; Gradus 1986), we refer to *core* as to a territorially and/or socially organized subsystem of society that has a high capacity for innovative change. It is the functional centre of development which spreads to periphery according to hierarchical diffusional patterns, and derives power from its ability to further centralize economic activity, decision-making and other functions related to the global development process. *Periphery* is a societal subsystem that is territorially and/or socially of low accessibility to the core and is characterized by limited access to markets, means of production, services, cultural facilities and sources of economic and political power. This implies varying degrees of economic and political dependency of the periphery on the core. The socio-economic and political relationship between core and periphery is characterized by dominance of the former and dependence on the part of the latter. This asymmetrical relationship is manifested through several major processes, such as decision-making and control, capital flow, innovative diffusion and migration.

In this respect, one useful conceptual frame of reference of a global nature is provided by world-system theory (Wallerstein 1974–80). According to this approach, nations form an interrelated web, constantly activated by numerous and diverse types of mutual relationships. The politically strongest and economically most developed countries can be viewed as standing at the system's core. Other countries, characterized by diminishing amounts of economic and political resources, can be viewed as increasingly peripheral belts around the core. Relative positions of countries in the world-system are assumed to reflect reciprocal ties of dominance and dependence. While we do not propose to accept the deterministic undertones often attached to world-system theory, or the assumption that relations within the system must necessarily be exploitative, a global perspective should take into account the conflictual nature of many interrelations between societies, and between different social groups within a given society, aimed at establishing their own hegemony over the world-system. The Jewish population in the world and Israeli society participate in, or are affected by, such conflicts.

Since the Jewish population we are dealing with is importantly defined by ideational categories – and not only by socio-economic terms of reference – we need to extend the conventional definition of core to the socio-cultural sphere. Core can, therefore, also be defined as the centre of a given ethno-religious group's cultural innovation, creativity and continuity, and the locus where the latter more clearly occurs within the recognizable cultural paradigm of the group itself. In terms of the group's socio-cultural distinctiveness and continuity, the periphery has a lesser capacity for maintenance of the original cultural contents and for innovation from within, and may depend on the support of cultural tools provided by the core. A further aspect of the socio-cultural relationship is the tendency of the periphery to loosen its identification and to experience diminishing contacts and similarities with the group's core, and eventually to drift away from recognizable belonging to the given ethno-religious group. In the cultural sphere, too, as in the more general political and socio-economic one, conflicts may arise between different competing centres, each trying to establish its own hegemony over the whole ethno-religious group.

In the rest of this paper, we consider the changing position of Jewish populations in Israel and in the Diaspora over the last fifty years as we try to apply a core/periphery framework to three different perspectives:

1 the world-system perspective, in relation to the general distribution of world population and the political and socio-economic significance attached to it;

2 the country-structure perspective, in relation to the geographical distribution of different ethnic groups, and its sociological implications,
within individual countries;
3 the Jewish peoplehood perspective, in relation to the significant cultural–
identificational differentials which exist within the world Jewish population.

WORLD-SYSTEM PERSPECTIVE

The first question we wish to examine is how the combined effects of very
different intervening processes – the *Shoah*, Zionism, international migration, differential rates of natural increase and differential rates of
assimilation – affected world Jewish population distribution as compared to
the general distribution of world population. The changing geographical
distribution of world Jewry provides a synthetic picture of the types of socio-
economic and socio-cultural environments within which Jewish life unfolds.
It reflects developments which run deep in history, and conveys the ultimate
sense of many-fold developments in Jewish population in the longer run.
Overall, did these changes bring contemporary Jewry closer to, or more
apart from, the core of the world geopolitical and socio-economic system of
nations than was the case before the Second World War?

To answer this question we need information on the position of each
country within the world-system, as well as data on the total and Jewish
populations in each country (see Table 1.3). Many different empirical
procedures may be followed to operationalize the position of each single
country within a global classification. In this study a simple one was chosen,
yet one we judge acceptable given the exploratory purposes of this analysis.
We built a composite index of a country's world-system centrality, based on
the sum of scores obtained by each country with regard to the following
five variables: gross national product per capita, energy consumption per
capita, infant mortality rate, adult literacy rate, political freedom/type of
governance. These indicators are hypothesized to represent good proxies for
each country's general standard of living, levels of industrialization and
modernization, public health, cultural development and political emancipation. Most of the data were originally collected by the World Bank (Camp
and Speidel 1987).

We consider the five chosen indicators to be not only of proven theoretical
relevance in general attempts to rank countries, but also especially suited
to a population, like the Jews, which has featured historically a unique
combination of high educational attainment and substantial socio-economic
specialization (Kuznets 1960). We assume that the different national levels
of economic development and quality of life, as reflected by the selected
variables, provide relevant criteria for an evaluation of the relative position of
countries on the global scene, as well as of the environments offered to the

Table 1.3 Estimated world Jewish population distribution, by socio-economic profile[a] of countries of residence, 1939 and 1988 (percentages)

Stratum of countries	No. of countries	1939		1988		Percent change 1939–88		Jews per 1,000 pop.	
		Jewish pop.	Total pop.	Jewish pop.	Total pop.	Jews	Total	1939	1988
Total number[b]	131[c]	16,600	2,216,700	12,979	5,101,655				
Total per cent		100.0	100.0	100.0	100.0	−22	+130	7.5	2.5
1 (highest)	21[d]	38.1	22.4	55.0	14.0	+13	+44	12.7	10.0
2	23[e]	55.8	17.5	42.3	12.5	−41	+65	23.8	8.6
3	27[f]	1.9	7.0	2.3	11.1	−6	+265	2.0	0.5
4	31[g]	3.9	46.5	0.3	52.7	−93	+161	0.6	0.0
5 (lowest)	29[h]	0.3	6.6	0.1	9.7	−67	+238	0.3	0.0
Dissimilarity index:		0.540		0.708					

a A composite index, based on the following five variables: Gross national product per capita, Enerqy consumption per capita, Infant mortality rate, Adult literacy rate, Political freedom/type of governance. Each variable was scored for each country on a scale between 0 and 10, from poorest to best, based on more detailed available data. The sum of scores for the five variables together could range between 0 and 50. Countries were regrouped into the following score strata:

$$1 = 40–9; 2 = 30–9; 3 = 20–9; 4 = 10–19; 5 = 0–9.$$

In the table, regrouping of countries was kept the same for both periods considered. Geographical divisions and index scores relate to the 1980s.
b All population figures in thousands.
c Not including thirty-nine countries or territories for which no sufficient data were available.
d Canada, United States, Trinidad and Tobago, Belgium, Denmark, France, Germany (Federal Republic), Ireland, Italy, Luxemburg, Netherlands, United Kingdom, Austria, Finland, Iceland, Norway, Sweden, Switzerland, Japan, Australia, New Zealand.
e Costa Rica, Jamaica, Argentina, Colombia, Uruguay, Venezuela, Greece, Portugal, Spain, Bulgaria, Czechoslovakia, Germany (Democratic Republic), Hungary, Poland, Romania, USSR, Yugoslavia, Hong Kong, Israel, Kuwait, Singapore, Thailand, United Arab Emirates.
f Cuba, Dominican Republic, Honduras, Mexico, Panama, Bolivia, Brazil, Chile, Ecuador, Guyana, Paraguay, Peru, Surinam, Turkey, Jordan, North Korea, South Korea, Lebanon, Malaysia, Mongolia, Oman, Philippines, Sri Lanka, Botswana, Libya, Mauritius, South Africa.
g El Salvador, Guatemala, Nicaragua, Albania, Burma, China, India, Indonesia, Iran, Iraq, Pakistan, Saudi Arabia, Syria, North Yemen, Vietnam, Algeria, Cameroon, Congo, Ivory Coast, Egypt, Kenya, Lesotho, Madagascar, Morocco, Sudan, Tanzania, Tunisia, Uganda, Zambia, Zimbabwe, Papua New Guinea.
h Haiti, Afghanistan, Bangladesh, Bhutan, Kampuchea, Nepal, South Yemen, Angola, Benin, Burkina-Faso, Burundi, Central African Republic, Chad, Ethiopia, Ghana, Guinea, Liberia, Mali, Malawi, Mauritania, Mozambique, Niger, Nigeria, Rwanda, Senegal, Sierra Leone, Somalia, Togo, Zaire.

Sources: Camp and Speidel (1987), Levy (1989), McEvedy and Jones (1978), Linfield 1942), DellaPergola (1987), Schmelz and DellaPergola (1990).

respective local Jewish populations. Countries with highest overall indexes are hypothesized to stand at the core of the world-system, while declining scores are to be associated with a country's more peripheral position.

International comparisons based on a similar set of variables at different dates are very problematic, since some of the criteria may not be applicable, or some of the relevant data may not be available for a significant number of countries at one point of time or another. Principally for this reason, the rather comprehensive country classification obtained for the late 1980s was kept unchanged for the earlier point in time considered here, the late 1930s. This procedure should *not* be construed as an assumption (which we consider unsustainable were it only for the limited purposes of our analysis) that changes in development levels cutting across nations do not imply any reordering in the ranking of countries over time. The only purpose here is to provide a consistent and analytically meaningful framework for a comparison of total and Jewish population distribution world-wide over a period of fifty years.

The 131 countries for which relevant data were available for the 1980s were divided into five strata, from most to least developed. The scores obtained were such that each stratum eventually included roughly the same number of countries. It should be noted that, in spite of the simple procedure followed by us, the resulting typology of countries is highly consistent with similar classification attempts that have used more refined tools (Snyder and Kick 1979; Shachar 1989).

Table 1.3 shows that both in 1939 and in 1988, the Jews tended to be far more concentrated in the more developed and stronger countries (Strata 1 and 2 in our classification) than the world's total population. Overall, the distribution of world Jewry was significantly different from the distribution of the general population at both dates examined. It should be stressed that over the last fifty years the share of world Jewry out of the total world population has declined to only one-third of what is was before the Second World War, from 7.5 per 1,000 in 1939 to 2.5 per 1,000 in 1988. This drastic decline of the relative demographic weight of the Jews on the world scene reflects the actual diminution of world Jewry, while the total world population more than doubled, largely as the result of the population explosion in developing countries where there are few Jews.

More than half of the world Jewish population is now located in Stratum 1, the group of most developed and strongest countries – or the core of the world-system – which include most of North America, Western Europe and Japan. The share of world Jewry found in this stratum increased from 38 per cent in 1939 to 55 per cent in 1988, against a decline from 22 per cent to 14 per cent in the stratum's share of the total world population. The Jewish population in this group of countries actually increased by 13 per cent in absolute numbers, yet its share of the total population in the same stratum slightly diminished from 13 to 10 per 1,000 because Jewish population growth was comparatively slower.

Before the Second World War, a majority of the Jewish people lived in Stratum 2, which we may define as the contemporary world-system's semi-periphery. The countries included in Stratum 2 feature either a somewhat weaker performance than countries in Stratum 1 on each of the indicators selected for our classification, or present a lack of equilibrium between some strong indicators and some much weaker ones. This second stratum includes most Eastern European countries, most of whose Jewish populations were destroyed during the Second World War; it also includes the state of Israel, whose rapid population growth only partly compensated for the destruction of East European Jewries. The overall Jewish population in Stratum 2 was 41 per cent smaller in the 1980s than it was in the 1930s. The share of this group of countries out of the total of world Jewry declined from 56 per cent in 1939 to 42 per cent in 1988. Its share of the world's total population declined, too, from 17 per cent to 12 per cent. The share of Jews out of the total population in Stratum 2 declined significantly, from 24 per 1,000 in 1939 to 9 per 1,000 in 1988.

Strata 3, 4 and 5 constitute the increasingly peripheral belts of the world-system, and include countries characterized by increasing dependency on a decreasing number of resources, or a lack of resources all together. The combined Jewish population in countries belonging to these three strata declined between 1939 and 1988 both in absolute and relative terms (–56 per cent). The decline was particularly strong in Stratum 4, which includes many Arab countries where important Jewish communities existed before the Second World War. The combined share of world Jewish population in Strata 3, 4 and 5 declined from 6 per cent in 1939 to 3 per cent in 1988, while the respective total populations, because of extremely high rates of natural increase, grew from 60 per cent of world population in the 1930s to 74 per cent in the 1980s. The share of Jews out of the total population in these strata declined to less than 1 per 1,000, and actually tended to zero.

The net effect of the various intervening processes on the overall distribution of world Jewry was approximate maintenance of the level of Jewish presence at the core of the world-system of nations, substantial decline at the semi-periphery, and virtual disappearance at the periphery. In 1988, the percentage of Jews out of total population systematically declined from the core to periphery countries. This contrasts with the situation before the Second World War, when the strongest relative Jewish concentration was still in countries that are today semi-peripheral in the world-system. Indexes of dissimilarity between the distributions of Jewish and total populations among the five strata of countries, shown in Table 1.3, indicate a substantial increase in the distinctiveness of world Jewish population distribution between the 1930s and the 1980s.

More specific country analyses not shown here (DellaPergola 1986; 1989b), especially focusing on the Western countries – the world-system's core – point to very high correlations between the number and percentage of Jews in individual countries, and detailed national indicators of socio-economic development, such as enrolment in higher education, number of scientific publications, investment in R&D, industrial productivity, energy consumption, communications networks, military investments and GNP per capita. The same variables also explain large amounts of the variance in international migration propensities (or lack of propensity) among Jews, including in particular rates of migration to Israel (*aliyah*) from developed countries. These analyses clearly indicate that, in spite of the variety of other intervening processes, including cultural and ideological factors, general socio-economic factors strongly underlay changing Jewish population distribution at the global level.

A final significant observation relates again to the position of the state of Israel in the framework of the world-system. According to the indicators chosen in our Table 1.3 classification, in 1988 Israel occupied twenty-fifth place in the ranking of 131 countries. This corresponds to one of the upper-most positions in Stratum 2 – which we have defined as semi-peripheral. It is perhaps symbolic that the structural position of contemporary Israel at the world level should be in the same category with those same Eastern European countries which hosted the largest sections of world Jewry before they were destroyed during the Second World War.

The second type of process we wish to examine concerns the changing structural position of the Jews in the framework of general population and society at the country-wide level. The internal stratification of national societies, whether considered in terms of simple differentiation, or with regard to possible inequalities and tensions, provides another relevant perspective to the evaluation of Jewish continuity and change. Taking into account the very significant structural changes that have occurred within Jewish populations and societies, does the socio-demographic structure of contemporary Jews continue to be substantially different from that of the majority populations of the respective countries, as it was before the Second World War? Are the Jews closer to the core or to the periphery of society in a given national context? Are changes that can be observed among the Jews convergent or divergent in comparison to similar changes among other relevant groups within the total population of the same countries?

Most of our exploration here concerns the United States – the largest and strategically most important component of world Jewry – but we assume that much of the analysis may apply as well to the smaller Jewries in many other Diaspora countries. An attempt is made, in the following, to assess the changing core/periphery position of the Jews within the American system of ethnic stratification. We focus on one fundamental aspect of population structure: the various groups' geographical distribution at the national level. The similarities and dissimilarities of national Jewish population distri-bution can be measured in relation to other groups before the Second World War and more recently. We assume, in general, that groups which are the more influential in determining overall national demographic, socio-economic or socio-cultural patterns, or in greater conformity with them, can be expected to be present in a greater variety of social frameworks, and therefore to be more geographically diffused. Conversely, groups that are territorially more concentrated, or tend to have a markedly different geographical distribution than that of the total population may be assumed to maintain a higher degree of cultural distinctiveness, as well as other patterns of socio-economic specialization. We assume these patterns of distinctiveness and specialization to be reflected in the social prestige and power ranking of the respective different ethnic groups. A pattern of greater and more complex diffusion and presence over the national territory – and, by implication, society – is therefore taken here as an indication of societal centrality; a limited or more specialized presence is taken as a proxy for societal marginality.

To test these assumptions, we present first a descriptive outline of the changes in the distribution of Jewish and total populations of the United States between the late 1930s and the late 1980s, based on the nine standard major regional divisions (see Table 1.4). Jewish population growth during the time interval considered was slower than among the total population (24 per cent versus 63 per cent), and therefore the share of Jews among total US inhabitants declined (from 36.2 to 24.6 per 1,000). Among both total and Jewish populations, the general trend was to move and redistribute to the Southern and Western regions; Eastern and Northern regions incurred slower growth rates among the total population, and actual population declines among the Jews. The special prominence of the Jewish population of the Middle Atlantic region, including New York, declined but did not disappear.

Similar geographical distribution data provide the basis for our attempt to evaluate the characteristics of the American system of ethnic groups around 1980. The materials for this analysis, based on the same nine regions as in Table 1.4, derive from US census data on ancestry (Lieberson and Waters 1986), and from the 1988 estimates of Jewish population size and distribution prepared by the North American Jewish Data Bank (Kosmin, Scheckner and Ritterband 1989). Figure 1.1 displays a Smallest Space Analysis (SSA) of the territorial distribution of thirty-six selected ethnic groups in the United States. With the SSA technique, each point synthesizes a full series of nine regional data for each ethnic group. The more similar the regional distributions for two groups, the closer the respective points appear on the diagram. The various groups' positions on the diagram are independent of the respective population sizes. The emerging display is the optimal graphical solution to the full matrix of intergroup correlations. Although the distances shown in the diagram cannot be interpreted as metric equivalents, the diagram is roughly indicative of the basic North–South, East–West orientation of the population distributions represented.

Most similar to the territorial distribution of the total US population (and, therefore, most diffused over the national territory), and highly visible

Table 1.4 Estimated Jewish and total population distribution in the United States, by regions, 1937 and 1988 (percentages)

	1937		1988		Percent change 1937–88		Jews per 1,000 pop.	
Region	Jewish pop.	Total pop.	Jewish pop.	Total pop.	Jews	Total	1937	1988
Total number[a]	4,771	131,669[b]	5,935[c]	214,078				
Total per cent	100.0	100.0	100.0	100.0	+24	+63	36.2	24.6
New England	8.3	6.4	7.1	5.3	+6	+51	47.2	33.2
Middle Atlantic	61.0	20.9	43.9	15.5	–11	+35	105.6	69.8
East North Central	15.6	20.2	8.9	17.3	–29	+57	27.9	12.7
West North Central	3.6	10.3	2.1	7.3	–28	+30	12.6	7.0
South Atlantic	4.0	13.5	16.8	17.0	+419	+130	10.8	24.3
East South Central	1.3	8.2	0.7	6.3	–40	+41	5.6	2.8
West South Central	1.6	9.9	2.0	11.1	+55	+106	6.0	4.5
Mountain	0.7	3.2	2.5	5.4	+368	+214	7.7	11.4
Pacific	3.9	7.4	16.0	14.8	+407	+267	19.3	26.6
Dissimilarity index:								
Total		0.420		0.314				
Without Middle Atlantic[d]		0.283		0.272				

a Thousands.
b 1940.
c Including small numbers of non-Jewish members of Jewish households.
d Based on 100 per cent distribution without Middle Atlantic.

Computed from: Linfield (1942); Kosmin, Schekner and Ritterband (1989).

for their central position within the whole system of American ethnic groups, appears to be a cluster of the four ancestry groups originating from the British Isles: England, Scotland, Wales and Ireland. A spatially close cluster includes the ethnic groups originating from Germany and neighbouring countries, such as the Netherlands, Switzerland and Bohemia. Keeping in mind what was assumed above about the relationship between territorial distribution and belonging to the more influential core of American society, Figure 1.1 appropriately designates what different analysts have described, at least in the past, as the societal role-model: the White Anglo-Saxon Protestants (WASP) (e.g., Gordon 1964).

On the other hand, several of the ethnic groups generally viewed as underprivileged and at the bottom of the American scale of social prestige – such as the blacks, the American Indians, the Mexicans, the Portuguese – occupy a ring of marginal positions in Figure 1.1. (The group labelled 'American' mainly refers to low-status whites in the southeast of the United States – see Lieberson and Waters 1988.) Further ethnic groups occupy intermediate positions in Figure 1.1, between core and periphery. This reflects the particular geographical distributions of these groups over the US

SERGIO DELLAPERGOLA

Figure 1.1 Smallest space analysis of territorial distribution of thirty-six selected ethnic groups, by major geographical divisions (United States, 1980)[a]

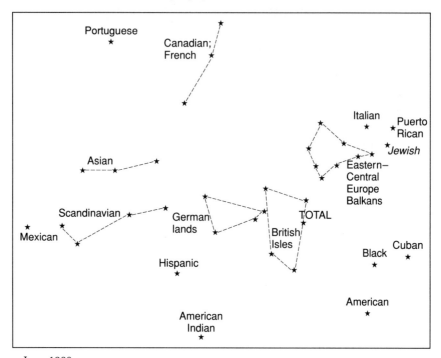

a Jews: 1988.

Sources: Lieberson and Waters (1988); *American Jewish Year Book* (1989).

territory, and possibly their position in the American social structure. These intermediate groups include several clusters of related ethnicities, such as a cluster of Eastern–Central European and Balkan countries of origin, or the strings formed by different Asian or Scandinavian countries, or by the French, French-Canadians and Canadians. Further individual ethnic groups occupy positions of their own, such as the Hispanics, the Italians and the Jews.

As might be expected, the geographical distribution of the Jews is most similar to those of Eastern European ancestry. Since the data for the Jews come from a separate source than those for the other groups shown in Figure 1.1, Jews are actually also included in the data relative to the various countries of origin. Such overlap is strongest with Russia and other countries which indeed represent the main places of origin of past Jewish immigration. Jews are also territorially close to Italians and Puerto Ricans, who share their strong concentration in the northeastern states, particularly in the New York metropolitan area. Further analyses, not shown here, also indicate that the regional geographical distribution of the Jews correlates

28

well with that of the total US labour force employed in economic branches, such as finances, whose share of Jews is relatively high.

On the light of these findings, we suggest that Figure 1.1 schematically reflects not only the physical distances between different ethnic groups over the US territory, but also the respective social distances. We may have here a graphic representation of quite a rigid and persistent system of ethno-social stratification in which social dominance tends to decline when moving from societal (and our diagram's) core, to the periphery. If this interpretation is correct, the position of the Jews in the American system of ethnic groups in the 1980s could be defined as semi-peripheral – indeed intriguingly close to the system's periphery.

Besides the inherent merits of these taxonomies, a major question concerns the amount of continuity or change in the position of the Jewish community within the American social structure. Important changes occurred between the late 1930s and the late 1980s in the geographical distribution of most ethnic groups in the US, including the Jews. As already shown in Table 1.4, the main geographical direction of these changes brought about absolute and relative population increases in the southern and western regions of the United States. The amplitude and main direction of these changes is schematically described in Figure 1.2, which shows a spatial analysis (SSA) of changes in territorial distribution of sixteen (out of the same thirty-six shown before) selected ethnic groups between 1940 and 1980; for the Jews, the comparison is between 1937 and 1988 (United States Bureau of the Census 1942; Lieberson and Waters, 1988; Linfield, 1942; Kosmin *et al.* 1989). It should be recalled that the distances shown in the SSA diagram cannot be interpreted as metric distances, but rather as the best possible graphic solution taking into account all of the data included in a given analysis.

The general trend emerging is not one of uniform convergence or divergence. We see, on the one hand, an initial cluster of mostly European ethnic groups becoming more dispersed between 1940 and 1980. Ethnic groups which we defined as associated with greater social dominance, such as the Anglo-Saxons, appear to have been more mobile than intermediate status groups, such as the Jews or the Italians. On the other hand, several of the socially weakest and more peripheral groups, such as the blacks or the American Indians, display definite patterns of convergence to the centre, implying greater integration in the mainstream of American society.

Geographical changes undergone by the Jewish population over the last fifty years appear to have been basically in the same directions as the total American population, namely westward and southward. These changes, however, did not necessarily lead to a full convergence with the majority of American society; there rather appears to have been a process of parallel geographical redistribution. Computation in Table 1.4 of a dissimilarity index between the regional distributions of Jewish and total populations

Figure 1.2 Smallest space analysis of changes in territorial distribution of sixteen
selected ethnic groups, by major geographical divisions
(United States, 1940 and 1980)[a]

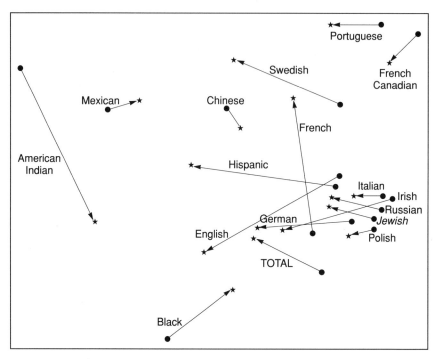

a Jews: 1937 and 1988.

Sources: US Bureau of the Census (1942); Lieberson and Waters (1988); *American Jewish Year Book* (1940; 1980).

shows that, between the 1930s and 1980s, Jews became geographically more similar to the rest of the population. However, once the particular effect of deconcentration from the New York area (Middle Atlantic) is accounted for, roughly the same amount of Jewish distinctiveness remained. The SSA analysis of geographical dissimilarity in Figure 1.2 confirms these findings by pointing to similar spatial – and perhaps also social – distances between Jews and non-Jews around 1940 and around 1980. Again, as should be expected, the one ethnic group behaving most similarly to the Jews was the Russians – most of whom were themselves Jewish. Further analyses indicate that, of the total change in country-wide geographical distribution experienced by the Jewish population over the last fifty years, nearly one-half can be attributed to the last ten or fifteen years, which points to an ongoing acceleration of social–structural changes among American Jewry. Generational and other cultural and socio-economic factors probably underlie these trends, whose momentum is far from exhausted at this point in history.

30

Although the examples reported here rely on extremely simple data classifications and processings, they quite efficiently illustrate the case of continuity and change in demographic trends, which also appears to extend to other aspects of the social structure. Another important example, illustrative of the same pattern, is the persistence over time of significant gaps between the levels of educational attainment and occupational distributions of Jews and non-Jews. Keeping in mind the deep differences which obtain in socio-economic levels attained and in patterns of occupational specialization in different periods and countries, nearly the same indexes of educational and occupational dissimilarity between Jews and non-Jews result in countries such as Germany, Hungary or Poland during the inter-war period, or for the contemporary United States, France or South Africa – in the latter case, even when occupations of Jews are compared to those of the total white population (Kuznets 1960; Goldstein 1981; Bensimon and DellaPergola 1984). Socio-economic specialization, however, should not be confused with economic dominance. There are clear costs, and not only benefits, in the concentration of many people of the same ethnic origin in a narrow – no matter how prestigious – range of occupations within the broader socio-economic context. Such concentration may involve more rapid upward mobility, in times of economic prosperity, but also greater vulnerability, in times of economic recession. It means, in any case, strong competition, and possible conflicts of interest among members of the group itself.

Summing up, the available evidence clearly points to the persistence of a strong social–structural distinctiveness of Jewish minorities over time, in comparison with other religious, national or socio-cultural minorities, or with the total population of the respective countries. This is true in spite of the extraordinary amount of geographical mobility, and of socio-economic and cultural changes experienced by the Jewish Diaspora over the last fifty years. The structural position of the Jews in the country-wide societal context rather consistently continues to be that of an intermediate group between the dominating core and the underprivileged periphery – as often depicted in the traditional role of the Jew as a middleman who fulfils a limited range of specialized functions.

JEWISH PEOPLEHOOD PERSPECTIVE

The third major type of social process we wish to consider is the changing position of the Jews with respect to the internal identificational framework of Jewish peoplehood itself. We refer to the visibility and frequency among Jewish populations of distinctly Jewish cultural and communal patterns. What conclusions can be drawn on the evolving balance of a core and a periphery *within* world Jewry from the observation of family patterns, Jewish education, religious identity, associationalism? The importance of these elements of Jewish continuity is tied to their ability to provide essential channels for the transmission of a viable community identity across generations.

We focus here on one among several indicators of socio-cultural change which can be shown to display similar patterns of evolution over time. We consider the rate of mixed marriage of Jews, i.e. Jews with non-Jewish spouses not converted to Judaism, to be an efficient indicator of ethnic cohesiveness – obviously in an inverse relationship. In doing so, the impact of other relevant structural variables, such as the size of Jewish communities and the availability of relevant marriage partners, should not be ignored in other more systematic analyses of Jewish family formation (DellaPergola 1989c).

According to classic ethnicity theory, one would expect that a substantial amount of structural assimilation is a necessary prerequisite for the subsequent stage of marital assimilation to occur (Gordon 1964). A large degree of residential and occupational proximity and similarity, and of institutional integration, would precede and facilitate the emergence of large-scale intermarriage The obvious corollary is that in the presence of strong social structural distinctiveness, other forms of assimilation would not have a great chance to develop among a given group (Goldscheider 1986). It would seem that both these propositions fail to be supported by recent empirical data. In spite of a considerable amount of Jewish social structural distinctiveness which still exists among Jews regardless of geographic location, the trend of Jewish family formation has worked its way towards ever-increasing levels of heterogamy (DellaPergola 1983).

Table 1.4 illustrates the changes that have occurred in the rates of mixed marriage among different Jewish populations over the last fifty years. World Jewish population is classified in Table 1.5 according to the rates of mixed marriage experienced in each country. The data presented are country-wide estimates, and therefore miss the significant amount of variation typical of different regions within the same country both in the past and present. It should be noted, as a word of caution, that the quality of the estimates presented varies from highly reliable to conjectural. Information on data quality is appended to Table 1.5. During the 1930s, rates of mixed marriage of around 1 to 5 per cent of all Jewish spouses that were marrying at that time were typical of a plurality (over 40 per cent) of world Jewry. This included, among other countries, the United States. Two other large sectors of world Jewry included, on the one hand, totally homogamous communities – such as Poland – with rates of mixed marriage below 1 per cent; or, on the other hand, somewhat more acculturated communities with rates of mixed marriage ranging between 5 and 14 per cent. The latter group of countries included the Soviet Union.

Clearly, extreme cohesiveness of the Jewish population, as expressed by very low mixed marriage rates, often reflected legal discrimination and separateness between Jews and non-Jews, and did not always adequately reflect more complex cultural and identificational trends that were developing within Jewish society. Yet, the prevalence of strong homogamy was a leading social fact among pre-Second World War Jewry. Jewish homogamy and ethnic cohesiveness was reinforced by the large diffusion of Jewish languages, religious practices and other cultural patterns among the Jewish public. Very few Jews – less than 3 per cent of the world total – lived in Jewish communities whose mixed marriage rates exceeded 15 per cent. This was the case in notoriously assimilated communities in Germany, Italy, the Netherlands, and even more so in small and isolated outposts, such as Australia.

What was exceptional then, turns out to be normal today. Towards the end of the 1980s, more than half of the world Jewish population lived in Jewish communities, including the United States and the USSR, where individual rates of mixed marriage range between 45 and 54 per cent. That is much above the uppermost extreme of Jewish assimilation that could be observed during the 1930s. New outposts of even more frequent heterogamy have emerged in the meanwhile, often in the same countries that have already witnessed the earlier spread of Jewish assimilation. While nearly everywhere rates of mixed marriage increased, correlation between rates during the 1930s and the 1980s was quite significant.

In recent years, the continuing increase in mixed marriage has stimulated an academic and public debate about the 'losses' or 'gains' resulting to the Jewish population from this phenomenon (Goldscheider 1986 and 1989: DellaPergola and Schmelz 1989b). The cumulative evidence of available social–scientific research rather indicates that these continuing developments can realistically be described as a slow, time-bound, chain-like process in which growing assimilation in one generation predicts and generates further assimilation in the next one. A measurable attrition to Jewish population results in the process (DellaPergola 1989d).

These mixed marriage data can be described as a process of diffusion of growing percentages of Jews from the identificational core of Jewish peoplehood towards its periphery. Such progression was scarcely affected by significant differences in the political and socio-economic environments that were available to Jews in the respective countries. Extreme differences in anti-Jewish prejudice and political discrimination that existed, for example, among the general societies of the USA and the USSR had very little effect on the eventual levels of mixed marriage in the two countries (Kosmin et al. 1991; Tolts 1991). Variation in mixed marriage frequencies rather seems to reflect broad historical and cultural patterns associated with the development of Jewish communities in different regions of the world, including whether or not legal provisions existed to limit the free interaction between different ethno-religious groups in a country. Significant social patterns underlying the increase in mixed marriage nearly everywhere include minority status of the Jews, diminishing cultural distinctiveness, often tied to the generational factor, and greater social acceptance of Jews

Table 1.5 World Jewish population distribution, by estimated frequency of current out-marriages, mid-1930s and late 1980s

Per cent of Jewish spouses currently marrying non-Jews[a]	Mid-1930s			Late 1980s		
		Jewish population			Jewish population	
	Country[b]	No. (000)	per cent of world Jewry	Country[b]	No. (000)	per cent of world Jewry
Total		16,600	100.0		12,979	100.0
0–0.9%	Poland,[1] Lithuania,[1] Greece,[2] Palestine,[2] Iran,[4] Yemen,[4] Ethiopia[4]	4,130	24.9	Israel[1]	3,659	28.2
1–4.9%	Latvia,[1] Canada,[1] United States,[2] United Kingdom,[4] Iberian pen.[4] Latin America,[4] Other Asia,[4] Maghreb,[2] Egypt,[1] Libya,[4] Southern Africa[4]	6,700	40.4	Africa (not stated elsewhere)[4]	19	0.1
5–14.9%	Switzerland,[1] France,[2] Austria,[1] Luxembourg,[1] Hungary,[1] Czechoslovakia,[1] Romania,[2] USSR,[1] Estonia,[1] Belgium,[4] Bulgaria,[4] Yugoslavia[4]	5,340	32.1	North Africa,[4] Asia (besides Israel)[4]	46	0.3
15–24.9%	Italy,[1] Germany,[1] Netherlands[1]	385	2.3	Southern Africa,[3] Mexico[3]	150	1.2
25–34.9%	Australia,[2] New Zealand,[4] Scandinavia[3]	45	0.3	Canada,[1] Australia,[3] New Zealand,[4] United Kingdom,[4] Brazil,[2] Other Latin America,[3] Europe (not mentioned elsewhere)[4]	944	7.3
35–44.9%				Argentina,[3] Italy,[2] France,[2] Belgium[4]	818	6.3
45–54.9%				United States,[2] USSR,[2] Austria,[1] Switzerland,[1] Netherlands[3]	7,186	55.4
55–64.9%				Scandinavia[3]	24	0.2
65–74.9%				West Germany,[1] Eastern Europe (besides USSR) [4]	132	1.0
75–84.9%					–	–
85–94.9%				Cuba[2]	1	0.0

Table 1.5 *cont.*

a Not Jewish at time of marriage. Out-marriage figures are country-wide or regional
  estimates. Within-country variation in out-marriage frequencies is ignored in this table.
b Data quality is rated as follows:
    1 Recent and reliable statistical data;
    2 Partial or less recent data of sufficient quality;
    3 Rather outdated or very incomplete data;
    4 Conjectural.

Source: adapted from DellaPergola (1972; 1976; 1983; 1989a), Linfield (1942), Schmelz
and DellaPergola (1990), and respective detailed references.

on the part of the non-Jewish majority. Continuing diffusion of mixed
marriage also entails a diminished opposition to it from the Jewish side. The
same centrifugal trend has probably not yet reached its terminal point:
the major explanatory factors of the growth in mixed marriage over the last
decades are still actively at work.

While this was the predominant pattern at the world level, it is quite
symbolic that by the late 1980s, the section of world Jewry featuring the
lowest level of heterogamy (less than 1 per cent) included a similar share of
world Jewry as during the 1930s (25–28 per cent). The countries included in
that section, though, had changed: modern Israeli society had replaced the
pre-war Eastern European and Middle Eastern Jewish population centres
as the proponent of a model of cohesive and almost entirely segregated
Jewish ethnicity. Here, again, we should warn against misreading a situation
supported by environmental segregation between Jews and non-Jews and the
legal absence of civil marriage, for one normatively chosen by the totality
or even the vast majority of Jewish Israelis. But, as long as the determinants
of the current patterns of Jewish family formation persist in Israel, they
constitute a significant link of continuity with a model of Jewish peoplehood
which does not exist any longer elsewhere – in any event, not as a generalized
behaviour.

To complement these data, two other important aspects of Jewish identity
maintenance should be briefly mentioned. The first one is the degree of
diffusion of Jewish languages among world Jewry. Here, two diametrically
opposed patterns appear. The knowledge and use of Jewish languages
(Yiddish, Judaeo-Spanish, Hebrew, etc.) was highly diffused throughout
Diaspora communities in the past. These languages once were important
vectors of Jewish cultural distinctiveness and creativity (Lestschinsky 1960).
It can be fairly estimated that, before the Second World War, an absolute
majority of world Jewry was fluent or at least could communicate in one of
these languages, especially Yiddish. Today, such knowledge and practice is
rapidly declining among Jews in the Diaspora, and is now the matter of
small minorities mainly confined to the elderly sections of the Jewish
population (Millman 1983). The opposite phenomenon has occurred in
Israel where along with Jewish population growth there has been a very

35

impressive revival and diffusion of the Hebrew language. Hebrew has achieved the status of the unquestioned main channel of communication, cultural integration and production among the previously heterogeneous Jewish immigrant communities in Israel (Schmelz and Bachi 1975). The area of Hebrew language and culture is actually expanding globally, mostly due to the growing share of Israel's population out of the total world Jewry.

The other and perhaps more significant aspect concerns the recent world distribution of formal Jewish education. According to the First World Census of Jewish Schools, during the early 1980s (1981–3) about 545,000 Jewish children aged 3 to 17 were currently enrolled in Jewish day (full-time) or supplementary (part-time) schools in the Diaspora. This represented a Jewish school enrolment rate of about 38 per cent of a total Diaspora Jewish school-age population estimated at 1.4 million (DellaPergola and Schmelz 1989a). At the same date, the Israeli state and private Hebrew school system had an enrolment of 973,000 Jewish pupils (Israel, Central Bureau of Statistics 1984). This means that out of the total world-wide Jewish school enrolment, a majority estimated at 64 per cent involved Jewish children in Israel; if we limit the observation of Jewish education in the Diaspora only to the more intensive day-school programmes, Israel Jewish pupils constituted 81 per cent of the world enrolment. In comparison, around 1983, the proportion in Israel out of the total world Jewish school-age population (3–17) could be estimated at 41 per cent.

Several possible channels and mechanisms of identity transmission have been outlined here – the homogamous Jewish family, use of Jewish languages and formal Jewish education. Each of the selected criteria indicates Israel's growing role as the core of Jewish ethno-religious identity maintenance and transmission among world Jewry.

SUMMARY AND DISCUSSION

Our exploratory overview suggests that the enormous changes undergone – often under the most stressful circumstances – by the Jewish people over the last fifty years resulted in different and somewhat conflicting types of development. Both the socio-economic and political position of the Jews facing world society at large, and the internal socio-cultural balance of world Jewry, emerged significantly changed in the context of the different core/periphery frameworks outlined here.

In the global perspective provided by the world-system, an absolute majority of the Jewish population gained access to economically affluent, politically stable and socially attractive environments. Central to our understanding of contemporary world Jewry should be the unprecedentedly favourable economic opportunity framework now available to most Jews in the world-system's core countries. This includes comparatively strengthened chances for higher income, high quality education and socio-economic mobility in a general environment of political freedom, technological innovation and secularization. In a sense, the *Shoah* tragically accelerated what might have been the normally expected course of affairs, namely a gradual concentration of the Jews towards the core of the world-system.

One implication of the presumed interest of those who enjoy a better socio-economic environment to preserve it, has been a growing overlap of interests between a substantial majority of contemporary world Jewry with the welfare, success and stability of the countries at the core of the world-system in which they live. In the past, when most Jews lived in semi-peripheral or peripheral countries in a world-system perspective, and in less attractive socio-economic positions from a more individual perspective, they may have been more prone to modify both their position in society, and to transform society at large. Another possible corollary of the much diminished Jewish presence in the numerically preponderant periphery of the world-system – where it once was visible, though often underprivileged – is a symmetric lack of interest of such societies towards Jewish culture or interests. This process of mutual estrangement may carry considerable social and political consequences in the longer run, as various processes involving the periphery may eventually be imported into the world-system's core, through international migrations or otherwise.

With regard to the position of Jews at the country level of national societies, conflicting mechanisms of continuity and erosion emerged. We have documented some important patterns of continuing Jewish distinctiveness. Distinctive socio-demographic and socio-economic characteristics persist today, in spite of massive changes in the actual social profile of the Jewish populations examined over the last fifty years. Significantly, social–structural diversity persists in spite of the removal of most of the legal constraints which promoted its initial emergence. Some recent American evidence indicates that, along with the progressive decline of ethnic groups' cultural distinctiveness, the choice of ethnic identification may increasingly reflect a person's socio-economic status, thus lending a different meaning to ethnic divisions and contents (Lieberson and Waters 1988). If this is true, one significant change in the current meaning of ethnicity among Diaspora Jews may be – at least in the US – its gradual transformation from sections of a world-wide confraternity of blood and creed, to a functional component of a country's system of social stratification.

Concurrently, internal transformations of unprecedented scope developed with regard to the perception, practice, contents and identity of Jewish peoplehood. With regard to Diaspora Jewries, these changes can be concisely described as a major trade-off between a very impressive strengthening in material conditions and opportunities, and an equally significant dilution of ethnic identity and continuity. Societal mechanisms – sometimes of a constrictive nature – which provided support for distinctive Jewish cultural content in the Diaspora, weakened over the last decades. Jewish group identity tends to constitute the primary focus of solidarity on the part of a diminishing share of the Jewish population, whose attention is increasingly attracted by the many available cultural and ideological alternatives. Integration of the Jews in the general society of the more developed countries exposes most of them to a pervasive and sophisticated network of cultural and social interaction. This enhances reception of a great volume of diverse cultural messages, and participation in many social contacts, some of which may support continuity of the cultural patterns of the Jewish group itself, but most of which propose challenges and alternatives to it. Mixed marriage – a significant intervening factor – may not imply total losses to the Jewish population but it reflects, and generates, a process of progressive disenchantment with Jewishness. One observes among growing sections of the Diaspora a slow downgrading of the ultimate meaning of Jewish group identity, from integral community to social group and ultimately to a mere statistical category.

Here come to mind the typologies suggested by Ruppin (1913) or Lestschinsky (1960) about the different strata of European or world Jewry during the nineteenth and early twentieth centuries, the respective degrees of acculturation and assimilation, and the chances for survival as a viable community. Many of the same criteria of classification – frequencies of secularization, heterogamy, conversion, linguistic and cultural environments – seem to be still relevant today, though perhaps they are no more sufficient. Contemporary societies may require further instruments for the assessment of Jewish cohesiveness and continuity. Theoretically, elements of the cultural construct may fall away, particularly those related to religious practices and beliefs, and new ones may emerge, without altering the basic robustness of Jewish identity. This transformation hypothesis has been prominently advanced in the context of the analysis of recent socio-demographic trends among Jews in the United States (Goldscheider and Zuckerman 1984). Recent empirical evidence, however, has so far failed to provide support for the transformation theory and rather points in the direction of erosion: no significant new patterns of Jewish identification have emerged to take the place of the weakening old ones (DellaPergola 1992).

On the other hand, in many respects the state of Israel has taken over from pre-Second World War East European Jewry the role of the core of Jewish demographic continuity and of identity preservation for the global Jewish people. Moreover, the emergence of the Israeli new core has been a strategically important factor of Jewish identification and cultural mobilization world-wide for a substantial part of the last fifty years. These major changes involving Israel's role among world Jewry go hand in hand with important typological similarities. As in the past, quite different socio-demographic patterns prevail today among different Jewish populations in Israel and in the Diaspora. The overall nature of contemporary Jewish socio-demographic processes results from the composition of these contrasting trends. To some extent, today's situation reminds one of the *West-Ostjuden* cleavages that existed among pre-1939 European Jewry (Mendelsohn 1987). Of course, we do not intend to confuse today's Israel with pre-war Poland; nor do we intend to confuse contemporary American Jewry, with its mixture of brilliant socio-economic and cultural achievements and its simultaneous demographic and identificational erosion, with interwar German Jewry. The internal and external socio-political contexts are entirely different. And yet, intriguingly, the global position of the new Israeli Jewish core is similar to what the pre-war Jewish core once was – it is at the semi-periphery of a world-system whose core countries also hold important but more acculturated Jewish communities.

The attempt to integrate these different aspects into one synthetic perspective reveals what is perhaps one of the main contradictions of the contemporary Jewish experience world-wide. Today, conflicting mechanisms of preservation and erosion affect world Jewry's material prosperity and ethnic group distinctiveness. To be part of the general society of countries at the world-system's core may guarantee – on the aggregate, if not to each individual – better chances for the preservation of freedom and security, as manifested by high standards of living, socio-economic mobility and political stability. To be part of the Israeli core of Jewish peoplehood may guarantee – again in aggregate terms – better chances for preservation of Jewish group identity and cohesiveness, as manifested by the full realization of a distinctive culture, particular institutions for the transmission of it, and homogamic family patterns. At the same time, exposure to the cultural environment of the world-system core's societies may result in a marked erosion of Jewish group identity, implying both demographic decline and growing dependency on the cultural reinforcements from Israel's Jewish core. Sharing Israel's semi-peripheral position in the world-system may result in painful socio-economic constraints and overall dependency on material resources only available at the world-system's core, as well as cultural insulation.

The various patterns of evolution, and the different poles of attraction just outlined, may be creating for the contemporary individual Jew a powerful dialectic tension, between wishing to be at the core of the world-system, and wishing to be at the core of Jewish peoplehood. One may even wonder whether these two goals are at all compatible. Renunciation of cultural distinctiveness and insulation may be, after all, one of the prices demanded of a human society in order to definitively achieve political and socio-economic power as well as stability. If the two goals are compatible, however, two major challenges appear to confront world Jewry: on the one hand, to bring the state of Israel into the more developed core of the world-system of societies; and on the other hand, to keep the majority or at least sizeable sections of the Diaspora within a recognizable pattern of identification with Jewish peoplehood.

Under the present circumstances, increasing differences may be developing between Jews in Israel and in the Diaspora, enhanced by patterns of selective international migration from and towards the two alternative cores outlined here. Moreover, the different sets of socio-economic and cultural opportunities and constraints naturally tied to each type of place and society are likely to generate different personal attitudes, socio-economic characteristics and demographic behaviour. Excessive stretching of the polarization between Israel and the Diaspora Jewries at the world-system's core much beyond what exists now, might eventually call into question the continuing relevance of a unitary frame of reference for the study and assessment of the contemporary Jewish people.

At the end of the 1980s, a fifty-year period of history seems to have reached completion, dominated by the Second World War and its long Cold War aftermath, and a new period has opened, marked by significant changes in the political structure of European countries and more generally in the global strategic equilibrium. As we noted at the beginning, our analysis was not meant to focus on process but rather on the end-product of fifty years of socio-demographic continuity and change in world Jewry. Such an end-product seems to reflect three major types of factors, in declining order of importance: the exogenous factor of *Shoah*; the factor of mass international migrations; and the endogenous factors of vital processes and identificational changes. Predictive theory, mostly focusing on the role of endogenous factors, would have missed, in the case dealt here, a crucial part of past realities. From the vantage point of what seems to be quite a momentous stage of transition between distinct historical periods, it can be asked whether we can really expect that in the foreseeable future the balance between the different types of factors just mentioned will continue to be basically similar to what it is now.

We hope to have shown that any systematic attempt to draw conclusions about the main thrust of the long-range changes affecting Jewish populations and societies requires an appropriate balance between theoretical formulations and documented substantiation based on extensive use of empirical data at the local, national and international level. A serious analysis of the qualitative contents of the Jewish experience should be put in the frame of reference that only an understanding of concrete demographic and sociological facts can provide. Some of the trends described and the questions raised in this paper may provide a rough blueprint which can help in monitoring the Jewish demographic and socio-cultural trends that will unfold within the newly emerging world context over the next fifty years and beyond.

ACKNOWLEDGEMENTS

This is a substantially revised version of the paper originally presented at the International Academic Conference on *A New Jewish World? Continuity and*

Change, 1939–1989, The Hebrew University of Jerusalem, The Institute of Contemporary Jewry, Mount Scopus, December 1989. I am grateful to Alice and Sidney Goldstein, Calvin Goldscheider, Robert Wistrich and Uziel O. Schmelz for providing thorough critiques of the original text, and hold sole responsibility for the paper's contents. The paper was revised during the author's stay at the Institute for Advanced Studies of the Hebrew University of Jerusalem.

REFERENCES

Bachi, R. (1976) *Population Trends of World Jewry.* Jerusalem, The Hebrew University, Jewish Population Studies, 9.

Bachi, R. (1977) *The Population of Israel.* Jerusalem, The Hebrew University and Prime Minister's Office, Demographic Center, Jewish Population Studies, 11.

Baron, S. W. (1952–83) *A Social and Religious History of the Jews,* 2nd edn. New York, Columbia University Press, 18 vols.

Ben-Sasson, H. H. (ed.) (1976) *History of the Jewish People.* London, Weidenfeld & Nicolson.

Bensimon, D. and DellaPergola, S. (1984) *La population juive de France: socio-démographie et identité.* Jerusalem, The Hebrew University, and Paris, Centre National de la Recherche Scientifique, Jewish Population Studies, 17.

Camp, S. L. and Speidel, J. J. (1987) *The International Human Suffering Index.* Washington, DC, Population Crisis Committee.

DellaPergola, S. (1972) *Jewish and Mixed Marriages in Milan, 1901–1968; with an Appendix: Frequency of Mixed Marriages among Diaspora Jews.* Jerusalem, The Hebrew University, Jewish Population Studies, 3.

DellaPergola, S. (1976) 'Demographic perspectives of mixed marriage', *Encyclopaedia Judaica Year Book, 1975/6,* pp. 198–210.

DellaPergola, S. (1983) *La trasformazione demografica della diaspora ebraica.* Torino, Loescher.

DellaPergola, S. (1986) '*Aliya* and other Jewish migrations: toward an integrated perspective', in U. O. Schmelz and G. Nathan (eds), *Studies in the Population of Israel in Honor of Roberto Bachi. Scripta Hierosolymitana,* vol. 30, pp. 172–209.

DellaPergola, S. (1989a) 'Changing patterns of Jewish demography in the modern world', *Studia Rosenthaliana.* Special issue published with vol. 23, 2, Proceedings of the 5th International Symposium on the History of the Jews in the Netherlands, pp. 154–74.

DellaPergola, S. (1989b) 'Mass *Aliyah* – a thing of the past?', *Jerusalem Quarterly,* 51, pp. 96–114.

DellaPergola, S. (1989c) *Recent Trends in Jewish Marriage.* Jerusalem, The Hebrew University, Institute of Contemporary Jewry, Division of Jewish Demography and Statistics, Occasional Paper 1989-07.

DellaPergola, S. (1989d) 'Marriage, conversion, children and Jewish continuity: some demographic aspects of "Who is a Jew"?', in W. Frankel and A. Lerman (eds), *Survey of Jewish Affairs 1989.* Oxford, Basil Blackwell for the Institute of Jewish Affairs, pp. 171–87.

DellaPergola, S. (1992) *New Data on Demography and Identification among Jews in the U.S.: Trends, Inconsistencies and Disagreements.* Jerusalem, The Hebrew University, Institute of Contemporary Jewry, Division of Jewish Demography and Statistics, Occasional Paper 1992-11.

DellaPergola, S. and Schmelz, U. O. (1989a) 'Demography and Jewish education in the Diaspora: trends in Jewish school-age population and school enrolment', in H. S. Himmelfarb and S. DellaPergola (eds), *Jewish Education Worldwide:*

Crosscultural Perspectives. Lanham, Md., University Press of America, and Jerusalem, The Hebrew University of Jerusalem, *Jewish Population Studies*, 21, pp. 43–68.

DellaPergola, S. and Schmelz, U. O. (1989b) 'Demographic transformations of American Jewry: marriage and mixed marriage in the 1980s', in P. Y. Medding (ed.), *Studies in Contemporary Jewry*. New York, Oxford University Press, 5, pp. 169–200.

Eisenstadt, S. N. (1985) *The Transformation of Israeli Society: An Essay in Interpretation*. London, Weidenfeld & Nicolson.

Goldscheider, C. (1986) *The American Jewish Community: Social Science Research and Policy Implications*. Atlanta, Scholars Press.

Goldscheider, C. (1989) 'American Jewish marriages: erosion or transformation?', in P. Y. Medding (ed.), *Studies in contemporary Jewry*. New York, Oxford University Press, 5, pp. 201–8.

Goldscheider, C. and Zuckerman, A. S. (1984) *The Transformation of the Jews*. Chicago, University of Chicago Press.

Goldstein, S. (1981) 'Jews in the United States: perspectives from demography', *The American Jewish Year Book*, vol. 81, pp. 3–59.

Goldstein, S. and Kosmin, B. (1991) 'Religious and ethnic self-identification in the United States 1989–90: a case study of the Jewish population'. Paper presented at the Population Association of America annual meeting, Washington, DC.

Gordon, M. (1964) *Assimilation in American Life: The Role of Race, Religion and National Origins*. New York, Oxford University Press.

Gradus, Y. (1986) 'Regional autonomy in Israel', in D. Morley and A. Shachar (eds), *Planning in Turbulence*. Jerusalem, The Magnes Press, The Hebrew University, pp. 97–106.

Israel, Central Bureau of Statistics (1984) *Statistical Abstract of Israel*, 35.

Kosmin, B., Scheckner, J. and Ritterband, P. (1989) 'Jewish population in the United States, 1988', *American Jewish Yearbook*, 88, pp. 233–52.

Kosmin, B., Goldstein, S., Waksberg, J., Lerer, N., Keysar, A. and Sheckner, J. (1991) *Highlights of the CJF 1990 National Jewish Population Survey*. New York, Council of Jewish Federations.

Kuznets, S. (1960) 'Economic structure and life of the Jews', in L. Finkelstein (ed.), *The Jews: Their History, Culture and Religion*. New York, Harper, vol. 2, pp. 1597–666.

Lestschinsky, J. (1960) 'New conditions of life among Jews in the Diaspora', *The Jewish Journal of Sociology*, 2, 2, pp. 139–46.

Levy, M. L. (1989) 'Tous les pays du monde (1989)', *Populations et sociétés*, 237.

Lieberson, S. and Waters, M. (1986) 'Ethnic groups in the flux: the changing ethnic responses of American whites', *Annals of the American Academy of Political and Social Science*, 487, pp. 79–91.

Lieberson, S. and Waters, M. (1988) *From Many Strands: Ethnic and Racial Groups in Contemporary America*. New York, Russell Sage Foundation (The Population of the United States in the 1980s – A Census Monograph Series).

Linfield, H. S. (1942) 'Statistics of Jews', *American Jewish Year Book*, 43, pp. 649–98.

McEvedy, C. and Jones, R. (1978) *Atlas of World Population History*. Harmondsworth, Penguin Books.

Martuzzi-Veronesi, F., Pettener, D. and Gueresi, P. (1990) 'Struttura biologica delle popolazioni', in M. Livi Bacci and F. Martuzzi-Veronesi (eds), *Le risorse umane del Mediterraneo*. Bologna, Il Mulino, pp. 41–70.

Mendelsohn, E. (1987) *The Jews of East Central Europe between the World Wars*. Bloomington, Indiana University Press.

Millman, I. I. (1983) 'Data on Diaspora populations from official censuses', in U. O. Schmelz, P. Glikson and S. J. Gould (eds), *Studies in Jewish Demography; Survey for 1972–1980*. Jerusalem, The Hebrew University and London, The Institute of Jewish Affairs, pp. 33–120.

Petersen, W. (1987) 'Politics and the measurement of ethnicity', in W. Alonso and P. Starr (eds), *The Politics of Numbers*. New York, Russell Sage Foundation, pp. 187–233 (The Population of the United States in the 1980s – A Census Monograph Series).

Ricci, R. (1990) 'Rapporti e scambi economico-sociali', in M. Livi Bacci and F. Martuzzi-Veronesi (eds), *Le risorse umane del Mediterraneo*. Bologna, Il Mulino, pp. 315–55.

Ruppin, A. (1913) *The Jews of Today*. New York, Holt.

Schmelz, U. O. (1989) *World Jewish Population in the 1980s: A Short Outline*. Jerusalem, The Hebrew University, Institute of Contemporary Jewry, Division of Jewish Demography and Statistics, Occasional Paper 1989-06.

Schmelz, U. O. (1991) *The Demographic Impact of the Holocaust on the Jewish People*. Jerusalem, The Hebrew University, Institute of Contemporary Jewry, Division of Jewish Demography and Statistics, Occasional Paper 1991-10.

Schmelz, U. O. and Bachi, R. (1975) 'Hebrew as everyday language of the Jews in Israel – statistical appraisal', in *Salo Wittmayer Baron Jubilee Volume*. Jerusalem, American Academy for Jewish Research, pp. 745–85.

Schmelz, U. O. and DellaPergola, S. (1990) 'World Jewish population, 1988', *American Jewish Year Book*, 90, pp. 514–32.

Schmelz, U. O. and DellaPergola, S. (1991) 'World Jewish population, 1989', *American Jewish Year Book*, 91, pp. 441–65.

Schmelz, U. O., DellaPergola, S. and Avner, U. (1991) *Ethnic Differences among Israeli Jews: A New Look*. Jerusalem, The Hebrew University, *Jewish Population Studies*, 22.

Schmelz, U. O., Glikson, P. and Gould, S. J. (1983) *Studies in Jewish Demography; Survey for 1972–1980*. Jerusalem, The Hebrew University, and London, The Institute of Jewish Affairs, *Jewish Population Studies*, 14.

Schnapper, D. (1987) 'Les limités de la démographie des juifs de la diaspora', *Revue Française de Sociologie*, 28, pp. 319–32.

Shachar, A. (1989) 'Israel among the nations: on determining Israel's position between developed and underdeveloped world', Paper presented at the Symposium on *Trends of Change in Israeli Society*. Jerusalem, The Hebrew University (in Hebrew).

Sharot, S. (1976) *Judaism: A Sociology*. London, David & Charles.

Shils, E. (1961) 'Centre and periphery', in *The Logic of Personal Knowledge: Essays in Honor of Michael Polanyi*. Glencoe, Free Press.

Snyder, D. and Kick, E. L. (1979) 'Structural position in the world system and economic growth, 1955–1970: multiple-network analysis of transnational inter-actions', *American Journal of Sociology*, 84, 6, pp. 1096–126.

Tolts, M. (1991) 'Jewish marriages in the USSR: a demographic analysis'. Moscow, Jewish Research Center, Soviet Sociological Association, USSR Academy of Sciences (mimeo.).

United States Bureau of the Census (1942) *Statistical Abstract of the United States*. Washington, DC, Government Printer.

Wallerstein, I. (1974–80) *The Modern World System*. New York, Academic Press.

Waters, M. C. (1990) *Ethnic Options. Choosing Identities in America*. Berkeley, University of California Press.

2

THE DEMOGRAPHIC IMPACT
OF THE HOLOCAUST

U. O. Schmelz

The Nazi mass murder of the Jews reduced their number in Europe from about 9.5 million on the eve of the Second World War to less than 4 million according to a rough estimate for mid-1948. This figure includes repatriates from the Asian territories of the USSR and those who would shortly leave Europe for the newly founded State of Israel.[1] This constituted a decrease of more than 5.5 million Jews in Europe – somewhat more than the corresponding decrease of about 5 million for the whole of world Jewry, which had numbered more than 16 million in 1939 and was still more than 11 million in 1948. The diminution of Jewry world-wide was smaller than in Europe, because of some natural increase that occurred outside that continent in the interval 1939–48.

Actually, the devastating losses attributable to the Holocaust surpassed the figure of 5.5 million since there had been a wave of Jewish births immediately after the Second World War, as part of the 'baby boom' in all the developed countries. The boom was very conspicuous among Holocaust survivors who sought to reconstitute truncated families and who comprised relatively high numbers of adults of reproductive age. Consequently, the direct losses of the Holocaust approached 6 million Jews, lending support to the usually accepted magnitude of this disaster. Speaking very broadly, the Holocaust reduced the number of European Jews by about two-thirds and world Jewry by about one-third.

However, this is not the full picture, because of further, albeit indirect, demographic losses. The Holocaust consisted not only of gassing, slaughter and infliction of death through starvation, other privations, exhaustion and resultant diseases – but expressed itself also in a drastic reduction of Jewish births. Most populations grew at that time through natural increase. Had it not been for the Holocaust, larger Jewish populations in Europe and in the world could have been expected after the middle of the 1940s than in the late 1930s (see Appendix I).

CHANGES OF SPATIAL DISTRIBUTION

Two processes operated to this effect – the geographically differential impact of the Holocaust and those Jewish migrations, especially intercontinental or international ones, that were wholly or partly due to the Holocaust.

The Holocaust took place almost exclusively in Europe. A part of the Jews of Germany, Austria and Czechoslovakia managed to escape in time, most of them leaving Europe. England and a few neutral states of Europe were not invaded. Of the countries occupied or dominated by the Nazis, the destruction of Jewish lives was greatest in Eastern Europe, with the exception of Romania and especially Bulgaria (as well as the unoccupied regions of the Soviet Union).[2] In continental Western Europe, Jewish losses were relatively heavier in Holland and Belgium than in France.

During the war years the intensity of Jewish migrations within Europe was quite extraordinary. Most Jews were on the move – and a great many repeatedly so – either seeking shelter or being transported to ghettos and camps. Only relatively few Jews managed to escape then from Europe, some by staying temporarily in Asian regions of the USSR.

However, soon after the war ended, an exodus from Europe of the Jewish survivors set in. Among the push-factors were the haunting memories of the Holocaust and dismal experiences of Jewish returnees (e.g. the Kielce pogrom). Among the pull-factors ranked foremost the frantic hope and eventual reality of a Jewish homeland in Eretz Israel, motivating what was termed 'illegal immigration' by the British Mandatory authorities, and which subsequently became the European share of the mass immigration in the earliest years of the State of Israel.

In consequence of the large-scale annihilation of European Jewry and the ensuing exodus from Europe, the relative distribution of the Jewish people according to continents of residence was radically changed. While the Americas had accounted for only a third of world Jewry before the Holocaust, they formed about a half afterwards. The share of Eretz Israel rose from less than 3 per cent of the Jewish people before the Holocaust to approximately 12 per cent by 1951, following the mass immigration to the newly founded Jewish State.[3] On the other hand the proportion of European among world Jewry dropped during 1939–51 from nearly 60 per cent to only 30 per cent.

Even within Europe, considerable movements of Jews from the Eastern to the Western regions of the continent took place in the wake of the Holocaust. A large part of the post-Holocaust *briḥah* (flight) soon moved on to Israel, while others settled in Western Europe. Instead of the previously flourishing Jewries of Central and East–Central Europe a void had been created. The Jewish survivors on that continent became geographically polarized – concentrating either in the USSR (and secondarily in Romania and Hungary) or else in France and England.

Neither were all these only geographical relocations. Actually they implied changed ethnic, linguistic, cultural, social and economic surroundings for the survivors and their offspring, leading to profound changes in the composition and characteristics of the remnants of European Jewry and of the Jewish people altogether. In particular the focus of the Diaspora shifted from the relatively backward setting of Eastern Europe, with its *shtetl* culture, to the USA that offered wide opportunities to Jews. Furthermore, Israel set out on its own course of statehood and development.

CHANGES IN AGE–SEX DISTRIBUTION

The age–sex distributions of the afflicted Jewish populations were also greatly affected by the Holocaust. Children and old people, the age categories of smallest physical staying power, suffered most. Both the mass destruction of Jewish children and the paucity of births during the Holocaust caused specific and serious deficiencies in the birth-year composition of the surviving remnants of the Jewish populations. On the other hand, the lesser mortality of young adults made itself felt by their increased proportions among the survivors. Forty-seven per cent of the approximately 350,000 immigrants from Europe to the new State of Israel during 1948–52 were then aged 20–44 years. At the time that the Holocaust had ended they had been even younger by several years. Moreover, children up to the age of 4 formed fully 10 per cent in this computation; they should however be omitted, as having been mostly born after the Holocaust and under the completely altered conditions of the 'baby boom'. If so, the proportion of 20–44-year-old immigrants from Europe to Israel during 1948–52 rises to 52 per cent.

The especially heavy losses of elderly people along with the large share of young adults among the immediate survivors caused severe departures from an ordinary, far more evenly spread age distribution. It could not fail to have its economic, social and specifically Jewish cultural effects. For some time the large proportion of young and (as the years advanced) of middle-aged persons probably caused enhanced representation of the survivors in the labour force and may have assisted their economic recuperation. Of late, forty-five to fifty years after the Holocaust, those who once were young adults are swelling the ranks of Jewish elderly with concomitant effects on the Jewish populations of their countries of residence.

Sex-differential and sex–age-differential losses of Jewish lives during the Holocaust seem however to have been irregular, depending on the particular fate of the Jewish group afflicted. In the Diaspora, the resulting age–sex imbalances may have sometimes operated as a demographic incentive to out-marriage by surviving Jews.

Despite incontestable great changes brought about by the Holocaust, some continuity of basic demographic peculiarities and trends among the Jews exists and will be analysed in the following sections.

46

FEATURES OF PARTIAL DEMOGRAPHIC CONTINUITY

Modern demographic trends

In order to understand the evolution of Jewish populations in the pre-Holocaust and post-Holocaust periods, and its relationship to the general demographic evolution of the developed countries, it is necessary to briefly characterize the latter.

(a) Some principal modern trends of population structure have been the following: urbanization and especially the formation of large metropolitan areas; great progress in formal education; occupational changes of the labour force associated with transformations in the economy, such as growing shares of commerce and services as well as of managerial tasks; ageing of populations.

(b) Regarding demographic dynamics: continual mortality reduction; but also strong limitation of fertility and of the rates of births and natural increase, assisted by innovations in contraceptive techniques; of late, decreasing propensity and stability of marriage (i.e., a rise in divorce); therefore declining – and by now even negative – prospects of intergenerational replacement.

(c) In our times, the ageing of populations is chiefly determined by prolonged low fertility. Demographic ageing, in turn, impairs the balance of natural movement and the prospects of intergenerational replacement, since elderly people have fewer children and obviously die at a greater rate than younger adults.

(d) Decline of fertility and replacement can go hand in hand with notable socio-economic success. In recent years the fertility of most of the economically very advanced nations, including the USA, has been below intergenerational replacement requirements; and the current balance of natural movement in Germany, despite that country's economic lead in Europe, has been outrightly negative (deaths outnumbering births).

(e) The modern evolution of populations – by now gradually extending, at least in part, from the developed countries to most of mankind – is viewed by demographers as largely consisting of a transition from traditional to the above-outlined novel patterns.

(f) While rather low natural increase (or possibly decrease) is likely to continue in the developed countries, its actual level – below minimal replacement needs, as at present, or perhaps somewhat above – had cautiously best be considered as an open issue which only the empirical future will decide.

Jews and demographic modernity[4]

In briefest outline it may be stated that in most of the above respects the Jews of the developed Diaspora countries have both preceded and exceeded their host population. For historical reasons the Jews have had a long record of urban or semi-urban residence, of concentration in non-manual occupations as well as of intellectual training, though the latter was in the past primarily of a religious character and beneficial to men rather than to women. Further, the Jews have preceded and outdone the corresponding general populations in the reduction first of mortality and then of fertility, and consequently in attaining low or negative rates of natural increase and intergenerational replacement.

In the twentieth century essential synchronization has prevailed between the Diaspora[5] and the general populations of the developed countries in the timing – though not the intensity – of the major phases in the evolution of fertility and natural increase: a prolonged downward trend during the first decades of this century, eventually exacerbated by the economic recession of the 1930s and the Second World War; a 'baby boom' after the war; and a drastic fertility shrinkage in recent decades. As stated, the latter was connected with changes in nuptiality and divorce patterns, and innovations in contraceptive techniques.

Besides, nearly everywhere in the Diaspora the Jews are now but relatively small sub-populations, mostly living in the midst of largely secularized and 'open' societies. As such they are exposed to the demographic challenges of assimilation and, in particular, of out-marriage. According to the fragmentary evidence available, out-marriages of Jews are frequent in the Diaspora today and consist increasingly of non-conversionary, overtly mixed unions, the majority of whose offspring are not raised as Jews. This adds another factor of demographic attrition for the contemporary Diaspora: very low fertility, intensive ageing as well as net losses through assimilation. It also necessitates a conceptual distinction between entire fertility (or, respectively, natural increase) in the Diaspora and its effectively Jewish scope – excluding those children of Jewish parentage who are not raised as Jews.

Moreover, the immigrations of Jews may not necessarily be a long-term remedy against negative trends of natural movement and of the assimilatory balance among the communities of destination. In the global context of world Jewry, migrations are initially no more than internal transfers (only in the longer run may they lead to a change in subsequent evolution). In a specific country of destination they will be no help in the long run against eventual decrease in the number of Jews, if the above-mentioned internal trends continue to be negative and demographically fritter away the migratory reinforcement.

THE HOLOCAUST AND DEMOGRAPHIC MODERNIZATION TRENDS AMONG THE JEWS

Consideration of these relationships requires some geo-cultural distinctions.

Eastern Europe

In the decades prior to the Holocaust, East European Jewry (including the Balkans), which then constituted the largest segment of the Jewish people, was undergoing a rapid transition from comparatively traditional to modern patterns. This applied not only to the spiritual and intellectual spheres but also to demographic aspects. Concentration in larger cities and the level of secular education increased, notable occupational shifts occurred towards more modern branches of the economy or more modern types of activity in branches customary among Jews. Mortality among the Jews continued to decline rapidly, boosting their natural increase up to a certain stage, although this increase slowed down later owing to the accelerated decline in fertility and the birthrate. During the period of greatest natural increase, which lasted until the beginning of the twentieth century, the East European Jews experienced strong economic pressures due to their natural increase. These were among the underlying determinants of mass emigration to the West, especially to the United States. Eventually, however, migration was largely barred: first by restrictive American legislation concerning immigration and then by a virtual ban on exits from the Soviet Union. The curtailment of the migratory outlet must have enhanced the economic motivation for demographic modernization in terms of birth control.

The establishment of the communist regime in what became the Soviet Union had far-reaching consequences for the Jews. For several decades until the end of the Second World War it divided the Jews into two sections, those inside and those outside the USSR. Within the Soviet Union freedom of movement was granted to the Jews, large numbers of whom left the 'Pale of settlement' of tsarist times – with its many *shtetls* and specific traditional culture – and moved to the largest and fast modernizing cities. New social, educational and occupational opportunities were opened to them but they were also exposed to cultural assimilation including secularization, low fertility trends and out-marriage. Besides, they did not fail to share the hardships of the general population during the 1920s and 1930s. In Eastern Europe, outside the Soviet Union, the trends of demographic modernization operated more gradually but also there the cumulative effects on the Jews became increasingly significant. In the 1930s, the economic recession, repressive and more or less overtly anti-Semitic regimes, and the spreading shadows cast by Nazi Germany led, on the whole, to lower fertility and ageing tendencies among the Jews, notwithstanding the continued existence among them of traditional sectors with high reproduction. According to official statistics, the natural increase of the Jews in Poland had already dropped below 1 per cent annually by the first half of the 1930s and reached 1 per 1,000 – virtually zero population growth – in Romania during the years 1936–8.

The Holocaust then exterminated physically the vast majority of East European Jewry. It was followed by the communist takeover in the Soviet satellite states. After the creation of Israel, most survivors outside the now enlarged territory of the USSR left Eastern Europe altogether, migrating primarily to the Jewish State. These major upheavals swept away the previously subsisting nuclei of traditionalism, both spiritual and socio-demographic, among East European Jewry.

In recent decades, a short-lived 'baby boom' directly after the Second World War was followed by very low Jewish fertility;[6] a birthrate insufficient to balance deaths; consequent natural decrease; very marked ageing; and high levels of out-marriage, especially in the Soviet satellite countries. To give just two illustrations of the extent of the ageing process, which, as already explained, has implications for natural increase/decrease: the Soviet population census of 1970 reported for the Jews of the Russian Republic (RSFSR), who then officially numbered 800,000, that only 7 per cent were in the ages 0–10 as against 16 per cent aged 50–59 and 26 per cent aged 60 and over. The Federation of Jewish Communities in Romania reported in 1979 (that is, after the majority of Jews had emigrated, particularly to Israel), 40 per cent who were aged 66 and above.

Comparing the present demographic situation with that at the beginning of the twentieth century, East European Jewry – or rather what is left of it – has moved from the top to a very low position in the ranking of European-American Jewish populations concerning levels of growth or decrease, while undergoing an opposite change (from low to high) with regard to demographic ageing.

If one were to hypothesize about the demographic evolution of East European Jewry had the Holocaust not occurred, it seems probable that these communities would in any event have moved in the direction of reduced fertility, ageing and intensified out-marriage, though more slowly and to a lesser degree than actually happened after the Holocaust and largely as a result of that catastrophe. This hypothesis seems likely, given the recent fertility and ageing trends among the general populations throughout the developed countries – including Eastern Europe – as well as among Diaspora Jewry as a whole (accompanied as it is among the Jews by rising out-marriage). Such a demographic pattern was already displayed by East European Jewry itself as early as the 1930s.

Central Europe

The other major branch of pre-Holocaust European Jewry lived mainly in the centre of that continent – in Germany, Austria (within its reduced borders after the First World War), the western parts of Czechoslovakia, Hungary and Italy. German Jewry was the largest and best documented. In all these countries the Jewish populations were reinforced by contingents of the large exodus from Eastern Europe at the turn of the nineteenth century. The majority of these arrivals were undergoing rapid acculturation, with its demographic implications, before the era of the Holocaust.

Central European Jewry prominently displayed, at a comparatively early period, advanced stages of demographic modernization. Structurally, it exhibited high urbanization and educational attainments, concentration in the tertiary sector of the economy (commerce and services) or in modern branches of production, with a growing proportion of persons in managerial positions or the liberal professions. Its demographic dynamics gave early evidence of very low Jewish fertility, rapid ageing and considerable out-marriage. Central European Jewry approached zero population growth already prior to the First World War. It arrived at a negative current growth (yearly deaths outnumbering yearly births) throughout the whole region as early as the middle of the 1920s – that is clearly before the onset of the great economic crisis and the seizure of power in Germany by the Nazis. Indifference to Jewishness and estrangement were widespread; out-marriages were growing rapidly. In all these respects no less than with regard to its conspicuous socio-economic rise and cultural success, Central European Jewry prior to the 1930s anticipated the demographic situation now prevailing throughout the Diaspora and especially in the Western countries – of course, in a different era and under historically very different circumstances.

Central European Jewry was destroyed through Nazi extermination, forced emigration and the dispersion of the survivors. But since its demographic characteristics still continue to manifest themselves in the Diaspora on a pervasive scale, one can find here a typological continuity, as distinct from physical and/or geographical continuity.

Western countries

In the mid-nineteenth century the Jewish populations both of the West European countries and outside the Old World were rather small and assimilated to their surroundings; by the turn of the nineteenth century they were being transformed by a large influx of East European Jews. The newcomers, who brought with them the traditionalism still extant in their regions of origin, initially retarded the overall socio-demographic evolution of the Western Jewries. Subsequently, in particular after the First World War, they became increasingly integrated and participated intensively in the processes we have characterized as modern – continuing to do so ever since. With the exception of the Jewish populations of Holland, Belgium and partly that of France, they were also spared Nazi extermination and therefore preserved physical continuity. The question arises whether the typological continuity of the modern socio-demographic trends among them was actually affected by the Holocaust, and if so – to what effect? It seems plausible that some Western Jews who lived during the Holocaust period outside Nazi control assimilated faster to their non-Jewish surroundings, and displayed higher out-marriage, than might otherwise have been the case. Among other Western Jews, on the contrary, the conscious resolve to maintain their Jewishness may have been strengthened. However, this must remain hypothetical in the absence of hard data from comprehensive investigations.

FROM 1939 TO THE PRESENT

In 1939 the Jewish people was socio-demographically more variegated than it appears at present. Besides the three geo-cultural and demographic types already outlined – those in Eastern Europe, Central Europe and in the Western countries – it comprised the still very traditional Jews in the Islamic countries of Asia and North Africa as well as the budding Jewish community of Eretz Israel. However, the latter, though endowed with the capacity for considerable growth as the future would show, amounted to merely 3 per cent of world Jewry by 1939. At that time it was primarily composed of East European Jews who were experiencing rapid fertility reduction in the 1930s. Yet, the age composition of the 'pioneers' was unusually youthful, the result being considerable natural increase even in that period.

The Holocaust virtually liquidated Central European Jewry and severely diminished that of Eastern Europe. Almost all Jews abandoned the Islamic countries and their great majority has been ingathered in Israel. Today only two major socio-demographic types stand out in world Jewry, one characteristic of the Diaspora and the other of Israel. The Jewish populations remaining in the Diaspora – which still constitute a majority of the Jewish people (about two-thirds by 1991) – are remarkably similar in their demographic features especially with regards to the trends operating among them. They all manifest advanced urbanization and educational attainments, modern occupational profiles, very low fertility and tendencies towards natural decrease, ageing and intensified assimilation associated with out-marriage. Nor are these commonalities surprising, for those very features (including intergroup marriages of various kinds) are now also common to the non-Jewish populations of the highly developed countries in which nearly all Diaspora Jews live. From the socio-evolutionary viewpoint it can be stated that most Jews remaining in the Diaspora are descendants, at a remove of two to four generations, of the historical Jewry of Eastern Europe.

The Jews living in Israel also constitute a structurally modern population but their nuptiality and especially their fertility patterns stand in sharp contrast to those among Diaspora Jewry and indeed among the other developed countries in the contemporary world. Though they share with others a very low mortality, their propensity to marriage and the stability of their marriages have so far been greater. Moreover they manifest considerable fertility and natural increase well above replacement needs, thus permitting natural growth regardless of the external migration balance. In this crucial respect for future population prospects they differ from the other developed nations and – with even greater differentials – from all major Diaspora communities. Unlike the latter, they are not handicapped by frequent out-marriages and net assimilatory losses. More interesting still, common demographic features are shared at present not only by the various often very distant Diaspora communities, but also by the several ethnic-origin groups within Israel's composite Jewish population. Thus, Jews of European-American and Asian-African origins in Israel generally share today a common demographic profile[7] which clearly differs from that prevailing in the Diaspora. Gone are the striking differentials in mortality levels, marriage patterns and fertility that obtruded themselves in the 1950s, after the mass *aliyah* in the early years of the State. In all these respects, an astonishing degree of uniformity has been reached between the major origin groups of Jews in Israel. This applies also to the marked wish for future children, i.e. to fertility expectations.[8] The substantial level of those expectations and the basic difference between having majority status in Israel as against minority status with contingent assimilatory losses in the Diaspora, are certain to perpetuate the demographic disparities between Israel and the Diaspora for decades to come. In fact, the only major sector of Jews that clearly deviates demographically from the general pattern in Israel are the ultra-orthodox, whose fertility far surpasses that of the rest.[9] It is true that even in Israel Jews are still considerably surpassed in fertility by their Arab neighbours; however, Arab fertility has gone down remarkably during recent decades and is now below that of the ultra-orthodox minority among Israel's Jewish population.

The existence of a considerable fertility level among Israeli Jews is abundantly and consistently documented. However, its causation, which is certainly complex, is far from being satisfactorily explained. In the context of this article the question inevitably arises: has the unforgettable trauma of the Holocaust had any effect, among other determinants, especially on the Jews of European origin, who have raised their fertility in Israel, whereas the Asian-African Jews have reduced theirs. The question deserves to be posed but in the absence of hard evidence, it cannot be answered on the empirical level.

One of the recurrent and arresting features in the long history of the Jews is their resilience following major crises. On the national level this can be followed over millennia: after each of the many calamities which have befallen this ancient people in the course of history, its remnants – often after great losses, physical and/or identificational – have rallied again for a phase of renewed vitality. Even after the catastrophe of the Holocaust which might have disheartened others, the Jews have impressively displayed this age-old capacity for recovery both in the establishment and defence of the State of Israel and in the spectacular socio-economic rise of Jewish individuals – indeed entire communities – in the Western world today, particularly in the United States. With regard to the Diaspora, however, it should be firmly realized that socio-economic success and the consequent sense of gratification are under current conditions no guarantee, in demographic terms, for reproductive replacement or for a positive net balance of assimilatory shifts between a minority group, like the Jews, and the 'open', receptive majority populations.

The estimated size of world Jewry which was more than 16 million prior to the Holocaust, has hovered somewhat below 13 million during recent years, in a state of virtually zero population growth. This recent situation has been the net result of two opposite tendencies: numerical decrease in the Diaspora was counterbalanced by growth in Israel. However, the natural increase of Israel's Jews will not be able to balance much longer the intensifying shrinkage of the Diaspora due to the fertility crisis, ageing and assimilatory losses. Strong *aliyah*, such as the recent wave from the Soviet Union, further accentuates the disparate trends in the Diaspora and in Israel.[10] The inevitable consequence will be a continuing diminution of the world Jewish population, as illustrated by demographic projections in Appendix II. The final point I wish to make is that there is no hope of recovering in the foreseeable future the pre-Holocaust size of world Jewry. Moreover, the relative magnitude of world Jewry is on the decrease *vis-à-vis* the still ongoing slow growth of most developed nations and especially the population explosion elsewhere, including in most Arab states. This brings us back to our starting point – the truncation of the Jewish people that was indeed wrought by the Holocaust.

APPENDIX I: ESTIMATION OF HOLOCAUST LOSSES

It is futile to attempt to establish the total of direct losses by compiling and summing up information on camp inmates, transports of designated victims 'to the east', etc. This is due to the obvious incompleteness of the available sources (there are also duplications among them).[11]

A demographic method for trying to assess fully the extent of direct as well as narrowly indirect losses – that is, of deaths inflicted and births missed[12] – might be computation of the difference between the estimated actual number of Jews in Europe on the eve of the Holocaust and a hypothetical expected number soon after the end of the Second World War, had the Holocaust not taken place. In order to arrive at such a hypothetical number, a method analogous to population projections ought to be used. Census data, or the best estimates obtainable from the 1930s for the Jews in the various European countries, should first be updated to a common baseline as of autumn 1939. Starting from that basis the probable net natural increase (or decrease) under 'normal conditions' should be accounted for until soon after the end of the Second World War.[13] Migrations of Jews during the Holocaust period between Europe and other continents should also be taken into account.

Yet, such an undertaking would encounter, apart from deficiencies of sources, the major difficulty of establishing levels of 'normal' natural increase (or decrease) of the Jews in the various European countries before and during the war years. In fact, the empirical data from the 1930s document a strongly downward trend of fertility among the general populations of the developed countries. For the Jews in Europe this trend was compounded with the intensifying implications, direct and indirect, of the Nazi persecutions. These demographic implications can, however, be viewed as anticipatory symptoms of the eventual Holocaust, whose influence this model is precisely intended to eliminate; therefore, they should be discounted in so far as possible. On the other hand, the post-war data can be of no help, since they reflect a completely changed situation: a 'baby boom' was then sweeping the developed countries, including their Jewish residents; besides, the age composition of those Jews who survived had been drastically altered as a result of the Holocaust itself. Under these complicated circumstances use of considerably differing alternative assumptions concerning the evolution of the various Jewish populations of Europe in the absence of the Holocaust would be inevitable. This in turn must lead to a considerable range of differing results for the hypothetical size of Europe's Jewish populations if the Holocaust had not taken place, intensifying the problematic character of such results. This laborious task has not yet been undertaken.

APPENDIX II: ESTIMATES AND PROJECTIONS OF WORLD JEWISH POPULATION

The current estimates co-authored by me relate ideationally to the 'core Jewish populations' – i.e. those persons who, if questioned in a census or survey, are reported as Jews (for whatever reason: religious, ethnic, cultural, etc.). The estimates for the end of 1989 were as follows: world Jewry – 12,810,000; Diaspora – 9,093,000; Israel – 3,717,000.[14] These figures were arrived at after correcting US Jewry by nearly 200,000 downwards according to the results of the National Jewish Population Survey of 1990–1 (we had explained in many previous publications that a reduction seemed indicated but its actual calibration should await the results of that meanwhile conducted national survey).[15]

Demographic projections do not pretend to be prophecies. They merely show the numerical results if a population of given size and composition evolves according to defined assumptions regarding the various factors of change (natural, migratory, identificational). Because of this conjectural character, it is usual to present alternative versions of projections (medium, high, low, etc.).[16] Elaborate projections are computed age–sex-specifically.

Projections of world Jewry, by major geographical regions, were published by me, based on empirical observation of trends in the preceding years.[17] According to the medium variant of these projections, world Jewry, which was estimated at roughly 13 million in 1975, would be reduced to 12.4 million in the year 2000 and would shrink further to 12 million by 2010. The above-mentioned downward correction for US Jewry according to the recent survey conducted there, diminishes the figures to approximately 12.2 and 11.8 million in the years 2000 and 2010, respectively. These figures quantify the wide gap *vis-à-vis* the estimate of more than 16 million Jews in the world before the Holocaust. They also indicate that this gap is not narrowing in our times but actually increasing.

Finally, the proportion of Israel among world Jewry is increasing. It amounted to about 23 per cent in 1975; at the end of 1989 it had grown to 29 per cent and by the middle of 1991 it approached 32 per cent, owing to both the demographic growth of Israel's Jews and the decrease of the Diaspora. Each of these trends has been intensified by the recent migration wave from the Soviet Union to Israel.[18] Furthermore, these trends will continue in the decades to come. Inversely, if Israel's Jews had behaved or would behave demographically like those of the Diaspora, the discrepancy with the pre-Holocaust size of world Jewry would even be augmented.

NOTES

The editorial assistance of Professor Robert Wistrich and Moshe Goodman is gratefully acknowledged.

1 Author's figures, based on estimates of the number of Jews in all countries; see also Ruppin (1946).
2 There too mortality was aggravated by wartime conditions.
3 The mass immigration to Israel at that time originated not only from Europe but also from the Islamic countries of Asia and North Africa. Entry to the USA remained virtually barred for Holocaust survivors during the immediate postwar years.
4 Bachi (1976); Schmelz (1981a, b; 1984; 1989a); Schmelz and DellaPergola (1988); DellaPergola and Schmelz (1989).
5 The Jews of Israel have behaved differently in recent decades regarding fertility and natural increase (see below).
6 Further reduced by loss of children through out-marriages.
7 Schmelz, DellaPergola and Avner (1990–1).
8 Peritz (in press).
9 Schmelz (1989b).
10 *Aliyah* reduces the number of Diaspora Jews and increases that of Israeli Jews.

In the short run, however, it is immaterial for the overall size of world Jewry since it consists of no more than geographical shifts. In the longer run, it may affect the size of world Jewry – when the *olim* adapt themselves to the demographic climate of Israel (virtual absence of out-marriage, greater fertility) and thus evolve demographically otherwise than they would have done in the Diaspora.

11 For a recent and comprehensive analysis of the available material see Benz (1991).

12 Accounting among others for children who both were born and died during the Holocaust years; also accounting for Jews whose health was so gravely impaired by the Holocaust conditions that they passed away within the first few months after the end of hostilities in Europe.

13 See second part of preceding note.

14 In 1991 the Jewish population of Israel passed the 4 million mark, mainly as a result of the influx of Soviet Jews.

15 Schmelz and DellaPergola (1991). Jewish population estimates (with some evaluations) for all the countries of the world have been published by these authors in the *American Jewish Year Book* since 1982.

16 A difficulty in formulating realistic assumptions, especially for Jewish populations, arises from irregularity of migrations – as illustrated by the strongly varying volume and direction of Jewish emigration from the Soviet Union since the beginning of the 1970s.

17 Schmelz (1981b and 1989a).

18 The above-mentioned downward correction of the estimated size of US Jewry operated to the same effect.

REFERENCES

Bachi, R. (1976) *Population Trends of World Jewry*. Jerusalem, The Institute of Contemporary Jewry.

Benz, W. (ed.) (1991) *Dimension des Völkermords*. Munich, Oldenbourg.

DellaPergola, S. and Schmelz, U. O. (1989) 'Demographic transformations of American Jewry – marriage and mixed marriage in the 1980s', and appended exchange of replies in P. Y. Medding (ed.), *Studies in Contemporary Jewry*, vol. V.

Peritz, E. (in press) *Fertility and Family Formation in Israel*. Jerusalem, The Institute of Contemporary Jewry.

Ruppin, A. (1946) 'The Jewish population of the world', *The Jewish People – Past and Present*, vol. I.

Schmelz, U. O. (1981a) 'Jewish survival – the demographic factors', *American Jewish Year Book 1981*.

Schmelz, U. O. (1981b) *World Jewish Population – Regional Estimates and Projections*. Jerusalem, The Institute of Contemporary Jewry.

Schmelz, U. O. (1984) *Ageing of World Jewry*. Jerusalem, The Institute of Contemporary Jewry.

Schmelz, U. O. (1989a) *World Jewish Population in the 1980s – A Short Outline*. Jerusalem, The Institute of Contemporary Jewry (Occasional Papers).

Schmelz, U. O. (1989b) 'Religiosity and fertility among the Jews of Jerusalem', in U. O. Schmelz and S. DellaPergola (eds), *Papers in Jewish Demography 1985*. Jerusalem, The Institute of Contemporary Jewry.

Schmelz, U. O. and DellaPergola, S. (1988) *Basic Trends in American Jewish Demography*, American Jewish Committee (Jewish Sociology Papers).

Schmelz, U. O. and DellaPergola, S. (1991) 'World Jewish population 1989', *American Jewish Year Book 1991*.

Schmelz, U. O., DellaPergola, S. and Avner, U. (1990–1) 'Ethnic differences among Israeli Jews – a new look', *American Jewish Year Book 1990*; reissued in the Jewish Population Series by the Institute of Contemporary Jewry.

3

EMIGRATION AND *ALIYAH*

A reassessment of Israeli and Jewish policies

Dalia Ofer

Jewish history is replete with emigrations of various kinds, including those which resulted from expulsions and those which expressed the desire of individuals or groups, who for economic or political reasons sought new places where they could be assured of a continued Jewish existence. In modern times, mass emigration has become a characteristic feature of Jewish life. After the Second World War, between a third and one-half of the Jewish people were either first- or second-generation emigrants. Between 1882 and 1914, some 2.5 million Eastern European Jews migrated to Western Europe or overseas. The 'great migration' was a mass movement resulting from economic, demographic and political factors. It was not planned by any public body, although Jewish organizations established for this purpose did assist by funding passports, by disseminating information regarding preferred countries of emigration and even covering travel expenses.[1]

Despite its wide scope and the changes it produced in the Jewish world, emigration up to the 1930s served as a 'pressure valve'. Jewish organizations engaged in aiding emigrants saw the process as a factor which would mitigate the economic and political hardships of the Jews of Eastern Europe and Romania by enabling the remaining Jews to integrate along lines comparable to that of the Jewish communities in Western Europe, enjoying equal rights in their respective countries.

Only after the *Kristallnacht* pogrom (9–10 November 1938), did the Jewish population of Europe and the Americas change their attitude towards emigration. With all hope lost for the continuation of Jewish life under the Nazi regime, emigration was now perceived as the means for an overall solution for the Jews of Germany and Austria. But political and economic realities in Western Europe and elsewhere together with the outbreak of the Second World War did not permit this approach to be put to the test.

I

After the Second World War many Jews wished again to emigrate from Europe and build their future in Eretz Israel and in the Americas. Many felt that a return to normal life in the countries of Central and Eastern Europe was neither possible nor desirable. Paradoxically, the Jewish condition after the Holocaust made the emigration of entire Jewish communities a viable option, due to both the considerable reduction of the Jewish population and the establishment of the State of Israel, which proclaimed and implemented a policy of unrestricted immigration. Thus it became possible to mobilize varied and even opposing groups within the Jewish community – Zionists and non-Zionists alike – for joint planning of policy.

The new policy created a basis for cooperation between the leaders of the State of Israel and Jewish leadership in the Diaspora, especially the American Jewish Joint Distribution Committee (hereafter Joint) and the American Jewish Committee (AJC).

In the 1950s, when the scale of the Jewish exodus from Europe and the Islamic countries numbered hundreds of thousands, the leaders of Israel and the heads of the Jewish organizations saw *aliyah* as the preferred solution. They cooperated in public and clandestine efforts to assert the right for free Jewish emigration, in the organization of such emigration and in financing *aliyah*. The question of an emigrant's personal choice and decision regarding the preferred country was not at issue where the mass emigration of the 1950s from Europe and the Islamic countries was concerned. Yet dialectically, when the success of this cooperation reached its height in the 1970s and 1980s, with the emigration of Jews from the Soviet Union, the ideological disparity between the partners emerged in full force. Emigration and *aliyah* appeared as conflicting concepts expressing opposing interests. Leaders of Diaspora organizations saw the granting of assistance for emigration as an expression of support for human rights in general and specifically for the individual right to determine one's place of abode. The emigration also served to strengthen the local Jewish community, expressing its status within the Jewish world as a whole. For their part, Israeli governments continued to view this *aliyah* as further proof of Zionism's power to guarantee the continued existence of the Jewish people and therefore maintained that *olim* (immigrants, in Hebrew) must start their new life in Israel. However, in 1990 when the scope of emigration enormously increased, the advantages of a political decision by a sovereign state again became clear and cooperation between the partners for *aliyah* to Israel was resumed.

In order to understand better the *aliyah* policies of the Israeli government we shall concentrate, in particular, on the decade after 1945 which was crucial in fashioning both Israeli and Diaspora Jewish attitudes. At the end of the war Jewish leaders in the Western countries and in Europe had confronted a totally changed situation. Leaders of the Zionist movement presented a policy based upon an ideological approach which demanded that all those who had been spared – the *She'erit ha-Peletah* or 'surviving remnant' (Jewish displaced persons after the Second World War) be brought to Israel. This demand became a political lever amongst the survivors themselves, among the wider Jewish public and governments which had decisive influence on the fate of the Middle East and Europe. The demand was reinforced by the claim that the survivors themselves wished to emigrate to Palestine. Since the Western allies argued that the refugees and displaced persons should be given a free choice as to whether they wished to return to their countries of origin or to emigrate elsewhere, Zionist leaders argued that the same policy should be applied to the Jewish survivors.[2]

The non-Zionist Jewish organizations were faced with a serious problem when they came to formulate their policy regarding the Jewish Holocaust survivors. Their ideological and political position led them to demand that the survivors should be returned to their countries of origin with full and equal rights and that all their property be restored. The American Jewish Committee had established the Research Institute for Peace and Post-War Problems towards the end of the war, which recommended guaranteeing the rights of Jews within a universal legal system through a declaration of civil rights which would be adopted by the United Nations and would be binding upon all its members (International Bill of Rights). However, political activities in the period prior to the end of the war and immediately after it failed to produce the hoped-for results.[3]

Unlike the Zionist leaders, who did not hesitate to speak on behalf of the survivors and declare their desire to emigrate to Eretz Israel, the leaders of the Jewish organizations did not propose any clear, unequivocal solution to the Jewish problem.

Relations between Jews and non-Jews in most of Europe during the war and immediately after liberation cast doubts on the possibility of rebuilding a full and secure Jewish life in the countries of eastern and southern Europe. For example, the pogrom of 4 July 1946 in Kielce, a city in southeast Poland, together with a series of other violent confrontations between Poles and Jews in which hundreds of Jews were killed, caused a mass flight of Jews from Poland to the American Zone of Occupation in Germany. This flight reflected the understandable Jewish distrust of the Poles and the need to find countries to which they could emigrate. Emigration was therefore not only the problem of displaced persons in the camps of Germany, Austria and Italy, but also that of many survivors from eastern and southern Europe. The leaders of the Jewish organizations attempted to formulate various solutions which would satisfy the desires of the survivors while also coping with political restraints. They wished to enforce neither a return to countries of origin, nor emigration, nor *aliyah* to Eretz Israel.[4]

The role of American Jewry in aid and assistance to the survivors was decisive because their economic and human resources were much greater than those of any other Jewish community. The political status of the United States and its role in determining the peacetime political order provided the American Jewish public with a convenient framework for combined Jewish activities. The liberation of Europe in stages served as an advantageous background for the planning and organization of aid to Jews in various sectors. France and the Balkan countries were the first in which the Jewish organizations had to deal with the hardships that prevailed after the liberation. The first problem which organizations like the Joint and the AJC had to confront was the provision of emergency aid to prevent further deaths resulting from inefficiency and difficulties in providing supplies. Thus they saw as their immediate and most important task the physical preservation of tens of thousands of Jews. However, they also had to care for the rehabilitation and reconstruction of the economic life of the Jewish community and to ensure their political rights. The economic and social situation of the Jews was far graver than had been anticipated, reflecting their weakness and vulnerability even by comparison with the suffering and economic havoc endured by the population in general. The leaders of the Joint and the AJC thought that in the long run the improvement of the Jewish situation depended upon the economic rehabilitation of the European countries. However, until such time, it was desirable to take specific steps to rehabilitate Jewish businesses and organize aid for those who had returned from the camps or were expelled and required assistance. In this they needed the help of the new governments and organizations such as UNRRA (United Nations Relief and Rehabilitation Administration).[5]

The first step in this direction was to demand the return of Jewish expropriated property. However, all over Europe the return of property to Jewish ownership was difficult, entailing considerable legal problems because the property had meanwhile passed through many hands. As the liberation of Europe proceeded it became clear to the representatives of the Jewish organizations that there was no single solution to the Jewish problem and that a variety of responses must be sought, based upon the specific experiences of the survivors in each area.[6]

Between 1946 and 1948 it became clear that the Jewish problem in Europe was much greater than had been anticipated. About a million survivors required aid (including 150,000 Jews who returned to Poland from the Soviet Union in 1947). Of these some 225,000 were in displaced person (DP) camps, a further 400,000 in Romania and the rest in other Eastern and Western European countries. By 1947 the aid supplied by Jewish organizations to communities in France, the Netherlands and Belgium was already reduced. The main problems were in the DP camps and Eastern Europe, where economic chaos was already rampant before the communist take-over. The Jews, who had been deprived of their livelihood and capital during the war and who were engaged mainly in commerce and crafts, were particularly hard hit by the communist economic policy of centralized control over capital, production and services.

Romania and Hungary had the largest number of penurious Jews. Until the end of 1947 the major objective of the Jewish organizations was to assist the Jews of these countries to integrate in the new economic system through a broad rehabilitation programme. The Joint initiated a successful large-scale operation in Poland by granting loans on easy terms, in the manner of the *Cassa* loan system developed by the Joint in the Soviet Union in the 1920s. These loans helped Jews to establish private enterprises or to set up partnerships which would employ a small number of workers, in collaboration with local organizations and institutions which were under government supervision. The resultant dependence upon the regime created suspicion and uneasiness amongst the Jewish organizations who carefully protected their autonomy regarding decisions on the use of monies transferred from North America. The matter was further complicated by the communist regimes' negative attitude towards the United States. Nevertheless, the Joint supported the establishment of productive cooperative enterprises which were more in line with the economic trends of the communist parties that dominated the economies of Eastern Europe. These production units employed between forty and 200 workers in such branches as textiles, footwear, carpentry and metals. By January 1948, 225 cooperatives had been established in Poland employing 5,000 heads of household. More than 16,000 people – i.e. one-fifth of the Jewish population – in Poland were supported by these cooperatives.[7]

In Hungary and Romania progress was much slower. At the end of 1947, many Jews still wanted to emigrate from Eastern Europe, despite the dynamic rehabilitation policy. After two years of drought and a continuing economic crisis, there was a famine in Romania. About 25,000 Jewish refugees illegally crossed the Hungarian and Austrian borders in order to reach DP camps near Vienna. Romanian Jews fled the country by every possible means, either to other European countries or in order to participate in the 'illegal' immigration to Eretz Israel. The large number of Romanian immigrants (more than 50,000 Jews in 1947 alone) can be attributed primarily to the dire economic situation.[8] This wave of refugees laid an even greater burden on the Joint budgets, and their European representatives stressed that while the policy of rehabilitation could not be terminated, it had nevertheless come to a critical point. At a meeting of the Joint's board of directors in January 1948, Professor Emanuel Stein, Chairman of the Reconstruction Committee, maintained that the policy of reconstruction and rehabilitation was the major objective of Joint activities but also emphasized that vocational training must be geared not only towards the needs of the resident country (Poland, Romania, Bulgaria, etc.) but also to those of Israel and other countries of emigration.[9]

At the beginning of 1948 it was clear that though the extensive aid had helped save thousands of Jewish lives, long-term solutions had been found only for the Jews of Western Europe who managed to integrate satisfactorily in the reviving economies of their respective countries. The problem of the DPs in Germany, Austria and Italy (some 250,000 people) continued however to weigh heavily upon the American Jewish community. Legislation regarding DP immigration, proposed by Senator William G. Stratton in the US Senate in April 1947, met with considerable opposition from various factions in the House and the Senate with anti-Semitic arguments being raised in the course of the controversy over changing immigration regulations. The DP camps were presented as a burden upon the American taxpayer and upon the army authorities supervising the camps.[10]

At the beginning of 1948, it was impossible to evaluate how the proposed legislation might affect the number of Jews from the camps that would be allowed to immigrate. Despite considerable achievements in rehabilitating the DPs through schools, workshops, cultural activities and the substantial cooperation with the Jewish Agency and its emissaries, the DPs were viewed negatively by the public at large and at times even by Jews themselves. Public relations efforts undertaken by the Jewish organizations in collaboration with non-Jewish groups which supported the legislative endeavour in the United States were of no avail. Moreover, Latin American countries, Australia, South Africa and Canada were equally unwilling to take in any significant number of DPs.

Emigration, more than any other issue, drove home the powerlessness of the Jewish community and the limits of political pressure that they could exert. In the 1930s and during the first years of the war they had been unable to influence the State Department's discriminatory immigration policy towards the Jews. Even the enormous efforts exerted in favour of the DP law in the years 1945 to 1948 had brought only limited results.[11]

Against the background of deteriorating relations between East and West, there was growing apprehension that the US government would prohibit the operations of Jewish organizations in the Eastern European countries and forbid the despatch of funds raised in the United States. Equally East European countries were likely to ban their activities in the new Cold War climate increasing the possibility of Eastern European Jewry's severance from the mainstream of Jewish life (as had occurred years earlier with the Jews of the Soviet Union), reinforcing the strong feeling of emergency that animated the leaders of the Jewish organizations.[12]

From November 1947 there was also a deterioration in the condition of Jews in Islamic countries, with persecutions and physical attacks on them in Aden, Iraq and North Africa. The heads of communities called upon the Jewish organizations to come to their aid and to intervene with the local rulers and with England and France. Though both the AJC and the Joint responded to these appeals, reports received from their local representatives heightened their sense that in this part of the world too, emigration provided the best solution for Jews. The beginning of 1948 saw the ripening of conditions which made massive emigration seem the optimal solution for destitute or suffering Jews in both Europe and the Islamic countries.

Such a policy could be implemented only by a Jewish state committed to free immigration and ready to invest all its resources in this task.[13]

Although the estimated number of potential emigrants was high, their *aliyah* appeared feasible if it were undertaken by a state framework, by Jewish capital and international aid. Israel's dependence upon the Jewish community in the United States both for the financial resources required for *aliyah* and for the preparation of an economic base for absorption, gave the Jewish organizations considerable influence on the Jewish State's *aliyah* and absorption policy. *Aliyah* thus became a factor for cooperation between the Jewish organizations and the government of Israel.

Though Israel was committed to the Zionist principle of free immigration for every Jew as a national right, attitudes were in practice more complex. The ideology of the 'ingathering of the exiles' admittedly found expression in Israel's Declaration of Independence, which proclaimed that the gates of Eretz Israel would be open to every Jew, and which received its formal affirmation in the Law of Return of 1950.[14] But there were also increasing doubts about the effect that this large unselective immigration would have on Israel's new society and whether the social and cultural absorption of the immigrants would be possible under the new conditions developing in the state. Furthermore, misgivings were voiced across the entire political spectrum, regarding the economic ability of the *yishuv* to absorb so many people in so short a period. Significantly, the first immigration regulations issued in May 1948 by the Minister of Immigration and Health, Moshe Shapira, embodied principles of selection which gave preference to immigrants who had a greater contribution to make to the Israeli economy, i.e. people of means or those who had desirable professions, while limiting immigration of those classified as undesirable for moral or social reasons or as unhealthy.[15] The new immigration regulations assumed a condition of true freedom of choice on the part of the immigrant, valid perhaps for Jews arriving from Western Europe and the United States, but inapplicable to the majority of immigrants to Israel who had arrived in the country because of distress or mortal danger. To meet these realities, procedures were instituted for the speedy and non-selective Jewish immigration to Israel.

On the political level, it was agreed by all the Jewish factions that the Jewish community in Israel had to be substantially enlarged in order to counter Arab notions that the existence of Israel was merely a passing episode. As a result of the War of Independence, many areas were added to the Jewish state, whose leaders declared in August 1948 that these regions would be retained as an integral part of the state and should therefore be speedily settled.

The first elected government of Israel declared in March 1949 that its aim was to double the Jewish population in the first four years of statehood.[16] This could be done only by large-scale immigration. The emigration of

She'erit ha-Peletah and the clearing of the DP camps, which had been proclaimed as the prime Zionist goal during the years of political struggle, were now perceived as a debt to be speedily repaid to the survivors, the United States government and the Jewish organizations. The DP camps held about 250,000 Jews who were the first target group for *aliyah*. However, since that number of immigrants was insufficient for the aforementioned 'demographic needs', the goals of the *aliyah* policy required the implementation of a planned policy which would guarantee the departure of Jews from those countries which forbade free emigration to its citizens. The assumption was that emigration would lead to *aliyah* to Israel. Nevertheless it was felt in Israel that a Zionist education had to be provided for the 'potential immigrants', through the youth movements and the Zionist Organization.

Israel's immigration policy was primarily concerned with the Eastern European countries where communist regimes had been established following the conquest of the region by the Red Army. Soviet support was obviously vital to endorse immigration from the Eastern European bloc. Although the USSR forbade Zionist activity in its own borders and insisted that the 'Jewish question' had been solved in the Soviet Union, they did approve the emigration of Holocaust survivors from Eastern Europe to Palestine before 1948. Indeed they permitted the repatriation of some 150,000 Polish Jewish refugees who later became a decisive factor in the mass flight (*Berihah* movement) to the DP camps in the West and the *Ha'apalah* ('trail blazing') to Eretz Israel. In their talks with Soviet officials the Israelis naturally avoided any mention of Jewish immigration from the Soviet Union, while stressing the importance of the *aliyah* from Eastern Europe.[17] Israel's foreign minister, Moshe Sharett, in discussions with the Soviet deputy Foreign Minister Andrey Vyshinsky (December 1948) and with Foreign Minister Andrey Gromyko in April 1949, stressed the political and strategic value of large-scale and high quality immigration to Israel, particularly from Eastern Europe. It would help to guarantee the demographic viability of the Jewish *yishuv* in Israel and its ability to cope with the problems of building a new state.[18] At the same time, the Israeli Foreign Ministry conducted negotiations with the governments of all the Eastern European countries in order to maintain emigration. It realized that some Eastern bloc countries hoped to benefit through receipt of direct foreign currency payments or preferential trade agreements while others intended to rid themselves of middle-class people, difficult to integrate into the new communist societies. These factors for a time outweighed the ideological and political opposition to Zionist *aliyah*, which was particularly strong among some of the Jewish communist leaders in Eastern Europe. The payment of ransom money to Bulgaria, beginning in 1948, resulted in the government agreeing, for example, to allow Jewish immigration to Eretz Israel.[19] Already before then, direct or indirect payments of ransom were used by members of the *Mosad le-Aliyah Bet* (the *yishuv* organization which dealt with 'illegal' immigration) in Romania and other Balkan countries.[20] Israeli policy would provide the method with a broader and more formal framework. According to various estimates, more than 5 million dollars were paid to Romania and Bulgaria for the immigration of about 160,000 Jews. Israel also used international trade and other economic interests of its own and of the Eastern European countries as a means of persuading them to allow Jewish emigration. Though the Israeli government had considerable success with this policy, the immigration from these countries remained unstable and made it difficult for Israel to plan for *aliyah*.

Between 1948 and 1952, the approximate figures for immigration from Eastern Europe were as follows: 101,000 from Poland, 18,500 from Czechoslovakia, 1,400 from Hungary, 170,000 from Romania and 37,000 from Bulgaria. In addition, some 6,000 immigrants arrived from the Baltic states and the Soviet Union and some 7,600 from Yugoslavia, which was already pursuing a fairly independent political policy. Eastern European immigration increased the population of Israel by more than 300,000 out of a total of approximately 700,000 who arrived during the first four years of statehood.[21] There is no doubt that *aliyah* was one of the central parameters in this period for determining Israeli policy towards the Eastern European countries, outweighing economic and other political factors.

The Israeli government and the Jewish Agency also acted to facilitate the immigration of Jews from the Islamic countries after 1948. In addition to the ideological motive of 'ingathering the exiles', Israeli leaders undoubtedly felt responsible for these communities which had suffered persecution from their Arab neighbours because of the Arab–Israel conflict and particularly because of the humiliating results (from the Arab point of view) of the War of Independence. Anti-Jewish feeling had increased in Iraq, where legislation excluded many Jews from traditional economic positions in commerce and banking, from the civil service and the professions. Youngsters were excluded from the universities and felt that their future in their country of birth was no longer assured. For the first time, the *Ha'apalah* and educational activities began to encompass thousands of children and adolescents while members of the Zionist youth movements succeeded in establishing extensive contacts with the non-Zionist Jewish public.

Israel now adopted a deliberate policy of continuing contacts with the Jews of Iraq by means of clandestine emissaries and *aliyah*, which was the major Zionist activity. Above all, the Iraqi government's surprise decision in March 1950 to allow the emigration of Jews created a new dynamic among the Jewish community in favour of leaving Iraq. To the surprise of the regime and the leaders of the Jewish community, the exodus encompassed about 90 per cent of Iraqi Jews.[22]

Violent anti-Jewish outbreaks accompanied by anti-Israel and anti-Zionist slogans occurred in other North African countries such as Libya,

Morocco, Algeria and Egypt. The State of Israel saw itself as bound to continue Zionist activity in these countries in every possible way. Its aim was to hasten the exodus of these Jews according to a timetable based on various factors such as the weakening position of the colonial regimes and the attainment of independence by the Magreb countries.[23] The major illegal activity was therefore diverted from Europe to the Islamic countries; its prime message was the need to prepare for *aliyah*, to study Hebrew and strengthen a modern Jewish identity based upon traditional values of love for the land of Israel and Zion, already well-rooted among the Jews of these countries. During Israel's first decade, the overwhelming majority of Iraqi Jews – about 120,000 – emigrated to Israel, as did about 48,000 from Yemen, 34,000 from Turkey and 31,500 from Libya. The Jews from Islamic countries constituted some 50 per cent of the immigrants who arrived during the first decade of Israel's existence as an independent state.

During this entire period, the debate concerning the scope of *aliyah* was always on the public agenda together with a questioning of Israel's policy of evacuating entire Jewish communities, including the sick and aged, who could not integrate into the workforce. In the Jewish Agency executive there was a difference of opinion between those who dealt with absorption and finance such as Zvi Hermon, Giora Josephthal and Levi Eshkol, and the *aliyah* emissaries in the various countries, Foreign Office officials and those in charge of the Aliyah Department, such as Yizhak Raphael. The absorption personnel, who had to cope with the daily flow of immigrants and their problems, found it difficult to mobilize professional personnel for work in the immigrant camps and in the various services required for initial absorption of immigrants. They also warned of the magnitude of the problems encountered by the immigrants.

Criticism of the unselective policy of mass immigration often reflected the lack of adequate conditions for the absorption of so many immigrants at so fast a pace. This problem already manifested itself upon the immigrants' arrival in the country, where they encountered inadequate facilities in the immigrant camps and houses, due to unsatisfactory sanitary and public health conditions. Even greater difficulties arose regarding food supplies and other basic necessities. The absorption authorities argued that the cumulative damage was very serious, both in the short and the long run. Immigrants would build up feelings of antagonism and opposition to society and the state, which would undermine their absorption for years to come. Another point of criticism related to the absorption of those immigrants who, because of their advanced age or disability, were unable to integrate into the Israeli workforce or to engage in physical labour.

Housing, too, was a major problem though more than 150,000 immigrants had settled in abandoned Arab towns and districts immediately after the War of Independence. However, once most of the buildings suited for habitation in these places were occupied, the problem of finding homes for the remaining immigrants proved insoluble. The pace of building was slowed by a lack of resources and of skilled labourers at all levels. In addition, there were also enormous difficulties in organizing the educational system for immigrant children and adapting the health services since some of the immigrants had brought with them diseases not previously encountered.[24]

The absorption personnel and the economists contended that 'the entire system was in danger of collapse' and that the state would face bankruptcy. Basing themselves upon reports from their emissaries, the *aliyah* personnel countered that one must not decrease the immigration from those countries where uncertainty existed regarding permission to leave. The lessons of the Holocaust figured prominently in these arguments and the *aliyah* personnel were often supported by Foreign Ministry officials.[25]

It was during this period that the public debate regarding mass immigration began. From 1949, the press started criticizing the irresponsible policy of the authorities, while reporting on *aliyah* from various places (even exotic ones like Shanghai) and describing the problems facing the immigrants. The subject received its fullest coverage in a series of articles by Aryeh Gelblum in *Ha'aretz*, entitled 'I was a New Immigrant for One Month', which opened the topic to broad public debate and criticism related to the very scale of the immigration, the lack of selectivity and the blunders of the absorption authorities.[26] Following the furore, two public opinion polls, commissioned in July and September 1949 respectively, showed that the majority of the Jewish population was in favour of mass immigration although many expressed the opinion that it should be better 'regulated'.[27]

In March 1950 news came of the Iraqi government's intention to permit Jewish emigration and of the change in Romanian policy, whereby Jews would be allowed to register for *aliyah*. According to the estimates of officials in these countries, Israel could expect a huge wave of immigration of over 250,000 people. In the spring of 1950, there were already over 150,000 people in camps in Israel. The Jewish Agency was unable to finance the *aliyah* and absorption budgets without massive help from the government and the need for coordination of decision-making by all of the responsible parties became essential. In May 1950 the *Mosad le-Teum* ('Coordinating Organization') was established with the purpose of formalizing cooperation between the government and the Jewish Agency. Headed by David Ben-Gurion, it was composed of four cabinet ministers, including the Minister of Finance Eliezer Kaplan and Minister of Labour Golda Meir, and four members of the Jewish Agency, including Yizhak Raphael, Head of the Immigration Department and Levi Eshkol, Treasurer of the Jewish Agency and the head of its Settlement Department.[28]

While the *Mosad le-Teum* had first and foremost to deal with the imminent wave of life-saving *aliyah* from Iraq and Romania, it also had to redefine more clearly the respective roles of the Jewish Agency and the government in the absorption process. Absorption needs grew and in addition to the problem of providing housing in the cities and in the rural settlements, educational, cultural, religious, social and health services had to be established. Though local authorities were to become more involved in the absorption process, many of them lacked the means and experience required to cope with such problems. In the face of these ever-growing difficulties, it was decided in November 1950 that the immigration quota for 1951 should not exceed 150,000 and that the number of elderly and social cases would be limited. But the immigration from Iraq and Romania thwarted this decision and in fact the target number of immigrants for 1951 was exceeded by 20 per cent.[29]

During 1951 the arguments in favour of more selective immigration gave way to concern at the negative selection of immigrants from among the general Jewish population, which was taking place in many countries. Eastern European governments, particularly Romania, as well as the Jewish communities of North Africa, chose to send to Israel the social cases, the sick and those unable to fit into the productive workforce. Many people began to question whether Israel should continue its policy of non-selective *aliyah*. In November 1951, when the operation of bringing the Jews of Iraq to Israel was completed, more stringent criteria were instituted in the choice of immigrants: the first restrictions, which related to medical problems, limited the immigration of families whose members suffered from various diseases prevalent in the countries of North Africa and Asia. Preference was also given to people who would be independent of assistance from the Jewish Agency, either because they could bring sufficient capital to see them through the initial absorption stage or because they had relatives in Israel who would help in their absorption. Younger people, under the age of 35, were given precedence, provided they undertook to engage in agriculture or in other work involving physical labour. In the event, the *aliyah* authorities proved unable to enforce these draconian regulations and at the beginning of the 1960s, faced with a mass life-saving immigration from Morocco, they were abandoned.[30]

The government of Israel realized its intention of doubling the population in four years: at the end of 1951 the country had a population of over 1.4 million Jews, half of them immigrants who had arrived since May 1948. However, the absorption problems – the budgetary restrictions, the scarcity of professionals in many fields and the lack of an infrastructure for a new population – created constant pressures to improve planning and the organization of immigration. At the end of 1952 there were over 300,000 people living in temporary accommodation of various kinds such as work camps or transit camps. About 37,000 people were in temporary transit camps, some 128,000 in settlement camps and 173,000 in *Ma'abarot* (transit camps or temporary settlements).[31]

Between 1952 and 1954 only about 54,000 Jews immigrated to Israel but after the beginning of 1955 there was an appreciable increase: 37,478 in

1955; 56,234 in 1956; 71,224 in 1957 and 51,598 in 1959–60. More than half of these immigrants came from North Africa (Tunisia and Morocco) or from Arab states such as Egypt and about 40 per cent from Europe and other countries. In July 1961 Israel celebrated the arrival of the one millionth immigrant. In 1962 there was a new wave of immigration from Morocco and Romania and from 1962 to 1965 more than 210,000 immigrants arrived in the country, half from North Africa (100,000 from Morocco) and the remainder from Romania and other countries.[32]

II

For Jewish organizations like the Joint and the AJC the first subject on the agenda after the establishment of the State of Israel was finance. The Joint, which received its funding from the United Jewish Appeal (UJA) operated according to the terms laid down by the United States Department of the Treasury regarding donations to philanthropic organizations, which forbade the transfer of funds for the purpose of covering budgetary expenditure of a foreign government.[33] It was, therefore, vital that the immigration and absorption activities should not constitute part of the Israel government's budget. The financial problems were further compounded by an internal Jewish issue which was also ideological for the Joint and other Jewish organizations, i.e. the status of the World Zionist Federation and the Jewish Agency in Israel and their relationship with the government of Israel.[34] These issues were likely to affect the working relations between the Israeli government and the non-Zionist Jewish organizations.

The Joint wished to operate in Israel and to be the sole partner in organizing *aliyah*. They maintained that they shared a common interest with the government of Israel and that this must find concrete expression in the organization of the *aliyah*. Joint representatives in Europe, headed by Joseph Schwartz, had cooperated with the leaders of the *yishuv* and the Jewish Agency during the Second World War and the *Ha'apalah*, prior to the establishment of the state. However, the leaders of the Joint feared that a situation might arise in which they would appear to be merely implementing the instructions of the Israel government. They therefore sought ways of ensuring that they could have an input even in aspects of their work on which the Israeli government's stand would be decisive – such as the immediate emigration of the Jews in the DP camps. On 18 May 1948 Harry Vitalis, who had spent extended periods in Palestine since 1944 and was one of the Joint representatives in the Middle East, was appointed their representative in Israel.[35]

In July 1948 Joseph Schwartz came to Israel to discuss with representatives of the government and the Jewish Agency, matters relating to the Joint's role in *aliyah*. He announced that the Joint would finance the *aliyah* of 10,000 immigrants a month and requested that priority be given to the DPs.

Questions arose regarding Israel's desire to give priority to young people from the camps who were of military age, even to the extent of separating married couples and families in which the husbands or sons were eligible for conscription to the Israel Defence Forces (IDF). Schwartz pointed out the sensitivity of American Jewish and non-Jewish public opinion on this subject. Other political aspects of *aliyah* were discussed, such as the prospects of immigration from Eastern Europe and the need for the *aliyah* of North African Jews. The Israelis put forward proposals for planning new operational centres for the Joint in Israel and requested an expansion of assistance to various institutions in Israel. Both sides emphasized the importance of increasing the extent of contributions to the UJA and the role of Joint activities in fundraising.[36] Schwartz reported on the discussions he had conducted in Israel at an executive meeting of the Joint in New York, asserting that members of the board must understand and accept the fact that all decisions regarding *aliyah* would be made by a sovereign government of Israel as was customary in all countries.[37]

In September 1948, when Schwartz announced at an executive meeting in New York that the Israel government had decided to bring in 15,000 immigrants per month, the Joint executive increased its monthly *aliyah* budget to $1.2 million. This resulted in a reduction of other budgetary items, such as the establishment of workshops and vocational training facilities in the DP camps and support to the cooperatives in the Eastern European countries. Furthermore, it was decided that the workshops would train people in those skills which were needed by the Israeli economy and that the supervision of the ORT ('Society for Manual and Agricultural Work among Jews') training programmes in the DP camps in Germany would be taken over by Israeli personnel. The aim was to transfer the workshops, the staff and the equipment to Israel.[38]

Despite the decisions of the government and the Jewish Agency, the number of immigrants exceeded 15,000 per month. In November 1948 more than 20,639 arrived and in December 27,829, with a further increase in the first months of 1949. In order to finance this large immigration the Joint increased its borrowings from private banks, thus supporting the Israeli government's mass immigration policy. During 1949 the Joint's public relations campaign concentrated on encouraging contributions to the UJA for the *aliyah* communities and not on aid and rehabilitation of Jewish communities in Eastern Europe and North Africa.[39] The visit to Israel in October 1948 of the adviser to the US Army in Germany and his very positive report on the absorption of DPs there, reinforced the policy of the Joint and also disarmed those critics who were doubtful or wary of over-involvement in Israel's *aliyah* activities.[40]

The scope and substance of the cooperation of the Joint and the AJC also expressed themselves in their dealings with the IRO (International Refugee Organization) which after May 1948 had ceased to cover the cost of transporting DPs to Israel. At the time, the organization was headed by the British representative, William Tuck, who was influenced by Britain's hostile policy towards Israel. The IRO justified its policy of opposing immigration by claiming that the war in Israel jeopardized the safety of the immigrants, adding that since Israel was not a member of the United Nations, the IRO did not have the authority to finance DP immigration.[41] The Israel government objected to any limitation on *aliyah* by an external agency, claiming that the *aliyah* policy was the sole provenance of a sovereign government. When its protests to the IRO proved of no avail, the government turned to the Joint, the AJC and other Jewish organizations, requesting that they lobby the American and other governments who were members of the IRO, to induce the organization to change its stand. Representatives of the Jewish organizations raised the issue in meetings with the US State Department, but although they received a sympathetic hearing there was no change in policy until after the War of Independence and Israel's acceptance into the UN in May 1949. Meanwhile, the Joint executive decided to finance the cost of emigration of all the Jewish DPs. Thus the Joint supported the Israel's government's stand in opposition to the decision of an international UN agency (IRO) and enabled the implementation of Israel's *aliyah* policy.[42]

In order to effectuate the *aliyah*, the Joint also had to reach an agreement with the American military authorities that they turn a blind eye to the DPs leaving the camps. At the request of the Israeli government, Joint representatives initiated negotiations on this matter with the military authorities.[43] When they proved unable to reach a firm agreement, the Joint emissaries in Germany agreed to a request that they ignore American army regulations and assist the *Mossad* (the Haganah underground movement for 'illegal' immigration) in transferring the immigrants under the pretence that their destination was France. (They did in fact go to France en route to their port of embarkation in Marseille.) The Joint also extended credit to the *Mossad* for the purchase of ships, thus facilitating the transport of emigrants.[44]

The Joint also participated in other political activities relating to *aliyah*, negotiating with national and municipal authorities in Italy, France and Cyprus regarding the disbanding of the camps as a result of the *aliyah*. In the autumn and winter of 1948–9, it was involved in negotiations with the Chinese government, the American consulate and the IRO for the evacuation of Shanghai's Jews in the face of approaching communist forces. Similarly, it was involved in efforts to persuade the governments of the Eastern European communist bloc to permit *aliyah*.

The Joint continued its activities in the Eastern European and Islamic countries in line with Israel's *aliyah* policy. While continuing to give aid and assistance to the Jewish communities in these countries, from May 1948 the Joint concentrated more and more on the planning of Jewish immigration. Medical services were expanded and educational activities and vocational training became more important in the light of impending *aliyah*. As the communist regimes consolidated their power in Eastern Europe, the work of the Joint took on a sense of urgency. In a meeting with State Department officials in March 1949, Herbert Katzki, one of the Joint leaders, found it necessary to clarify the Joint's activities in Hungary by pointing out that its only interest there, as in other Eastern bloc countries, was to bring the Jews to Israel.[45] These statements illustrate the clear change in the agenda of the Jewish organizations, which abandoned hope of restoring Jewish life in Eastern Europe and now aspired to transfer entire communities to Israel.

The Joint's political activity in the Islamic and North African countries was of particular importance in the absence of diplomatic relations between them and Israel. The Joint served as an umbrella organization for local political activity, provided aid to needy families, assisted in medical services, organizing treatment for thousands of people who were waiting to emigrate to Israel. It also financed the camp in Marseille which was the assembly point for the North African immigrants.[46]

As a result of the overwhelming immigration from Iraq and Romania, the annual *aliyah* budget was already expended by the end of September 1950. The Joint considered paying only part of the cost for the *aliyah* from Iraq, Romania and Poland, the other part to be paid by the Israeli government and the rest to be obtained in special fundraising or from a loan.[47] The budgetary problem raised doubts in the Joint regarding its financial ability to continue supporting the mass immigration policy. There were those in the organization who viewed Israel's *aliyah* policy as irresponsible, particularly since the Joint's input in the decision-making was limited to finance. Consequently it was agreed with the heads of the Jewish Agency that from the beginning of 1951 the Joint would revert to its traditional activities of social welfare, care for sick and aged immigrants and the economic rehabilitation of the disabled immigrants in the framework of small businesses. In February 1951 it was agreed that the entire *aliyah* organization would be transferred to the Jewish Agency, together with all the *aliyah* facilities in Europe. Accordingly, the amount of money transferred to the Joint from the UJA was reduced, the balance being transferred directly to the Jewish Agency for *aliyah* purposes. By the end of 1950, the Joint had financed about 86 per cent out of a total of 499,000 immigrants. The Joint's activities also expanded in those Jewish communities targeted for *aliyah*, particularly North Africa which had now become one of the most important sources of immigration to Israel.[48]

But though in the 1950s it achieved maximal coordination with Israeli government policy, the flexibility, improvization and constant readjustment to changing situations which the Israeli government's *aliyah* policy required, proved too much for the Joint. It therefore withdrew from the organization of the *aliyah* even before the mass wave of immigration ceased and concentrated instead on its traditional and practical functions of aid and rehabilitation. Until the beginning of the 1970s there was no change in the nature of Joint activities relating to *aliyah* and social welfare. Its activities expanded in Israel and in North Africa because of the mass immigration from Morocco at the end of the 1950s and particularly in the 1960s. The AJC also assisted in the negotiations with the Moroccan government regarding Jewish immigration to Israel. Other organizations which played a considerable role in arranging the *aliyah* from North Africa were the World Jewish Congress and HIAS (United Hebrew Sheltering and Immigrant Aid Society).[49] The majority of Jews who left North Africa in the large wave of emigration reached Israel. Only Algerian Jews, who had French nationality, emigrated *en masse* to France.

III

At the beginning of the 1970s, the wave of immigration from the Soviet Union led, however, to a substantial change in the relationship between the Jewish organizations, the Jewish Agency and the government of Israel. The figures show that from the establishment of the Jewish State in May 1948 until 1989 about 210,000 Jews had emigrated from the Soviet Union to Israel. The majority (about 182,000) arrived after the Six Day War. In 1990, 185,242 Jewish immigrants came from the Soviet Union and during the first half of 1991 about 180,000. During the years 1971–89, 363,740 Jews left the Soviet Union, of whom 176,747 came to Israel, but the remaining 186,995 had emigrated to other countries, primarily the United States. This 'dropping-out' aroused both disappointment and sometimes anger in Israeli government circles and among the Israeli public. It also caused a serious conflict between Israel and the Jewish organizations in the United States – the Joint, the AJC and above all HIAS. Table 3.1 gives a statistical breakdown of *aliyah* from the Soviet Union from 1971 to 1989.[50]

In the opinion of Daniel Elazar, an authority on contemporary Jewish policy, a serious confrontation between two political policies emerged for the first time. There was the original pre-sovereign state approach that one must help Jews who are in distress to settle wherever they choose and assist them in improving their condition as human beings. The opposing approach – a Zionist one which became the norm after 1948 – held that, with the exception of very special cases, Jews who seek new homelands with the aid of world Jewry should be settled in Israel. According to Elazar, the drop-out phenomenon 'paved the way for a dispute, the first of its sort since the rise of Nazism, the first that tested the new framework [i.e. the cooperation between the various Jewish organizations and the Israeli government] which was established upon the renewal of Jewish sovereignty'.[51]

One cannot understand the nature or intensity of feelings that permeated this subject without a general awareness of the struggle for free emigration from the Soviet Union and the participation of the various parties in this struggle. Soviet support for Israel had declined as early as 1949 once the

Table 3.1 Statistical breakdown of *aliyah* from the Soviet Union, 1971–89

Year	Emigrants from USSR	Immigrants to Israel	Drop-outs in Vienna
1971	12,877	12,819	58
1972	31,903	31,652	251
1973	34,933	33,477	1,456
1974	20,695	16,816	3,879
1975	13,459	8,531	4,928
1976	14,283	7,279	7,004
1977	16,831	8,348	8,483
1978	29,059	12,192	16,867
1979	51,547	17,614	33,933
1980	23,056	7,595	15,461
1981	9,481	1,806	7,675
1982	2,708	756	1,952
1983	1,320	390	930
1984	896	340	556
1985	1,144	352	792
1986	914	208	706
1987	8,147	2,064	6,083
1988	19,251	2,231	17,020
1989	71,238	12,277	58,961
Total	363,742	176,747	186,995

Soviets had achieved their main objective – the expulsion of the British from Palestine. Thereafter, the relative importance of the Arabs increased, while Israel appeared to the Soviet Union as a predominantly pro-Western state. The receipt of the American loan at the beginning of 1949 and Israel's strong ties with American Jewry were understood by the Soviets as creating an Israeli dependence on the United States which (in the context of the Cold War) was interpreted as antagonistic to the communist East.[52] This negative attitude continued to deteriorate as a result of virulent anti-Zionist and anti-Semitic propaganda in the Soviet Union during the last years of Stalin's regime, arousing deep concern in Israel for the fate of the Jews in the Soviet Union. Israel's diplomatic delegation in Moscow was restricted in its contacts with the Jewish community. The telephones of its personnel were tapped by the secret police and all their movements were known to the authorities. But only after the death of Stalin and Khrushchev's revelations at the Twentieth Party Congress in 1956 was the full extent of the Jewish plight revealed. Western newspaper reports and accounts by various visitors describing the situation of Soviet Jews motivated the Israeli government to adopt a more dynamic policy to secure Jewish rights in the Soviet Union and to demand free emigration for those who chose to leave.[53]

The demand to allow Jews to leave the Soviet Union could be based on two principles: either repatriation or family reunification. These were the criteria which the Soviet Union applied when it agreed to allow various ethnic populations to leave the country immediately after the Second World War. In this way more than half a million Poles returned to Poland in two waves, from 1945 to 1948 and from 1957 to 1960. (These included some 150,000 Jews in the first wave and about 25,000 in the second.) But the Soviets claimed that the Israeli government was not entitled to demand the return of the Jews to Israel because it was not their birthplace. A limited number of Jews were allowed to emigrate to Israel on the grounds of family reunification, but only if they could prove that they had first-degree relatives there. Until Stalin's death in 1953, only eighteen visas were issued. However, from 1957 there were those in the Soviet government who advocated emigration of Soviet Jews for reasons of family reunification. During the eleven years of Khrushchev's regime (1953–64) 2,418 Jews received visas to Israel. This trend continued and from 1965 to mid-1968 more than 4,000 visas were issued. In 1966 *Izvestia* actually printed a speech by the first secretary of the Polish Communist Party, Wladyslaw Gomulka, which related positively to the desire to emigrate of those Jews who did not see themselves as citizens of the communist homeland.[54]

The gradual change in Soviet policy regarding Jewish emigration accelerated at the beginning of 1970. From then until 1991 the Soviets issued exit visas to more than 600,000 Jews, the majority as a result of Israeli demands. Scholars generally attribute the change in Soviet policy to a combination of three factors: the struggle of Jews within the USSR for the right to emigrate, which expressed their national identity and allegiance, a trend which gathered momentum after 1968; the accelerated international pressure on the Soviets regarding human rights and especially the right to emigrate; finally the impact of *détente* with the West and the subsequent thaw in East–West relations.[55]

Israel initiated the struggle for free emigration for Jews of the Soviet Union at the end of the 1950s and thus gave *aliyah* priority over its political relations with the Soviet Union, which had continued to deteriorate from the mid-1950s. From Israel's standpoint the rationale for the struggle was the demand for repatriation, family reunification and human rights. In the UN the subject was raised by the Israeli delegation, chiefly before the Commission on Human Rights. International public opinion was mobilized through a large-scale public relations campaign about the lack of rights of Jews in the Soviet Union. The international media, and famous intellectuals, were major targets of this campaign because their protests to the Soviet leadership and their influence on Western public opinion were particularly important. Harnessing Jewish public opinion to activate public figures and politicians was also a central strategic element in the struggle for free emigration. A special role was reserved for the Jewish communities and organizations, since they led organized Jewry.

In 1959 the Israeli government instructed its representatives in the United States to inaugurate a formal public relations campaign on the subject. The campaign included approaching politicians who were favourably inclined towards Israel and also human rights activists; requesting the Jewish organizations to use their contacts with the State Department and the White House; and to ask their members all over the country to request their representatives in Congress to act on behalf of Jewish rights. On 15 September 1960 the First International Conference was convened in Paris to discuss the hardships of the Jews in the Soviet Union. Israel initiated the Conference and played an important role in its organization. Participants included intellectuals and human rights activists from many countries; Martin Buber spoke at the opening session. Daniel Mayer, chairman of the Conference and president of the French League for Human Rights, submitted the resolutions passed at the conference to the Soviet ambassador in Paris. These resolutions included an appeal to the Soviet government to cease persecuting Jews and denying them their rights, and to allow free emigration on grounds of family reunification and for humanitarian reasons. The ambassador's refusal to accept the document containing the resolutions prompted the publication in the press of protest letters to the Soviet authorities in Moscow. Since the signatories included Jean-Paul Sartre, Bertrand Russell and other prominent intellectuals, the action had a resounding effect upon public opinion in the West.[56]

In April 1964, the National Conference for Soviet Jewry was established by the Council of Jewish Federations, the AJC, the World Jewish Congress, the Anti-Defamation League and others. On 24 January 1969 the leaders of the AJC met with Soviet representatives to present their demand for free emigration. A similar demand was made in January 1969 by the Anti-Defamation League and representatives of the World Jewish Congress. During this period similar committees were established in Argentina and Uruguay while in Europe the activities on behalf of Soviet Jewry's right to emigrate increased among Jewish communities, scientists, intellectuals and representatives of the trade unions.

Following the Six Day War the Soviet Union severed diplomatic relations with Israel and for over a year the Soviet authorities forbade the submission of requests for emigration. The absence of Israeli representation in Moscow made it difficult to maintain contact with Soviet Jewry, a task which now fell to the Jews of the Diaspora. Many Jewish students, community activists and ordinary people started visiting the Soviet Union on planned tours, bringing with them information and various kinds of study material. This activity became a cornerstone in Diaspora Jewry's political strategy. Concurrently, widespread educational activities were undertaken in Jewish communities and public protests were organized in all kinds of Jewish frameworks. Meanwhile the Jews in the Soviet Union intensified their struggle for free emigration. In addition to their repeated applications to the Soviet authorities and appeals to international bodies, they initiated Jewish cultural activities which included the study of Hebrew and Jewish knowledge. They were dismissed from their jobs and suffered from intense social pressure, which presented them as enemies of the Soviet society. Their children and relatives were also roundly condemned. The authorities even resorted to violence and in the summer of 1970, following an attempt to hijack a plane from Leningrad and fly it to Israel, many *aliyah* activists from Vilnius, Riga, Kishinev, Tiblisi and other places were arrested.[57] The trial of the hijackers in December 1970 generated extensive international repercussions and the heavy sentences (including two death sentences) aroused vehement world reactions.

A world conference of the many organizations engaged in activities for the right to emigrate held in Brussels on 23 February 1971 was prompted by the increase in persecution of the *aliyah* activists in the summer of 1970. Israel had a major role in initiating this conference and David Ben-Gurion participated as a guest of honour together with a large contingent of Knesset members. The conference received extensive media coverage.[58] This strategy of combining open and covert Jewish and Israeli activities in the recruitment of international forces to support the struggle of the *aliyah* activists continued throughout the years of the fight for the immigration of the Soviet Jews. The demand for their release was based on the human rights argument, while the *aliyah* activists themselves were motivated by distinct Zionist nationalism, i.e. a demand to return to the historic homeland. This combination of various emigration motives was effective and reflected the genuine interests and attitudes of the parties concerned. The Israeli government combined the two aspects in its policy, although ideologically and pragmatically it identified with the motives of the *aliyah* activists. The pressure on the Soviet Union increased in proportion to its political effort to integrate itself in the international structure without the tension and hostility of the Cold War period. Another aspect of Jewish strategy was to convince American statesmen that it was appropriate to link issues relating to *détente* with Jewish emigration. The pinnacle of Jewish success was the Jackson–Vanik amendment to United States legislation regarding trade, which made the granting of most favoured nation status to the Soviet Union conditional upon its improving human rights in the country.[59]

It is against the background of these events and attitudes that one must measure the Israeli shock and disappointment when the number of drop-outs from the Soviet Union first equalled the number of immigrants (1976 and 1977) and then rose to more than 90 per cent. Research shows that most of the drop-outs had decided in advance that they preferred to emigrate to the United States and requested visas to Israel only because this was the sole method of leaving the Soviet Union. Upon arriving in Vienna they turned to the representatives of HIAS and the Joint, who assisted them in obtaining entry visas to the United States on special quotas for refugees from communist countries. Their travel expenses were covered by the US government, while the Jewish organizations which dealt with their initial absorption in the country also received government aid.[60] From the American Jewish point of view, this was an opportunity to help Jews in need, to enlarge the American Jewish community and to operate according to the laws and values of American society in general. Organizations like HIAS and other refugee aid groups were able to revive their activities on a broad and dynamic scale after long years of inaction. One must again stress that this situation grew out of a political struggle by and on behalf of Soviet Jews, while a forceful Jewish public relations campaign (that also involved non-Jews in the American public) was based upon principles of human rights, including freedom to choose one's way of life and country of residence. Furthermore, the arrival of so many Soviet Jews in the United States was an expression of the achievements of the American Jewish community and of its ability to absorb needy Jews, actions that went far beyond mere assistance to Israel in its political struggle or contributing money for immigrants in Israel.[61]

Nevertheless, many American Jewish leaders expressed an ambivalent attitude to the drop-out phenomenon because, as Daniel Elazar pointed out, the norm in the Jewish community regarding *aliyah* to Israel had been challenged. The dispute was part of a renewed ideological debate in world Jewry, regarding the respective responsibility of Israel and the American Jewish community for the well-being of all of Jewry.[62] On 3 April 1978 the absorption committee of the Knesset issued a statement which reflected its approach to the subject. The section relating to the drop-outs and efforts to prevent this phenomenon stated:

> The committee is convinced that dropping-out causes great damage to Israel and may well weaken our basic Zionist struggle to enlist world public opinion to act on behalf of the emigration of Soviet Jews. It provides the Soviet Union with propaganda weapons to be used against us at some appropriate time, sows demoralization amongst the western Jewish communities, and 'spreads calumnies about the land.' The committee is convinced that the activities of the HIAS and Joint offices in Vienna which deal with the drop-outs are a direct factor in encouraging the dropping-out. ... The committee views with great disfavor the fact that part of the UJA money earmarked for Israel is being used by the communities in the United States to assist drop-outs – an act likely to encourage dropping-out – and it therefore recommends a change in this policy.[63]

In contrast to this stand, one should note the statement of the AJC nearly eighteen months earlier, in December 1976:

> It is imperative that Jews who wish to leave the Soviet Union should have a free choice as to the place in which they choose to live. Nothing should be done that might cause the cessation of Soviet Jewish

emigration. Soviet Jews will receive assistance to settle in whichever country grants them entry visas.[64]

In July 1976 an *ad hoc* committee was established with the participation of representatives from Jewish organizations, including HIAS, the Joint, AJC, the Jewish Federations and social welfare organizations, the Jewish Agency, UJA and the Israeli government, to discuss means of resolving the conflict between Israel and the Jewish organizations. Israel's wish was that Jews leaving the Soviet Union with Israeli entry visas should receive assistance only if they came to Israel. Against this wish stood the principle of the immigrant's freedom of choice. Israel argued that the assistance provided by HIAS and the Joint in Vienna acted as an encouragement to emigrate to the United States. This argument was countered by pointing out that the considerations for choosing between Israel and the United States were not symmetrical, because once in the United States the drop-outs could always decide to emigrate to Israel, whereas if they first emigrated to Israel they would be denied refugee status.

Israel rejected the argument that the drop-outs were entitled to refugee status since they possessed entry visas to Israel and therefore in fact held Israeli citizenship (under the Law of Return). Furthermore, Israel expressed fears that the drop-outs would cause the Soviet authorities to curtail emigration on the grounds that the emigrants were acting fraudulently. Israel proposed that aid to the drop-outs in Vienna should be given only in cases of family reunification. Those Jews who wished to emigrate to the United States should say so from the outset and would receive their entry visas in the Soviet Union. Israel also attempted to propose to the Soviets that there should be direct flights from Moscow or via Bucharest, where there was no HIAS representative. These steps were taken in order to minimize the contact between the Soviet Jewish emigrants and the representatives of HIAS and the Joint. The Israeli proposals proved unacceptable to the Jewish organizations, who considered the idea of turning to the Soviet authorities regarding the travel arrangement as an act which would sabotage Soviet Jewish emigration. The conflict between Israel and the Jewish organizations had taken on the character of an ideological dispute between Israel and the Diaspora, the content of the quarrel recalling some of the formulas of the pre-state period. From the viewpoint of Zionist ideology, the wheel had come full circle.

NOTES

1 Aryeh Gartner, 'The mass emigration of European Jews 1881–1941', *Jewish Emigration and Settlement in Israel and Other Countries* (Jerusalem, 1981), pp. 343–85 (Hebrew).
2 On Zionist policy after the war, see Joseph Heller, *The Struggle for a State. Jewish Zionist Policy, 1936–1948* (Jerusalem, 1981), pp. 61–113 (Hebrew).

3 Naomi W. Cohen, *Not Free to Desist: The American Jewish Committee 1906–1966* (Philadelphia 1972), pp. 265–75. Henceforth, Cohen (1972); and Menahem Kaufman, *An Ambiguous Partnership, Non-Zionist and Zionist 1939–1948* (Jerusalem and Detroit, 1991), pp. 186–242.

4 YIVO Archive (YIVO) AJC Record Series FAD-1 Box 80 Partition Israel Palestine 1937–48, Morris Waldman to John Slawson, 26 August 1946.

5 Michael R. Marrus, *The Unwanted European Refugees in the Twentieth Century* (New York, 1985), pp. 298–346.

6 JDC Archive (JA) AR 4564/3249 Staff conference, 17–18 February 1945.

7 Israel Gutman, *The Jews of Poland after World War II* (Jerusalem, 1985), pp. 60–106 (Hebrew).

8 Yehuda Bauer, *Out of the Ashes: The Impact of the American Jews on Post-Holocaust European Jewry* (Oxford, 1989), pp. 133–58. Henceforth, Bauer (1989); and Ze'ev Hadari and Ze'ev Zahor, *Ships or a State, The Story of the Large 'Illegal' Immigration Ships, Pan York and Pan Crescent* (Tel Aviv, no date) (Hebrew).

9 JA AR 4564/331 National Council Session and Board of Directors of JDC, 4 January 1948. In Bauer (1989), pp. 133–58.

10 For further amplification see: Leonard Dinnerstein, *America and the Survivors of the Holocaust* (New York, 1982), pp. 117–63. Henceforth, Dinnerstein (1982).

11 A total of 100,000 DPs emigrated to the United States between 1945 (Truman Directive) and 1951. Ronald Sanders, *Shores of Refuge, A Hundred Years of Jewish Immigration* (New York, 1988), pp. 586–7.

12 JA AR 4564/3331 National Council Session and Board of Directors of the AJDC, 4 January 1948, in particular the report of Moses A. Leavitt.

13 Ibid.

14 Dalia Ofer, 'The dilemma of rescue and redemption: mass immigration in the first year of statehood', *YIVO Annual*, 20, (New York, 1991), pp. 187–212. Henceforth, Ofer, 'Dilemma'. The Law of Return guaranteed the right of every Jew to emigrate to Israel and immediately receive Israeli citizenship.

15 See David Ben-Gurion, *The Restored State of Israel*, vol. I (Tel Aviv, 1969), pp. 210–11 (Hebrew). Henceforth, Ben-Gurion (1969). 'The Minister for Immigration stressed that so long as the war has not ended we are interested in a selective immigration, which will enhance our military and economic capacity, and not in sick people or social cases nor in children and the elderly.' Ben-Gurion (1969).

16 Regarding the boundaries, see Central Zionist Archives (CZA) S5/324, Moshe Sharett at a meeting of the Zionist Executive on 22 August 1948. Regarding doubling the population, see Ben-Gurion (1969) pp. 371–2.

17 Uri Bialer, *Between East and West. Israel's Foreign Policy Orientation 1948–1956* (Cambridge, Mass., 1989), pp. 68–76. Henceforth, Bialer (1989).

18 Ibid., pp. 70–1.

19 Ibid., p. 81.

20 Regarding Transnistria, see Dina Porat, *The Blue and Yellow Stars of David: The Yishuv and the Holocaust 1942–1945* (Cambridge, 1990), pp. 164–74; Dalia Ofer, *Escaping the Holocaust – Illegal Immigration to the Land of Israel 1939–1945* (Oxford, New York, 1990), pp. 180–8.

21 An estimate of the number of immigrants according to countries from which they emigrated is particularly difficult for the 1950s and especially for Eastern Europe. The population registry and the statistical tables indicate the country of birth, but during this period the congruency between country of birth and

country of emigration is deficient. For example, a large number of the DPs are registered as immigrants from Poland. The children of Polish immigrants who were born in the Soviet Union during the war are registered as immigrants from the Soviet Union even though they emigrated from Poland. I have used figures from the following sources: (1) Aliyah Department of the Jewish Agency as filed in the State Archives, Prime Minister's Office; *Ha-Mosad le-Teum lamed/gimel* 5388/536. (2) Moshe Sikron, *Aliyah to Israel 1948–1953* (Central Bureau of Statistics) (Jerusalem, 1957), Statistical Appendix, p. 23 (Hebrew). (3) Ernst Stock, *The Chosen Instrument. The Jewish Agency in the First Decade of the Jewish State of Israel* (New York and Tel Aviv, 1988), pp. 128–34. Henceforth, Stock (1988).

22 Esther Meir, *The Policy of the Jewish Agency and the Israel Government Regarding the Jews of Iraq, 1941–1954*, unpublished doctoral dissertation (Tel Aviv University, 1991) (Hebrew). Dafna Zimhoni, 'The activities of the *yishuv* on behalf of the Jews of Iraq, 1941–1948', *National Solidarity in Modern Times* (Beesheva, 1988), pp. 221–60 (Hebrew). Also *idem*, 'The Iraqi government and the mass immigration of Iraqi Jews', *Pe'amim*, 39, pp. 64–101(Hebrew).

23 The Israel State Archives (ISA), Golda Meir files, *Ha Mosad le-Teum*, gimel/5795, statement by Yizhak Raphael (head of the Immigration Department of the Jewish Agency) at a press conference on 8 November 1951 (Hebrew).

24 CZA, S100/55a. Jewish Agency Executive (JAE) from 2 November 1948, 10 January 1949, 29 March 1949 (Hebrew) and note 14 (Ofer, 'Dilemma').

25 ISA, Golda Meir files, *Ha-Mosad le-Teum*, gimel/5975, Yizhak Raphael to Moshe Sharett, 5 and 14 September 1950; the secretary of the Immigration Department to *Ha-Mosad le-Teum*, 6 October 1950. See also Sharett's memorandum to *Ha-Mosad le-Teum* regarding the urgency of *aliyah* from Iraq, 28 August 1950. CZA S6/6768 (Hebrew).

26 Aryeh Gelblum, 'I was a New Immigrant for One Month', *Ha'aretz*, articles from 13 April to 20 May 1949.

27 *The Problems of Aliyah as Perceived by the Residents of Israel*, Institute for Public Opinion Research (Institute for Applied Social Research – mimeograph publication) Jerusalem, August 1949 (Hebrew). *The Scope of Aliyah*, Institute for Public Opinion Research (Institute for Applied Social Research – mimeograph publication) Jerusalem, October 1949 (Hebrew).

28 CZA, S30/446, Summary of establishment of *Ha-Mosad le-Teum* on 14 May 1950; ibid. S41/101, Meeting of the Executive of the Zionist Actions Committee, 11 May 1950; CZA S30/3055, April 1949. A decision to establish a body whose work was less organized to coordinate the activities of the government and the Jewish Agency. S41/100, 22 January 1950. The Jewish Agency Executive decided to propose to the government that an Agency representative should attend cabinet meetings as an adviser on matters of *aliyah*.

29 ISA, *Ha-Mosad le-Teum*, gimel/5388/536. See also the changes in the laws of selection, 21 November 1951.

30 ISA, *Ha-Mosad le-Teum*, gimel/5388/536, 15 February 1954. Health problems were on *Ha-Mosad le-Teum* agenda many times, becoming more acute as health service proved inadequate to the growing number of immigrants requesting complex medical treatment. See also Avraham Steinberg, *Absorbing a People* (Tel Aviv, 1972) (Hebrew).

31 ISA, *Ha-Mosad le-Teum*, gimel/5388/536 'summaries', 15 May 1948, 14 May 1952, the Jewish Agency, statistical section of the Immigration Department.

32 The figures are taken from the *Israel Government Yearbook*, 1990 (Central Bureau of Statistics, Jerusalem, 1991).

33 JA AR 4564/3042, meetings of the Administrative Committee of the Joint (ADCOM) 18, 25 and 27 May 1948. Ibid. 4564/3374 ADCOM 29 June 1948 for Lessing Rosenwald's statements. Stock (1988), pp. 35–62. CZA, S30/3055. See letter from the Cabinet Secretary to the Jewish Agency Executive, 9 August 1948, informing the executive of the Provisional Government's decision of 17 July 1948 to fund all ministerial expenditures and all functions related to defence from the state budget, which derived from taxes and loans which the government would receive. The ministries received instructions forbidding them to accept Jewish Agency funding for the services for which they were responsible.

34 Stock (1988), pp. 63–73. Also Charles Liebman, *Pressure without Sanction: The Influence of World Jewry in Shaping Israel's Public Policy* (Rutherford, 1977).

35 JA AR 4564/3374 (ADCOM), 25 May 1948, Harold F. Linder. 'In effect we are faced with a decision to determine the extent to which we are prepared to change the basic character if not the existence of the JDC in order to meet the needs for Israel which are real and urgent but which cannot be met in terms of philanthropic funds in six weeks or two months.' JA AR 4564/3374 (ADCOM), 29 June 1948, in particular Harold Glasser's statement.

36 JA AR 4564/640, Joseph Schwartz on his meeting with Israeli representatives in Talpiot on 31 July 1948.

37 JA AR 4564/3374 (ADCOM), 1948.

38 JA AR 4564/3402 (EXCOM), 21 September 1948.

39 Ibid. Meeting of Board of Directors.

40 JA AR 4564/640, 2 November 1948, memorandum of William Haber. The dissenting votes were mainly those of members of the Council for Judaism whose chief spokesman at the Joint meeting was Lessing Rosenwald.

41 JA AR 4564/64, Joint office in Paris to Joint office in New York. Memorandum on a meeting with the IRO, 27 August 1948; ibid., 1 October 1948, Joseph Schwartz to New York.

42 Ibid. Joseph Schwartz to Joint office in New York, 3 August 1948. Kurt Grossman, World Jewish Congress (WJC) directive to WJC representatives in countries which participated in IRO activities, urging them to lobby for a change in the IRO decision, 3 August 1948.

43 JA AR 4564/640 (EXCOM), 21 September 1948; JA AR (ADCOM), 564/3374, 17 August 1948; (EXCOM), 12 December 1948.

44 JA AR 4564/640, 9 November 1948; JA AR 3344/468, 21 December 1948; and additional discussions regarding loans to the Jewish Agency and the *Mossad* for the purchase of ships.

45 United States National Archives 864.48/10/2648. Discussion between Moses Beckelman and Israel G. Jacobson with the American representative in Budapest, 26 October 1948.

46 Michael Laskier, 'Immigration of Moroccan Jews.: the attitude of the French protectorate and the stand of the Jewish organizations in the world, 1949–1956', *Shorashim Ba-Mizrah*, 2 (1990), pp. 315–67 (Hebrew).

47 JA AR 4564/3372, Memorandum of the discussion at a sub-committee meeting of the Administration Committee regarding the problem of emigration to Israel and other matters to be discussed at the forthcoming meeting in Israel on 3 September 1950 and a meeting of the Joint Executive on 31 October 1950.

48 Michael Laskier, 'The Jews of Morocco during the reign of Muhammad V', *Skira Hodshit*, 9 (1986), pp. 34–5 (Hebrew).

49 Yaron Zur, '"Illegal" immigration from Morocco and the building of the national community: the effects of the clandestine immigration from Morocco on the relationship between Moroccan Jews and Israel', *Ha-Ziyyonut*, Supplement 15 (1990), pp. 145–74 (Hebrew); Hayyim Sa'adon, 'The immigration from Tunisia during the period of Tunisia's struggle for independence', *Pe'amim*, 39 (1988), pp. 103–25 (Hebrew).

50 The source for these figures is the government's Central Bureau of Statistics and *The Statistical Yearbook for Israel 1990*, vol. 41 (Central Bureau of Statistics, Jerusalem, 1990), p. 175 (Hebrew). See note 21 for an explanation of some of the classifications. Regarding the motives for *aliyah* and dropping-out and the role of ideological factors amongst Soviet Jews see Ludmilla Dymerskaia-Tsigelman, 'The ideological motivation of Soviet *aliyah*', in Tamar Horowitz (ed.), *Soviet Man in an Open Society* (New York and London, 1990), pp. 49–55. Henceforth, Horowitz 1990). Also ibid., Elazar Leshem, Yehudit Rosenbaum and Orit Kahanor, 'Drop-outs and immigrants from the Soviet Union' (Research Report, 1990), pp. 49–55. Henceforth, *Drop-Outs* (1990).

51 Daniel Elazar, 'The drop-outs: testing point for a comprehensive Jewish policy', *Tefuzot Yisrael* (April–June 1978), pp. 5–8 (Hebrew).

52 Bialer (1989), pp. 133–72.

53 Zvi Alexander, 'The immigration of Soviet Jews', Yoram Dinstein (ed.), *Israel Yearbook of Human Rights*, vol. 7, (Tel Aviv, 1977), pp. 268–334. Henceforth, Alexander (1977). In particular note page 275 containing quotations from an article in the Yiddish newspaper *Forverts* of 4 April 1957 by Leon Crystal, 'Unser Weitig und unser Treist' ('Our pain and our consolation'), who had visited the Soviet Union in February of that year. Also an article in the Jewish Polish newspaper *Folksshtime*, April 1956.

54 In order to establish the number of Jews who left the Soviet Union, one must check the number of exit visas to Israel that were issued. See note 21.

55 Zvi Nezer, 'The *aliyah* from the Soviet Union, 1981', *Shevut*, 9 (1983), pp. 7–15 (Hebrew).

56 Alexander (1977), pp. 276–7.

57 Nezer (1983), pp. 8–9.

58 Alexander (1977), p. 277.

59 Alexander (1977), pp. 297–303.

60 Statement by HIAS director-general on aid to the drop-outs, 1976; statement by the HIAS director-general about dealing with the drop-outs, 1976. A letter from the director of the HIAS research department to the editor of *Tefutsot Yisrael* (1978), pp. 10–11, 13–15.

61 Leonard Fine, 'Let my people go – where?', *Tefutsot Yisrael* (1978), pp. 16–25. Originally published in *Moment* (January 1977).

62 Calvin Goldschneider, *The American Jewish Community: Social Science Research and Policy Implications* (Atlanta, 1986). Charles E. Silberman, *A Certain People, American Jewry and Their Lives Today* (New York, 1985).

63 *Tefutsot Yisrael* (1978), pp. 9–10.

64 Ibid., pp. 11–12.

4

THE NEW JEWISH POLITICS
IN AMERICA

Peter Y. Medding

To appreciate what is distinctive about the contemporary politics of American Jews (as well as what it has in common with the political behaviour of Jews in other times and other places), we begin with an analysis of different patterns of Jewish politics. These are broad models – theoretical approximations combining the essential elements of these different patterns that serve as measuring rods for understanding and comparing diverse and complex particular historical situations. While three such patterns are identified, and discussed here – traditional Jewish politics; modern Jewish politics; and the new Jewish politics – the major part of the article is devoted to the latter.

Pattern of Jewish politics

The characteristic pattern of politics of the corporate Jewish communities in Europe from the medieval period until emancipation – traditional Jewish politics – never existed in the United States. Commonly referred to as *shtadlanut* (intercession), traditional Jewish politics consisted in the main of personal intercession on behalf of the corporate community by individual Jews who had access to the authorities, often arising out of the latter's economic needs or dependence. These intercessors utilized their elite connections or influence to plead for the Jews – entreating, requesting, persuading (and sometimes bribing) the rulers to grant them residence permits, protection, toleration, or to reduce taxes, but always as a matter of grace or favour. In return, the Jews would show their gratitude in various ways.[1]

The key elements of traditional Jewish politics were a Jewish political status that was devoid of rights, had constantly to be renegotiated, and was therefore fundamentally insecure and permanently vulnerable; a strategy of political action that relied upon personal, behind-the-scenes influence, the hope or expectation of acquiring a grant of favour or grace; and the fear and reality of expulsion, increased taxation, and other sanctions if the intercession failed.

Emancipation gave rise to a new pattern. While most developed in democratic societies, modern Jewish politics was not confined to them. It involved
the pursuit by Jews of the benefits of citizenship and, where present, of
liberty and equality as a matter of right, and for the removal of impediments
to their enjoyment of those benefits – particularly those arising from prejudice and discrimination, and from restriction upon the maintenance of
Judaism, Jewish cultural life and communal institutions. Such claims were
generally pressed by the leaders of Jewish organizations. This reflected the
political mobilization of the Jewish mass public in the pursuit of Jewish
political concerns, a process that was further promoted by the development
of a Jewish press.[2] Although resort was sometimes made to personal, non-
public representations by Jewish notables or members of various elites,
this was no longer the main or sole mode of activity, but was auxiliary
to organizational modes of representation, and the public airing of issues of
Jewish concern.

Towards the end of the nineteenth century in Eastern Europe, modern
Jewish politics took a turn in the direction of auto-emancipation. Jews as
a group now sought to determine and take responsibility for their own
political fate, as evidenced by various movements for autonomism; and,
most notably, Zionism.[3] Over time, sympathy for these movements among
Jews in Western democracies gave modern Jewish politics in these countries
an international dimension. It now included the seeking of governmental
action to ameliorate the plight and secure the rights of oppressed Jews in
other countries, and support for the national rights of the Jewish people.
Thus Jewish communities in various countries became involved in activities
to influence their governments' conduct of foreign relations.

Modern Jewish politics was thus characterized by a formally equal Jewish
citizenship status even if not always secured in practice; by resorting to rights
in order to secure, maintain, protect or improve that status; and by the
political mobilization of Jews and the public pressing of Jewish concerns by
organizations and communal bodies seeking to persuade political, executive
and judicial authorities, as well as other groups and the public at large of the
validity of Jewish claims.

By and large, such politics sought to influence public policy from the
outside – without getting directly involved in the formal structure that
exercised power and possessed authority.[4] While in general such a stance
characterizes interest groups in democracies, among Jews it was reinforced
by the sense of being a vulnerable minority, and social outsiders who lacked
full acceptance, and who either suffered or feared social rejection.

The new Jewish politics does not completely replace modern Jewish
politics of an earlier era, rather it builds upon, and enhances it. While most
fully developed only in the United States, some of its features can also
be found elsewhere. In brief, the new Jewish politics reflects the recent
political transformation of American Jewry. Over the past two decades, both

as individuals, and as a group, American Jews have assumed a more active role, enhanced their status and increased their influence within the American political system.

Previously, American Jews were politically weak and insignificant. They were hampered in the pursuit of their political interests by an inhospitable social and cultural environment that tended to make them and their leaders somewhat equivocal in asserting their claims and in giving public prominence to them. As a group, their needs were not always viewed sympathetically, and on occasion their legitimacy was questioned, if not denied outright.

Today, American Jewry is widely regarded as a significant and influential political force that exercises considerable political power. Issues of direct and immediate concern to Jews figure prominently on the American political agenda, engaging the continuous and close attention of the White House, the Administration, Congress and the media. Jewishness, *per se*, has become politically salient. Once political outsiders, American Jews have become political insiders.

The development of the new Jewish politics has involved a transformation in American Jews' perception and ordering of their basic ethnic concerns – consolidating and improving Jewish social, economic and cultural status in America; enhancing relations between the United States and Israel; and ensuring Jewish survival[5] – and an even greater transformation in how these concerns are pursued.

Social, economic and cultural status

American Jews believe that to conserve and enhance their status in American society they must defend it from two major hostile pressures – the threat of anti-Semitic prejudice and discrimination; and the threat of Christianity, that is, the incorporation into American society and public life of Christian symbols, practices and values.

Even though discrimination and prejudice against Jews in America have declined, especially since the 1950s, those manifestations that continue to exist, together with the experience of Jewish history, led many American Jews to believe that anti-Semitism is endemic in America (as it is in other Western societies), and affects all sections of the population, including elite groups. However benign conditions seem, therefore, and however open the institutional structures of society are, and however great their actual participation in those structures even at the highest levels, American Jews do not feel completely secure because the potential always exists for things to become worse, particularly if economic and social conditions deteriorate.[6]

American Jews perceive a second threat to their group status in the direct and indirect social and cultural pressure of Christian America. Christianity is the formative cultural system for the vast majority of Americans, in terms of both values and emotions. In this sense, Jews regard American society as Christian, despite the formal constitutional guarantees aimed at ensuring the neutrality of the state with regard to religion.

Consequently, for American Jews, Christianity is not merely the religion of the majority of their fellow Americans – a relatively neutral aspect of social diversity – but is rather a fundamental feature of their own status definition. Jews reject Christianity at the rational level as essentially false, and even more strongly at the affective level as the theological source of a long history of anti-Semitism and persecution. Under such conditions, they define their Jewishness, in part, in terms of its distinction from, and rejection of, Christianity. To be Jewish in America, therefore, means, among other things, to be *not* Christian.

This translates politically into a strong commitment to the separation of church and state. While many other Americans share this conviction, its meaning to American Jews is fundamentally different. No other identifiable group in America has a greater investment in separation than the Jews. For them – but not for others – the separation of church and state constitutes and defines their individual and group status in American society, because to breach separation – to Christianize America – would relegate the Jews to second-class citizenship. Thus, a prime concern of Jewish politics in America is to ensure that this does not occur by support for the maintenance of a society that is strictly neutral in matters of religious affiliation.

America may be the most tolerant, welcoming, pluralistic and opportunity-laden society in Jewish history. Jews may be freer, more accepted, more integrated and more successful there than in any other country in the Diaspora. Yet, the threats of anti-Semitism and Christianity both continue to jeopardize Jewish equality. As a result, American Jews suffer from a permanent sense of insecurity and vulnerability, that is heightened by the fact that they have come so far, and have so much to lose. Much of their political activity seeks to overcome such threats.

Relations with Israel

In common with many ethnic Americans who maintain a sense of national, linguistic and cultural identification with their homelands, American Jews care deeply about Israel and seek to enlist the support of the United States for it. At first, this concern was tinged with ambivalence. In the 1950s pride in and support for Israel were accompanied by a distinct sense of separateness and distance, and some apprehension that too close an identification might harm Jewish status in America. Eventually, however, commitment to Israel became a central element in American Jewish identification and self-definition, and a focal point of its organizational and political activity. This process has gone so far that today, the future strength and vitality of American Jewish life are thought to be dependent upon Israel.[7]

American Jewish pride in Israel has focused particularly on the existence of sovereign Jewish political power, which contrasted so dramatically with the situation of Jewry during the Holocaust. Israel also enhanced Jewish status in America, by placing American Jews in the same category as other ethnic groups, which have homelands to which they relate, instead of being treated as a dispersed and rootless people. That Israel was a progressive, democratic, pioneering, egalitarian society, embodying universal prophetic moral and social values, and at the same time was self-reliant, and courageous, and had proved that Jews could fight to defend themselves against much greater odds, added to their enhanced status in America, and reinforced their positive self-image. Israel then is a prime focus of American Jewish self-worth and shared identity, simultaneously affirming common roots, individual personality needs, and collective aspirations. Caring for Israel, supporting it, involvement in its life and its problems, are self-evident to Jews, and an extension of caring and concern for one's family.

But the dominant element in American Jews' relations with Israel has been concern with its security, which since the end of the 1960s has to a great extent become dependent upon the political, economic and military assistance of the United States. Their primary goal, therefore, has been to ensure American support for Israel. Any indication of a weakening of that support generates anxiety and apprehension, as well as intensive political activity.

The elemental issue of survival

These two ethnic concerns – ensuring equality, and support for Israel – spill over into the third: Jewish survival. The concern with status in America is set against a long history of anti-Semitic persecution, culminating in the Holocaust. The constant threat to Israel's security directly raises fears about the physical survival of its Jews, as well as doubts about the future of American Jewry should Israel go under.

For about a generation after the Holocaust, its meaning as a historical event had little impact upon the political behaviour of American Jewry.[8] By the mid-1960s, however, it began to have an effect. In 1967, when a beleaguered Israel faced a battle for survival just prior to the Six Day War, the lesson of the Holocaust was dramatically imprinted on the consciousness of American Jews. Established in order to provide a safe haven for Jews from the ineradicable evils of anti-Semitism, by some twist of historic irony the independent Jewish state suddenly seemed the likely scene of another Holocaust. And, once more, the Jews appeared to stand alone.

Neither the swift Israeli victory of 1967, nor the slower, more costly military success of 1973, weakened the influence of the felt analogy with the Holocaust. American Jews came to recognize that Israel's survival was permanently in question, since the loss of one war would mean the annihilation of its Jewish inhabitants. As a result, concern with survival came to pervade American Jewry's collective identity, affecting its perception of its status and role in American society and becoming the central focus of American Jewish politics.[9]

Modern Jewish politics in America in the 1950s and 1960s was informed by the liberal politics of individual rights, which reflected the predominant concern of American Jews with securing equality of social, economic and cultural status in America. Having witnessed and been affected by the rise in anti-Semitic prejudice and educational, economic, residential and social discrimination during the 1920s and 1930s, and spurred on by the events of the Second World War, the major defence organizations of American Jewry made it their main goal to seek conditions that would enable Jews fully to enter American society as equal citizens. From the mid-1940s until about the mid-1960s the central problem confronting Jews in America was defined in individual terms – the full integration of individual Jews into society, where they could enjoy their rights as citizens free of discrimination. The National Jewish Community Relations Advisory Council (NJCRAC) put it this way in 1953:

> The overall objectives of Jewish community relations are to protect and promote equal rights and opportunities and to create conditions that contribute to the vitality of Jewish living. . . . These opportunities can be realized only in a society in which all persons are secure, whatever their religion, race or origin. . . . Freedom of individual conscience is a basic tenet of American democracy. The right of each person to worship God in his own way is the keystone in one of the major arches of our national edifice of personal liberties. Government must protect this right by protecting each in the pursuit of his conscience and by otherwise remaining aloof from religious matters.[10]

Jews regarded established and advantaged groups – business, religious, academic and social elites – as the major source of anti-Jewish prejudice. Their discriminatory activities, however, ran counter to the liberal and egalitarian values of the Constitution. In seeking to right such wrongs, therefore, Jews sought to have America live up to, and practise, its own highest ideals. American Jews also manifested support for these ideals in elections, and in public-opinion surveys. They preferred the Democrats – in presidential elections by margins of 18 to 36 per cent more than the population at large – and in congressional elections by even more. Such stable Jewish partisan loyalty was closely associated with strong support for liberal political, social, economic, moral and cultural values. Identification between liberalism and Jewishness was very high. To be sure, some Jews voted Republican, but even they, generally, supported the liberal ideals of economic and social justice. Thus, they viewed Republican candidates such as Eisenhower as liberals, and were attracted to the liberal wing of the

Republican Party. What distinguished them from Jews who voted Democrat was not, therefore, opposition to liberalism, but greater social integration with non-Jews.[11]

This political pattern dominated because it provided individual Jews and the organized Jewish community in America with a coherent world-view that simultaneously met particular Jewish ethnic concerns and more universal goals. It joined together the American liberal ideals, Jewish values, Jewish partisan affiliations and Jewish coalition partners in the belief that the achievement of individual liberal values and goals would necessarily satisfy Jewish concerns. In practice, Jews were allied with others in a universal struggle for a better society for all, as exemplified in Jewish support for the civil rights movement.

The coherence of this political approach began to disintegrate at the end of the 1960s due to the impact of ethnic pluralism, whose two main features were the legitimation of claims upon American society in group terms, and the rise of public and militant ethnic assertiveness. The resulting change in the focus of American Jewish politics is evident in the striking contrast between the NJCRAC 1953 statement cited above, and the following statement by the same organization in 1984:

> Jewish community relations activities are directed toward enhancement of conditions conducive to secure and creative Jewish living. Such conditions can be achieved only within a societal framework committed to the principles of democratic pluralism; to freedom of religion, thought and expression; equal rights, justice and opportunity; and within a climate in which differences among groups are accepted and respected, with each free to cultivate its own distinctive values while participating fully in the general life of the society. . . . The Jewish community has always been profoundly aware that maintaining a firm line of separation between church and state is essential to religious freedom and the religious voluntarism which foster the creative and distinctive survival of diverse religious groups, such as our own.[12]

The social legitimation of distinctive group values and diversity reinforced and heightened American Jews' already growing particularistic concerns with Israel and with Jewish survival, and the urgency of these issues tended to divert attention from their universal concerns, a process that was reinforced by a growing lack of sympathy for basic Jewish ethnic concerns among some liberal groups. In addition, direct conflicts of economic interest between Jews and other ethnic groups weakened or broke up long-standing coalition arrangements; erstwhile liberal and ethnic allies now became political opponents.

To be sure, American Jews as individuals did not move far from their previous pattern of liberal political attitudes and Democratic partisan loyalties. But as a group they developed a new political approach. The liberal politics of individual rights gave way to a pluralist politics of group survival that formed the basis for the new Jewish politics.

THE NEW JEWISH POLITICS

Some of the main features of the new Jewish politics are well captured in the following excerpts from an address by a key official to the 1985 Annual Policy Conference of the American Israel Public Affairs Committee (AIPAC):

40 years ago – April, 1945 – we had failed. We didn't know then the extent of our failure, but we knew we had failed. And, for many of us . . . that failure has haunted us and driven us and provided us with the internal fuel needed to create a politically active people pledged to survival. . . .

In our modern world, Jews have been torn between a desire for maximum integration in the general culture on the one hand and the will for Jewish survival on the other. But, the aftermath of the Holocaust, the creation of the State of Israel, and then in 1967 and 1973 the experience of almost losing what it took the murders of six million to create, drove home the urgency of putting Jewish survival first. I believe that today we recognize that if we fail to utilize our political power we may be overwhelmed by our adversaries throughout the world. We understand that if that happens, Jewish existence itself is endangered. . . . As we have bitterly learned, it is when we assume too low a profile and fail to develop economic and political power, that we are perceived as having no vital societal role. That is what makes us dispensable – that is what made Polish Jewry dispensable in the 1930s. *NEVER AGAIN*. . . .

The specter of *dual loyalty* still haunts our community. . . .

But here, in this country of ours, we ought not be shy about our interest in Israel. This is a pluralistic society and our survival here is dependent upon that pluralism. . . . Our concern for Israel does not erase our concern for America's domestic policies nor, in fact, does it mean that we do not have such concerns. . . . We care to the depths of our souls about what happens to both the United States and Israel – that caring is not inconsistent – it is not un-American and *it is not dual loyalty*. It is part of democracy.[13]

The primacy accorded group survival – focused upon but not confined to Israel – has led directly to a group demand for political power as the only way to ensure that survival. Such a quest for power is made possible by the pluralism of American society and its democratic political system.

The group demand for power which lies at the heart of the new Jewish politics requires American Jewry as a group actively to participate in the making of public policy on matters that affect it. To exercise power in this context means to have an input into the decision-making process, and thereby to gain some influence over the content and direction of political outcomes. While power in this sense can be exercised without occupying public office or possessing formal authority, it cannot be attained without organization and ongoing and direct involvement in the political process. Thus a distinctive feature of the new Jewish politics and a striking indication of its interaction with the political system is the integration of the Jewish political agenda and organizational framework into the mainstream of American politics. Jewish issues have become interwoven into America's routine political agenda. Jewish concerns have become Americanized. They are adopted, promoted, shaped and responded to, by leading American political figures, including the president, cabinet members, key administration officials and congressional leaders, and not just by Jews.

The most prominent Jewish concern embedded in American politics is Israel. Following the marked increase in the level of American foreign aid and defence assistance to Israel, particularly after the Yom Kippur War of 1973, such appropriations have become regular items on the congressional agenda. This tendency is reinforced by the United States' continuing role as Israel's main source of military supplies, and by its increasingly active part in Middle East peacemaking since 1967. Israel has thus became important in both congressional and presidential legislative and electoral politics, and its problems receive constant and disproportionate media coverage.

From the early 1970s until 1989 Soviet Jewry was a second significant Jewish concern demanding political and executive decisions at the highest level. Jewish political activity succeeded in making it part of the more general question of America's response to the situation of human rights in the Soviet Union, and a litmus test of Soviet behaviour in the larger context of American–Soviet relations. Soviet Jewry's right to emigrate and its freedom to maintain its cultural and religious life in the Soviet Union were major discussion items at Reagan–Gorbachev Summit meetings, and those between the American secretary of state and the Soviet foreign minister. The issue was dramatically highlighted by symbolic gestures such as Secretary Shultz's Seder with refuseniks at the US embassy in Moscow, and President Reagan's meetings with prominent refuseniks such as Natan Sharansky after their release. In 1989, the Soviet Union, in no small part due to previous US pressure and its desire for good relations with the USA, relaxed emigration restrictions for Soviet Jews. As a result of a quota for the admission of Soviet Jews as refugees set by the Bush administration, in the ensuing years hundreds of thousands of Soviet Jews emigrated to Israel.

Such US actions and policies were in no small measure the outcome of discussions by American Jewish leaders with the president and the secretary of state, and with State Department officials, reinforced by congressional contacts. A broad bipartisan Congressional Coalition for Soviet Jews was established in the 99th Congress to keep members and their staffs informed on developments in the Soviet Union, while there was also an active group of Congressional Wives for Soviet Jewry.

Commemorating the Holocaust in American public life has also become interwoven with the domestic American political agenda, although in a somewhat more sporadic manner. Thus we have seen the establishment of the President's Commission on the Holocaust (now called the United States Holocaust Memorial Council) and the erection of a United State Holocaust Memorial Museum in Washington. The Holocaust issue erupted into a major public debate and controversy in 1985 when President Reagan announced his intention to visit the German military cemetery at Bitburg and place a wreath there honouring the war dead of both countries. His refusal to change these plans after it became known that SS officers were buried there raised questions about America's relationship to the victims of the Holocaust, on the one hand, and their Nazi oppressors, on the other.

Israel, Soviet Jewry and Bitburg also illustrate the militant public self-assertiveness of American Jews that characterizes the new Jewish politics. The Soviet Jewry Mobilization Rally of 6 December 1987, on the Washington Mall, attended by some 250,000 American Jews and a large number of government officials, congressmen and presidential candidates, was the most dramatic example in a long string of public Jewish rallies for such causes. It was distinguished only by its national scope, the extent of Jewish political mobilization, the sophistication of organizational coordination, the scale of the media coverage and the public impact.

The integration of the Jewish and American political agendas was clearly reflected in the address to the rally of the then Vice-President George Bush, who declared, with what turned out to have been considerable political foresight, that he did not want to 'see five, six, ten released at one time, but tens or hundreds of thousands of those who want to go'. Although, in his view, for the United States it would be 'easier and more diplomatic to drop the human rights issue' in US–Soviet negotiations, this 'would be untrue to ourselves and break our promise to the past'. His address also indicated that these issues were interrelated, not just for Jews but in his mind as well. In a poignant and pointed reflection on the events of the 1940s, he added, 'I came away from Auschwitz determined not just to remember the Holocaust, but determined to renew our commitment to human rights around the world'.

Integrating into the structures of American politics: becoming professionals and insiders

The presence of Jewish issues and concerns on the American political agenda goes only part of the way in meeting American Jews' quest for power – the pursuit of influence over the content and direction of political outcomes that matter to them. An essential contribution to that goal is made by the direct, ongoing and increasingly professional participation of American Jews in the political process at many levels, thus increasing their input into political decisions and policy-making.

Prior to the advent of the new Jewish politics, American Jews as a community were by and large political outsiders, only intermittently involved in the political process, and mobilized on an *ad hoc* basis to meet the various crises that erupted. On such occasions, entry into the White House was generally gained via individual Jews who were major contributors and fundraisers for the political parties, often personal friends of the President, and sometimes leaders of major Jewish organizations. The overall pattern, therefore, was one of sporadic representations mainly to the White House and the administration, followed by an exit from the political arena when the issue was resolved, and concentration upon internal ethnic pursuits and community relations, until the next critical issue arose.

Now, Jewish organizations and professionals involved in the pursuit of Jewish ethnic concerns are professionals and insiders in American politics. For them, the political process is a day-to-day operation, very complex, fast-moving and fluid, subject to short-term and shifting coalitions and alliances, as well as to longer-term loyalties. To keep abreast of politics under such conditions necessitates full-time, skilled, sophisticated and professional organization, both in Washington and across the country, that is able to keep on top of complicated and sometimes obscure legislative procedures, stratagems and manoeuvres. It must be capable of dealing with a whole range of complex policy questions, often demanding a high level of scientific or technological expertise, a grasp of politics that comes only with direct and intimate political experience, and the capacity to make decisions quickly in the light of these considerations. This is no game for amateurs.

The most striking illustration of the development and practise of the new Jewish politics is AIPAC. Attempts to muster American support for Israel were initiated in the early 1950s by I. L. Kenen on behalf of the American Zionist Council. Although it registered with Congress as a domestic American lobby, pro-Arab and State Department circles exerted pressure on it to register as an agent of a foreign government, perhaps the ultimate symbol of outsider status. In response to this pressure, in 1954 the American Zionist Committee for Public Affairs was established as an independent and separately funded entity, which in 1959 changed its name to the American Israel Public Affairs Committee in order to strengthen its organizational base by gaining the support of non-Zionists.[14] Its goal remains today as it was formulated then: 'promoting strong and consistently close relations between our country and Israel'.[15]

Today, AIPAC has a nation-wide grass-roots membership of over 50,000, and its budget and full-time professional staff have grown dramatically.

Until 1973, Kenen was the only registered lobbyist, and the organization could be described as a tiny shoestring operation. By the end of the 1980s, there were six lobbyists, a staff of over 100 and a budget of over $10 million.[16] It monitors congressional activity relating to Israel and this, too, has expanded over the years. Thus, in 1987 an AIPAC report noted that forty-seven separate Israel-related items were then at various stages of the congressional process.[17] Of particular significance in keeping abreast with these issues is close and ongoing cooperation with congressional staff members. This is in line with the established pattern in Congress whereby much legislative activity is transacted by the staff, with elected representatives often becoming involved only at the last stage, when a decision or a vote is required.[18]

The transformation of AIPAC's status in Washington is epitomized in the different career patterns of the three leading officials it has had since its inception. Its founder, Kenen, served as an official of the American Zionist movement. His successor, Morris J. Amitay, had worked for the State Department as a foreign service officer, and subsequently served as a legislative aide to Senator Abraham Ribicoff. He was succeeded by the current executive director, Thomas Dine, who had been a Peace Corps volunteer and then worked in the Senate for ten years as an aide to Senator Edward Kennedy, Edmund Muskie and Frank Church. Before coming to AIPAC he had no known Jewish affiliations and few even knew that he was Jewish. Similarly, many people who have served as AIPAC lobbyists had previously worked as congressional aides and have gone back to such work, or established themselves as political consultants and private lobbyists after leaving AIPAC. Here, too, AIPAC is similar to the many Washington-based lobbying and consulting firms whose staff members follow the same career pattern.[19]

To supplement its Washington lobbying, AIPAC uses grass-roots organization in congressional districts to mobilize 'key contacts' – AIPAC members who have direct and prompt access to congressmen and senators through political, professional or personal connections. AIPAC members or leaders from particular regions or areas will often come to Washington during the year to lobby their representatives, and these activities peak during the annual AIPAC Policy Conference, when the 1,500 or more activists present meet with their representatives in Congress. This pattern has recently been emulated by many other Jewish organizations, which undertake missions to Washington on a local or regional basis, or hold national meetings there. In each case the scenario is repeated: Jews from all over the country call on their congressmen and senators to make them aware of the Jewish political agenda.

The process also works the other way. A major feature of AIPAC's Policy Conference are addresses by senior Cabinet members, and a high turnout of legislators. For example, at the 1987 Conference 307 legislators attended, including eighty-six Senators (forty-eight Democrats and thirty-eight Republicans) and 221 Representatives (134 Democrats and eighty-seven Republicans). During presidential primary season, most candidates attend, make known their views on Israel and contact potential campaign contributors. Such meetings are common also in major cities (particularly New York) where Jewish community relations councils host functions with leading politicians and candidates. This is, in some cases, an expression of gratitude for past support on issues of Jewish concern, but often it also serves to introduce candidates to the Jewish community. Even congressional candidates from all over the country make the rounds of such Jewish organizational events – often very distant from their constituencies – in order to make themselves and their views known to American Jewry.

The new Jewish politics is further integrated into the structures and rhythm of the American political system through an extensive network of PACs (political action committees) which maximize Jewish electoral influence. Currently, over eighty PACs seek to generate congressional support for Israel by raising funds and allocating them to candidates who have supported or are pledged to support pro-Israel policies. The largest and most significant of these is NATPAC situated in Washington, which is nationally organized; most of the others are local.[20]

In all, pro-Israel PACs raised $6.2 million in the 1985–6 electoral cycle, and contributed about $3.2 million to candidates for Congress. This represents approximately 2.9 per cent of the total given by PACs in 1986 and less than 1 per cent of the cost of electing a Congress ($450 million). But the significance of the pro-Israel PACs is greater than these proportions indicate. First, although the maximum that each PAC can contribute to a candidate is $5,000, PACs tend to concentrate on specific candidates in crucial races, particularly in the Senate, thereby magnifying the PAC impact. Thus, for example, the leading recipient of pro-Israel PAC money in 1986 received over $200,000. Second, PAC contributions to candidates are only part of the total picture. The same candidate may for the same reasons attract individual contributions and personal independent expenditure. Third, because Democrats generally are less well-funded than Republicans, the traditional liberal Jewish pro-Israel contribution can be crucial. According to one analysis it assisted the Democrats in unseating six incumbent Senate Republicans in 1986, despite the fact that the latter outspent the Democratic challengers by margins as wide as two-to-one. Pro-Israel PACs, then, helped shift control of the Senate from the Republicans to the Democrats.[21]

The recent proliferation of the PAC phenomenon has significantly facilitated the development of the new Jewish politics. By limiting the amount of money that individuals may contribute to electoral expenses, whether to candidates, parties or PACS, and limiting also the amounts that PACs may contribute to candidates, the electoral laws have lessened, but not eliminated, the influence of large contributions by very wealthy individuals, which used to be a key aspect of Jewish involvement in American politics. At the same time, these laws confer a relative advantage upon those who can mobilize many small contributions, such as the existing Jewish fund-raising network which specializes in soliciting contributions from many individuals. This network can thus be utilized to tap political contributions for the promotion of Jewish concerns.

PACs reinforce the new Jewish politics in three ways. First, they integrate the organized Jewish community structure into the ongoing operations and structures of the American political system by giving the group a direct say in the electoral process, as voters, contributors and activists. Second, they directly mobilize large numbers of Jews into politics as individuals. The process may begin with a campaign contribution, but it often leads to campaign activity, lobbying, party membership, and so forth. Third, the laws that structure PAC activities make the new Jewish politics truly national. The focus on concerns that can be met only in Washington and the possibility of supporting candidates anywhere in the country, based on their positions on issues, give American Jews influence even in states and districts where there are few Jews. This also encourages Jewish organizations to think more on national lines, and less in terms of their own organizational, local or regional interests. One obvious manifestation is the increasing tendency of Jewish organizations and umbrella bodies to open Washington offices.

The Jewish members of Congress clearly demonstrate the integration of Jews into the structures of American politics that is central to the new Jewish politics. These individuals palpably meet the community's demand for power – the desire for control over policy outcomes on matters of ethnic concern – by direct participation in the policy-making process. They also symbolize Jewish achievement of insider status in the political system. Particularly striking has been the numerical increase of such office-holders. In 1971 there were twelve Jewish members of the House of Representatives, and two Jewish senators, but in 1991 this had increased to thirty-three Jewish House members, many from districts without any appreciable Jewish constituencies, and eight Jewish senators. Moreover, there has been a degree of partisan realignment among them. In the past, the great majority were Democrats, but recently about a quarter have been Republicans.

What is more, the Jewish members of Congress today generally have deep, strong and public Jewish commitments that are integral to their political style and their conception of their role. A survey in the mid-1970s of the twenty-four Jewish members of the 94th Congress found most of them actively and openly identified with the Jewish community. They publicly acknowledged and pursued Jewish interests. Not surprisingly, they were more sympathetic to Israel than their non-Jewish colleagues: in fact, their view about the Arab–Israeli conflict were well within the mainstream of opinion in the organized American Jewish community. For that reason one scholar described them as an 'in-house lobby' for Israel.[22]

A more extensive and detailed survey in 1986/7 of the Jewish members of the 99th Congress showed a similar pattern.[23] It demonstrated that almost all of them attached great importance to their Jewishness, and were highly committed to Israel. Sixty per cent had a background of leadership and strong organizational involvement in the Jewish community before their election, and five out of six belonged to a synagogue or temple both before election and currently. About nine in ten observed some Jewish rituals (Passover Seder and Hanukkah candles), and stayed home from work on the High Holidays. All contributed to the UJA/Federation and subscribed to a Jewish periodical. About eight out of ten said that all or most of their closest friends are Jewish.

Approximately 75 per cent of these congressmen believed that being Jewish had a positive impact on their political careers, and only one perceived a negative effect. Close to a third reported that they had become more Jewish and more positive about Israel since their election: none reported a weakening of these commitments. All had visited Israel – about half of them for the first time after their election – and regarded issues specially affecting Jews as important aspects of their congressional role. About half reported that such issues sometimes created conflict in their fulfilment of their congressional role, but none felt that this conflict was constant or even usual. They tended to resolve such conflicts through informal consultations with each other, and with Jewish organizational leaders.

Unlike the black and Hispanic members of Congress, the Jewish members do not have a formal caucus. On the one hand, this indicates the high degree of consensus among them on Jewish concerns, and the effectiveness of informal consultation, which preempts the need for a formal caucus. On the other hand, it reflects the belief of Jewish congressmen that they should personally fulfil their public role in a manner that broadly integrates general and Jewish interests and confirms the balance between them, a strategy that would be disturbed by a formal Jewish caucus. As one put it, 'It would be an unwanted element, unfortunately; others are expected to have a caucus, we are not'. It could, another believed, 'harm Jewish interests by narrowing rather than broadening congressional support of Jewish causes'. According to a third legislator, there is a 'fear of antisemitsm'. Overall, however, Jewish congressmen believe that there is less anti-Semitism in Congress than in the United States as a whole: just over one-third agreed that there is 'little or no antisemitism in the United States today', but nearly three-quarters found little or none among members of Congress.

These Jewish commitments of Jewish members of Congress help maintain congressional support for Israel. By and large, since congressmen are overloaded with work, they concentrate on areas that interest them and on matters for which they are responsible. On other subjects they tend to be guided by congressmen who are considered experts, irrespective of party. Two groups that are particularly influential on matters affecting Israel are the Jewish members of congress in general, and the members of the House Foreign Affairs Committee – particularly its Middle East sub-committee. There is significant overlap between the two groups: in 1984, 30 per cent of the middle East sub-committee was Jewish, and by 1987 this had risen to 38 per cent.

Congressional support for Israel is reinforced by the electoral impact of identifiable Jewish communities in over 380 congressional districts. Though Jews are only a very small proportion of the electorate, their commitment to Israel is intense, and actively mobilized. What is more, public opinion polls generally indicate greater sympathy and support for Israel than for the Arabs, and very little outright opposition to Israel. Under such conditions, members of Congress stand to benefit greatly by supporting Israel, and to gain nothing – if not lose a great deal – by opposing it.[24]

The success of the new Jewish politics in generating and maintaining congressional support for Israel must be set within a broader context of factors that encourage effective Jewish political activity. Over 80 per cent of Jewish members of the 99th Congress said that three factors – 'shared moral and democratic values'; 'Israel as a strategic asset'; and 'shared foreign policy interests and objectives: Israel as an ally', were 'very important in determining U.S. support of Israel'. These factors were marked higher than 'considerable sympathy for Israel within the American public', 'the activities of AIPAC and the Israel lobby', 'the electoral significance of Jews and campaign financing' and 'sympathy for Jews because of the Holocaust'.[25]

Creating community consensus

Policies on issues of Jewish concern can be pursued most effectively if they are within the parameters of Jewish community consensus. In practice, on matters relating to Israel this means close organizational coordination between AIPAC and other major organizations, especially the Conference of Presidents of Major American Jewish Organizations. Until recently there was a general division of function between them: the Presidents' Conference represented the view of the organized Jewish community on Israel to the White House and the executive branch, whereas AIPAC worked through Congress to promote strong and close relations between Israel and the USA.

To ensure the necessary coordination, AIPAC is a member of the Presidents' Conference. Even more significantly it has in recent years widened its own executive committee to include the top leaders of major national Jewish organizations, many of whom also sit on the Presidents' Conference, and on the executive bodies of other leading umbrella organizations such as the Council of Jewish Federations, NJCRAC and the National Conference of Soviet Jewry. Some are also well-known leaders, major donors and fund-raisers in large Jewish communities. This overlapping of organizational leadership, the close collaboration between AIPAC's professionals and lay officers in formulating major policy decisions, and good informal relations between them and lay leaders and professionals of the major agencies and umbrella organizations, have made AIPAC representative of the community consensus and provide widespread American Jewish support.

The system does not always work, however, and on occasion sudden changes of policy by AIPAC have caught some other major Jewish organiz-ations (and members of Congress) unawares and left them pursuing policies that AIPAC no longer supported. This occurred in March 1986 over a proposed arms sale to Saudi Arabia.[26] Whatever the substantive justification for AIPAC's sudden change of attitude, a number of Jewish leaders and organizations felt aggrieved that they had not been consulted prior to the decision, which was made after Secretary of State Shultz promised AIPAC executive director Tom Dine and some of AIPAC's officers that the administration would attempt no further arms sales to Saudi Arabia that year. These problems of insufficient consultation and of policy differ-ences were aired in October 1988 in a letter to the head of AIPAC from the three major community relations agencies, the American Jewish Committee, the American Jewish Congress and the Anti-Defamation League.[27]

The professionalization of AIPAC, on the one hand, and its crucial role in creating and representing Jewish communal policy consensus, on the other hand, have led it in recent years to go beyond its focus upon Congress, and to extend its formal and informal ties with the administration, particularly the Departments of State and Defense, and the National Security Council. Meetings are often initiated, not by AIPAC, but by government officials: rather than American Jewry making representations to the administration, the Secretary of State might meet with the AIPAC executive director in an attempt to persuade him to moderate opposition to certain administration proposals, thus increasing the chances of congressional approval. Similarly, the administration has often used the promise of significant foreign aid to Israel as a means of helping it overcome Congressional opposition to various unpopular aspects of the overall foreign aid bill.

Over the last decade or more, strategic, defence, trade, communications and other relationships between the United States and Israel have widened and deepened. Often expressed in written agreements, they are structured in formal and informal mechanisms of consultation, cooperation and joint activities between various departments within the administration and Israeli government ministries. The need to routinely monitor policy proposals both to maintain these relationships and to extend them, led AIPAC in 1987 to establish a separate department to maintain contact with the executive branch. Its staff consisted mainly of professionals who had worked for or had close relations with the administration or the Republican Party that controlled it. The formal involvement of AIPAC in routine administration policy-making signified a further stage in the ongoing professionalization that characterizes the new Jewish politics.

Dual loyalty, divided loyalties and single loyalty

Another key aspect of policy coordination derives from frequent consultation with representatives of Israel, both in Washington and Jerusalem. Such contacts ensure that, in seeking and maintaining American support for Israel, and in lobbying for strong and close relations between the two countries, American Jews and their organizations – particularly the Presidents' Conference and AIPAC – know the views of the Israeli government. It is simply self-defeating for American Jews to promote policies that conflict with those of Israel.

Of course, the two communities may, and sometimes do, differ, particularly over what is feasible on the American political scene. But such differences must be worked out before action is taken. The American Jewish input in this process has been considerable, and Israel has learned a lot from the professional practitioners of the new Jewish politics about the realities of American politics. Although Israel is the dominant partner, and in the nature of the relationship has the last word, American Jewry makes an independent contribution, exerting influence upon the Israeli government at both the substantive and the tactical levels. American Jewish organizations are not, as they are sometimes perceived, simply another conduit for the Israeli government. One recent example was the question of Israel's relations with South Africa, where American Jewish views had a significant impact on Israel's decision to cut back its ties with that country.

Such close, routine and open contacts with Israeli officials point to another distinctive characteristic of the new Jewish politics – that contemporary American Jewish political leaders and activists are generally less fearful of being accused of dual loyalties than were their predecessors during the 1950s.[28] This largely reflects the greater overall receptivity of the American political system to the involvement of foreign governments and their diplomatic representatives in the policy-making process. Officials of many countries, particularly allies of the United States, frequently discuss issues of shared interest with members of Congress and their staffs. Similarly, it is not unusual for American citizens – especially those with ethnic ties – to promote concerns that involve their ethnic homelands. Neither is it uncommon for American citizens to be retained as paid lobbyists on behalf of foreign governments.

Thus, issues necessitating a choice between the interests of two countries friendly to the United States may pit groups of Americans against each other, as in the administration proposal to supply AWACs to Saudi Arabia in 1981. The battle to gain congressional approval put the White House and the administration, paid lobbyists for Saudi Arabia, oil companies, other major corporations and groups of Arab-Americans, on the one side, with AIPAC and the major Jewish organizations, on the other.

What is clear in the case of the AWACs – and in other proposed arms sales to Arab countries – is that for the practitioners of the new Jewish politics there exists a clear distinction between dual loyalties and divided loyalties. American Jews, concerned for their ethnic homeland, act to promote its interests by securing it American support, in the belief that America's foreign policy and defence requirements are best served by such support. Ties to Israel do not create divided loyalties that set off American Jews from America: on the contrary, they provide American Jews with an opportunity to weld these two loyalties into one. In the new Jewish politics, then, 'dual loyalties' have been replaced by a single integrated concern for strong American–Israel relations.

Such a stance assumes an Israel that upholds democratic and moral values shared by the United States. If that assumption turns out to be mistaken, the capacity of American Jews to weld the two loyalties together will be undermined. By the same token, the possibility that American Jewish leaders and political activists might disagree with Israeli leaders about appropriate policies for Israel, and about their impact in America, on the grounds that they fail to live up to those common values, is inherent in the new Jewish politics.

The broader agenda, coalitions and issue networks

Although Israel and the other international issues capture the most prominence, the agenda of what we termed above the pluralist politics of group survival is much broader. Based on the assumption that participation in the processes of democratic pluralism in the United States will enhance Jewish security, many Jewish organizations are active on a host of domestic political issues, entering into relationships of mutual support and understanding with other groups, which may later be reciprocated in support for Jewish group concerns.

These organizations actively pursue a broad political agenda in the national capital, and in many state capitals and major cities as well. Prominent among them are the American Jewish Committee, the American Jewish Congress, the Anti-Defamation League, NJCRAC, the Council of Jewish Federations and the major synagogue and religious bodies, many of which maintain Washington offices in addition to their national offices, usually situated in New York.

Thus the organized Jewish community addresses many issues that are not directly related to Jewish survival. *On the Issues*, a December 1988 publication of the American Jewish Committee, describes that agency's 'multi-issue agenda' based on AJC testimony to the Democratic and Republican platform committees in 1988. It includes specific policy recommendations on human rights, South Africa, separation of church and state, civil rights and civil liberties, poverty, family policy, energy, immigration and acculturation, public education and campaign finance reform. Even more detailed positions on these matters are presented in NJCRAC's 1988/9 *Joint Program Plan*, as well as on the housing crisis, long-term care for the elderly, the minimum wage, the right to reproductive choice, broadcast deregulation and AIDS.

Steady informal consultations among the professionals working for Jewish organizations in Washington over common concerns, ideas and tactics, keep the major organizations and leaders in touch with developments in the capital, make them aware of each other's positions and contribute to the formation of community consensus. On particularly complex or critical issues, the list of participants may be extended to include a wider range of Washington political actors involved in or informed about these issues.

One result, then, of such pluralist group politics has been the formation of loose but extensive issue networks on major Jewish ethnic concerns, and their integration into the larger issue networks that have recently become significant features in American politics.[29] An issue network cuts across all the formal structures to bring together individuals and groups that are particularly concerned with an issue area in a loose, informal set of relationships that have no clear boundaries or are easily permeable. Involvement in such a network is an increasingly significant form of participation in the policy-making process that confers the capacity to influence policy outcomes.

Thus the pro-Israel community would include members of Congress, their staffs, some White House and administration officials, leaders and professionals in Jewish organizations, academics, journalists, policy planners who work for think-tanks like the Washington Institute for Near East Policy, lobbyists, PAC officials, party-affiliated bodies such as the National Jewish Coalition, and more. They intersect with various independent bodies such as the Brookings Institution, with those promoting pro-Arab policies, and with groups concerned with general foreign policy and security questions, to form a Middle East issue network. Similarly, one can identify a Soviet Jewry issue network. Both it and the pro-Israel network intersect or overlap at one time or another with networks concerned with US–Soviet relations, human rights or South Africa, to name but a few.

Ideological differentiation

Somewhat paradoxically, the emphases on pluralism and group survival in the new Jewish politics have been accompanied by, and in many ways

105

encouraged, the development of marked ideological differences within American Jewry.

When the liberal politics of individual rights was the dominant ideological approach of American Jews, it was believed that answers to the problems of the Jews as a group would be provided by solving those of all individuals. Although Jews had certain collective concerns, these were to be promoted in terms of what was good for *all* Americans, and not in separate group terms. The specific Jewish aspects of public issues therefore tended to be consciously understated and kept out of the limelight.

But the rise of ethnic pluralism led to the recognition that the protection of ethnic concerns was a matter for groups and would be determined by the outcome of political competition between them. Ethnic politics is based upon the expectation of group conflict rather than the harmonious resolution of concerns in terms of individual rights and the general interest. American Jews, in common with other ethnic groups, began to pursue their concerns in a more openly particularistic manner. 'Is it good for the Jews?' was now a legitimate and public question, one that became urgent and inescapable when Israel and Jewish survival became central to the Jewish political agenda.

However, while forging an impressive consensus on their major international ethnic concerns, American Jews have become more and more divided on other political questions. The range of political responses among American Jews to the question of what is really 'good for the Jews' is ideologically more varied than in the past, even if the vast majority of American Jews are still to be found on the liberal side of the political divide. Generally, about two-thirds of American Jews support Democratic presidential candidates over Republican candidates. No Republican candidate for president has ever received as high as 40 per cent of the Jewish vote. Even a highly popular and extremely pro-Israel President Reagan received only 32 per cent when running for re-election in 1984, and George Bush did not fare any better in 1988. In congressional, gubernatorial, state and local government elections Jewish support for the Democrats has by all accounts generally been even higher. (The New York mayoralty election in 1989 is a striking exception, but analysis of this race and its impact upon Jewish voters is beyond the scope of this article.)

Similarly, attitude surveys have found American Jews to be predominantly liberal on a whole range of issues, including welfare and social justice, civil rights and civil liberties. One might say that Jews have not so much abandoned liberal individualism as adapted it to incorporate pluralistic group politics, while organizationally and individually continuing to give strong support to many, if not all, of the traditional liberal principles. Indeed, they continue to support issues in which the liberal response is cast in terms of individual rights or liberties, such as welfare policies, social problems and separation of church and state, but oppose those in which the liberal response is cast in terms of group rights, such as affirmative action programmes that involve preferential treatment for disadvantaged ethnic groups.[30]

At the same time, however, there are now significant groups of politically active Jews who express ideological support for conservatism and the Republican Party, on Jewish as well as on general grounds. Particularly prominent among them are a small but influential group of Jews, mainly academics, intellectuals and writers, who have taken a leading role in the formulation of neo-conservatism. Jewish neo-conservatism is the mirror image of Jewish liberalism: it seeks answers for Jewish ethnic concerns in broad general political principles that are applied to the whole spectrum of issues on the American political agenda.

Neo-conservatives are generally characterized by a liberal past and a continuing allegiance to older liberal principles which in their view have been radicalized and betrayed. Thus, neo-conservatives oppose affirmative action programmes as reverse discrimination; generally take a hard line with regard to communism and the Soviet Union; advocate increased American defence expenditure; and support monetarist economic policies. In general, they have tended to sympathize with the Reagan and Bush administrations. On Jewish issues, they are particularly disturbed by anti-Semitism and anti-Israeli policies on the Left, among some Democrats – mainly blacks and other minorities – and among pro-Arab and pro-Third World groups. They anchor their concern for Israel's security and survival in a strong American defence posture. Before the dismantling of Soviet control and communism in Eastern Europe and the internal changes in the Soviet Union, they adopted hardline policies towards arms limitation agreements with the Soviet Union, which they regarded as the major enemy of the free world and of Israel.

A very different conservatism characterizes many Orthodox Jews, particularly the ultra-Orthodox of New York City. Here the catalyst is different, stemming mainly from their opposition to liberalism in personal morality – abortion, homosexuality, pornography, the sexual revolution, the permissive society – which threatens fundamental Jewish religious values. Indeed, it may also stem from a deep-seated rejection of modernity and secularism as a whole. The overwhelming electoral support in these circles for Reagan and Bush in the 1980s, was more a matter of religious conservatism than of Republican partisanship. In congressional, state and local politics, these Jews have also generally voted Democrat.

Jewish Republicanism took root institutionally in the 1980s with the formation of the National Jewish Coalition. This organization sought to channel Jewish conservatism – and Reagan's popularity – into steady and solid ideological, financial, organizational and electoral support for the Republican Party, in the hope of making it the majority party within the Jewish community. Its leaders expected, as a result, to increase support for Jewish concerns in the Republican Party and in Republican administrations. The appointment to positions in the Bush administration of a number of Jews connected with the National Jewish Coalition, indicates its success in cementing Jewish links with the Republicans.

The current ideological differentiation within American Jewry has also led to conflicting perceptions of Jewish political interest. For example, does strict separation of church and state continue to serve Jewish interests? Although Jews generally oppose all attempts to Christianize America, the Orthodox community, in particular, which runs an extensive network of Jewish day schools, supports various forms of government aid to parochial schools, such as tuition tax credits. Significantly, their spokesmen argue that a rigid interpretation of the establishment clause banning direct and indirect governmental financial assistance to private religious schools conflicts with the constitutional guarantee of free exercise, since it makes the provision of traditional Jewish education extremely difficult.

Ultra-Orthodox groups, motivated by traditional Jewish values, have joined like-minded Christian groups in active opposition to the liberal position on abortion, gay rights and constitutional protection of pornography. Some have expressed support for silent prayer in public schools on the grounds that religion in general has positive effects on society. One Hasidic group has sought to use governmental property for the display of a religious symbol, the Hanukkah menorah, thereby breaking ranks with major Jewish organizations that are active in opposing such display of religious symbols. The extent of disagreement over what is the Jewish interest on such issues is illustrated by the decision of the American Jewish Congress and the American Jewish Committee to litigate against displays of menorahs on government property, and by the survey finding that the same proportion of American Jews (about 63 per cent) opposed displays on government property of menorahs, and Christmas manger scenes.[31]

Quite aside from Orthodox/non-Orthodox disagreements, conflicting perceptions of Jewish interest also figure in differences over affirmative action. Does the Jewish interest lie in support for equality of opportunity as measured by the old liberal standard of individual merit and achievement, which enabled Jews to overcome discrimination and quotas that excluded them? How should Jews react to programmes that seek to end discrimination against minorities and undo the accumulated effect of past wrongs by departing from individual merit criteria and giving preference on the basis of group membership? How should Jews react to the possibility that preference for less qualified people on group grounds in the name of social justice and equality might disadvantage some Jews personally and directly?

Even if individuals are disadvantaged in the short term, might not these programmes be supported on grounds of a longer-term Jewish interest in a society free of all discrimination, and the benefit to Jews of resolving the social and economic problems that produce much anti-Semitism?

Most Jews respond by supporting what they consider economic and social justice through affirmative action programmes, but not quotas. Some on the political left support more radical programmes including quotas, while others on the right adhere rigidly to the standard of individual achievement, opposing all affirmative action initiatives. Each of these responses is framed in terms of both what is good for American society, and what is good for Jews.

New threats, new allies, split coalitions

The new Jewish politics has made relations with other groups in America more complex. As long as the liberal politics of individual rights prevailed, American Jews participated in broad liberal coalitions sharing common goals and aspirations with other groups on a wide range of issues. But the pluralist politics of group survival has generated internally conflicted or split coalitions. On some issues, American Jews find themselves in partnership with groups that, on other issues, reject basic Jewish ethnic concerns. Managing split coalitions poses constant tensions and dilemmas for American Jews. It is one thing to disagree with others, but partial rejection by coalition partners is an entirely different political experience. This has occurred recently in Jewish relations with blacks, Protestants and Catholics.

Since the mid-1960s black–Jewish relations have deteriorated significantly. Growing black anti-Semitism has found public expression in statements by some black leaders. A 1982 survey of American anti-Semitism found that the mean level of anti-Semitism among blacks had risen since 1964 – it had fallen among whites – and in 1981 it was 20 per cent higher than among whites.[32] Studies of Jewish opinion indicate that American Jews are keenly aware of black anti-Semitism.

Nevertheless, the vast majority of American Jews support vigorous enforcement of civil rights and anti-discrimination laws, social welfare programmes to improve the situation of blacks and other minority groups, and initiatives to improve a black–Jewish relations community.[33] The efforts of a number of major Jewish organizations to accomplish these objectives are made difficult by the overwhelming Jewish opposition to quotas and preferential hiring, policies which are supported by most blacks.[34]

Jewish–black cooperation is further set back by the widespread Jewish perception that blacks are not particularly sympathetic to Israel, and are much more likely than whites to think that Israel is not a reliable ally, and that American Jews are more loyal to Israel than to the USA.[35] Israel's relations with South Africa also hurt its standing in the black community.

Jewish apprehensions about blacks were reinforced by the prominence and political success of the symbolic leader of American blacks, the Reverend Jesse Jackson. His own publicly quoted anti-Semitic remarks, and his refusal to denounce or disassociate himself from the outspoken anti-Semitism of the black Muslim preacher Louis Farrakhan, and other black officials, led to a widespread Jewish perception that he was anti-Semitic. His denials, his actions in favour of Soviet Jewry, dialogues with Jewish organizations and the presence of a number of Jews on his campaign staff, have not entirely managed to dispel this image. In Cohen's 1984 and 1988 surveys of American Jews, only 8 per cent and 10 per cent, respectively, said that he was not anti-Semitic, while 74 per cent and 59 per cent said that he was. This, together with his pro-PLO views and widely publicized meetings with Yasser Arafat, were perceived by Jews as a direct threat. The vast majority of American Jews were extremely uneasy about Jackson's influence within the Democratic Party, at the head of a potentially broad liberal coalition of blacks, other minorities and whites, as witnessed by the events at the 1988 Democratic Party Convention.

In seeking, nevertheless, to maintain what they can of the old alliance with blacks by supporting their claims to social and economic justice, American Jews act partly out of shared values, but also out of the need for defence and self-protection. Black anti-Semitism threatens Jews from below. Their socio-economic disadvantage makes blacks available for mobilization by demagogic political leaders if economic and social conditions worsen, with the Jews as targets for outbreaks of urban disorder and violence.

Alliances with some major Christian groups in America have also been impeded by the latter's approach to basic Jewish concerns. Any lack of sympathy for Israel and its survival on the part of Christians is, for many Jews, indistinguishable from anti-Semitic prejudice. Thus relations between American Jews and American Catholics are affected by the Vatican's refusal to grant Israel diplomatic recognition. Similarly, American Jews have since 1967 been disturbed by the indifference of some leading mainline liberal Protestant bodies to threats to Israel's survival, which recall Christian silence during the Holocaust.

A second complication in Christian–Jewish coalition-building comes from the pressure for a Christian America. Many of the Evangelicals associated with this movement strongly support Israel, seeing it as part of an overall divine plan. Yet, these same Christians are among the most determined opponents of the separation of church and state, and of a liberal, pluralist, open and secular society – all of which Jews espouse. Nevertheless – as is the case with blacks – major Jewish organizations seek to maintain a dialogue and form stable alliances with Christians. Some Jewish agencies relate specifically to those denominations with political and social outlooks roughly comparable to their own. Others engage in the pursuit of common interests with Christians on such matters as welfare, housing and assistance for the poor and aged, thereby avoiding areas of disagreement. Jews seek these coalitions not only to move towards policy agreement, but also in the hope that they may eventually lead Christians towards greater understanding of Jewish concerns. But until this occurs, the new Jewish politics will be characterized by many split coalitions involving only partial and temporary cooperation with other groups. Maintaining such arrangements is fraught with the constant tension of avoiding sensitive issues and of handling disappointed expectations.

Conclusion: politics without authority

The authority structure of American Jewry has changed little since the advent of the new Jewish politics. It is still characterized by diversity and organizational autonomy. To be sure, rationalization and unity at the top levels of the Jewish community structure have increased somewhat, but lines of authority remain more implicit than explicit, existing more in informal organizational arrangements than in formal agreements or institutional structures.

At the same time, American Jewry remains united around the principle that no single body speaks on its behalf as a whole. It constitutes a community without formal authority, lacks a defined membership, clear boundaries and contested democratic methods for choosing leaders. It has no mechanisms for reaching binding majority decisions, for setting priorities or for penalizing dissidents.

So far, this informal and unstructured process for reaching decisions on issues has held up, largely because of the community's strong consensus on key issues such as Israel. But what will happen if disagreements emerge within American Jewry over the policies of the Israeli government? Already there is controversy over whether American Jewish organizations have a right to disagree with Israel's course, whether it is prudent to express such disagreements publicly in the United States rather than privately to Israeli leaders, and whether the answers to these questions would be any different if the Israeli government and public themselves were united rather than fundamentally divided.

The American Jewish community may not be able to settle such problems. How, then, will dissension among American Jews over Israeli policies affect the new Jewish politics? On the one hand, a variety of American Jewish opinions about Israeli actions may signal the further Americanization of Jewish concerns, adding Israel to the list of political issues about which Jews can disagree. Indeed, such dissent may buttress claims for greater American support for the Jewish State by showing that American Jews reach their pro-Israel position through mutual discussion and persuasion, not through automatic, reflex reactions. On the other hand, failure to resolve this and other questions could very well undermine the capacity for united action to secure Israel's survival which is so central an element in the new Jewish politics.

At the moment, the threat of the loss of political effectiveness that would ensue if different Jewish groups promoted opposing policies towards Israel within Congress and the administration is a powerful incentive for the organized Jewish community in America to maintain unity on this issue. Whether it will continue to do so in the future remains to be seen, and until that issue is resolved the future path of the new Jewish politics will remain unclear.

Many other Jewish communities in democratic societies (Britain, Australia, Canada, France) have adopted some of the key elements of the new Jewish politics, including a public and often militant assertion of Jewish interests and concerns with particular emphasis on the centrality of Israel and Jewish survival. These communities, however, remain within the broad parameters of what we have termed modern Jewish politics. What makes American Jewry unique are other elements such as the incorporation of Jewish concerns and the professionalized integration of Jewish organizations and individuals into structures and processes of the American political system. It is features like these that have helped to make American Jewry insiders in the American political process and thereby to fulfil its search for greater influence over its own fate.

NOTES

1 See the treatment of these issues in Eli Lederhandler, *The Road to Modern Jewish Politics: Political Tradition and Political Reconstruction in the Jewish Community of Tsarist Russia* (New York, Oxford University Press, 1989) pp. 11–35, 154–7.

2 I have dealt with the issue of political mobilization in Peter Y. Medding, 'The politics of Jewry as a mobilized Diaspora', in William C. McCready (ed.), *Culture, Ethnicity and Identity: Current Issues in Research* (New York, Academic Press, 1983) pp. 195–207.

3 See Jonathan Frankel, *Prophecy and Politics: Socialism, Nationalism and the Russian Jews, 1862–1917* (Cambridge, Cambridge University Press, 1981).

4 The existence of Jewish political parties contesting parliamentary elections in Poland and Romania between the wars are something of an exception to this general rule.

5 According to John Higham such concerns are common to most ethnic groups in America. He adds a fourth – the group's internal integrity and cohesion – which we do not deal with here, although it is dealt with below in a somewhat different context. See his 'Introduction: the forms of ethnic leadership', in John Higham (ed.), *Ethnic Leadership in America* (Baltimore, Johns Hopkins University Press, 1978), p. 4.

6 Steven M. Cohen's studies for the AJC conducted almost annually since 1980 consistently show that between two-thirds and three-quarters of American Jews believe that 'Anti-Semitism in America may, in the future, become a serious problem for American Jews'.

7 I have examined this development in some detail in Peter Y. Medding, 'Segmented ethnicity and the new Jewish politics', in *Studies in Contemporary Jewry*, vol. III (New York, 1987), pp. 26–48.

8 See Leon A. Jick, 'The Holocaust: its use and abuse within the American public', *Yad Vashem Studies*, vol. 14 (1981), pp. 303–18, for an analysis of the development of the awareness of the Holocaust in the United States, for both Jews and non-Jews. See also Stephen J. Whitfield, 'The Holocaust and the American Jewish intellectual', *Judaism*, 28 (1979), pp. 391–401.

9 For a more detailed analysis of the development of Holocaust consciousness and the question of Jewish survival, see Medding, 'Segmented ethnicity . . .', pp. 26–45.

10 *Joint Program Plan, 1953*, pp. 3, 21. This is the annual statement by NJCRAC setting out the full spectrum of political and social issues confronting American Jews, with guidelines and recommendations for action. It is without a doubt the most comprehensive and authoritative statement of the political agenda of the organized Jewish community in America, as NJCRAC is the roof body of eleven national and 111 local Jewish community relations bodies.

11 Lawrence H. Fuchs, *The Political Behavior of American Jews* (Glencoe, Ill., Free Press, 1956), ch. 6.

12 *Joint Program Plan, 1984/5*, pp. 3, 29.

13 Unpublished typescript made available by the speaker, Arthur Chotin, who was then a key AIPAC official.

14 See I. L. Kenen, *Israel's Defense Line: Her Friends and Foes in Washington* (Buffalo, Prometheus Books, no date), for a personal history of AIPAC's early years by its founder and long-time executive officer.

15 AIPAC Policy Statement, *Near East Report*, 29 April 1985.

16 Mitchell Geoffrey Bard, *The Water's Edge and Beyond: Defining the Limits to Domestic Influence on United States Middle East Policy* (New Brunswick, Transaction Publishers, 1991), p. 12.

17 AIPAC *Congressional Report*, to: AIPAC Officers, Executive Committee, National Council and Key Contacts (mimeo., 17 May 1987).

18 See Michael J. Malbin, *Unelected Representatives: Congressional Staff and the Future of Representative Government* (New York, Basic Books, 1980), for a critical analysis of the pivotal and burgeoning role of congressional staff.

19 Ibid.

20 On PACs in general see Larry J. Sabato, *PAC Power: Inside the World of Political Action Committees* (New York, W. W. Norton, 1984).

21 The data in this paragraph are derived from Herbert E. Alexander, 'Pro-Israel PACs: a small part of a large movement', a paper for the International Conference on the Domestic Determinants of US Policy in the Middle East (Tel Aviv University, 1987), 19pp. He also indicated that the total number of such PACs is hard to determine, and could be as high as ninety.

22 Marvin C. Feuerwerger, *Congress and Israel: Foreign Aid Decision-making in the House of Representatives, 1969–1976* (Westport, Greenwood Press, 1979), p. 97.

23 This was conducted by the present author with the assistance of the Center for Modern Jewish Studies at Brandeis University. A mail questionnaire was sent to all Jewish members of the 99th Congress in December 1986, with follow-ups in 1987. As a result of electoral defeat, retirement and death, the total possible return was thirty-four. Of these, nineteen responded. No clear pattern could be detected among the non-respondents as far as their known Jewish affiliations could be ascertained.

24 Feuerwerger, op. cit., pp. 77–90.

25 Feuerwerger's survey of all members of the 94th Congress reached similar findings, emphasizing Israel's democratic character, the tradition of friendship between the two countries, shared foreign policy interests and public awareness of the Holocaust.

26 See AIPAC *1986 Legislative Report*, pp. 13–16 for a detailed analysis of the long congressional battle, the successful whittling down by AIPAC of the size of the arms package, the continuing congressional opposition to the President's proposals even after they had been whittled down, and even after AIPAC (backed

by the Presidents' Conference, NJCRAC and ADL) decided not to fight, because 'Israel would not be significantly threatened by the proposed package', a 'major fight against this sale was not worth the expenditure of political capital', 'and given the marginal threat of the weapons involved, an effort against the missiles alone would not be worth risking the overall favorable state of U.S.–Israel relations', and finally the President's eventual success in overriding the congressional veto margins only after tremendous personal pressure on senators and congressmen, including an attempt to get Jewish leaders to lobby senators in support of the sale.

27 *New York Times*, 12 October 1988.
28 See Ben Bradlee Jr, 'Israel's lobby', *Boston Globe Magazine*, 29 April 1984, pp. 8. 9, 64, 66, 70, 72, 73, 76, 78, 80, 82; William J. Lanouette, 'The many faces of the Jewish lobby in America', *National Journal*, 13 May 1978, no. 19, pp. 748–59; Wolf Blitzer, 'The AIPAC formula', *Moment*, November 1981, vol. 6, no. 10, pp. 22–8.
29 See Hugh Heclo, 'Issue networks and the executive establishment', in Anthony King (ed.), *The New American Political System* (Washington, DC, AEI, 1981), pp. 87–123.
30 See, for example, Steven M. Cohen, *The Dimensions of American Jewish Liberalism* (New York, American Jewish Committee, 1989), especially the tables, pp. 42–7.
31 Cohen, *Dimensions of American Jewish Liberalism*, p. 44.
32 See Gregory Martire and Ruth Clark, *Anti-Semitism in the United States* (New York, 1982), p. 42.
33 Steven M. Cohen, National Survey of American Jews, 1984, 1985, AJC.
34 Ibid.
35 See, for example, the reports on the February 1987 and April 1988 Roper Polls, prepared for the American Jewish Committee by David Singer and Renae Cohen.

5

THE SKILLS AND ECONOMIC STATUS OF AMERICAN JEWRY

Barry R. Chiswick

I INTRODUCTION

The past half-century has witnessed dramatic changes in the structure of the American economy and in the opportunities open to American Jews in the classroom and in the workplace. Has the opening of opportunities accelerated the rate of improvement in skills and economic status among American Jews in comparison with other Americans? Has the growth in higher education across the board in America reduced the relatively advantageous situation of American Jews with non-Jews catching up to the educational and occupational achievements of Jewish Americans? Has the greater Americanization of the Jewish population resulted in a regression to the mean of their skills and economic status?

There have been several quantitative and qualitative studies of the relative educational attainment and economic status of American Jewry at various points in time over the past century.[1] The pattern that emerges from these studies is that after an initial immigrant adjustment period, Jews have achieved higher levels of schooling, occupational status and earnings than non-Jews. It is not possible to discern, however, whether there has been a trend in relative Jewish achievement since the Second World War. The studies present a picture at a moment in time, but they differ in research methodology and the data are not strictly comparable. This paper is able to examine the level and trends over time in Jewish educational and economic status relative to non-Jews by using survey data collected over a period of years using the same survey research methodology.

The data required for this study and that form the basis for the analysis are described in Section II. The empirical analysis is in Section III. Section III begins with a discussion of the method of analysis. It then includes three substantive sections on patterns of educational achievement, occupational attainment and labour market earnings. Section IV closes the paper with a summary and conclusion.

115

II DATA REQUIREMENTS AND AVAILABILITY

This section discusses the data problems inherent in a systematic quantitative analysis of the skills and economic status of American Jewry over time. Part A discusses the general data problems for social science research on American Jewry and the particular requirements for this inquiry. Part B identifies the General Social Survey (GSS) as the best data available for the purpose of this study. The study population and variables are defined in Part C.

(A) Data requirements

Certain quite specific data are required to analyse the trends over time in the skills and economic status of American Jewry. First, the data must include measures of skill and economic status. For the purposes of this study, educational attainment, occupational status and labour market earnings can be used as widely accepted useful indices of the concepts relevant for skill and economic success.[2]

Second, the data must include both Jews and non-Jews, and a way of distinguishing between them. Jews cannot be studied in isolation; a reference group is required. If a reference group is not explicitly identified, the reader will implicitly evaluate the data relative to his or her own subjectively defined reference group. For this reason Jewish communal surveys are not useful for this project. The communal surveys are limited to Jews and their questions and survey methodology do not permit easy comparisons with general population surveys and censuses.[3]

Much of the data used for the study of racial and ethnic minorities in the United States, such as blacks, Hispanics, Asians and immigrants, are derived from censuses (e.g., decennial Census of Population) and surveys (e.g., the on-going Current Population Survey, the Survey of Income and Program Participation, and the 1976 mid-decade Survey of Income and Education) conducted by the US Bureau of the Census. Census Bureau policy, however, precludes asking a question on religion and precludes coding any response to an ethnic ancestry question that might reveal a person's religion (e.g., a response of 'Polish Jew' would be coded 'Polish' and a response 'Jewish' would be coded as 'Other').[4]

A third requirement is that there be a sufficiently large number of Jews in the data for a statistically meaningful analysis. Some privately conducted surveys and certain federally sponsored fertility surveys do ask religion and often 'over sample' minorities. These surveys are generally relatively small and do not include Jews among the minorities oversampled.[5] Since American Jews are only about 2.5 per cent of the population, even if Jews are separately identified the number of observations is generally too small for a statistically meaningful analysis.

For the purposes of this project there is a fourth data requirement. It is not possible to analyse trends over time by a study of data that refer to a point in time. If, for example, the 1980 Census of Population had included a question on religion it would have been possible to analyse the earnings of Jews relative to non-Jews in 1980. It would not have been possible from such data to analyse trends over time. What is ideally required are data drawn from many different points in time using the same questions and survey methodology. The relative patterns from these many points in time can then be used to study trends over time.

(B) The general social survey

The four data requirements discussed in Part A are extremely demanding. There is apparently only one data set for the United States that satisfies each of these requirements, the General Social Survey (GSS).

The GSS is a national probability sample (random sample) of the population of the United States conducted by the National Opinion Research Center (NORC), which is affiliated with the University of Chicago. The GSS has been conducted during February to April in nearly every year since 1972.[6] Each survey is an independently drawn sample of English-speaking individuals 18 years of age and over, living in non-institutional arrangements within the United States. Each respondent is asked a lengthy series of questions about himself or herself, the respondent's parents and household members. The questions elicit information about the demographic, economic and sociological characteristics of the respondent, the parents and spouse. The median length of the interview is about one and a half hours. Because the primary objective of the GSS was to develop time-series data, the basic questions and survey methodology did not change over time.

The most recent cumulative data file includes a total of 21,975 completed interviews for the fourteen surveys conducted from 1972 to 1987. This is about 1,500 interviews per survey. The GSS asked religion at the time of interview of the respondent and, for those currently married, the respondent's spouse. Since 1973 the survey has also asked the religion of the respondent and the respondent's spouse at age 16. These questions on religion permit an identification of Jews.

The GSS asked many other questions of the respondent relevant to this study. These include age, education, marital status, region of residence, size of place of residence (e.g., metropolitan area), occupation and labour market earnings. Furthermore, the GSS asked certain questions about the respondent's parents. These include parental education, father's occupation and mother's labour force status when the respondent was age 16.[7]

The GSS permits an analysis of the respondent's schooling, occupational status and earnings at the time of interview. The multi-year nature of the survey allows for an analysis of trends over time for the period 1972 to 1987.

Two features of the data on the respondents that constrain the analysis can be mitigated by utilizing the data on father's education and occupation. First, the time period is only about fifteen years.[8] Second, for the analysis of men the total sample size of Jews is about 250; a larger sample would be desirable. The data on father's educational attainment and occupational status at age 16, together with data on the respondent's age at time of interview (a proxy for father's age) and the year of the interview provide important parental information at a known point in time. This extends the data back in time by about two decades. Furthermore, the data on father's education and occupation can be used for both the male and female respondents, thereby nearly doubling the sample of males in the parental analysis compared to the respondent analysis.

Thus, the GSS satisfies each of the four requirements specified above. It includes data on the relevant variables for the study of skills and economic status, it includes an explicit identification of Jews, the Jewish sample is sufficiently large and the time-series nature of the survey and retrospective data on parents permit the analysis of trends in differences between Jews and others.

(C) Defining the study population and variables

The General Social Survey includes data for non-institutional individuals age 18 and over. For the purpose of this study only those 25 to 64 years are considered. Many of those age 18 to 24 years are still in school or making relatively large investments in on-the-job training and job search. For those 65 years and older the impact of retirement on earnings and labour market status becomes dominant. The study population is further limited to whites; the white population is a more appropriate comparison group for a study of Jews than is the total population. The analysis of educational attainment is performed for both men and women, but the analyses of occupational attainment and earnings are limited to males.[9]

Jewish respondents in the General Social Survey can be identified by two questions on religion (see Table 5.1). One is self-reported religious preference at the time of interview and the other, asked since the 1973 survey, is religious preference at age 16. As would be expected there is a very high degree of correspondence between the two methods for identifying Jews. The question on religion during childhood is used for this study, largely because these responses are less likely to be influenced by the person's current educational and economic status than is religion at the time of interview. Under either definition Jews are about 2.5 per cent of the sample. There are too few cases of individuals who are Jewish under one definition but not under the other for a statistically meaningful analysis of this group.

The three measures of skill and labour market status studied here are educational attainment, occupational prestige and earnings. Educational attainment refers to the highest grade of schooling the person finished and

Table 5.1 General social survey: questions on respondents' religion

Question	Years
'What is your religious preference? Is it Protestant, Catholic, Jewish, some other religion or no religion?'	1972 to 1987
'In what religion were you raised? (Religion at age 16)'	1973 to 1987

Source: National Opinion Research Center, *General Social Survey Cumulative File, Code Book*, Chicago, NORC, 1987.

for which he or she received credit. The father's educational attainment is defined in the same way.

The respondents were asked a series of questions to elicit the information needed for the coding of an occupation variable. The GSS used the US Bureau of the Census three-digit occupation classification and converted this to an occupational prestige score.[10] A similar procedure was used to develop the occupational prestige score of the respondent's father.

For each of the eleven GSS surveys from 1974 to 1986 the respondents were asked to report their labour market earnings, before taxes and other deductions. Interval mid-points were used to approximate the respondent's earnings in that interval.

III   DATA ANALYSIS: DIFFERENCES IN LEVELS AND TRENDS OVER TIME

This section presents the method of analysis and the substantive analysis.

(A)   Method of analysis

For each dependent variable the analysis follows the same four-step pattern. First, the statistical analysis estimates the average difference between Jews and non-Jews for the variable under study, controlling only for survey year.[11] This has only a trivial effect on the observed difference in means. It will be shown below that in each instance the Jewish respondents, and the parents of the Jewish respondents, have significantly higher achievements.

Second, the analysis is performed adding statistical controls for demographic and skill variables. For example, Jews may have higher levels of education, occupational status and earnings because they are more likely to live in metropolitan areas outside the south where these measures tend to be higher in general. Or, their higher level of occupation and earnings may be due to a greater educational attainment. The effect of being Jewish when the analysis controls for differences in demographic, skill and survey year variables, indicates the remaining unexplained average Jewish–non-Jewish difference. It will be shown below that, although the Jewish–non-Jewish differences diminish when these variables are held constant, Jews still have significantly higher levels of schooling, occupational status and earnings.

Third, a variable is added to the analysis to test for a trend over time in the Jewish–non-Jewish differential. It will be shown below that among the respondents there is no trend in the Jewish advantage in schooling, occupational status and earnings in the survey period.

Fourth, for education and occupation there is an analysis of the intergenerational change in the Jewish–non-Jewish differential. It will be shown that the differential in favour of Jews increased from the father's to the son's (respondents') generations.

The explanatory variables are defined for the respondent at age 16 for the study of education and at the time of the interview for occupation and earnings. The situation is more complex in the analysis of father's educational attainment and occupational status. Data on the father's demographic characteristics are not available, so it is assumed that the father's race and religion are the same as that of the respondent and that the father was married and living in the same place as the respondent when the latter was age 16. For the analysis of fathers it is also necessary to control for the point in time when the respondent was age 16. Was it ten years ago or forty years ago? Obviously, the older the respondent the further back in time was the respondent age 16. This influence is held constant by including the respondent's age as a proxy for father's age in the analysis for father's education and occupation.

(B) Educational attainment

The analysis of educational attainment is performed separately for the respondents, both male and female, and for the respondents' fathers.

(i) The respondents' education

There are 316 Jewish observations (2.7 per cent) in the sample of 11,873 observations for which all of the variables are available for the analysis of the educational attainment of male and female respondents. The mean educational attainment in the sample is 12.6 years for the non-Jews and 15.1 years for the Jews (see Table 5.2). Controlling for the survey year, the Jewish observations have 2.5 more years of schooling than the non-Jews, and the difference is highly statistically significant.

Statistical controls are added to the analyses for the respondent's age, sex and residence at age 16.[12] This is important because educational opportunities and attainment vary systematically across these variables and Jews are more likely than others to live in the urban north. Controlling for these factors the Jewish educational advantage is 2.0 years and is still highly

Table 5.2 Means and percentages for variables in analyses of education[a]

Variables	Jews	Non-Jews	Total
Education (years)	15.1	12.6	12.6
Education of father (years)	11.6	9.7	9.8
Lived in south at age 16 (per cent)	12.0	29.0	28.0
Lived in city at age 16 (per cent)	87.0	36.0	38.0
Age (years)	43.0	42.0	42.1
Female (per cent)	52.0	55.0	55.0
Lived outside US at age 16 (per cent)	7.0	4.0	4.0
Sample size (respondents)	315	11,549	11,864
Sample size (fathers)	246	9,037	9,283

a All of the variables refer to the respondent, except father's education.

Source: National Opinion Research Center, *General Social Survey, 1972–1987, Cumulative Data File*, Chicago, NORC, 1987.

statistically significant. That is, place of residence at age 16 explained about one-fifth of the simple differential of 2.5 years. The advantageous effect of region is due to residence in the urban north, rather than in rural or southern areas. The effect of a larger proportion of Jews among adult immigrants (i.e., those living outside the United States at age 16) is associated with a slight lowering of their average level of schooling.

The substantial Jewish educational advantage is greater for men than for women. Jewish men have 2.5 more years of schooling than non-Jewish men, while Jewish women have 1.6 more years of schooling than non-Jewish women. Women have less schooling than men in both groups, but the difference is 0.5 years for non-Jews and 1.3 years for Jews.[13]

The data indicate that within the survey period there is no significant trend over time among the respondents in the Jewish–non-Jewish educational differential.

Another way of testing for a trend is to ask whether the educational attainment of the children relative to that of their fathers has grown over time. Because of missing data on father's education, when this variable is added to the analysis the sample is reduced to 9,275 observations of which 246 are Jewish (2.7 per cent).

As would be expected, father's education is the most important determinant of children's education. An extra year of father's schooling is associated with a statistically significant 0.30 years of additional schooling among the children. Controlling for father's education has little effect on the Jewish/ non-Jewish differential. Jews still have a higher level of education; the difference is greater for men than for women (by 2.10 years for men and 1.33 years for women), and both differences are highly significant. The time-trend variable within the GSS survey period remains small and positive, but not statistically significant. These findings indicate that there was a sharp increase in the relative education of Jews from their parent's generation to their own.

(ii) The father's education

When the analysis shifts to the study of the father's educational attainment, the 247 Jewish observations are 2.7 per cent of the sample. The fathers in this sample had 9.8 years of schooling among non-Jews and 11.6 years for the Jews (see Table 5.2). Controlling for the respondent's age and the survey year, the Jewish fathers had 1.85 years more than the non-Jewish fathers, and the difference is highly significant.[14] When variables are added for the father's residence, the Jewish educational advantage is smaller, 1.04 years, but is still statistically significant.

The analysis indicates that Jewish and non-Jewish fathers had about the same number of years of schooling, other variables the same, among the respondents 52 years of age in the mid-point of the sample period (1980). That is, parental schooling was about the same for those born in 1928, or with fathers born at the turn of the century. Younger Jewish respondents, however, had fathers with increasing educational advantages over non-Jews – by one year of schooling for each ten years of age.

Thus, the analysis indicates that adult American Jews in the 1970s and 1980s experienced a sharp increase in educational attainment, both absolute and relative to non-Jews, in comparison to their father's generation, particularly for the younger cohorts. An educational advantage of about two years persists among adults reporting in the 1970s and 1980s. There is no evidence that this differential is widening or diminishing.

(C) Occupational status

The analysis of occupational status is based on the occupational prestige score as coded in the General Social Survey. Table 5.3 reports the prestige scores of selected occupations. This section first examines the occupational prestige scores of the respondents and then that of the respondents' fathers.

(i) The respondents' occupational status

The occupational prestige scores for male respondents are available for 5,314 observations of whom 147 (2.8 per cent) are Jewish. The mean occupational prestige score in the sample is 42 in the non-Jewish sample (see Table 5.4). This is the equivalent of the occupational prestige scores (41 to 43) of photographers, inspectors (construction and non-construction), railroad conductors and engravers. The mean prestige score in the Jewish sample, however, is 53 which is the equivalent (51 to 55) of industrial engineers, surveyors, social workers, opticians, librarians and locomotion

Table 5.3 Prestige scores of selected occupations

Occupation	Score
Physicians	82
Teachers, college and university	78
Lawyers and judges	76
Aeronautical engineers	71
Mechanical engineers	62
Accountants	57
Librarians	55
Editors and reporters	51
Bank tellers	50
Sales representatives, manufacturing	49
Policemen and detectives	48
Real estate agents and brokers	44
Construction inspectors, public administration	41
Railroad conductors	41
Welders and flame cutters	40
Restaurant, cafeteria and bar managers	39
Cranemen, derrickmen, hoistmen	39
Automobile mechanics	37
Farm foremen	35
Dispatchers and starters, vehicles	34
Bakers	34
Plasterers	33
Bus drivers	32
Truck drivers	32
Cashiers	31
Boilermakers	31
Drill press operators	29
Sales clerk, retail	29
Carpenter's helpers	23
Taxi cab drivers and chauffeurs	22
Vehicle washers	20
Messengers and office boys	19
Clothing ironers and pressers	18
Farm labourers, wage workers	18
Construction Labourers, except carpenter's helpers	17
Baggage porters and bell hops	14

Source: National Opinion Research Center, *General Social Survey Cumulative File, Code Book*, Chicago, NORC, 1987, Appendix F, pp. 544–55.

engineers. Controlling only for the survey year, the Jewish observations have an occupational prestige score 11.3 points greater than non-Jews.

As was shown above, however, Jews have a significantly higher educational attainment than non-Jews, and educational attainment is the most important determinant of the occupational score. Since each additional year of schooling raises the prestige score by 2.64 points, the Jewish male educational advantage of 2.5 years of schooling, all else the same, could

Table 5.4 Means and percentages for variables in analysis of occupational prestige scores and earnings[a]

Variables	Jews	Non-Jews	Total
Prestige score	53.2	41.9	42.2
Father's prestige score	46.6	40.5	40.6
Earnings ($)	27,322	19,750	19,969
Education (years)	15.8	12.8	12.9
Labour market experience (years)	22.4	24.2	24.2
Married (per cent)	69.0	76.0	75.0
Living in the south (per cent)	20.0	31.0	30.0
Living in a metropolitan area (per cent)	78.0	43.0	43.0
Sample size (respondent, except earnings)	147	5,161	5,308
Sample size (father's prestige score)	246	9,962	9,208

a All of the variables refer to the male respondent, except for father's occupational prestige.

Source: National Opinion Research Center, *General Social Survey, 1972–1987, Cumulative Data File*, Chicago, NORC, 1987.

account for a 6.6-point differential, or over one-half of the observed 11.3-point simple differential. Jews are also more likely to be currently married and living in a metropolitan area, both of which are associated with higher prestige scores. On the other hand, Jews are less likely to live in the south, and southern residence is associated with higher prestige scores.

Controlling for education, labour market experience, marital status and residence, the occupational prestige score of the Jews exceeds that of the non-Jews by 3.79 points, and the difference is statistically highly significant. Although education explains nearly half and the other variables explain another one-sixth of the observed simple difference, about one-third of the differential remains. There is, however, no trend over time within the sample period in the difference in prestige scores.

The father's occupational prestige score can be added to the analysis of the respondent's occupational status. When this is done, due to missing data, the sample of Jews is reduced to 138 men (2.9 per cent) out of 4,728 observations. Other variables the same, father's occupational status has little effect on the son's occupation. A unit increase in the father's score raises the son's score by only 0.08 points, although the effect is statistically significant.

Education remains the most important variable. Among adult white men one year of their own schooling is worth the equivalent of 32 points in their father's occupational prestige score. A difference of 32 points is very large; it is the equivalent of a difference between a father who is a lawyer or judge (score 76 points) and one who is a real estate agent (score 44 points). When combined with the small effect of father's educational attainment on the son's educational attainment, this demonstrates the meritocracy of America. That is, a person's own educational attainment is far more important in determining his occupation than is his father's occupation.

Controlling for father's occupation, Jews have an occupational prestige score that is 3.49 points higher than non-Jews at the mid-point of the survey interval. That is, controlling for father's occupational prestige results in only a small reduction (from 3.8 to 3.5 points) in the Jewish–non-Jewish differential, but the differential remains substantial and significant. This implies an increase from the fathers' to the sons' generation in the differential in prestige scores.

(ii) The father's occupational status

The sample size is larger for the analysis of father's occupational status than for the male respondents. The increase arises because the data on fathers used for both the male and female respondents more than offsets the losses due to the non-reporting of father's occupation. Of the 10,474 observations for the analysis of father's occupational prestige, 283 (2.7 per cent) are for Jews.

The mean occupational prestige score in the analysis of father's occupation is 40 overall and among the non-Jews, and 47 among the Jews (see Table 5.4). A score of 40 is the level of sales representatives (wholesale trade), floor layers (except tile setters), and carpenters, while 47 is the level of carpet installers, aircraft mechanics, machinists and dental laboratory technicians. When the survey year and the age of the respondent (a proxy for the father's age) are held constant, the Jewish fathers had an occupational prestige score 6.0 points higher than the non-Jews, a highly significant difference.

Controlling for father's education and place of residence when the respondent was age 16, the occupational prestige score of the Jewish father's exceeded that of other fathers by 3.06 points. These variables explain about one-half of the gross differential of 6 points. The occupational prestige differential did not narrow or widen over time among the fathers.

(D) Earnings

The analysis of the respondent's earnings is for his primary occupation, before deductions and taxes.[15] The analysis is performed using the data from the eleven samples taken during the period 1974 to 1986. The 124 Jews in the data that can be analysed constitute 2.9 per cent of the sample of 4,297.

The average earnings over the sample period was less than $19,800 for non-Jews and over $27,300 for Jews (Table 5.4).[16] This implies 38 per cent higher earnings among the Jews. Controlling for only the survey year, the Jews have about 40 per cent higher earnings.

Jews have higher earnings in part because they have more schooling, are more likely to be currently married and are more likely to live in the urban north. Controlling statistically for these effects substantially reduces the earnings differential from about 40 per cent to 16 per cent higher earnings among Jews. There does not appear to be a trend over time in the observed earnings differential. The differential of 16 per cent is consistent with other studies that have examined Jewish/non-Jewish earnings using single cross-sections of data in the post-war period (Chiswick 1983; 1985; in press).

IV SUMMARY, CONCLUSIONS AND IMPLICATIONS

This paper has been concerned with the economic status of American Jews in comparison with non-Jewish Americans. It focuses on trends over the past few decades in the levels of schooling attainment, occupational status and earnings. Trends in these differentials are important for understanding the Jewish experience in the United States, and the experience of the diverse racial and ethnic minorities in the United States, as well as for assessing the future needs of the Jewish community and viability of its institutions.

The General Social Survey (GSS) appears to be the only source available that satisfies the essential data requirements for this study. The GSS includes data on schooling, occupation and earnings, as well as a variety of demographic variables essential for the analysis. It also includes a variable for identifying Jews, and there are a sufficient number of Jews for a statistically meaningful analysis. A key feature of the GSS is that the same survey methodology was used in each of the fourteen surveys from 1972 to 1987, thereby permitting an analysis of trends in schooling and economic status over time. Furthermore, the GSS includes selected information on the respondent's father. This permits extending the analysis of Jewish–non-Jewish differentials back in time and examining the inter-generational change in the differentials in schooling and occupation.

The mean educational level of the male and female respondents in the GSS was 15.1 years among the Jews and 12.6 years among the non-Jews, a difference of 2.5 years. Adjusting statistically for the respondent's age, sex and residence, the Jewish educational advantage declines to 2.0 years, but is still statistically significant. The educational advantage of Jews, other things the same, is greater for men (2.5 years) than it is for women (1.6 years). There was no trend in the difference in schooling levels between Jews and non-Jews across the survey years.

For the respondents' fathers, there was no Jewish–non-Jewish differential in schooling among those born at the turn of the century, but there was a growing educational differential in favour of Jews the more recently born is the father. And the increase in educational attainment from father to child was larger among the Jews. Furthermore, even after controlling for their own characteristics and their fathers' education, the Jewish respondents had a higher level of schooling (2.1 years among the men, 1.3 years among the women).

The occupational status of the male Jewish respondents, as measured by the occupational prestige score, is significantly greater than that of non-Jews both overall (11.3 points greater) and when other variables are controlled (3.8 points greater). Other things the same, the Jewish fathers also had a greater occupational attainment (by 3.1 points). The statistical control for the father's occupation had only a small effect on the Jewish/non-Jewish differential, lowering it from 3.8 points to 3.5 points. These findings imply an inter-generational increase in the relative occupational status of the Jews. The data, however, show no significant change within the survey period for the respondents.

The analysis also indicates that overall the Jewish men earned about 40 per cent more than the non-Jewish men. Other things the same, including schooling, the Jewish respondents have about 16 per cent higher earnings. This is comparable to findings in other studies for the post-war period. There is, however, no significant trend in this earnings differential over the period under study.

The analyses indicate a dramatic increase in the educational and occupational attainment of the Jewish respondents relative to their fathers, in comparison with non-Jews. Within the survey period (1972 to 1987), however, there is no significant trend in the Jewish advantage in schooling, occupational status and earnings. This could arise because the steepening Jewish advantage among the immigrant and first-generation American Jews has reached a plateau for their more Americanized descendants. It is possible, however, that it reflects offsetting trends and that the forces for convergence to the American norm may be gaining ascendancy. Yet, other data suggest that the differentials will not narrow significantly in the next generation. The very low fertility, high rate of marital stability, and large investment of parental time and other resources per child on the part of contemporary American Jews can be expected to result in continued high levels of achievement among their children.

NOTES

1 These single-period studies include Chiswick (1983; 1985; 1989; 1990), Dinnerstein (1982), Goldstein (1969), Kahan (1986), Kephart (1949), Kuznets (1972; 1975) and Ruppin (1913), among others. Chiswick (in press) compares data at four points in time in the post-war period. For studies of other countries, see Altshuler (1987), Elazar (1983), Prais and Schmool (1975) and Tomes (1983).

2 Although it would be desirable to expand the analysis to include assets, income from assets (rents, interest and pensions) and public income transfers, these data are generally not available, and when they are available are subject to much more reporting error than the three measures under investigation.

3 The Jewish communal surveys have been very fruitful for addressing many questions that require data solely on Jews, and comparisons among Jews. The

1990 National Jewish Population Survey is being designed to permit meaningful comparisons with data from the 1990 Census of Population of the United States.

4 A notable exception is the March 1957 Current Population Survey which included a question on religion. Although some cross-tabulations have been released from this survey, the data have not been made generally available. The cross-tabulations have been studied in Chiswick (1985; in press), Goldstein (1969) and Kuznets (1972).

5 The oversampling of minorities is generally limited to those who are disadvantaged, blacks and more recently also Hispanics. The religion question frequently asks respondents to identify whether they are Protestant, Catholic or Other, with no separate identification of Jews, or Jews are combined with others during data reduction.

6 The cumulative data file, 1972 to 1987, includes fourteen surveys, with a survey conducted annually except for 1979 and 1981. Most of the analyses in this study are based on the thirteen surveys from 1973 to 1987.

7 For understandable reasons, respondents generally cannot report parental earnings when they were teenagers.

8 While age cohorts can, in principle, be used to look 'backward' to study trends over time for schooling, this cannot be done for occupational status or earnings, which vary over the working life.

9 The labour market variables, occupation and earnings, can be studied only for those currently employed. Because adult women have about half the labour force participation rate of adult men, the sample of Jewish women becomes too small for a statistically meaningful analysis. A study of female labour supply is beyond the scope of this paper.

10 For further details on the construction of the occupational prestige scores, see *General Social Surveys* (1987).

11 Controlling for the survey year adjusts for changes over the period in the average levels of schooling, occupational status and earnings. Earnings, for example, are particularly affected by annual variations in rates of inflation and real wages. The survey-year variables also help to hold constant the effects of subtle differences in the survey that may influence the variables from year to year.

12 Residence at age 16 is more appropriate than current residence in an analysis of the determinants of educational attainment among the adult population. However, as a test the equations were also computed using current place of residence. The substantive findings are the same.

13 It appears that differences in educational attainment in the United States vary across racial and ethnic groups by more for men than for women. The male-to-female educational ratio is greater the higher the mean level of education for the group.

14 The older the respondent the earlier in time was he or she age 16 and the lower the educational level of the father.

15 Occupational prestige scores are not included in the earnings analysis. Earnings and occupational status are two measures of the same phenomenon, the outcome of the labour market process.

16 Earnings increase sharply in the sample period due to the increase in skill level, real wages for workers of the same skill, and inflation. Average earnings among the respondents for 1985 were about double the earnings in 1973.

REFERENCES

Altshuler, M. (1987) *Soviet Jewry since the Second World War: Population and Social Structure*. New York, Greenwood Press.

Chiswick, B. R. (1983) 'The earnings and human capital of American Jews', *Journal of Human Resources*. Summer, pp. 313–36.

Chiswick, B. R. (1985) 'The labor market status of American Jews: patterns and determinants', *American Jewish Year Book, 1985*. New York, American Jewish Committee, pp. 131–53.

Chiswick, B. R. (1989) 'Jewish immigrant wages in America, 1909', Department of Economics, University of Illinois at Chicago, photocopy.

Chiswick, B. R. (1990) 'Jewish immigrant skill and occupational attainment at the turn of the century', *Explorations in Economic History* (October).

Chiswick, B. R. (in press) 'The post-war economy of American Jews', *Studies in Contemporary Jewry*, vol. 8.

Dinnerstein, (1982) 'Education and the achievement of American Jews', in Bernard J. Weiss (ed.), *American Education and European Immigration, 1840–1940*. Urbana, University of Illinois Press.

Elazar, D. J., with Medding, P. (1983) *Jewish Communities in Frontier Societies: Argentina, Australia and South Africa*. New York, Holmes & Meier.

General Social Surveys, 1972–1987: Cumulative Codebook (1987). National Opinion Research Center, University of Chicago.

Goldstein, S. (1969) 'Socioeconomic differentials among religious groups in the United States', *American Journal of Sociology* (May), vol. 74, no. 6, pp. 612–31.

Kahan, A. (1986) *Essays in Jewish Social and Economic History*. Chicago, University of Chicago Press.

Kephart, W. M. (1949) 'Position of Jewish economy in the United States', *Social Forces* (December), vol. 28, no. 2, pp. 153–64.

Kuznets, S. (1972) *Economic Structure of U.S. Jewry: Recent Trends*. Jerusalem, Institute of Contemporary Jewry, Hebrew University.

Kuznets, S. (1975) 'Immigration of Russian Jews to the United States: background and structure', *Perspective in American History*, vol. 9, pp. 35–126.

Prais, S. J. and Schmool, M. (1975) 'The social-class structure of Anglo-Jewry, 1961', *Jewish Journal of Sociology*, June, vol. 16, pp. 5–15.

Ruppin, A. (1913) *The Jews of To-Day*. New York, Henry Holt & Co.

Tomes, N. (1983) 'Religion and the rate of return on human capital: evidence from Canada', *Canadian Journal of Economics*, February, pp. 122–38.

6

MODERNIZATION, ETHNICITY AND THE POST-WAR JEWISH WORLD[1]

Calvin Goldscheider

Two radical and complex revolutions have characterized the Jewish people in the post-Second World War, post-Holocaust, period. The first is more conspicuous and well known – the establishment of the Jewish State of Israel, the immigration *and* integration of over 1.5 million immigrants from diverse Jewish communities around the world, and the social–economic–political–cultural development of Israeli society. The impact of the State of Israel on the condition of the Jewish people world-wide has been, and continues to be, overwhelming; and can be described accurately as a critical turning point in Jewish history. The State of Israel is the ideological, cultural, emotional and historical centre of Jewish peoplehood.

A second revolution has also emerged clearly in the second half of the twentieth century and it too has profoundly altered the nature of the Jewish people. It is less well appreciated and some have been sceptical about its revolutionary nature: it is the emergence of large, cohesive and powerful Jewish communities in modern, Western, pluralist societies. Jews in these societies define themselves and are comfortable both as Jews and as full citizens of the states that they live in. These Jews are part of legitimate and accepted ethnic–religious communities, consider themselves a significant part of their societies but distinctly identify as Jews, with long-term roots in their countries, as well as with strong linkages to the State of Israel. They have developed complex local, national and international institutions, life-styles and cultural forms that enrich their ethnic and religious expressions.

These multi-generational Jewish communities outside of the State of Israel do not appear to be ephemeral. Their Judaism and their Jewishness are expressed in diverse and new ways that challenge the simple assumptions about the demise of religion and the total assimilation of ethnic and religious minorities in modern society. For while Jews have assimilated and become secular in some ways, their communities have become stronger and more viable in other ways. They have developed creative responses to their Jewishness and new expressions of Judaism in a secular context, at the same time that they have experienced some forms of assimilation. They are well integrated into and share much of the broader national culture and society in which they live; yet they remain distinctive communities. While most are committed to the State of Israel and the continuity of the Jewish people, they are not in their own view and in their behaviour in 'exile' or in Diaspora. Their 'home' is where they live, where they expect to continue living and where they are raising the next generation to live.[2]

Both of these Jewish revolutions inside and outside of the State of Israel are rooted in the historic pre-Second World War past. The Israeli Jewish community, its structure and institutions, are very much continuous with the Jewish settlement and institution building in Palestine; most Jewish communities outside of the State of Israel have roots that are several generations deep in their societies and did not emerge simply out of the ashes of the Holocaust in a destroyed Europe. Both of these revolutions are unfolding in our days and are most likely to continue to change in the future. While rooted in the past, these communities are strikingly different from any previous pattern in modern Jewish history.[3]

These two revolutionary developments are also linked to each other in complex ways: the State of Israel is a powerful source of Jewish continuity and identity for Jews and their communities elsewhere; Jewish communities outside the State of Israel have been critical economic and political resources for the State of Israel. The web of interrelationships between these communities is symbiotic, such that mutual dependencies have developed. These dependencies have also undergone revolutionary changes in the post-Second World War period, as each of the communities is changing, as both respond to each other and to the world community, and as technology and communication bring together geographically separated communities and foster the increasing exchange of ideas, culture *and* people. And these exchanges between the communities flow in both directions, such that a radically different relationship is emerging between Israeli society and Jewish communities elsewhere.

What are the major features that these revolutions share? What are the consequences of these revolutions for the whole Jewish people in the last half of the twentieth century? How can we explain these revolutionary developments in the Jewish world and provide guidelines to interpret the research findings on these developments that have rapidly accumulated in the last two decades?

The answers to these questions may be drawn from general social scientific theories in the comparative–historical examination of ethnic and religious groups in the modern world. In this regard, the analytic master-theme of social science can be formulated as follows: under what conditions do modernization and its associated processes lead to the dissolution of ethnic and religious particularism and when does modernization result in the reformation of ethnic communal cohesion? Translated into concrete and

Jewish terms, the question for the Jewish people in the post-Second World War era becomes: Are modernization processes supportive, or destructive, of the continuity of Jewish communities?[4]

This question about modernization, on the one hand, and Jewish continuity and change, on the other, can be *directly* applied to those Jewish communities where Jews are a minority ethnic and religious group. Then the question is addressed to the structural and cultural dimensions of Jewish communal life, how they have changed, which features of Judaism and Jewishness have declined and which have increased, what newer forms of ethnicity and religion, if any, have emerged as substitutes for older forms. In short, what are the sources of cohesion within the community and how have they changed over time? This analytic question can also be addressed to the situation where Jews are a national, socio-political majority. Here, the question of ethnic continuity among Jews relates to the relative integration of Jews from different national origins into the national Jewish Israeli society and the sources of ethnic and religious communal cohesion in the Jewish state. In turn, changes in ethnic cohesion among Jews in Israel and in Jewish communities outside of Israel have consequences for the relationships between these communities.

The question of whether ethnicity is diminished or enhanced in modern society and the dialectic between state formation and ethnic group integration are of course not strictly Jewish questions nor did they first emerge in the aftermath of the Holocaust. What is specifically Jewish about them that is distinctively associated with the post-Second World War era? A combination of factors – economic and demographic developments in Israel, affluence and assimilation in America, and the emergence of third- and fourth-generation Jews distant from their traditional Jewish communities of origin in both societies – has brought into clearer focus issues about the future of the Jewish communities inside and outside of the State of Israel. These changes have reduced the threat of the annihilation of Jews and their communities and redirected concerns away from the demographic survival of the Jewish people. It has become clear that the Jewish community in the State of Israel is politically, demographically and socially viable as a new state; it has also become clear that Jewish communities outside of the State of Israel (those in Western, modern, pluralistic, largely democratic states) are viable as well, socially, institutionally, culturally and demographically. So the twin threats of the pre-Second World War period – whether a Jewish state would be politically, economically and demographically viable and whether there would be a demographic and socio-cultural future for the third and later generations of Jews in communities outside of the State of Israel – are no longer dominant concerns.

Our questions can therefore be framed about the *inner* dynamics of religious and ethnic group cohesion, rather than the continuity of community that flows from disadvantage, inequality, discrimination, the absence of opportunities for total assimilation, or the lack of equal access to the resources and rewards of the society. Ethnic and religious pluralism among Jews inside and outside of the State of Israel can be assessed in contexts of individualism and choice; Jewish continuity can be linked to the availability of alternatives, options and opportunities. Thus, the contemporary situation contrasts sharply with the pre-Second World War period when Jews inside and outside of Palestine were characterized by fewer options, greater discrimination, fewer economic and social opportunities, and greater external constraints on assimilation.

I shall use the concept 'transformation' to refer to the ways modernization has eroded the older bases of ethnic communal cohesion and has at times, under some conditions, substituted alternative bases for that cohesion. My examples will be drawn from the Jewish communities both in the United States and in Israel. The first example, Jews and their communities in the United States, is the ideal–typical case of a Jewish community in a large, open, pluralistic, secular, Western society. The other, Jews in the State of Israel, is our only test case of a total, secular Jewish society where modernization and development are vigorously pursued. My goal is to review in outline form several major aspects of the transformations associated with ethnic–religious change and continuity of the Jewish people and in the process specify theoretical guidelines for the social–scientific study of contemporary Jewry.

SOCIAL–ECONOMIC MOBILITY AND JEWISH CONTINUITY

We begin our review by examining how social and economic mobility affects group cohesion for American Jews and Jews in the State of Israel. We begin with the social mobility of American Jews. The increase in educational attainment, occupational achievement and income level has been among the best documented aspects of American Jewish life. As never before in Jewish history, Jews have benefited from the expansion of opportunities and the access to them which America has offered. The social and economic mobility of Jews over the last century, through four and moving towards five generations, has made the Jews one of the great American success stories. Research has documented the generational mobility of Jews, particularly the ways in which the immigrants and their children have moved out of the working classes towards the middle and upper social classes. Patterns of Jewish upward mobility have often been compared to other immigrant groups, and the more rapid changes among Jews have been noted.[5]

These changing social class patterns have resulted in the concentration of younger Jews among the college educated, high white collar and upper middle classes. Moreover, socio-economic changes have resulted in a stronger Jewish community in some ways and have created the potential for further enhancing the quality of American Jewish life.

But does occupational change imply assimilation or continued occupational segregation and concentration? The high concentration of Jews in certain industries, as workers and owners, has been documented for early periods of twentieth-century America, as has the movement into diversified occupations. The shifts from traditional skilled and unskilled labour into white-collar jobs have been linked to the occupational assimilation of Jews. However, as occupational levels increase, new forms of occupational concentration have developed at high socio-economic levels. Thus, an understanding of Jewish stratification patterns emerging in America requires a focus on these new types of concentration, not only on the loss of the 'older' forms of cohesion.

The 'new' occupational concentration has not resulted in stratification convergences between Jews and non-Jews. Indeed, the evidence suggests that occupational differences among white American ethnic groups have crystallized, rather than converged, with Jews located in a very small number of occupations (e.g., professionals in education, medicine and law). This concentration of young American Jews in particular occupations has meant that increasingly they share life styles, work patterns, neighbourhoods and family orientations. These similarities provide a foundation for powerful associational and contextual ties linking Jews to each other, forging structural bonds and economic networks among Jews. The period of rapid changes, for example in the generations between the immigrants and their children, is over, ending the conflict that weakened generational and family ties and diminished the cohesion of the group as a whole. Ties within the community have been strengthened between recent generations, since both contemporary younger and older age cohorts share greater occupational similarities.

Viewed dynamically, the long-term pattern is from low to high socio-economic status, with a shift from high levels of occupational concentration to occupational diversity and then *back* to high levels of concentration. The transition *to* occupational homogeneity has rarely been stressed. Past research has focused on occupational mobility as the basis for the assimilation of Jews in America, emphasizing almost exclusively the transition *from* occupational homogeneity and the role of occupational mobility in the process of integration. An alternative view stresses the occupational re-concentration emerging among third- and fourth-generation American Jews, different from the earlier forms characteristic of immigrants, but with similar consequences for group cohesion.

A detailed comparison of self-employment patterns among Jews over time and among Jewish communities leads to similar conclusions. Jews continue to be disproportionately concentrated among those who work for themselves. This characterizes both Jewish men and women, nationally and in local communities, and reinforces the patterns of occupational concentration, linking Jews to each other economically, in terms of life-style and prestige, and via family and kinship networks.

An examination of educational attainment reveals a similar picture. The high levels of, and increases in, educational attainment have been noted in every study of American Jews. Increased education has often raised even more concern than pride, since the educational experience is viewed as liberalizing and secularizing, resulting in increased contacts with non-Jews, and the separation of young adults from the control of family and from the constraints of ethnic particularism. Hence, as more Jews become college educated, it is argued, the greater is their assimilation. Such a view misses three important points: first, in modern societies, most parents, families and kin facilitate educational attainment, economically, socially and normatively. Only in isolated communities, or perhaps sometimes for daughters, would a break with family of orientation result from increases in educational attainment. Second, ethnic clusters develop among students in universities. While options to increase contacts with non-Jews are available, colleges and affiliated institutions and organizations also facilitate interactions among Jews, formally and informally. As the number of young Jews attending particular colleges in a limited number of areas of the United States increases, Jewish densities within institutions have also increased, resulting in new bases of in-group interactions. (The number of Jewish students attending the elite universities on the east coast of the United States is around 25 per cent; Queens College and other New York-based universities are between twice or three times that proportion.)

A third and final point emphasizes the fact that most Jews have some college exposure and very high proportions graduate from college. These educational commonalities, like the occupational commonalities noted earlier, develop peer and age-connected bonds that are ethnically related. Education was a source of generational conflict when the generational gap in educational attainment was wide, but educational similarities of third- and fourth-generation American Jewish men and women have become sources of communal cohesion. Educational homogeneity, inter- and intra-generationally, has become an important basis of communal bonds, family ties and social linkage.

There is also every indication from the evidence available of continuing socio-economic exceptionalism among Jews. If for no other cultural or structural reason, the commonality of class and status among Jews, of occupational concentration and educational achievement at high levels, would result in social bonds, economic networks and common life-styles and interests. When other structural and cultural factors are added, including commonalities associated with residential concentration and religious and communal sharing, the socio-economic pattern may be viewed as reinforcing and cementing the bases of Jewish cohesion in America. Socio-economic commonality among fifth-generation Jews in America is likely to be as distinctive as earlier generations, even as it will be different from past patterns.

Thus, the common assumption that the increased levels of education and occupation would lead to the assimilation of the American Jewish community and, in turn, to the erosion of the quality of American Jewish life seems to be unfounded. An examination of the empirical evidence has pointed to the very opposite conclusion. The uniqueness of the stratification profile and the distinctive social mobility patterns of American Jews mark Jews off from others and bind Jews to each other. The emergent social class distinctiveness of American Jews has important consequences for the structure of the Jewish community. The concentration of Jews in particular jobs and in college and post-graduate educational categories link Jews to institutions, networks, families, neighbourhoods and political interests and therefore has become a powerful basis of ethnic continuity. Indeed, ethnic cohesion among American Jews finds its most concrete expression in the structural conditions of social class and life style. Since one of the major strengths of an ethnic group is the overlap of ethnicity and social class, fourth-generation American Jews are characterized by powerful sources of structural continuity.

Are there parallel patterns among ethnic Jewish groups in Israel? The similarities in ethnic processes are striking. Recent research using both census and survey data, employing cross-sectional and longitudinal designs, has documented the enormous educational expansion and occupational diversity of the Jewish population in the State of Israel from the 1960s to the 1980s.[6] Did economic mobility and expansion result in ethnic integration and greater ethnic similarities among Jews from different ethnic origins? A systematic examination of the nature of educational expansion and the extent of occupational concentration shows clearly and unambiguously that the educational gap has *increased* among second-generation Asian and African Jews compared to Jews of European-American origins. While there may be some convergences between ethnic groups in life style, there is every indication of increasing ethnic inequality by education and occupation among Israeli Jews.

As among American Jews, increases in education and occupational mobility among ethnic Jewish groups in Israel do not necessarily imply the reduction of the ethnic–social class overlap. Among young adult males, socialized in Israel, the proportion of Asian-Africans with post-high school degrees is significantly lower than among European-Americans, and even lower than comparable Muslim and Christian Arabs in Israel. Since the expansion of the occupational structure during the last twenty years in Israel reduced opportunities for those with only a high school education, improvements in the general educational level of Asian and African Jews did not improve their occupational structure. Thus, the occupational structure of the younger and older generation of Asian and African Jews are *similar* despite the higher educational attainment of the second generation; in contrast, the occupational structure of the younger generation of European-American origins is significantly *different* from the older generation. Under these circumstances, remaining at the same socio-economic level means moving backwards in terms of status relative to their peers of the same cohort. The expansion of the educational system seems to have duplicated the ethnic gap and moved it from lower to higher socio-economic levels. The increasing ethnic gap extends to self-employment patterns in Israel as among American Jews.

Two further observations are relevant about the ethnic Jewish stratification picture in Israel. First, over time, there has been an increasing *similarity* in the educational levels attained by the diverse ethnic groups *within* the two broad ethnic categories of European-American and Asian-African. In earlier generations, there was considerable educational variation within these two ethnic categories, with overlaps between these two broad ethnic groups. In contrast, the ethnic groups of the second generation, socialized in Israel, have become more clearly dichotomized into two major groups, with little internal variation in educational attainment within each group. Such ethnic–educational polarities have increased in recent cohorts. There is considerably more analytic justification for examining the educational attainment of the two new emerging ethnic groups in Israel (European-Americans and Asian-Africans) among the younger generation than ever before.

A second observation is that the growing disadvantage of Asian and African Jews in terms of occupation and education is complicated and aggravated by the location–ecological factors which define where new opportunities are located. There is substantial evidence that ethnic residential segregation among Jews in Israel, within urban areas and in towns peripheral to the major cities, is a persistent feature of ethnic stratification. Residential concentration of ethnic groups reinforces educational and occupational disparities between the groups and also generates sources of communal cohesion. These residential patterns resemble in important ways the residential segregation of ethnic and religious groups in the United States.

These stratification patterns of the Jewish communities inside and outside of the State of Israel imply that new forms of education and occupational concentration have become sources of cohesion. In the United States the exceptional social class patterns of Jews mark Jews off from other groups and result in greater commonalities among Jews than between Jews and others. In Israel, the increasing ethnic inequalities among the native born of the two major Jewish ethnic groups leads to internal ethnic commonalities and life styles that are emerging to further distinguish the groups. Increasingly, the occupational bonds, economic networks and educational linkages define the nature of ethnic Jewish communities in Israel more so than cultural distinctiveness. The emphasis on understanding these patterns in the context of discrimination and disadvantage and in the framework of culture misses the complexities of ethnic group formation and the social structural underpinnings of ethnic distinctiveness, particularly the role of social class and economic–ethnic enclaves.

JEWISH INTERMARRIAGES IN AMERICA AND IN ISRAEL

Intermarriage symbolizes perhaps more than any other indicator the conflict between universalism and particularism, between ethnic continuity and total assimilation. High rates of out-marriage threaten directly the demographic survival of a small minority and the cultural and social basis of ethnicity. Since marriages are a major form of intensive and extensive interaction, changing levels of intermarriage may imply alterations in group cohesion. Demographically, socially and culturally intermarriage patterns are of critical importance in assessing ethnic changes.

How are patterns of intermarriage affecting group cohesion in the United States and Israel? Let us start again with Jews in the United States.[7] Until the 1960s, Jews in America had been accurately described as the classic illustration of voluntary group endogamy, i.e., most married other Jews. However, evidence has accumulated of increasing levels of intermarriage in every community in the United States. There has certainly been an increase in the numbers of those intermarrying over the last decades and there has been a concomitant increase in the number, but not necessarily the rate, of conversions to Judaism.

The key question is, what will be the Jewishness of the children and grandchildren of the intermarried as they grow up and have families of their own? We of course do not know, but there are important clues in the research studies available. While the intermarried are less connected Jewishly than born Jews, their ethnic and religious identification does not reflect complete disaffection from the community or from Judaism. Communal bonds and networks continue to link the intermarried to the Jewish community. Intermarriage is therefore not necessarily the final step towards total assimilation.

The evidence available shows that almost all of the converts to Judaism raise their children to be Jewish, provide Jewish educational experiences for them, and have as strong a religious basis for their Jewish identity as born Jews. As such, converts are qualitative and quantitative additions to the Jewish community and are increasingly accepted as Jews in the formal and informal networks that define American Jewish communities. The religious component of Jewishness is significantly less pronounced among those households where the non-Jewish-born partner identifies as a Jew, but has not converted in a religious ceremony. But in close to half of these 'mixed marriages', the children are raised as Jewish and ethnic (non-religious) elements of Jewishness are more central in their Jewish identity.

There is every basis for concluding that intermarriage results in a gain to the Jewish community when it involves conversions. There are gains as well among those non-Jews who marry Jews and identify themselves as Jews, along with a significant proportion of the children of these households who are raised as Jews. In total, there is likely to be a net quantitative and qualitative gain through Jewish intermarriage in many American Jewish communities. Usually the Jewish partner remains attached to the Jewish community and in many cases the partner not born Jewish becomes attached to the Jewish community through friends, family, neighbours, organizations, secular and religious. Most of the friends of the intermarried are Jewish; most support the Jewish State of Israel; most identify themselves as Jews. The Jewishness of the non-Jewish-born partner in an intermarriage is understandable in large part because few come from traditional or ethnic–religious-based families. Most are well educated and 'secular' in origin. Hence, they are more likely to be incorporated into a cohesive, secular, well-educated ethnically Jewish community, particularly when they are more welcomed.

Clearly we cannot infer the loss of the intermarried to the Jewish community from the increasing level of intermarriage; even the declining importance of religious conversions at the time of marriage does not neces- sarily mean that there will not be a formal conversion at a later stage of the life course. A systematic look at the evidence points to the changing meaning of intermarriage for the assimilation of Jews; unlike in the past, when the rates of intermarriage were lower, the costs to Jewish communal cohesion of increasing intermarriage rates are lower than had been considered by social scientists in research during the 1960s and 1970s and the benefits for Jewish continuity considerably higher.

Do these conclusions about group cohesion in the face of high intermarriage among American Jews have any parallels in the analysis of inter-ethnic marriages among Jews in Israel? The answer, I think, is surprising. A review of rates of inter-ethnic marriages among Jews in the State of Israel shows that there has been a systematic increase from the 1950s to the 1980s of marriages between Jews from Asian-African origins and from European- American origins. These increasing rates have been often used to indicate the 'assimilation' of the Jewish ethnic groups in Israel, and the 'melting' together of Israeli Jewish ethnic groups and their eventual disappearance. But these conclusions are premature and miss the complexity of ethnic cohesion and the role of intermarriage within that complexity.

First, we have not systematically studied the ethnic identity of the children of inter-ethnically married Jewish families in Israel. So long as we treat intermarriage in the context of the 'integration' of ethnic groups, there is no reason to go beyond the increasing rate. But we have just shown that inferring ethnic 'assimilation' from increasing intermarriage rates is inadequate. In the context of ethnic cohesion, we need to ask, to what ethnic-class sub-group do the children of the ethnically intermarried belong, in terms of their own goals and those others have for them?

We do know that there are direct educational–ethnic trade-offs in these intermarriage patterns. Data from the Israeli censuses show that the proportion marrying out among Asian-African Jews in Israel *increases* with education, while among the European-American group the higher the education, the *lower* the ethnic intermarriage rates. If the less educated Asian-Africans do not intermarry, they are likely to be the more ethnically committed and therefore the selectivity of out-marriages reinforces ethnic continuity. Some have predicted therefore that the rates of ethnic inter-marriage will decline over time and level off. More importantly, the different ways that education relates to ethnic intermarriages point unmistakably to the increased polarization that will emerge between these ethnic groups over time as inter-ethnic marriages will reinforce the ethnic–social class overlap. In this sense, and paradoxically, the educational selectivity of ethnic intermarriages in Israel may represent one of the structural conditions that reinforces ethnic group cohesion and the continuity of Jewish ethnic patterns in Israel.

There are also indications that girls from Asian and African origins are more likely to be enrolled in academic programmes than are boys. This gender–education gap is also likely to distort marriage selection patterns, as more educated Asian and African Jewish women will be seeking spouses among the more educated and the market of eligibles among educated Asian and African Jewish men is relatively small. This should further lead to selective inter-ethnic marriages and further polarize the social class basis of the two ethnic groups. It is not clear which ethnic communities are gaining demographically from inter-ethnic marriage, but in the context of these educational–ethnic trade-offs it is unlikely that the children will be simply raised as 'Israeli Jews'! They have cousins and grandparents, neighbours and friends, and these kin are all part of ethnic networks. They are exposed to an educational system that clearly differentiates by ethnic origin, will join a labour force that is characterized by ethnic-based jobs, ethnic–economic networks and will live in neighbourhoods that are defined in part ethnically. Taken together, therefore, the ethnic factor among Jews in the State of Israel, while changing, is likely to remain salient for at least another generation.

IMPLICATIONS OF JEWISH ETHNIC CONTINUITY

For both the Jewish communities in the United States and in Israel, communal institutions and networks are the basis for ethnic continuity.

These networks include the overlap of ethnicity with a variety of statuses – family, economic, cultural, political, residential and social. While individuals can enter and exit the boundaries of the ethnic community, the community *per se* can remain cohesive. Intermarriage involves the exiting and entering of persons in a complex web of networks that form communities. Communities can remain powerful sources of identity even when persons leave and enter them.

American Jews interact with other Jews in schools, jobs, places of residence, at family-holiday occasions, as well as in the synagogue several times a year. While there is a clear trend in all the studies of American Jewry of the growing secularization of religious observances and rituals, there is, as well, clear documentation of new ethnic linkages, defining Jewishness beyond, and in addition to, Judaism. Those not affiliated religiously, for example, have a multiplicity of ties within the Jewish community, most have mainly Jewish friends and neighbours, and are involved with Jewish culture and are Israel-centred. There is no basis for concluding that the decline of religious observance means the absence of ethnic Jewish continuity. For almost all American Jews, Israel is an anchor of communal life and their personal identity as Jews.

The distinctive social class patterns of American Jews are reinforced by religious activities and observances which have themselves become family–community based. While religion has lost its centrality and dominance in modern, secular, educated America, Judaism continues to play a supportive role in linking educational, family, economic and life-style issues to broader communal and ethnic (including Israel) issues, and therefore to Jewish continuity in America. Most Jews, educated and non-educated, middle and upper class, have a wide range of ties to Jewishness. The overwhelming majority have some connections to Judaism and religious institutions. Among these ties and linkages are commonalities of socio-economic status. Jobs, education, careers and money link Jews to each other in an intricate web of social, family and economic networks, as much as the external concerns with Israel as a state binds Jews to each other within the American Jewish community and to other Jewish communities around the world.

On both quantitative and qualitative grounds the American Jewish community is characterized by multiple bases of cohesion. The changes and transformations over the last several decades, including the social class transformations, have resulted in greater ties and networks among Jews. Social change has reinforced ethnic-community identification. The modernization of the socio-economic distribution of the Jewish community does not threaten Jewish continuity. As a community, Jews are surviving in America, even as some individuals enter and others leave the community.

Religious observances have also declined in Israel, as part of a general secularization pattern. But because religion has been part of political institutions, few creative pluralistic religious forms have developed that can integrate Israelis as Jews. Religious reforms that have become conspicuous and powerful institutional and cultural expressions of American Jews, have been conspicuously absent in the State of Israel. Religious conflict dominates Israeli society rather than the development of religious pluralism. Therefore Judaism 'Israeli style' has not become a major basis of ethnic cohesion. The meaning of ethnic cohesion among Israeli Jews is clearly not a simple cultural link to national origins. Even the cultural base has been transformed within the context of Israeli society as distances from communities of origin increase. Ethnicity among Jews in Israel is emerging as an Israeli-based and Israeli-formed product that has weakening roots to the past. Ethnic distinctions in Israel mean residence and job, education and economic networks, family, neighbours and friends. Therefore, it means community. In Israel, as among American Jews, culture and life style often cement the structural bases of ethnic communities.

Ethnic communities are unlikely to disappear in the next several generations in the modern societies of America and Israel. What becomes the basis of their cohesion may change and conflict and competition may reinforce ethnic solidarity. But the basis for continuity is also deeply rooted in the contemporary patterns of family and education. The argument that modernization results in the demise of ethnicity, that ethnicity remains salient only when attached to disadvantage and discrimination, that over time occupational mobility and increased levels of educational attainment result in greater ethnic equalities cannot serve as a framework for the understanding of ethnic Jewish patterns in Israel or Jewish change and continuity in Western countries. Modernization reforms the old and creates new forms of Jewish expression and new forms of family, economic, political and cultural relationships. For Jews in the post-Second World War era, modernization has created new forms of ethnic identity and communal cohesion.

The trajectories of these two revolutions among Jews inside and outside the State of Israel are moving in directions that are likely to polarize the relationships between the communities. As each moves through its own developments, each is moving further away from the other. The commonalities of the past, Yiddish language, European culture and religion, Western, democratic, pluralistic, secular values, are less binding between communities of Israel and elsewhere in the last decade of the twentieth century than they were in the past.

The question of the Jewish people towards the end of the twentieth century cannot mean the emergence of 'one people' (Am Eḥad) in the sociological sense. The retention of social structural and cultural differences among communities, the emergence of new Jewish communities and the importance of context for understanding communities reduce the oneness of the Jewish people. In the short run, the differences between Jews inside and outside of Israel are likely to become accentuated. At the same time, there is a strong basis for developing new alliances and new relationships between the communities. It is most unlikely that the old pattern of relationships can be sustained within the contexts of the transformed Israeli society and American Jewish community.

There are remarkable parallels between the ethnic change and continuity among American Jews and among Israeli Jews of different ethnic origins. In both cases, modernization has resulted in the transformation of ethnic groups and the development of new forms of ethnicity; in turn, this has resulted in greater polarization between the two communities. Since these revolutions could not be and were not imagined by our grandparents, the future shape of these communities for our grandchildren's generation is unlikely to be imagined by us. As we have built on the legacy of our grandparents, so our grandchildren will build on our legacy. What will emerge is 'a new Jewish world' that will reflect new forms of Jewish expressions and new relationships between communities; it will be a world that recognizes the distinctive features of communities in the core and on the periphery, and appreciates the value of new forms of interdependencies that will regenerate the creative energies of both types of Jewish communities.

NOTES

1 Frances Goldscheider read an earlier version and helped reshape the analysis.
2 See C. Goldscheider and J. Neusner (eds), *Social Foundations of Judaism*, Prentice-Hall, 1990.
3 See C. Goldscheider and A. Zuckerman, *The Transformation of the Jews*, University of Chicago Press, 1985.
4 This is the fundamental theme of C. Goldscheider and A. Zuckerman, *The Transformation of the Jews*, University of Chicago Press, 1985.
5 See, for example, C. Goldscheider, *Jewish Continuity and Change*, Indiana University Press, 1986; T. Kessner, *The Golden Door*, Oxford University Press, 1977; S. Lieberson, *A Piece of the Pie*, University of California Press, 1985; S. Cohen, *American Modernity and Jewish Identity*, Tavistock Publications, 1983.
6 See C. Goldscheider, *Israel's Changing Society: Population Development and Ethnic Group Formation*, Westview Press, 1991, for documentation of these patterns in Israel.
7 For a discussion of intermarriage in the United States see the review in C. Goldscheider, 'The unaffiliated Jew in America: sociological perspectives', *Humanistic Judaism*, vol. 18, no. 2, Spring 1990, pp. 15–22, and the references cited therein.

Part II

7

THE POLITICAL PROFILE OF AMERICAN JEWRY

Seymour M. Lipset

American Jews have been deeply involved in their country's politics since the time of the Revolution, almost always predominantly on the left, liberal or progressive side. The encouragement to American Jewry to play a full role in society and polity is endemic in George Washington's message to the Jews of Newport in 1790, that in the new United States 'all possess alike liberty of conscience and immunities of citizenship'. Even more significantly, the first President emphasized that the patronizing concept of 'toleration . . . of one class of people . . . [by] another' has no place in America, that Jews are as much Americans, and on the same basis, as anyone else.[1] He recognized that tolerance denotes second-class citizenship. Jefferson and Madison also noted that America was different from Europe, that the discrimination against Judaism prevailing there did not exist here, where in Jefferson's words all are 'on an equal footing'. He 'rejoiced over the presence of Jews in the country because they would insure that religious diversity which, in his judgement, was the best protector of Liberty'.[2]

There were relatively few Jews in the United States before the Civil War. They totalled only 15,000 in 1825, increasing to 50,000 in 1848. The record suggests they largely were staunch Democrats, backing Jefferson, Jackson and Van Buren, as the more liberal and anti-nativist party.[3] Some were able to reach high places in the American military and political systems, including a number of Congressmen and local elected officials. The most prominent of the latter, Mordecai Noah, served at different times between 1813 and 1841 as US Consul to Tunis, High Sheriff of New York, Surveyor of the Port of New York, Associate Judge of the New York Court of Sessions, and editor of six different New York newspapers. He also headed a number of Jewish communal organizations.[4] August Belmont, a Jewish banker who had once represented the Rothschilds, was Chairman of the Democratic National Committee from 1860 to 1872. At a time when Jews were still barred from public office in almost all of Europe, two highly assimilated Jews, David Yulec (née Levy) of Florida and Judah P. Benjamin of Louisiana were elected to the US Senate, the former in 1844, and the latter in 1854. Benjamin, of course, is better known as Secretary of War and later of State of the Confederate States, and President Jefferson Davis's closest adviser during the Civil War.[5]

The period from 1848 to the late 1890s was one of dominance by German Jewry. They constituted the bulk of the 250,000 Jews in the country in 1890, and were very successful. As of that time, 'bankers, brokers, wholesalers, retail dealers, collectors, and agents accounted for 62 percent of their occupations. In addition, 17 percent were professionals'.[6] In the post-Civil War period, a number of Jews of German origin developed some of the leading banking houses of the country. They, together with New England scions of the Puritans, dominated investment banking.[7]

Although socializing and marrying largely among themselves, these extra-ordinarily successful people were opposed to social separatism. Some were among the founding members of the high status social clubs formed in many cities immediately before and after the Civil War. They 'generally had become Republican Progressives, because the Democratic party had been the party of slavery', and subsequently its leading turn-of-the-century populist figure, William Jennings Bryan, 'was perceived to be an anti-Semite'.[8]

The late nineteenth century witnessed the steady mass immigration of poor Jews from Eastern Europe, which, by the First World War, produced a population of over 3 million, mostly concentrated in the tenement districts of the major northern cities. They worked mainly in the garment industries or in trade, often initially as peddlers, the lowliest form of self-employment.[9] Living in crowded slums, in areas marked by high crime rates and red-light districts, speaking Yiddish, frequently looking unkempt and outlandish, they helped to produce new anti-Semitic stereotypes. These fed nativist prejudices. Considerable tensions developed between the Jews and other immigrant groups, which presaged some of the more serious working-class-based anti-Semitic movements of the 1930s. These hostilities, particularly with the Irish, who dominated Democratic politics in many cities, helped to keep many Jews loyal to the Republicans, viewed as Progressives, before the First World War.[10]

The Republican appeal to Jews on the Presidential level seemingly ended in 1912, when the conservative GOP Presidential incumbent, William Howard Taft, faced three rivals with attractions to different segments of American Jewry; former President Theodore Roosevelt, who had strong links to the community, running as a Progressive; Woodrow Wilson, as a liberal Democrat; and Eugene Debs, as the Socialist nominee. From then on, a combination of the Democratic and left third party nominees, or the Democratic one alone, secured a clear majority among Jews.

While a minority of the East European Jews were devout, many rejected religion entirely, and arrived supporters of radical politics. Facing anti-Semitic regimes and societies, they could not simply enter the majority cultures. Barred from being members of conservative parties, they supported left-wing movements.[11] They came to America as socialists and tried to remain such as workers. The major Yiddish newspaper, the *Daily Forward*, was socialist. The predominant Jewish unions in the garment and other industries joined in the United Hebrew Trades, backed the Socialist Party.[12] The only two Congressmen that party elected before the First World War, Meyer London from the East Side of New York and Victor Berger from Milwaukee, were both Jewish. The Socialists constituted the second largest party in many Jewish districts in New York until the New Deal, when they voted for Franklin D. Roosevelt, often on a third, American Labor, party line. As the foremost student of the subject, Arthur Liebman notes: 'American Jewry has provided socialist organizations and movements with a disproportionate number – at times approaching or surpassing a majority – of their leaders, activists, supporters.'[13] Similar statements can be made about the supporters of subsequent other left third parties, including the La Follette Progressive Party in 1924, the Communist-dominated Progressive Party in 1948 and the Anderson Independent candidacy in 1980.[14]

Zionism constituted an alternative secular political strand among Jews in Eastern Europe and North America. (The religiously Orthodox opposed the movement, believing that only God could redeem the promised land for the Jews.) In the USA, it was much weaker than socialism, with only 12,000 members in 1914, and, in any case, included a socialist wing. The immigrant generation could not accept the idea that they should uproot themselves once more, while the more affluent natives felt at home.[15]

Jews of German descent retained their Abe Lincoln born Republican attachments until the 1930s, but on the whole they backed the liberal or progressive Republicans who were an important force in the party. The one important genuinely conservative segment among Jews came from the Orthodox minority. Their journalists felt that in a country in which the right was not anti-Semitic, religious 'conservatism in Jewish matters could best be complemented by conservatism in politics'. But the circulation of their papers 'was small in comparison with the *Daily Forward*'.[16]

The left orientation of American Jews expressed in their support of the Socialist and Democratic parties and the trade union movement was reinforced by the events at home and abroad from the 1930s on. To reiterate the obvious, the period from the start of the Great Depression and the rise of Nazism to the end of the Second World War witnessed the greatest transformation in world Jewry since the destruction of the Second Temple. The prolonged economic collapse stimulated the growth of extremist movements, some of which in Germany, the United States and elsewhere, focused on blaming the Jews for all that went wrong. The German developments, as we know, led to the Holocaust and the murder of 6 million Jews, one-third of the world's Jewish population.

In the United States, assorted anti-Semitic right-wing movements, the most important of which was Father Coughlin's National Union for Social

Justice, as well as a number of smaller ones which appealed to evangelical Protestants, gained strength. There is no reliable estimate of their support; they failed miserably at the ballot box. On the other hand, national opinion polls suggest that as much as a quarter of the population approved of the anti-Semitic demagogue, Charles Coughlin, who broadcast every Sunday on a national radio network. That support dropped to one-seventh by 1940. Assorted surveys designed to estimate the degree of anti-Semitism among the American public by responses to various prejudicial statements about Jews, conducted by Jewish defence groups, reported that roughly one out of two had some anti-Jewish views. This pattern lasted through the Second World War.[17]

Franklin Roosevelt strongly appealed to the Jews. His pro-trade union and welfare state policies and direct links with major Jewish socialist and labour leaders, like David Dubinsky and Sydney Hillman, his strong opposition to Nazi Germany and endorsement of aid to the Allies from the start of the war on, unified the vast majority of Jews in the New Deal–Democratic camp. Even the old Socialists moved over to vote Democratic.[18]

For Jews, the politics of the immediate post-war period was centred first around the plight of the Holocaust survivors and then support for the creation of the State of Israel and its struggles with its Arab neighbours. Again the Democrats and the left backed the Jewish cause. Harry Truman supported a special quota for Displaced Persons entering the country and then gave immediate recognition to the new Jewish state and backed it in international forums. Three-quarters of the Jews voted for him in 1948, while another 15 per cent backed the leftist third party candidate Henry Wallace.[19] His Republican successor, Dwight Eisenhower, who had a strong appeal to Jews as the leader of the Allied military effort, secured close to two-fifths of their votes. But his turning against Israel in the 1956 Sinai War, while the Democrats continued their support, helped to refurbish the Jewish attachment to Democratic and liberal politics. In the 1960s, Jews gave over 80 per cent of their votes to John F. Kennedy, Lyndon Johnson and Hubert Humphrey.

At the same time, American Jewry as a group was reaching new heights of social and political acceptance and of economic affluence. A study in the early 1970s of national-origin and religious groups, using census and sample survey data, found that 'Jews, regardless of ethnic ancestry, attain higher levels of education, occupation and income than all other subgroups. . . .'[20] A national survey of American Jews and non-Jews completed for the American Jewish Committee in April 1988 by Steven M. Cohen led to the conclusion that 'Jews are among the wealthiest groups in America . . . [that] per capita Jewish income may actually be almost double that of non-Jews.' More than twice as many Jews as non-Jewish whites report household incomes in excess of $50,000. At the other end of the spectrum, almost twice as many non-Jews as Jews indicate incomes of less than $20,000.[21] As

Calvin Goldscheider and Alan Zuckerman note, 'the pace of socioeconomic change and the levels attained are exceptional features of Jews compared to non-Jews'.[22]

These generalizations have been abundantly documented for various high-level groups. An analysis of the 400 richest Americans, as reported by *Forbes* magazine, finds that two-fifths of the wealthiest forty are Jews, as are 23 per cent of the total list.[23] Jews are disproportionately present among many sections of elites, largely drawn from the college educated. These include the leading intellectuals (45 per cent), professors at the major universities (30 per cent), high-level civil servants (21 per cent), partners in the leading law firms in New York and Washington (40 per cent), the reporters, editors and executives of the major print and broadcast media (26 per cent), the directors, writers and producers of the fifty top grossing motion pictures from 1965 to 1982 (59 per cent), and the same level of people involved in two or more prime-time television series (58 per cent).[24]

On the behavioural level, dramatic changes developed as well. Almost all the restrictions against Jews, such as limited access to advantages, or restrictive quotas, have declined or disappeared. By the end of the 1980s, it is hard to find any area of American life in which discrimination is still a problem.[25] And public opinion has changed in tandem with behaviour, that is, anti-Semitism as measured by opinion polls is at the lowest point since such surveys were first taken in the 1930s.[26]

Given these developments, various commentators, both Jewish and non-Jewish, anticipated that the group would turn conservative in tandem with its high position. Beyond the effects of upward mobility, a shift to the right could be anticipated as a consequence of the growing conflict between Jews and other minority groups – the blacks, the Hispanics, as well as the feminist movement – backed by liberals and Democrats over issues of affirmative action. Many Jewish organizations actively moved into the camp of the defenders of the traditional American emphasis of competitive meritocracy, in opposition to any efforts which suggest preferential treatment for the underprivileged or those who have been discriminated against. The concept of quotas, even affirmative ones, frightened Jews who remembered the efforts to hold down their numbers in various areas of life by proportionate quotas. The shift in Israel's international position to that of a pariah state – particularly defined as such by various international left-wing tendencies, the communist movements and most Third World countries – also seemed to press Jews to the right.

There is, however, a major problem with these analyses, namely that the evidence we have on mass Jewish behaviour simply does not sustain the suggestion that Jews as a group are becoming more conservative. American Jews continue to present an anomaly, the wealthiest ethno-religious group in the country by far, and the most liberal in attitudes and behaviour.[27] Studies of voting behaviour indicate that American Jews remain more committed to the Democratic Party than any other religious or non-black ethnic group. 'In every Presidential election since 1924, Jews have voted Democratic by an average of some 25 percent more than the electorate as a whole.'[28] As of the end of the 1980s, three-fifths of all Jews identify as Democrats, only 15 per cent are Republicans. Other whites divide evenly between the parties, 37 per cent each. Only blacks have shown a higher proportion Democratic.

In 1972, George McGovern, a left liberal, perceived by many Jews as an isolationist who, if elected president, would weaken American support for Israel, was still able to secure close to two-thirds of the Jewish presidential vote. This was noted as a setback for the Democratic Party, since Hubert Humphrey had won over 80 per cent of the Jewish ballots in a three-party race in 1968. But the almost two-thirds who voted for McGovern were more than the support he obtained from any other white group. In 1976, Jews again led among whites in overwhelmingly backing Jimmy Carter against Gerald Ford, 72 to 28 per cent. Ronald Reagan, who had been a strong public supporter of Israel, secured a higher vote among Jews, 35 per cent (or more) in 1980, running against Jimmy Carter, who, in office, had shown himself to be a less than enthusiastic supporter of Israel's foreign policy. The latter received less than 50 per cent among Jews; one-sixth opted for a third liberal Independent candidate, John Anderson, three times his vote among the entire electorate. But four years later, when the Democrats nominated Walter Mondale, a protégé of the Israelophile Hubert Humphrey and a consistently strong supporter of the Jewish state, Reagan's support among Jews actually declined to 30 per cent. Jews were the only group to shift against Reagan when he was gaining among all others, except for blacks, whose vote distribution did not change.[29]

It may also be noted that the results of the 1988 elections, as indicated in many opinion polls, confirm Milton Himmelfarb's generalization that while Jews earn more than any ethno-religious group for whom data exist, including Episcopalians, they are still more liberal or left in their opinions than other white groups, and vote like Hispanics. In November 1988, over 70 per cent of the Jews backed Dukakis. Republican presidential support among them has declined slightly, but steadily, since 1980. Well over 80 per cent back Democrats for Congress. The only identifiable sub-set that is conservative and Republican is composed of the Orthodox (less than 10 per cent), particularly the more extreme and less affluent among them.[30] George Bush received over 85 per cent of the vote in areas in Brooklyn and elsewhere inhabited by Hasidic sects.

Beyond electoral habits, which are not necessarily the best indicator of liberal or conservative thought, analyses of polls of Jewish attitudes towards various social and political issues indicate that the overwhelming majority of Jews take very liberal, often extreme, positions. Jews remain more consistently left on economic, political and social issues than any other group in the country, with the possible exception of blacks, who, race-related issues apart, are not particularly liberal on social matters, such as abortion. Though it is true that Jews, almost to a person, are supporters of Israel against the Arabs, and favour giving military and economic aid to Israel, they, more than any other identifiable ethno-religious group, also tend to be against a strong American military posture and a high spending level for American armaments. Thus most Jews advocate anti-militarist, often isolationist, policies, usually associated with more liberal-to-left orientations, while at the same time backing a country highly dependent on American aid.

Jews are the most supportive of activist politics on behalf of the less fortunate, including maintenance or expansion of government welfare programmes, relying on the state as an employer of last resort for the un-employed, wage and price controls in inflationary periods, and government regulations to remedy assorted ills for which business or other large organizations are held responsible; and various social concerns, such as attitudes towards the death penalty, abortion, gun control, nuclear freeze proposals, and the like.[31] In spite of their relative affluence, Cohen reports, as of 1988, 'more Jews than whites or blacks endorse raising taxes as a way of cutting budget deficits', and oppose reductions in domestic spending. Jews are also much more likely than others to approve of liberal and civil rights organizations such as the National Association for the Advancement of Colored People (NAACP), Planned Parenthood, the National Organization for Women (NCW) and the American Civil Liberties Union (ACLU).[32]

The most recent opinion surveys continue to find that 'In no [opinion] area are Jews significantly more conservative than non-Jewish whites. . . . [I]n many issue domains, the Jewish center is well to the left of the Gentile centre.'[33] Black mayoralty candidates, such as Bradley in Los Angeles, Green in Philadelphia, and Washington in Chicago, have received a much higher proportion of votes among Jews than from any other definable white group other than academics.

> In 1983, the Chicago mayoral election pitted a black, Democrat Harold Washington, against a Jewish Republican. . . . [S]lightly less than half the Jews voted for Washington. But slightly less than half was still two and a half times as high a percentage as other whites in Chicago gave the Democratic candidate, even though Democratic loyalty in Chicago had long seemed a fact of nature.[34]

Clearly, Jews continue to be among the principal supporters of organized liberal-to-left tendencies in the country, i.e., they give heavily and dispro-portionately to liberal political candidates and various liberal-to-left organizations.

The much publicized discussion of a supposed shift of Jews to the right in recent years is largely left intellectuals who cite the appearance among their stratum of an allegedly predominantly Jewish group of neo-conservatives as evidence of Jewish behaviour generally. The proof is very weak, as an indicator of Jewish increased conservatism, for a number of reasons: the number who have been so labelled is a tiny proportion of the total group of Jewish intellectuals; Jews are also to be found in disproportionate numbers among those associated with various left-wing journals and causes. Studies of Jewish elites, including intellectuals, academics and media personnel, indicate they are 'considerably more liberal than elite non-Jews as reflected in their voting behaviour, self-identified ideological position, and their responses to a wide variety of social, economic, and political attitude questions'. They have 'consistently supported the Democratic candidate [for president] by margins of more than four to one'.[35] Close to one-third, '31 per cent of elite Jews think that the U.S should move toward socialism'.[36] In any case, the majority of those originally described as neo-conservatives are still Democrats, and have never backed Ronald Reagan or George Bush.[37]

What those labelled neo-conservatives have had in common, in addition to retaining an identification with welfare state policies and support for trade unions, is a deep suspicion of the Soviet Union (pre-Gorbachev), advocacy of hard-line foreign military programmes and a passionate concern for Israel's security. Almost all had reacted strongly against the New Left movement of the 1960s and early 1970s. Identifying with democracy as an end in itself and strongly attached to the values of scholarship, they argued that the attacks by the New Left on the university and on the democratic political system were not only unwarranted, but played into the hands of anti-Democratic extremists, both of the left and the right.

Most of the Democratic neo-conservatives now reject the term because it has also been widely applied in Europe and Canada in recent years to mean Reagan–Friedman classically liberal *laissez-faire* free market policies, as distinctive from (for these countries) traditional Tory communitarian *noblesse-oblige* ones, and this usage has spread to America. They identify much more with *The New Republic* than with *Commentary*. They would prefer to be identified as 'neo-liberals'. This label, however, has been taken over by others who are somewhat more fiscally conservative on domestic policies, but much more dovish on foreign issues. Morton Kondracke, past executive officer of *The New Republic*, solved the dilemma by referring to himself as a 'Neo-Lib–Neo-Con . . .'.

Most American Jews have remained adherents of the social democratic values of their parents, as evident in the results of a national telephone survey taken by the *Los Angeles Times* in April 1988. When asked which among three 'qualities do you consider most important to your Jewish identity', over half, 57 per cent, replied 'a commitment to social equality'; about a fifth chose 'support for Israel' or 'religious observance'.[38] When queried in the same poll as to whom they preferred in the then upcoming Israeli elections, 'Peres, the Labor candidate' won out by over two-and-a-half to one over

'Shamir, the Likud candidate' among those with opinions. As with their behaviour in American politics, the Orthodox were the only denominational group to prefer Shamir – by two to one. There is relatively little difference among the others related to religious preference or degree of affiliation. Cohen's 1989 survey also found 'Labor (or its allies)' considerably ahead of 'Likud (or its allies)'.

Extant survey data also indicate how American Jews react to the policy debate as to whether Israel should negotiate giving up control of the West Bank and Gaza as part of a peace settlement and deal with the Palestine Liberation Organization. Nine months *before* Arafat agreed to recognize Israel and reject the use of terrorism, in December 1988, both the *Los Angeles Times*'s and Cohen's surveys indicated more American Jews favoured an agreement which involves giving up territories for peace, than believed the country should hold on to them indefinitely. Cohen found that 67 per cent agreed with the statement: 'If the PLO recognizes Israel and renounces terrorism, Israel should be willing to talk with the PLO', while only 16 per cent disagreed. By a plurality, 42 to 33 per cent, they favoured 'territorial compromise . . . in return for credible guarantees of peace'. Not surprisingly, the Cohen survey taken in February 1989 reports that they *reject* by 63 to 23 per cent the statement: 'American Jews should not publicly criticize the politics of the government of Israel', and by 73 to 13 per cent *agree* that 'Jews who are severely critical of Israel should nevertheless be allowed to speak in synagogues and Jewish community centers'.

The explanation for Jewish adherence to liberal-left politics, while having become astonishingly affluent, is obviously complex.[39] Without trying to tease out all the factors, it may be suggested that the behaviour is related to the continued effect of leftist political values imported from Eastern Europe, noted above, deep concern about anti-Semitism, still linked in the minds of many American Jews much more to the political right than to the left, secularized intellectuality and an accompanying impulse to universalism and the impact of norms underlying *tzedekah*, the obligation of the fortunate to help individuals and communities in difficulty. The latter norm became general among European Jews during the Middle Ages, when it was literally a condition for survival, given that some communities were generally experiencing severe persecution, while others were doing well. The political values derived from *tzedekah* are communitarian and imply support for the welfare state.[40] Beyond this, historic experience with discrimination seemingly leads many Jews to favour civil rights legislation for other minorities.

Apart from the fact that most Jews agree with most liberal positions on both domestic and foreign policy, they still have a historically-based visceral feeling that they belong in the company of political liberals. They were released from the medieval ghettos by 'the liberals'. They were joined in the fight against Nazism by 'the liberals'. Anti-Semitism, religious intolerance and immigration restrictions, in their memory, have been associated with 'the conservatives'. Cohen has found in polls taken in the mid- and late 1980s that, when asked what proportion of a number of groups in the United States is anti-Semitic, by a ratio of four to one, they are more likely to say many or most conservatives and Republicans are as liberals and Democrats.[41] The latter are seen as more friendly. Whether for these reasons or not, a plurality, by 44 to 31 per cent, told Cohen that 'Jewish values, as I understand them, teach me to be politically liberal'. The Democratic Party is perceived as 'the liberal' party and the Republican Party as 'the conservative' party. Jews are still more comfortable in the Democratic Party than in the Republican Party. They are more at ease with the kinds of people they find in the Democratic Party – their fellow ethnics with whom they grew up in America – than with the White Anglo-Saxon Protestants (WASPs) still predominant in the Republican Party. As Alan Fisher notes, 'Jews identify the Democrats as friends, and, by and large, they stay with their friends. The Democratic Party is home to them.'[42]

It is important to recognize that, in spite of the extent to which the United States has been open to Jews, and the clear evidence of a sharp fall-off in social and economic restrictions on them since the Second World War, they remain fearful of anti-Semitism, still see themselves as marginal, as outsiders in a Gentile society.[43] Only 14 per cent of those responding to Cohen's questionnaires in 1988 and 1989 agreed: 'Antisemitism in America is currently not a serious problem for American Jews.' Over-whelming majorities, 76 per cent in 1988 and 73 per cent in 1989, replied that it is a serious problem. The fact that they feel this way contributes to an identification with the left against the right.

The reluctance of Jews to accept evidence that anti-Semitism has declined or to shift their image as to the relative contribution of the left and the right, given the reality of their progress in American society and the strong efforts on behalf of Israel by the most recent Republican administrations, those of Nixon and Reagan, is striking testimony to the long-term effects of historical experience and collective memory. San Francisco provides an example of how some Jews can totally ignore reality. Polls taken among contributors to the San Francisco Jewish Community Federation have found that one-third believe that a Jew cannot be elected to Congress from San Francisco. A poll reported such results in 1985 when all three members of Congress from contiguous districts in or adjacent to the city were Jewish, as were the two State Senators, the mayor and a considerable part of the city council. San Francisco is not unique, although its record of electing so many Jews in an area with a small Jewish population outdoes all others. The evidence is clear from many parts of the country that non-Jews will vote for identifiable and avowed Jews to represent them in high public office. There are now thirty-one Jews in the House of Representatives and eight in the Senate.[44] During the past decade there have been Jewish senators from such unlikely states as Minnesota, Nebraska, Nevada and New Hampshire, while others have been elected to important state and municipal positions by voters who are overwhelmingly non-Jewish.

The religious emphasis on learning has been transmuted among American Jews into an emphasis on intellectuality and on secularized learning and education which in turn is closely linked to liberalism. Close to 90 per cent of all their youth go to universities. As noted earlier, they constitute close to one-third of the professoriate at major universities and an even larger proportion of leading intellectuals.[45] In discussing 'the intellectual pre-eminence of the Jews' shortly after the First World War, Thorstein Veblen commented on the fact that they not only contributed 'a disproportionate number' of leaders of 'modern science and scholarship', but that they 'count particularly among the vanguard, the pioneers, the uneasy guild of pathfinders and iconoclasts, in science, scholarship, and institutional change and growth'.[46]

Creative intellectuality, as Veblen and many others have recognized, includes an emphasis on innovation, on newness, on rejection of the old, of the traditional.[47] It is also linked to universalism, to reacting to knowledge independently of the background of its exponents. Secularized Jews, in their desire to be treated like others, to become part of the larger society, support a universalistic ethic, which emphasizes equality for groups and individuals. Intellectuality and universalism predispose American Jews to liberalism. Thus Charles Liebman notes: 'The basic [Western] Jewish commitment ... is to the Enlightenment, the optimistic faith that the application of human intellect can create a constantly progressing universal cosmopolitan society. Internationalism, libertarianism, and welfarism are consequences of this basic commitment.'[48] These values also predominate in the liberal arts in the leading institutions, the very places in which the large majority of American Jewish youth spend four to six years on the threshold of their adult lives.

The continuity of adherence to liberal and left politics does not mean there has been no change in the views or behaviour of American Jews in response to events. The Six Day War was a particularly notable turning point in their orientation. It seems evident that, in the USA at least, there were many Jews who, while being pro-Israeli, were not dedicatedly so. The Six Day War, however, won many of these people over, first by activating their concern for Israel, and then by giving them a tremendous sense of pride in its accomplishment. As Nathan Glazer puts it, 'After 1967, Israel became the religion of American Jews.'

There is no need to detail here the story of American Jewry's support for Israel in funds, but even more importantly in exercising whatever clout and influence it has been able to develop on behalf of the Jewish State. And the politicians have listened. The domestic political game played around the activity of the United States in the Middle East has had only one major player, the organized Jewish community, who, with campaign contributions, activism and media influence constitute a major force. The pro-Arab forces are much weaker both in political resources and among the public as a whole. Support for Israel, therefore, has not been an issue between the major parties, although every administration and the majority of Americans, including most Jews, have believed since 1967 that Israel in its own interests, as well as by conforming to the liberal principle of national self-determination, should exchange most of the territory it occupies on the West Bank and Gaza for a peace treaty incorporating security guarantees.

Tensions within the New Left and anti-war movements of the late 1960s pressed some Jews out of the radical left, where they had been heavily present.[49] Following the Six Day War, Israel, now seen as a powerful state linked to imperialist America, became anathema to the international left. Support for the PLO and the Palestinian cause emerged as one of its major causes. At the same time, hostility towards the USA was stimulated by support for the Viet Cong and opposition to the country's role in the Vietnam War. This antagonism was also turned against Israel as a satellite-ally of the USA. As a result, many people active in the anti-war left in America and elsewhere became openly anti-Israeli and pro-Palestinian. This phenomenon put a serious strain on the loyalties of various Jewish leftists who felt both Jewish and left. They were faced with the choice of giving up their attachments to Israel or dropping their ties to the left. At this juncture a significant and visible number of Jewish leftists dropped out of the New Left.[50]

Another set of factors which has affected Jewish politics has been relationships with blacks. There is no question that real tensions have emerged between the two groups, despite the fact that Jews were the main white supporters of the civil rights and racial equality causes – both in terms of participation and funding of organizations such as the NAACP from their inception at the beginning of the century down to the present. The strains which developed between Jews and blacks stem from a number of sources. Both sociological and political factors are involved.

The history of recent urban change in residential patterns has involved in some part the succession of blacks into what were once Jewish neighbourhoods. Many black districts around the country – Harlem and Bedford Stuyvesant in New York, the South Side of Chicago, the Downtown Washington District, Roxbury in Boston, the Fillmore area in San Francisco, Watts in Los Angeles, and others – were once Jewish ghettos. To some degree, the changes occurred because Jews were more ready to welcome blacks, or at least not treat them with the same degree of physical hostility as other white groups. But often when Jews moved out as residents they remained on as landlords and storekeepers and in some cases as civil servants, particularly as school teachers in local schools and social workers. Hence, blacks frequently found that the whites with whom they have had to deal in power situations were largely Jews. Such relationships not unnaturally led many blacks to define their exploiters or enemies, not just as whites, but as Jews, and to accept various anti-Semitic stereotypes.

This situation did not give rise to manifest political conflict until the 1960s, in part because blacks were not politically active and militant prior to that time, and in any case there were no obvious political issues and demands that pitted blacks against Jews. Such issues did arise, however, with the emergence of the concept of affirmative action, of setting aside positions, quotas, for blacks. In New York City, the demand was voiced that Jewish school teachers in black districts be fired and replaced by blacks, and that, in general, preference for government jobs be given to blacks. The highly publicized and prolonged 1968 New York teachers' strike was viewed as a black–Jewish struggle.[51] Many blacks now regard Jews as the principal group trying to stop them on the issue of affirmative action. With the growth of race consciousness from the 1960s on has come concern about black Africa and identification with the Third World, which includes the Arabs. Blacks have become sensitive to tensions between Israel and Africa and the Third World and tend to side more with the Palestinians than any other group in America.

The organized Jewish community has reacted negatively to these developments. Many Jews feel they have been betrayed by blacks, whom they see as a group they tried to help and whose causes they have supported for much of this century. In this context, many Jews have withdrawn their financial support from black organizations. This is one reason that some of these groups are having severe financial difficulties and have declined, developments which have exacerbated the blacks' resentment of Jews. The division between the Jewish and black leadership has pushed some Jews to look for other coalition allies, such as the rapidly expanding Asian populations. It is noteworthy that these differences now show up clearly in opinion poll findings: blacks are the least pro-Israel and the most anti-Jewish ethnoreligious group in the USA, and Jews perceive them as being so.[52] Conversely the level of support for black-related issues among Jews has declined. Although survey research still reports that Jews have more liberal attitudes towards black rights than whites as a whole, they now appear less sympathetic than some other well-educated whites.

Will most American Jews remain bound to the Democratic Party for the foreseeable future? Does this close and stubborn relationship mean that Jews have little leverage with the Republicans, who have won five of the last six presidential elections?

To deal with these questions, it must be understood that American Jewish strength in politics has only partly been a function of their voting preferences. The chief influence of the Jews comes from the fact that they have been hyperactive on the political scene.[53] Power bases may be distinguished among 'expert power', 'reward power' and 'coercive power'. The Jews, of course, have no *direct* coercive power.

For some time, the main Jewish reward power has been related to their political hyperactivism. Although less than 3 per cent of the citizenry, they register and vote in almost twice the proportion of the rest of the population. As the percentage of Americans exercising their franchise goes down – 50 per cent in the 1988 presidential elections, much less in Congressional contests and party primaries – the proportion of the electorate formed by Jews, who always vote, goes up. Since the great majority of them are Democrats, they can be especially important in determining the party's nominees in many areas. They have at times contributed as much as half of the Democratic Party coffers nationally, and a disproportionate amount to the Republican Party as well.[54] They also have comprised a significant number of political activists, to a considerable degree as 'expert' volunteers, as well as 'expert' professionals – important to candidates and elected officials of both parties.

Several reasons continue to be advanced by those anticipating an eventual shift to the Republican Party. In spite of the record presented here, some suggest that a sizeable number of Jews are close to becoming Republicanized because of shifting viewpoints on the domestic agenda. The argument is not that Jews will turn away in any large numbers from a bias towards economic liberalism, towards support for the underdogs, but that more of them are ready, along with many other Americans, to move away from New Deal liberalism, perceived as having produced welfare dependency.

The record does not sustain these expectations.[55] The many national polls conducted during the Reagan and Bush eras have documented the seemingly contradictory pattern that the majority of Americans (and an even larger proportion of Jews) favour maintaining or increasing expenditures for the assorted welfare state measures identified with the Democratic Party, and oppose most of the specific cuts proposed by Ronald Reagan and, to a lesser extent, George Bush. At the same time most Americans seek to lower taxes, and identify long-term economic prosperity and favourable personal financial prospects with Reagan–Bush policies. That majority voted with their pocketbooks in 1984 and 1988. Most Jews, however, who, as we have seen, are among the well-to-do, still opt for their communitarian ideals rather than their pocketbooks.

The links of Jews to the Democratic Party continue to be strongly related to foreign policy concerns, beginning, as noted, with the struggle against Nazism identified with Franklin Roosevelt, whose efforts to resist Hitler were met with opposition by the Republicans, seen as isolationists and neutralists. The Democratic Party has been seen by Jews as the particular political friend of Israel. This may be a circular reality and a circular perception: Democratic Party leaders being closer to and supported by the Jews have been seen as, and for the most part actually have been, extremely sympathetic to Israel. In this sense, Hubert Humphrey epitomized the Democratic Party for American Jews. It was obvious that he was intellectually and sentimentally as committed to Israel as the most Zionist Jew.

At some point, perhaps during the 1970s, it began to be clear to some Jewish observers that American support of Israel would finally rest less and less on personal and sentimental commitments and more and more on hard-headed evaluations that Israel was important for America's national interest. Such an evaluation would depend on a global view of the East–West conflict, and on the total context of American foreign policy.

Starting with the struggle against the Vietnam war, a substantial number of Democrats formulated an isolationist and anti-militarist position, seeking to reduce America's militant anti-Communist posture and overseas commitments. Although most liberal Democrats who adopted this position, such as George McGovern and his campaign manager, Gary Hart, Alan Cranston, Edward Kennedy, and to a considerable degree Jimmy Carter, continued to advocate strong support for Israel, their position could be seen as political opportunism, not rooted in a logical commitment. And more recently a visible anti-Israel Democratic left led by Jesse Jackson has emerged, whose Middle East views had considerable backing among the delegates to the 1988 Democratic National Convention. According to various media polls taken at the convention, many who supported Dukakis agreed with Jackson's position on the Israeli–Palestinian conflict.

Conversely, a number of prominent conservatives, including Ronald Reagan and various Christian fundamentalist ministers, strongly backed Israel. In addition to different personal and religious reasons, they viewed the alliance with the Jewish State as part of the larger struggle against Communist expansionism and the rise of radical anti-Western Third World leaders.

These developments put many American Jews in a dilemma. Israel's most militant supporters internationally and to some degree nationally are on the right. Its overt enemies are disproportionately to be found on the left in the ranks of Communists, Socialists, Third World nationalists, and, to a growing, though still small, extent, American liberals and Democrats.

These changes logically should lead to a move towards the Republicans by American Jews. Yet, as we have seen, they have not. The immediate answer to this conundrum may be that in spite of their concern for Israel's security, most Jews are not only liberals on domestic issues, but, as noted, they are also in the forefront of foreign policy dovishness. Although clearly not pacifists, they are remarkably anti-militarist. For example, various polls have consistently found that a much larger proportion of Jews than non-Jews say that the USA should reduce military spending. Israel, however, complicates Jewish foreign affairs liberalism. In the 1984 National Survey of American Jews, the Jews approved by a 61 to 24 per cent ratio the statement that 'in order to be a reliable military supporter of Israel, the U.S. should maintain a strong military capacity'. But they also agreed by a 59 to 27 per cent ratio with the opinion that 'to help reduce deficits and relieve world tension, U.S. military spending should be cut'. And almost all white liberal

Democratic politicians, publicly at least, take the same positions, sometimes even criticizing the Republican administrations whenever they appear to waver in support of Israel, thus reducing the strain for Jews.

The argument repeatedly raised by some Republican Jews in their missionary activity is that the Democratic Party – with its neo-isolationist, excessively anti-militarist, even a visible minority of anti-American and politicized Third World elements – is leading the country in directions which are deleterious to both Israel and the USA. The Jewish activist corps in the Republican Party continues to try to build a foreign policy bridge away from the Democratic Party, largely in the name of Israel's interests.[56] They will continue to reinterpret in Republican terms the current Jewish state of confusion about foreign policy liberalism. It is at least conceivable that if there is no Humphrey-like nominee in the Democratic Party future, if there are more Jesse Jacksons and George McGoverns, if the Democratic Party's foreign policy becomes further factionalized in a radical direction, if the party's economic liberalism does not become more modernized, and if the Republican Party repudiates the effort to saddle it with politicized Christianity, that a more substantial movement towards the Republican Party can ensue.

But these are a lot of 'ifs'. As recent election results suggest, it will take more than a single bridge for the Jews to cross over in large numbers. And their hesitancy on that score must finally be assessed on some measure other than those used in election surveys.

Basically, identification with liberalism, the L word, which, most analysts agree, has been a liability for the Democrats since the 1960s, remains a crucial asset in retaining Jewish support. 'Liberalism', of course, is a matter of some imprecision. It is historically compounded of several dimensions. But, however it is defined, the fact is that the Jews are much more disposed than others to identify as liberals. In most polls taken in recent years, on the average twice as many Jews describe themselves as liberals rather than conservatives, and about twice as many Jews call themselves liberals as do Americans generally. One long-term analyst has even referred to Jewish conservatism as a form of 'deviant' behaviour.[57]

Substantive issues could eventually make a difference, but it will take an emotional wrench, or more generational distance, to eliminate the Democratic Party advantage in Jewish voting. It is at the level of cultural liberalism that we still find the deepest source of Jewish reluctance to make the change.

A COMPARATIVE NOTE

The country most similar to the United States, whose Jews have comparable backgrounds to those across the border, is Canada.[58] As in America and other Western countries, Jews there contributed heavily to the Communist and early Socialist movements. A comprehensive log-linear analysis of their party preferences in the post-Second World War era shows that in a three-party situation, Jews are more likely to support the socialist party, the CCF/NDP, which normally secures between 15 and 20 per cent of the national vote, than the other two, and disproportionately prefer the centre-left Liberals rather than the Conservatives by a substantial margin. In trying to account for this outcome, Jean Laponce suggests that

> in democratic countries of immigration such as Canada and the United States, centre-left parties became particularly attractive to the groups and communities that are not at the cultural core, that are not part of the dominant historical stream of the society – groups that may have been persecuted or harassed or subject to discrimination (Jews in Canada, Protestants and Jews in France). . . .[59]

I will not try to relate interpretations of the North American pattern to those of Jews elsewhere. I would note, however, that in almost all Western countries, prior to the last two decades, Jews had given Labor and Socialist parties heavy support, and also contributed significantly to the ranks of the Communists. These patterns are no longer the case, with the exception of continued socialist strength in France.[60] Symbolic of the change to conservatism is the fact that, throughout her period as Prime Minister of Great Britain, Margaret Thatcher represented the most heavily Jewish constituency in the UK, Finchley. The majority of Jews who once voted Labour now support the Conservatives. Some have explained these changes as derivative from Jews having achieved a high level of acceptance and affluence in recent decades. But then why are American Jews different? Why do they remain on the left?

There is no simple answer to this question, but in large measure the shifts can be traced, particularly in Australia and Britain, but in much of Europe as well, to the fact that the socialist left, especially its youth affiliates and intellectuals, turned openly and vigorously in support of the Palestinian Liberation Organization in the 1970s and 1980s. As noted, Israel has become anathema to ideological radicals, as a collaborator with imperialist America against the Third World. This development resulted in efforts to push Jewish supporters of Israel out of socialist organizations, and even to efforts to deny them, as 'Zionist racists', free speech on university campuses.

The conservatives, on the other hand, whose historic record was likely to have included anti-Semitism and opposition to Zionism, have in recent decades become friendly to the Jewish State and have made overtures to their Jewish electorates.[61] In effect, Jews outside of North America and, to some degree, France, have been rejected by the left and courted by the right, an inversion of traditional relationships. As noted earlier, except among the now tiny Marxist left movements and militant blacks, the dominant left forces in the United States (and Canada) have not behaved in the same way; although I believe many American left-Liberals share the same predispositions as their European ideological soul-mates, as the polls of the delegates to the 1984 and 1988 Democratic national conventions reveal. Basically Jews are too important to the liberal and Democratic forces for them to risk alienating their support by turning against Israel. Democratic leaders, who oppose military spending and American involvement abroad, back military and other forms of aid to Israel. Hence relations with blacks apart, American Jews, unlike their European brethren, have not been pressed to choose between their commitment to Israel and their traditional ties to the left. They have been able to remain liberals and Democrats.

NOTES

1 'Washington's reply to the Hebrew congregation in Newport, Rhode Island', *Publications of the American Jewish Historical Society*, no. 3 (1895), pp. 91–2.
2 John A. Hardon, *American Judaism* (Chicago, Loyola University Press, 1971), pp. 32–3.
3 Lawrence H. Fuchs, *The Political Behavior of American Jews* (Glencoe, Ill., Free Press, 1956), pp. 25–30; Nathaniel Weyl, *The Jew in American Politics* (New Rochelle, NY, Arlington House, 1968), pp. 37–8; William R. Heitzmann, *American Jewish Voting Behavior: A History and Analysis* (San Francisco, R&E Research Associates, 1975), pp. 21–4.
4 Peter Wiernik, *History of the Jews in America* (New York, Hermon Press, 1972, third edition), pp. 128–34.
5 Henry L. Feingold, *Zion in America* (New York, Hippocrene Books, 1974), pp. 89–90; Eli N. Evans, *Judah P. Benjamin: The Jewish Confederate* (New York: Free Press, 1988), pp. 23–48, 115–58.
6 Calvin Goldscheider and Alan S. Zuckerman, *The Transformation of the Jews* (Chicago: University of Chicago Press, 1986), p. 116. For details, see Nathan Glazer, 'Social characteristics of American Jews, 1654–1954', *American Jewish Year Book*, 56 (1955) (New York: American Jewish Committee, 1955), pp. 9–10.
7 Barry E. Supple, 'A business elite: German–Jewish financiers in nineteenth-century New York', *Business History Review*, 31 (Summer 1957), pp. 143–78; Vincent P. Carosso, 'A financial elite: New York's German–Jewish investment bankers', *American Jewish Historical Quarterly* (September 1976), pp. 67–87.
8 Stephen D. Isaacs, *Jews and American Politics* (Garden City, NY, Doubleday, 1974), p. 153; Fuchs, *The Political Behavior of American Jews*, pp. 41–57; Weyl, *The Jew in American Politics*, pp. 63–76, Heitzmann, *American Jewish Voting Behavior*, pp. 27–39.
9 Chaim L. Waxman, *America's Jews in Transition* (Philadelphia, Temple University Press, 1983), pp. 49–51.
10 Fuchs, *The Political Behavior of American Jews*, pp. 55–7; Isaacs, *Jews and American Politics*, pp. 153–5.
11 Werner Cohn, 'The politics of American Jews', in Marshall Sklare (ed.), *The Jews: Social Patterns of an American Group* (Glencoe, Ill., Free Press, 1958), pp. 615–18.
12 Ronald Sanders, *The Downtown Jews* (New York, Dover Publications, 1987), p. 56–180; Melech Epstein, *Jewish Labor in the U.S.A.* (New York: Trade Union Sponsoring Committee, 1950).

13 Arthur Liebman, *Jews and the Left* (New York, John Wiley & Sons, 1979), p. 1, see also pp. 20–33; Irving Howe, *World of Our Fathers* (New York, Harcourt, Brace, Jovanovich, 1976), pp. 287–324.

14 Isaacs, *Jews and American Politics*, pp. 151–2; Fuchs, *The Political Behavior of American Jews*, pp. 151–69. On the heavily disproportionate support which the American Communist Party drew from Jews, see Nathan Glazer, *The Social Basis of American Communism* (New York, Harcourt, Brace & World, 1961), pp. 130–68.

15 Nathan Glazer, *American Judaism* (Chicago, University of Chicago Press, 1972, second edition), p. 71; Howe, *World of Our Fathers*, pp. 204–8.

16 Cohn, 'The politics of American Jews', p. 621.

17 Seymour Martin Lipset and Earl Raab, *The Politics of Unreason: Right-Wing Extremism in America 1790–1970* (New York, Harper & Row, 1970), pp. 171–89; Charles Stember et al., *Jews in the Mind of America* (New York, Basic Books, 1966), pp. 110–35.

18 Fuchs, *The Political Behavior of American Jews*, pp. 71–81, 129–30.

19 Isaacs, *Jews and American Politics*, p. 152.

20 David L. Featherman, 'The socioeconomic achievement of white religio-ethnic subgroups: social and psychological explanations', *American Sociological Review*, 36 (1971), p. 207.

21 Steven M. Cohen, *The Political Attitudes of American Jews, 1988: A National Survey in Comparative Perspective* (New York, American Jewish Committee, forthcoming); Andrew M. Greeley, *Ethnicity, Denomination and Inequality* (Beverly Hills, Sage, 1976), p. 39.

22 Calvin Goldscheider and Alan S. Zuckerman, *The Transformation of the Jews* (Chicago, University of Chicago Press, 1986), p. 183.

23 Data from Gerald Bubis as reported in Barry A. Kosmin, 'The dimensions of contemporary Jewish philanthropy' (unpublished paper, North American Jewish Data Bank, Graduate School, City University of New York, 1988), p. 13.

24 The data for leading intellectuals are from Charles Kadushin, *The American Intellectual Elite* (Boston, Little, Brown, 1974), pp. 23–4, 35–6. Those for professors are from Seymour Martin Lipset and Everett Carl Ladd, 'Jewish academics in the United States: their achievements, culture and politics', *American Jewish Year Book*, 72 (1971) (New York, American Jewish Committee, 1971), pp. 89–128; the other elite groups, see Stanley Rothman, Robert Lichter and Linda Lichter, *Elites in Conflict: Social Change in America Today* (forthcoming).

25 Lucy S. Dawidowicz, *On Equal Terms: Jews in America 1881–1981* (New York, Holt, Rinehart & Winston, 1982), p. 51.

26 Seymour Martin Lipset, 'Blacks and Jews: how much bias?', *Public Opinion*, 10 (July/August 1987), pp. 4–5, 57–8.

27 Charles Liebman, *The Ambivalent American Jew* (Philadelphia, Jewish Publication Society of America, 1973), pp. 136–7.

28 David Singer, 'Still liberal', *AJC Journal* (Spring 1989), p. 5.

29 Stephen J. Whitfield, 'The Jewish vote', *The Virginia Quarterly Review*, 62 (Winter 1986), pp. 1–20. See also Seymour Martin Lipset and Earl Raab, 'The American Jews, the 1984 elections, and beyond', in Daniel J. Elezar (ed.) *The New Jewish Politics* (Lanham, Md., University Press of America, 1988), pp. 33–50.

30 Martin Hochbaum, *The Jewish Vote in the 1984 Presidential Election* (New York, American Jewish Congress, 1985), p. 6.

31 Alan Fisher, 'The myth of the rightward turn', *Moment*, 8, no. 10 (1983), p. 25.
32 Cohen, *The Political Attitudes of American Jews, 1988*.
33 Ibid.
34 Fisher, 'The myth', p. 26.
35 Robert Lerner, Althea K. Nagai and Stanley Rothman, 'Marginality and liberalism among Jewish elites', *Public Opinion Quarterly*, 53 (Fall 1989), pp. 335, 338–9.
36 Ibid., pp. 339–40.
37 Seymour Martin Lipset, 'Neoconservatism: myth and reality', *Society*, 25 (July/August 1988), pp. 29–37.
38 In their study of Jewish elites, Lerner, Nagai and Rothman 'find a distinctive *political* tradition that Jewish parents pass down to their offspring, . . . a tradition of political liberalism', 'Marginality and liberals among Jewish elites', p. 348.
39 Reviews of various hypotheses may be found in Peter Y. Medding, 'Toward a general theory of Jewish political interests and behaviour', *Jewish Journal of Sociology*, 19 (December 1977), pp. 117–18, 123; and J. A. Laponce, 'Left or centre? The Canadian Jewish electorate, 1953–1983', *Canadian Journal of Political Science*, 21 (December 1988), pp. 694–6. For an innovative presentation, see Irving Kristol, 'The liberal tradition of American Jews', in Seymour Martin Lipset (ed.), *American Pluralism and the Jewish Community* (New Brunswick, NJ, Transaction Books, 1990), pp. 109–16.
40 Fuchs, *The Political Behavior of American Jews*, pp. 180–2, 187–8.
41 Cohen, *The Political Attitudes of American Jews* (1984 and 1988).
42 Fisher, 'The Myth', p. 26.
43 Alan M. Fisher, 'Where the Jewish vote is going', *Moment*, 13 (March 1989), p. 43. Summaries of changing and improving attitudes towards Jews may be found in Geraldine Rosenfield, 'The polls: attitudes toward American Jews', *Public Opinion Quarterly*, 46 (1982), pp. 431–43, and Lipset, 'Blacks and Jews: how much bias?', pp. 4–5, 57–8. See also Gregory Martire and Ruth Clark, *Anti-Semitism in the United States: A Study of Prejudice in the 1980s* (New York, Praeger, 1982).
44 Peter Y. Medding, *The Transformation of American Jewish Politics* (New York, The American Jewish Committee, 1989), p. 15.
45 Lipset and Ladd, 'Jewish academics . . .', and Kadushin, *The American Intellectual Elite*.
46 Thorstein Veblen, *Essays on Our Changing Order* (New York, Viking Press, 1934), pp. 221, 223–4. The essay on the Jews was first published in 1919.
47 For a review of the literature and an application of this type of analysis to the politics of intellectuals, see Seymour Martin Lipset and Richard B. Dobson, 'The intellectual as critic and rebel', *Daedalus*, 101 (Summer 1972), pp. 137–98.
48 Liebman, *The Ambivalent American Jew*, pp. 149–50; Fuchs, *The Political Behavior*, pp. 189–90.
49 Stanley Rothman and S. Robert Lichter, *Roots of Radicalism: Jews, Christians and the New Left* (New York, Oxford University Press, 1982).
50 For a discussion of these developments, see Seymour Martin Lipset, *The Left, The Jews and Israel* (New York, Anti-Defamation League of B'nai B'rith, 1969).
51 Isaacs, *Jews and American Politics*, pp. 164–6; Louis Harris and Bert E. Swanson *Black–Jewish Relations in New York City* (New York, Praeger Publishers, 1970), pp. 131–58; Mark Levy and Michael Kramer, *The Ethnic Factor* (New York, Simon & Schuster, 1972), pp. 109–14.

52 Charles Silberman, *A Certain People* (New York, Summit Books, 1986), pp. 339–40, 351–2.
53 Isaacs, *Jews and American Politics*, pp. 6–10.
54 Medding, *The Transformation*, pp. 13–14; Michael V. Malbin, 'Jewish PACs: a new force in Jewish political action', in Elezar (ed.), *The New Jewish Politics*, pp. 51–63.
55 Leonard Fein, *Where Are We? The Inner Life of America's Jews* (New York: Harper & Row, 1988), pp. 227–41.
56 They derive hope from the fact that for over two decades younger Jews, aged 18–29, have been more likely to vote Republican than older generations. They also have exhibited less enthusiasm for Israel than their elders. But seemingly as they mature and presumably become more involved in the Jewish community as parents, their cohort shows up as more Democratic and pro-Israel. Fisher, 'Where the Jewish vote is going', pp. 41–2.
57 Fisher, 'The myth', p. 5.
58 See Seymour Martin Lipset, *Continental Divide: The Values and Institutions of the United States and Canada* (New York, Routledge, 1990).
59 Laponce, 'Left or centre?', pp. 713–14.
60 See Geoffrey Alderman, 'Not quite British: the political attitudes of Anglo-Jewry', in Ivor Crewe (ed.), *British Political Sociology Yearbook*, vol. 2, *The Politics of Race* (New York, Wiley, 1975), pp. 188–211; *idem*, *The Jewish Community in British Politics* (New York, Oxford University Press, 1983); *idem*, 'London Jews and the 1987 general election', *The Jewish Quarterly*, 34, no. 3 (1987), pp. 13–16; *idem*, *London Jewry and London Politics* (London, Routledge, 1989); 'Jews and socialism: the end of a beautiful relationship?', symposium, *The Jewish Quarterly*, 35, no. 2 (1988), pp. 7–19; Peter Medding, 'Factors influencing the voting behaviour of Melbourne Jews', in Medding (ed.), *Jews in Australian Society* (South Melbourne, Macmillan, 1973), pp. 141–59; Bernard Wasserstein, 'The Jews, the left, and the 1973 elections in France', *Midstream*, 19 (August/September 1973), pp. 41–54; Dominique Schnapper and Sylvie Strudel, 'Le "vote juif" en France', *Revue française de science politique*, 36 (December 1983), pp. 933–61; Jacky Akoka, 'Vote juif ou vote des juifs', *Pardes*, 1 (1985), pp. 114–36.
61 See W. D. Rubenstein, *The Left, The Right and the Jews* (London, Croom Helm, 1982), pp. 77–173, for discussion of the effect of the behaviour of the left on the shift to the right among Jews in a number of countries, excepting the United States and France, which he analyses as well. This book is the most comprehensive comparative work on Jewish political behaviour in recent decades.

8

AMERICAN JEWS AND UNITED STATES FOREIGN POLICY (1945–90)

Steven L. Spiegel

American Jews have experienced dramatic changes in their relationship to US foreign policy in the post-1945 period. Issues of concern to the Jewish community, especially relating to Israel, were initially considered peripheral to Washington's central global objective of containing the USSR. Few Jews were engaged in American diplomacy and Jews were widely regarded as biased in favour of the Zionist quest. By the 1980s, however, the treatment of Soviet Jews had become a bench-mark in judging Moscow's human rights record and the degree to which America could trust the Kremlin. Israel had come to be seen as a 'strategic asset' and Jewish views towards Israel were generally regarded as one important perspective of American policy in the Middle East. Individual Jews increasingly played a prominent role in American diplomacy towards both the USSR and the Middle East as bureaucrats and negotiators, and did so in a balanced and unbiased manner.

This paper will examine how these dramatic changes occurred. It will do so by investigating the process from four different perspectives: (1) the evolving definition of American national interests; (2) the Jewish role *vis-à-vis* Congress and the political parties; (3) the participation of individual Jews in the executive branch; and (4) the changing focus of American Jewry. It will conclude with some predictions about future directions in the relationship between US Jews and American foreign policy.

THE EVOLVING DEFINITION OF AMERICAN NATIONAL INTERESTS

When American Jews attempt to influence United States foreign policy, they do not operate in a vacuum. The Jewish role in American foreign policy must be viewed in the light of the evolving definition of American national interests. The most important determinant of the influence of American Jewish organizations and prominent figures is whether they are pressing the government in ways similar to or different from the direction in which the administration in power seeks to move.

Often what is viewed as influence is actually receptivity. When the administration and the Jewish leadership have opposing conceptions of the direction in which American foreign policy should move, the receptivity of an administration to Jewish concerns and influence is low. In such cases successful strategies to influence an administration will be limited to efforts to constrain it from taking all the actions it would otherwise pursue, efforts to convince key officials to make compromises in some of their policies, and efforts to gain the release or transfer of officials viewed as particular adversaries. On the other hand, when the administration and the Jewish leadership have similar conceptions of American national interests, Jewish organizational activities are directed at reinforcing administration policies and changing policy positions where tactical differences exist. In the first case, Jewish influence is limited; in the second, it is less a matter of influence and more a convergence of interests.

The Middle East

American policy towards Israel can be evaluated on the basis of three criteria: (1) The importance of the Middle East in an administration's global priorities and the extent to which Arab–Israeli problems are a matter of interest or concern; (2) whether Israel is viewed as a strategic asset or burden; and (3) whether key policy-makers reject the appropriate involvement of the Jewish community in foreign policy, see it as a crucial target of their own efforts to gain public support on important policy matters, or see Jewish leaders as allies with similar objectives.

For differing reasons, the Truman and Eisenhower administrations are examples of low receptivity to Jewish concerns. In the years immediately following the Second World War, when Jews were fighting in Palestine for a state, American leaders were focused on the effort to develop a global policy for the perceived Soviet threat, with particular attention devoted to Europe and the Far East. Arab–Israeli issues were peripheral. Thus when Britain declared its intention to abandon involvement in Greece and Turkey in early 1947, the Truman administration prepared a major programme of foreign aid and the President declared the Truman Doctrine. About the same time, the British announced their plans to leave Palestine and the administration was relieved to be able to hand the unwanted issue over to the fledgling United Nations. In 1948, as violence developed between the Arabs and Jews, Truman and his aides were not worried about Palestine, but about a possible communist victory in Italy, the future of Germany and the Berlin blockade.[1]

To a unanimous national security bureaucracy, the concept of a Jewish state in the Middle East was a terrible idea, injurious to American interests.

In an autumn 1947 memorandum addressed to Secretary of State George Marshall, Loy Henderson, the director of the State Department's Near East bureau, argued that a Jewish state would alienate the Arabs and large sectors of the Muslim world, endanger oil supplies to an impoverished Europe, and even threaten Jewish security in the United States when Americans realized the perils of US support for a Jewish state.[2] Most bureaucrats in the executive branch thought the Jews could not win after an inevitable Arab attack, and America's demobilized army could not rescue them. Even if the Jews miraculously emerged victorious the communists would benefit as the Arabs would hold the West, and especially the US, responsible. Some even thought Israel would be an ally of the Soviets, as many of its leaders had emigrated from Russia and held socialist beliefs. In short, supporting a Jewish state was seen as either a disaster or at best a luxury America could not afford.

Eisenhower and Dulles proceeded one step further and thought the Arabs were essential to blocking the advance of international communism in the area. Unlike their predecessors' preoccupation with Asia and Europe, the 'new look' in American policy assumed that the Middle East would be an imminent battleground in the expansive Soviet threat.[3] True believers in the vision of a future Middle East organized in the image of Europe, they proceeded to distance American policy from Britain, France and Israel; to push for the Baghdad Pact – a Near East NATO – meant to contain the Soviets through cooperation with the 'northern tier' of Turkey, Iraq, Iran and Pakistan; and to promote 'technical' solutions to the problems of the area, such as the equitable sharing of the Jordan waters. When Khrushchev simply leapfrogged their political Maginot line by offering arms to Egypt and Syria, Eisenhower and Dulles produced a new version of the Marshall Plan – the Aswan Dam project. Their strategy exploded in the Suez Crisis. The Eisenhower Doctrine of 1957, which offered assistance to governments threatened by communism, was a makeshift response still embedded in the idea of organizing the states of the area to withstand the perceived communist onslaught. The cathartic experience of the 1958 intervention in Lebanon convinced the administration that Nasserism had been effectively thwarted.

Thus, during the 1950s, Jewish concerns were of a low priority in American policy towards the Middle East, and Jewish community efforts on behalf of Israel were often perceived as a nuisance.[4] In the Kennedy era, the Arab–Israeli problem – now temporarily quiescent – was again relegated to a back-burner and receptivity to Jewish concerns remained low, but for reasons of lack of attention. Issues such as Cuba, Berlin and defence policy made headlines and absorbed policy-makers' time.[5] Under Johnson America's vistas narrowed to a perilous preoccupation with Vietnam, but the President's personal foreign policy orientation increased interest in Israel and receptivity towards Jewish concerns. The Six Day War reminded

Washington that the Middle East was crucial to its strategic interests and that the region's instability could lead to a Soviet–American confrontation. Johnson was too overwhelmed by the war in Indo-China to deal with the implications of these conclusions, but in Nixon's first press conference he called the Middle East a 'powder keg' demanding American attention.[6]

In the Nixon first term, policy towards the Arab–Israeli issue was inconsistent and therefore the receptivity to Jewish concerns was mixed. Nixon's problem was that he thought other matters, such as relations with the USSR and China, ending the Vietnam War, were more critical than the Middle East.[7] His administration was united in its determination to reassert American influence in the Arab world, which was perceived as having been lost in the wake of the Six Day War, and thus embarked on a serious effort to reach an Arab–Israeli settlement. The Nixon policy team was, however, irreparably divided about how to achieve the objectives of an Arab–Israeli settlement and enhanced relations with the Arabs. On the one hand, Secretary of State William Rogers sought to improve American–Arab relations by pressuring Israel towards territorial and political concessions. On the other hand, National Security Adviser Henry Kissinger believed that before any pressure was placed on Israel, Egypt and Syria, the major Arab states which remained clients of the USSR, must first turn to Washington for assistance in efforts to reach a settlement. Otherwise, Moscow would be the beneficiary of any Arab political gains at Israel's expense. Rogers was weakened by the failure of his Mid-East diplomatic efforts in the wake of the Egyptian and Soviet breach of the August 1970 cease-fire ending the War of Attrition and the Jordan crisis one month later, which Nixon saw as being provoked by the Soviets.[8]

The differences between Kissinger and Rogers concerning policy towards the Middle East were part of a wide range of conflicts between the two men, which ultimately led to Rogers's resignation in 1972; as a result, Kissinger became both Secretary of State and National Security Adviser. Ironically, after the Yom Kippur War, Kissinger adopted the step-by-step policy Rogers had pioneered. By taking advantage of the changed regional conditions and by employing rare diplomatic skill he was able to achieve the breakthroughs which had eluded his predecessor.[9]

Kissinger devoted unusual time and effort to the problems of Arabs and Israelis after the 1973 war because the Middle East had become the focal point of American global concerns. The region was viewed as central to relations with the USSR; to the security of energy supplies and thus the economic vitality of the West; and to amicable relations with America's allies. It was also seen as a model of the dangers of severe Third World instability and the potential for their leading to superpower confrontation. Washington had thus come full circle from the days of Harry Truman. Now all major problems the United States confronted in foreign affairs seemed to be interpreted in Arab–Israeli terms.[10]

Under Nixon and Ford, Kissinger had tried to juggle conflicting interests in a constant struggle to avoid linking a comprehensive settlement of the Arab–Israel conflict with problems like the energy crisis, the shaky *détente* with the Soviet Union and strained relations with allies. The Carter team reversed the premises of the Kissinger era: they assumed that the resolution of the Arab–Israeli dispute would bring with it a resolution of the energy crisis and would lessen the potential for tensions with the USSR, the allies and the Third World.[11] Not surprisingly, after eighteen months the President commented that he had spent more time on this issue than any other. Truman would have been astonished at the centrality of the Middle East during the Carter administration, even more by the certainty and unity with which it approached the area. He would, however, have empathized with Carter's low receptivity to Jewish attempts to influence his policy.

The Carter administration's premises collapsed over an area of the Middle East the President had hitherto seen as an 'island of stability' – Iran.[12] Although with the Camp David Accords and subsequent peace treaty he had achieved a settlement between Egypt and Israel, another energy crisis occurred anyway, this time due to the fall of the Shah – not the frustration of the Palestinians and their Arab patrons. In 1979 it was Persian rather than Palestinian policy which precipitated repeated crises with the allies. In the end, the *détente* of the 1970s did collapse, but over the Soviet invasion of Afghanistan – not over another Arab–Israeli war. Like Eisenhower, Carter was preoccupied with a future threat to American interests, but failed to produce a policy which would prevent it, in part because he misunderstood the nature of the region. Eisenhower thought the Middle East was another Europe; Carter forgot there was more to the area than Arabs and Israelis.

Reagan entered office committed to righting what he viewed as Carter's wrongs. The Soviet Union would be confronted on all levels of potential competition – global and regional – and if possible its gains would be reversed.[13] The Truman Doctrine was essentially reactive; the Reagan Doctrine envisioned a dynamic policy of rolling back Soviet influence. In the Middle East, Reagan was determined not to repeat Carter's miscalculations, and the Arab–Israeli issue was accorded less emphasis. This president ultimately intervened unsuccessfully in Lebanon and failed to gain the hostages' freedom, but could claim to have achieved his goals in both the Persian Gulf and Afghanistan.

One of Reagan's reactions to the fall of the Shah and to Carter's perceived misguidedness was to see Israel as an important strategic asset to the United States in the confrontation with the USSR, in the fight against terrorism, and in the protection of American interests in the area. Here too Truman was turned on his head. To the 'man from Missouri', support for Zionism was based on humanitarian, not political, reasons. Palestine was viewed as a haven for Jewish refugees: a state was unnecessary. Before 1948, only Special Counsel to the President Clark Clifford argued that the establishment of a democratic Jewish state would be a bulwark against communism; he was overwhelmed by opposition in the State Department, the Pentagon and the CIA. Eisenhower had assumed Israel was a deficit; Kennedy and Johnson viewed Israel as a positive democratic force but still a burden in terms of American interests, which were perceived to lie in the Arab world. Nixon and Kissinger had been the first officials at the pinnacle of power to see Israel in strategic terms as an asset, a view that had been strengthened by the Jordan crisis of September 1970, in which Israel aided in saving the Hashemite kingdom.[14]

But Israel's prestige plummeted in the aftermath of the Yom Kippur War. Its respected deterrent capability had not prevented an Arab attack and its vaunted intelligence services had proven fallible. As Arab influence over American financial and energy security increased under Ford, American policy towards Israel appeared as bait to entice Arab cooperation with the United States. According to this approach, the US would pressure Israel to offer concessions, the Arabs would be satisfied, and America would benefit. In turn, an Israel grateful for American *largesse* would gain a measure of peace and security. To this Machiavellian definition of Israel's role Carter had added a zealous conviction that the US had to 'save Israel in spite of herself'.[15] The 1950s view of Israel as a deficit to American interests resurfaced with a vengeance.

Reagan reversed Carter's assumptions. Particularly reacting to the fall of the Shah, many on his team regarded Israel as a country of special value in the area. The two Secretaries of State of the period, Alexander Haig and George Shultz, believed that strategic cooperation with Israel would bring important benefits to the USA. Shultz had entered office with different views but quickly became disillusioned with Arab rejection of his diplomatic initiatives and pursued a policy of exceptionally close relations with Israel from 1983 onwards. Although Secretary of Defense Caspar Weinberger advocated the opposite approach, stressing the drawbacks of close collaboration with Jerusalem for US–Arab relations and in the conflict with Islamic fundamentalism, President Reagan's strong commitment to strategic cooperation contributed to the ultimate victory of those who favoured this policy direction.

From this brief review of the record of eight administrations, we can extract several lessons for the role of American Jews in the formulation of American policy towards the Middle East, and particularly Israel. First, when the priority of the Arab–Israeli issue is extremely high, due to American interest in gaining support in the Arab world, tensions with Jerusalem increase. We can see a large range of disputes between Jerusalem and Washington under Eisenhower in the late Nixon period and again under Ford and Carter. When the priority of this issue is extremely low, in the main because the USA is preoccupied with other global issues that are more pressing, as under Truman and Kennedy, it is difficult to gain the attention of high ranking policy-makers and the national security bureaucracy has particular influence, which works against Israel. In this case, relations with Israel remain moderate. Israel seems to do best either when there is a president ideologically sympathetic to the Jewish state, such as Johnson and Reagan, or when a president sees Israel as playing a positive role in the region, as with Nixon and Reagan. Not surprisingly, the receptivity of an administration to Jewish community efforts was especially high in periods in which the administration favoured Israel for its own reasons, or at least had no major policy differences with Jerusalem. Receptivity was low when the priority was on using Israel as bait for the Arabs or when Israel was seen as a burden to American interests in the region.

Second, united administrations are rarely open to American Jewish efforts to influence policy. United administrations are more likely to be opposed to Israeli policies and to exhibit a low receptivity to Jewish concerns, as demonstrated under Eisenhower, late Nixon and Ford, and then Carter. Only in the second Reagan term was a united administration receptive to advocacy in support of Israel. On the other hand, divided administrations, such as those of Truman, Kennedy, Johnson, Nixon and during Reagan's first term, offered opportunities to counter opponents of closer relations between Jerusalem and Washington.

Third, the political party of the President does not help in predicting his attitudes towards the Arab–Israeli issue. Thus, the greatest divergence in perspective between the American Jewish community and individual administrations occurred with one Republican (Eisenhower) and one Democrat (Carter). The closest areas of agreement on Arab–Israeli matters also occurred with one Republican (Reagan) and one Democrat (Johnson). Even past ties to the American Jewish community are not predictors of the policies a president will pursue once in the White House. Thus, Ford had closer ties to American Jews than Nixon, but the ideas of the latter proved more compatible with American Jewish views. Carter had more Jewish support than Reagan, but the latter proved more sympathetic to American Jewish perspectives on Israel. In an earlier period, Roosevelt had exceptionally strong ties to American Jews, but they did not translate into gains in foreign policy.

Despite the closeness of the relationship between the United States and Israel, only three men have become president who had previously established a strong record advocating enhanced ties between Washington and Jerusalem: Johnson, Ford and Reagan. Only Ford, who was less interested in foreign policy and who assumed office during a severe domestic crisis, did not follow through on his previously advocated policies.

The key factor affecting an administration's receptivity to American Jewish efforts is the fundamental approach of the key players – especially the President – while they are in office. Thus, Truman and Kennedy were not particularly interested in the issue, which led to the greater involvement of other parties, in the main the bureaucracy. Eisenhower's mind was made up, and priority was placed on improving relations with the Arabs. Johnson had a romantic attachment to Israel but differentiated between emotional sympathy and security calculations. Nixon restricted himself to the latter, but frequently changed his mind in the light of the advice of competing aides (Rogers and Kissinger) and altered circumstances (September 1970, October 1973). Ford genuinely feared growing Arab power and thought the Israelis in an hour of American need owed him and the United States a debt for past support.[16] He believed Jerusalem should have been more forthcoming in negotiations. In genuinely Christian terms, Carter saw himself as a friend (who would solve the problems of Israel and America) ultimately to be praised for his sacrifices. Reagan seems to have had a romantic vision of Israel, a country he has never visited, which was part biblical, part Hollywood-style reincarnation of the Wild West fighters, part anti-communist crusader.

Whatever the attitudes of any president, he and his team set the agenda and American Jews can only react. We can see from the brief historical review that presidents are more receptive to Jewish organizations and leaders when they are interested in their issues and they agree with them. One particularly dramatic example summarizes the point: even though Carter needed Jewish votes and Reagan did not, the Carter White House saw Jewish organizations as an obstacle to implementing foreign policy aims while the Reagan White House and State Department often viewed Jewish organizations favourably because Jewish leaders basically agreed with them on policy towards the Middle East. Johnson had a close relationship with many Jews until Vietnam, but still saw Israel in paternalistic terms. Once he complained to Jewish war veterans that Jews should support what he was doing in Indo-China because the cause of South Vietnam was similar to that of Israel.[17] Truman spent much of his time in the White House before 1948 annoyed with Zionist groups; Eisenhower ignored them; Nixon and Kennedy treated them with respect because of their perceived political clout. Ford assumed Jews would understand why it was important to build new ties with Arabs.

Where is Jewish influence in foreign policy? The United States Jewish community has indeed affected administrations on the margins, at times coaxing presidents into making statements they might not otherwise have made. Often this influence has been more important in affecting the timing rather than the substance of policies. Thus, Zionist lobbying forced Truman to pay more attention to the Palestine issue than he would have preferred, encouraged support for partition, helped save the Negev for Israel, gained White House opposition to the 1948 Bernadotte Plan, and led to an earlier *de facto* recognition of Israel than might have occurred otherwise. Indeed, recognition is remembered as an important example of Jewish influence precisely because it took a gargantuan effort to gain what was in reality a relatively minor victory. Not surprisingly, Truman continued to rely on the State Department rather than external authorities for major elements of his Middle East policy. This approach led to major delays in actions supporting the Zionists and a host of anti-Israel policies including the refusal to accept the UN enforcement of partition, brief support for the trusteeship plan, and the arms embargo in 1948.[18]

The timing of arms deals to the Middle East, and in particular to Israel, has clearly been influenced by Jewish concerns. In 1962, Kennedy approved the first major sale of arms to Israel – Hawk anti-aircraft missiles. In 1968 Johnson announced the sale of fifty Phantom jets. In 1972 Nixon concluded the first long-term aid agreement with Israel. In all three cases, the deals were concluded prior to US elections, congressional in 1962 and presidential in 1968 and 1972. Timing clearly influenced why the deals were consummated when they were. In all cases, however, there were solid national security grounds for reaching agreements: the Hawk and Phantom sales to counter advanced Soviet weapons sold to Egypt, upsetting the balance between it and Israel; the long-term aid agreement because short-term agreements caused constant tension with Israel, which precipitated domestic pressures and confused efforts to move the peace process forward.

Carter was constrained in dealing both with the Russians and the PLO by the pressure of Jewish organizations and Congress and prior agreements, such as Kissinger's 1975 assurance that the USA would not meet with the PLO until it recognized Israel's existence and accepted UN Resolutions 242 and 338, but he was also limited by fears that Begin's Israel would not enter into negotiations if he 'went too far' in pressing for Israeli concessions.[19]

Thus, the Jewish community can try to restrain a president from doing what he wants to do, as it did with limited success under Carter. Sometimes Jewish groups can quicken a policy's pace (e.g., on aid for Israel) or slow it down (e.g., on arms for Arabs). It is not accidental, however, that supporters of Israel appeared particularly powerful in the 1980s. On most issues, they were preaching to the converted.

The Soviet Union

In policy towards Israel, some administrations have seen the American Jewish community as special pleaders; others as allies. In every case, however, the community – at least until recently – has been viewed as united, single-minded and focused on specific issues. The American Jewish community's position on the Soviet Union has always been more complex. In the 1940s, 1950s and 1960s, Jews were known for being represented on the far left in greater numbers than their proportion of the population. Jewish activism has been well-documented among communists, supporters of Henry Wallace in 1948, opponents of Dulles's hardline policies, advocates of nuclear disarmament and opponents of the Vietnam War.

Several factors occurred in the late 1960s to mute traditional Jewish universalism. First, the traumatic experiences surrounding the lead up to the Six Day War convinced many American Jews that Israel should receive stronger support and greater attention. Second, the war coincided with a period of increased ethnic identification in American life. Many American Jews who had participated actively in the civil rights movement in the early 1960s were thereby propelled to become more vocal in advocating Jewish causes. It would not be much of an exaggeration to claim that the indirect effect of a movement led by Martin Luther King made many Jews more active in matters of special concern to the Jewish community.

Third, many Jews were disillusioned when other groups with which they had been aligned – the American left, the Christian ecumenical movement, blacks – did not share their new-found identification with Israel and indeed often expressed sympathy with the Palestinians and opposition to specific Israeli policies. Bitterness at the perceived failure of these groups to co-operate and support issues of concern to Jews, especially in regard to Israel, reinforced the determination of many in the American Jewish community to place greater emphasis on matters defined as Jewish, with less attention devoted to other problems.

Fourth, and probably most important, the Soviet Union emerged in the post-1967 period as a vociferous and ardent opponent of Israel. This opposition was demonstrated by the severing of diplomatic relations with Jerusalem in June 1967, the intensified spreading of anti-Zionist and anti-Semitic propaganda, and the arming of Arab states and Palestinian terrorists. Based on the previous dovish policy attitudes that had once prevailed in the American Jewish community, it could have been expected to support moves towards *détente* with Moscow. Vociferous opposition to Jewish causes by the Kremlin helped drastically weaken the backing many Jews might have provided to improved relations with the Soviet Union.

Thus, the focus for American Jewish activity towards Moscow became how the Soviets handled their own Jews. In the period following the May 1971 summit meeting in Moscow, this concern became a major factor in Soviet–American relations. Senator Henry Jackson, a prominent Democrat from Washington state, mobilized American Jews and forced the Kremlin and the White House to concentrate on the problem through his efforts to link Soviet Jewish emigration to the issue of relations between the United States and the Soviet Union. These positions were codified in late 1974 with the passage of the Jackson–Vanik Amendment, which precluded the extension of most-favoured-nation status for imported Soviet products until Soviet Jewish emigration was allowed on a wider scale. For the first time since the onset of the Cold War, a non-Israeli Jewish issue was tied directly to Soviet–American relations. The concerns of Jewish organizations now focused on central problems in the contacts between the superpowers, providing Jewish leaders with unprecedented involvement in matters at the core of US diplomacy.

On Soviet Jews, Nixon, Ford and Kissinger preferred quiet diplomacy to the public approach advocated by Senator Jackson and the Jewish community. On the other hand, both the Carter and the Reagan administrations were prepared to deal with the issue openly and energetically. To both presidents and to their chief aides, Soviet Jews became a top priority as a cause in their own right. It was also clear that the Soviets would be judged in part by their treatment of their Jewish citizens after the 1975 Helsinki accords placed emphasis on individual rights, including that of emigration. The Jewish community was strongly supportive of Carter's human rights campaign, which tended to emphasize the fate of Soviet Jews, among others. Reagan continued this tradition, differing from Carter only in the role Soviet Jews played. To Reagan, the issue was initially part of his confrontation of the evil empire; to Carter, it was a test of Soviet goodwill in the context of a policy designed to promote better relations between Moscow and Washington. Ironically, both presidents achieved the opposite of their initial intentions: Carter's policies resulted in renewed confrontation, Reagan's in renewed *détente*.

THE JEWISH ROLE *VIS-À-VIS* CONGRESS AND THE POLITICAL PARTIES

We have thus far examined the manner in which various administrations' definition of US interests affects the role of American Jews in the foreign policy process. In the United States, however, Congress also plays a critical role in foreign policy formulation, a role which has increased in the wake of the greater openness ushered in by Vietnam and Watergate. Election campaigns also become arenas in which candidates make commitments and pronouncements, which often come back to haunt them once they have reached Washington. American Jews early found Congress and the political parties avenues available for pressing issues about which they were concerned.

This pattern can be seen as early as the second decade of the twentieth century when the Russian Jewish question and the Jewish quest for a homeland in Palestine received prominent support in Congress but restricted backing in the executive branch. Individuals outside the executive branch who had close political ties to President Wilson, such as Rabbi Stephen S. Wise and Louis Brandeis, contacted him in support of Zionist objectives. The State Department, however, was a bastion of opposition.[20]

Similarly, in the 1920s and 1930s, prominent congressmen supported Zionist aspirations in Palestine, which the State Department opposed. Despite the aversion in Congress to loosening immigration restrictions into the United States, it was easier to gain sympathy for Jewish suffering at the hands of the Nazis among Congressmen than in the State Department. Jewish ability to lobby for Nazi victims and Zionism was still inhibited by a weak, divided and insecure community, the pressures of the war effort, and the State Department's ability to manipulate politicians such as Sol Bloom, the chairman of the House Foreign Affairs Committee. While prominent congressmen lobbied the White House for support of the Zionist enterprise, President Roosevelt was able to deflect these efforts and the State Department buried them in promises to Arab leaders that the United States would do nothing without consulting the Arab states.[21] In the wake of the Holocaust, growing American Jewish sympathy for Zionism led to strong congressional support, the backing of both major party platforms in the 1948 campaign, strong press and public interest, and pressure on a reluctant administration.

As the years passed after Israel's establishment, it became clear that Jews could have considerable impact on issues affecting Israel and which were at least partially in the domain of Congress. Economic – and later military – aid were the prime examples. Jewish organizations were less effective in halting aid to Arabs and even less able to influence policies which were conducted solely within the executive branch, particularly US diplomacy towards the peace process. In the Eisenhower period, the strength of the President's convictions offset Congressional criticism that he was not treating Israel properly, even though several congressmen were particularly active in support of Israel in the wake of the Suez crisis. After 1967 it was easier to focus public attention on the deficiencies of an administration's posture towards Israel because of the expanded media and press coverage of Israel and the Arab states.[22]

The role of American Jews is enhanced when the two parties control different branches of government, as was the case throughout the Nixon presidency. This process was accelerated when one of the Senate's most respected leaders, Henry Jackson, emerged as the chief spokesman for Israel and American Jewish causes in opposition to the administration. Jackson's anti-communist, pro-Israeli positions legitimized Jewish analysts who offered alternative policy perspectives to those espoused by the State Department, whether under William Rogers in the first term or Henry Kissinger in the second. Unlike the Truman and Eisenhower eras, Jackson's efforts suggested it was possible to herald the importance of Israel without being embarrassed that merely domestic political or parochial ethnic concerns were at the centre of one's intentions.

During this period, the 1972 political campaign included prominent Jewish participation in both parties. On the one hand, many liberal Jews were active in the McGovern campaign, which was energized by opposition to the Vietnam War. On the other hand, Nixon made an unprecedented effort to bring Jewish voters and contributors under the Republican wing. The Committee to Reelect the President (CREEP) had a special Jewish unit,[23] and the president's political backers (aided indirectly by Israeli Ambassador Rabin) argued that Nixon was a stronger supporter of Israel than McGovern and, unlike the Democrat, could be trusted to aid Israel in a crisis.

Although Jewish voters still usually supported the Democratic candidate strongly, Jews became more active in Republican politics in ensuing years.[24] It was no longer possible to assume that the Democrats could take the Jewish community for granted and the Republicans could ignore them. Rather, candidates of either party who became strong supporters on issues considered central to Jews (e.g. Israel, Soviet Jews) could anticipate backing, whereas those who were considered major opponents (e.g. Senator Charles Percy, Representative Paul Findley) could expect opposition. The result was that Jews began to have more influence politically, especially in Congress. As the Congressional leadership weakened and power on Capitol Hill became diffused in the 1970s, the influence of groups which were able to lobby the rank-and-file was enhanced. Gradually, the Jewish community became such a force.

Thus, in the Carter era, major criticisms of the President's Mid-East policies were voiced by Congressmen. Yet, despite intense activity by Jewish organizations and lobbyists, the pro-Israeli forces suffered two major defeats in the 1978 arms sale to Saudi Arabia by Carter and the sale of AWACS jets to the Saudis in 1981 by Reagan. The bitterness of this second defeat proved a traumatic development for many involved Jews. The consequence was a significant expansion of the budget and organization of the pro-Israeli lobby (the American–Israeli Public Affairs Committee – AIPAC) which now became a national unit with branches across the country. Taking advantage of the post-Watergate election funding reforms, pro-Israeli political action committees (completely separate from AIPAC) were created around the country. They offered an opportunity for individuals to contribute as a group to particular candidates. As PACs made it easier for incumbents to win congressional elections, the strength of the pro-Israeli community was dramatically strengthened in the 1980s.

By the end of the Reagan era, the pro-Israeli community was in its strongest position ever. Impressive victories had become commonplace on issues such as foreign aid to Israel, arms sales, dealings with the United Nations and the disposition of PLO offices in the United States. While an increased number of Jewish legislators facilitated pro-Israeli activities, the pro-Israeli coalition was bipartisan, crossed ideological lines (including conservatives and liberals), and encompassed prominent representatives from all of the country's geographical regions and many ethnic groups represented in Congress. Even many foreign governments began to assume that the Jewish community was a vehicle by which they could improve relations with the United States.

Although there were no signs of erosion of support for Israel at the end of the 1980s, many Washington observers cited a variety of factors which could lead to an increased criticism of specific Israeli policies: the intifada, tense black–Jewish relations, reports of Israeli collaboration with South Africa, frequent negative media portrayals of Israel, the expansion of settlements on the West Bank. While positive attitudes towards Israel remained among many congressmen, most analysts anticipated that the strictures of the Gramm–Rudman budget deficit-cutting law, the huge American deficit, and competing claims by fledgling democracies in East Europe and Latin America would soon lead to cuts in aid to Israel. Meanwhile, Israel's positive reputation and the strength of pro-Israeli PACs were keeping Jewish efforts intense and influence strong on behalf of Israel. The Persian Gulf War (1991) at least temporarily reversed the decline in Israel's popularity and reversed any talk of decreasing aid to Israel. Yet, the growing preoccupation with budget cutting at the very time Israel's needs were growing because of increased Soviet Jewish immigration represented a clear danger signal for supporters of Israel.

PARTICIPATION IN THE EXECUTIVE BRANCH

By the 1980s American Jews had become more active than ever *vis-à-vis* Congress. A subtle change had also occurred in their involvement in the executive branch. Since the administration of Teddy Roosevelt, Jews had served as informal advisers who helped politically and financially with campaigns. This was the traditional role of the '*shtadlan*', the 'court Jew' who intervenes with 'the palace' on behalf of issues considered critical to the community. At first, these issues were largely domestic, but they became more oriented to foreign policy as Jewish interests shifted to this arena. Many of the names of informal advisers and friends of presidents are legendary: Louis Brandeis, Stephen S. Wise, Felix Frankfurter, Samuel Rosenman, Eddie Jacobson, Bernard Baruch, Abraham Feinberg, Arthur Krim, Abe Fortas, David Ginzburg, Max Fisher, among others.

Under Franklin D. Roosevelt Jews began to play a role as experts and officials who contributed to the formulation of US domestic policy. In foreign policy, however, their progress was much slower. Presidents at times filled a 'Jewish portfolio' in the White House. This individual was usually a domestic policy specialist who also handled the President's 'Israel problem' by representing the Jews to the administration and the administration to the Jews. Thus, David Niles played a critical role in gaining the President's support for partition and early recognition of the Jewish state. Myer Feldman under Kennedy was important in the decision to sell Israel Hawk anti-aircraft missiles.

Under Johnson there were several Jews in key domestic posts who were also favourable towards Israel, because the President had a long and close relationship with many American Jews during his period in Congress.[25] He had been one of the champions of Israel during the 1956 Suez Crisis in

opposition to the Eisenhower administration, and he had carefully cultivated contacts with liberal Jewish Democratic Party activists, especially
many associated with the labour unions. Not surprisingly, this experience
was reflected in several appointments which he made at the White House
– most of which involved individuals engaged in domestic policy.

Nixon also had several Jewish aides, e.g. Leonard Garment and William
Safire, as did Carter in Stuart Eizenstat who was the chief domestic policy
adviser, Philip Klutznick, his second Secretary of Commerce, and Neil
Goldsmith, the second Secretary of Transportation. The pattern of prominent Jewish officials serving in the domestic sphere began to weaken with
the Carter administration, although no Jews had served on the Supreme
Court since Abe Fortas resigned in 1969. There had been at least one Jew
serving on the Court for the previous fifty years.

In foreign policy, by contrast, another pattern was slowly developing
from the Johnson period onward. The State Department had once been an
'aristocratic club', but as most institutions in American society gradually
broadened, the State Department and the rest of the national security
bureaucracy began to be affected as well. Ben Cohen, who was best known
for his work as a Roosevelt 'brain truster' on domestic policy in the 1930s,
served for a time as the Counsellor of the State Department in 1947 and
1948, but he had little influence over actual foreign policy decisions. Once
Jews began to be members of the foreign policy bureaucracy on a regular
basis, however, it was only a matter of time until they would also deal with
the Middle East.

Thus, Johnson appointed three Jews to prominent foreign policy posts:
Arthur Goldberg was ambassador to the United Nations and two brothers
also served – Walt Rostow was the National Security Advisor, and Eugene
Rostow was the Under Secretary of State for Political Affairs. Eugene Rostow
and Arthur Goldberg were well-known active supporters of Israel, and all
three had influence over parts of Mid-East policy.

Unlike Johnson, Richard Nixon did not have close ties to the Jewish
community, but he appointed a Jew, Henry Kissinger, to be his National
Security Advisor and closest foreign policy aide. Kissinger, the product of an
observant home and a refugee from Germany, had never closely associated
himself with the American Jewish community. His rise to power was in spite
of, not because of, his Jewishness, and he was clearly insecure among a
Nixon inner circle not known for its close ties to Kissinger's 'co-religionists'
as he often called them. In contrast with Walt and Eugene Rostow or
Goldberg, Kissinger was at first explicitly excluded from dealing with the
Middle East. Since he was responsible for nearly all other major issues
– Soviet policy, arms control, China, Vietnam – this decision seemed to
make sense. Secretary of State Rogers had to be given responsibility for
something and the Assistant Secretary of State for Near East policy, Joseph
Sisco, was regarded as especially able. However, at the time, Kissinger's

Jewishness was generally regarded as a further reason why he was not explicitly engaged in the issue.[26]

Yet, despite the hostile atmosphere which surrounded Nixon, Kissinger survived and ultimately took charge of Mid-East policy *en route* to becoming secretary of state. He therefore became a vehicle for increased participation of individual Jews in the foreign policy process by inadvertence rather than by design. Certainly Kissinger's role as the most important foreign policy official in the administration dramatically demonstrated that Jews could contribute to the implementation of America's global agenda and even to Arab–Israeli matters. Although Kissinger may have distanced himself from the Jewish community, it was never again possible to argue that 'being Jewish' necessarily ruled someone out of the foreign policy process or that Jews could not pursue American national interests towards the Middle East in a balanced manner.

As we have seen, by the mid-1970s the Jewish community's preoccupation with foreign policy issues was growing and Jewish attention to both the Middle East and Soviet–American relations was intense. Two of the most prominent journals contributing to the United States foreign policy debate, *Commentary* and *The New Republic*, were accurately identified as dominated by Jews. Some of the most articulate critics of the Nixon/Ford administrations' foreign policy in the Senate, such as Henry Jackson, Walter Mondale, Hubert Humphrey and Edward Kennedy, were closely identified with the Jewish community. In the 1976 presidential campaign both liberal and conservative candidates criticized the administration as insufficiently supportive of Israel.

The growing Jewish activity and support for Israel, represented by the fact that American Jewish organizations were becoming more involved on a daily basis with foreign policy issues, came at a time of growing uneasiness in the American foreign policy elite about the situation in the Middle East. Through the use of the oil weapon and wealth generated thereby, the Arab states were simultaneously attaining powerful instruments of leverage over the United States. The pressures of increased energy dependence on Arab oil producers and the sluggish pace of the peace process intensified criticism of Israel during the late 1970s. In the press and other media, talk was rampant of an 'erosion' of support for Jerusalem. Many anticipated the public at large would blame Israel for America's energy and economic problems, resulting in a possible growth of anti-Semitism.[27]

Since he was a Democrat, the election of Jimmy Carter to the presidency in 1976 may have led to expectations of stronger support for Israel and greater Jewish involvement in the foreign policy process, but the Jewish relationship with the Democratic Party is complex. Many American Jews frequently have had difficulties with Democrats in dealing with foreign policy issues because Democratic presidents have also had control of Congress and have therefore been freer to act against Israel; because after

Vietnam, parts of the left wing of the party became critical of Israel; and because Jews have higher expectations of Democrats than of Republicans. Since American Jews tend to be strongly aligned with Democrats on domestic policy issues, they expect a comparably strong level of agreement in the foreign policy sphere, which does not always occur.

The seminal events of 1976–7 epitomized this split. Deep divisions had emerged in the American intellectual and political elite about the meaning of the Yom Kippur War and the energy crisis and what the United States should do about it. The Jewish community had vociferously entered the fray. If Henry Jackson or Hubert Humphrey had won the Democratic nomination in the primaries, the views being expressed in such journals as *Commentary* and *The New Republic* might well have emerged as highly influential. Instead, Carter turned to a different group of advisers, who were chastened by the Vietnam experience and thus determined to seek better relations with the Third World. They perceived international economic issues as of greater import than the competition with the Soviet Union, and were impressed by the new-found power of the Arabs. The Carter team thus tended to be critical of Israel. There were no Jews among this group, with the single exception of Secretary of Defense Harold Brown, who was neither close to the Jewish community nor a major player in the administration's Mid-East policy. There were no Jews in the American delegation to Camp David. The classic pattern harking back to the days of Roosevelt and Truman had been reasserted – Jewish participation in domestic, not foreign policy.

Carter only began to appoint Jews when tensions with Israel and her supporters mounted to a crisis point, especially after political aide Mark Siegel resigned over the President's decision to sell advanced F-15 fighter jets to Saudi Arabia. In mid-1978, Edward Sanders, a Los Angeles attorney, was appointed to the 'Jewish portfolio' post in the White House, with added responsibilities in the State Department. After the signing of the Egyptian–Israeli peace treaty, two Jews were chosen as special negotiators for the Middle East as Carter tried to limit the amount of time he would have to spend on the issue. First, he appointed Robert Strauss, who had been trade negotiator and was noted for his skills in political manipulation. When Strauss became chairman of his re-election campaign late in 1979, Carter appointed Sol Linowitz, who had distinguished himself for his diplomatic activity towards Latin America and especially in his efforts to negotiate the Panama Canal Treaty. These appointments suggested a new wrinkle in the American approach to the Arab–Israeli scene. If a president wished to take controversial actions, it might be an asset to have a prominent Jew as the chief negotiator, thereby eliminating one possible basis for criticism from Jewish organizations. Nixon's concern about placing Kissinger in such a role had been completely reversed. Now being Jewish was considered a benefit, not a drawback.

184

However, this role of Jews in the executive branch was still limited to the highest and lowest of bureaucratic levels. Jews had begun to serve in the foreign service in greater numbers. By the late 1970s it was considered acceptable for individual Jews to serve in Mid-East posts as barriers began to break down in the wake of improved Egyptian–Israeli relations. Jews could now be sent to some parts of the Arab world, particularly to Egypt and North Africa, although by 1990 Jews still were not stationed in such countries as Saudi Arabia and Syria.

Until the Reagan administration, Jews were still not prominent in the national security bureaucracy and were generally absent from high-level policy-making posts dealing with Middle East related issues. Beginning in the 1980s Jewish bureaucrats for the first time were elevated to positions of influence in the foreign policy process, including posts dealing with both Soviet and Middle East policy. There are several reasons for this change. First, the increased role of individual Jews in policy formulation was in large measure due to the fact that the Reagan coalition included a strong pro-Israeli grouping, many of whom were former Democrats from the Jackson wing who had been ignored or shunted aside during the Carter period. Second, it was not surprising that as more American Jews entered positions in universities and think-tanks which dealt with national security issues, they would also be tapped for government posts. Third, because Jews were active in the neo-conservative movement which emerged victorious in the 1980s, many were logical candidates for positions of authority. Fourth, the success of Kissinger, Strauss and Linowitz at the highest levels of the Middle East peace process legitimized American Jewish involvement at lower levels. The general fear of assigning Jews to these tasks turned out to be unfounded. Finally, once Israel was accepted in the 1980s as a strategic asset for the United States, it was easier for American Jews to work in this area.

We have now reached the 1990s. In the Bush administration, the pattern of Jewish involvement changed totally from the Roosevelt and Truman eras. The process which began with Reagan solidified, and there were no Jewish cabinet members and no one occupied the Jewish portfolio in the White House, although Max Fisher assumed his old post of informal Jewish intermediary. There were also no Jews prominent in major domestic policy posts. Instead, individual Jews were present in the administration's second tier of national security officials, especially those dealing with the Middle East. Many officials who had served in the Reagan administration either retained their positions or moved to higher posts.

Dean Acheson and John Foster Dulles would be astonished to discover the new constellation of forces operating within the bureaucracy in Washington. It is exactly the opposite of what they experienced: Jews are involved in foreign, not domestic, policy. The Jewish passion for domestic policy of the 1920s and 1930s, which once translated into positions in the

US government, has been replaced by a passion for foreign policy in the 1970s and 1980s, now also translated into bureaucratic posts.

Yet what should be clear is that while individual Jews have become progressively involved in the foreign policy apparatus, and at higher levels, it has not necessarily been to the benefit of Israel. The pro-Israel stance of the Reagan administration was due to its global strategy of confronting the Soviets, the fact that the peace treaty between Israel and Egypt decreased Arab pressure on the USA, and the diminished influence of the Arab states in the wake of the fall in oil prices and the Iran–Iraq war. Rather than individual Jews influencing policy in a pro-Israel direction, the pre-existing policy facilitated the increased involvement of individual Jews. Acheson and Dulles would be truly astonished by the frequently strained relations between the USA and Israel during the early part of the Bush years, notwith-standing the prominence of individual Jews in the bureaucracy. Many of these individuals have even been criticized by elements of the Jewish community for the critical stance the Bush administration has taken towards Israel.[28]

The Bush administration

The Bush administration entered office after a period of high profile activity by Jewish organizations towards both the Arab–Israeli dispute and the Soviet–American relationship. Indeed, many Jews feared the close relation-ships established during the previous eight years would not be continued. The Bush administration was widely expected to be less sympathetic towards Israel. Reagan and Shultz would be a tough act to follow, and the cautious bureaucratic approach of the new administration implied decreased attention to and a lower profile on the Middle East in comparison with other issues, and a more cerebral approach to foreign affairs generally. Gone was the emotion and romanticism expressed towards Israel by former leaders. None of the highest ranking officials in the administration were noted for their closeness to the Jewish community nor were they regarded as having particular sympathy or antagonism towards Israel. Instead, these were Washington veterans who gained their key experiences in the Ford and Reagan administrations. The only exceptions were two peripheral figures on this issue – Vice-President Dan Quayle was a strong supporter of Israel and Chief of Staff John Sununu was known as a strong backer of the Arabs.

The prime orientation of the new team was for successful deal-making. The end of the Iran–Iraq War, the continuation of the intifada, and the US dialogue with the PLO all encouraged renewed attention to the Arab–Israeli peace process. Meanwhile, dramatic developments in the communist world (including the improvement in the conditions for Jews in the USSR, increased emigration and improved ties between Moscow and Jerusalem) helped to dilute the focus of American Jewish energies *vis-à-vis* Washington on global foreign policy concerns. In contrast with the 1970s, the major foreign policy problems confronting the administration (e.g., Europe, the environment, economics, trade, deficits, debt, Central America, China, etc.) were not those which centrally concerned Jews as Jews.

For reasons of lessened involvement and attachment and competing interests, the receptivity to Jewish concerns had dropped, although the Bush administration was unique in its ability to avoid major tensions with Israel in its first year. Serious tensions had even occurred under Reagan in 1981. The experience of the Bush team helped it to avoid an early confrontation with Jerusalem, but other factors were at work as well. Attention to the region was declining because of the decreased importance by comparison to other world problems. The unusual complexity of the Palestinian question muted Washington's optimism concerning a quick solution, often a factor in American–Israeli tensions in the past. The special importance the new administration accorded to confidence-building measures between Arabs and Israelis accentuated long-term efforts.

Yet, the administration's initial temptation to devote itself to a relatively gradual effort towards Israeli–Palestinian negotiation was soon aborted. By late 1989, it was clear that pressing forward with Prime Minister Shamir's plan for Palestinian elections on the West Bank and a transition period of autonomy would require increased involvement by the United States or any progress towards a settlement would be stifled. Egypt and officials of the Israeli Labor Party – then members of an Israeli National Unity government – were also pressing for intensified US engagement. The administration began to use interpretations of Shamir's basic proposal, adapted and expanded in Egypt's 'Ten Points' and Baker's 'Five Points' to convene a meeting in Cairo between Israelis, Egyptians, Americans and a mutually approved Palestinian delegation in early 1990. The idea collapsed when Shamir balked at the idea of including in the Palestinian delegation residents of East Jerusalem, lest Israel appear to be relinquishing its claim to all of Jerusalem. Disputes also occurred over whether the Palestinian delegation could include members identified as affiliated with the PLO, lest Israel appear to be accepting the legitimacy of that organization.[29]

In frustration at these steps and Shamir's earlier comments about the need for a 'big' Israel, the President sealed Shamir's opposition when he criticized Israel for settling any Soviet Jewish immigrants in the West Bank and East Jerusalem. He thereby seemed to be questioning Israel's right to control all of Jerusalem.[30] The prospect of talks soon collapsed, as did the national unity government. A lengthy Israel political crisis ensued, putting the peace process on hold.

In the spring of 1990 two events created a new environment guaranteed to make movement towards peace more difficult. In May, the PLO refused to condemn a large terrorist attack against Israel, forcing the USA to break off the dialogue in June. Also in June, the most right-wing Israeli government in the country's history was formed. In frustration, Secretary of State Baker suggested before a congressional sub-committee that if Shamir wanted to resume discussions about his plan he could phone the White House. He proceeded in a rather insulting manner to give the phone number. While American Jewish organizations protested vehemently about the administration's apparent backslide on Jerusalem and increased tensions with Israel, they could only watch with growing apprehension the advent of a nationalist Israeli government whose stated policies seemed destined to precipitate a major confrontation.

Then Saddam Hussein invaded Kuwait, an earthquake that altered the fundamental conditions facing all parties. On the one hand, the Bush administration made special efforts in the period between the 2 August invasion of Kuwait and the 15 January deadline for Iraqi withdrawal to keep Israel at arm's length lest the anti-Saddam Arab coalition it was forging be negatively affected. When, in October 1990, a violent incident at the Temple Mount in Jerusalem killed twenty Palestinians, the administration seemed to go out of its way to join the criticism and even led the effort at the UN Security Council to condemn Israeli actions. On the other hand, as the domestic American debate over how to handle Hussein's occupation of Kuwait increased, both American Jews and Israel emerged as important supporters of the President's determination to reverse Iraq's aggression. While many Jews worried anew about Israel's survival in the wake of Saddam Hussein's threats, some were also concerned that Israel could some-how be blamed if the results of the Persian Gulf crisis were not completely successful.

Such fears proved to be unfounded once the American-led forces won a quick victory, in which Iraq's unconventional weaponry and long-range missiles, the major identifiable threats to Israel's security, were largely destroyed. Israel's restraint in the wake of repeated Scud missile attacks on its territory also reversed the trend of declining support in the United States for the Jewish state. Public opinion polls demonstrated unprecedented support for Israel, even higher than at the time of the Six Day War, while Palestinians, and especially the PLO, were derided for their support of Saddam Hussein. The Jewish community, unified in its concern over the threat to Israel's security and mobilized in support of the increasing influx of Soviet Jews, had apparently improved its links with a victorious adminis-tration whose own relations with Israel had markedly improved. Yet, these developments only demonstrated more dramatically than ever that while American Jews are not passive actors, they remain peripheral players on America's foreign policy stage.

Looking towards the late 1990s, it is possible to predict that the concerns of American policy-makers on the one hand and Jewish organizations and leaders on the other are moving in different directions. The era which began with the Six Day War, when issues concerning Jews were of growing interest to the President and his entourage, is ending. Jewish leaders may find that it will become more difficult to meet with presidents and secretaries of state as often as in the past, or to develop as close relations. The pressure of events will most likely lead presidents to focus attention on different problems. The receptivity of American administrations to Jewish concerns is likely to decline in the late 1990s, if for no other reason than that the salience of the Arab–Israeli dispute will diminish by comparison with domestic issues, concern about America's economic decline, and the 'new world order'.

THE CHANGING FOCUS OF AMERICAN JEWRY

Jews have achieved their comparatively prominent role in foreign policy formulation in the United States in both the executive and legislative branches by following paths previously pursued by other groups. They have written articles in journals and magazines. They have lobbied, contributed to candidates and PACs, established close ties with individual politicians and been active in Washington think-tanks.

Yet just as many American Jews had begun to fulfil long-cherished dreams about foreign policy participation, they were beginning to move on to new interests. The Jewish leaders who rushed to Jerusalem in December 1988 went to urge Israel's parties not to form a coalition committed to passing the 'Who is a Jew?' legislation.[31] They were expressing a new-found willingness to attempt to change policy in Jerusalem as well as in Washington.

The result was that two approaches to Israel emerged in the late 1980s among American Jews – one Jerusalem-oriented, the other Washington-oriented. Both were equally involved with Israel, but their agendas and tactics differed markedly. The Washington-oriented approach was pursued by the right, the Orthodox and mainstream traditionalists who were still concentrating on the familiar issues of aid to Israel, strategic cooperation, arms sales to Arabs, terrorism, basic support for Jerusalem and improving Israel's image. The Jerusalem-oriented approach was adopted by the left, the younger generation and even some centrists. They were increasingly focused on the Palestinian question and the peace process as well as such specific issues as Israeli policy towards South Africa, electoral reform, human rights and civil liberties inside Israel. Generally more willing to be critical of Israeli policies, the proponents of a Jerusalem-oriented focus believe that Israel has failed to seize the diplomatic initiative. They argue that the Shamir government has been insufficiently prepared to compromise, even with moderate Arabs.

This process of intensified debate within the American Jewish community was accelerated by the export of the Likud–Labor competition to the American Jewish community and by the growing questions about the policies of Israel raised by the Lebanon War in 1982, the Pollard affair, settlement policy on the West Bank, and especially the intifada. The constant efforts by Likud and Labor officials and representatives visiting the United States to deride the views of their opponents inside Israel and to raise funds for their own party had a gradual, insidious impact on respect for Israeli leaders among the American Jewish elite. Jewish energy was in the process of being transformed from an exclusive effort to influence American and Soviet policy as had been the case in the 1970s and 1980s to an attempt to influence both the United States and Israel. Increasingly on the left side of the Jewish community, there was a greater preoccupation with changing Israeli policy than with changing American or Soviet policy towards the region.

Thus the American Jewish role in the US foreign policy process has become progressively complicated. Greater opportunities are now available to individuals who are Jewish to participate in the policy process and American Jewish organizations have become more sophisticated in monitoring the policy-making scene. On the other hand, the divisions within the Jewish community have grown and the objectives of individual American Jews and organizations have become more varied, more complex and more divided. The consequence of these increased divisions may result in a diminished influence in future policy disputes within the United States. However, if an administration were again, as in the Carter case, to express views strongly critical of Israel, the American Jewish community would likely rally. The extent of the rally, however, would largely depend on whether the Israeli government were seen to be unreasonable or intransigent. Except in extreme cases where Israel's vital security appears to be at stake, as was the case with the Scud attacks, Jerusalem is not likely to receive universal and uncritical support for all of its diplomatic actions as was frequently the case in the past.

The absorption process of Soviet Jewry is an example *par excellence* of the new era. While the influx was first greeted by American Jews as the latest Israeli miracle requiring major contributions, generated by 'Operation Exodus', when the Shamir government began to experience difficulties in providing the new immigrants with housing and employment many in the American Jewish community began to question the perspicacity of its economic policies. Nor was criticism limited to the Likud: Labor institutions, including the Histadrut, also came in for their share. Some American Jews believed the answer to Israel's problems lay in increased American public and private assistance and the end of the Arab boycott; others argued that Israel should revamp its economic system quickly. As with the 'Who is a Jew?' and other issues, American Jews have become increasingly vocal in advocating policy changes in Israel.

If American Jewry is indeed entering a new period where it focuses on internal developments inside Israel and the possibility of increased disagreement with the policies pursued by Jerusalem, it will have been reached as a result of a dialectical process. Concerns about US domestic policy, US foreign policy, and Israel's internal and external policies will coexist uneasily.

190

More American Jews are likely to find themselves weighing trade-offs uncomfortably in their voting and philanthropic decisions and in their decisions over how to become involved with Israel-related activities. Of one conclusion, we can be certain. The simple post Second-World War period is over, when all Israelis were seen as heroes and all Soviet Jews as oppressed, when memories of the Holocaust united American Jews in a determined consensus to avoid future tragedy, and when most American Jewish leaders thought they knew precisely what Washington should do.

Adjustment to the new complexities will not come easily. For all their added experience and involvement in the United States foreign policy process, Jewish organizations remain unprepared to adapt to changing global and domestic conditions. Few Jewish professionals or lay people have formal training in foreign policy formulation or diplomacy. The social science literature is replete with material on discerning analogies, historical lessons, case studies. Few Jewish activists even know these tools exist. Instead, lawyers, businessmen and social workers who compose the majority of lay people and professionals in the Jewish community are taught by their experience and training to believe that the successes of the 1980s are applicable to the future. Such a conclusion may be premature. As in the case of the Jewish role in domestic policy and participation in the United States Supreme Court, recent achievements based on such mechanisms as PACs, financial contributions, and 'key contacts' with major politicians may be fleeting or cyclical.

Is a pattern now emerging in which Jews are active in the Democratic Party in domestic policy and in the Republican Party in foreign policy? It is difficult to answer this question because Republicans until very recently have been in control of the White House during all but five years since 1967. Certainly, individual Jews who are particularly interested in foreign policy, especially as it relates to Israel, gravitated in the late 1970s and 1980s towards the Republican Party. Jews were especially active in the anti-war movement of the Vietnam years, particularly in the Democratic Party, but they were not able, as the neo-conservatives were, to translate that activity into a coherent global policy perspective which included Israel.

The coming to power of the Democratic Party in the United States and of Labor in Israel, along with the current breakthrough in negotiations on the Palestinian question, have undoubtedly transformed all these perspectives in ways that lie beyond the scope of the present essay. However, unlike the Republican Party during the late 1970s, it is worth noting that the Democrats have not developed a dominant and comprehensive foreign affairs philosophy which includes a central place for Israel. Despite the changing world scene, President Clinton has focused his attention overwhelmingly on America's domestic problems. It remains to be seen whether the Democrats can generate a compelling and convincing vision, global in scope, and capable of pushing the Middle East peace process to a successful conclusion.

A rarely noted key ingredient in Jewish success in the foreign policy process has been the contribution of particular ideas to the debate which could be adopted by conservatives and liberals for their own purposes. In the 1950s and 1960s the idea of Israel as a vibrant democracy appealed to some liberals seeking a moral basis for United States foreign policy and to some conservatives looking for countries 'on our side' of the free world. In the 1970s, the focus on Soviet Jews appealed to both liberal human rights advocates and conservative anti-communists producing a powerful coalition in favour of pressure on the USSR. In the 1980s, the concept of Israel as a strategic asset appealed to conservatives anxious to counter Soviet moves in the Middle East, to a bipartisan consensus concerned about terrorism and the growth of Islamic fundamentalism and to liberals seeking to adapt Israeli methods to achieve savings in the United States defence budget. A major task facing the Jewish community at the start of the 1990s is to contribute fresh ideas, with general appeal, that address the changing world-order, and the place of America and Israel therein. In the absence of such a contribution, issues of concern to American Jews are likely to suffer even if Jewish political strength remains intact. The competition for American attention and engagement elsewhere will be too great to overcome without new and appealing foreign policy ideas.

Given changing world conditions, the prognosis of continued American Jewish foreign policy success must be very guarded. While the gains of American Jews in the United States foreign policy process have been real, they are unstable and continued achievement is by no means guaranteed. Many Jews are not so sure what Washington should be doing towards Israel. Many are beginning to conclude that they should begin to pay more atten-tion to decision-making in Jerusalem. This struggle is itself news. The ways in which this new uncertainty among American Jews, and the new divisions between them, is played out will determine the manner in which American Jewry influences US foreign policy in the post-Cold War, post-Persian Gulf War period.

NOTES

1 Arthur Abramson, *The Formulation of American Foreign Policy towards the Middle East during the Truman Administration, 1945–1948*, ch. 1, pp. 101–4.
2 Director of the Office of Near Eastern and African Affairs Loy Henderson to Secretary of State George Marshall, 22 September 1947, *Foreign Relations of the United States, 1947*. Vol. V: *The Near East and Africa* (Washington, DC, Government Printing Office, 1971) pp. 1153ff.
3 Judah Nadich, *Eisenhower and the Jews* (New York, Twayne Publications, 1953) p. 18.
4 Robert J. Donovan, *Eisenhower: The Inside Story* (New York, Harper & Row, 1956), p. 67; Robert H. Ferrell (ed.), *The Eisenhower Diaries* (New York, W. W. Norton, 1981), pp. 220–1; Dwight D. Eisenhower, *Waging Peace* (Garden City, NY, Doubleday, 1965), pp. 74 and 99.

5 Chester Bowles, 'A look at the Middle East today', *Department of State Bulletin* (Washington, DC, 7 May 1962), pp. 765–6.
6 *Personal Papers of the President*, 27 January 1969, p. 18.
7 Henry A. Kissinger, *The White House Years* (Boston, Little, Brown & Co., 1979), pp. 178, 453–4, 763, 1103; Richard Nixon, *RN: The Memoirs of Richard Nixon* (New York, Grosset & Dunlop, 1978), p. 345.
8 See Richard Nixon, *Memoirs*, p. 483.
9 Nixon, op. cit., p. 786.
10 On American concerns about the Middle East at the time, see Henry Kissinger, *Department of State Bulletin (DSB)* (Washington, DC), 29 October 1973, p. 535; 10 December 1973, p. 701; 21 July 1975, p. 90; 6 October 1975, pp. 473–500; 27 October 1975, p. 609 ; also, Richard Nixon, *DSB*, 7 July 1974, p. 3; and Joseph Sisco, *DSB*, 8 July 1974, p. 56.
11 Zbigniew Brzezinski, 'Recognizing the crisis', *Foreign Policy*, Winter 1974–5, p. 67.
12 Speech by President Carter in Tehran, 31 December 1977, *Public Papers of the Presidents of the United States: Jimmy Carter, 1977 (Book II)* (Washington, DC, Government Printing Office, 1978), p. 2221.
13 Ronald Reagan, *Public Papers of the President* (Washington, DC, US Government Printing Office, 8 March 1983), p. 369. President Reagan was addressing the National Association of Evangelicals in Orlando, Florida.
14 William B. Quandt, *Decade of Decisions* (Berkeley, University of California Press, 1977), p. 127; Kissinger, op. cit., pp. 618 and 631.
15 George W. Ball, 'How to save Israel in spite of herself', *Foreign Affairs*, April 1977. See also Stanley Hoffman, 'A new policy for Israel', *Foreign Affairs*, April 1975.
16 Gerald R. Ford, *A Time to Heal* (New York, Harper & Row, 1979), p. 457.
17 Harry McPherson, Lyndon Baines Johnson Library, Oral History Interviews (Austin, Tex., 16 January 1969), tape 4, pp. 36–7; author's personal interviews with Harry McPherson and Herman Edelsberg.
18 *Foreign Relations of the United States Diplomatic Papers*, (Washington, DC, US Governmental Printing Office, 1948), p. 1007; Robert J. Donovan, *Conflict and Crisis, the Presidency of Harry S. Truman, 1945–1948* (New York, W. W. Norton, 1977), p. 386; John Snetsinger, *Truman, the Jewish Vote and the Creation of Israel* (Stanford, Calif., Hoover Institute Press, 1974), p. 132.
19 Zbigniew Brzezinski, *Power and Principle* (New York, Farrar, Straus, Giroux, 1983), pp. 53–4.
20 See Peter Grose, *Israel in the Mind of America* (New York, Knopf, 1983).
21 See David Wyman, *The Abandonment of the Jews: America and the Holocaust, 1941–45* (New York, Pantheon, 1984).
22 Steven L. Spiegel, *The Other Arab–Israeli Conflict: The Making of America's Middle East Policy, from Truman to Reagan* (Chicago, University of Chicago Press, 1985), p. 120.
23 Stephen Isaacs, *Jews and American Politics* (New York, Doubleday, 1974), p. 152.
24 *New York Times*, 5 November 1981, p. 1.
25 Author's interview with Ephraim Evron and Harry McPherson.
26 On the reasons Kissinger was initially excluded from Middle East policy, see Nixon, op. cit., p. 477; and Henry Kissinger, *White House Years* (Boston, Little, Brown, 1979), pp. 348, 559.
27 See *Washington Post*, 22 December 1973, p. 1.
28 For example, see Eric Rozenman, 'Jewish Arabists at the State Department', *Moment*, April 1991.

29 *New York Times*, 4 March 1990, p. 3.
30 *New York Times*, 9 March 1990, p. 8.
31 *New York Times*, 3 December 1988, p. 6.

9

SOVIET JEWRY – A COMMUNITY IN TURMOIL

Mordechai Altschuler

Mikhail Gorbachev's rise to power in 1985 marked the beginning of the final chapter in the history of the USSR. Though the process by which a new political, economic and social order is being shaped out of the ruins of that country is still continuing, all agree that the USSR, with its governmental and socio-political structure, is a thing of the past. The dismantling of the USSR at the end of 1991 can, therefore, be regarded as representing the end of Soviet Jewry.

Three major themes will be the focus of this essay: the changes which the Jewish community underwent during the final years of the Soviet Union; the relationship between Soviet Jews and non-Jewish society; and, finally, the issue of emigration. Whereas for the first theme we will follow a chronological exposition, for the other two a typological analysis will be attempted with special emphasis on regional differences.

CHANGES IN THE JEWISH COMMUNITY

On the eve of Gorbachev's ascendancy to power

During the period immediately preceding Gorbachev's rise to power, Jewish emigration was at its lowest level for the past fifteen years.[1] Even the number who considered emigrating was almost negligible.[2] Compared to the preceding decade, Soviet officials adopted a most lenient attitude towards prospective emigrants, i.e. those who had received an invitation from relatives in Israel, and even to persons who applied for exit permits. They were generally not fired from their places of employment, nor were they castigated in public or made into social outcasts. At worst they were given to understand that their 'mistake' would be forgiven and that the way was open for their return to the fold and to their former standing. Indeed, the majority of those Jews who in the 1970s had seriously thought of emigrating no longer considered that option to be relevant and once more sought to become a part of Soviet society. Thus, emigration seemed to be more of a hypothetical question, though it was not completely ruled out as an option for the distant future. Two factors, however, kept emigration alive as a distant option, even if it was not immediately relevant: (a) many Soviet Jews had relatives, friends and acquaintances among the 260,000 who had already emigrated (mainly in the 1970s)[3] – this was a kind of Soviet Jewish Diaspora with whom Jews in the USSR constantly corresponded; (b) the Soviet media's continuous condemnation of Jewish emigrants[4] indirectly contributed to keeping many Jews, who might otherwise not have given emigration a thought, aware of that possibility.

Anti-Israeli propaganda – which adopted a definitely anti-Semitic character – equating Zionism with Nazism, and embracing allegations that the Jews had supported Hitler's rise to power, had also increased in the early 1980s.[5] Most Jews, however, learned to live with such propaganda, especially since wide circles within the intelligentsia (the social group with which most Soviet Jews came into contact) became increasingly sceptical of anything printed in the Soviet press. Despite the anti-Jewish propaganda, there was a certain 'moderation' in the practice of restricting the access of Jews to the universities. There was a slight increase in the percentage of Jews among Soviet students in the 20–29 age group and in the number of Jews who graduated with a Master's degree.[6] The 'silent majority' of Soviet Jews, it seems, were fully absorbed in the daily problems of earning a living, becoming eligible for an apartment, or enrolling their children in universities. This shift in orientation was admitted by a Moscow Jewish activist in the emigration movement in March 1985:

> Over the past few years . . . even among the 'refuseniks' themselves we have discerned . . . certain people who have reconsidered their original intent to emigrate to Israel, finding it to be an unachievable objective, and are now setting out on that most painful path of reintegration into Soviet society.[7]

Simultaneously with some slackening of the pressure on Soviet Jews, the policy of the authorities towards the activist hard core was to combine repression[8] with the grant of exit permits to a small number of them. Twenty Jewish activists were in jail in July 1985;[9] since the beginning of 1984 ten of them had been tried in court and two more were awaiting trial.[10] The minority of those tried had been charged with spreading malicious lies against the government and anti-Soviet propaganda,[11] while the majority were convicted on various criminal charges.[12] Apparently, the Soviet security police preferred to play down the political implications of the trials and present them as criminal cases in order to discourage the Jewish population from identifying with the activists.

Only a miniscule minority spoke for Soviet Jews at this time, and it too had split into two mutually antagonistic groups, neither of which enjoyed any real support among the Jewish population of the USSR.[13] The first of the two might be described as activists who had generally applied for and been refused exit permits. They either could not or would not try to re-integrate into Soviet society, which had expelled, demeaned and condemned them. They had crossed the Rubicon, were cut off from their former environment and for many years had been subject to persecution. Though they carried the brunt of the stubborn, drawn-out and unceasing struggle for the right to leave the Soviet Union, they did not greatly influence the outlook of those who actually emigrated.[14] The vast majority of these activists, whether by choice or by circumstance, lived in a world apart from other Jews who did not accept their spiritual and cultural values. One of the Moscow activists admitted in March 1985 that 'for the past five years . . . the efforts of our movement have been primarily expended in educational and cultural endeavours.'[15]

This group of activists, generally speaking, was divided into three sub-groups, the lines dividing them not always being clearly discernible.

(a) Members of the first sub-group were religious activists, mostly former secular Jews who had become disenchanted with Communist ideology and had turned to religion. This sub-group gained influence primarily during the 1980s, when the number of emigration permits greatly diminished, most of the Zionist activists had left the country and the likelihood of having to remain in the USSR while being completely cut off from Soviet society, seemed to be its only prospect. The majority of this group was not Zionist in outlook; its main objective was to enable its members to lead a religious life, conduct religious study, ensure the supply of kosher meat, ritual baths, etc.[16]

(b) The second sub-group, which also included some secular Jews who had turned religious, concerned itself primarily with the provision of a cultural atmosphere: learning Hebrew, educating the children of the 'activists' and preserving some semblance of intellectual life.

(c) Those who belonged to the third sub-group considered the *political* struggle (disseminating information abroad, appealing to world opinion, demonstrations, hunger strikes, etc.) to be their major concern. This was by now the smallest sub-group, since some had already been granted exit permits, others were in jail or detention camps and many had grown tired of the struggle over the years and were no longer very active.[17]

The major source of support for those whom we termed activists did not come from Soviet Jews (on whose behalf they claimed to speak), but rather from world Jewry, especially the American Jewish community, which largely supplied the funds for their daily needs. The strategy adopted by American Jews on behalf of Soviet Jewry had undergone some transformation in the 1980s. Over the years, the groups within the American Jewish community that were actively supporting Soviet Jews had become institutionalized, professional organizations[18] which sought the most efficient tactics to keep the plight of Soviet Jewry in the public mind. One of these was 'personification' of the struggle by bringing to public attention the sufferings of specific individuals. Thus, by the mid-1980s, the slogan 'Let my people go!' had given place to lists of those imprisoned for their Zionism or for being 'refuseniks', the major objective being to force the Soviet authorities to grant these Jews exit permits. American Jewish organizations now concentrated on transferring lists containing tens, or even hundreds, of names of 'refuseniks' and their families to the American government for individual attention.

However, it was precisely then that relations between the USA and the USSR had become tense once more; consequently, not much effective American influence could be brought to bear on the Soviets. Since the American groups were aware of the situation, their major effort was to keep the issue on the public agenda and raise it once more at a more propitious time. However, the fact that the refuseniks themselves showed no inclination for dramatic action that could gain public attention did not add to the success of Jewish activity on their behalf in the USA. It is not surprising, therefore, that the emotional involvement of American Jews in this struggle (over and above the organizations for whom it was a *raison d'être*) began to wane.[19]

Two additional major factors contributed to this state of affairs. First, during the early stages of the large-scale emigration of Soviet Jews to the United States, many American Jewish communities and organizations had expected this influx to lead to a revival of Jewish activity. They hoped that various communities across the continent would be reinforced by groups of Jews thirsting for Jewish culture and values. However, following direct contact with the new immigrants, many American Jews came to realize that this assumed Soviet-Jewish yearning for Judaism had been greatly exaggerated. Furthermore, it also became evident that soon after their arrival in the USA, having availed themselves of the aid tendered by Jewish organizations, many of the immigrants cut themselves off from the local Jewish community, preferring to integrate directly into American society. In addition, the public image of certain segments of this wave of immigration as being involved in illegal or, at best, quasi-legal activities, dampened the enthusiasm with which American Jews first received them.

Second, most American Jews believe that Israel is the primary haven for persecuted Jews everywhere and this certainly applies to Soviet Jewry as the oppressed Jewish community *par excellence*. At the same time, American Jews had successfully organized a broad front of support for Soviet-Jewish emigration based on the principle of the human right to unrestricted movement and freedom to choose one's place of residence. Due to this duality, many American Jews faced a difficult dilemma which became more severe as Israel increasingly became a secondary, or even marginal, destination of the Soviet-Jewish emigrants.

A growing sense of frustration was felt in Israeli official circles which for several decades had led the struggle on behalf of Soviet Jewry.[20] The great majority of those who had left the USSR bearing Israeli visas were now choosing to emigrate to the USA,[21] where they received the status of stateless refugees. As a result, Israeli officials expended much time and energy on drafting proposals that would reduce the number of emigrants to countries other than Israel. They engaged in protracted and tiring negotiations with American Jewish organizations to reach agreement on a common policy. Their proposals included direct flights to Israel; flights to points of transit in communist countries rather than to Vienna where Soviet Jews could choose their own destination; the supply of 'invitations' from Israel only to those who, with a high degree of certainty, would be likely to stay.

The Israeli public, too, appears to have been disappointed by the wave of Soviet-Jewish immigration once it became clear that most Russian Jews (including many who had expressed strong Zionist sentiments while in the USSR) preferred the United States. For years their image in Israel had been that of fervent Zionists whose only aspiration was to return to the historic homeland. A few former Soviet Jews in Israel, not part of the 'establishment', unsuccessfully tried to increase public interest in the fate of Soviet Jewry by claiming that the majority faced the danger of deportation and exile. Thus by the mid-1980s both the activists and their supporters abroad had good reason to feel some fatigue and disenchantment.

The other diametrically opposed group which claimed to speak for Soviet Jewry was looked upon with favour by the Soviet authorities who perhaps even encouraged their public activity. It, too, can be divided into at least three sub-groups, which overlapped to some extent. The first included political figures and journalists who were members of the 'Anti-Zionist Committee' established in 1983 at the initiative of the KGB. They sharply opposed nationalist tendencies among Soviet Jews and emigration to Israel, reinforcing the official anti-Zionist and anti-Semitic propaganda.[22]

The second sub-group included authors, poets and journalists connected with the Yiddish journal, *Sovyetish Heymland*. A few of them tried to take advantage of the small space left by the authorities for activities of a Jewish nature, introducing some Jewish themes into their writing. The majority of this group, in their sixties or older, had lived through the Stalinist persecutions (most of them had been imprisoned in the late 1940s and were released in the mid-1950s) and were extremely careful never to exceed the bounds of what was permissible.

The third sub-group included a few rabbis, foremost among them the rabbi of the Moscow synagogue. Wishing to see religious institutions continue to function, even in a limited fashion, they served the Soviet propaganda machine, whether by condemning Israel, denying the existence of anti-Semitism in the USSR, or by serving the Soviets as a showcase for its continuation of Jewish religious life.

199

There is little doubt that Soviet Jewry as a whole was disgusted by the activities of the 'Anti-Zionist Committee' which was considered to be a slavish tool of the authorities. The same can also be said of the Jewish public attitude towards the literary personalities connected with *Sovyetish Heymland*, personified by its editor, Aaron Vergelis, also a member of the 'Committee'. As for the rabbis and the leaders of the few surviving synagogues, they were frequented primarily by small numbers of elderly Jews. Even those secular Jews who had become religiously observant objected to them, while the great majority of Soviet Jews exhibited little interest in religion. Hence, this sub-group had little, if any, influence on Soviet Jewry, drawing whatever little power it had directly from the authorities.

The first years of Gorbachev's rule

The appointment of the relatively young and energetic Mikhail Gorbachev as First Secretary of the Communist Party of the Soviet Union in 1985 was a sharp change from the elderly, pokerfaced Communist leaders of the previous decade. In his first appearances in public and before senior officials he expressed criticism in such an outspoken manner as to raise reservations against him in wide circles of the party's higher echelons.[23] Nevertheless, Gorbachev's twin slogans of *glasnost* and *perestroika* became part of the popular vocabulary, people interpreting them as they saw fit. Despite his different style, during the first years of his rule Gorbachev initially behaved like his predecessors, appointing loyal members of his entourage to positions throughout the party bureaucracy.

But Gorbachev had clearly come to the conclusion that should the USSR wish to remain a world power, it could no longer afford to lag behind in its economy, technology and modernization programme. Already in 1985, both he and his prime minister spoke of 'radical reforms', of the need for innovative economic doctrines, modern technology, scientific research and development, in order to create a considerable growth in national income.[24] Freedom of speech was seen as essential for the utilization of human creativity, to encourage criticism of past mistakes and also of the socio-economic classes which had become accustomed to routine. This new emphasis gained him the support of wide segments among the intelligentsia,[25] including its Jewish members.

Another necessary precondition of economic transformation was an improvement in relations with the Western powers, which had deteriorated after the Soviet invasion of Afghanistan. Gorbachev knew that structural changes in the Soviet economy could not be achieved without massive technological aid from the West and a reduction in the armaments race. The renewed dialogue with the West which resulted provided an opportunity to place once more the issue of Soviet Jewry, especially its right to emigrate, on the agenda. These new conditions encouraged Jewish activists to increase their appeals to international bodies and to the Soviet authorities, demanding exit permits for the refuseniks. Demonstrations once more became common and Jewish organizations in the West also stepped up their activity on behalf of Soviet Jewry.[26]

The Soviet Union, more desirous than ever of improving its international image, now displayed a greater inclination than in the past to reconsider its 'Jewish problem'. Anti-Zionist and anti-Jewish propaganda, while denouncing Zionists and Jews as the ultimate source of imperialism, as demonic forces or as organizers of a secret conspiracy to gain world domination, was now denounced in some quarters as contrary to Lenin's class theory.[27] Such publications now appeared less often in the major centres of the USSR. There was also a certain waning in anti-Israel propaganda, though it did continue to some extent from force of habit. During 1987, some of the Jews who had been imprisoned for their public activity were released, and 8,155 permits to leave the USSR were granted as compared to only 904 in 1986. As in previous years, 75 per cent of the emigrants chose as their destination countries other than Israel.[28]

Greater leniency towards Jewish emigration, like the more intensive negotiations of the Soviets with international Jewish organizations, were not, of course, new in themselves. Many Soviet leaders were aware of the international implications of the 'Jewish problem', and had taken this into account in the past. But the more liberal Gorbachev policy did enable Jewish activists to expand their cultural activities. The clandestine, uncensored Jewish publications (*Samizdat*) which had almost ceased appearing were now circulated in larger editions than at any time in the past.[29] Seminars and study circles on Jewish topics became more common, without any interference on the part of the authorities. Participants included persons who in the past had not been connected with the activists or had abandoned their ranks over the years.

Even the official Jewish publications, sensing winds of change in the higher echelons of Soviet government, hesitantly began to deal with topics that had previously been avoided. They now openly discussed the persecution of Jewish culture in the final years of Stalin and hinted at the existence of anti-Semitism in the USSR. This was more true of the *Birobidzhaner Shtern* than of the conservative *Sovyetish Heymland*,[30] which echoed Gorbachev's anti-Zionist statement to the French paper, *L'Humanité*, in February 1986: 'I believe that there is no place in a civilized society for anti-Semitism or for Zionism, nor, in fact, for any expression of nationalism, chauvinism and racism.'[31] *Sovyetish Heymland*, however, in dire straits because most of its writers were quite elderly, had to attract younger authors, who did not adhere to the strict party line.[32] The younger generation included authors and poets in Yiddish as well as young students of Jewish topics who wrote in Russian. On the whole, they did not identify with the journal's traditional ideology. This young cadre of writers was more attuned to the changed atmosphere and found a common language with some of the Jewish activists.

A new type of Soviet Jew had meanwhile emerged during the past few decades, influenced by the general tendency to search for roots prevalent both in the West and in the USSR. Many of these young persons were unfettered by the fears, trepidations and ideological conceptions typical of the older generation. But they preferred not to overtly identify with any of the activists. Some probably feared persecution or the loss of their jobs; others may have been deterred by the radical ideological and cultural concepts espoused by some of the activists, such as the absolute negation of Yiddish or of Jewish life in the Diaspora. Moreover, it was not yet clear that Soviet policy to the Jews had fundamentally changed and some observers even foresaw the strict limitation of Jewish emigration, given the new needs of the Soviet economy.[33]

The time of change

The central government, which culled most of its information from its own functionaries throughout the USSR, has strikingly failed to assess the importance of the ethnic element, at least before 1988.[34] Soviet leaders before then still believed that a few empty slogans favouring the unhampered development of national groups or calling for 'brotherhood among nations' would suffice to keep things under control. They assumed that economic interest and mutual interdependence would blunt ethnic antagonisms. But they had overlooked both Russian nationalism and the nationalist sentiments of other ethnic groups in the USSR, which had been ripening for years, and which now became a major source of tension in the country. Events in the Baltic republics and the Caucasus as well as open expressions of Russian national sentiment were obvious signs of this development. Moreover, national issues were not limited to territorial conflicts between the republics, they also came to the fore within them. The traditional assumption, that as the level of education rose and the process of acculturation progressed, so nationalist sentiment would wane were proven to be false. This was even admitted by two Soviet scholars who noted that

> the increasing process of acculturation is not bringing about a decrease in internal ethnic solidarity and in the intensity of national sentiment. The level of cultural development introduces certain mechanisms which help to preserve and intensify ethnic solidarity.[35]

This phenomenon also influenced ethnic groups who lived outside their own republic and even those who possessed no territorial framework at all. Millions of Ukrainians, Byelorussians, Tatars, Armenians and members of other national groups in the former USSR reside outside of their respective republics. Even though these groups generally speak Russian and their life style is, at least in part, similar to that of the society within which they live, they identify with their own unique national heritage. In 1987, Galina Starovoitova, who later became an adviser on ethnic problems to the President of the USSR, drew the following conclusion from one survey conducted among Armenians, Tatars and Estonians in Leningrad:

> The dispersed ethnic groups are an integral element of the big city ... their members have adopted the all-Soviet culture in the Russian language, but many of them simultaneously maintain strong ties with the nucleus of their nation, ties which encourage them to preserve their own ethno-cultural identification. ... Part of the dispersed ethnic group became a special cultural sub-group within the big city, having unique needs and fields of interest of its own.[36]

In the face of growing ethnic tensions, coupled with increasing criticism from the press and academic circles, the central government finally admitted the seriousness of the problem and created a Centre for the Study and Research of Ethnic Relations within the Soviet Academy of Sciences. The ethnic problem was a central issue at the 19th Conference of the CPSU in July 1988. The resolutions adopted by the congress refer not only to those ethnic groups which possess a national republic within the USSR but also to other national groups.[37]

On the face of it, they seemed to legitimize cultural, religious and organizational activities by Jews, who are recognized as an ethnic group in the Soviet Union. However, in many cases local officials found it difficult to digest the idea that the Jews have the right to ethnic self-expression like other 'dispersed ethnic groups'. Thus, the establishment of officially recognized Jewish organizations was to a great degree the result of initiatives and public pressure on the part of the Jewish communities, though the final decision remained with the local bureaucracy. In May 1987, for example, a club was established in the city of Bukhara (in Uzbekistan) to study the history of the Jewish quarter of that city. In November 1987 courses for Hebrew and Yiddish were opened in Baku, on the premises of the Communist youth movement. In mid-1988, the authorities in Kiev, capital of the Ukrainian Soviet Republic, decided to establish a 'Jewish Theatrical Studio'. Its director, Giorgy Malesky, announced that it was not to be merely a theatrical company performing in Yiddish but rather a Jewish theatre.[38] Utilizing the right to establish private cooperatives, troupes which presented Jewish audiences with selections from their national folklore mushroomed throughout the country.[39] Though most of them were very amateurish, they filled a widely-felt need and almost always performed before capacity audiences. This sporadic cultural activity, with the official approval of the local authorities, was one small expression of the revolutionary transformation which Soviet Jewry was undergoing.

A characteristic sign of the Gorbachev era was the increasingly public involvement of many people who had in the past submissively acquiesced to government directives. This was especially true of the intelligentsia, the social group to which a large segment of Soviet Jewry belongs. This involvement was particularly evident in the nationalist movements, especially in the Baltic republics, where oppositional elements joined hands with members of the CPSU and with leading figures in the literary, artistic and academic worlds.[40] A similar process took place among the Jews. Persons who in the past had in some way been connected with activists wishing to leave the USSR now cooperated with people who until recently had been an integral part of the Soviet cultural establishment, to revive Jewish cultural activity in the USSR. Increasing national consciousness in Soviet society was in effect also encouraging national sentiment among many Jews.

The first public meeting called to further the establishment of a Jewish cultural association in Lithuania was held on 2 December 1987, while a similar organization was officially proclaimed in May 1988 in the conference hall of the Estonian Ministry of Culture. In July of that year a meeting was held in Riga (Latvia) to establish the local Association for Jewish Culture and a similar association began to function two months later in Lvov (the Ukraine).[41]

It is no coincidence that the new initiatives for local Jewish cultural activity began on the periphery, before becoming openly manifest in the Russian republic as well. This was connected with the nationalist stirrings in the Baltic republics and western Ukraine as well as the support of local authorities who wished to show some degree of independence by permitting such Jewish activity without prior sanction from Moscow. This is also the background against which one should view the special resolution adopted by the Central Committee of the Communist Party of Lithuania (even before that passed by the 19th Congress of the CPSU) outlawing discrimination against ethnic minorities and calling for the encouragement of Jewish and Polish culture.[42]

Whereas authorities in the periphery were prepared to officially recognize Jewish cultural organizations and even to provide them with a legally-registered status, this was not yet the case with the central authorities who refused to grant such recognition and status to an all-Soviet Jewish cultural organization.

In September 1988, the constituent meeting of the Association for Jewish Culture (*Asotsiatsia evreiskoi kultury*) was held in Moscow. Among the objectives adopted by the Association were the diffusion of Jewish culture, coordination of efforts by various organizations active in this field, maintenance of ties with the Jewish people throughout the world (including Israel), combating anti-Semitism etc.[43] However, the Soviet government refused to register the Association even though its stated objectives were compatible with the resolution adopted at the 19th Congress of the CPSU. They still preferred to relate to the 'Jewish problem' as part of the USSR's foreign policy rather than as a movement which had sprung up from within the Soviet Jewish community itself. It is not surprising, therefore, that simultaneously with their refusal to recognize the Association for Jewish Culture, the Soviet authorities signed an agreement with representatives of Australian Jewry (and indirectly with the World Jewish Congress) for the establishment of a Jewish cultural centre in Moscow. This centre, which bore the name of Solomon Mikhoels – the famous Jewish actor and spokesman for Soviet Jewry who was murdered in January 1948 – began to operate in Moscow in February 1989. The dedication ceremony was attended by representatives of Jews throughout the USSR and delegations from Jewish communities from abroad. It soon became clear that the Mikhoels Centre was little more than a continuation of the traditional Soviet policy of dealing with Jewish issues as part of its foreign and international relations.[44]

Certain elements in the Soviet government began to develop Jewish organizational frameworks over which they could retain influence as a counterweight to Jewish organizational activity which openly declared its independence from the central authorities and its connections with organizations of Jews from abroad and with Israel. Whereas official circles referred to 'Soviet Jewish culture', harking back to the 1920s and 1930s, those who led the independent movement spoke of Jewish culture as a whole, without defining its specific character. This dichotomy did not stem from ideological differences alone. It also flowed from the increasing reservation expressed by the Soviet intelligentsia in general, and the Jewish intelligentsia in particular, concerning organizational frameworks which were suspect of having any connection with the authorities. Additional misgivings were raised by the fact that these new pro-Soviet Jewish organizations were led by personalities who in the past had been the symbol of acquiescence to the authorities.[45] For all these reasons, the official organizations were not popular among the masses of Jews in the Soviet Union, and the conception that called for independent Jewish organizations gained the upper hand. It should be borne in mind, however, that this competition between official and independent organizations – often also marked by personal competition – was more characteristic of Moscow than of the periphery and was mainly limited to the struggle over the shape which the all-Soviet framework for Jewish culture would take.

Tension in the periphery, which had suffered greatly from a lack of local leadership and was the scene of almost no legitimate Jewish activity prior to the Gorbachev era, was not as intensive as in Moscow. As was the case with other national movements, Jewish organized activity was generally marked by cooperation between avowed Communists or Communist supporters and oppositionist elements. Here and there, differences of opinion arose as to the preference to be given to the study of Yiddish or Hebrew, but these, as a rule, were arguments of an academic nature, since cultural activity was conducted in Russian, and the decision to provide instruction in

Hebrew or Yiddish was primarily contingent upon the availability of qualified teachers and prospective students.

The Baltic republics, engaged in a struggle for their independence, sought allies among various ethnic national movements in the Soviet Union. Their official newspapers prominently reported what the Soviet authorities were doing in Georgia, Azerbaijan and Armenia. They were also prepared to host national entities unable to convene in their own republics, such as one of the first conventions of the Byelorussian national movement which was held in Vilna in June 1989. It is not surprising, therefore, that these republics provided the territorial basis for the fledgling independent Jewish national movement. The first printed Jewish newspaper appeared in Estonia; published in Russian, it was actually intended to be a national Jewish organ. Riga, capital of Latvia, hosted the 'Round Table' which discussed the problems of Soviet Jewry and laid the ideological and institutional foundations for an all-Soviet Jewish organizational framework.[46] It led to a national meeting in December 1989 of representatives of Jewish organizations and communities from all parts of the USSR.[47]

This meeting, attended by almost as many observers from abroad as representatives of Soviet Jewry, was marked by great enthusiasm, but also by differences of opinion. One group claimed that the objective of cultural activity among Soviet Jews was to prepare them for emigration to Israel, while the majority held the view that variegated cultural activity was important *per se*. Representatives from republics outside of Russia were apprehensive lest Moscow become the focal point of Jewish organization in the Soviet Union, stressing the need to preserve the independence of each group and to assure representation of Jewish organizations in every republic. An executive body, comprising three chairmen from different republics, was elected and named 'the Council', to emphasize continuity with 'the Council of the Four Lands' that directed the affairs of Polish Jewry during the sixteenth to the eighteenth centuries. The 'Council' had little practical value in relation to actual activity among the Jews throughout the Soviet Union; it did have a special status *vis-à-vis* international Jewish organizations and the Soviet authorities, claiming to represent Soviet Jewry as a whole. To the best of our knowledge, the authorities did not take much account of the 'Council'. Its greatest contribution was to local groups who were encouraged by the fact that they now had a central body to which they could turn. Despite the limited practical value of the 'Council', the very existence of an independent, representative, central organ for Soviet Jewry was a revolutionary development in the USSR.

The USSR on the verge of disintegration

Two major phenomena characterized Jewish life in the last two years of the USSR's existence: the multiplicity of organizational frameworks and the growing identification with the decentralist tendencies of the majority ethnic groups within the republics. There were almost 500 Jewish organizations established at this time without any interference on the part of the authorities. Among the causes of this multiplicity were the general atmosphere in the USSR, differences of opinion among the active members in the community, and the involvement of Jewish organizations and individuals from abroad. Ideological controversy played a relatively minor role in this development.

Every group in the fragmenting USSR tended to create its own organization and to publish its own organ.[48] This was no less true of Soviet Jewry. Several Jewish organizations were established in cities having an appreciable Jewish population. The tremendous increase in the number of Jewish organizations took place precisely during a wave of mass Jewish emigration so that there was a very large turnover both in participants and organizers. The activities of these organizations focused on the study of Hebrew, basic knowledge of Jewish history in general (and of Russian Jewish history in particular) and the celebration of Jewish festivals, etc. For most of the participants, such activities helped prepare them for emigration, while for a minority, enhancement of their knowledge of the Jewish cultural heritage was a spiritual necessity. What emerged was a radically new development – the attempt to fashion a Jewish cultural milieu from the foundations up at a time of emigration and great turnover of the target populace. It is not surprising that most of this activity depended, to a lesser or greater degree, on 'imported' human resources.

In time, however, very small groups of local Jewish intelligentsia emerged whose members were not contemplating immediate emigration. They took the first steps to establish a semi-academic base for Judaic studies. During the early stages of this cultural–educational activity, Soviet Jews flocked to every Jewish or Israeli event. Once the innovation had worn off, each person chose the areas best suited to his or her own level and field of interest. Thus, there was a decrease in the number of participants in events of Jewish interest, though not necessarily in the number of organizations that provided them, which at times even increased.

The second phenomenon which became increasingly noticeable in the last years of the USSR was the growing emphasis on membership in regional, as opposed to national, Jewish bodies. As the Soviet republics exhibited a growing inclination for independence, so Jewish organizations began to place greater emphasis on local patriotism. We find Jews in Lithuania claiming to be Lithuanian Jews, though most of them had emigrated from other parts of the USSR. The same held true for Jews in the Ukraine and elsewhere. This necessarily led to a further decline in the importance of the all-Soviet Jewish Organization. A clear tendency emerged to divide Soviet Jewry into regional Jewish communities that emphasized their loyalty and allegiance to the republic in which they resided.

Jewish organizations could find themselves in problematic situations, however, when there was tension between their 'home republic' and neighbouring ethnic territories. This was especially true in the Moldavian Republic after the Pridnestrovie region seceded, proclaiming its independence. Most Moldavian Jewish organizations declared their support for Moldavia, while those of Pridnestrovie stood up for the local secessionist authorities. In such cases the 'Organization' in Moscow generally preferred to remain neutral, a stance which removed it even more from the concrete problems faced by Jewish organizations throughout the disintegrating USSR. As the Soviet Union came apart at the seams the 'Organization' ceased to exist altogether as an all-Soviet coordinating framework. Its demise marked the end of Soviet Jewry as a single entity. The Jewish communities of the former USSR entered a new phase in which the fate of each of them would be intimately connected with that of the new states.

SOVIET JEWRY AND NON-JEWISH SOCIETY

For several decades the manner in which Soviet society related to its Jewish population has tended to be neglected and attention has been focused on the discriminatory policy of the Soviet authorities. This is not a very useful approach for our period, when discrimination against Jews as an official policy virtually disappeared, despite scattered cases here and there within the government bureaucracy. However, as Soviet citizens became increasingly involved in all facets of public life, their attitudes towards the Jews became a social factor with which political figures and government officials had to contend. Our discussion will be confined here to four regions of the former USSR: Russia, the Ukraine, the Baltic republics and the Muslim region.

Russia

According to the last census (January 1989), 38 per cent of Soviet Jews lived in the Russian Federated Republic, 68 per cent of them in the two capital cities, Moscow and St Petersburg.[49] The highest rate of intermarriage by Jews in the USSR was in the Russian Republic.[50] Furthermore, during the past decades, the role played by Jews in Russian cultural and intellectual life has been substantial and proportionally higher than their involvement in the culture of any other ethnic group in the USSR.[51] At the same time, with the collapse of Marxist–Leninist ideology, certain circles within the Russian intelligentsia sought a firmer foundation in their own historic past. This search for roots was manifested by collecting icons and reviving Russian Orthodoxy, or through sentimental attachment to the landscapes of old Russia as expressed in paintings that included the symbols of pagan Russia alongside churches, saints and crosses. These patriotic circles sought out information concerning monuments of the past which had been destroyed by the Soviet authorities in the process of 'constructing a socialist society'. Such concerns, which influenced wide segments of the intelligentsia, filtered down into the literature produced by some of the authors whose views of life and whose literary styles were taking shape in the 1950s and 1960s.

Siberian-born Vladimir Chivilikhin was one such author whose work has become the symbol of an outspokenly anti-Semitic movement. During his youth, the sights and scenes of Russia had made a lasting impression upon him. He remained faithful to them long after completing his studies at the Faculty of Journalism at Moscow University in 1954. In his massive work, *Pamiat*, which he wrote over a period of fifteen years (from 1968 to 1984), Chivilikhin's main protagonists are the Decembrists, Russia's first revolutionaries at the beginning of the nineteenth century. They, however, form but a loose framework for the novel, into which the author selectively and very freely weaves historical documentation on various subjects and from different periods of time. What is most striking is the wish to glorify the noble traits of the Russian people and their primordial roots which date back to the pre-Christian era. These unique Slavic–Russian traits and values, antithetical to those of the West, are not a thing of the past. They live on in contemporary Russian society and in each individual Russian. It is significant that Chivilikhin's *Pamiat* was widely acclaimed when the first chapters were published in literary journals, the author receiving thousands of letters from his readers. The entire novel itself went through many printings running into hundreds of thousands of copies and was awarded many literary prizes.[52]

The word *Pamiat* (memory) soon became a socio-cultural catchphrase around which rallied many of those who sought to promote Russian historical consciousness and longed to restore Russia's ancient past, old buildings and primeval landscape. In associations inspired by the conservationist ideology expressed in Chivilikhin's epic novel, oppositionists joined hands with Soviet bureaucrats. Together, they launched campaigns against grandiose government schemes that could seriously damage the natural environment, while simultaneously trying to preserve and restore monuments of the past.[53]

Even if Chivilikhin's novel did not include overtly anti-Semitic passages, his subtle fingering of those responsible for the destruction of the spirit and historical consciousness of Russia coupled with his reservations concerning Western culture, helped to prepare the ground. The Jews were the chief culprits. Thus, it is not surprising that from the very outset, 'The Historical and Literary Society Pamiat' was marked by increasingly militant anti-Semitic undertones. As life in the Soviet Union became less rigorously controlled, so the influence grew of those circles identified with 'Pamiat', who spoke in the name of historical Russia and Russian patriotism.[54] Pamiat was able to organize a mass demonstration and its representatives were received by Boris Yeltsin, then First Secretary of the Communist Party in

Moscow.[55] Seeking popular support, Yeltsin apparently realized that it was good policy to show an interest in the association which, at that time, seemed to be the leading voice of Russian nationalism.

Within a short period of time, similar organizations were established, all emphasizing the unique history and character of Russia but without specifically alluding to the Jews. Pamiat, in contrast, continued and increased its anti-Semitic propaganda. Accusations to the effect that the Jews had murdered millions of Russians during the period of Soviet rule, that they had desecrated Russian cultural treasures and destroyed the Russian Church, became the leitmotif that ran through all this propaganda. Different groups, sometimes holding directly opposite opinions, joined ranks in Pamiat, only hatred of the Jews keeping them together, at least for some time. There were those who held on to pagan concepts, claiming that the Russian nation must be freed of Christianity, which was no more than a Jewish plot to control the Russian spirit. They were active within Pamiat, side by side with others who believed that restoration of Eastern Orthodoxy to its primacy would be the most authentic expression of the Russian national spirit. Pamiat also attracted imperialistic elements who admired Stalin for extending the area of Russian power to Central Europe after 1945. They identified with Stalin's views on the superiority of the Russian people and its history, and with his steps to purge Russian culture of any Jewish influence.[56]

Virulent anti-Semitism, then, was the primary bond that enabled the strange bedfellows who made up the membership of Pamiat to work together. Not for long, however. Pamiat, and similar organizations, fell apart at the seams as a consequence of leadership struggles and ideological controversies. The various splinter-groups, many of which stubbornly stuck to the use of 'Pamiat' in their new titles and accused each other of treason and collaboration with the authorities, did sometimes manage to hold a united anti-Jewish demonstration, but the differences between them gained the upper hand over what they held in common.[57] As vulgar demagoguery increasingly became its hallmark, and with the advent of other 'patriotic' organizations, Pamiat's influence decreased, especially among the Russian intelligentsia. Any self-respecting person tended to keep his distance from that organization, whose ranks were filled more and more by young persons from marginal social classes. The Pamiat groups were soon commonly accepted as the lunatic fringe of Russian society. Since the Pamiat phenomenon was quite an innovation in Russia, it received much attention from the Western media, and caused Russian Jews no small amount of trepidation. In time, however, many of them learned how to live with this phenomenon and how to combat it (like in the West) by appealing to the authorities, influencing public opinion in the media and turning to the courts.

Side by side with the vulgar, militant anti-Semitism of the Pamiat variety, a more sophisticated anti-Jewish movement emerged, which gained some support among the Russian intelligentsia. Its roots, too, must be sought in

Russian *belles-lettres* of the 1970s and 1980s, especially in that genre which has been termed 'rustic prose' (*derevenskaia proza*). In the hallowed tradition of nineteenth-century Russian literature, authors are expected – both by themselves and by their public – to lead and educate the masses, and thus to fulfil a social mission in their writing. The rustic prose school intended to make Russian society aware of past and present ecological destruction, which is not limited to nature alone but is also evident in the social sphere.

The founders of the rustic prose genre were Viktor Astafe'ev (born 1924) and Vasilii Belov (born 1932). Both moved to the northern city of Vologda, situated in a region where one can still sense the authentic soul of Russia, far from the centres of literary activity. Their works focused on the village and the peasant, who lives in perfect harmony with Mother Earth. The harm man brings upon nature and the destruction of the village, they believe, are what caused the deterioration of this harmonic life, leading to Russia's decadence. Their works – especially those of Belov – served as a catalyst for literary–philosophical deliberations on the intrinsic nature of the Russian national character, on the fate of the Russian village and on the conflict between 'land and asphalt' (asphalt was at times defined as 'a Jewish amalgam' – *Zhidovskaia smes*). Valentin Rasputin (born 1937) can also be considered part of this school of literature. In his works he emphasizes that instead of integrating into nature man ruins it with his own hands, thus corrupting the noble traits of the Russian people.

The authors of this school candidly portrayed the truth, painful as it may be, using the language and idioms of Russia's northern rural areas. These characteristics, together with the opposition expressed in their pages to the destruction of natural landscapes and indirect criticism of the havoc wreaked upon the Russian village by collectivization, made their works immensely popular among the intelligentsia, including the Jewish intelligentsia.[58] Preservation of nature's gifts and opposition to the destruction caused by the march of civilization – concepts which are by no means foreign to intellectuals and literary people in the West – have acquired a special significance in Russia. Here they have frequently been juxtaposed with the alleged intellectualism, scepticism and counterfeit moderation of the West. Furthermore, these artistically gifted Russian authors did not refrain from pointing to the culprit guilty of destroying these 'unique' Russian values, i.e. the decadent, pampered and opportunist intelligentsia, especially the Jews. Several Jews wrote these authors widely circulated letters, pointing to the anti-Jewish, or even anti-Semitic, undertones in their works.[59] In his response to one such letter, sent by scholar and critic of Russian literature Nathan Edelman (1990), Astafe'ev wrote:

> Every movement of national revival, especially the Russian one, must have its opponents and enemies. In the process of our revival we are able to achieve that stage where we sing our own songs, dance our own

dances, and write in our mother tongue, not in the 'Esperanto' forced upon us, which they term 'a literary language'. By our chauvinistic aspirations we might even reach the point when our academic studies of Pushkin and Lermontov will be written by Russians; it is frightening to even think that we ourselves will edit the collected works of our classic authors, and that we will 'take in hand' encyclopedias and other facets of cultural expression such as the theatre and the cinema. Oh, how horrifying! What a nightmare! To think that we ourselves will interpret Dostoevski's journals![60]

Elsewhere in his response, Astafe'ev accuses the Jews and the Zionists, among other things, of murdering the tsar, the symbol of Russia's historical continuity. He also compared Russians to Jews: the former are magnanimous, lovingly accepting the Jews despite all the calamities which they have brought upon the Russian nation. The great chasm that seemingly exists between the Jew – even the one steeped in Russian culture – and the original essence of the Russian spirit is also portrayed in literary works. The only Jew in Vasilii Belov's novel *All is Ahead of Us* is Misha Brish, a wholly unscrupulous character bent upon raising the money he needs to begin life anew overseas. To gain his own selfish purposes he exploits the love of an innocent Russian woman. But the day of reckoning will come, hints the novelist; the future lies with the novel's Russian protagonists who have been refined in the melting-pot of suffering and manipulation by negative types such as Misha Brish. When they finally understand the tactics used by such satanic forces, they will unite and free themselves.[61]

Russian mathematician Igor Shafarevitch committed himself to the same objective. For twelve years he worked on the final draft of his volume, *Russophobia* (1989), in which minority groups, called by him 'little nations', interfered with the organic development of human societies. The 'little nation' is a minority that lives its own cultural life, hating and ridiculing that of the 'big nation', the majority population within which it resides. Such were the Huguenots in France and the Puritans in England who left their mark on sixteenth- and seventeenth-century Europe; the intellectuals and the Masonic lodges in eighteenth-century France who laid the foundations for the French Revolution; and 'Young Germany' in the 1830s. In Russia, it was the liberal and nihilistic movements as well as terrorist and revolutionary groups, who expressed their ridicule and derision of Russian history, worshipping anything that originated in the West.

Today, 'Russophobia' is the dominant expression of this fear and hatred within the 'little nation', in which Jews play a catalytic role. Penetrating Russian culture, the Jews are influenced by the concept of their being a 'chosen people', by hatred of non-Jews and by a desire to wreak revenge upon the Russian nation. That is why they were prepared to sacrifice the lives of millions of Russians upon the altar of the Revolution and the Civil

War. Similar motivations caused liberal Jews in the West to purposely shut their eyes to the suffering that was the lot of the Russian people during the decades of Soviet rule. Shafarevitch's meaning is that Russian society must spew out the Jews and purge Russian culture of foreign, Judaeo-Western ideas. He calls upon Russian society – especially the intelligentsia – to return to the true fount of Russian culture and pave the way for the organic development of the nation.[62]

In such ideologies, which can be loosely termed 'Russian national fundamentalism', one finds variations on the theme of safeguarding Russia against the harmful and decadent influences of Western culture. They are widely accepted in the Russian intelligentsia, both in 'patriotic circles' and among those who call for far-reaching reform of the economy and the system of government. This means, in effect, that they are more widespread and have greater influence than the ideas propagated by the Pamiat splinter-groups.

Among the intelligentsia, however, there are many who do not adhere to 'Russian national fundamentalism', objecting to the exploitation of historical myths and the emphasis placed on the uniqueness of Russian culture. They generally point out that throughout the centuries this culture was influenced by diverse nations and ethnic groups. They object to excessive idealization of Russian history and are prepared to admit its negative aspects. Since they believe the individual to be the focus of national life, they recognize the advantages of Western culture. Not surprisingly, therefore, these circles praise the Jewish contribution to Russian culture and are unwilling to accept anti-Semitism, even if it was espoused by Russian literary geniuses. Elena Starikova, a literary critic and scholar of the works of Dostoevski (born 1924), wrote in her reply to Astafe'ev: 'Dostoevski, who was guilty of such expressions [of anti-Semitism] at least did not, and could not, know about Auschwitz and Dachau. But we, Astafe'ev, we know.'[63]

Thus, the attitude towards the Jews in Russia – not always identical with the attitude towards Israel – became an integral part of the internal conflict waged within the intelligentsia over the shaping of the new Russian national consciousness. Until very recently, it had been grounded in the concept of empire. The Russian knew that he was the overlord of the entire Soviet empire and considered his language and culture to be superior to those of all other nations and ethnic groups in the USSR. His country's status as a world superpower added to national pride. This national consciousness was shaken even before the formal disintegration of the Soviet Union, the intelligentsia being forced to redefine its national identity. Thus, the controversy over the Jewish contribution to the shaping of Russian culture during the past century is more than just an expression of how Russians relate today to the Jews who live among them. It may also point to the various tendencies in present-day Russia which will shape the new Russian nationalism.

The Ukraine

According to the last census (January 1989), about 34 per cent of Soviet Jews lived in the Ukraine, some 20 per cent of them in the capital city of Kiev. About 60 per cent of them, not including those in Kiev, lived in areas in which Russians accounted for at least one-quarter of the population. The rate of Jewish intermarriage in the Ukraine in the late 1980s was about three-quarters of that in Russia and – in so far as this can be ascertained on the basis of incomplete data – more mixed marriages were with Russians than with Ukrainians. The same holds true for a university education: the rate among the Jews of the Ukraine is about two-thirds of that among Russian Jews. In the last census, when asked about the languages they spoke, only about 2 per cent of this republic's Jewish residents gave Ukrainian as their mother tongue, while another 46 per cent replied that they had a good command of that language. In other words, about one-half of them do not speak Ukrainian, Russian being their only language. This socio-demographic portrait indicates some of the dilemmas which Ukrainian Jews have traditionally faced.[64]

The overriding elements in the renewed Ukrainian nationalism have been sovereignty and independence. The Ukrainian nation, some 45 million strong, has known only short periods of sovereignty; the move towards independence, therefore, was accompanied by a sense of liberation from colonial rule. The Ukrainian intelligentsia has successfully rallied almost all of that republic's populace around nationhood. A poll conducted in November 1991 showed that 90 per cent of the Ukrainians, 65 per cent of the Russians and 92 per cent of the Jews voted for independence.[65] The Jews, then, expressed their unhesitating support for Ukrainian national aspirations.

Since the Jews played but a minor role in Ukrainian culture – as compared to their status in Russian culture – it would have been irrelevant to demand that Ukrainian culture be purged of Jewish elements. Furthermore, much of the local intelligentsia was aware of the fact that during the short periods of Ukrainian independence in the past, marked by harsh oppression of the Jews, their own national vulnerability had increased. In addition, a not inconsiderable part of the intelligentsia felt a moral debt towards the Jewish nation because many Ukrainians actively participated in the mass murder of Jews during the Holocaust. For all of these reasons, many members of the Ukrainian intelligentsia evinced much consideration and understanding for their Jewish neighbours. It was no coincidence that from the outset the Ukrainian national movement, *Rukh*, was highly considerate of the special needs of ethnic minorities, first and foremost among them being the Jews. Anti-Semitism was publicly condemned as being detrimental to Ukrainian interests; voices that raised the slogan 'Ukraine for the Ukrainians' were silenced. Attempts by *Pamiat* splinter-groups to extend their activities into the Ukraine in the name of pan-Slavic solidarity were an utter failure. One group of *Rukh* members even came to Moscow in December 1989 to defend a conference of Jewish organizations against possible physical attack by extremist anti-Semitic elements. Such elements within the Ukrainian intelligentsia consider good relations with the Jews and recognition of their special needs to be an integral part of their humanistic outlook on life and their nationalist ideology.[66]

Most political personalities, too, make it their business to favourably consider special Jewish needs and to condemn anti-Semitism. This is also seen as an effective and necessary means for establishing good relations with the West in general, and the United States in particular. It is all the more important in view of the widely-accepted image of the Ukrainians as an anti-Semitic nation that had been created over the years. True, anti-Jewish stereotypes are still very much alive on the lower levels of government bureaucracy and among the general public, though this is more evident in small towns and villages than in the larger cities. Here and there extreme nationalist and anti-Semitic groups have begun to organize, but this is a marginal phenomenon which has been condemned in no uncertain terms by the intellectual and government establishments.

Ukrainian, the official language of the republic, is the second foundation of Ukrainian nationalism. It is intended to replace Russian in public affairs and as the language of instruction in the school system and the universities. In this sphere, too, the authorities have been progressing carefully and wisely in order to avoid resistance on the part of one-quarter of the populace (Russians and other ethnic groups) whose first language is Russian. However, for many Jews the language policy of the Ukrainians poses difficult problems with which they will have to deal if they wish to remain in the Ukraine and improve their social standing.

The third foundation upon which nationalism rests is a historical consciousness that emphasizes unique elements which differentiate between Ukrainian and Russian history. It is only natural that the Ukrainians stress the periods of their independence and the struggle against the Russian empire in general and the Soviets in particular. As part of these historiographical efforts, national heroes of the past are raised from oblivion, many of whom are indelibly inscribed in Jewish collective memory as cruel oppressors. This tendency places many Jews, especially of the older generation, in a rather untenable position, whenever it touches upon the Second World War.[67] Since the intelligentsia is aware of this situation, it has tried to lessen the tension created when the blood-soaked annals of Jewish history on the soil of the Ukraine encounter the record of Ukrainian history. Ukrainian intellectuals stress that throughout most of the lengthy history of the Jews in the Ukraine, the two nations in fact lived in symbiosis and that the violent outbursts against the Jews were generally instigated by foreign elements (Poles or Russians) who manoeuvred the uneducated masses of Ukrainians to further their own interests.

The new reality which is taking shape in the Ukraine, then, poses awkward dilemmas for the Jews of that country, despite the efforts of the intelligentsia, the authorities and the media. It should also be borne in mind that widespread, deeply rooted hatred of the Jews is still prevalent, fed by Christian tradition and by folklore.

The Baltic states

The great majority of the approximately 40,000 persons in the Baltic states who gave their nationality as Jewish in the last census (about 3 per cent of the Jews in the former Soviet Union) were not residents, or the children of residents, of these states before the Second World War. They or their parents emigrated to the Baltic states during the past forty-five years as part of the general wave of migration of Soviet citizens, especially Russians. Their language, culture and life style were more identical to those of the Russians than of the Lithuanians, Latvians and Estonians; furthermore, they had very little in common with the Jewish communities who lived in these three countries during the inter-war period. Only about 35 per cent of the Jews acknowledged that they spoke Latvian, Lithuanian or Estonian, whether as their mother tongue or as a second language.[68]

Under such conditions, it would be reasonable to expect that the great majority of Jews would join the Russian minorities in these republics in strong opposition to the nationalist aspirations of the majority populations, whose final objective was independence. However, most Jews in the Baltic republics refrained from supporting the Russian minority, whether due to the anti-Semitism that characterized it or because of the positive attitude towards the Jews displayed by the Baltic national movements. These movements, and the governments of the Baltic states, well knew that the demands of the Jewish minority were infinitesimal in comparison with those of other ethnic minorities, such as the Poles in Lithuania, not to mention the Russians. Realizing that refusal of the Jews' demands might push them into the camp of the Russian oppositionists, they adopted a policy meant to show that the Jewish residents of the Baltic states enjoyed freedom of expression and received state support for the development of their own institutions and cultural activities. The purpose of this policy, held in common by both the Communist authorities in the Baltic republics and the nationalist opposition movements, was to gain a favourable public image.[69]

Not surprisingly, therefore, the media in the Baltic republics and those of the Lithuanian, Latvian and Estonian communities in the West did their best to publicize Jewish activity in these countries, especially in comparison to the restrictions imposed in Moscow. The great majority of Jews in the Baltic republics adopted a stance of positive neutrality towards the national-ist movements while a few of their leading spokesmen even became actively involved.[70] Whereas the Russians were held to be agents of a foreign oppressor,[71] the official attitude towards the Jews portrayed them as heirs of the pre-Second World War Jewish communities of Lithuania, Latvia and Estonia, though it was a well-known fact that most of them were comparatively recent arrivals, just like the Russians.[72] As tension increased between Moscow and the Baltic countries, the majority of their Jewish populations emphasized more and more that they were Lithuanian, Latvian or Estonian Jews, concealing the fact that they, or their parents, had actually migrated from other areas within the Soviet Union.

It should be borne in mind, however, that during the struggle for independence – and even more so after it was achieved – the seccesionist movements stressed the national character of these states. Preference was given to members of the majority ethnic group, while speedy practical steps were taken to transform the languages spoken by these ethnic groups into the official languages of the government bureaucracy and of cultural activity. Russian language and culture were expressly frowned upon, since they represented the oppressor. From the little data available, it would seem that in this matter, too, the authorities have been more lenient towards the Jews, probably because they formed such a small minority and also in view of the negative repercussions which harsh discrimination against Jews was likely to have upon public opinion throughout the world. Despite this tendency, many Jews in these republics sensed that they had become second-rate citizens; moreover, they now had to acquire fluency in a language with which they had been completely unacquainted in the past.

Official circles and members of the intelligentsia in the Baltic republics emphasized the thriving Jewish cultural and organizational activity during the previous period of independence, completely overlooking the anti-Semitic policy of the authorities during the late 1930s.[73] Furthermore, several of the leaders in the period that preceded the Soviet invasion of Lithuania, Latvia and Estonia had been elevated to the rank of national heroes. Many of those who fought against Soviet rule when it was first established in 1940 and again when it was re-established in the final stages of the Second World War, who had been directly or indirectly involved in the murder of Jews during the Nazi period of occupation, now became symbols of resistance to Soviet oppression. Their graves were marked by memorial plaques and covered with flowers; they themselves were declared martyrs of Communist dictatorship.

Glorification of persons who had directly or indirectly participated in the murder of the Jewish populace placed many Jews in an awkward position.[74] Whereas part of the younger generation was prepared to acquiesce in this state of affairs, demanding only that a commission investigate each case *ad hoc*, this was not the case with those who had lived through the Holocaust. Furthermore, a not inconsiderable number of publications (the majority in

Latvian and Lithuanian, with only a few in Russian) noted that the manner in which the majority populations, at least in part, had treated the Jews during the period of Nazi occupation was a way of revenging themselves for the collaboration of many Jews with the Soviet oppressors in the pre-1941 years. These publications often greatly exaggerated the role of Jews in the Soviet administration of the Baltic states, completely overlooking the fact that the Soviet authorities had put an end to most Jewish organizations and activities, while many individual Jews were jailed or exiled because of their political views or because they belonged to a 'hostile' social class.[75]

The primary objective of the newly independent Baltic states is to further the interests and well-being of the majority ethnic groups in these republics. For the Jews who live in them, who wish to preserve their cultural heritage but also to be allowed to advance in accordance with their capabilities (not on the basis of ethnic origin), such a condition presents many difficult problems.

The Muslim republics

Some 200,000 Jews live in the predominantly Muslim areas of the ex-USSR. About 35 per cent belong to Jewish communities indigenous to the area for centuries, such as the Mountain Jews and the Bukharian Jewish community, while the other 65 per cent emigrated to the area during the past century, especially since it came under Soviet domination.[76] Whereas the behaviour patterns of the indigenous communities do not vary greatly from those of the majority populations, that of most of the newcomers – Ashkenazic Jews who emigrated from European USSR – is greatly similar to the behaviour pattern of the Russian minorities in these republics. The same can be said for the languages they speak. The older Jewish communities, as a rule, are fluent in the language of the majority ethnic groups, while the Ashkenazic Jews converse in Russian. The Ashkenazic Jews also have a higher rate of university-educated among them, than do the indigenous Jewish communities. It is only natural that the majority populations have generally differentiated between the older Jewish community and the newcomers, who at best have lived among them only since the beginnings of the Soviet Union.

Generally speaking, national movements similar to those which arose in the European parts of the USSR have not yet made much headway in the Muslim areas. Under the surface, however, there was a widespread feeling of discrimination by the Russians and hostility towards them, expressed in part in religious revival and a return to traditional symbols. This religious revival did not generally take the form of Islamic fundamentalism, which aims to unite the Muslim world. It was rather a way of expressing opposition to outside rule and of stressing national traits. The majority of the population belongs to nations whose civilization is to a great extent steeped in Muslim religious practice. This also caused those who live in these areas to react to events within the USSR in a manner different from the European part of the Soviet state, a tendency no less influenced by traditional intra-tribal relationships, not unlike those of the Mafia in some respects. This is the background against which one must view the relationship of the majority populations to the Jews.

Hostility towards the USSR, and especially towards Russians who emigrated to the Muslim region, is characteristic of the area. Notwithstanding this hostility, the majority populations were wise enough to realize to what degree they were economically dependent upon Russia and that they also needed the skills of the Russian educated class, which included the Ashkenazic Jews. The general tendency is to slowly but surely check the 'Russians' and replace them by members of the native ethnic groups. It was this policy that influenced the relationship of the majority populations, and at times of the authorities, towards the Ashkenazic Jews, often further aggravated by the Arab–Israeli conflict and emotional support of the Arabs. This was diametrically opposed to their relationship with the older Jewish communities – the 'Mountain Jews' and the Bukharian Jews – who were not considered 'foreigners'. Such hostility as was expressed towards these Jews was a result of their superior economic status, for they were generally better off in comparison to the average income of the majority population. Since violence is a trait more common to the populace (not necessarily the authorities) of the Muslim republics than to that of other areas of the former USSR, hostility sometimes took a violent turn, but there is no evidence of specifically anti-Jewish violence.

The complexities of the ethnic problems that plagued the USSR in the final years of its existence and the breakdown of central government, which could not effectively cope with these problems, created situations in different regions of the USSR that forced the Jews living there to make momentous decisions. Many had to adapt to a situation in which they now owed allegiance to the new national entities instead of loyalty to the Soviet Union, to which they had been accustomed for over seven decades. They were forced to recognize the primacy of indigenous cultures over that of Russia, of which they had been an integral part, and in certain regions even active agents of its diffusion. They were compelled to learn the languages spoken in their places of residence which were now given priority over Russian, the language in which most Jews were fluent. They bore the brunt of popular – and at times ideological – anti-Semitic outbursts which became more frequent as mass involvement in public affairs increased and freedom of speech and organization became more prevalent. As a result, some of the Jews sought a solution to these problems in emigration.

EMIGRATION FROM THE USSR AND
IMMIGRATION TO ISRAEL

Many segments of Soviet Jewry always kept in mind emigration from the USSR, at least as a hypothetical possibility, though it generally remained no more than that. Like the Russian intelligentsia in general, during the first years of the Gorbachev era the Jews were intoxicated by the more liberal policy of the authorities and the decline in official discrimination, eagerly awaiting to see speedy improvements in the country's economy. As time passed without tangible evidence of practical positive developments in the economy, and as the central government grew weaker, with an attendant deterioration in personal security, the tendency to emigrate increased. To this was added the fear of mass anti-Semitism, a new phenomenon to which Soviet Jews were unused, which even reached the stage where rumours were spread that pogroms were possible. In 1988, Soviet Jewry was hit by an emigration mania, there being almost no family in which at least the possibility of leaving the USSR was not discussed.

In that very year, the process by which Jews could leave the USSR also became much more simplified. The regulation which made exit permits available only to those who had received an invitation from relatives of the first degree was rescinded in February 1988. In addition, the Soviet authorities adopted a much more lenient policy towards Jewish emigrants. Pavel Abramovich, a leading Jewish activist, wrote:

> I was in the Dutch Embassy [which issued Israeli visas at the time] and spoke with the people who had come there, mostly Jews from Kharkov. They said that anyone who had not been involved in secret projects now receives an exit permit within about a month and a half.
> ... The administration is forbidden to place obstacles in the way of those who wish to emigrate, such as firing them from their place of employment.[77]

Even if the manner in which prospective emigrants were treated in Kharkov was not universally applied throughout the USSR, there is no doubt that at this time the attitude of the Soviet authorities to Jewish emigration had undergone a fundamental transformation. In contrast to past years, when emigration was equated with treason both by public opinion and in official circles, a more tolerant attitude was now evident towards the emigrants. In some cases, those who remained in the USSR were prepared to continue their ties with those who left even after their emigration.

This new attitude did not completely put an end to the former policy by which exit permits were refused for reasons of security (not always clearly defined) or because a close member of the family objected. Applications for exit permits had to be accompanied by a writ of agreement from the applicant's parents, if they were unable to work and provide for themselves, or from the divorced spouse, if the couple's under-aged children were in that person's custody. Such stipulations laid prospective emigrants open to pressure by parents or former spouses, so much so that in 1988 a group which called itself 'miserable relatives' petitioned the authorities to change this procedure.[78] In that same year, emigration on the basis of Israeli visas dramatically increased (19,251 as compared to 8,155), but there was no appreciable change in the emigrants' destination: 25 per cent reached Israel in 1987 and only 12 per cent in 1988.[79]

The desire to emigrate, on the part of Jews and non-Jews alike, snowballed. It soon reached the stage, according to certain estimates made by Soviet sociologists, when it encompassed some 20 to 22 million Soviet citizens, with the authorities inclined to grant permits to most of them. This new situation called for a re-evaluation of the emigration question. Four major elements were involved, in so far as the re-evaluation related to Soviet Jews: (a) the American administration; (b) American Jewish organizations; (c) the Israeli authorities; (d) the Soviet government. We shall briefly deal with each of them.

(a) As East–West relations substantially improved, Jewish emigration from the Soviet Union lost its effectiveness as an element in the Cold War. Moreover, the claim could no longer be made that the Jews were an oppressed ethnic and religious minority, suffering from discrimination, who should therefore be afforded the status of political refugees. In addition, in view of the fact that members of many ethnic groups in the Soviet Union aspired to emigrate to the USA, it was no longer convenient for the American government to grant preferential treatment to the Jews. Above all, the United States was wary of an immense wave of unselective immigration, in direct contradiction to American immigration policy, and was under no circumstances willing to cover the immense costs involved in granting refugee status to masses of immigrants from the Soviet Union. Administration policy, therefore, tended more and more to relate to immigration from the USSR, including that of Soviet Jews, within the framework of existing immigration legislation, not as an exception to the rules.

(b) In past years, American Jewish organizations had been torn between the principle that Israel should be the destination for Jewish emigration and their demand that the US administration increase the number of entry permits for Soviet Jews. Now they were unwilling to come out openly against the administration's new policy. In addition, it had become increasingly apparent that Jewish emigration from the USSR did not bring about the hoped-for revitalization of Jewish organizations in the USA, since many of the emigrants preferred to integrate into the wider American society and after a year or two refrained from active participation in Jewish community affairs. Thus, the American Jewish organizations made no special efforts, being content with the administration's obligation to continue issuing about 50,000 entry permits per year for Soviet Jews.

(c) The Israeli government pressured American Jewish organizations to acquiesce in the US administration's new immigration policy. For the State of Israel and its government, mass immigration from the Soviet Union was a historical opportunity to strengthen the country, increase its Jewish population and somewhat rectify the demographic balance between Jews and Arabs. The Israelis were even willing to promise explicitly that Soviet Jews would not be encouraged to settle in the occupied territories.

(d) The Soviet authorities, for their part, adopted a policy of almost complete freedom of emigration. They were now willing to forgo the fiction that exit was allowed only to those who held Israeli visas which, in turn, were issued only to those who claimed that they intended to unite with their families and return to their homeland. They now agreed that visas to the United States be issued in the American Embassy in Moscow and Israeli visas by the recently established Israeli diplomatic mission in the Soviet capital. As a result of improved relations between Israel and the USSR – part of the extensive changes in Soviet foreign policy in general and its Middle Eastern policy in particular – direct flights to Israel were no longer out of the question.

On 1 October 1989, new emigration procedures came into effect. All who held Israeli visas on that date would still be allowed to choose their destination while those who would be issued Israeli visas in the future would be obligated to emigrate to Israel. At first, only a few American visas were issued in Moscow since the quota was almost filled by thousands of Soviet Jews in transit camps in Italy awaiting entrance permits to the USA and by many others from among those who had received Israeli visas prior to 1 October. It is probably correct to assume that the Israeli representatives in Moscow, aware of the new regulations which would take effect at the beginning of October, slowed down the issuance of visas in the months immediately preceding the change of policy and then accelerated the processing of requests during the last three months of 1989. The change is reflected in the statistics for that year. Of the 71,238 Jews who left the USSR holding Israeli visas, over 17 per cent emigrated to Israel, especially during the months of October to December.[80] The first day of October 1989, then, was certainly a turning point at which emigration from the Soviet Union was transformed into immigration to Israel. This change, however, was not the doing of the Soviet Jews nor of their representatives. From then until the end of 1991, when the Soviet Union was formally disbanded, Jewish emigration to destinations other than Israel was marginal.

The new regulations did not diminish the number of Jews who wished to leave the USSR. To the best of our knowledge, there were even no complaints raised against Israel and its policy, which obstructed emigration to the United States and additional countries, turning the flow towards Israel. In 1990, 185,242 Soviet Jewish immigrants reached Israel while only 5,056 emigrated directly to the USA (excluding those who had left the USSR prior to the enforcement of the new regulations and reached America from transit camps in Italy). The number of Jewish emigrants to other countries, such as Germany, South Africa, etc., was rather scanty. The figure of 192,000 is therefore a reasonable estimate of the number of persons who left the Soviet Union as Jews during 1990.[81]

There was a slight decline in these numbers for 1991, the last year of the USSR's existence. Israel was the destination of 147,839, another 34,715 reached the United States, while a fair estimate of those emigrating to other countries is 3,000, for a total of about 185,000. In the three-year period under discussion (1989–91), therefore, about 448,000 Jews emigrated from the USSR, a mass movement when one remembers that in the census conducted during January 1989, about 1.5 million Soviet citizens registered as Jews. If all of these emigrants were included among those 1.5 million Jews, this would mean that about 30 per cent of Soviet Jewry left the country in that three-year period. It is a well-known fact, however, that among the emigrants were some (we have no way of even estimating how many) who do not appear in the 1989 census as Jews, whether because they are non-Jewish members of Jewish families, or for other reasons.

The decision to emigrate is a difficult and intricate one, influenced by many elements, though made easier by the new Soviet policy which no longer cuts the emigrant off from all contact with his relatives and friends who remain in the USSR. Different considerations of varying intensity influenced the decision of each individual family. In general, though, deteriorating economic conditions, government instability and social unease, together with anxiety about the future, provided the major motives for emigration. To this one should add specific apprehensions caused by the rise of national sentiment in some of the republics and fear of becoming second-class citizens there. Anti-Semitism was generally but one – and not always the most important – cause of emigration.

The republics where Jews emigrated at a rate at least 150 per cent higher than the national average included Armenia, Moldavia, Azerbaijan, Tajikistan and Byelorussia. In the first four, general acts of violence and threats to personal safety were the likeliest reasons that raised Jewish emigration far above the national level, while the 'Chernobyl syndrome' obviously caused many Jews to have second thoughts about living in Byelorussia. Uzbekistan, Lithuania, Kirghizia, Latvia and the Ukraine fell into a second category, in which the rate of emigration ranged between a maximum of 150 per cent and a minimum of 80 per cent of the national average. The nationalist tendencies of the majority populations in these republics was almost certainly one of the weightiest considerations that led their Jews to opt for emigration. In the Ukraine, one should add the fear concerning long-term effects of the Chernobyl nuclear disaster.

The republics with the lowest rate of Jewish emigration were Kazakstan, Estonia, Russia, Turkmenistan and Georgia. Interestingly enough, the Russian republic, which is the scene of the most virulent anti-Semitism anywhere in the USSR, had a rate of Jewish emigration just slightly higher than one-half of the national average. There were differences between the major cities of this vast republic. Whereas the rate for Leningrad (now St Petersburg) almost reached the national average, that for Moscow was much lower.

The wave of mass emigration, which continues even after the disbandment of the USSR, albeit at a lower level of intensity, poses new challenges for Israel and world Jewry. It also has far-reaching implications for the Jewish community in the former USSR. Many of its most active members (those relatively young in age, having initiative and more easily able to adapt to new conditions) – and perhaps also those with a more highly developed Jewish national consciousness – have left or are in the process of leaving. Their emigration has raised the age level of the Jewish community in the former Soviet republics and has also greatly affected the extent of cultural activity.

Throughout the Gorbachev period (1985–91), especially during its final three years, Soviet Jews underwent a process of accelerated change from every point of view. They have been able to engage in unrestricted educational, cultural and religious activity to a degree unknown since the revolution of 1917. Simultaneously, this community has participated in a wave of mass emigration from the USSR and immigration to Israel, all this against the backdrop of unstable political and social conditions at home, which have been changing at an accelerated pace. Intricate problems emerged concerning relations with the majority populations, some grounded in traditional, centuries-old anti-Semitism and others resulting from the new nationalist sentiments of ethnic groups and their aspirations for sovereignty and independence.

Under such conditions, it is not surprising that one finds diametrically opposed opinions in relation to the future of Soviet Jewry, or Russian Jewry as it is commonly called today. There are those who claimed that the history of Russian Jewry is drawing to a close. Others expressed their conviction that out of the ranks of this community, with its glorious heritage and extraordinary vitality, will arise a spiritual and cultural elite that will attract many new adherents. But even these opinions have been changing rapidly, depending on the prevalent mood in Russian society in general and among the Jews in particular. Russian Jewry stands today at a crossroads; its future will be shaped to a very great extent by increasingly unpredictable events in the new states that have arisen out of the ruins of the Soviet Union.

NOTES

1 The average number of Soviet Jews who left the USSR bearing Israeli visas during the decade from 1970 to 1980 was 24,669 per year, but during the five-year period of 1981–5 it dropped to 3,098. The lowest figure was for 1984 when only 894 exit permits were issued.

2 In order to apply for an exit permit, a Soviet citizen needed an invitation from a close relative in Israel. The authorities were well aware that a great proportion of these invitations came from fictitious relatives, but they preferred to ignore this anomaly. A central office in Israel, which collected information concerning the number of Soviet Jews contemplating emigration, handled the expedition of invitations. However, invitations were sometimes sent twice, and even three times, to the same person. Hence, the figure of 400,000 prospective emigrants was received with some scepticism within Soviet Jewry and by Jewish organizations in the West. Even the Israeli central office pointed to a sharp decline in the number of Jews who asked for invitations, from about 23,000 in 1981 to 6,000 in 1984.

3 During fifteen years (1971–85) 262,175 Jews emigrated from the Soviet Union. Some 159,671 of them, 60.9 per cent, reached Israel.

4 The following is a small and random selection of articles against emigration, all from 1985: 'Each lives and dies by himself' (Yiddish), *Birobidzhaner Shtern* (23 January); Ts. Solodar, 'Lovushka s pozolochennymi reshetkami', *Rabochaia Gazeta* (15 January); S. Fridmanis, 'Rodina odna – SSSR', *Sovetskaia Litva* (17 January); S. Ostrouszchenko, 'Lovushka prostakov', *Sotsialisticheskaia Industriia* (2 February); 'O chem givoriat pisma', *Argumenty i Fakty* (9 July); 'Dorogaia tsena prozreniia', *Rabochaia Gazeta* (23 July); 'Krakh', *Ogonek*, no. 8; La. Akshin, 'Igra v repatriantov', *Komsomolskaia Pravda* (22 October).

5 An incomplete listing shows that during the four-year period from 1981 to 1984, forty anti-Semitic and anti-Zionist books and pamphlets were published in the Ukrainian SSR alone, having a total run of about 750,000 copies. See N. Bibichkova and M. Kipnis, 'A list of Anti-Judaic and Anti-Zionist books published in the Ukrainian SSR in 1960–1984', *Jews and Jewish Topics in Soviet and East-European Publications*, nos 2–3 (June 1986), pp. 47–58.

6 See V. Konstantinov, 'Jewish population of the USSR on the eve of the Great Exodus', *Jews and Jewish Topics in the Soviet Union and Eastern Europe*, no. 3 (16) (Winter 1991). pp. 18–20.

7 'Soviet emigration activists think', (Hebrew), in D. Prital (ed.), *Yehudei Brith Ha-Moatsot*, 9 (Jerusalem, 1985), p. 140.

8 Several amendments were made to the Soviet criminal code in January 1984, increasing the kinds of act for which one could be charged with anti-Soviet activity. See *Vedemosti Verkhovnogo Sovieta*, no. 3 (1984), pp. 91–3.

9 The eight who had been tried and jailed prior to 1984 were Iosif Begun, Boris Kanevsky, Feliks Kochubievsky, Valery Senderov, Anatoly Shcharansky, Lev Shefer, Simon Shnirman and Yuri Tarnopolsky.

10 At this time, Leonid Volvovski and Roald Zalichonok were awaiting trial.

11 The following activists were charged with violating Paragraph 190–1 of the Criminal Code of the RSFSR and similar sections of the criminal codes of other republics: Yakov Levin, Zakhar Zunsheyn, Mark Nepomnyashchy and Evgeny Aizenberg.

12 The following were convicted on various criminal charges: (1) Moshe Abramov, sentenced to three years of labour in a public institution for 'wanton hooliganism'; (2) Iosef Berenshteyn, four years in prison for resisting arrest; (3) Yuly Edelshteyn was given a three-year sentence on a charge of drug possession;

(4) Nadezhda Fradkova was sentenced to two years after being found guilty of being a 'parasite'; (5) Aleksander Yakir, two years for evading conscription to the army; (6) Aleksander Kholymansky was sentenced to a year and a half for illegal possession of arms. See 'Trials of Soviet Jewish "refuseniks" and "activists", 1980–July 1985', Institute of Jewish Affairs, *Research Report*, no. 5 (September 1985).

13 M. Altshuler, 'Changes in Soviet Jewry', *Jews and Jewish Topics in the Soviet Union and Eastern Europe*, no. 2 (9) (Summer 1989), pp. 5–29.

14 This seems to be borne out by the statistics of Soviet Jewish emigrants in 1987, who included a high percentage of refuseniks from previous years. In 1987, 8,155 Jews left the Soviet Union, only 2,072 of them (25.4 per cent), reached Israel. See M. Altshuler, 'Who are the "refuseniks"? A statistical and demographic analysis', *Soviet Jewish Affairs*, 18, no. 1 (Spring 1988), pp. 3–15.

15 'Soviet emigration activists think' (above, n. 7), p. 141.

16 B. Pinkus, 'The *Hazara bitshuva* phenomenon among Russian Jews in the post-Stalin era', *Jews and Jewish Topics in the Soviet Union and Eastern Europe*, no. 2 (15) (Fall 1991), pp. 15–30; K. Lourie, 'Religious-refusenik networks in Moscow and Leningrad', ibid., pp. 31–47; I. J. Liebler, *Soviet Jewry – Report on Visit to Moscow* (September 1987).

17 On this subject see *Dvatset dva*, no. 38 (October 1984), pp. 126–67.

18 Two national organizations in the USA were active on behalf of Soviet Jewry: 'The Union of Councils for Soviet Jewry' and the 'National Conference for Soviet Jews'.

19 See the remarks of Izzie Liebler, Vice-President of the World Jewish Congress and one of the leading personalities active on behalf of Soviet Jewry. I. Liebler, 'Soviet Jewry – a turning point', *Jerusalem Post* (23 May 1985).

20 Y. Ro'i, *The Struggle for Soviet Jewish Emigration, 1948–1967* (Cambridge, 1991).

21 Only 25.7 per cent of those who left the USSR between 1981 and 1984 bearing Israeli visas emigrated to Israel. Based on the statistics supplied D. Prital (ed.), *Yehudei Brith Ha-Moatsot*, 13 (Jerusalem, 1990), p. 149.

22 'Eight Soviet Jews appeal for creation of an anti-Zionist committee', Institute of Jewish Affairs, *Research Report* (April 1983); 'Fulfilling a restricted role: the Soviet anti-Zionist committee in 1984', ibid. (December 1984); S. Ycikas, 'Soviet public anti-Zionist committees', *Jews and Jewish Topics in the Soviet Union and Eastern Europe*, no. 2 (18) (Summer 1992), pp. 40–5.

23 D. Doder and L. Bramson, *Gorbachev – Heretic in the Kremlin* (New York, 1991); I. Zemstov and D. Ferrar, *Gorbachev – Chelovek i sistema* (London, 1987).

24 N. Ryzhkov, *Perestroika: Istoriia predatel'stva* (Moscow, 1992).

25 E. Evtushenko, *Politika – privilegiia vsekh* (Moscow, 1990).

26 For a collection of appeals to Soviet and international bodies see D. Prital (ed.), *Yehudei Brith Ha-Moatsot*, 9 (Jerusalem, 1985), pp. 223–30; 10 (Jerusalem, 1987), pp. 227–367; 11 (Jerusalem, 1988), pp. 199–240.

27 See A. Romanenko, *0 klassovoi sushchnost sionizma* (Leningrad, 1986), and the critical review in the major journal devoted to the history of the CPSU: L. Dadiani, S. Mokshin and E. Tadovosian, '0 nekotorykh voprosakh istoriografii proletarskogo internatsionalizma', *Voprosii istorii KPSS* (1987), no. 1. For an analysis of these publications see L. Dymerskaya-Tsigelman, 'Party criticism of the racist interpretation of Zionism', *Jews and Jewish Topics in Soviet and East European Publications*, no. 5 (Summer 1987), pp. 3–19.

28 Based on the statistics supplied by D. Prital (ed.), *Yehudei Brith Ha-Moatsot*, 13 (Jerusalem, 1990), p. 149.

29 The Jewish 'samizdat' was almost non-existent on the eve of Gorbachev's ascendance to power, with the exception of *Leningradskii evreiskii almanakh*, which was printed in issues of about 100 copies and dealt only with cultural topics, steering clear of political subjects. In 1987, by comparison, two additional uncensored Jewish periodicals appeared in Moscow. These were *Evreiskii istoricheskii almanakh*, most of whose contributors were not veteran 'activists', and *Informatsionnyi biulletin po problemam repatriatsii i evereiskoi kultury*. The latter was a fully fledged periodical, though produced by old-fashioned techniques. It had a circulation of about 2,000 copies, and included information from all parts of the Soviet Union. M. Beizer, 'Contemporary Jewish periodicals in the USSR', *Jews and Jewish Topics in the Soviet Union and Eastern Europe*, no. 2 (12) (Fall 1990), pp. 71–2.

30 See, for example, L. Dadiani, 'What purposes are served by the Zionist slogan "dual loyalty of Jews"?' (Yiddish), *Sovyetish Heymland*, no. 4 (1986), pp. 128–30; A. Belyaev, 'Only two years . . .' (Yiddish), ibid., no. 9, pp. 97–113; no. 10, pp. 49–71; no. 11, pp. 100–30.

31 Quoted in *Pravda* (8 February 1986). One of Gorbachev's closest advisers, too, considered both Zionism and anti-Semitism to be among the most negative expressions of chauvinistic nationalism. A. Iakovlev, *Muki prochteniia bytiia* (Moscow, 1991), p. 13.

32 Ch. Shmeruk, 'Twenty-five years of *Sovetish Heymland*: impressions and criticism', in Y. Ro'i and A. Beker (eds), *Jewish Culture and Identity in the Soviet Union* (New York, 1991), pp. 191–207. See also *Sovyetish Heymland*, no. 11 (1986), pp. 56–83, and no. 3 (1987), pp. 102–12. Issue no. 7 for 1987 was also devoted to young writers.

33 L. Hirszowicz, 'The Twenty-seventh Congress of the CPSU', *Soviet Jewish Affairs*, no. 2 (1986), pp. 6–9; R. Wistrich, '"Glasnost" and the Jews' (Hebrew), in D. Prital (ed.), *Yehudei Brith Ha-Moatsot*, 12 (Jerusalem, 1989), pp. 40–5.

34 During a visit to the Hebrew University of Jerusalem in 1992, Alexander Iakovlev was asked why, during the early years of the Gorbachev era, the Soviet authorities ignored the ethnic problem in the USSR. He said that since the leaders of all republics repeatedly stressed their loyalty to the USSR, the central authorities did not realize just how acute the problem was.

35 V. Artunian and L. Robizhev, *Mnogoobrazie kul'turnoi zhizni narodov SSSR* (Moscow, 1987), p. 278.

36 G. Starovoitova, *Etnicheskaia gruppa v sovremennom sovetskom gorode* (Leningrad, 1987), p. 149.

37 *Pravda* (5 July, 1988).

38 V. Chernin, 'In a propitious hour – "Mazal Tov"' (Yiddish), *Birobidzhaner Shtern* (21 October 1988).

39 For Jewish theatrical activity during 1988–9 see *Birobidzhaner Shtern* (6 March; 9, 30 April; 1, 4, 15, 20 May; 5, 17 July; 23 November and 13 December 1988); 'The birth of a new Yiddish troupe' (Yiddish), *Sovyetish Heymland* (1988), no. 9, pp. 157–9; no. 12, p. 151; (1989), no. 4, p. 83.

40 W. C. Clemens, *Baltic Independence and Russian Empire* (New York, 1991); J. Vollmer and T. Zulch, *Aufstand der Opfer: Verratene Völker zwischen Hitler und Stalin* (Hannover, 1989), pp. 198–228; M. Butenschon, *Estland, Lettland, Litauen: das Baltikum auf dem Weg in die Freiheit* (München, 1992).

41 *Sovyetish Heymland* (1988), no. 10, p. 159; no. 12, p. 90; (1989), no. 6, pp. 57, 119; no. 9, p. 65.

42 *Folks-shtime* (10 June 1988).

43 D. Prital (ed.), *Yehudei Brith Ha-Moatsot*, 12 (Jerusalem, 1989), pp. 203–8.

44 Ibid., pp. 209–21.

45 A. Vergelis, 'Prognosis for the twenty-first century' (Yiddish) *Sovyetish Heymland* (1988), no. 7, pp. 114–23; 'National Readers' Conference of Sovyetish Heymland' (Yiddish), ibid. (1990), no. 1, pp. 16–30; no. 2, pp. 5–6; no. 5, pp. 144–7; no. 7, p. 85; *Perestroikas i evreiskii vopros* (Moscow, 1989), pp. 10–13.

46 For the 'Round Table' conference, held in May 1989 with representatives from forty-nine Jewish organizations, see *VEK*, no. [2], (1990), pp. 1–5; and also *Informatsionnyi biulleten po voprosam repatriatsii i evreiskoi kul'tury* (1989), no. 8 (31), p. 9; no. 9 (32), pp. 4, 49; no. 11 (34), p. 9; nos. 12–13 (35–6). p. 8.

47 For the establishment of the all-Soviet Jewish organization see ibid. (1990), nos. 2–3 (38–9), p. 61 and also D. Prital (ed.), *Yehudei Brith Ha-Moatsot*, 13 (Jerusalem, 1990), pp. 150–6.

48 During 1990 and 1991 about ninety Jewish newspapers and periodicals were published. M. Beizer, 'Jewish periodicals in the USSR, 1990–1991', *Jews and Jewish Topics in the Soviet Union and Eastern Europe*, no. 3 (19) (Winter 1992), pp. 62–77.

49 *Natsional'nyi sostav naseleniia SSSR* (Moscow, 1991).

50 *Nasaeleni SSSR, 1988* (Moscow, 1989).

51 For the Jewish contribution to Russian culture during the Soviet period see J. Miller (ed.), *Jews in Soviet Culture* (London, 1984).

52 Chapters of Chivilikhin's novel appeared in the periodical *Nash sovremennik*, which as early as the 1970s had attracted authors with Russian nationalist tendencies. This was during the celebrations marking the 600th anniversary of the Russian victory over the Tatars and Mongolians (*Kulikovskaia bitva*). Part II was also published in 1982 in *Roman gazeta*, which had a circulation of 2.5 million copies, the very year in which both parts were published in a first printing of 150.000 copies and Chivilikhin was presented with a government literary award. In 1983, a year after the novel was published in book form, *Nash sovremennik* – with a circulation of 200,000 – published further excerpts. All in all, this book, or parts of it, were distributed in about 6.5 million copies, a tremendous number by any standard.

53 Responding to the widespread ardour for the preservation of historic monuments, the 'Organization for the Preservation of Historic Monuments and Places' was established in the late 1960s under the leadership of Lev Korelev. This society, with a membership of about 10.5 million, was an all-Soviet organization and thus did not meet the nationalist interests of the Russians, so that specific circles which emphasized Russian nationalism soon developed within it. See *Insight* (July 1987), pp. 4–5.

54 See 'A meeting of the historical and literary association "Pamiat"', *Jews and Jewish Topics in the Soviet Union and Eastern Europe*, no. 5 (Summer 1987), pp. 51–4. For Pamiat activities in Leningrad see M. Beizer, 'The situation in Leningrad today', ibid., pp. 54–7. See also H. Spaier, 'Soviet antisemitism unchained: the rise of the "Historical and Patriotic Association 'Pamiat'"', Institute of Jewish Affairs, *Research Report*, no. 3 (July 1987).

55 Yeltsin's meeting with representatives of 'Pamiat' has been widely discussed and analysed. See *Moscow News* (17 May 1987); V. Solov'ev and E. Klepikova, *Boris Eltsin* (Moscow, 1992), pp. 58–67.

56 This was most clearly evident when Dimitri Vasil'ev became the leader of Pamiat and when that organization changed its name from 'Historical and Literary Society' first to 'The Patriotic Union Pamiat' and later, in May 1988, to 'The National-Patriotic Front Pamiat'. See *Informatsionnyi biulletin po problemam repatriatsii i evreiskoi kultury*, no. 4 (1987), p. 15; '"Pamiat" kak ona est', *Soglasie*, no. 4 (14 March 1989).

57 For the various splinter-groups of Pamiat see *Khronograf,* no. 30 (15 September 1989), pp. 2–3; *Konsensus,* no. 13 (6 November 1990), pp. 1–2; *Novaia zhizn,* no. 6 (15) (March 1990); *Panorama,* no. 3 (February 1990) and no. 8 (July 1990); *Novaia ganzenskaia gazeta,* no. 4 (August 1990); *Karetnyi riad,* no. 15 (44) (August 1991); *Situatsia,* no. 6 (September 1990); *Soglasie,* no. 4 (14 March 1989); *Daidzhest,* no. 14 (21) (1990); *Admoda* (April 1990); *Izmailovskii vestnik,* no. I (1990).

58 In December 1984, R. Zelichonok published an open letter to author Vasili Belov, in the pages of the semi-clandestine Jewish periodical *Leningradskii evreskii almanakh,* in which he criticized Belov because of the anti-Semitic overtones of his short story 'Education according to Dr. Spock', published in 1982. See *Evreiskii samizdat,* vol. 27 (Jerusalem, 1992), pp. 64–6. In 1986 Edelman wrote an open letter to Astafe'ev expressing astonishment at the anti-Semitic elements in his story *All is Ahead of Us.* See *Jews and Jewish Topics in Soviet and East-European Publications,* no. 5 (Summer 1987), pp. 32–4.

59 Evidence of the wide circulation of this exchange of letters is the fact that it was even mentioned in an article in *Pravda,* at the time still the most important official newspaper. See A. Mikhailov, 'Pozitsiia i ambitsii', *Pravda* (30 January 1987).

60 *Strana i Mir* (1986), no. 12.

61 Vasili Belov, *Vse v peredi* (Moscow, 1987).

62 I. Shafarevich, *Rusofobiia i dve dorogi k odnomu ovragu* (Moscow, 1991).

63 *Voprosy literatury* (1986), no. 11.

64 Based on *Natsional'nyi sostav naseleniia SSSR* (Moscow, 1991); V. Konstantinov, 'Jewish population of the USSR on the eve of the Great Exodus', *Jews and Jewish Topics in the Soviet Union and Eastern Europe,* no. 3 (16) (Winter 1991) pp. 5–23.

65 On the Jewish vote for Ukrainian independence see E. Golovakha and N. Panina, 'Jewish cultural activity in the Ukraine: public opinions and the attitudes of local authorities', *Jews and Jewish Topics in the Soviet Union and Eastern Europe,* no. 2 (18) (Summer 1992), pp. 5–12.

66 'Protiv Antisemitisma (Rezoliutsia uchreditel'nogo s'ezda RUKHa)', *Informatsionnyi biulleten po voprosam repatriastsii evreiskoi kul'tury* (1988), no. 16, pp. 48–9; *Molodii natsionalist,* no. 1 (July 1990). An organization called 'The Anti-chauvinist Action' issued a call to combat anti-Semitism. See *Ekspres Novini,* no. 11 (March 1990). In February 1990, *Rukh* urged the Ukrainian public to ignore broadsheets calling for pogroms against Jews and Azaris, ibid. (February 1990). The views of part of the Ukrainian intelligentsia concerning Jews were expressed at a conference on 'Relations between Jews and Ukrainians' held in Kiev in June 1991. See *Svit,* nos. 3–4 (1991), and Ludmila Tsigelman, 'Sovereign Ukraine and the Jews' (Hebrew), in D. Prital (ed.), *Yehudei Brith Ha-Moatsot,* 15 (Jerusalem 1992), pp. 71–83.

67 For articles which uncritically praise the Ukrainian national movement during the Second World War without mentioning its fascist and pro-Nazi aspects and utterly disregarding its relationship to the Jews, see 'Chim byla UPA v nashikh vizvol'nykh zmaganniakh', *Postup,* no. 6 (23) (April 1990); 'OUN', *Krok,* no. 9 [1990?]; S. Bandera, 'z istorii OUN i UPA', *Moloda Ukraina,* nos. 3–4 (1990); 'Do pitannia istorii OUN i UPA', *Dzvin,* no. 2 (5) (February 1990). See also: *Poklik Voli* (1990); M. P., 'Strakh Pered Istorichnoiu Pravdoiu', *Suchasnist* (1989), no. 4, pp. 90–9.

68 Based on *Natsional'nyi sostav naseleniia SSSR* (Moscow, 1991); V. Konstantinov, 'Jewish population of the USSR on the eve of the Great Exodus', *Jews and Jewish Topics in the Soviet Union and Eastern Europe,* no. 3 (16) (Winter 1991), pp. 5–23.

229

69 See 'Doklad La. Petersa na uchreditel'nom sezde narodnogo fronta Latvii', *Sovetskaia Latvia* (11 October 1988); 'Programma Litovskogo dvizheniia za perestroiku po natsional'nomu voprosu', *Sovetskaia Litva* (11 October 1988); G. Kobetskaite, '"National" noe menshenstvot pravo na samobytnost' *Vilnius* (1991), no. 11, pp. 3–14.

70 A. Shvelnis. Deputy Director-General of the Lithuanian Department for Ethnic Affairs, said in May 1991: 'Lithuanian Jews were almost the first to realize [what was happening] and supported the Lithuanians' aspirations for independence.' M. Erenburg, 'Sotvorenie legendy', *Golos Litvy* (29 May 1991).

71 For such a view of the Russians, see Lu. Kuuskemaa, 'Pribaltam – ravnye s palestintsami prava', *Novaia ganzeiskaia gazeta*, no. 3 (July 1990); A. Tukhkamen, 'My ili oni', *Daidzhest Materialy estonskoi pressy*, no. 11 (18) (1990).

72 See: 'Vil'niuskie evrei v istorii Litvy', *Sovestskaia Litva* (30 November 1989).

73 'Dolgi put'k normal'noi zhizni', *Baltiiskoe vremia* (4 June 1990).

74 *Ha-Aretz* (6 September 1991) (Hebrew); *Yediot Aharonot* (13 September 1991) (Hebrew).

75 See the articles signed by K. Lakickas (*Kauno Tiesa*, 11 December 1991), N. Paulaskas (*Gimtasis Krastas*, 25 July 1991), P. Stankeris (*Lietuvos Aidas*, 1 January 1992), V. Anulionis (*Panevezio Balsas*, 21 November 1991) and A. Smailys (*Kauno Aidas*, 4 December 1991). I am indebted to Professor Dov Levin who placed summaries of the Lithuanian press at my disposal. See also S. Ycikas, 'Lithuanian–Jewish relationships in the shadow of the Holocaust', *Jews and Jewish Topics in the Soviet Union and Eastern Europe*, no. 1 (11) (Spring 1990), pp. 33–66.

76 Based on the sources cited above, n. 68.

77 *Problemy otkaza v vyezd iz strany*, no. 3 (May 1988), p. 66.

78 Ibid., pp. 50–2.

79 Y. Florsheim, 'Emigration of Jews from the Soviet Union in 1988', *Jews and Jewish Topics in the Soviet Union and Eastern Europe*, no. 2 (9) (Summer 1989), pp. 30–9.

80 Y. Florsheim, 'Emigration of Jews from the Soviet Union in 1989', *Jews and Jewish Topics in the Soviet Union and Eastern Europe*, no. 2 (12) (Fall 1990), pp. 22–31.

81 Y. Florsheim, 'Emigration of Jews from the Soviet Union in 1990', *Jews and Jewish Topics in the Soviet Union and Eastern Europe*, no. 2 (15) (Fall 1991), pp. 5–14.

10

ETHNICITY AND THE JEWISH VOTE

The French case

Dominique Schnapper and Sylvie Strudel

The notion of a 'Jewish vote', used commonly in ordinary life as well as in many scientific works, is often inexact and ambiguous. It was developed in the United States for the American case, and before it can be applied to another country, it is important to discuss it critically. Indeed, it is not enough to say that, as citizens of different countries of the free Diaspora, the Jews vote in order for there to be a 'Jewish vote'. The 'Jewish vote' is not simply the vote of the Jews. The idea implied in the notion is that the Jewish vote has an *effect* on political life.

In all liberal democracies, the Jews represent a small minority. In France and in Argentina they make up for about 1 per cent of the population and less than 3 per cent in the United States, to take the example of the largest Jewries. In consequence, it becomes clear that there cannot be a 'Jewish vote', that is, a specific political effect due to the voting behaviour of the Jews, unless certain conditions are met.

THE CONDITIONS OF THE 'JEWISH VOTE'

When scattered between different candidates, a small number of votes can have no effect on the results. The first condition for there to be a 'Jewish vote' is that a strong majority emerge within the Jewish electorate. This is the case in the United States, where, according to S. M. Lipset's recent work, 80 per cent of the Jews continue to vote for the Democratic Party, even though they now belong to social categories where the majority vote for the Republicans.

However, given the small number of Jews, the concentration of the votes on the same party or on a single candidate is not enough. There must also be sufficient geographic concentration so that the small electorate's weight can be felt at the constituency level.

Finally, the ballot and the electoral system must be so organized as to confer a decisive role to certain districts. We know that this is again the case in the United States, where the East Coast states have, for historical reasons, a particularly prominent role related to the American nation's constitution. Whereas the President of the United States must obtain 270 electoral college votes in order to be elected, the six states of New York, New Jersey, Illinois, Ohio, Pennsylvania and California count 181 presidential electors, i.e., more than two-thirds of the total necessary in order to assure the election. Seeing that 70 per cent of the Jews, whose rate of voting turnout is higher than the other ethnic groups, live in these states, they acquire an electoral weight that is disproportionate to their number. For example, their role in the very close election of President Kennedy could have appeared to be a decisive one.[1]

The concentration of Jewish votes on the same candidate or on the same party; the grouping together of Jews in certain districts; and the particular role given to these districts by the political system: it must be stressed that it is only if these three conditions are met *at the same time* that there can be a 'Jewish vote'. That is, moreover, the reason why the American 'Jewish vote' is fragile: if only one of these conditions was not met – if, for example, the Jewish population spread out throughout the American territory – that would be enough for it to no longer exist.

'ETHNIC GROUPS' AND THE CONSTITUTION OF THE NATION

In so far as it is a particular case of the 'ethnic vote', the 'Jewish vote' cannot be disassociated from the 'ethnic vote' in its entirety. An essential methodological rule of the study of contemporary Jewries in the Diaspora must always be respected: never isolate the case of the Jews from the national situation which gives it meaning: the Jews constitute part of a national society.

The very notion of 'ethnic group', developed in the society and sociology of the United States, is tied to the specificity of the American experience. The 'ethnic vote', by definition, only makes sense in countries that admit and recognize both the social existence and political expression of particular groups or communities as defined by their national, religious or racial origin (or a combination of these factors). This is the case of the United States, land of immigration, founded on the one hand on the common adhesion to the Constitution and to political institutions and, on the other, on the social recognition of 'communities', who share the same national and/or religious origin and the same culture. These 'communities', recognized on the social level, also intervene in political life in the form of 'ethnic groups', defined by their will for collective action. These 'ethnic groups' openly defend the interests of their members in American life. The Greek, Turkish or Jewish *lobbies*, officially seated in their Washington offices, intervene as such in the definition of American domestic and foreign politics. Under the condition that they respect the legal, institutional and ideological American context, it seems normal for the Jews, as for the Indians (natives of the Indian Union), or Greeks, when it concerns their country of origin, to participate through their efforts in the definition of American politics in favour of the State of Israel.[2] The 'Jewish vote', both real and avowed, used in the battles of American democracy, intervenes as one of the normal expressions of social and political life, by the same right as the black vote, the Greek vote, etc., because the Jewish, black or Greek 'ethnic groups' are constituent elements in the way American democracy functions.

This is not true of the old European nations. France, from this point of view, is an exemplary case. More than any other European country, France tends, *par excellence*, towards the nation-state: the confusion of political and cultural unity is driven as far as possible. French political tradition, whose origins go back far earlier than the Revolution, to the history of the nation's constitution set up around the monarchy, rejects any 'ethnic' dimension. The citizen of the Republic abstractly defines himself through an ensemble of rights and duties. There are no intermediary groups with a recognized and accepted political existence. Particular religious, national or regional identities can and should only be expressed in the private domain: the public realm does not acknowledge them. In school, in companies, in unions, in the occupation of the urban space, French politics has always refused to take the 'ethnic' dimension into account. Furthermore, there are only very few examples of the grouping together of the Jewish population. The Parisian neighbourhood of the Rue des Rosiers, a symbol of the Jewish presence in an urban neighbourhood, is comprised of about 25 per cent Jews. This is also the case of the 'Jewish neighbourhoods' of Strasburg that we will look at later. The only exceptions involve the two new cities of the Parisian suburbs, Créteil and Sarcelles, where the Jewish population reaches up to 38 per cent (from a polling station of Sarcelles). Areas reserved for a national or religious 'community' do not exist in European cities, and in any case, not in French cities, because France ignores ethnic identities and, even more so, 'ethnic groups', which belong in the private domain.[3]

That is why acknowledgement of political representation of 'national' groups as such has always been, and still is, rejected. The 'second generations', natives of Poland, Italy, Portugal or of the Maghreb countries, who have become French citizens, are active within the existing political parties. They have never created a party nor political or union-type organizations in order to defend their specific interests in political life. The 'SOS-Racisme' movement does not defend one group. It militates in the name of general principles ('anti-racism' or equal opportunities) and its activities are intimately related to those of the Socialist Party. The 'France-Plus' association, made up primarily of French citizens with origins in the Maghreb countries, see that those who are called *beurs* (young French whose parents migrated to France from the Maghreb countries) take part in French political life like other citizens: they ensure they are registered on ballot lists, fight for electoral participation and the presence of *beurs* in the political parties. French citizens of Polish origin react perhaps more strongly to political events in Poland, yet it is unimaginable for them to express themselves as such, and even less so for them to try to secure a specific action from the French government on behalf of their native country. Emigrant associations have a cultural and philanthropic role, as well as one of identification – they do not intervene on the political level. A tradition that does not acknowledge particular groups as such, forbids *political* expression of ethnic specificities. The 'Jewish vote', if it existed, would constitute a break with political tradition and would ignite feelings of shock.

THE 'JEWISH VOTE' IN FRANCE

If we go back to the problem of the 'Jewish vote', we must ask a twofold question: (1) Is the electoral system likely, in the way it is organized, to give political weight to a small number of voters disproportionate to its size? (2) Do the Jews vote as a majority for one or another of the parties and its candidates? We will examine these questions based on two surveys, one carried out in Strasburg in 1983,[4] the other in 1988–9,[5] in the Parisian suburb of Sarcelles.

The choice of these two areas is justified by the way the Jewish population is composed in France. In the case of Strasburg, we are dealing with a Jewish community that has been settled for generations, even if diverse waves of immigration have renewed it: the immigrants inserted themselves within structures and institutions already rooted in local life. The community of Sarcelles, however, is new. It is made up of recent migrants, with the majority from North Africa who settled during the 1960s. The city and the area of Sarcelles are of recent construction. The comparison of the two allows us to take into consideration the intensity of religious practice, migration and the duration of presence in France.

The electoral system

It is important to distinguish two types of elections: presidential elections and diverse local elections, of which the most important are the legislative elections. Since 1965, the central element of French political life has been the election of the President of the Republic through a universal direct vote. The ensemble of the electorate makes up one single college. The Jews represent, in accordance with their number, 1 per cent of the electorate (approximately 300,000 voters). Voting turnout being high in France, the Jews, even if they vote in large numbers, do not vote more than others. They therefore correspond to their mathematical weight. If we take an extreme hypothesis and say that 80 per cent of them vote for the same candidate on the second round (when only two candidates remain on the lists), 240,000 people would vote for candidate A and 60,000 for candidate B – a difference of 180,000 votes. Arithmetically, we can therefore assume that if the difference of votes between candidates A and B was inferior to 180,000 votes in favour of candidate A, the vote of the Jews, if pronounced in favour of candidate B, could have a decisive role.

But this arithmetic possibility remains abstract for three reasons: (1) the difference of votes in the closest elections has been at the smallest (1974) 424,599 votes, and more than 1 million in 1981 and more than 2 million in 1988; (2) the Jews do not massively choose one of the two candidates or one of the two parties; (3) the Jewish vote does not go in a contrary direction to the movements of the whole, but slightly accentuates it given the small number of Jews.

Concerning the results in local elections, the possibilities of a Jewish vote are even slighter, except for two or three exceptions. Because 'ethnic groups' are not recognized, as we have stated, 'ethnic neighbourhoods' do not exist. Scattered in geographical space, the Jews, even if they massively voted for one of the candidates, could not have an effect on the results. It is only in the case of dense concentration, like in the Rue des Rosiers, in certain Strasburg areas (25 per cent Jews in one polling station) and especially in Sarcelles (38 per cent), and of a hypothetically massive vote in favour of one of the candidates, that the Jews could have an effect on the electoral results on the local level.

Let us take an example to illustrate this proposition, the case of Thionville.[6] The sources of the organized community register 350 homes, which corresponds to an approximate potential of 1,000 voters, or 800 expressed votes. However, these votes are divided in two voting districts, West Thionville and East Thionville. In the first, during the legislative elections of 1978, the Communist deputy was re-elected with 39,233 votes against 26,317 for his UDF rival; in the second, on the contrary, the UDF deputy was re-elected with 36,308 votes against 27,219 for the Communist candidate. It is easy to establish that the 800 Jewish votes, whatever their division between the two districts, even if they had voted massively for one or the other candidate, would have had no effect on the results. The local exceptions can only be exceptional (two or three).

If we can consider it proven that there is no 'Jewish vote', the voting behaviour of the Jews – as individual citizens, independent of a collective effect of their vote – remains to be examined.

The vote of the Jews

It is not easy to study how the French Jews vote. The clarification of the methodological difficulties is not a simple academic exercise. It is intimately related to the Jewish condition in France. There are major difficulties, well known by demographers, in localizing Jews within the national population.[7]

Sources of national statistics, particularly the census surveys from 1872 (requested by a Jew), do not ask for religion because of the separation of the church and the state and of the rigorously applied principle of *laïcité* (laicism). Even more so, 'ethnic identification', which does not have an acknowledged existence, is not requested. Statistical data are also a product of social life. France is founded on the constitution of a population unified by a political will and citizenship/nationality. Thus, everything within national statistics is done so that distinctions cannot be made among the French between diverse religious or national origins within the population of French citizens.[8]

Unlike other countries, where the majority of the Jewish population is organized, it is not possible to use Jewish sources since only a small number of Jews belong to an organization, be it consistorial, cultural or political. It is estimated, and this is only an approximation, that one-quarter, at the most one-third, of the Jews have some kind of rapport with a Jewish organization. Any survey based on Jewish sources would end up overestimating the most aware and active part of the population and would bring in a systematic bias.

These apparently technical difficulties are intimately related to the very definition of the Jewish population, which in France today is not defined by any objective and measurable character, but by a personal declaration of identity that statistical tools do not easily grasp. Since there is neither a legal nor a religious definition of the Jews, one does not 'belong' to a Jewish population. From the sociological standpoint, it is not the number of Jewish grandparents that sets the majority of the Jews apart from the non-Jews, but the will to continue to affirm, in one way or another, the Jewish identity of their grandparents. Hence, there is only one possible sociological definition, adopted by sociologists and demographers: Jews are those who say they are Jewish. But to make this definition operational in research is a long and difficult enterprise.

We strove to pinpoint the Jewish population in the Strasburg survey from the lists of registered voters. Voters were identified by one of the leaders of the organized community: Alsacian Judaism is, in fact, one of the most organized in France. A city in the province makes for an environment small enough so that an active member of the milieu, who has held responsible functions in the organizations of the city for a long time, can designate all those who have said they were Jewish, according to our definition, on a voting list. This way we can attain the equivalent of self-designation. This method allows us to avoid the hazards of picking names by the use of onomastics: given the diversity of the origins of Jews in France, these risks are particularly great. There was another advantage in Strasburg: the Jewish population is large enough so that in two of the polling stations the vote of the Jews could be compared to that of the non-Jews who come from the same social milieu.

In order to pinpoint the Jewish population of Sarcelles, Sylvie Strudel completed the count from the voting lists, as she did in Strasburg, with two other techniques. She took a poll at the exit of the voting stations during the second round of the presidential elections held in 1988. The Jews were identified from their response to a general question on religion.[9] The population thus localized, this survey also allowed for the precision of its relationship to Judaism through a question on the different forms of practices and adherence to the Jewish religion.[10] She then wrapped up these givens with a series of interviews among the Jewish population.

It is indeed essential to start from the objective fact that the Jewish population in France is extremely heterogeneous. French Jews differ by their national origins. Some are of French origin that goes back generations. Others descend from the Ashkenazim who arrived in the periods between 1880 and 1914 or between the two world wars. The Sephardic Jews arrived *en masse* from North Africa in the 1950s and 1960s. Even though the relationship between the Ashkenazim and the Sephardim is not full of strong tensions, it is certain that origin is a major factor of differentiation. The Jews also differ in their occupations. The massive migration from North Africa brought the social differentiation population closer to the whole of the national population by increasing the numbers of the whole of the lower-income population of workers and employees in such a way that the Jews belong to all social groups. Finally, they differ in their relation with Judaism. Some, a growing minority, or 'practising' Jews, uphold the rules of Jewish tradition more or less strictly. The majority, or 'militants', concentrate the expression of its Jewishness on its relationship with Israel. Some 'assimilated Jews', who have renounced religious practices or social solidarity, none the less maintain a feeling of identity essentially founded on the claim to belong to a community of fate.[11]

To appreciate the specificity of the Jewish vote, one must simultaneously take into account: (1) occupation; (2) the date of settling/migration; (3) the relationship with Judaism. The Strasburg survey brought a first response concerning the effect of occupation, the Sarcelles survey on the effect of the other two variables.

THE STRASBURG SURVEY OR THE VOTE OF THE ESTABLISHED JEWS

The survey permitted the comparison of the vote of the Jews with the vote of the non-Jews *belonging to the same social milieux.* To do this, we compared the ballot results of four polling stations, chosen according to the following thinking: (a) two polling stations of upper-class composition (wealthy and established 'haute bourgeoisie'), including one (bureau 403) with about 24 per cent Jews and the other (bureau 410) with between 4 and 5 per cent Jews; (b) two polling stations of less elevated social composition ('petite bourgeoisie', storekeepers, employees), including one (bureau 109) with about 24 per cent Jews and the other (bureau 110) with about 9 per cent Jews.

The results of this comparison permitted the following conclusions: (1) The abstention rate of the Jews is very slightly inferior to that of non-Jews within the same polling station, i.e. 13.4 per cent against 14.8 per cent. One can conclude that Jewish voting turnout is very slightly higher than that of the non-Jewish population. Chantal Benayoun obtained similar results in her survey of the community of Toulouse.[12] (2) The effect of occupation is preponderant in all types of elections. The votes of the Jews and the non-Jews are identical or very close in the socially homogeneous polling stations (bureaus 403 and 410 on one hand; 109 and 110 on the other). In consequence, if one compares socially different polling stations (bureaus 403 and 109), but includes the same proportion of the Jewish population, the votes differ. During the elections to the European Parliament, Simone Veil's list obtained 48.5 per cent in bureau 403 and 41.6 per cent in bureau 109, which are made up of the same proportion of Jews: she obtained the same percentage of votes in the polling stations of the same social level: 48.5 and 46 per cent in bureaus 403 and 410, respectively; 41.6 and 41.5 per cent in bureaus 109 and 110, respectively (see Table 10.1). We have voluntarily brought up the example of Madame Veil's list, since she herself is Jewish and particularly popular among Jews as well as non-Jews, which demonstrates how little the Jewish dimension influences the results. Even if, of course, the social homogeneity of the neighbourhood does not authorize a comparison as rigorous as the comparison of populations classified according to their socio-professional group, the occupation appears as determinant (see Tables 10.2 to 10.6). In Strasburg, the firmly established Jews vote like the non-Jews who belong to the same social groups.

THE SARCELLES SURVEY OR THE VOTE OF THE RECENTLY MIGRATED JEWS

The Sarcelles survey permitted an analysis of the vote of a very different population: 74 per cent of the Jews polled were born outside France, 47 per cent of which were born in Tunisia, 15 per cent in Algeria, 9 per cent in Morocco and 3 per cent in other foreign countries. In spite of the differences of method, the comparison of the results of the two surveys allows for the measuring of the effect of *migration* on political attitudes and behaviours. It also measures the effect of the *intensity of Jewish religious practices*, since the question on practices permits the differentiation within the population of those who 'practise regularly' (30 per cent),[13] 'practise irregularly' (38 per cent), [14] 'practise at Yom Kippur' (11 per cent),[15] and the 'non-practising' (18 per cent)[16] and 'detached' (3 per cent).[17]

Table 10.1 European Parliament elections, 10 June 1979 (Strasburg) (per cent)

	Mitterrand	Hallier	Marchais	Laguiller	Fernex	Veil	Servan-Schreiber	Chirac Debré	Poujade Malaud	Bouchardeau	Tixier-Vignancour
Bureau 403: Jewish population of 23.5% to 24.5%	14.3	0	1.4	1.0	12.1	48.5	5.2	14.8	0.9	0	1.8
Bureau 410: Jewish population of 4% to 5%	14.2	0	2.0	2.5	12.7	46.2	4.1	15.3	0.5	0	2.5
Bureau 109: Jewish population of 23.5% to 24.5%	21.5	0	4.2	1.9	12.2	41.6	3.2	13.0	0.8	0	1.6
Bureau 110: Jewish population of 8.5% to 9.5%	20.2	0	4.3	2.3	12.2	41.5	4.5	11.2	1.0	0	2.8

Table 10.2 Presidential election, first round, 26 April 1981 (Strasburg) (per cent)

	Laguiller	Garaud	Crépeau	Bouchardeau	Lalonde	Mitterand	Giscard	Marchais	Debré	Chirac
Bureau 403: Jewish population of 23.5% to 24.5%	0.3	2.8	1.2	1.8	5.1	20.7	37.5	1.6	2.5	26.5
Bureau 410: Jewish population of 4% to 5%	0.8	3.3	2.8	2.0	5.6	20.0	38.7	2.1	3.5	21.2
Bureau 109: Jewish population of 23.5% to 24.5%	1.8	2.0	4.0	2.9	5.6	31.0	33.0	2.0	1.7	16.0
Bureau 110: Jewish population of 8.5% to 9.5%	1.2	1.6	3.5	2.4	7.5	25.1	34.8	2.6	2.0	19.3

Table 10.3 Presidential election, second round, 10 May 1981 (Strasburg)
(per cent)

	Mitterand	Giscard d'Estang
Bureau 403: Jewish population of 23.5% to 24.5%	32.9	67.1
Bureau 410: Jewish population of 4% to 5%	31.9	68.1
Bureau 109: Jewish population of 23.5% to 24.5%	44.9	55.1
Bureau 110: Jewish population of 8.5% to 9.5%	42.8	57.2

Unlike in Strasburg, where occupation is the variable that explains, for the most part, the votes, a specificity of votes of the Jews is found in Sarcelles. Greater numbers, in fact, vote for leftist candidates than non-Jews who belong to the same socio-professional groups (see Table 10.7). It should be noted that this entails a vote in favour of the moderate left and that it goes hand in hand with a strong refusal to vote for the candidate from the extreme left, particularly the Communist Party candidate (see Table 10.8).

How can these votes be interpreted? The Jews who voted for François Mitterrand during the second round of the presidential elections were asked to position themselves on the left–right axis.[18] Twenty-five per cent placed themselves in the 'centre', 40 per cent as 'centre-left' and only 24 per cent to the 'left'. The other voters of François Mitterrand placed themselves in lesser numbers in the 'centre' and the 'centre-left' (47 per cent Catholic and 35 per cent 'with no religion'. They were more numerous in placing themselves to the 'left' (36 per cent Catholic and 54 per cent 'with no religion') (see Table 10.9). As Mitterrand and the Socialist Party have been in power for about the last ten years, we are talking about a vote that is essentially centrist. In a local election, two-thirds of them preferred to vote for a candidate from the right than for the Union of the Left candidate, a member of the Communist Party.

Whereas, the intensity of religious practice among Catholics can be correlated with a vote to the right,[19] the same correlation concerning the Jews of Sarcelles cannot be found. On the contrary, the more intense their religious practice the more they vote for the leftist candidate: 91 per cent of those who practise regularly, 87 per cent of those who practise irregularly, 84 per cent of those who practise at 'Kippur', 80 per cent non-practising declared having voted for François Mitterrand during the second round of the 1988 presidential elections (see Table 10.10). Those who practise regularly also reject the candidates of the extreme left and of the Communist Party more sharply than the others.

The Strasburg survey, which shows a rate of voting that turns out to be very slightly higher than that of the non-Jews, along with Chantal Benayoun's results, led us to conclude that the Jews have a strong political consciousness. This hypothesis was encouraged by the well-known results of the high voting turnout of the American Jews. One might think that the

Table 10.4 General election, first round, 14 June 1981 (Strasburg) (per cent)

	Rennemann (Independent)	Hornus (PSU)	Olivier Utard (PC)	Ries (PS)	Joseph (Ecology)	Koehl (UDF)	Bilger (Independent)	Meyer (Independent)	Liger (PFN)	Zind (MPA)
Bureau 403: Jewish population of 23.5% to 24.5%	0.5	1.6	2.5	22.7	5.8	38.7	27.1	0.8	0	0.3
Bureau 410: Jewish population of 4% to 5%	0.6	1.3	2.3	23.1	5.5	43.7	22.8	0.2	0	0.5
Bureau 109: Jewish population of 23.5% to 24.5%	0.6	1.5	3.3	38.2	4.5	38.3	13.2	0.2	0	0.2
Bureau 110: Jewish population of 8.5% to 9.5%	0.6	2.1	1.8	34.7	5.6	38.0	15.6	1.0	0	0.6

Table 10.5 General election, second round, 21 June 1981 (Strasburg) (per cent)

	Koehl (UDF)	Ries (PS)
Bureau 403: Jewish population of 23.5% to 24.5%	65.2	34.8
Bureau 410: Jewish population of 4% to 5%	65.7	34.3
Bureau 109: Jewish population of 23.5% to 24.5%	53.6	46.4
Bureau 110: Jewish population of 8.5% to 9.5%	53.7	46.3

conditions imposed on the Jews over the centuries in the Christian Western world or in the Muslim world preclude political indifference; that the imposed migration of the 1960s, the presence of genocide in the collective memory, the threatened existence of the State of Israel compelled them to place their personal destiny into a historical perspective. Furthermore, in 1983, we hypothesized that the strong political bent of the Jews led them, in the French elections, to be part of the 'unstable' or 'mobile' voters who vote for one party or another, according to the stakes and the polls (always with the exception of extremes).[20]

The Sarcelles survey shows that the high rate of voting turnout in Strasburg applies to deeply-rooted Jewish communities and *not* to Jews as a whole.[21] The participation of the recently immigrated Jews in the first round of the presidential elections is inferior to that of non-Jews by five points and equal during the second round (see Tables 10.11 and 10.12). Moreover, contrary to the hypothesis made following the Strasburg survey, Jewish voters do not appear to be particularly mobile.[22] The Jews of Sarcelles are firmly anchored to the left: whatever the election, the vote for the moderate left remains unstable, between 67 and 87 per cent depending on the type of election. The only exception concerns the already mentioned local elections where, during a partial municipal poll held in October 1993, because of the alliance between the Communist and the Socialist parties, the common list of the left was led by the outgoing mayor, a Communist Party member. Here the majority of the Jews voted for the moderate right candidate, who was not with a party (he then registered with the Jacques Chirac's Gaullist RPR).

CONCLUSION

These two surveys confirm the hypotheses made about the non-existence of a 'Jewish vote'. The vote of the Jews does not have an effect on the national electoral results. The possible effect of the vote of the Jews is limited to local elections in two or three constituencies, where the Jewish population is highly concentrated. This conclusion is obviously related to the notion of French citizenship and the absence of the 'ethnic' dimension in political life. The votes of the Jews appear like those of all French citizens closely tied to, though not being determined as much, by their occupation and education.

Table 10.6 Borough elections, 6 March 1983 (Strasburg) (per cent)

	Oehler (PS)	Bord (RPR diss.)	Monschenross (Independent)	Rudloff (UDF-RPR)	Dreysse (autogest.)	Reyer (Extreme Left)	Peter (Ecology)
Bureau 403:	14.5	10.2	1.8	66.4	1.9	0.2	5.0
Bureau 410:	19.3	10.4	1.9	61.4	1.8	0.3	4.9
Bureau 109:	22.6	7.7	1.6	57.7	3.0	1.2	6.2
Bureau 110:	20.7	8.2	2.7	55.1	4.5	1.3	7.5

Table 10.7 Vote in favour of François Mitterand in the second round of the 1988 Presidential election, by occupation and religion (Sarcelles) (percentages followed by actual numbers in brackets)*

	Jews	Catholics	No religion	Total
Farmers	–	–	–	–
Storekeepers and craftsmen	77% (39)	50% (10)	71% (7)	71% (61)
Intelligentsia and entrepreneurs	80% (88)	63% (51)	96% (25)	76%(178)
Intermediary professions	98% (55)	63% (71)	88% (26)	80%(160)
Employees	93% (31)	68% (98)	85% (26)	78%(169)
Blue-collar workers	100% (6)	84% (31)	100% (9)	87% (52)
No professional activity	85%(154)	43%(129)	78% (58)	68%(364)
Total	86%(373)	59%(390)	85%(151)	74%(964)

* Because of the small numbers involved, results should be interpreted with caution

Even the most 'practising' French Jews, for whom Jewish identity is an essential dimension of existence, do assume other identities and other social roles, particularly in terms of political participation. The Jews do not constitute a ghetto in the concrete city space, nor in the abstract space of political life. They participate fully, as citizens, in the democratic process.

Concerning the Jewish vote, the results appear to differ depending on whether deeply rooted or recently migrated Jews are involved. In the first case, no specificity of electoral behaviour is to be found. It is true that the Jews, even the most settled, maintain a singular kind of sensibility: the awakening of identity and the renewal of affirmation of Judaism, at least in the middle and intellectual classes; a common sensibility to anti-Semitism and to all forms of racism; finally, the constant concern over the survival of the State of Israel, which unites Jews from all walks of life, irrespective of

Table 10.8 Vote in the first round of the 1988 Presidential election, by religion (Sarcelles) (percentages, with actual numbers in brackets)

	Jews	Catholics	No religion	Total
Boussel (EG)	–	–	–	–
Laguiller (EG)	1%	1%	2%	1%
Juquin (EG)	1%	3%	17%	5%
Lajoinie (PC)	2%	7%	17%	7%
Mitterrand (PS)	75%	34%	40%	51%
Total left	79%	45%	76%	64%
Waechter (Ecologist)	1%	3%	5%	2%
Barre (UDF)	6%	13%	5%	9%
Chirac (RPR)	8%	19%	6%	13%
Le Pen (FN)	1%	13%	5%	7%
Total right	15%	45%	16%	29%
Abstentions	5%	7%	3%	5%
Total	100% (373)	100% (390)	100% (151)	100% (984)

Key: EG, Extreme left; PC, Communist Party; PS, Socialist Party; UDF, Union pour la Démocratie Française; RPR, Rassemblement pour la République; FN, Front National.

Table 10.9 Autoposition on the left–right axis, by religion, among the second-round electors of François Mitterand in the 1988 Presidential election (Sarcelles) (percentages, with actual numbers in brackets)

	Catholics	Jews	No Religion	Total
Left	36%	24%	54%	34%
Centre-left	30%	40%	24%	33%
Centre	17%	25%	11%	20%
Centre-right	2%	3%	2%	2%
Right	2%	1%	-	1%
No reply	13%	7%	9%	10%
Total	100% (230)	100% (320)	100% (128)	100% (732)

Table 10.10 Vote on the second round of the 1988 Presidential election by the intensity of Jewish practices (Sarcelles) (percentages, with actual numbers in brackets)

	Mitterrand	Chirac	Blanc	Total
Regularly	91%	9%	–	100% (111)
Irregularly	87%	12%	1%	100% (143)
Kippur	84%	14%	2%	100% (43)
Non-practising	80%	17%	3%	100% (66)
Detached	(7)	(3)	(1)	(11)
Total	86%	13%	1%	100% (374)

Table 10.11 Voting turnout of the Jewish and non-Jewish population in the first
round of the 1988 Presidential election (Sarcelles)
(percentages, with actual numbers in brackets)

	Participation	*Abstention*	*Total*
Jewish population	76%	24%	100% (632)
Non-Jewish population	81%	19%	100% (1020)
No information	(10)	(1)	(11)
Total	79%	21%	100% (1663)

Table 10.12 Voting turnout of the Jewish and non-Jewish population in the
second round of the 1988 Presidential election (Sarcelles)
(percentages, with actual numbers in brackets)

	Participation	*Abstention*	*Total*
Jewish population	83%	17%	100% (632)
Non-Jewish population	83%	17%	100% (1020)
No information	(9)	(2)	(11)
Total	83%	17%	100% (1663)

their identification or religious practices. But this shared sensibility can
translate itself in the French political space by a variety of options, with the
exception of voting for the Nationalist Party of the extreme Right (Front
National) or in more recent times for the Communist Party which remains
one of the last 'Stalinist' parties of Western Europe. As one of those inter-
viewed put it: 'We asked ourselves what was best for Israel: the result was
that the family split in two. Half voted for the majority, the other half for
the opposition.' On the other hand, the results of the Sarcelles survey show
that the vote for the moderate left dominates in the case of the more recent
Jewish immigrants. These results can be interpreted in two ways, which are
not, by the way, exclusive of each other. On the other hand, as they
progressively establish themselves within French society, the vote of the
French Jews becomes less and less specific. However, it is not excluded that
in the case of Sarcelles, the new phenomenon of an ethnic vote, tied to an
evolution within national citizenship, may begin to make itself heard. This
would make room for the 'ethnic' factor, but in the case of Jews it would
still affect very few constituencies.

The results of these surveys enter into Peter Medding's theory.[23] Even if,
in France, the majority of the recently migrated Jews vote in favour of the
moderate left, Judaism does not have a universal vocation for the left. The
settled Jews vote like the non-Jews in their same social categories. In so far
as their vote is not exclusively determined by their being Jewish, it can be
expressed through different electoral choices. Since the beginning of modern

times, historical circumstances have led the Jews to believe that the right, tied to Catholicism and to traditional society in France, was their enemy and the left was their ally. Moreover, under most historical conditions, immigrants have, no doubt, voted favourably for the left. The vote for the left by the Jews is tied to history. The weight of Jewish variables on the vote of Jewish citizens is, however, less important as the population becomes more settled and where the national political tradition makes less room for ethnicity.

NOTES

1 M. Kramer and M. Levy, *The Ethnic Factor, How American Minorities Decide Elections* (New York, Simon & Schuster, 1972), p. 104.

2 M. Wiener, 'Asian-Americans and American Foreign Policy', *Revue européenne des migrations internationales*, vol. 5, no. 1, pp. 97–113.

3 These analyses are developed in D. Schnapper, *La France de l'intégration, sociologie de la nation en 1990* (Gallimard, Paris, 1991).

4 D. Schnapper and S. Strudel, 'Le "vote juif" en France', *Revue Française de Science Politique* (December, 1983), pp. 933–61.

5 S. Strudel, *Les juifs et la politique, un exemple: attitudes et comportements politiques de la population juive à Sarcelles* (The Jews and politics, an example: political attitudes and behaviour of the Jewish population in Sarcelles) (Thesis of the Institut d'Etudes Politiques de Paris, 1991).

6 Discussed in D. Schnapper, *Juifs et israélites* (Gallimard, Paris, 1980). English translation, *Jewish Identities in Contemporary France* (Chicago University Press, 1983).

7 D. Bensimon and S. DellaPergola, *La population juive en France: socio-démographie et identité* (The Jewish population in France: socio-demography and identity) (Jerusalem and Paris, 1984). See also D. Schnapper, 'Les limites de la démographie des juifs de la diaspora' (The limits to the demography of the Jews in the Diaspora), *Revue Française de Sociologie*, XXVIII (1987), pp. 319–32.

8 D. Schnapper, 'Un pays d'immigration qui s'ignore', *Le genre humain* (Paris, Seuil, 1989), pp. 99–109.

9 By the answer to the question: 'Are you – Catholic – Muslim – Jewish – Protestant – other: which one? – no religion – does not wish to say.'

10 See notes 13–17, below.

11 This typology is borrowed from D. Schnapper, op. cit.

12 C. Benayoun, *Les juifs et la politique* (Paris, CNRS, 1984).

13 Having checked item: 'I go to synagogue very regularly and strictly observe the rules of kosher and Shabbat'.

14 Having checked item: 'I go to synagogue especially during the holidays and am not too strict about keeping kosher or the Shabbat'.

15 Having checked item: 'I only go to synagogue at Yom Kippur and rarely keep kosher or Shabbat'.

16 Having checked item: 'I feel Jewish without any religious observance'.

17 Having checked item: 'None of this applies'.

18 The text of the question is as follows: 'The French are customarily represented on an axis that goes from the left to the right. Would you situate yourself on this axis by circling the number that corresponds to your personal position?

Left, 1, 2, 3, 4, 5, 6, 7, right. Answers 1 and 2 were classified "left", 3, "centre-left", 4, "centre", 5, "centre-right", 6 and 7, "right"'.

19 G. Michelat and M. Simon, *Classe, religion et comportement politique* (Class, religion and political behaviour) (Paris, Presses de la Fondation Nationale des Sciences Politiques, 1977).

20 D. Schnapper and S. Strudel, article quoted in note 4, above.

21 These analyses are developed in S. Strudel, 'De Strasbourg à Sarcelles: les logiques de la participation électorale des juifs' (From Strasburg to Sarcelles: the analysis of electoral participation of the Jews), in P. Birnbaum (ed.), *Histoire politique des juifs de France*, (Paris, Presses de la Fondation Nationale des Sciences Politiques, 1990), pp. 278–95.

22 D. Schnapper and S. Strudel, article quoted in note 4, above.

23 P. Medding, 'Toward a general theory of Jewish political interests and behavior', *Jewish Journal of Sociology*, vol. 19, no. 2, 1977, pp. 111–44.

11

JEWISH POLITICAL ATTITUDES AND VOTING PATTERNS IN ENGLAND 1945–1987

Geoffrey Alderman

Political attitudes and allegiances are the outcome of a complex dynamic, the precise nature of which is the subject of intense academic dispute. The influence of the home environment, and of parental example, have been identified as important in the process of political socialization in the United Kingdom. Peer groups and geographical location also play a part, as does exposure to the media. Above all, there is the impact of socio-economic class. Until the 1970s class was reckoned to be the single most important predictor of political attitudes in Great Britain. 'Class is the basis of British politics [the author of a standard textbook wrote]; all else is embellishment and detail.'[1] 'The most significant division in electoral loyalties [another author explained] is that the well-to-do . . . predominantly vote Conservative, while those of a lower social status and a lower income group tend to vote Labour.'[2]

These assertions, though undoubtedly sweeping and oversimplified, embodied a basic truth. And while the extent of this truth is questioned even in relation to the 1950s and 1960s, there is also general agreement that, through a variety of sociological and economic changes which the country has undergone, the bases of political identity and voting habits have become much more varied and complex over the past fifteen or so years. The class structure of Britain, in particular, has experienced a fairly massive realignment, as the old Victorian heavy industries (labour-intensive and dependent upon a reservoir of unskilled manual workers) have contracted and decayed; in their place have come new technologies demanding a skilled and educated workforce, and prompting new methods of marketing and selling. On the evidence of the 1987 general election Britain is indeed 'two nations': prosperity has come to those willing and able to move with the times.[3]

Class has not disappeared as a prime factor in the shaping of political attitudes in Britain; rather, a new class structure has emerged, more complex than before and more subtle in its relationship to the act of voting. This

249

development, added to a number of political factors (such as the re-emergence of 'issue' voting), has materially assisted in the growth of 'third parties' (such as the nationalist parties in Scotland and Wales and the Liberal, Social-Democratic and Green parties in England). Above all, it has dealt a heavy blow to the Labour Party in the form in which it has existed hitherto.

The Labour Part was established in 1900 as the political arm of the trade union movement; it served – quite deliberately and unashamedly – the interests of the manual working classes and, in the course of time, it adopted the rhetoric and (to a limited extent) the dogmas of socialism. The general election of 1945 which swept Labour into power represented a genuine expression of the popularity of 'Labourism'. More than forty-five years later the constituency which Labour addressed no longer exists; the class it was created to serve has disappeared; the collectivist policies its constitution proclaims resulted in electoral catastrophe.

In considering the development of Anglo-Jewish political attitudes it is necessary to bear these trends and these considerations in mind because the political partisanship of English Jews in modern times (and certainly since 1945) has reflected in large measure the alignments of the greater socio-economic and occupational groups of which the Jews have formed but a small part.[4] None the less, two other interactive considerations have impinged upon the political attitudes of Anglo-Jewry. First, Anglo-Jewry has been affected inevitably by the comportment of political parties and of individual politicians towards matters of Jewish interest and concern. Second, and consequentially, Jewish political behaviour has been modified by the reaction to this comportment at specific times. To put the matter bluntly, there have been occasions on and circumstances in which a 'Jewish vote' has manifested itself, sometimes in marked contrast to secular trends. It was to be seen at work at the general election of 1906, when it was orches-trated to good effect against a Conservative Party widely perceived (because of the passage of the Aliens Act by Balfour's government the previous year) to be anti-Jewish.[5] It was at work again during the Whitechapel by-election of 1930, this time against the Labour government whose White Paper on Palestine had evoked the most hostile reactions on the part of the Jewish masses of East London.[6] It survived the Second World War intact, and there are politicians today who know that they cannot afford to ignore it.

Anglo-Jewry has always been an urban community. When peace came to Europe in 1945 this community consisted of not more than 450,000 persons.[7] Roughly two-thirds lived, as roughly two-thirds have always lived, in London and its immediately surrounding areas; by 1985 (when the total estimated Jewish population of the UK had fallen to 330,000) the proportion living in Greater London and the 'Home Counties' was about 67 per cent, or roughly 219,000.[8] But in the intervening forty years a great change had come about in the specific location of the London population.

Before 1939 the bulk of London Jewry lived in the 'East End', a deprived area of poor housing and chronic overcrowding into which the refugees from tsarist persecution had poured in the quarter-century following the assassination of Alexander II.

The political orientation of East End Jewry was decidedly left-wing. Jews were active in Labour politics. Many Jews and Jewish trade unionists were among the founders (in 1918) of the Stepney Central Labour Party, the secretary of which was the formidable Oscar Tobin, a Rumanian Jew who played a key role in the political education of Clement Attlee. Attlee's biographer has rightly described Tobin as 'the East End's most influential political "boss"' at that period.[9] Within a few years the mantle had devolved upon M. H. ('Morry') Davis, who combined the Labour leadership on Stepney Borough Council with the presidency of the Federation of Synagogues, then the largest synagogal body in Britain.

I have dealt elsewhere with Davis's extraordinary political and communal careers, both of which came to an abrupt halt when he was sent to prison at the end of 1944.[10] Here I wish only to remark upon some aspects of the significance of his tenure of power. His combination of intense Zionism, socialist fervour and cynical (not to say rebellious) attitude towards the ruling elites of Anglo-Jewry reflected views widely held by working-class Jews and the Jewish petty-bourgeoisie. Prime Minister Ramsay MacDonald's defection from the Labour Party in 1931 helped the party overcome the negative image it had acquired through the Passfield White Paper. The party stood by the Balfour Declaration (however that might be interpreted), was robust in its denunciation of the appeasement of Nazi Germany (in spite of its opposition to remarmament) and was steadfast in its support of working-class aspirations.

All these factors made it acceptable in the eyes of the Anglo-Jewish proletariat, and it was a party towards which Jews with political ambition naturally gravitated.[11] Of the twenty-eight Jews elected to Parliament in 1945 – a record – no less than twenty-six took the Labour whip. Of the remaining two one was Daniel Lipson, a rebel Conservative who, in a celebrated incident in 1937 had run successfully against the official Conservative candidate in Cheltenham, where Lipson's Jewishness had caused him to be passed over by the local party.[12] The other was the Communist Phil Piratin, who had snatched the much-depopulated Stepney seat from Labour to become (as it turned out) Britain's last Communist MP.

I have calculated that about half Piratin's vote was Jewish.[13] His victory was a potent reminder of the intensity of the Jewish infatuation with communist politics in East London in the 1930s and 1940s, and it was followed by others. At the Stepney Borough Council elections of 1946 the party won ten seats, all in heavily Jewish wards and seven of them by Jewish candidates. In the same year Jack Gaster, son of the late Rabbi Dr Moses

Gaster (*Haham* of the Spanish and Portuguese Jews) was elected as one of the two Communist councillors on the London County Council for the Mile End division.[14] As late as 1957 every one of the four Communists elected to Stepney Council was a Jew.[15]

But the love-affair between Jews and Communism in East London was based upon a combination of circumstances that could not outlive the era of its birth. Alone of the political parties in the capital, the Communists had taken the menace of the British Union of Fascists seriously from the start; for this reason even Jewish capitalists (admittedly modest capitalists) had supported them financially.[16] Communists were very prominent in organizing tenants facing eviction from rack-renting landlords; and they took a stand against, and benefited from, the iniquities of the Davis regime in Stepney.[17] The reputation of the Labour Party in East London suffered as a result of the misdeeds of Davis and his associates, and the Communists reaped a rich and predictable harvest. However, with the end of Anglo-Soviet cooperation against the Nazis, and the onset of the Cold War, the relationship rapidly deteriorated. Whatever sentimental attachment Jews might have harboured towards Communism was killed off by news of Soviet anti-Semitism (under Stalin), proof of Soviet anti-Zionism (in 1956 and 1967), and disenchantment with the realities of East European totalitarianism.[18] There could be no question of replanting the seeds of Jewish Communism in the London suburbs to which Jews were moving in large numbers in the immediate post-war period.

Daniel Lipson's presence in Parliament from 1937 to 1950 was a potent reminder of the strength of anti-Jewish prejudice then to be found in the Conservative Party. Official Conservative MPs who were Jewish did not reappear at Westminster until 1955, when Sir Henry D'Avigdor Goldsmid was returned for Walsall South; the following year he was joined by Sir Keith (now Lord) Joseph, elected for Leeds North-East. Sir Henry and Sir Keith had both been educated at Harrow and Oxford; neither was remotely typical of Anglo-Jewry. In due course Sir Keith was to play a central part in alerting his party colleagues to the advantages to be gained from harnessing the power of the Jewish vote for the Conservative cause. But in the 1950s the hostility with which sections of the party regarded Jews was still strong, and had indeed been rejuvenated in the aftermath of the Holocaust by the popular anti-Semitism that had accompanied the last and most bloody years of the Palestine Mandate.

It is worth recalling that those who led the Conservative Party at the time of Suez (1956) were not friends of Israel, and that the mood of the party as a whole, if it was anti-Egyptian, was certainly not pro-Israeli.[19] It must also be emphasized that although anti-Semitism was rampant in some Conservative associations in rural areas, it was by no means confined to the countryside. In post-1945 Britain the most blatant example came from Finchley, in north-west London. Briefly, at the London borough council elections of 1957 Liberals alleged that the Finchley Golf Club, 'officered by prominent Conservatives', was implementing a policy of excluding Jews from membership.[20] The allegations turned out to be true, and they were followed, three years later, by revelations of Jewish quotas operated by other golf clubs, in such prominently Jewish areas as Hendon and Stanmore.[21]

These events were subsequently held to have been responsible for a swing of Jewish voters away from the Conservative Party and towards the Liberals. There is some statistical support for this view, and it is also the case that Liberals did well in Jewish wards.[22] In 1956 there was not one Liberal member of Finchley Council; by the time of the 1959 general election there were seven (all elected at the expense of the Conservatives), and at the 1962 local polls the Liberals advanced still further. It must be added at once that these Liberal victories were essentially the result of protest votes, and that they owed something to the national Liberal revival at this time. None the less, their relationship to Jewish sensitivities could not be ignored. When the young Mrs Thatcher was first elected at Finchley, in 1959, she quickly embarked on a pro-Jewish policy from which – in broad terms – she rarely deviated.

At the general election of 1945 only eight of the thirty-four Jewish Labour candidates had failed to secure election, whereas all five official Jewish Conservatives and all sixteen Jewish Liberals had been defeated; indeed, the 1945 election was the first since Emancipation at which no Jewish Liberals were returned. The evidence of the fate of parliamentary candidates, therefore, points to a very strong attachment on the part of Anglo-Jewry to the Labour Party. But the situation in reality was not nearly as straightforward as this parliamentary analysis might suggest. The vast majority of constituencies where Jews were to be found in large numbers (the two seats at Bethnal Green, the three in Hackney, two of the three in Stepney, the Stoke Newington seat, Hendon North, the two seats at Ilford, Central and North-East Leeds, North Salford, South Tottenham, the two Walthamstow seats, the two at Wembley, the two at Willesden, and Glasgow Gorbals) had indeed all returned Labour MPs. This did not of course mean that all or nearly all Jews had voted Labour.

Evidence relating to the make-up of Anglo-Jewish political preferences at this time is largely qualitative. In 1947 the research unit of the Jewish Fellowship conducted a wide-raging survey of 40,000 Jews; 22.5 per cent of the respondents identified themselves as Conservative supporters, 33.1 per cent as Liberals, 32.9 per cent as Labour supporters or 'socialists', and 2.3 per cent as Communists.[23] These percentages, as indications of any overall pattern, must be treated with a great deal of scepticism, because the number of respondents who answered the question dealing with party preferences amounted to less than 8 per cent of those to whom the questionnaire was sent. What is important, however, is that even in 1947 Jews were fully prepared to identify themselves as Conservative supporters. In 1964 a much more reliable survey was carried out by Dr Bernard (now Lord) Donoghue in the Finchley constituency. In a random sample of 130 electors, two-fifths voted Conservative and only one-fifth Labour; in 1959 the ratio had been three Conservatives to one Liberal and one Labour.[24]

The survival and careful nurturing of a tradition of Jewish support for the Conservative Party was to pay handsome dividends in the outer-suburban areas of the large conurbations, Jewish migration to which (already under way before 1939) was to become a key feature of communal settlement after 1945. In London this tradition had remained intact during the inter-war period; to the Toryism of the established Jewish gentry was added, at this time, the Toryism of the Jewish *nouveaux riches*.[25] Even in an area as strongly working-class as Hackney had become by the 1950s, Jews could be found standing as Conservatives; five Jews stood in the Conservative interest in the Hackney Borough Council elections of 1953.[26] In the following year a Jew secured election as a Conservative in the Cricklewood ward of Willesden, then an area of expanding Jewish settlement in north-west London. In 1930 and again in 1946 Herman Courlander was elected Mayor at Richmond-upon-Thames, J. L. Freeman became Mayor of Hendon in 1950 and Emil Grant served as Mayor of Finchley in 1952–3.[27] All were Conservatives. It is also worth observing that at the 1945 general election there were a few constituencies, already heavily populated with Jews, which were held by the Conservatives: Hendon South, Finchley, Leeds North and Middleton & Prestwich (north Manchester). Significantly, these were all marginal seats situated in outer suburbs.

During the 1950s and 1960s two quite separate but complementary processes eroded the foundations of the inter-war alliance between Anglo-Jewry and the Left. One was political, grounded in developing Labour attitudes towards Zionism and the State of Israel; the other was sociological and demographic. In driving a wedge between the Jews and Labour the second process was far more important than the first, the broad outlines of which are well known.

In November 1945, barely four months after an election victory that was celebrated widely in Jewish circles, the Labour government announced its intention to uphold the terms of the 1939 White Paper on Palestine. So began the last and most unhappy phase of the British Mandate – unhappy not merely for the *Yishuv* but for an Anglo-Jewish community now seen to be at odds with an elected government, and which suffered in consequence from renewed fascist activity against Jews and Jewish property. The resulting sense of shock was compounded by the evident helplessness of the Jewish Labour MPs, few of whom were willing to step out of line and publicly oppose government policy. In April 1946 only six Jewish Labour MPs, 'after desperate "lobbying" by the *Poale Zion*' could be persuaded to venture the slightest parliamentary opposition to Ernest Bevin's Palestine policy.[28] The blowing-up of the King David Hotel in Jerusalem on 22 July

1946 lost Zionism many friends in the British Labour movement; a number of MPs whose approach to the Palestine problem had previously been regarded as 'even-handed' now openly supported Bevin's policy. Significantly, a proposal to outlaw anti-Semitism was rejected by the Labour Party Conference in 1946; a similar proposal in the House of Commons in 1948 failed to get past its first reading.[29]

Israel was recognized *de facto* by the Labour government in February 1949, and *de jure* in March 1950 – but only after a general election (February 1950) in which the Labour Party had seen its majority slashed from 146 to just five seats. Some Jewish Labour supporters hoped that, with Bevin's death (1951) and the State of Israel already a fact of life, relations between the Labour Party and British Jews could be restored to something like their former level. But the Suez crisis of 1956 thwarted efforts at reconciliation, the more so because Labour was then out of office, and so could not plead the burdens of government in defence of its attitude towards Israel.

Within Anglo-Jewry (and judging by the many communal gatherings held in October and November 1956) there was general unanimity that Israel had been justified in attacking Egypt in order to bring to an end years of terrorist incursions across the Gaza Strip; the Israeli conquest of Sinai was a further source of pride and, if this had been facilitated to some extent by an Anglo-French intervention, so much the better. The seventeen Jewish Labour MPs returned in the 1955 election were therefore expected to support Israel's position. This expectation was natural but most naive. All seventeen obeyed the three-line whip and voted against the government on 1 November 1956, and all but one (Emanuel Shinwell, then in Australia) behaved similarly a week later.[30] On 30 October, in an unexpected division that had not carried a three-line whip, seven Jewish Labour MPs had abstained; of these only Shinwell and Harold Lever (who sat for the Jewish constituency of Manchester Cheetham) made it clear that their abstentions had been deliberate.

The standard response of Jewish Labour MPs to criticism from the community was to state that in Parliament they represented their constituents, not their fellow Jews. This was constitutionally correct, but was widely regarded within the community as nothing more than an excuse. The failure of the *Poale Zion* activist and MP for East Willesden, Maurice Orbach, to even accidentally abstain, caused deep resentment, and was certainly a factor in his defeat there at the 1959 general election.[31] The failure of Barnett Janner (in 1956 President both of the Board of Deputies and of the Zionist Federation) to abstain gave rise to a communal furore. But of more fundamental significance for the future relationship between Jews and Labour was the attitude of the new Labour leader, Hugh Gaitskell. Gaitskell's previous record had been that of a friend to Israel. At the time of Suez, however, he had likened the British Prime Minister, Anthony Eden, to a policeman who had determined 'to go in and help the burglar [i.e. Israel] shoot the householder [Egypt]'.[32]

This comparison was not easily nor quickly forgiven, and it had certainly not been forgotten by the time of the Six Day War (1967), when the Labour government of Harold Wilson (again, regarded hitherto as a good friend of Israel) went to great lengths to distance itself from Israeli policy. It is, I think, generally recognized that the Six Day War marked an ominous turning-point in the history of left-wing anti-Semitism in Britain.[33] With the capture of East Jerusalem, the West Bank and Gaza, Israel, till then the underdog of the Middle East, could henceforth be regarded as an imperialist, colonial power, ruling by force of arms over a downtrodden Palestinian Arab population.

This aspect of Israeli policy can of course be criticized without questioning the legitimacy of the Jewish State or the justice of its re-establishment; many Jewish citizens of Israel have done so over the years. However, elements of the left in Britain (as elsewhere in Western Europe) used the events of 1967 as an excuse to attack the very fact of Israel's existence and, by scarcely-concealed implication, the entire basis of the movement for Jewish self-determination – that is, Zionism. The force of this attack was made all the greater by the resolution of the General Assembly of the United Nations (10 November 1975) equating Zionism with racism (more recently rescinded). Those who supported the Zionist cause could henceforth be branded as racists, and racism could be portrayed as part of a new 'world Jewish conspiracy' that was already alleged to embrace capitalism and imperialism.[34]

However vigorously left-wing anti-Zionists denied that their motives were in any way anti-Semitic, the reaction of Anglo-Jewry was one of justifiable scepticism and disbelief. Following Labour's defeat at the 1979 general election, the 'hard' – or 'outside' – left began to make very significant inroads into the machinery of Labour policy-making at all levels. In September 1979 Councillor Arthur Super, a former Jewish mayor of Hackney, leaked news of a motion passed in secret by the Hackney North & Stoke Newington Labour Party the previous July, declaring its opposition to the very existence of the State of Israel.[35] Super blamed the affair on a 'small, but virulent, anti-Semitic element'; but a year later this element was evidently still very much in control, condemning the 'Zionist State of Israel' and (as before) urging recognition of the Palestine Liberation Organization.[36]

The Israeli invasion of the Lebanon in 1982 whipped the anti-Zionism of the left to fever-pitch. In May 1982 the Labour Party's National Executive Committee, which had already endorsed Palestinian self-determination and urged participation of the PLO in peace talks, passed a motion criticizing Israeli policies on the West Bank and the bombing of the Lebanon. Anti-Zionist motions had, by then, become standard items on the agenda-papers of many Constituency Labour Parties.[37] The Manifesto prepared by the Labour Party for the 1983 general election proclaimed the right of Israel to exist within 'secure internationally recognized borders', but at the same time urged the establishment of a Palestinian state.[38] Labour lost that election in disastrous fashion. But in London the party, dominated by the hard left, had won control of the Greater London Council in 1981, and, under the leadership of Ken Livingstone, embarked upon a five-year period of intense anti-Zionist activity that brought it and the Jewish community of London to a state of conflict unprecedented in British or Anglo-Jewish history.[39]

These developments (of which I have of necessity given only the barest outline) were of course of the profoundest significance for the relationship between Jews and Labour politics. But – by themselves – they would not necessarily have caused an irreparable rupture, and they would not – by themselves – have driven Jews into the arms of any other party. During the White Paper crisis of 1930 there had been a state of virtual warfare between East London Jewry and the Labour government; but the crisis passed.[40] In the years immediately following the 1967 war it was the Young Liberals who carried the banner of anti-Zionism with most enthusiasm.[41] Both anti-Zionism and unadulterated anti-Semitism were to be observed at work in the Conservative Party at this time. Left-wing politics certainly pushed Jews into seeking political camps other than those of Labour in which to dwell. What pulled them towards the Conservatives was a quite different set of circumstances.

In the quarter-century that followed the 1945 general election Anglo-Jewry relocated itself geographically and socio-economically. The many small provincial Jewish communities of Victorian England fast contracted as Anglo-Jewry became concentrated in a limited number of urban centres. But within these centres, and pre-eminently within the Greater London area, the Jews moved out of the original quasi-ghetto areas of settlement (often badly war-damaged) into the suburbs where, as we have already noted, a significant Jewish presence had already established itself before 1939. Thus by the mid-1970s London's East End, which at one time accounted for two-thirds of London Jewry, contained less than a quarter, while the outer London area accounted for over 70 per cent. More specifically, five outer London boroughs (Barnet, Brent and Harrow in the north-west and Enfield and Redbridge in the north-east) came to contain over half the Jewish population of London (see Table 11.1). The pattern has been repeated, albeit on a lesser scale, in other cities. In Leeds Jews have moved out of the Leylands and Chapeltown into the newer suburban districts of Moortown and Alwoodley, and even further afield – just as in London they are moving beyond the county boundary into areas of south Hertfordshire and south-west Essex.[42] In Greater Manchester (the second-largest 'Jewish' city in the UK, accommodating about 10 per cent of Anglo-Jewry) and its surrounding districts the bulk of the community is now to be found in the northern and north-western suburbs, such as Crumpsall, Cheetham Hill and Prestwich.[43]

In moving out, from the city centres to the suburbs, the Jews also moved upwards, from the ranks of the working classes and the petty bourgeoisie into a more comfortable middle-class existence. Self-perception is as important in this regard as any objective measurement of social-class composition. In his study of the Jewish community of Edgware (now part of the London Borough of Barnet) Professor Ernest Krausz showed that although Edgware Jewry in the early 1960s was thoroughly working class in origin (53 per cent of his sample having been born in London's East End) over 80 per cent regarded themselves as belonging to the middle class, while only just over 8 per cent said they belonged to the working class.[44] From the point of view of occupation, moreover, Jewish men in Edgware were to be found predominantly in the professional, managerial, skilled and self-employed groups – the exact opposite of the picture for the general population of the district.[45]

The trends illuminated by Professor Krausz have been confirmed by both aggregate analysis and other surveys carried out since his work was completed. Estimates prepared by Professor S. Prais and Mrs M. Schmool of the social-class structure of Anglo-Jewry in 1961 emphasized the tendency for British Jews to be found among the higher social classes (see Table 11.2). Their work suggested that in the early 1960s over 40 per cent of Anglo-Jewry was located in the upper two social classes, whereas these categories accounted for less than 20 per cent of the general population. A survey of Sheffield Jewry (south Yorkshire) carried out in 1974, demonstrated that over half the male sample fell within the categories of employers, managers, professional and middle-ranking non-manual workers, compared with less than one-fifth in the city of Sheffield as a whole.[46] The survey of Jews in Hackney, inner-north London (1974–5) put about a third of the economically active Jewish sample in these categories; in the general working population of the borough as a whole only 12 per cent were within these groups.[47] The analysis of Redbridge Jewry (north-west London), carried out in the winter of 1977–8, showed that no less than 70 per cent of the Jews there belonged to the professional, managerial and skilled non-manual occupational classes; for all economically active males in the borough the proportion was about 50 per cent.[48]

In Greater London as a whole it seems that Jews in the 1970s were roughly twice as numerous as non-Jews in these socio-economic groups. It is also worth noting the heavy representation of Jews in self-employed occupations: 55 per cent of Edgware Jewish males were found to be self-employed, 44 per cent in Sheffield, 34 per cent in Redbridge and 21 per cent in Hackney; in Great Britain as a whole the 1971 Census placed less than 8 per cent of the economically active population in this category.[49]

The demonstrable upward social mobility of British Jews has undoubtedly played a central role in their movement away from Labour and toward

Table 11.1   The pattern of Jewish settlement in London, 1974

Anglo-Jewry	408,311
London Jewry (GLC area)	259,100
Outer London	184,200
Barnet	58,100
Brent	20,400
Enfield	11,000
Harrow	18,000
Redbridge	29,300
Inner London (LCC area)	74,900

Source: Adapted from B. A. Kosmin and N. Grizzard, *Geographical Distribution Estimates of Ethnically Jewish Population of the UK 1974* (Board of Deputies of British Jews, mimeo., 1975).

Table 11.2   Estimated social-class distribution of the live Jewish population, 1961

	Population distributions (%)	
Social class	Jews	General
I Professional	10	4
II Intermediate	34	15
III Skilled	36	49
IV Partly skilled	10	19
V Unskilled	–	8
Other	8	5

Source: S. J. Prais and M. Schmool, 'The social-class structure of Anglo-Jewry, 1961', *Jewish Journal of Sociology*, xvii (1975), p. 11.

Conservative politics. The class structure of Anglo-Jewry – and especially of suburban Anglo-Jewry – marked it out as a group that would be particularly receptive to Conservative ideologies as these were redeveloped first under Edward Heath (1965–75) and then under Margaret Thatcher who succeeded him as Conservative leader. We must bear in mind in this connection that in 1970 about 64 per cent of the 'A', 'B' and 'C1' occupational groups (embracing professional, administrative, managerial and non-manual occupations) over the country as a whole voted Conservative, and that although this proportion fell somewhat over the five subsequent general elections, it has not since then dropped below 50 per cent; whereas the percentage of the combined A, B and C1 categories supporting Labour has contracted fairly steadily from 25 per cent in 1970 to just 18 per cent in 1987.[50]

One particular aspect of British electoral sociology in the 1980s has been the relationship between voting behaviour and housing tenure. At the general elections of 1983 and 1987 about half of all owner-occupiers (that is, people who had bought or were buying their homes, as opposed to those who lived in rented accommodation) voted Conservative; only about a quarter of owner-occupiers voted Labour, and about the same proportion supported the Social-Democratic/Liberal 'Alliance'. We know that in Redbridge at the end of the 1970s over 90 per cent of Jews were owner-occupiers, and that in those parts of Barnet, Brent and Harrow where Jews reside in large numbers the proportion of owner-occupiers is not less than a half and often much higher.[51]

It should come as no surprise, therefore, that Anglo-Jewish political attitudes and loyalties, which were substantially Liberal for much of the nineteenth century and substantially Labour in the mid-twentieth, are now substantially Conservative in orientation. That this is so can be demonstrated by reference to both quantitative and qualitative data. During the general election of February 1974 I began collecting data relating to the voting preferences of Jews in selected London parliamentary constituencies. The series is summarized in Table 11.3.[52] In respect of the Hendon North, Ilford North and Finchley results, and for comparative purposes, I have inserted, in parentheses, the proportions of the combined A, B and C1 categories found (by national opinion surveys) to have supported the political parties at each election.[53] It will be readily apparent that the broad trend of Jewish electoral behaviour in north-east London (Ilford) and the north-west of the capital (Hendon and Finchley) has been in line with that of the top social classes; usually, indeed, the Jews have proved somewhat more Conservatively inclined, which is what one would expect. At Finchley in 1983 the Jewish result, which showed an abnormal degree of support for Labour, probably reflected a short-term antipathy on the part of Jewish voters directed against aspects of Mrs Thatcher's foreign policy – specifically, British support for PLO participation in a Middle East peace settlement.

In the Hackney North result for 1979, the percentages in parentheses refer to the national pattern of the C2, D and E categories – that is, skilled and unskilled manual workers, casual workers and state pensioners. Again, the remarkable similarity between the Jewish pattern and that of these lower social classes needs no further emphasis, and reflects the social-class composition of Hackney Jewry – an ageing community drawing its political inspiration from memories of the vibrant left-wing Jewish tradition with which the area was once saturated.

One aspect of Jewish political sociology not touched upon in these surveys is the relationship (if any) of partisanship to degree of religiosity. It is tempting to suppose that the more 'right-wing' a British Jew is in religious terms, the more likely he or she is to be a Conservative supporter. The Conservative Party has a long history of support for denominational schools, and its emphasis on the centrality of religious commitment (Christian or otherwise) in the moral and ethical underpinning the state is (it is argued) likely to enhance its attraction for the right-wing orthodox.

Table 11.3 Jewish political preferences in London, 1974–87

	Conservative (ABC1)	Labour (ABC1)	Liberal/All (ABC1)
Hendon North (February 1974)	59%	16%	25%
(N = 150)	(53%)	(24%)	(23%)
Hendon North (October 1974)	68%	22%	10%
(N = 178)	(51%)	(24%)	(25%)
Ilford North (1979)	61%	35%	4%
(N = 143)	(59%)	(22%)	(16%)
Finchley (1983)	52%	24%	24%
(N = 120)	(55%)	(17%)	(28%)
Finchley (1987)	60%	22%	18%
(N = 205)	(54%)	(18%)	(26%)
	(C2DE)	(C2DE)	(C2DE)
Hackney North (1979)	36%	49%	13%
(N = 130)	(35%)	(50%)	(14%)

Note: Hendon North, Ilford North and Finchley percentages are based on those who stated an intention to vote; Hackney North percentages are based on those who actually voted.

It is certainly true, as I have shown elsewhere, that Hackney's 'ultra-orthodox' community is strongly identified with Conservative politics. In May 1978 Josef Lobenstein won, in a heavily ultra-orthodox ward, the only seat on an otherwise entirely Labour-controlled Hackney Borough Council; councillor Lobenstein, a leading member of British Agudas Israel and of the Union of Orthodox Hebrew Congregations, is now President of the North London Adass Yisroel Synagogue (the founding synagogue of the Union) and Conservative leader on the Hackney Council.[54] The other centre of ultra-orthodoxy in London is situated in Hendon and adjacent to Golders Green. In a survey of a small number of members of the Hendon Adass Yisroel Synagogue (also a constituent of the Union), carried out in 1976, Dr Sabine Roitman found that 70 per cent of her respondents identified themselves as Conservative supporters.[55] But what one does not know is whether these pieces of evidence reflect a true correlation between religious and political commitment, or whether they are simply reflections of other criteria, such as socio-economic group or even housing tenure. It is worth pointing out that aspects of *chassidism* – especially its teachings concerning the duties owed by those who happen to possess wealth – incline more to a socialist than to neo-liberal political philosophy.[56] It is also certain that strictly orthodox Jews are to be found supporting and even being members of the Labour Party. In May 1982, in what is believed to be the first occasion on which a rabbi has gained election to a local authority in Britain, Rabbi Avroham Pinter topped the poll – for Labour – in Hackney's Northfield Ward.

It is also possible that such well-known local Jewish celebrities as Lobenstein and Pinter polled a personal vote, or that they polled a specifically

Jewish (and perhaps Yiddish-speaking) vote. In England local election contests are held in multi-member divisions known as wards; in Hackney there is unmistakable evidence of Jews performing much better than non-Jews belonging to the same party and contesting the same wards.[57] Being Jewish, and particularly being an orthodox Jew in an orthodox Jewish area, gives a candidate a distinct and perhaps decisive advantage, at least at local election level, where Jewish electors are concerned.

In relation to parliamentary elections the evidence is less clear. On the one hand there are plenty of instances of well-known Jews being defeated in Jewish areas: Barnett Janner (then Liberal) at Whitechapel in 1930, for instance, and Dr Bernard Homa (Labour) at Hendon South in 1951 and 1955. On the other, there is very strong circumstantial evidence that Janner's excellent performance in 1930 (he cut Labour's majority from 9,180 to just 1,099, on a swing of over 18 per cent against Labour) was due largely if not entirely to the operation of a Jewish vote.[58] More recently, the success of the late Mrs Milly Miller (Labour) in snatching the Ilford North seat from the Conservatives at the general election of October 1974 by a mere 778 votes, was ascribed by both Labour and Conservative Party workers to her ability to capitalize upon her local popularity with her fellow Jews at a time when the Conservatives were still being heavily criticized for the embargo on arms shipments to Israel imposed during the Yom Kippur.[59]

The Conservative government of Edward Heath suffered in a number of Jewish constituencies as a result of its 1973 arms embargo. But local Conservative MPs and candidates who criticized or condemned the embargo reaped an advantage thereby. The most dramatic instance of this was at Hendon North at the election of February 1974, where the sitting MP, John Gorst, who had voted against the embargo and had secured the support of the Reverend Saul Amias (the outspoken and extrovert minister of the Edgware United Synagogue) as a result, secured a movement of Jewish voters to him that substantially offset the anti-Conservative swing in Greater London as a whole.[60] At the election of October 1974, in which Reverend Amias spoke in support of Gorst from the pulpit on the Sabbath before polling, the number of Jewish electors declaring a definite intention of voting for Gorst actually rose (see Table 11.3) and (at a time of growing unpopularity for the Conservative Party nationally) he suffered not merely the lowest anti-Conservative swing in any of the constituencies in the Borough of Barnet, but an adverse swing less than half that registered by the Conservatives in the entire Greater London area.[61]

Mrs Thatcher won the Conservative leadership contest in 1975 and entered upon her record-breaking tenure of the premiership in 1979. It is not my intention here to explore in any detail Mrs Thatcher's own relationship to the Jewish people, for whom I believe her respect is quite genuine. At the same time this respect dovetailed most conveniently with other of her preoccupations, more particularly her overriding concern to promote entrepreneurship, self-help and a spirit of independence among the entire citizenry of the United Kingdom; British Jewry is often held up as a prime example of these characteristics at work, materially assisting in overcoming prejudice and adversity. Finchley is the only constituency Mrs Thatcher ever represented in the House of Commons and, as we have seen, she entered upon this inheritance at a time of acute local tensions between the Jews and sections of the Finchley Conservative hierarchy; it was therefore in her interest to foster good relations with Jews, both locally and nationally. The influence of Sir Keith Joseph upon her economic thinking was enormous. Nor do I believe that her promotion of so many Jews to ministerial and Cabinet positions was entirely fortuitous.[62]

In the early 1980s, when Lord Carrington was in charge of the Foreign Office, the relationship of the Conservative government with Anglo-Jewry underwent a period of strain, following Carrington's statement (March 1980) that the PLO was not a 'terrorist organization'. There were a number of well-attended protest meetings in synagogues in north-west London; in letters to the local newspaper (the *Hendon Times*) and to Rabbi B. J. Gelles of the Finchley United Synagogue, the Prime Minister carefully distanced herself from the policy of her Foreign Secretary.[63] None the less, Finchley was not then considered the safest of Conservative-held seats and the Jewish vote could not be relied upon. So soundings were taken with a view to moving the Prime Minister to safer territory.[64]

These events took place before the Falklands conflict (1982), which dramatically changed the fortunes of the Conservative administration and which (fortuitously from the point of view of relations with Anglo-Jewry) resulted in Lord Carrington's resignation. After 1983 Mrs Thatcher arguably pursued a foreign policy more pro-Jewish than that of any prime minister since Lloyd George. It is true that her government concluded an arms deal with Saudi Arabia, and called upon Israel to negotiate with the PLO. But the Prime Minister and the party she led went out of their way to support Soviet Jewry. The Foreign Office ended its complicity in the Arab boycott (through the certification of signatures on boycott documents), and the then Prime Minister visited Israel, taking the trouble to distance herself from some of the more extreme pro-PLO utterances of her ministers.[65] She also showed sensitivity to other Jewish concerns, such as *shechita* (the Jewish method of slaughtering food animals).[66]

The peerage which she bestowed at the beginning of 1988 upon Immanuel Jakobovits, Chief Rabbi of the United Synagogue, has a significance the importance of which can hardly be overestimated. Lord Jakobovits's admiration for Mrs Thatcher, and for the encouragement of wealth creation and acquisition, are well known.[67] As early as 1977 he had condemned the welfare state for undermining individual responsibility and for encouraging a 'get something for nothing' attitude.[68] In particular, he faithfully reflected a feeling of antipathy towards the aspirations of Britain's black communities that is undoubtedly widespread within Anglo-Jewry.

Most British Jews resent the 'race-relations industry', and many object to being termed an 'ethnic minority'; they realize that the 1976 Race Relations Act can protect them (and are occasionally grateful for it), but nevertheless they feel uncomfortable in its presence. During the 1970s many Jews blamed the blacks for the resurgence of racist politics and for the rise of the National Front.[69] Sir Keith Joseph's plea to the Jews of Ilford North, during the 1978 by-election there, to support Mrs Thatcher's policy of tight immigration control, was condemned by the *Jewish Chronicle*, but caught the communal mood exactly. The Tories won back Ilford North on a swing of 6.9 per cent, but among Jewish voters the swing to the Conservatives was no less than 11.2 per cent.[70]

Sir Keith's intervention was itself a landmark: for the first time in over half a century, a leading Conservative politician had appealed to Jewish voters to support the party on a major issue, and had met with resounding success. Since then the growing anxieties of the Anglo-Jewish community surrounding the quality of urban life have served only to strengthen its support for Thatcherite values. During the 1980s Mrs Thatcher found herself under increasing attack from within the Established Church of England on fundamental questions of social policy, especially in relation to inner-city areas. Her most consistent theological support came from within the circle of orthodox Jewry.

In a pamphlet published by the right wing Social Affairs Unit in 1985 Rabbi Dr Jonathan Sacks, the Principal of Jews' College, London, contrived to offer thinly-veiled support from the Old Testament for major elements of Conservative domestic legislation; Rabbi Sacks's selected texts (the political commentator Hugo Young argued) served to confer 'ethical legitimacy on a series of economic policies that Christian churchmen have denounced'.[71] Nowhere were such denunciations more eloquently expressed than in the pages of the report (*Faith in the City*) of the Archbishop of Canterbury's Commission on Urban Priority Areas. It was Immanuel Jakobovits who came to Mrs Thatcher's rescue, exhorting the disadvantaged not to insist upon public help ('self-reliant efforts and perseverance eventually pay off'), and criticizing the blacks for wishing to change the character of British society into 'a new multi-ethnic form'.[72]

These views were themselves controversial, and did not represent the opinions of all orthodox Jews, or even of all orthodox Jewish clergy. But they did accurately mirror a feeling widespread within an Anglo-Jewish community that was rapidly turning its back on the welfare state and its face against collectivism. Some features of the general election of June 1987 reflected these developments. Reverend Amias once again signed the nomination papers of John Gorst at Hendon North, while Cecil Parkinson (a self-confessed adulterer, later promoted back into the Cabinet) received the endorsement of Alan Plancey, Rabbi at Elstree & Borehamwood (since elected chairman of the Rabbinical Council of the United Synagogue). Martin Savitt, a former vice-president of the Board of Deputies and at that time a vice-chairman of the British Zionist Federation, assisted the campaign of the Conservative Harriet Crawley (whom *The Times* of 3 June 1987 described as 'pregnant and unmarried') against former GLC leader Ken Livingstone, the Labour candidate at Brent East. The Livingstone candidature was always controversial, and his election to Parliament, on a much reduced Labour vote, entirely predictable. Mr Savitt is, however, entitled to claim a little credit for the narrowness of Livingstone's victory.

Sixty-three Jewish candidates stood at the 1987 election: twenty-five for the Conservatives, fifteen for Labour, twenty-one for the Alliance and two independents. Of these there were returned sixteen Conservative and seven Labour MPs. The number of Jewish Labour MPs reached its peak (thirty-eight) in 1966; the Jewish Labour contingent at Westminster in 1987 was smaller than at any time since 1935. The Jewish Conservative total returned in 1987 was smaller by one than in 1983, but was still the second-largest ever, and the pattern established in 1983, of the political balance among Jewish MPs lying with the Conservative Party, was maintained and indeed strengthened.

As I have stressed in relation to 1945, we must be wary of drawing too many conclusions from the success or failure of Jewish parliamentary candidates. None the less, the fact that a third of all Jewish candidates in 1987 stood for the Alliance, that over a third were Conservatives, and that, while the number of Jewish Labour candidates declined (there were twenty in 1983), the number of Jewish Conservative candidates (eighteen in 1983) increased, does, I think, tell us something about the changing political balance within Anglo-Jewry as a whole. The strength of the picture increases, and its definition is sharpened, when considered in conjunction with the Jewish voting pattern in Finchley. Compared with 1983, the Prime Minister increased her share of the total poll in 1987 by just 2.8 per cent; but her share of the Jewish poll (see Table 11.3) increased by nearly three times that amount. At Finchley there was in fact a (conventional) swing *from* the Conservatives *to* Labour of 1 per cent. Mrs Thatcher clearly owed some of the increase in her own share of the vote to her Jewish supporters: the Jewish vote there swung heavily (5.0 per cent) against the trend. Of course – as the Finchley statistics themselves indicate – there are still Jews who vote Labour, and the centre parties (the merged Social & Liberal Democrats and the rump SDP) can expect some Jewish support. Equally clearly, however, the very strong rapport that existed between Anglo-Jewry and Labour a half-century ago is no longer to be found.

When the bulk of Anglo-Jewry lived in areas of deprivation in the inner cities, this relationship was bound to be strong, and it was made stronger still by the anti-Jewish prejudice then to be found in large measure within the Conservative Party. It matters little that this prejudice has not entirely disappeared. The Labour Party no longer serves what are regarded as Jewish interests. I have in mind not merely the anti-Israeli foreign policy of the Greater London Council under Labour control from 1981 to its abolition in 1986, or the enthusiasm expressed in certain quarters for Louis Farrakhan, or even the opposition of the Labour-controlled Inner London Education Authority to the granting of voluntary-aided status (i.e. financial support) to Jewish schools. From a purely socio-economic point of view the Labour Party and the Anglo-Jewish community now inhabit worlds which barely touch each other.

A writer in *The Times* of 10 October 1987 described Mrs Thatcher's social policy as 'the Jewish ethos of practical charity'. I did not hear any communal protest at this turn of phrase, and I suspect that many Jews regarded it as a mark of honour, a sign of social and political assimilation and also of acceptance by the ruling Conservative Party.

NOTES

1 P. J. G. Pulzer, *Political Representation and Elections in Britain* (3rd edn, London, Allen & Unwin, 1975), p. 102.

2 R. M. Punnett, *British Government and Politics* (3rd edn, London, Heinemann, 1976), p. 70.

3 See generally G. Alderman, *Britain: A One-Party State?* (London, Christopher Helm, 1989), ch. 1.

4 I use the term 'English Jews' throughout this paper. In 1918, of the 300,000 or so Jews in the UK, over 95 per cent lived in England; in 1985 the proportion was about the same (out of 330,000).

5 G. Alderman, *The Jewish Community in British Politics* (Oxford University Press, 1983), pp. 75–6.

6 Op. cit., pp. 112–13; J. Gorny, *The British Labour Movement and Zionism 1917–1948* (London, Frank Cass, 1983), pp. 91–6.

7 H. Neustatter, 'Demographic and other statistical aspects of Anglo-Jewish population, 1960–65', in M. Freedman (ed.), *A Minority in Britain* (London, Vallentine Mitchell, 1955), p. 76.

8 S. Waterman and B. Kosmin, *British Jewry in the Eighties* (London, Board of Deputies of British Jews, 1986), p. 21.

9 K. Harris, *Attlee* (London, Weidenfeld & Nicolson, 1982), p. 42.

10 G. Alderman, *London Jewry & London Politics, 1889–1986* (London, Routledge, 1989), pp. 83–9; G. Alderman, *The Federation of Synagogues 1887–1987* (London, Federation of Synagogues, 1987), pp. 55–7, 64–8.

11 See, for example, the views of the veteran Manchester Jewish politician Sir Sidney Hamburger, quoted in S. Brook, *The Club: The Jews of Modern Britain* (London, Constable, 1989), p. 271.

12 Alderman, *Jewish Community*, p. 120.

13 Op. cit., p. 118.

14 Alderman, *London Jewry*, p. 98.

15 *Jewish Chronicle* (hereafter *JC*) (11 January 1957), p. 9.

16 Alderman, *Jewish Community*, p. 117.

17 Alderman, *London Jewry*, pp. 95 and 97.

18 Op. cit., p. 146.
19 L. D. Epstein, *British Politics in the Suez Crisis* (London, 1964), pp. 176–8.
20 B. Donoghue, 'Finchley', in D. E. Butler and A. King, *The British General Election of 1964* (London, Macmillan, 1965), pp. 241–53; *JC* (3 May 1957), p. 10. See also Board of Deputies of British Jews, Minutes of the Metropolitan Area committee of the Defence Committee: C6/1/2/5 (10 July 1957).
21 *Hendon Times* (1 April 1960), p. 6.
22 Donoghue, 'Finchley', pp. 250–2.
23 *JC* (2 September 1949), p. 9.
24 Donoghue, 'Finchley', p. 251.
25 Alderman, *London Jewry*, pp. 107–8.
26 *JC* (1 May 1953), p. 25; (25 May), p. 11. Out of a total of fifty-one Jews elected to London borough councils in 1953, no less than twelve were Conservatives.
27 *JC* (15 November 1946), p. 15; (24 March 1950), p. 6; (21 March 1952), p. 7; *Richmond Herald*, (14 November 1931), p. 10; (3 November 1934), p. 6; (16 November 1946), p. 4.
28 *JC* (26 April 1946), p. 5.
29 A. Sharf, *The British Press and Jews under Nazi Rule* (London, Oxford University Press for Institute of Race Relations 1964), p. 203.
30 *JC* (9 November 1956), p. 8; Epstein, op. cit., pp. 188–9.
31 Alderman, *Jewish Community*, pp. 133, 139–41.
32 This remark, made in the House of Commons on 3 November 1956, is quoted in Epstein, op. cit., p. 192.
33 On the origins and development of left-wing anti-Semitism in Britain see S. Cohen, *That's Funny, You Don't Look Anti-Semitic* (Leeds, Beyond the Pale Collective, 1984).
34 Ibid., pp. 38–49.
35 *JC* (25 September 1979), p. 6; *Hackney Gazette* (25 September 1979), p. 6.
36 *JC* (23 November 1979), p. 22; (11 July 1980), p. 22.
37 *JC* (7 May 1982), p. 10; (28 August), p. 6.
38 *The New Hope for Britain* (London, The Labour Party, 1983), p. 38.
39 See, generally, Alderman, *London Jewry*, ch. 5.
40 D. Cesarani, 'Zionism in England, 1917–1939' (unpublished Oxford University D.Phil. thesis, 1986), ch. 2.
41 Alderman, *London Jewry*, p. 117.
42 On Leeds see E. Krausz, *Leeds Jewry* (Cambridge, 1964), pp. 24–5.
43 Alderman, *Jewish Community*, p. 136.
44 E. Krausz, 'A sociological field study of Jewish suburban life in Edgware 1962–63 with special reference to minority identification' (University of London Ph.D. thesis 1965), pp. 93 and 103. A few years later a similar pattern on response was found among Jewish Hackney: J. W. Carrier, 'Working class Jews in present-day London: a sociological study' (University of London M.Phil. thesis, 1969), p. 346.
45 Krausz, 'A sociological field study', p. 67.
46 B. A. Kosmin, M. Bauer and N. Grizzard, *Steel City Jews* (London, Board of Deputies of British Jews, 1976), p. 22.
47 B. A. Kosmin and N. Grizzard, *Jews in an Inner London Borough* (London, Board of Deputies of British Jews, [1975]), p. 27.
48 Waterman and Kosmin, op. cit., p. 45; Alderman, *Jewish Community*, p. 158.
49 Waterman and Kosmin, op. cit., p. 44; B. A. Kosmin and C. Levy, *The Work and Employment of Suburban Jews* [Redbridge] (London, Board of Deputies of British Jews, 1981), p. 19.
50 Alderman, *One-Party State?*, p. 8.

51 B. A. Kosmin, C. Levy and P. Wigodsky, *The Social Demography of Redbridge Jewry* (London, Board of Deputies of British Jews, 1979), p. 25; R. Waller, *The Almanac of British Politics* (3rd edn, Beckenham, Croom Helm, 1987), pp. 40–2, 46, 70.

52 The methodology of the Hackney, Hendon & Ilford surveys is explained in Alderman, *Jewish Community*, pp. 202–5; the methodology of the Finchley surveys follows that employed at Ilford.

53 The full data may be found in Alderman, *One-Party State?*, and D. Butler and D. Kavanagh, *The British General Election of 1979* (London, Macmillan, 1980), p. 343.

54 Alderman, *Jewish Community*, pp. 159–60.

55 S. Roitman, 'Les juifs anglais de 1966 à 1976 – pratiques, mentalités, comportements' (Strasburg, Université des Sciences Humaines Ph.D. thesis, 1978), p. 220.

56 A. L. Patkin, *The Origins of the Russo-Jewish Labour Movement* (Melbourne, 1947), p. 17.

57 Alderman, *Jewish Community*, p. 206.

58 Ibid., pp. 112–13.

59 Ibid., p. 147.

60 Ibid., pp. 144–5.

61 Ibid., p. 145.

62 Alderman, *One-Party State?*, pp. 118, 135.

63 Alderman, *Jewish Community*, pp. 170–1.

64 Ibid.; I. Bradley, 'A Finchley problem for Mrs Thatcher', *The Times* (29 October 1981), p. 14. A proposal was mooted to move the Prime Minister to the adjacent Hendon South constituency.

65 *Jewish Herald* (20 January 1989), p. 1; *JC* (20 January 1989), p. 10.

66 On this issue see G. Alderman, 'London Jewry and the 1987 general election', *Jewish Quarterly*, vol. 34, no. 3 (1987), p. 16.

67 See, for example, his interview with Walter Schwarz in the *Guardian* (29 December 1988), p. 20.

68 *Jewish Tribune* (17 June 1977), p. 4.

69 Alderman, *London Jewry*, pp. 118–24.

70 Alderman, *Jewish Community*, pp. 148–9.

71 J. Sacks, *Wealth and Poverty* (London, Social Affairs Unit, 1985); *Guardian* (27 May 1986), p. 23.

72 Sir I. Jakobovits, 'From doom to hope', *JC* (24 January 1986), pp. 26–8.

12

ANTI-SEMITISM IN EUROPE AFTER 1945

Robert S. Wistrich

The German National Socialists lost the Second World War but by destroy-ing 6 million Jewish men, women and children during the Holocaust they struck a devastating blow at European Jewry and brought a millennial Ashkenazic Jewish culture on European soil virtually to an end. Yet anti-Semitism, which all over Europe had attained a hitherto unprecedented genocidal savagery during the war years, did not simply vanish with the end of the Third Reich. In Germany, itself, despite the Allies' efforts at de-Nazification (somewhat half-hearted on the British and American side), many Germans in the immediate post-war era clearly maintained a strong prejudice against Jews, even as they denied all knowledge of Hitler's mass murder. In 1947, for example, three-quarters of all Germans considered Jews 'to belong to a different race than ourselves' and nearly as many opposed intermarriage. At the end of 1948 nearly half of all Germans still approved the Nazi seizure of power and in 1952 a third of the population had preserved a positive opinion of Hitler. Also in the same year, 65 per cent of Germans agreed that the Nazis had largely succeeded in spreading aversion to the Jews, 37 per cent that it was better for there to be no Jews in Germany and no less than a third of all West Germans felt that anti-Semitism was primarily caused by Jewish characteristics.[1] At the same time in Communist-ruled East Germany where much firmer action had been taken against ex-Nazis and Jewish 'victims of fascism' were relatively well treated, the country was engulfed at the end of 1952 by an 'anti-Zionist' campaign emanating from the USSR which had unmistakably anti-Jewish overtones.

The Soviet Union, which during the Second World War had saved millions of Jewish lives and in 1948 had strongly supported the creation of Israel, had begun in the very same year to systematically implement (for the first time in Soviet history) explicitly anti-Jewish policies. There was the campaign against 'rootless cosmopolitans' and against Jewish bourgeois nationalism which began in 1948; there was the murder of Soviet Jewry's leading figure, Solomon Mikhoels, by the secret police in Minsk in January 1948; other leading Jewish cultural figures were also arrested and many of the leading Soviet Yiddish writers would eventually be executed in 1952; all the main Jewish cultural institutions were closed down; Jews found admission to higher education much more difficult than before, and they began to be removed systematically from top positions in academic life as well as from influential posts in state, party or bureaucratic apparatuses. The 'Black Years of Soviet Jewry' culminated in Stalin's attempted Soviet-style 'final solution' to the Jewish problem – the notorious Doctors' Plot in which a group of prominent Soviet Jewish physicians were accused of seeking to poison several top Soviet leaders. According to this wholly fabricated scenario, the Jewish doctors had received their criminal instructions from the American Joint Distribution Committee and had also collaborated with Western and Zionist intelligence agencies. The hysterical anti-Semitic denunciations in the media were clearly a prelude to Stalin's planned massive deportation of virtually all Soviet Jews to Siberia, which was only halted by his unexpected death in March 1953.[2]

Elsewhere in the Soviet bloc, the influence of Stalin's anti-Semitic paranoia could also be felt, particularly in Czechoslovakia, which in 1948 had been the conduit for implementing the Soviet dictator's pro-Israel and anti-British policy in the Middle East. It was in Czechoslovakia, where in 1950 there were fewer than 20,000 surviving Jews (out of a pre-1939 population of 357,000) that the most notoriously anti-Jewish Stalinist show-trial of post-war Eastern Europe would be held. The General Secretary of the Czech Communist Party, Rudolf Slansky, a veteran Communist of Jewish origin, was tried and sentenced to be hanged in 1952 along with eleven other leading 'Jewish' Communists accused of treasonous collaboration with Western imperialism, Zionism, Titoism and Trotskyism. The proceedings, orchestrated by Soviet advisers from Moscow, inspired an ugly burst of anti-Semitic incitement in the Czech Communist media. The fictitious charges against Jews as subversive intriguers, 'petty-bourgeois' Zionist spies, 'fifth columnists' and counter-revolutionary agents would be repeated after August 1968 when Soviet tanks crushed Dubczek's Prague Spring and with it the hopes of socialism 'with a human face'. The interesting fact to note, however, is that anti-Semitism as a neo-Stalinist and 'anti-Zionist' masquerade was successfully grafted onto Communist Czechoslovakia in the post-war period, penetrating into a country which before 1939 had a distinctly better record than its neighbours in East–Central Europe with regard to its Jewish minority.[3]

In Poland and Hungary, too, the ghastly slaughter of Jews during the war years did not prevent the immediate revival of anti-Semitism after 1945, though the historic background was rather different to that of Czechoslovakia. Poland, before 1939, had of course held the largest Jewish community in Europe – over 3 million Jews who represented more than 10 per cent of the total population. They had suffered throughout the 1930s from an increasingly violent, xenophobic anti-Semitism instigated by

Poland's largest opposition movement, the National Democrats (Endeks), from economic boycotts, from government discrimination, the hostility of the Catholic church and popular allegations that they were agents of Soviet Communism.[4] These charges were revived by Polish claims that Jews in Eastern Poland welcomed the invading Red Army with open arms in September 1939 and that Jewish Communists who had spent the war years in the USSR had returned to Poland in 1945 to dance on the country's grave together with the new Soviet conquerors.[5]

After the Polish Communist seizure of power in 1948 there were indeed a number of Jews, like Jakob Berman, Hilary Minc and Roman Zambrowski, who did play key roles in the party, the security services and economic planning. No doubt they were considered by Moscow as being less susceptible than the Catholic majority to Polish nationalist feelings, though in the eyes of many Poles they were little better than agents of a foreign, semi-colonial, power. This was one important reason for the intensification of Polish anti-Semitism after the Holocaust (some testimonies have argued that it was actually worse in the 1945–8 period than it had been before 1939!), especially since the anti-Communist underground was convinced that Jews were deliberately betraying Poland. But Jews returning from the Soviet Union were also killed simply for claiming the return of their property, for trying to open stores or workshops, or found themselves attacked in their homes, on the streets or on public transport.[6] Incredibly, there were several pogroms in post-war Poland – the worst of these at Kielce in July 1946 led to forty-one Jewish deaths and more than seventy-five were wounded in the wake of a local blood-libel.[7] About 100,000 surviving Jews left Poland in the following year and a further 50,000 emigrated between 1948 and 1950.

In Hungary, too, there were anti-Semitic pogroms immediately after the war despite the fact that over half a million Hungarian Jews had been killed by the Germans in collaboration with the local gendarmerie and police, during the final year of hostilities.[8] As in Poland, the pogroms reflected the general brutalization engendered by the Nazi occupation, the fact that life itself had become cheap, general fear of a Communist coup, and protests against the payment of reparations to Jews who had suffered losses during the war. Anti-Semitism in post-war Hungary was also influenced by the central role which Communists of Jewish origin like Matyas Rakosi (General Secretary of the Hungarian Communist Party and a faithful ally of Stalin) played in the Sovietization of the country. Many of Rakosi's leading lieutenants were Jews and they were particularly prominent in the political police and security services, a fact which strengthened the popular pre-war identification of Jews with Communism. Nevertheless, the revolution against Stalinist rule in Hungary in October 1956 did not lead to pogroms or virulent anti-Semitism, perhaps because Jews were also well represented among the reform Communists.[9] Assimilation was also more deeply entrenched in Hungary, whose Jewish population, significantly perhaps, constitutes the largest surviving community in Eastern Europe today.

In neighbouring Austria, the number of Jews had been drastically reduced from its pre-war level, following Nazi measures of forced emigration and mass murder during the Second World War. Between the *Anschluss* of March 1938 and 30 November 1939, 126,445 Jews had been driven out of the country and a further 65,000 were killed as a result of wartime deportations to the death camps.[10] A mere 5,700 Jews survived in Vienna by 1945 compared to the 250,000 Hungarian Jews still in Budapest when the Red Army entered the city. Official Austrian government policy towards the survivors or Jewish refugees wishing to return was far from friendly, reflecting a surprising degree of congruence with unsympathetic popular attitudes.[11] Any affirmative action on behalf of Jews was ruled out and there were various manoeuvres and delays by government officials to avoid paying financial compensation to Jewish victims of Nazism.[12] De-Nazification was even more superficial than in the Federal Republic of Germany, primarily due to the fact that former Nazis formed a substantial part of the Austrian electorate. By 1949 many of the lower-level ex-Nazis had been given the vote and by 1955 even prominent National Socialists like Anton Reinthaller (who had become president of Austria's post-war Freedom Party) had been fully integrated into the political process.[13] The dominant political parties – the Socialists and the Conservatives – were interested in attracting the former Nazi vote and in making political deals, when expedient, with the Freedom Party. As a result, anti-Nazi traditions within Austria were played down, those who had fallen while serving in the wartime German Wehrmacht were honoured and even cases against proven mass murderers of Jews were thrown out by Austrian courts with noticeably less hesitation than in neighbouring West Germany. Collective amnesia about Austria's role during the Third Reich was further encouraged by the support of the Western Allies for the myth that brave little Austria had been its first 'victim' and by the obvious need to develop a separate and distinctive Austrian national identity which had nothing further to do with Germany. Thus, public consciousness about Austrian responsibilities in the atrocities against Jews was much less developed than in West Germany. Anti-Semitic stereotypes at a social level could flourish unchecked under the cover of a good conscience, though they did not play a major role in public life during the early post-war years.[14]

In post-war France, popular hostility to the Jews was still quite tenacious – a 1946 opinion poll indicating, for example, that over a third of the French population felt that Jews could never become loyal French citizens.[15] In the same year the philosopher Jean-Paul Sartre published his remarkable *Réflexions sur la question juive* which critically noted the silence of his countrymen about the sufferings of the Jews, about the deportations and the gas chambers, about the Jewish role in the Resistance and the liberation of

France. 'For four years French society has lived without them', Sartre ironically observed. 'It is just as well not to emphasize too vigorously the fact that they have reappeared.'[16] The silence over the complicity and collaboration of Vichy France in the German 'Final Solution' would, in particular, remain a feature of post-war French society until the end of the 1980s. Many eminent Frenchmen continued to pretend that Pétain's Vichy regime sought to protect the Jews, despite the strict racial laws, the institutional anti-Semitism and daily vilification in the French wartime media, not to mention the complicity of the French police and judicial system in the deportation of Jews to the death camps.[17]

Political anti-Semitism, particularly on the nationalist and Catholic Right, also remained a continuing feature of French society in the first decade after the Second World War, especially after the appointment of Pierre Mendès-France as Prime Minister in 1954. Some of the anti-Semitic invective which greeted Mendès-France's decolonization policy was reminiscent of the campaigns led by the Action Française against the Popular Front government of 1936 and its Jewish Socialist leader Léon Blum, though without reaching quite the same pitch of ferocity.[18] In the mid-1950s some of the classic anti-Semitic themes directed against the Jewish role in the French State and in financial capitalism were also revived by the populist, lower-middle-class Poujadist movement.[19] Nevertheless, in contrast to many other European societies like Austria and Poland, there was, in France, alongside the familiar racism and anti-Semitism, a vigorous tradition of anti-racism and anti-anti-Semitism which had retained its vitality in the post-war period, especially with the reassertion of the republican legacy of 1789. Unlike Poland, where anti-Semitism after 1945 had never really been discredited, in France as a result of a campaign of patient education by the churches, the schools and the media, it was partially though far from completely marginalized, in the post-war years.[20]

In post-war Britain, as in neighbouring France, popular prejudice against Jews had by no means disappeared after 1945. Indeed, despite the British war for survival against Nazi Germany, there is evidence to suggest that even during the war years, anti-Semitism had actually increased as a result of the strains and stresses provoked in British society by the external threat.[21] Though Oswald Mosley's pre-war fascist movement had been banned by the British government in 1940 (it never regained its strength after 1945) the Jewish terrorist war against British colonial rule in Palestine gave a temporary new impetus to anti-Semitism. In 1947 there were anti-Jewish riots in several British cities following the execution of two British army sergeants in Palestine by the Irgun. In the occupying British army in Palestine during this period anti-Semitic sentiments were fairly rampant. Nor were they altogether absent, in a more genteel form, in the higher echelons of the Arabophile British Foreign Office where the creation of Israel and the 'behaviour' of Israeli Jews were often regarded with profound distaste, down to and beyond the Suez War of 1956. On the other hand, anti-Semitism had little if any significance in British domestic politics, where the representation of Jews as Members of Parliament (especially in the Labour Party from 1945 until the mid-1970s) was constantly growing.[22] Moreover, Anglo-Jewry, while still suffering periodically from the ingrained social snobbery of the British class system, began to enjoy unprecedented affluence and acceptance by the late 1950s. As in the Scandinavian countries and in Holland during this period, Jews benefited from a mixture of compassion, guilt and shame over the Nazi atrocities and from the goodwill of most liberal and socialist opinion towards the new State of Israel.[23]

The following decade between 1956 and 1967 was one of the most 'philo-Semitic' in European and Western history, much more so than the immediate post-war era where anti-Semitism had been especially rampant in Russia and Eastern Europe during Stalin's final years and was still tenaciously present just beneath the surface in the Western democracies. Jews, above all in North America but also in Western and Central Europe, were living under conditions of unprecedented affluence and enjoying a level of comfort, personal security and self-esteem unknown to their parents or grandparents. They were prominent in the arts and sciences, respected as free and equal citizens of their respective countries. Traditional religious hostility, particularly in Catholic countries, had been somewhat attenuated by the Second Vatican Council's document *Nostra Aetate* (1965), finally lifting the blame for the crucifixion of Christ from the Jewish people as a whole and in particular from contemporary Jewry. The Gentile sense of guilt for the Holocaust, stimulated by the Eichmann trial in Jerusalem (1961) and similar trials in Germany, was more palpable than in the previous decade. Israel, before its extraordinary successes in the 1967 Six Day War (which not only substantially enlarged its boundaries, negatively changed its image to that of a conquering, occupying power but also reopened the issue of Palestinian self-determination) was still regarded with considerable sympathy throughout the Continent, west of the Iron Curtain.[24]

Even in the Communist bloc, though Zionism was routinely attacked as a 'bridgehead' of Western imperialism, diplomatic relations with Israel were maintained until the June 1967 war. Anti-Semitism, too, was relatively mild in the USSR during these interim post-Stalin years, despite the militant atheistic campaigns against the Jewish religion and the implication of Jews in economic crimes under Khruschev. When an openly anti-Semitic book by the Ukrainian academician Trofim Kychko, *Judaism without Embellishment* (1963), aroused international protest (and provoked intervention by Western Communist parties) it was criticized by Soviet party authorities and silently withdrawn from circulation, though the author was not accused of violating any articles in the Soviet legal code. (A few years later such publications had not only become widespread but were officially encouraged in the USSR). Another sign of a temporarily more positive attitude was the speech of Soviet Prime Minister A. N. Kosygin in July 1965 at a large rally in Riga, where he denounced manifestations of nationalism, chauvinism, racism and anti-Semitism as 'absolutely alien to and in contradiction to our world view'.[25]

In Hungary, too, under the new regime of Janos Kadar, anti-Semitism was now to be avoided as a means of establishing popular legitimacy. But as in the USSR, the prevailing tendency was to deny the existence of a 'Jewish Question' and to suppress discussion of other embarrassing questions like Hungarian collaboration during the Holocaust.[26] Kadar's policy of sweeping the Jewish issue under the carpet was, however, less easily achieved in Poland, where so-called 'Jewish' Stalinists had already been targeted as a convenient scapegoat for popular wrath during the crisis of October 1956. During the next ten years under Gomulka's rule, anti-Semitism was relatively quiescent on the surface but behind the scenes it was already becoming a political factor in an internal Communist Party factional struggle.[27] From the early 1960s Jews (who by this time numbered only a little more than 30,000 or less than 0.1 per cent of the population) were being weeded out of the party and state administration as well as the security apparatus. A full card-index for the remnants of Polish Jewry was already being prepared as a step towards the complete purge of *all* Jews planned by General Moczar as a lever in his struggle to overthrow Gomulka and institute an even more nationalist form of Polish Communism.

In Germany, Austria and France, in the decade before the Six Day War, anti-Semitism was not a major issue despite Jewish concern at the persistence of right-wing radicalism. In newly independent and neutral Austria, the case of Taras Borodajkewicz, an anti-Semite and a former Nazi who held a chair at the Vienna College of Economics but was forced to resign in 1965 as a result of anti-Nazi demonstrations, seemed, if anything to bode well for the future.[28] The election of a Jewish-born Marxist, Bruno Kreisky, to head the Austrian Socialist Party in 1967 (he led it to its first post-war victory in the 1970 elections) was seen by some as another signal that Austria finally wished to liberate itself from the Nazi legacy, though as we shall see this hope proved to be somewhat illusory.

In West Germany, where Konrad Adenauer had been Chancellor from 1949 to 1963 and early on inaugurated a reparations policy towards Israel and Jewish Holocaust survivors, 'philo-Semitism' had at an official level become almost obligatory, though it by no means reflected popular attitudes.[29] There was for example, a brief flurry of support for the neo-Nazi NPD party in the mid-1960s which had included a somewhat diluted anti-Semitism in its general anti-democratic platform, but this soon ebbed and it would take another twenty years for this type of radical-right extremism to revive in a significant way.[30] On the other hand, the German New Left, reacting in the wake of the Six Day War to what it saw as an artificial, hypocritical philo-Semitism of the West German Establishment, became increasingly drawn to a rabid anti-Israelism and hostile to Jews in general. According to one young radical, Dieter Kunzelmann, who had planted a bomb in West Berlin's rebuilt Fasanenstrasse synagogue, his New Left comrades simply had to get over 'their thing about the Jews', i.e. their paralysing post-war liberal philo-Semitism.[31] In France, though anti-Semitism had seemed politically unimportant in the 1960s, an opinion poll in 1966 revealed that about 20 per cent of the French population still held 'seriously anti-Semitic opinions'.[32] The Six Day War and the November 1967 press conference of French President Charles de Gaulle was in many ways a watershed in legitimizing a new form of anti-Semitism in France, whatever the General's personal intentions. De Gaulle had not only criticized Israel's 'arrogance' and aggressiveness but referred to the Jews in general as an 'elite people, sure of itself and domineering'. This was the first time that a Western head of state had publicly conjured up such a stereotypic image of the Jewish people since the end of the Second World War. While De Gaulle himself was probably no anti-Semite, such utterances undoubtedly gave a new respectability to both right- and left-wing traditions of anti-Semitism in France, especially when expressed under the mask of anti-Zionism.[33]

In the 1970s it was mainly the 'anti-imperialist' attacks from the left on Israel and Zionism – whether they came from the French Communist Party, the left wing of the Socialists or the many *gauchiste* sects in France – which seemed to many Jews to ooze an unadulterated anti-Semitism.[34] If the Gaullist right tended to focus on alleged Jewish 'dual loyalties', the anti-Zionist left denounced Jews for acting as accomplices of so-called Israeli 'racism', colonialism and repression of the Palestinians. Such accusations could easily slide over into anti-Semitism, as they sometimes did during the Lebanon war of 1982 when for several months the French media unleashed an unprecedented frenzy of denunciations directed at Israeli 'fascism' and a purely fictional 'genocide' allegedly perpetrated against the Palestinian and Lebanese peoples.[35]

Similarly, malicious attempts to morally delegitimize Israel (for many Jews today one of the most dangerous and novel forms of Judaeophobia, though such a definition is inevitably controversial) could be found in Holland, the Scandinavian countries, Britain and the United States.[36] Such attacks which in the pre-1989 Communist world were either a cynical instrument of State policy in home and external affairs or else a thinly disguised cover for blatant anti-Semitism, did not always signal anti-Jewish sentiments in the West. Indeed, many anti-Zionist polemicists in Europe today insist that they are motivated by *anti-racism* and the struggle against anti-Semitism – this being especially true of liberal Left, left-wing socialist, Trotskyist and Third World oriented positions. But for European and American Jews, delegitimizing Zionism as 'racism' or even worse as Nazism, is seen as an attack on the right of Jews to collective emancipation as a people, and as a deliberate slur and as a peculiarly wounding accusation when directed against a national grouping (in this case the Jews) who more than any other has suffered from genocidal racism in this century. Such stigmatizing of Israel seemed designed and bound to create a pariah status for the Jewish State reminiscent of the uses of anti-Semitic stereotypes against European Jewry before the Holocaust. In the 1970s and 1980s across Europe, the obsession with Holocaust analogies, the use of double standards to condemn Israel (while playing down much greater Arab and other Third World infringements of human rights) and the often hate-ridden language gave to this anti-Zionist rhetoric – especially on the left and in but also within the liberal centre – a distinctly unpleasant flavour, often indistinguishable for Jews from classical anti-Semitism.[37]

On the other hand in the USSR and the former Soviet bloc between 1967 and the end of 1986 the seeds of the current wave of anti-Semitism had been planted by massively orchestrated state propaganda campaign against Zionism. It is no accident that this was the period of apprenticeship for many of the leading lecturers and writers of Pamyat (Memory), the Russian nationalist and anti-Semitic organization. At that time, a paranoid image of the global 'Zionist corporation' controlling finance, the media and politics in the Western capitalist world, was developed in the Soviet media and echoed to a greater or lesser degree in the satellite nations of Eastern Europe.[38] An almost cosmic omnipotence was attributed to 'world Zionism' which was depicted in Manichean terms as a perfidious, reactionary monster locked in a death struggle with the mighty Soviet State, with the forces of peace and progress and with national liberation movements throughout the world. The theory of the World Jewish Conspiracy as laid out in the *Protocols of the Elders of Zion* (itself a Russian secret police fabrication from the turn of the century) was revived in a suitably Sovietized version to suggest that Zionist Jews were seeking global domination; that they were animated by the concept of the 'chosen people'; that they regarded the *goyim* as sub-humans to be exploited and controlled; and that together with Freemasons they were collaborating to subvert and overthrow the Socialist system.[39]

This campaign, whose seeds had been sown in Stalin's Doctors' Plot of 1953 (officially repudiated after his death as an aberration) would continue unabated for at least two decades after the Six Day War, beamed at the Arab and Third Worlds no less than at Russian or European public opinion. It was used in Czechoslovakia from the summer of 1968 as a means of undermining the short-lived experiment to humanize and liberalize Communism, by depicting the Prague Spring as a counter-revolutionary, 'Zionist' and capitalist conspiracy against the socialist camp. In Poland, it led to an extraordinary witchhunt in 1968 which forced two-thirds of the country's remaining Jews into emigration. The Polish Army was made *judenrein*, the Foreign Ministry and other government departments, the universities, the press and party schools were purged of the allegedly dangerous 'Zionist fifth column'. 'International Zionism' was blamed for inciting Polish students to anti-government protests in March 1968.[40] The ringleaders were denounced as being of 'Jewish origin' or 'Jewish nationality' and their 'real' Jewish names put in brackets after their Polish-sounding names – an echo of Stalin's campaign against the 'rootless Jewish cosmopolitans' twenty years earlier. The Polish Communist Party leader, Gomulka, in order to beat off the challenge of his anti-Semitic rival General Moczar, condemned those Polish Jews who were supposedly agents of Zionism, cosmopolitan 'national nihilists' or ideologically 'alien' to Polish culture.[41] A leading Party theorist, Andrzej Werblan, further explained in a notorious essay of 1968 that Jews were particularly prone not only to Zionist intrigues but to other ideological heresies such as 'Trotskyism' and Social-Democratic 'revisionism'. The forced exodus of the remnants of Polish Jewry was justified as an act of correcting the 'ethnic imbalance' in Communist Party cadre policy, since no society could tolerate undue influence exercised by a national minority 'coming from an outside cosmopolitan background'.[42]

In the Soviet Union, theoreticians like Yuri Ivanov and Vladimir Bolshakov developed at the beginning of the 1970s the equally ominous theory that Zionism was a prime enemy of the Soviet people, rooted in bellicose chauvinism, anti-Communism and a long history of collaboration with counter-revolutionary forces.[43] Vicious anti-Semitic novels, like those of Ivan Shevtsov, published in huge editions and sponsored by state publishing houses, further elaborated on the sinister, covert role of 'Zionism' in undermining Soviet power. For Shevtsov and writers of a similar ilk, 'Judas Trotsky (Bronshtein)' was a 'typical agent of Zionism' and of the international Jewish conspiracy. A vast industry of Judaeophobic and anti-Zionist literature was created – according to one expert the number of books of this type officially sponsored during the late 1960s and 1970s reached a total of 112.[44] It was given international legitimacy by Soviet sponsorship of the United Nations resolution defining Zionism as 'a form of racism and racial discrimination', which encouraged a further escalation of this propaganda. By the late 1970s and early 1980s Zionism was being widely equated in the Soviet Union with German Nazism, and Zionist leaders were constantly accused of having collaborated with the Germans in the mass murder of European Jewry – a monstrous lie that found a ready echo not only in the Arab world but also in some Western leftist (and even Jewish) circles.[45]

A number of publicists like Yevgeny Yevseev, Valery Emelyanov, Lev Korneyev, Skurlatov, Vladimir Begun and Aleksandr Romanenko (some of whom would become closely involved with Pamyat in the 1980s) developed a particularly racist and anti-Semitic form of 'anti-Zionism' under Communist Party auspices at this time. As early as 1974 Emelyanov was telling Moscow audiences that Zionism aimed at world mastery toward the year

2000', that it desired to conquer and destroy the *goyim* with the help of world-wide Freemasonry. In his book *De-Zionization* (1980), Emelyanov traced in classic Protocols fashion the origins of the Zionist–Masonic conspiracy back to King Solomon 3,000 years ago. Emelyanov, Begun, Zhukov, Skurlatov, and other Soviet anti-Semites, saw the roots of the Zionist danger in Judaism and the Torah itself, depicted as the blackest, most criminal book in history which had legitimized a 'chosen people' ideology of racial superiority. This was a favourite theme of Yevseev's *Fascism under the Blue Star* (1972) and of subsequent writings that attributed to 'racist' Judaism the 'genocidal' policies supposedly implemented by Zionist Israel against the Arabs.[46] Such works had support in the highest party circles and the cachet of 'academic' approval by prestigious scholarly institutions like the Soviet Academy of Sciences. As late as 1986, Romanenko's *On the Class Essence of Zionism*, officially published in Leningrad, accused Zionism and reactionary Judaism of claiming that 'the Jews are superior to other peoples and their vocation is to rule over the whole of mankind'.[47] The echo which these and other similar works expounding on Masonic–Zionist and Jewish conspiracies have found in the USSR, testify to the strength of anti-Semitism at both the official and popular levels. The mushrooming of this literature since 1967 has coincided with consistent discrimination against Jews in higher education (the enrolment figures for Jewish students have fallen drastically in the past twenty years), not to mention their near-total exclusion from military, political or diplomatic careers. Moreover, the long official anti-Zionist campaign of the Brezhnev years paved the way for the even more vicious populist anti-Semitism that has, ironically enough, blossomed since Gorbachev's more liberal policy of *glasnost* was instituted after 1985. Though the Kremlin has retreated from the old-style anti-Zionist vituperation, it has found itself confronted with a Frankenstein monster of Black Hundred anti-Semitism, largely of its own creation.[48]

Pamyat and other Russian nationalist organizations like Otechestvo are simply more open and direct in their use of 'Elders of Zion' propaganda – claiming that the satanic Zionist–Mason conspiracy has already systematically destroyed historic monuments and churches, the natural environment and the moral fabric of Russian society and culture. They blame the 'Zionists' for Chernobyl, for alcoholism, crime, drugs, pornography and the infiltration of Western-style rock music.[49] The 'Zionists' are behind the disintegration of Russia as a great power, its manifold military and economic failures, its loss of internal cohesion. Above all they [i.e., the Jews] are responsible for the catastrophe brought about by the Russian Revolution of 1917, the Gulag system and the 'genocide' of the Russian people during the years of Soviet terror.[50]

The new anti-Semitism, especially in the Russian Republic, is by no means a marginal protest phenomenon. The leader of Pamyat, Vasiliev, claimed in 1989 that his organization had 20,000 members in Moscow alone and many more in other major Russian cities. Their meetings are well attended and attract people from a wide spectrum in Soviet society. Since 1987 they have had control of the Moscow section of the All-Russian Society for the Restoration of Historical and Cultural Monuments, the Russian Republic Culture Fund and a number of environmental movements. They have many sympathizers in the Russian Writers' Union, including one of its presidents, Yuri Bondarev and a number of popular novelists like Valentin Rasputin, Victor Astafiev and Vasily Belov, whose widely read books have disseminated some ugly anti-Jewish stereotypes. Even more disturbing is the fact that at least three prominent conservative Soviet monthly publications – *Nash Sovremennik* (Our Contemporary), *Molodaya Gvardiya* (Young Guard) and *Moskva* – as well as the newspaper *Sovietskaya Rossiya* and the weekly *Nedelya*, promote anti-Semitism as part of their nationalist ideology. These newspapers and periodicals reach millions and given the vacuum created by the failure of Communism, anti-Semitism thereby provides the new Russian Right with a crucial component in its anti-Communist and Great Russian chauvinist platform. It is, moreover, given additional credibility by the anti-Jewish writings of renowned academicians like Igor Shafarevich, whose *Russophobia* (1989) sums up the intellectual paranoia of the new anti-Western, anti-Socialist and anti-Semitic gospel, obsessed as it is with finding scapegoats for the spiritual crisis of Soviet society.[51]

There were undoubtedly powerful conservative forces within the Communist Party hierarchy and the KGB, interested in using anti-Semitism as a weapon against Gorbachev's liberalization and *perestroika*. The Soviet authorities appeared to have belatedly understood this, in so far as some major Soviet journals published articles sharply critical of Black Hundred and Nazi-style anti-Semitism in the USSR.[52] But matters were not helped by occasional statements from Mikhail Gorbachev even-handedly linking Zionism and anti-Semitism as nationalist aberrations which have no place in a civilized society. Nor do conciliatory steps like those of Boris Yeltsin, when he was still Communist Party head in Moscow and spent two hours with Pamyat leaders, signal strong opposition or even understanding of the threat which anti-Semitism represents to Soviet society. Since Yeltsin became the first democratically elected President of Russia, it is true that anti-Semitism has not been promoted in any way from the top. Like Gorbachev, before him, Yeltsin is well aware that some of his most fanatical opponents are hard-core anti-Semites or willing to use this weapon to attempt to discredit him as a 'lackey of the West' and of world Zionism. They include disaffected military officers, embittered Communists, marginalized proletarians and hooligan elements and, most dangerously, the xenophobic nationalists led by Vladimir Zhirinovsky. Economic chaos, street violence, intellectual and working-class disaffection, a disintegrating ethnic situation, political instability, the impotence of the authorities, and a strong sense of national humiliation provide the background for the unravelling of Russian society, following the collapse of the USSR.[53] In the midst of this deep spiritual, economic and political crisis, the pre-revolutionary traditions of Russian anti-Semitism have been reactivated and long bottled-up ethnic and religious hatreds projected against Jews, Caucasians and other vulnerable minorities.

In Poland, too, in recent years, anti-Semitism has once again been on the rise despite the fact that there are barely 10,000 Jews left in the country, most of them sick and elderly. During the 1980s with the rise of the powerful trade union movement Solidarity, the beginnings of a Catholic–Jewish dialogue involving liberal Catholic Polish intellectuals and a general movement towards democratization and the West, it seemed that perhaps the ghosts from the past would finally be laid to rest.[54] True, the Communist regime tried in the early 1980s to discredit Solidarity by charging that it was manipulated by 'Jewish' advisers and dissident intellectuals like Adam Michnik, Bronislaw Gieremek and Karol Modzelewski.[55] Even labour activists like Kuron and Lipski, who had no Jewish ancestry at all, were tarred with fictitious 'Zionist' links. But despite the cynical efforts of the Communist government and the anti-Jewish Grunwald Patriotic Association, there was no sign that public opinion would swallow a re-run of the 1968 'anti-Zionist' crusade.

Paradoxically, it was the fall of Communism in 1989 which revived the language of raw, popular anti-Semitism and the search for 'hidden' Jews in Poland in an electorate embittered by economic mismanagement, poverty and the soured promises of democracy.[56] The return of old pre-war slogans like 'Judaeo-Communism', of xenophobia towards minorities and anti-democratic sentiments suddenly came to the surface, along with attempts to revive the National Democrat tradition of Poland as a purely Catholic and Polish nation.[57] The controversy over the Carmelite monastery in Auschwitz sparked an anti-Semitic homily from the Primate of Poland, Cardinal Jozef Glemp, delivered in Czestochowa on 26 August 1989, in which he warned Jews not to 'talk to us from the position of a people raised above all others'. The Cardinal, Poland's leading churchman, seemed to be presenting anti-Semitism as a legitimate form of national self-defence against Jewish 'anti-Polonism'. Deploring the attacks of 'world Jewry' on the poor nuns at Auschwitz, he admonished Jewish leaders in terms that seemed to echo the words of the pre-war National Democratic leader Roman Dmowski (one of Glemp's heroes): 'Your power lies in the mass media that are easily at your disposal in many countries. Let them not serve to spread anti-Polish feeling.'[58]

In the Polish elections of 1990, such atavistic sentiments took a new turn when Lech Walesa's supporters (half-encouraged by their leader) began to smear his opponent, the liberal Catholic Prime Minister, Tadeusz Mazowiecki, as a crypto-Jew who was soft on Communism. The Walesa camp played on the theme that Mazowiecki's government was allegedly controlled

by Jews and that the time had come for 'real Poles' like Walesa to govern.[59]
This was an even cruder version of the Communist smear campaign ten years
earlier against Solidarity, only this time former advisers of Walesa like
Michnik and Gieremek were on Mazowiecki's side. Walesa himself was
highly equivocal, suggesting that he admired Jews who were open about
their ancestry and Jewish culture, but why did Michnik, Gieremek and
others hide under Gentile names? It was such behaviour, he argued, that
created anti-Semitism in Poland! The campaign was quite successful and
seemed to demonstrate that anti-Semitism was alive and well in a Poland
that was virtually *judenrein* – a legitimate political opinion and religious or
cultural stereotype which had become wholly divorced from reality. In
contrast to pre-war Polish anti-Semitism it no longer related – be it in a
rational or irrational manner – to the presence of a coherent, organized
Jewish community or to an objective national minority problem. But it did
reflect the climate of anxiety and disorientation, fear of the future and doubts
about national identity that had been opened up by the collapse of the hated
Communist system.[60]

In Hungary, too, pre-war chauvinist and anti-Semitic tendencies
which had been frozen for more than forty years under Communist rule,
have risen to the surface since Hungary's 'quiet revolution' of 1989. As in
Poland, the overthrow of Communism has been beneficial in terms of
human rights, the rule of law and a revival of interest in Jewish culture,
but it has also brought with it greater political instability, inflation and
growing unemployment. Those searching for scapegoats and simplistic
answers can find them, as many Hungarians did before 1939, by blaming
the Jews for their problems.[61] Once more one can hear Budapest referred to
in some circles as Zydapest, a symbol of urban, rootless cosmopolitans
against the national and 'Christian' countryside.[62] During the last elections,
the victorious, populist Democratic Forum called on its electors to vote for
'true Hungarians' and stars of David were daubed on some posters of the
Social Democratic Party, in which Jewish intellectuals were known to play
an important role. The presence of between 80,000 and 100,000 Jews in
contemporary Hungary means that anti-Semitism, if it were to be
unleashed, would have more of a target than in neighbouring Poland or
Slovakia. This is already partly the case in Romania, the only East European
Communist state not to have broken off diplomatic relations with Israel
after the 1967 war. Paradoxically, under the hard-line Stalinist dictatorship
of Ceaucescu, Romanian Jews had enjoyed greater autonomy and freedom
to emigrate that any other Jewish community in the Eastern bloc and some
resentment was stirred by the misperception that they enjoyed better
conditions than other Romanians or ethnic minorities in the country.
Though Ceaucescu was scarcely philo-Semitic, he found it financially and
politically advantageous to trade his Jews off against a 'most favoured nation'
status in the United States.[63] The fall of Ceaucescu has brought with it,

however, a revival of the visceral anti-Semitism that was endemic to pre-war Romania, as part of the historic tradition of the country. Articles have appeared in the Romanian press depicting the Jews as Satan or Anti-Christ and blaming them for imposing the Communist scourge on Romania. The 'diabolical' role of the post-war 'Jewish' Stalinist foreign minister of Romania, Ana Pauker, is commonly recalled, while at the same time there are efforts to rehabilitate Marshal Antonescu, the nation's wartime fascist leader. Remnants of the pre-war Iron Guard (one of Europe's most fanatically anti-Semitic movements in the 1930s) have returned to the country from abroad or revived inside Romania, though they are scarcely a major force and today there are only 20,000 Jews left against whom they can direct their wrath. Nevertheless, the former prime minister of Romania, Petre Roman, who was of Jewish origin (or a 'hidden Jew' in anti-Semitic parlance) was frequently vilified and the slogan 'Roman is not Romanian' featured prominently at one time among graffiti in Bucharest.[64] The fact that another Jew, Silviu Brucan, was the leading ideologist of the ruling National Salvation Front in Romania, is further grist to the paranoid world-view of a resurgent Romanian chauvinism – directed against Jews, Hungarians and gypsies.

In what was formerly East Germany, with its tiny Jewish community, anti-Semitism has also raised its ugly head in street demonstrations and in the violence that has accompanied the rapidly burgeoning fascist skinhead youth culture. Neo-Nazi slogans and symbols have grown in popularity since the collapse of Communism and German reunification. Even the tomb of a non-Jew in East Berlin, like the Communist playwright Bertolt Brecht, has been smeared with the words 'Jew-pig'. Cemetery desecrations and swastika daubings on Jewish graves have occurred in Poland, France, Britain and many other countries over the past two or three years with growing frequency. But in a newly united Germany, currently suffering all the economic, social and psychological stresses of reunification (especially in the East) such a development is potentially more troubling. According to figures published at the beginning of 1991, the number of neo-Nazi activists in the whole of Germany had doubled in the previous year, again due mainly to their success in the East.[65] Admittedly, the radical right-wing Republikaner, led by a former Waffen-SS soldier, Franz Schönhuber, suffered some reverses in the 1990 all-German elections, not least because the main plank in its platform, German reunification, had been realized by the Christian-Democrat Chancellor Helmut Kohl. But the Republikaner, with their 'Germany first' watchword, their xenophobic racism (for electoral reasons their anti-Semitism is muted), their national sentiment and the desire for 'normalcy', including, above all, normalizing the German past have grown popular since the early 1980s.[66] Shortly before reunification, opinion surveys indicated that in West Germany alone, some 6 or 7 million Germans (between 10 and 15 per cent) could be classified as having anti-Semitic prejudices. This was, as in Poland, Romania or Austria, an 'anti-Semitism without Jews', no longer related to real or imagined social conflicts with a Jewish community of any significant size but rather one which has thrived on abstract stereotypes and unresolved complexes pertaining to the Holocaust and the 'unmastered' German past.[67]

We have already seen how the German left, despite its anti-racist and anti-Semitic declarations, had already attacked Germany's Holocaust and 'Judenkomplex' in the late 1960s. In the 1970s and 1980s the radical left in West Germany relieved its own feelings of anxiety and guilt in two different directions with regard to Jews, both of them having unmistakably anti-Jewish connotations. One direction, perhaps best symbolized by the play *Garbage, the City and Death* (written in 1975 by the radical film-maker, Rainer Werner Fassbinder and banned in 1985 from public performance after vehement Jewish protests) stereotypically linked Jews to wealth and power, insisted that they could not be immune from criticism and reduced the problem of anti-Semitism to that of popular anti-capitalism.[68] Fassbinder's stereotype of the anonymous 'rich Jew' (whatever his actual intentions) coincided with a widely held prejudice in Germany that Jews are cunning and rapacious, successful in business, greedy and clever. His portrait of the vengeful Jew also corresponds to the insistent German desire to draw a line over the Nazi past and the feeling that the Jews will not permit this since they wish to extract the maximum financial and political benefit from the Holocaust. This is a motif that finds expression as much on the right as on the left, with a Christian Social-Union deputy, Hermann Fellner, publicly complaining in 1985 that 'Jews are quick to speak up when they hear the tinkling of money in German cash-registers'.[69]

The other direction for coming to terms with German guilt, pioneered on the left but today no less fashionable on the radical right, is the demonization of Israel and Zionism, as if they were actually worse than the Nazis and hell-bent on exterminating the Palestinian people. This was a favourite theme of the Baader-Meinhof 'Red Army Faction' in the early 1970s, which a decade later had found wide acceptance among the pacifist Green Party on the one hand and on the neo-Nazi right on the other.[70] If the Greens felt a 'special responsibility' to the Palestinian victims of Israeli occupation, this was because, in the words of one Green Party Euro MP in 1984, 'The genocide of the Jews created the psychological prerequisites for setting up Israel as an internationally recognized state. The expulsion of the Palestinians is therefore indirectly the result of the Nazi persecution of the Jews.'[71] The neo-Nazis, by contrast, cynically juxtaposed the 'real' Holocaust inflicted on the Palestinians by Israel with the purely 'fictive' Holocaust, which they denied that Germans had ever perpetrated against Jews.

These may be extreme fanatical views, but in an era of heightened German national consciousness and fading awareness of the Nazi era, as well as a growing public desire to distance Germany from Israel and world Jewry, they can provide fertile soil for anti-Semitism. The most recent opinion polls from the beginning of 1991 showed that 57 per cent of West Germans rejected the idea of any 'special relationship' with the Jewish State and no less than 33 per cent agreed strongly or somewhat that 'Zionism is racism' (so did a similar percentage of East Germans). Moreover, as many as 65 per cent of West Germans felt that it was time to put the Holocaust behind them.[72] The survey revealed widespread resentment at what was seen as 'Jewish' pressure for Germans to constantly remember, take responsibility and atone for their murderous past.[73]

The recent Gulf War provided some chilling reminders of what this irresponsibility might mean in practice. It was German firms who in the 1980s provided the criminal Iraqi dictator Saddam Hussein not only with the best bomb shelters and the technological know-how to increase the range of Soviet-supplied Scud missiles (which in January–February 1991 would descend on Israel's civilian population) but also with the poison gas that once again threatened the lives of Jewish men, women and children. It was almost certainly pure greed rather than residues of anti-Semitism that explained the German (as well as the French, Soviet, American, British, Austrian and Italian) involvement in heavily arming the Iraqi regime, but for many Israeli Jews the prospect of poison-gas attacks could only revive the terrible spectre of the Holocaust, with Europe – led by Germany – helping once more to supply the technology of mass destruction. Moreover, the Gulf War did help to fuel anti-Semitism across Western Europe, especially among young people in countries like Britain, Germany, Italy and France, gullible enough to believe either radical left- or right-wing propaganda about the 'Jewish War' or the 'Zionist *Diktat*' that supposedly pushed the Allies into confrontation with Saddam Hussein.[74]

In Austria, the level of *hard-core* anti-Semitism has been ostensibly similar to that of Germany (7 to 10 per cent) but the percentage of 'moderate' anti-Semites has tended to be significantly higher. In the mid-1970s, at a time when the Jewish-born Socialist Chancellor Bruno Kreisky was at the peak of his popularity, 32 per cent of Austrians were considered as either virulently or moderately anti-Semitic (25 per cent for the latter), 35 per cent as having weak prejudices and only 15 per cent as wholly unprejudiced. In 1976, 64 per cent of Austrians felt that Jews had excessive influence in international finance and business, 48 per cent believed that they controlled international politics, 45 per cent that they had too much power in Austria, 42 per cent that they were alien to Austrians, 33 per cent that they were responsible for many catastrophes in history and 20 per cent wished to restrict their access to important positions. The most prevalent stereotypes – held by more than a third of the population – signalled that Jews were averse to physical work and dishonest in their business dealings. The notion of a Jewish *Geldmacht* (money-power) was particularly tenacious though it had little practical meaning in a post-war Austria that was almost *judenrein* after the Holocaust.[75]

As in Germany, resentment about reminders of the Holocaust has been consistently high (57 per cent in 1976) and Kreisky's long reign as Chancellor between 1970 and 1983 did nothing to diminish entrenched anti-Jewish sentiments or the desire to repress the Nazi past. Indeed, Kreisky's attacks on Nazi-hunter Simon Wiesenthal, whom he branded as a 'Jewish fascist', his courting of the Freedom Party leader, Friedrich Peter (who had been involved in war-crimes on the Eastern Front as an SS Obersturmbannführer) and his unrestrained vituperation against 'Zionst racism', probably gave a new legitimacy to such feelings in the Austrian population – the more so since they came from an Austrian Jew who had lost most of his family in the Holocaust.[76]

The election campaign of Kurt Waldheim, the former UN Secretary-General, who in 1986 was the successful Conservative candidate for the Austrian presidency, brought to the foreground all the latent anti-Semitic prejudices which had previously been publicly taboo in post-war Austrian politics. The investigations by the World Jewish Congress into Waldheim's Nazi past (he had served as a Wehrmacht staff officer in the Balkans with a unit that supervised mass deportations of partisans and Jews) provoked a strong reaction by members of Waldheim's own party. Its secretary-general, Michael Graff, declared that unless Waldheim could be personally shown to have strangled five or six Jews with his own hands, he must be considered blameless. He denounced the 'mafia of slanderers' who had stopped at nothing to blacken Austria's good name. Many Austrians appeared to agree that World Jewry was guilty of unwarranted interference in Austria's internal affairs, that Waldheim had only done his 'duty' as an Austrian patriot and was being unjustly persecuted by the all-powerful Jewish interests that allegedly dominated the world media.[77] The former vice-mayor of Linz even compared the 'persecution' of Waldheim to the Jews handing over Jesus for crucifixion to the Romans (*sic!*) and attacked the vengeful Old Testament attitudes displayed by the World Jewish Congress. The majority of the Austrian press also indulged in anti-Semitic stereotyping of World Jewry, with its nerve-centres in New York, vigorously condemning the campaign against Austria and its democratically elected president led by malevolent foreigners. The effects of this campaign were no doubt reflected in an opinion poll conducted in January 1989, which showed that 37 per cent of all Austrians still exhibited anti-Jewish prejudices (10 per cent could be described as hard-core anti-Semites) – the confirmation of long-standing and persistent attitudes that had never been uprooted after the Second World War.[78] The more radical anti-Semites were generally to be found in the Freedom Party (led today by a charismatic, ultra-nationalist young politician, Jörg Haider) which has done consistently well in Austrian elections since 1990.[79]

In France, as we have already seen, anti-Semitism remained active into the 1970s though it had to confront a more militant anti-racist tradition of political mobilization in favour of republican ideals. The past decade, beginning with the terrorist attacks on the Rue Copernic synagogue (October 1980), followed by the assault on a Jewish restaurant in the Rue de Rosiers (August 1982) and culminating in the desecrations of the Carpentras cemetery (1990), has however been considerably more traumatic for many French Jews.[80] Though anti-Semitism has not been a *major* political issue since 1945 (and even today one could not describe it as such, despite the understandable anxieties of some French Jews) and the intellectual and moral atmosphere is quite different from that prevailing in the 1930s, nevertheless there are signs of its growing respectability as memories of the Holocaust fade.[81] Already in the 1970s, the existing taboo on public Jewishness and the critical preoccupation with Jewish problems was being challenged by fierce criticism of Israel and also by the growing self-assertiveness of Europe's largest Jewish community (west of the USSR) – many of them fairly recent Sephardi immigrants of French culture, who had emigrated from North Africa in the 1950s and 1960s. This influx, along with the impact of the Six Day War and the sensitivity to anything smacking of anti-Semitism after the Holocaust, provoked a reawakening of Jewish consciousness in France at many levels. Jews also became prominent in French politics first under Giscard d'Estaing (Simone Veil, Lionel Stoleru, Jacques Wahl) and even more under François Mitterand's presidency since 1981 (Laurent Fabius, Robert Badinter, Jacques Attali, Jacques Lang and others) – a fact which has inevitably attracted much adverse comment on the radical right.[82] Admittedly, such negative sentiments seem to waning in the French population as a whole and are far weaker than the rampant prejudice against the North African Arab influx into France over the past two decades.

But the danger for Jews in this generalized racism and xenophobia is evident as France has become home to what until recently was Europe's largest post-war radical right movement, the National Front led by Jean-Marie Le Pen.[83] Le Pen is a politician who has built his career on vocal opposition to Arab and Muslim immigration (which did not prevent him admiring Saddam Hussein as a 'great Arab patriot') while being more quietly and insidiously anti-Jewish. His movement, which today represents between 10 and 15 per cent of the electorate, thrives on the cynical exploitation of real social problems provoked by immigration, unemployment and urban neglect as well as a growing anxiety about the religious and national identity of France. The 650,000 French Jews are, at first sight, a secondary target compared to the Arab–Islamic 'peril', but increasingly in National Front literature the classical imagery of anti-Semitism has found a populist voice. The Jews are identified by their wealth, their power and influence, their prominence in the Socialist government, their 'cosmopolitanism' and hostility to Catholic morality. The 'Jewish International' or the 'Judaeo-cosmopolitan *médiocratie*' is depicted as controlling the press, television, radio, international communications and high finance. The Jews are seen by the radical right as stateless nomads, part of a shadowy international which has seized real power in France and aims at extending it on a global scale.[84]

These classical pre-war themes of French anti-Semitism are reinforced by the nationalist and fundamentalist cult of monolithic Catholic civilization, which is extremely intolerant of liberalism, pluralism or dissent. Thus, many conservative catholic *intégristes*, convinced that there is a Judaeo–Masonic–Republican conspiracy against the true faith, can find their political home in the National Front.[85] The traditional Catholic theology of the Jews as a God-rejected people can be seen as once again fusing with xenophobic racism of the radical right, as it often did before the Holocaust. The same obsessions with the '*complot juif*', with the Protocol's mythology of Jews seeking to wreak revenge on the Christian world and to attain world domination, have resurfaced along with another pre-war image – that of '*le juif belliqueux*' (the Jewish war-monger). During the 1991 Gulf War, the radical right, echoed by Arab voices and those of the extreme left, pictured the Allied liberation of Kuwait from Iraqi aggression as a 'Jewish war' or the 'vengeance of Yahweh', orchestrated by world Zionism to remove its most dangerous enemy. As in 1938–9, pacifist sentiment was often overlaid with more than a whiff of anti-Semitism by those who urged the appeasement at any price of Saddam Hussein.[86]

The only truly novel element in radical right anti-Semitism since 1945 has been its espousal of so-called 'revisionism' or the denial that the Holocaust took place. This trend is not confined solely to the right nor indeed to France (the United States, Britain and Germany are also centres for such literature) but it gained significantly more *pseudo-academic* currency in France and has a longer pedigree than in any other European country. Already in the early 1950s it was being propagated by a former French socialist, Paul Rassinier, and it gained notoriety when it was espoused by Professor Robert Faurisson at the end of the 1970s in the French media. According to Faurisson, 'the claim of the existence of gas chambers and the genocide of the Jews constitute one and the same historical lie, which opened the way to a gigantic political fraud of which the principal beneficiaries are the State of Israel and international Zionism'. This statement, made in 1980, was followed five years later by the successful defence of a 'revisionist' dissertation by Henri Rocques at the University of Nantes, whose main thrust was also to deny the existence of the Nazi gas chambers.[87] A year later, in 1986, the National Front (which has with increasing openness supported 'revisionist' claims) won thirty-five seats in the French parliamentary elections. Le Pen, who was initially equivocal over the Rocques affair, would later go on record as saying that the Holocaust was 'just a detail in the history of the Second World War.'[88] For many of his supporters, denial, trivialization or merely casting doubt on the Holocaust, is at one and the same time a way of undermining Jewish legitimacy, implying immense Jewish power (to perpetrate such a colossal fraud over so many years) and rehabilitating fascism from the taint of mass murder.[89] It also forges a link with pro-Palestinian militants and Arab governments (Libya and Saudi Arabia are known to have financed Holocaust-denial literature in the West) who claim that Jews 'invented' the *Shoah* to protect Israel and to neutralize the injustice done to the Palestinians.

France is not, of course, an anti-Semitic state and the existence of such currents should not blind one to the important changes which have occurred here, and in many other European countries, since 1945, which have undoubtedly been to the benefit of the Jewish community. A fuller and more successful Jewish integration has taken place in French society, especially since the 1960s, than was the case thirty years earlier. France, like Germany and other West European countries, has become a more mobile, industrially modern and technological society, reconciled to the 'spirit of capitalism' and less prone to the kind of anti-modernist backlash associated in the nineteenth century with anti-Semitic ideologies. Its intelligentsia no longer throws up anti-Jewish ideologues and writers of the calibre of Barrès, Maurras, Céline, Brasillach or Drieu la Rochelle. The tone of the French press, even on the radical right (where caution is dictated by the anti-racist legislation) is nothing like as incendiary or hysterically violent in its anti-Semitism as it used to be in the 1930s. The political elites are thus far resolutely opposed to anti-Semitism, and incidents like Copernic or Carpentras did after all lead to spontaneous mass demonstrations of Frenchmen and women against such racist acts of violence. Moreover, it is clear from opinion polls that French people today have a notably stronger antipathy to Arabs, Africans and sometimes even Corsicans or Spaniards, than to Jews – suggesting a decline in the intensity of popular anti-Semitic feeling.

Does this mean, however, that viewed in a European-wide perspective and through the prism of modern political anti-Semitism, Jews in 1994 are indeed living in a new world? Certainly, if such an extreme and unprecedented event as the Holocaust itself were to be our sole measure, then we are still far away from the repeat of such a horrific scenario, though not from the real danger of pogroms materializing in the USSR and individual acts of anti-Jewish violence in parts of Eastern Europe. But leaving the Shoah itself aside, what has been happening in Europe in recent years does seem to represent a definite loosening of the taboos that temporarily held anti-Semitism in check during a part of the post-war period and to constitute a resurgence of many classical anti-Jewish themes from before 1939. This is particularly obvious in the ex-Soviet Union, in Poland, Hungary, Slovakia, Romania and East Germany where a state-controlled Communist anti-Semitism which had been rather carefully dosed has given way to a popular Jew-hatred from below, that is deeply chauvinist and anti-Communist, reviving some of the ugliest features of older national traditions.[90] Ancient prejudices embedded in the popular psyche have come to the fore in these societies, even where there are scarcely any Jews left, intensified in some cases by the very abstractness of the anti-Jewish stereotypes and by their protean nature, which can be readily transformed and adapted to new situations. Moreover, from a political standpoint, anti-Semitism in Russia and Eastern Europe has always had a wide variety of functions, some of which are still relevant today, in those circles striving for an authoritarian, monolithic alternative to Western liberalism, political democracy, cultural and religious pluralism.[91]

Nor have the older, more traditional forms of stereotyping disappeared from the democratic societies of Central and Western Europe. In Germany, France and Austria one still finds Christian Judaeophobia alongside racism and xenophobia, not to mention the more modern forms of 'anti-Zionist' anti-Semitism, though the specifically religious component has declined in importance. The unresolved problems of national identity in these countries as well as their difficulties in living with the burdens of the Nazi past, suggest that there is a still a living potential for anti-Semitism which adverse economic conditions and political instability could easily activate. Such a cultural or political anti-Semitism would probably be less concerned with the Jewish communities in their midst (though they would be the first to suffer) and more with Israel and American Jewry, seen as the two main arms of a world Jewish power that was antagonistic towards them. In France, as in the former Soviet Union, the revival of a 'Jewish question' is more directly related to the physical presence and security of large Jewish communities. What is going on in Russia with the recent electoral success of Vladimir Zhirinovsky is, of course, by far the most dangerous of all the present examples of a renewed anti-Semitism in Europe. With the collapse of the empire and of the economy, popular anti-Semitism has reached a point unprecedented in Russian history since Stalin's abortive war against the Jews in the early 1950s. In France, on the other hand, one might argue that despite steady support for Le Pen's National Front, Jews have never enjoyed such outward acceptance, security and success, even if they themselves frequently do not perceive their situation in these terms. But even in France, anti-Semitism has hardly disappeared as a popular prejudice, as a semi-respectable sentiment or even as a potential political weapon in domestic or foreign affairs. It may as yet appear as relatively benign when compared with the pathologies of hatred unleashed in communist or ex-communist societies, but it still stems from similar religious roots, cultural stereotypes, socio-economic resentments and political manipulation.[92]

The new Europe of the 1990s, while providing great potential opportunities for Jews to consolidate their post-war achievements, their prosperity and revived culture after the incomparable devastation of the Holocaust, also contains within itself all the dangers of a resurgent, inward-looking nationalism leading to fragmentation, ethnic unrest and growing anti-Semitism. The horrors of genocide in the Balkans, the sensational upsurge of support for neo-fascism in the south of Italy and the growth of xenophobia even in the stable democracies like Sweden, Holland and Belgium are a reminder that no society is immune to this virus in hard times. As we have seen, European anti-Semitism never went away after 1945, even though it was no longer openly espoused as an ideological world-view by serious politicians. Since the early 1970s it has slowly gained ground, as the Holocaust receded into memory, as anti-Zionism began to provide a new political framework, and new challenges to liberal democracy, especially from the radical right, have emerged in the West. Throughout this period (and this is too frequently overlooked) anti-Semitism was also deliberately exploited for political ends throughout the Soviet-controlled part of Europe, preparing the ground for the explosion of popular resentment in the East that we have seen unfold more recently. The decade of the 1980s also saw an upsurge of violent acts against Jews and Jewish institutions all over Europe, whose origin came not from within Western countries or indigenous anti-Semitic traditions, but from the Arab Middle East. This anti-Jewish terrorism was and is an offshoot of the Arab–Israeli conflict and a reminder that what happens in the Middle East can directly affect the security and well-being of Jewish communities in Europe. While technically extraneous to the phenomena we have been discussing, it is obvious that the reverberations of Israel's existence, its wars, its policies and its impact on Diaspora Jewry, cannot be divorced from the future prospects of anti- Semitism. As with the Lebanon war, the intifada or the Gulf crisis, events in the Middle East may provoke a sudden new flurry of anti-Jewish feeling as well as expressions of solidarity or support for Israel. In this respect, the mutual recognition between Israel and the PLO and the progress of reconciliation with the Arab states is however a hopeful sign, which may well diminish one of the external causes of anti-Jewish sentiment in Europe. But in the last analysis, the future of Jews in the new Europe will depend on whether or not it succeeds in containing xenophobic nationalism and moving forward to a harmonious, prosperous and more tolerant society towards minorities in general, across the continent as a whole.

NOTES

1 Elizabeth Noelle and Erich Peter Neumann (eds), *The German Public Opinion Polls 1947–1966* (Westport, Conn., 1981), pp. 185–92, 202, 206, 219, 311–16, 333. The surveys were carried out by the Institut für Demoskopie, Allensbach.

2 See Yehoshua A. Gilboa, *The Black Years of Soviet Jewry* (Boston, 1971); and, more recently, Louis Rapoport, *Stalin's War against the Jews. The Doctors' Plot and the Soviet Solution* (New York/Toronto, 1990).

3 Artur London, *L'Aveu* (Paris, 1969); Euegen Loebl, *Sentenced and Tried: The Stalinist Purges in Czechoslovakia* (London, 1969); Robert S. Wistrich (ed.), *The*

Left against Zion: Communism, Israel and the Middle East (London, 1979), pp. 57–64, 72–85, 156–60.

4 Celia S. Heller, *On the Edge of Destruction. Jews of Poland between the Two World Wars* (New York, 1977); Pawel Korzec, *Juifs en pologne: la question juive pendant l'entre deux guerres* (Paris, 1980); and Yisrael Gutman, Ezra Mendelsohn, Jehuda Reinharz and Chone Schmeruk (eds) *The Jews of Poland between Two World Wars* (University of New England Press, 1989), pp. 97–140.

5 Michal Borwicz, 'Polish–Jewish relations, 1944–1947', in C. Abramsky, Maciej Jachimczyk and Antony Polonsky (eds), *The Jews in Poland* (Oxford, 1986), pp. 190–8. Also the controversy sparked by Norman Davies's assertions, 'Poles and Jews: an exchange', *New York Review of Books* (9 April 1987), pp. 40–4.

6 Lucjan Dobroszcki, 'Restoring Jewish life in post-war Poland', *Soviet Jewish Affairs*, 3 (1972), p. 66.

7 See Borwicz, op. cit., pp. 195–6; and S. E. Schneiderman, *Between Fear and Hope* (New York, 1947).

8 On inter-war anti-Semitism in Hungary, see the articles by Nathaniel Katzburg and C. A. Macartney in Bela Vago and George L. Mosse (eds), *Jews and Non-Jews in Eastern Europe 1918–1945* (New York/Toronto/Jerusalem, 1974), pp. 113–56. Also the article by Randolph L. Braham, ibid., pp. 137–56 and his *The Politics of Genocide: The Holocaust in Hungary*, I (New York, 1981).

9 Paul Lendvai, *Antisemitism without Jews: Communist Eastern Europe* (New York, 1971).

10 See Gerhard Botz, *Wien vom 'Anschluss' zum Krieg* (Vienna/Munich, 1978) for the immediate pre-war period.

11 George E. Berkley, *Vienna and its Jews. The Tragedy of Success, 1880–1980s* (Boston, 1988), pp. 352ff.

12 This has been extensively documented from Austrian government sources by Robert Knight (ed.) *'Ich bin dafür, die Sache in die Lange zu ziehen': Die Wortprotokolle der österreichischen Bundesregierung von 1945 bis 1952 über die Entschädigung der Juden* (Frankfurt a.M., 1988).

13 Anton Pelinka, 'The great Austrian taboo: the repression of the civil war', *New German Critique*, no. 43 (Winter 1988), pp. 69–82.

14 See John Bunzl and B. Marin (eds), *Antisemitismus in Österreich* (Innsbruck, 1983) for facts and figures about anti-Semitic attitudes in post-war Austria. See also Marin's article in Ivar Oxaal, Michael Pollak and Gerhard Botz (eds), *Jews, Antisemitism and Culture in Vienna* (London/New York, 1987), pp. 216–33.

15 For post-war opinion polls in France concerning attitudes to Jews, see Doris Ben-Simon and Jeannine Verdès-Leroux, 'Les Français et le problème juif: analyse secondaire d'un sondage de l'Institut Français d'Opinion Publique (IFOP)', *Archives de sociologie des religions* 19 (1970), pp. 53–91.

16 Jean-Paul Sartre, *Antisemite and Jew* (New York, 1976), p. 71.

17 See the standard work by Michael A. Marrus and Robert O. Paxton, *Vichy France and the Jews* (New York, 1981). For an apologia of Vichy, see Alfred Fabre-Luce, *Pour en finir avec l'antisémitisme* (Paris, 1979); and for the broader context of post-Six Day War anti-Semitism, Henry H. Weinberg, *The Myth of the Jew in France, 1967–1982* (New York/London, 1987).

18 See Pierre Birnbaum, *Un mythe politique. La 'République juive' de Léon Blum à Pierre Mendès-France* (Paris, 1988), pp. 382–92.

19 Ibid., pp. 334–9.

20 See E. Roditi, 'Antisemitism in France', *Midstream* (November 1980), pp. 9–14, Shmuel Trigano, *La République et les juifs* (Paris, 1982); Michael R. Marrus, 'Are the French antisemitic? Evidence in the 1980s', in Frances Malino

and Bernard Wasserstein (eds), *The Jews in Modern France* (University of New England Press, 1985), pp. 224–41 for opposing views on this issue. According to Marrus, anti-Semitism has steadily declined in France since the late 1940s. I doubt whether one could make this claim with quite the same confidence today.

21 Tony Kushner, *The Persistence of Prejudice. Antisemitism in British Society during the Second World War* (Manchester, 1989). See my review in *Shofar*, vol. 8, no. 4 (Summer 1990), pp. 96–8.

22 See W. D. Rubinstein, *The Left, the Right and the Jews* (London/Canberra, 1982).

23 This began to change in the 1970s and 1980s, due in part to the alienation that many Jews felt as a result of left-wing and liberal attacks on Israel's legitimacy and on Diaspora Jewry's support for it. See Geoffrey Alderman, *London Jewry and London Politics 1889–1986* (London, 1989), pp. 111–42. Also the interesting chapter on British anti-semitism today, in Stephen Brook's popular survey, *The Club. The Jews of Modern Britain* (London, 1989), pp. 382–98; the comments by Angela Lambert, 'In the shadow of the Swastika', *The Independent* (25 March 1989); and the symposium in *The Jewish Quarterly* (no. 141) (Spring 1991), pp. 33–43. For the hostile attitude of the Swedish media to Israel, Zionism and Jewish topics in general during and after the Lebanon war, see Per Ahlmark, 'Sweden and the new antisemitism', in Leo Eitinger (ed.), *The Anti-Semitism in Our Time* (Oslo, 1984), pp. 63–9.

24 See the articles in Robert S. Wistrich (ed.), *Anti-Zionism and Antisemitism in the Contemporary World* (London, 1990), pp. 46–52, 171–7, 181–94 by J. Gould, Shlomo Avineri and the present author.

25 Lionel Kochan (ed.), *The Jews in Soviet Russia since 1917* (Oxford, 1970).

26 See Ferenc Feher's notes on the 'Jewish Question' in Hungary, in A. Rabinbach and J. Zipes (eds), *Germans and Jews since the Holocaust* (New York, 1986), pp. 333–6.

27 Michael Chechinski, *Poland. Communism, Nationalism, Anti-Semitism* (New York, 1982).

28 Heinz Fischer (ed.), *Einer in Vordergrund: Taras Borodajkewycz: Eine Dokumentation* (Vienna, 1966).

29 Robert S. Wistrich, *Between Redemption and Perdition. Modern Antisemitism and Jewish Identity* (London/New York, 1990), pp. 121–32.

30 Eva Kolinsky, 'Nazi shadows are lengthening over Germany', *Patterns of Prejudice* (November–December 1978), vol. 12, no. 6, pp. 25–31. Also M. Ellerin and S. Rabinove, 'Does neo-Nazism have a future?', *Midstream* (October 1983) pp. 1–6.

31 Quoted by Gould, op. cit., p. 181.

32 Meyer Weinberg, *Because They were Jews. A History of Antisemitism* (New York, 1986), p. 78.

33 Raymond Aron, *De Gaulle, Israel et les juifs* (Paris, 1968), p. 18.

34 See the remarks of Pierre Goldman in *Libération* (Paris) (31 October 1978). Goldman, a French Jewish left-wing militant, declared that the atmosphere of visceral hostility in the pro-Palestinian discourse prevented him and many Jewish leftists from identifying with the Palestinian cause.

35 Bernard-Henri Lévy, *L'Idéologie Française* (Paris, 1981); and Alain Finkielkraut, *La Réprobation d'Israël* (Paris, 1983).

36 See Robert S. Wistrich (ed.), *Anti-Zionism and Antisemitism*, op. cit., pp. 46–62, 155–70, 178–94.

37 Robert S. Wistrich, *Anti-Zionism as an Expression of Antisemitism in Recent Years* (Study Circle on World Jewry in the Home of the President of Israel, Jerusalem, 1985).

38 For the effects in Eastern Europe, see Lendvai, *Antisemitism without Jews*, op. cit.

39 Wistrich, *The Left against Zion*, op. cit., pp. 272–300.

40 L. Hirszowicz, 'The Jewish issue in post-war communist politics', in Abramsky et al. (eds), *The Jews in Poland*, op. cit., pp. 199–208.

41 Josef Banas, *The Scapegoats* (London, 1979).

42 Andrej Werblan, 'Przyczynek do genezy Konfliktu', *Miesiecznik Literacki* (June 1968).

43 Y. Ivanov, *Ostrozhno! Sionizm!* (Moscow, 1969). V. Bolshakov, 'Antisovietizm – professiya sionistov', *Pravda*, (18–19 February 1971); and ibid. (17 January 1984). Also Robert S. Wistrich, *Hitler's Apocalypse* (London, 1985) for an analysis of the 'Protocols of Zion' in their Sovietized version.

44 William Korey, *Glasnost and Soviet Antisemitism*. Working Papers on Contemporary Antisemitism (New York, 1991).

45 Robert Wistrich, *Hitler's Apocalypse*, op. cit. pp. 205–25.

46 Y. Yeveseyev, *Fashizm pod goluboy zvezdoy* (Moscow, 1972); V. Skurlatov, *Sionizm i aparteid* (Kiev, 1975); V. Begun, *Polzuchaya Kontrrevolutsiya* (Minsk, 1974); L. Korneyev, 'Sami sionistkii byzness', *Ogonyok* (8 July 1978).

47 On Romanenko, see 'What is patriot?', *Moscow News* (28 May 1989) and 'Fighting the enemy within', *IJA Research Report*, no. 5 (1989).

48 L. Dymerskaya-Tsigelman, 'Anti-Semitism and opposition to it at the present stage of the ideological struggle in the USSR', *Jews and Jewish Topics in the Soviet Union and Eastern Europe* (The Hebrew University of Jerusalem, Summer 1988), pp. 3–27. Also personal interviews conducted in the USSR with Oleg Kalugin, Sergei Lezov, Mikhail Chelnov and a number of other Jewish activists at the end of 1990.

49 Yitzhak M. Brodny, 'The heralds of opposition to perestroyka', *Soviet Economy* (1989), 5, pp. 162–200; Walter Laqueur, 'From Russia with hate', *The New Republic* (5 February 1990), pp. 21–5.

50 'Antisemitism in the USSR and the reactions to it', *Jews and Jewish Topics*, op. cit. (Spring 1989), pp. 5–44.

51 Andrei Sinyavsky, 'Russophobia', *Partisan Review* (1990), 3, pp. 339–44.

52 For documents relating to Pamyat and criticism of it, see the Summer 1988 issue of *Jews and Jewish Topics*, ibid., pp. 30–88.

53 For an overview, see Robert S. Wistrich, *Antisemitism. The Longest Hatred* (London, 1991).

54 Henryk Grynberg, 'Is Polish antisemitism special?', *Midstream* (August/September 1983), pp. 19–23.

55 'Blaming the Jews again', *Newsweek* (15 February 1982).

56 Abraham Brumberg, '"The problem that won't go away": antisemitism in Poland (again)', *Tikkun* (January/February 1990), pp. 31–4.

57 D. Warzawski (Konstanty Gebert), 'The convent and solidarity', *Tikkun*, vol. 4, no. 6 (1989), pp. 30ff. Personal interview in Warsaw (October 1990).

58 *New York Times* (30 August 1989); *The Guardian* (31 August 1989).

59 'Bez maski', *Gazeta Wyborocza* (Warsaw) (22 September 1990). B. Lecomte, 'Walesa après Walesa', *L'Express* (28 September 1990).

60 Z. Ben-Shlomo, 'Boiling cauldron', *Jewish Chronicle* (15 February 1991).

61 'Alarm in Hungary', *Jewish Chronicle* (20 April 1990).

62 Neal Ascherson, *The Independent on Sunday* (11 November 1990), pp. 3–5.

63 Glen Frankel, 'Saving Jews: Ceaucescu's high price', *International Herald Tribune* (22 February 1990).

64 'Nasty writing on the wall for Jews', *Observer* (11 February 1990). Also *Newsweek* (7 May 1990), pp. 22–3.

65 'Fascists consolidate in Western Europe', *Searchlight* (January 1991).
66 'Germany United: democracy or danger?', ibid. (October 1990).
67 Werner Bergmann and Rainer Erb, 'Aspekte der gegenwartigen Antisemitismus', *Semit*, No. 2 (March/April 1989), pp. 46–7.
68 Heiner Lichtenstein (ed.), *Die Fassbinder-Kontroverse oder Das Ende der Schonzeit* (Konigstein, Ts. 1986); Johann N. Schmidt, *These Unfortunate Years: Nazism in the Public Debate of Post-war Germany* (Indiana University, 1987), Public Lecture Series.
69 R. S. Wistrich, *Between Redemption . . .*, op. cit., p. 126.
70 Rabinbach/Zipes (eds), *Germans and Jews . . .*, op. cit., pp. 12ff.
71 Quoted by Micha Brumlik, '"Fear of the father figure" Judeophobic tendencies in the new social movements in West Germany', *Patterns of Prejudice*, vol. 21, no. 4 (1987), p. 34.
72 David A. Jodice, *United Germany and Jewish Concerns. Attitudes towards Jews, Israel and the Holocaust* (New York, 1991). Working Papers on Contemporary Antisemitism, pp. 5–6, 15–16, 23–5.
73 Ibid., pp. 3, 5, 12–13, 17–19. See also Jennifer L. Golub, *German Attitudes Towards Jews. What Recent Survey Data Reveal* (New York, 1991), who maintains that about 15 per cent of all West Germans can be classified as anti-Semitic.
74 'The global fallout from Desert Storm', in *Response* (Los Angeles, Spring 1991), vol. 12, no. 1, pp. 9–13. Also Pierre Birnbaum, 'Retro. Le complot juif', *L'Arche*, no. 404 (March 1991), p. 62.
75 For the empirical survey material, see John Bunzl and B. Marin (eds), *Antisemitismus in Österreich*, op. cit.; and Hilde Weiss, 'Antisemitische Vorurteile in Österreich nach 1945. Ergebnisse empirischer Forschungen', in J. H. Schoeps and A. Silbermann (eds), *Antisemitismus nach dem Holocaust* (Koln, 1986), pp. 53–70.
76 Robert Wistrich, 'The strange case of Bruno Kreisky', *Encounter* (May 1979), pp. 78–86.
77 *'Wir sind alle Unschuldige Täter!' Studien zum antisemitischen Diskurs im Nachkriegsösterreich* (Wein, 1989), 2 vols., documents the Waldheim presidential campaign, media responses and the anti-Semitic discourse that developed in Austria.
78 'Antisemitic attitudes in Austrian society, 1973–1989', *Institute for Conflict Research* (Vienna, July 1989). According to this survey, following the Waldheim Affair, anti-Semitism had returned to its 1973 levels with 'more than a third of the Austrians representing a propagandist movable antisemitic potential'.
79 Ibid. In the 1989 survey, over 30 per cent of the FPÖ supporters could be described as hard-core racist anti-Semites, the highest level for supporters of any mainstream Austrian political party. The FPÖ leader, Jorg Haider, was forced to resign as governor of Carinthia over his publicly expressed admiration for the economic policies of the Third Reich.
80 S. Trigano, *La République et les juifs*, op. cit., p. 37, claimed in 1982 that the Rue Copernic bomb revealed the 'terrible precariousness' of the Jewish situation in France. For a sharp rejection of this view, see Dominique Schnapper, 'Perceptions of antisemitism in France', in M. Curtis (ed.), *Antisemitism in the Contemporary World* (1986), pp. 261–71.
81 According to Marrus, 'Are the French antisemitic?', in Malino and Wasserstein (eds.), *The Jews in France*, op. cit., p. 234: 'there is nothing whatever to match the 1930s' obsession with Jews seen in writers like Céline, Robert Brasillach or Pierre Drieu la Rochelle'. But while literary anti-Semitism has lost much of its lustre, Le Pen's populist movement has clearly helped to make anti-Semitism more commonplace since the 1980s.

82 E. Plenel and A. Rollat, 'The revival of the far right in France', *Patterns of Prejudice*, vol. 18, no. 2 (1984), pp. 26ff.
83 'L'Extreme droîte', *Passages* (December 1987), pp. 8–18. 'L'antisémitisme en France', *L' Evénement du jeudi* (15 to 21 October 1987), pp. 58–86.
84 Jérome Jaffré, 'Des sombrages', *L'Express* (1 June 1990), p. 23, who points out that 88 per cent of the Front National members polled, agreed that Jews have too much power.
85 David Selbourne, 'French Jews begin to feel alien all over again', *Sunday Times* (3 June 1990).
86 Henri Raczymow, 'D'une guerre à l'autre', *L'Arche*, no. 404 (March 1991) pp. 62ff.
87 Henry Weinberg, 'Revisionism: the Rocques affair', *Midstream* (April 1987), pp. 11–13.
88. 'Les fourriers de l'antisémitisme', *L'Express* (25 May 1990).
89 For the attraction of Holocaust 'revisionism' to the extreme left, see in particular Alain Finkielkraut, *L'Avenir d'une négation. Réflexions sur la question du génocide* (Paris, 1982).
90 Dr Leon Volovici, 'A Jewish and Russian tragedy', *SICSA Report* (Vidal Sassoon Center for the Study of Antisemitism, The Hebrew University of Jerusalem), Winter 1991.
91 Konstanty Gebert, 'Poland: antisemitism without Jews', *The Jewish Quarterly* (Winter 1990–1), pp. 26–9.
92 Robert S. Wistrich, *Antisemitism. The Longest Hatred*, op. cit.

Part III

13

RELIGIOUS TRENDS AMONG AMERICAN AND ISRAELI JEWS

Charles S. Liebman

There is a major definitional problem in describing religious trends among Jews. Is it appropriate to confine the description to Jews who identify themselves as 'religious'? If so, are they the *datiim* (religiously Orthodox) in Israel and the Orthodox in the United States or do they include *datiim* as well as *masoratiim* (traditional) in Israel and Orthodox, Conservatives and Reform in the United States? Should we inquire about changes in the number of affiliates to each group – surely this is one measure of religious trends – or about changes in the religious life of each sub-group or of all of them, taken together? An entirely different alternative, though not necessarily an exclusive one, is to enquire about non-religious Jews – Jews who evince no commitment to religion and/or define themselves as non-religious. One may ask how they conceive of religious symbols and ideas and how they relate to religious Jews. Are they antagonistic or simply indifferent to religion and/or religious Jews? This is also part of a study of religious trends.

RELIGIOUS TRENDS AMONG JEWS IN THE UNITED STATES

American Judaism, like American religion in general, is adaptationist rather than radical. American Judaism takes its physical as well as its cultural environment as a given. It is, as a rule, non-judgemental about broad social and cultural norms though it may be very judgemental about specific norms and values, especially if they bear an overt relationship to Jews and Judaism. In other words, Jews in general and their religious and communal elite in particular may have something to say about particular government policies or legislation, or about an anti-Semitic incident. But they will accept general social norms and values, for example rising divorce or intermarriage rates, or new sex codes, as facts of life to which they must learn to adjust. They do not adopt the radical stance which would argue that if the cultural environment is inimicable to Jewish norms and values, Jews must either change that environment or withdraw from it. They do not even ask the kinds of question which might lead to a radical posture. In other words, they do not seek to weigh the norms and values of contemporary American culture against the norms and values of their religious tradition. This characteristic of American Judaism is not a recent one. It, nevertheless, merits attention because, as we shall see, it does not characterize religious Jews in Israel.

Adaptationism seems to be the opposite of what one might expect from a 'religious' point of view. At least upon first reflection, I would anticipate a religious perspective to dictate that the only given, the only norm or value that one must take for granted, is God and God's commands. After all, it is He who must be obeyed. Therefore, religious perspective, I would expect, would be quite judgemental about the cultural environment; measuring it by standards of religious propriety and impropriety. It strikes me, therefore, that those who accept their cultural environment as a given are those who do not take religion as seriously as they sometimes pretend.

Radical religion is the opposite of religious adaptationism. By radical religion I mean the insistence that there is no ultimate authority other than the imperatives of religion. Furthermore, those who espouse radical religion are likely to believe that knowledge about these imperatives is available to human beings. Therefore, radical religionists will judge their cultural environment and, to the extent that its norms and values are opposed to those of religion, will either seek to change them or withdraw from their environment.

Paradoxically, the adaptationist stance is characteristic of religion in traditional society. The great religions of the world have, in general, adjusted to the rhythms of their environment rather than insisting upon hegemony or withdrawal. As long as human beings could not imagine alternatives to their own culture (that, after all, is one way of defining traditional society), an adaptationist posture was not inconsistent with a high degree of religious commitment. Today, this is less likely to be the case. Modern man and modern society are peculiarly conscious about the self-made nature of reality. Some celebrate and others bemoan but few deny that our culture is at least as much our creation as our heritage. From a purely religious perspective one might suggest that traditional society's passive acceptance of prevailing cultural patterns represents, at worst, a sin of omission whereas, in contemporary society, it is a sin of commission.

Adaptationism means that Judaism is interpreted as malleable rather than fixed. The Jewish tradition is not something that compels, it is not a body of law or a set of norms which one is obliged to observe. Consistent with that characteristic, levels of observance of Jewish law among American Jews who claim religious affiliation are very low. It has been argued with regard to some rituals, such as the *seder*, that levels of observance among the present generation of American Jews is no less than among their parents. My response has been that whereas many Jews participate in a ceremonial meal which they may call a *seder* they are not celebrating a ritual in accordance with Jewish law.[1] In fact, I suspect that an analysis of the *seder* celebration in most American Jewish homes would confirm the adaptation of that ceremony to contemporary middle-class, liberal, urban, American cultural norms.

The nature of adaptationism, the redefinition of Judaism in accordance with the prevailing cultural norms and values of American society, or at least that portion of American society with which Jews are identified, effects both the structure of Jewish life as well as its content. The two are interrelated but I want to distinguish them, if only for heuristic purposes.

STRUCTURE OF RELIGIOUS LIFE – PLURALISM

If pluralism is defined as the right of individuals to organize themselves in the pursuit of whatever purpose they deem proper and is not patently illegal, then pluralism is a requisite of democracy. America is a peculiarly pluralistic society in the sense that not only is the organization of such groups deemed lawful, it is a positive virtue. This is a characteristic of religion in the United States and of Judaism as well. Hence, Jews find nothing disturbing or exceptional about the fact that there are a variety of religious 'denominations' that differ over the nature of Judaism or the obligations which Judaism imposes. This is not a new feature of American Jewish life. But in the last fifty years the pluralist nature of Jewish religious life has been intensified in two respects. First, a fourth denomination, Reconstructionism, has been added to the previous three – Orthodoxy, Conservatism and Reform. The pluralist nature of American Judaism is evident in the relative ease with which Reconstructionism was accepted as an independent denomination. It had only to declare its independence, and the principle of pluralism, despite the objections of the Orthodox, assured its legitimacy. The other denominations did not welcome Reconstructionism. But they had no principled basis upon which they could challenge its acceptance into the mosaic of Jewish religious life in the United States. They might have argued, for example, that Reconstructionism cannot be labelled a religious denomination because its very definition of God departs rather radically from that which is generally meant by God in American culture in general and Judaism in particular. Indeed, Reconstructionist leaders have argued that atheists can feel at home among them.[2] But if the other denominations were to object to Reconstructionism on these grounds they would be suggesting that it is appropriate to examine everyone's belief and that there are objective criteria for determining what is or is not legitimately religious.

This relates to the second component of pluralism in religious life – a component which has also been significantly deepened in the last generation. It is a small step from conferring legitimacy on any group which calls itself a religious denomination regardless of what it espouses, to legitimating the individual's right to remain a member of any denomination regardless of what he or she believes or practices. In other words, structural pluralism, at least in religious life, leads to the assertion of an endless variety of religious interpretations. Eighty-one per cent of all Americans agree that 'an individual should arrive at his or her own religious beliefs independent of any churches or synagogues' – a finding that ought not surprise us since as John Wilson observes:

> Pluralism . . . encourages the view that one's level of commitment to a religion is also a matter of choice. Worse, it opens the door to the idea that if none of the religions on the shelf are satisfactory, one can create one's own religion.[3]

This is, in a sense, what many American Jews have been doing with increasing frequency, although the unit for creating or reinterpreting their religion tends to be the synagogue or a sub-synagogue unit such as the *havurah*.

THE CONTENT OF JUDAISM

The principles through which Jews have redefined the nature of their religion are: personalism, voluntarism, moralism and universalism. The first two are closely interrelated to pluralism.

Personalism refers to the tendency to transform and re-evaluate the tradition in terms of its utility or meaningfulness to the individual. 'The best assurance of Jewish survival,' say two contemporary observers of American Jewish life, 'is the development of a community that offers its members opportunities for personal fulfillment not easily found elsewhere.'[4]

Voluntarism refers to the absence or devaluation of *mitzvah* (commandment). The individual is urged, encouraged, cajoled into performing certain acts of a ceremonial nature and is constantly reassured that what one does is legitimate if that is what one chooses to do. Personal choice is endowed with spiritual sanctity and is in all cases (contrary to the Jewish tradition), considered more virtuous than performing an act out of obedience to God.

Universalism refers to two ideas: that the Jewish tradition has a message for all people, not only for Jews; and that Judaism is open to the messages of other traditions and cultures. Moralism is the tendency to explain Judaism as a moral or ethical system. Since ethics are generally viewed as universal, examples of universalism and moralism tend to overlap. I have sought to illustrate all these principles with a variety of examples elsewhere.[5] I confine myself, here, to illustrating how these principles work themselves out in the celebration of Purim.

Personalism, voluntarism and universalism are reflected in the statement of a Conservative rabbi on how the Book of Esther is read in his synagogue.

The Hebrew text will be wrapped around with song, dance and narrative in musical revue format – a folk art pageant involving the entire congregation. . . . We present Esther in this way in order to bring out its ever-current as well as its ancient meaning. . . . A point like this is brought out through the songs of such composers as Spike Jones, Cole Porter and George Landry, late voodoo chief of New Orleans. . . . [6]

An example of the transformation of Purim in moralistic terms is its celebration at the largest Conservative synagogue in the New Haven area. The Congregation printed a pamphlet called *Purim Service* which is recited instead of the Book of Esther. The synagogue's version of the story excises all violence. The villain Haman does not meet his end by being hung from (or impaled on) a tree. Instead, 'when the King found out that Haman plotted against the people of Esther, the Queen, he removed him from office and appointed Mordekhai in his place.' The moral of the story is formulated as follows: 'Our story is important because it is about people who had courage and who risked their lives to help others. That's what we celebrate on Purim.'[7]

DISSENT FROM RELIGIOUS TRENDS AMONG AMERICAN JEWS

There are exceptions to our description of religious trends among Jews in the United States. To some extent the exceptions prove the rule. The left wing within the Reform movement is unhappy because the tradition retains positive symbolic value and generates nominal allegiance even though its content is transformed. The right wing within the Conservative movement created the Union for Traditional Conservative Judaism to challenge the continued adaptation of the tradition to prevailing cultural norms. (In 1990 it dropped the word Conservative from its name.) The Conservative movement seems to have lost a sense of the binding nature of tradition. This is less evident in the rationale behind its decisions on such major issues as the ordination of women as rabbis but rather in the tendency at all levels of the movement to ignore the detailed prescriptions of Jewish law. What is less clear is the extent to which these trends extend to Orthodox Jews in the United States and to their religious leaders.

If we confine our view to the religious elite, to the statements of the leading Orthodox rabbis and heads of yeshivot in the United States, then Orthodoxy has not only resisted the trends we have described but has responded to them by strengthening tendencies in the opposite direction. This results in less personalism and voluntarism as the scope of Jewish law is expanded and fewer matters are left to individual judgement, and greater Jewish particularism rather than universalism. On the other hand, it would appear that large numbers of Jews who define themselves as Orthodox have been affected by the trends described above. In a private communication, Steven M. Cohen reports that in his surveys of American Jews, about one-third of those who define themselves as Orthodox deviate considerably from the canons of Jewish law. Jews of New York are, as a group, more observant than their counterparts in other sections of the United States, but Heilman and Cohen find that even among New York Jews, rates of non-observance are surprisingly high. For example, even among men under 35 who define themselves as Orthodox, and this is the most observant age group among the Orthodox,[8] only 82 per cent report that they attend services weekly, 79 per cent that they handle no money on the Sabbath, and 63 per cent that they abstain from eating on the Fast of Esther.[9] American Jews who call themselves Orthodox also deviated from Orthodox norms in the past. But it is more surprising today because an increasing proportion of youngsters from Orthodox homes are socialized in Orthodox day schools and youth movements and an older generation of permissive and adaptationist Orthodox leaders, rabbis in particular, are being replaced by a younger generation of more zealous rabbis and scholars. It might be expected, therefore, that those who continue to call themselves Orthodox would, in fact, behave in accordance with Orthodox norms.

There are two ways of looking at emerging trends among Orthodox Jews in the United States. Both probably contain elements of the truth. One view is that Orthodox Judaism resists accommodation to American culture. Evidence that accords with this view include: the greater rigour in religious observance that characterizes the behaviour of most Orthodox Jews compared to their parents, the growing authority of the religious elite and of Talmudic sages at the expense of the communal rabbi, and the widespread challenge by Orthodox leaders to the legitimacy of non-Orthodox rabbis and their unwillingness to cooperate with them. These trends point to the growing insulation of Orthodox Judaism in the United States and may be understood as a reaction to tendencies among the majority of American Jews.

A second view is that Orthodox Jews have accommodated themselves to American culture. In accordance with this view, one can find traces of voluntarism, personalism, universalism and moralism among Orthodox Jews in general, as the Heilman and Cohen study shows, and even among the religious elite – although such tendencies find their expression in rather subtle form and within a basically *halakhic* framework. I will not attempt to demonstrate the adequacy of this view in the present paper. It not only would take me too far afield from the topic but requires more basic research than anyone, as far as I know, has undertaken.[10] I raise the point here in the hope that others will pursue it in depth.

IMAGES OF ISRAEL AMONG JEWS IN
THE UNITED STATES

These trends have an impact on the image of Israel among American Jews. I refer to images of *Israel* rather than the State of Israel or the people of Israel or the land of Israel deliberately. Lines between state, community and land are quite blurred among American Jews.

The trends in the religious life of American Jews as described here serve to undermine the religious significance of Israel among American Jews. As religion becomes more personalistic, as it is viewed as a set of acts voluntarily undertaken rather than as a set of obligations imposed from without, and to the extent that the religious tradition is interpreted in a universalistic and moralistic mode, Israel becomes increasingly irrelevant. This is true for two reasons. First, the kind of behaviour generated in support of Israel – collective activity, political demonstrations, the necessity to achieve consensus, the high premium on deferring to institutional needs rather than individual self-fulfilment – runs contrary to what many American Jews increasingly regard as the essence of their Judaism. Second, developments within Israeli life itself, to which we will allude in the following section, make it increasingly difficult to interpret Israel in universalistic and moralistic terms – something that was much easier and indeed was done fifty years ago, when the symbol of the *yishuv* was pioneers and *kibbutz* members whose altruism and courage on the one hand and social and technological achievements on the other were projected as a model for new societies.

One reason that synagogues and rabbis served as the rallying point and centre of concern for Zionism and the nascent state fifty years ago was that synagogues and rabbis constituted the institutional base of American Jewish life. But it was entirely appropriate for them to rally Jews in support of Zionism because their support for collective Jewish concerns, their insistence that support for the establishment of a Jewish state and help for Holocaust survivors, was an 'obligation' of American Jews, made sense in terms of that which Jews believed about the nature of the Jewish religion.

Nowadays, activity on behalf of Israel has shifted to the Conference of Presidents and to the Federations. This does not necessarily mean that Israel is less important to American Jews. In one respect, this shift is both a cause and effect of the rising importance of secular leaders and organizations at the expense of the religious ones. But there is more to it than this. Israel is the centrepiece of Jewish public life, but Jewish public life does not define the totality of Jewish life in the United States.

American Jews' concern for Israel is limited in a number of ways that observers of American Jewish life often overlook. In quantitative terms, the commitment to Israel varies considerably. Steven Cohen, in his survey of American Jews on behalf of the American Jewish Committee, finds that about a third of American Jews are passionately dedicated to Israel but another third are relatively indifferent to it.[11]

The limited commitment to Israel is reflected in the recently published credo of the Conservative movement. According to that document, a good Conservative Jew supports Israel but sees no compelling reason to live there and denies the primacy of Israel for Jewish life. The relevant sentences read:

> Wherever we were permitted, we [Jews] viewed ourselves as natives or citizens of the country of our residence and were loyal to our host nation. Our religion has been land-centered but never land-bound; it has been a portable religion so that despite our long exile (*Galut*) from our spiritual homeland, we have been able to survive creatively and spiritually in the *tefutzot* (Diaspora).[12]

The vast majority of American Jews do support Israel, if not passionately then at least wholeheartedly. But with some notable exceptions, American Jewish involvement with Israel has relatively few consequences for the construction of Jewish identity in the private sphere. This presupposes a distinction between public and private Judaism, each with its own orientation.

Private Judaism is built on a cultural–religious–spiritual model which takes the individual as its starting-point and which understands Judaism as a system of meaning oriented towards questions of ultimate concern. Public Judaism is built on a political–secular model which takes the Jewish people as its starting-point and concerns itself with its collective existence. Public Judaism is that which is conducted by communal organizations, primarily in the philanthropic or political spheres. Political and financial support for Israel is the dominant feature of this sphere, the one constant and commanding cause of public American Judaism. But the massive philanthropic and political lobbying apparatus has had relatively little impact on the private Jewish lives of most American Jews. Israel – as a society, culture, state, language or sacred symbol – has little meaning for most American Jews at the times in their private lives when they feel most keenly Jewish: at life-cycle events (birth, bar- or bat-mitzvah, marriage, divorce, bereavement) and family celebrations (Rosh Hashana meals, the Passover Seder, Hanukkah candle lighting).

Furthermore, the vast majority of American Jews have no familiarity with the currents of Israeli cultural and even political life. Israeli culture, in other words, is not integrated into the cultural life of most American Jews, even in an English-language version. An informal scan of the adult education programmes sponsored by synagogues and Jewish community centres reveals few lectures and classes devoted to Israel. Those that are devoted to Israel generally focus on the external threat rather than the internal features of Israeli society.

Others have expressed similar ideas. Writing in *The Jerusalem Post*, a Conservative American Jewish educator, now working in Israel, observes:

> Today, while support for Israel is conceived of as an integral part of being Jewish, it stands somewhat apart from American Judaism. It is

as if the influences of American life have exorcised the spiritual meaning of Zion from the political reality of Jerusalem.

What remains is an urgent sense of obligation to support Israel, with only faint echoes from the tradition as to the reasons why. Israel in American Jewish education has become an entity to be learned about, to be supportive of and devoted to, and to identify with. But it is not a reality with implications for Jewish self-understanding.[13]

This tendency is strengthened by the dramatic increase in mixed marriage – marriage between a Jew and a spouse born non-Jewish who does not convert to Judaism. As one authority on the topic observes, even when the non-Jewish partner converts to Judaism, children of such marriages are less likely than children of parents who were both born Jewish to feel that 'Jews have a special responsibility for one another and a special responsibility toward Israel.' And, he goes on to add, this is even more common among children raised in homes where the non-Jewish spouse has not converted.[14]

A consequence of this development, in my opinion, is that as religious currents are strengthened among American Jews, support for Israel will weaken. It will not weaken in the sense that American Jews will become hostile to Israel but in the sense that they will become increasingly indifferent to it. This is a serious consideration to someone like myself who also believes that, the present strength of 'secular' Jewish communal institutions and the relative weakness of the synagogues and rabbis to the contrary notwithstanding, the survival of Jewish life in the United States depends on the strength of its spiritual component.

But there is another side to the coin that cannot be ignored. Many American Jews, and this may be true of other Diaspora communities as well, have created their own conception of Israel. This is the chunk of Israel that they see and/or they imagine they see or they are shown when they visit Israel. Even when they stay for extended periods I am impressed by how vivid this partial image remains. It is not an Israel of self-serving and inept leaders, of a rude populace, and, as we shall see in the next section, an increasingly xenophobic culture. Rather, it is a society that exudes universalist sentiment wrapped in the symbols of Jewish particularism. It is an Israel where Jerusalem looms more centrally than in the Israel which its citizens know. It is a society in which creative intellectuals and rabbis, many of them *olim* from America, whose names are barely known by the mass of Israelis, play a prominent role. It is an Israel of universities, youth seminars, Jewish Agency tours and kibbutzim. Above all else, it is an Israel filled with spirit and spirituality and it speaks with special poignance to the young. It is this Israel which is a rallying point and a locus for travel and study for many Jewish-American youngsters and serves as an instrument to further their Jewish identification. Over 40,000 Jewish youth from North America participate in educational programmes of long or short duration in Israel each year. According to Jonathan Woocher, head of JESNA (Jewish Education Service of North America), 'the Israel experience is regarded as among the most successful educational tools in our arsenal – an experience that reaches thousands of young people of high school and college age who might otherwise have no Jewish education at all'.[15] But adults, especially among those who are active in Jewish public life, are also 'turned on' to Judaism by visiting Israel or dedicating themselves to activity on behalf of Israel. What I suspect is happening here, and this suggests a more hopeful scenario than the one I outlined above, is that some American Jews have transformed Israel into a cultural centre and integrated it into their own conceptions of Judaism.

RELIGIOUS TRENDS AMONG JEWS IN ISRAEL

The discussion of religious trends in Israel begins with the *datiim*, the Orthodox, although their proportion of the Israeli Jewish population is estimated at less than 20 per cent. Nevertheless, it is the Orthodox who have gained increasing recognition as the legitimate interpreters of Judaism in Israel. Herein, therefore, rests the contrast between religious trends in Israel and the United States. The Orthodox in the United States differ from *datiim* in Israel. I have already advanced the possibility that one can detect American currents in the behaviour and belief of Orthodox Jews in the United States. These are of academic interest but they may be of little more than academic consequence. The difference between religion in Israel and the United States is in the relative influence of Orthodoxy in each society. In the United States, Orthodox Judaism is the religion of the dissenters. In Israel it is the religion of the society, although, as might be anticipated, it effects secularists differently than it does *datiim*.

Pluralism is not a norm, certainly not a religious norm in Israeli society. This does not mean that Israeli Orthodox Judaism is monolithic. It does mean that the varying Orthodox interpretations of Judaism are judged on their merit, on the proof texts offered in their support, on the linkage of each interpretation to an older tradition, on the scholarly reputation of the rabbis who represent them. Orthodoxy tolerates plural interpretations of the tradition but only within a limited set of parameters and only when the interpretations are anchored in the text. Variant interpretations of the Jewish tradition are not legitimate just because some principle such as freedom of religion requires the state to allow its practice. Instead, from an Orthodox point of view, each variant interpretation must demonstrate that it is linked to an authentic Jewish tradition. Non-*datiim* in Israel are generally sympathetic to this point of view. They are not, therefore, sympathetic to religious pluralism in the way that is true of American Jews. We must not confuse anti-clericalism – which most Israelis share – with a sympathy for non-Orthodox interpretation of Judaism. Israelis assume that there is some body of beliefs and practices which constitutes Judaism. While there may be differences over what Judaism really is, not everyone has the authority to say what it is.[16]

This is evident in a recent incident. In April 1989, the Reform movement sponsored a twelve-day trip of seven Knesset members (all secularists) to the United States to expose them to institutions of Reform and thereby convince them to oppose any amendment in the 'Who is a Jew?' law. After visiting two Reform synagogues, M. K. Ruby Rivlin of the Likud, outspoken in his defence of secularist positions in Jerusalem, said, 'I am shocked. This is idol worship, not Judaism.' And, he went on to say, 'Until now I believed that the Reform were a denomination within Judaism. After visiting two of their synagogues here, I am convinced that this is a new religion entirely, with no connection to Judaism. Total assimilation.'[17] He added that he continued to harbour reservations about amending the law to exclude conversions by Reform rabbis. These reservations stemmed from the fact that Reform was a Zionist movement. 'They sing Hatikva; Habad [followers of the Lubavitch *rebbe*] don't do this', he said.

The Orthodox in Israel, as we noted, are quite divided.[18] The basic division is between *haredim* and religious-Zionists. Within each of these camps are sub-groups whose animosity towards one another (at least among the *haredim*), sometime leads to outbreaks of violence. Furthermore, the standard division of Orthodox Israelis into the *haredi* and religious-Zionist camps is complicated by the growing religio-political strength of Sephardi Jewry which does not fit neatly in either camp. But the question here is whether one can point to the development of religious trends common to all the Orthodox. I think it very clear that, dissenting voices to the contrary notwithstanding, most major trends are the opposite of what one finds among American Jews.

Religion in Israel, which is represented by Orthodoxy, is neither pluralistic in outlook nor adaptationist. It is increasingly identifiable as radical in its interpretation of religion and its rejection of its cultural environment. *Haredim* always adopted a radical stance of withdrawal. But, fifty years ago, religious-Zionists could have been characterized as adaptationist. Aryei Fishman has shown how the religious-Zionists integrated both Zionism and modernity into their religious formulations.[19] This is no longer the case. Or, more properly, the mood of adaptationism no longer predominates within Orthodox circles in Israel. Instead, a new form of religious radicalism now plays an important role – a form of messianism which seeks the expansion of religious control over the entire society. The strongest expression of this tendency is found among many supporters of Gush Emunim and among leaders of almost all religious-Zionist yeshivot. They do not favour religious coercion in the same way that *haredim* might coerce the population if they had the wherewithal to do so. Instead, this new form of religious radicalism insists that public policy, especially that concerned with Israel–Arab relations, be formulated in accordance with their religious world-view which attributes a central religious role to the land of Israel and identifies the present era as a critical one in the process of Redemption.

Many, perhaps even most religious-Zionists, do not conduct their own lives as if they lived in a period of imminent Redemption any more than all those identified with the *ḥaredi* community observe the *halakha* with the kind of punctiliousness that the *ḥaredi* elite insists upon. But, the *ḥaredi* elite on the one hand, and the religious-Zionist elite to which we referred on the other, dominate their respective religious communities to the point where those who dissent from them run foul of accepted norms. It is they who find they must express themselves defensively and with great caution.

There is one exception to the observation that religious tendencies among the *datiim* in Israel are opposite to those found among American Jews. Like Americans, Israelis too – even Orthodox Israelis – have absorbed elements of personalism. The opposite of personalism would be interpreting the tradition without regard to the relevance or meaning it has for the individual. I find no such tendency among Israeli *datiim*, although it is a charge that non-*datiim* often level against the rabbis. Efforts on the part of the religious sector to attract *ba'alei t'shuvah* (penitents), has sensitized their leadership to the need to reformulate Judaism in terms that speak to the personal needs of the individual in addition to collective societal concerns. What has happened, however, is that these needs are often formulated in terms that are only meaningful to that segment of the population, Sephardim in particular, with a high incidence of pathological behaviour.

The voluntarism which is found among American Jews, even among the modern Orthodox who do pick and choose among those elements of Jewish law which they observe, is eschewed by religious Jews in Israel. Orthodoxy in Israel has sought to enhance the place of *halakha* in the interpretation of Judaism and the authority of the rabbis who rule on the details of the *halakha* thereby diminishing the element of subjectivity, choice and personal interpretation.[20] This tendency encapsulates a number of currents. The law is defined as rigid and very precise in its demands. It leaves no room for subjective interpretation. In addition, the law is increasingly interpreted as strict, imposing greater and greater demands on its adherents.

Universalism, a central component in the American Jewish understanding of Judaism, one that extends to many Orthodox as well, is deliberately rejected by mainstream Orthodoxy in Israel. The signs of Jewish particularism are quite noticeable. Everything is perceived from within a Jewish prism and judged from within a Jewish perspective. And the rise of particularism has implications for the interpretation of 'moralism' as well. Emphasis on law (and ritual) means a de-emphasis on the centrality of ethics. But, in addition, religious Jews in Israel have redefined the very term 'morality' in particularistic rather than universalistic terms. According to the rabbi who pioneered the establishment of extremist education within the religious-Zionist school system, Jews are enjoined to maintain themselves in isolation from other peoples. Foreign culture is a particular anathema when its standards are used to criticize Jews.[21] There is no place in Judaism for 'a humanistic attitude in determining responses to hostile behavior of the Arab population' says one of them.[22] An article in *Tkhumin*, the most distinguished annual dealing with matters of Jewish law and public issues from an Orthodox perspective, published a learned essay on the status of Muslims in Israel according to Jewish law.[23] The author seems to phrase himself carefully and there is no trace of polemic in the tone of the article, a fact that makes the conclusions all the more striking. According to the writer, under the ideal conditions envisioned by Jewish law, non-Jews in the Land of Israel ought to live in servitude to Jews. In fact, their very right to live in the Land of Israel is problematic. It is permitted though not required to save their lives when they are endangered. However, they ought not to benefit from free public services. These, the author stresses, are basic principles according to which we want to build our society. The *halakhic* imperative to subjugate non-Jews living under Jewish rule may be relaxed because of political constraints, but we ought never lose sight of the ideal society to which we should aspire.

This de-emphasis on universal standards of morality extends to areas other than the Jewish–Arab dispute. The chief rabbi of Ramat-Gan, for example, decries the practice of childless Israeli couples adopting Brazilian children who then undergo conversion. Such children, he says, will be raised as Israelis but not all of them will identify with the Jews. 'After all, it is clear that children inherit characteristics from their parents,' he states. He then cites proof texts to prove that non-Jews are not blessed with the quality of mercy with which Jews are blessed, but on the contrary are cruel by their very nature.[24]

The penetration of these tendencies into Israeli society is due, in good measure, to the influence of the Orthodox on the non-religious. This is not the place to describe the reasons for that influence.[25] I simply observe here that the affirmation of religion (Orthodoxy), has become synonymous with good citizenship among an important segment of Israeli society, especially within the political right. Ariel Sharon is quoted as saying, 'I am proud to be a Jew but sorry that I am not *dati*.'[26] It does not matter, as far as we are concerned, whether he was expressing what he really believes, or saying what he thought would further his political career. In either case, the statement reflects the deference the secular political right pays to Orthodoxy.

In the last few years, as divisions between doves and hawks have sharpened, one hears increasingly that fidelity to religion and loyalty to the state are associated. Thus, for example, in December 1987, the then prime minister Yitzhak Shamir is quoted as saying:

> The left today is not what it once was. In the past, social and economic issues were its major concern. Today, its concern is zealousness for

311

political surrender and, on the other hand, war against religion. It is only natural that someone whose stance is opposed to the Land of Israel will also oppose the Torah of Israel.[27]

What most non-religious Israelis seem to share is the sense that Judaism is concerned with either narrowly ritualistic matters, primarily prohibitions (what one cannot eat, what one cannot wear, or what one cannot do on the Sabbath), or with a limited set of public issues. They have little conception of Judaism as addressing one's personal problems. Although Israelis disagree over whether religion and state ought to be separated, those who do believe in separation do not advance a 'private' conception of Judaism that is especially relevant to them. The debate over separation of religion and state in Israel does not occur, as it did in some Protestant countries, with religious protagonists on both sides. On the other hand, most of those who favour the privatization of Judaism, those who would restrict it to the home rather than the street, feel this way because they find public Judaism bothersome and oppressive. They take it for granted that the Orthodox interpretation of Judaism is authoritative and it is from this interpretation which they wish to escape.

Judaism has personal meaning for religious Jews in Israel. But for the non-religious, especially for the secular, the explicit message of authentic religious leaders is almost exclusively confined to public life. It is about the state (whether it is or is not a signal of the beginning of Redemption), about which territories are or are not part of the land of Israel, about obligations of Jews to live in the land of Israel, about one's responsibilities to other Jews and the nature of relationships between Jews and non-Jews. It is also about what public life ought to be like on the Sabbath or holidays. But it is rather irrelevant to the individual's 'spiritual' or transcendent concerns.

This perception of Judaism by the non-religious – the notion that Judaism is concerned with public and not with private life, or with the narrowly ritualistic rather than with life as the individual experiences it – may stem from their own ignorance or rejection of the Jewish tradition. It may also stem from the fact that public and collective problems are far more troublesome to Israelis than they are to American Jews. Immersion in questions of 'meanings' and existential problems of self-fulfilment may be a luxury no one in a besieged society can afford. Whatever the reasons, it does tell us about how Judaism in Israel has been projected by Orthodox spokesmen and, because there are no serious alternative projections, about what Judaism means to the Israeli Jew.

DISSENT FROM RELIGIOUS TENDENCIES AMONG JEWS OF ISRAEL

We can distinguish two forms of religious dissent from these prevailing trends in Israeli religious life. Both trends are adaptationist. One comes from within the *dati* community and one from outside it.

Among the religious adaptionists there is some, albeit very little, inclination to favour greater voluntarism and subjectivity in religious interpretation. But one does find emphasis on the ethical imperatives of the Jewish tradition in relationships with non-Jew. It is expressed symbolically in the phrase, 'man was created in the image [of God]'. Whereas the alternate and better known tradition has argued that the essence of Torah is the obligation to love one's neighbour as oneself, with the term 'neighbour' implying only 'Jew', the tradition which the religious adaptationists favour expresses a distinctly universal conception of the essence of Judaism. According to Yehezkel Cohen, a leading spokesman for this point of view, those whom he represents differ from the rest of the Israeli religious world by 'a deeply philosophic question – whether to place emphasis on those *mitzvot* directed towards divine service or those guiding relations with one's fellows'.[28]

Among the non-religious, one also finds those who are committed not only to Judaism but to what borders upon a religious interpretation of the Jewish tradition. This is a new development; a significant departure from the past. Whereas the religious adaptationists really reaffirm what was essentially an earlier religious-Zionist tradition, the non-religious who now affirm important elements of the religious tradition have departed from their own past. The Zionist-socialists, for example, affirmed Judaism but disassociated Judaism and the Jewish religion. Today, however, Yehoshua Rash of Mapam criticizes a book on religion and nationalism because the author insists that clericalism is identical to the Jewish religion. Rash argues that the religious tradition can be distinguished from anti-liberal and anti-humanist currents that he associates with clericalism. Rash calls the author a 'Hellenist' and cites with approval Shulamit Har-Even's dictum that religion need not be separated from the state, only from policy formation.[29]

The late Abba Kovner was a representative figure of this strand,[30] as is Eliezer Schweid. Like Kovner, Schweid is concerned by the growing tensions between secular and religious Jews in Israel because he fears the consequence of a purely secular culture devoid of religious values.[31]

IMAGES OF ISRAEL IN ISRAELI SOCIETY

What changes, if any, have taken place in conceptions of land and/or state of Israel among religious Israelis?

In the discussion of Israel among American Jews, it was argued that distinctions between state of Israel and land of Israel are blurred and are subsumed under the image 'Israel'. This image, it was suggested, is a political rather than a religious conception and has become fairly irrelevant to the religious life of American Jews. In Israeli society, land of Israel and state of Israel are distinctive categories. In general, but among *datiim* in particular, land of Israel has assumed special religious significance. The state of Israel is a more problematical religious category. It was generally of little religious relevance to *haredim* except among those for whom it assumed a negative religious valence.[32] Among religious-Zionists, at least among the mainstream represented by the National Religious Party and the rabbinical elite, the state is probably less significant than it was in the past. This is in part a result of disappointment with the negligible accomplishments which the establishment of the state has wrought in increasing the proportion of *datiim* or the level of public observance of *halakha* and in part a result of the rising importance of the land of Israel (*eretz yisrael*) which has replaced the state as a central focus of religious concern.

Among religious-Zionists, the concept *eretz-yisrael* has assumed enormous significance. There can be no question that this is related to the political threat which mainstream religious-Zionists fear – Israeli withdrawal from Judaea and Samaria. But there can also be no question that the tremendous concern which religious-Zionists feel about the occupied territories stems from the central role which the land of Israel has assumed in their theology. The attribution of mystical properties and the central significance of the land are by no means new notions. They can be traced to important strands within the Jewish tradition and already find reflection in statements by the individual whose books, in the last two decades, have turned into central texts for religious-Zionists. Rabbi Avraham Yitzhak Hacohen Kook wrote:

> In the impure lands of the gentiles, the word view of unity is imperceptible, and the divided world rules with force. . . . The impure soil that is everywhere outside the land of Israel is thus suffused with the stench of idolatry, and the Jews there are worshippers of idols in purity. The only way in which we may escape the disgrace of idolatry is for the Jewish people to gather in the land of Israel, as it is written, 'to give you the land of Canaan, to be your God.' (Lev. 25:38) . . . enlightened wisdom is to be found only in the land of light; there is no Torah like that of the Land of Israel.[33]

This belief was shared by his son, Rav Zvi Yehuda Kook (1891–1982), spiritual leader of Gush Emunim and Israeli ultra-nationalists in general. He wrote:

> This is a land 'whose fruit is holy' and the working of the land is equivalent to the command of putting on phylacteries. . . . This is how matters have been determined: this is a holy land and this is a holy people.[34]

The change in the religious importance attributed to the land of Israel is not primarily in new theological conceptions formulated during the past fifty years but rather in the rise to prominence, indeed in the very dominance of the teaching of Rav Kook as interpreted by his son and his son's pupils over the world of religious-Zionism. Rav Kook, the father, was always admired, indeed one might say revered, by religious-Zionists. The admiration, if not the reverence, was shared by many non-religious. But until most recently it was his personality that was cherished along with value conceptions about Rav Kook's emphasis on *ahavat yisrael* (love of Israel) – which was understood to mean the obligation of religious Jews to love their fellow Jews even if they were not religious – and the notion that secular Zionists were acting as an instrument of God, even if they were unaware of it. Whatever Rav Kook might have intended, both his image and his message served as convenient instruments in a strategy of religious adaptationism. Since the 1960s this has changed very dramatically. Rav Kook's message is no longer understood as legitimating adaptationism but rather as the core of radical religion which seeks to control Israeli society.[35]

It is in the new interpretation of Rav Kook, that one understands the determination of the religious settlers in Judaea and Samaria to resist any form of territorial concession, even in exchange for peace. For in the words of one leader, 'the wholeness of the Jewish people cannot be obtained without the wholeness of the land'.[36]

Not every religious-Zionist shares this extreme position. Rabbi Yehuda Amital, leader of Meimad, the moderate religious-Zionist party that almost won a seat in the 1988 elections, has stated that whereas the people of Israel, the Torah of Israel and the land of Israel are all central components in Judaism, there is an order of priority among them and land comes last. But this is not a position which wins much sympathy from mainstream religious-Zionists. More typical is the notion expressed by Rabbi Moshe Buchko in reply to an article by a leader of Meimad on the pages of the moderate religious-Zionist journal *Emdah*. Buchko claims that the only purpose of Meimad was to justify territorial concessions. He distinguishes between tactics, which are instrumental, and strategy which is concerned with ultimate goals. According to Rabbi Buchko:

> For me, the wholeness of the land [i.e. maintaining the Greater Land of Israel under Jewish control] is a matter of strategy. The land of Israel is the heart and soul of the Jewish people, it is the purpose, and everything else is secondary to it.
>
> Of course, the lives of our soldiers are important .. and peace in the area is an important need for every Jew. Even the concern about moral consequences is not the monopoly of Meimad. All these are in the realm of tactics. We must struggle, day and night, to find a peaceful solution, to minimize as far as possible the threat to human life and to preserve the morality of our battle. But we musn't reverse priorities.
>
> This is the difference between the two views. In Meimad's view, the matter of the territory of *eretz yisrael* is a marginal matter, whereas for me it is a matter of principle.[37]

This orientation is absent among significant segments of *ḥaredim* but not, by any means, among all of them. Elements within Agudat Israel, some elements of Shas, and the Lubavitcher hasidim, while not as extreme as the religious-Zionists, are sympathetic to this point of view. Among this element, the land of Israel has assumed a far more prominent place in their religious thinking than was previously true.

The religious-Zionists and *haredim* differ more significantly on the sanctity to be attributed to the State of Israel. Rav Zvi Yehuda Kook, for example, not only argued for the sanctity of the State but for all its instrumentalities, including the army.[38] But these ideas, in turn, stemmed from the fact that the State of Israel was endowed with purpose. Hence, according to the resolution adopted by the Council of Jewish Settlements in Judaea, Samaria and Gaza, if Israel surrenders sovereignty over Judaea or Samaria, it would:

> represent a *prima facie* annulment of the State of Israel as a Zionist Jewish state whose purpose is to bring Jews to the sovereign Land of Israel, and not, perish the thought, to remove them from the Land of Israel and replace them with a foreign sovereignty.[39]

This is not the statement of a group to whom the State of Israel is unimportant but of a group with a particular image of what the State of Israel represents. They, as we indicated, are religious radicals rather than adaptationists. The State becomes a major instrument in securing religious goals.

Among the moderate religious-Zionists, heirs to the older religious-Zionists' adaptationist orientation, the State also assumes a sacred character, but in their case it is virtually an end in itself. Indeed, religion becomes an instrument in service of the State. For example, according to one spokesman:

> Education for military service. study of science, and respect for the rule of law must serve, in a principled manner, as the basis for all religious values. . . . That is the purpose of religious-Zionism which finds its expression in expanding the concept of religion until it includes service to the needs of the national state.[40]

This adaptationist attitude commands less and less allegiance among the religious-Zionists. Its decline is associated with a general decline in the centrality of the symbols of the State as foci of loyalty and reverence among Israeli Jews. This is a trend which may have far-reaching implications as the Jewish State confronts the real possibility of making major territorial concessions in the occupied territories for the sake of peace with the Palestinians.

NOTES

1 Charles S. Liebman, 'The quality of American Jewish life: a grim outlook', in Steven Bayme (ed.), *Facing the Future: Essays on Contemporary Jewish Life* (New York, KTAV, 1987), pp. 50–71.

2 Although this is implied in Reconstructionist doctrine I have no evidence that anyone has ever written this. I heard a prominent Reconstructionist rabbi say this to a group invited to consider whether they ought to join his congregation.

3 John Wilson's review of Wade Clark Roof and William McKinney, 'American mainline religion', *Journal for the Scientific Study of Religion*, 27 (September 1988), pp. 442–3.

4 Steven M. Cohen and Leonard J. Fein, 'From integration to survival: American Jewish anxieties in transition', *Annals of the American Academy of Political and Social Science*, 480 (July 1985), p. 88.

5 For a detailed description of these characteristics of American Judaism see Charles S. Liebman, 'Ritual and ceremonial in the reconstruction of American Jewish life', in Ezra Mendelson (ed.), *Studies in Contemporary Jewry: An Annual*, VI (New York, Oxford University Press, 1990). This article is an expanded version of material found in Charles S. Liebman and Steven M. Cohen, *Two Worlds of Judaism* (New Haven, Yale University Press, 1990), where these same conceptions are also described.

6 *The Connecticut Jewish Ledger* (12 March 1987), p. 13.

7 Congregation B'nai Jacob, *Purim Service* (Woodbridge, Connecticut, Congregation B'nai Jacob, mimeo., n.d.).

8 Both more intense socialization which characterizes contemporary American Orthodoxy in comparison to American Orthodoxy in the past, and nearness in time to yeshiva education may account for this fact.

9 Samuel Heilman and Steven Cohen, *Cosmopolitans and Parochials: Modern Orthodox Jews in America* (Chicago, University of Chicago Press, 1989).

10 Liebman and Cohen, op. cit., offers a few examples but does not treat the topic with the depth it merits. Samuel Heilman is currently engaged in a study of the attitudes of American rabbis that may be helpful in this regard. In a very important essay, David Singer has developed the point with respect to a small group of Orthodox theologians. But the question is the extent of their influence on any but a handful of others within the Orthodox camp. See David Singer, 'The new Orthodox theology', *Modern Judaism* (February 1989), pp. 35–54.

11 Steven M. Cohen, *Are American and Israeli Jews Drifting Apart?* (New York, Institute on American Jewish-Israel Relations, American Jewish Committee, 1989).

12 *Emet Ve-Emunah: Statement of Principles of Conservative Judaism* (New York, Jewish Theological Seminary, 1988), p. 38.

13 David Breakstone, 'Woeful neglect of the vital center', *The Jerusalem Post* (29 July 1988), p. 11.

14 Egon Mayer, 'Intermarriage research at the American Jewish Committee: its evolution and impact', in Steven Bayme (ed.), op. cit., p. 173.

15 Jonathan Woocher, 'Mountain high, valley low: the state of Jewish Education Today', in Steven Bayme (ed.), op. cit., p. 118.

16 A recent poll of Israelis reports that 51 per cent favour giving Reform and Conservative rabbis equal privileges with the Orthodox in matters of marriage, divorce and conversion (*Jerusalem Post*, 8 May 1989). I do not believe that these and similar polls should be interpreted to mean that Israelis favour religious pluralism. They do reflect acute dissatisfaction on the part of many Israelis with the behaviour of the Orthodox rabbinate. Since only 16 per cent of the sample, in this report, defined themselves as either religious or very religious, I am surprised that only a bare majority from among all those sampled favoured the proposal.

17 *Yediot Aharonot* (10 April 1989), p. 20. Spokesmen for the Reform movement,

reported, in private conversation, that Rivlin later retracted these statements and that he was the only member of the delegation who reacted in this manner. That may be true. It is all the more significant, therefore, that it was Rivlin's original statement which the press chose to highlight and without approbation.

18 The section that follows is adapted from Charles S. Liebman and Steven M. Cohen, op. cit.

19 Aryei Fishman, "'Torah and Labor": the radicalization of religion within a national framework', *Studies in Zionism*, no. 6 (August 1982), pp. 255–71; 'Tradition and renewal in the religious-Zionist experience', in Abraham Rubinstein (ed.), *In the Paths of Renewal: Studies in Religious Zionism* (Ramat-Gan, Bar-Ilan University Press, 1983), pp. 127–47 (Hebrew); and Fishman's introduction and the collection of documents in *Hapoel Hamizrachi: 1921–1935* (Tel-Aviv, Tel-Aviv University, 1979) (Hebrew).

20 Charles S. Liebman, 'Extremism as a religious norm', *Journal for the Scientific Study of Religion*, 22 (March 1983), pp. 75–86; and Menachem Friedman, 'Life tradition and book tradition in the development of ultra-Orthodox Judaism', in Harvey Goldberg (ed.), *Judaism Viewed From Within and From Without* (Albany, State University of New York Press, 1987), pp. 235–55.

21 Cited in Charles S. Liebman, 'Jewish ultra-nationalism in Israel: converging strands', in William Frankel (ed.), *Survey of Jewish Affairs, 1985* (Rutherford, Fairleigh Dickinson University Press, 1985), p. 46.

22 Ibid.

23 Elisha Aviner, 'The status of Ishmaelites in the State of Israel according to Halakha', *Tkhumin* 8 (1987), pp. 337–59 (Hebrew). The editor of the annual demurred from the author's conclusions.

24 *Hatzofeh* (20 June 1988), p. 4. I have deliberately eschewed citing individuals known for their political extremism or forums which encourage the expression of extremist positions. Among the most horrendous in this regard are the anthologies *Tzfiya*, three of which have appeared to date. In the last issue a rabbi from Merkaz Harav writes on the differences between Jews and non-Jews (David Bar Haim, 'Israel is called – 'Man'", *Tzfiya*, 3, n.d., pp. 45–73 (Hebrew)). After bringing proof texts he concludes that, '. . . non-Jews are considered as animals . . . the status of non-Jews in Jewish law resembles the status of animals and there is generally no distinction between them' (p. 61). A number of articles in the anthology are overtly racist, some of them written by rabbis of some distinction. The most depressing aspect is not that there are learned rabbis who hold such views but that the religious establishment finds no cause to condemn them.

25 Eliezer Don-Yehiya and I have attempted this in Charles S. Liebman and Eliezer Don-Yehiya, *Civil Religion in Israel: Traditional Judaism and Political Culture in the Jewish State* (Berkeley, University of California Press, 1983). An interesting essay that notes the general decline of secular Jewish legitimacy and the increased association of Judaism with religious, indeed with the *haredi*, interpretation of Judaism is Yosef Dan, 'The Hegemony of the black hats', *Politika*, no. 29 (November 1989), pp. 12–15.

26 *Ma'ariv*, 'Weekend supplement' (10 March 1986), p. 12.

27 *Ma'ariv* (20 December 1987), p. 6.

28 *The Jerusalem Post Magazine* (4 December 1987), p. 6.

29 Yehoshua Rash, 'Left, right, religion – the political view', in Yehoshua Rash (ed.), *Regard and Revere – Renew Without Fear: The Secular Jew and his Heritage* (Tel-Aviv, Sifriat Poalim, 1987), pp. 194–209 (Hebrew).

30 Abba Kovner, 'Controversy – a foundation stone in Israeli culture', *Rash*, ibid., pp. 279–84.

31 Eliezer Schweid, 'Relations between religious and secular Jews in the State of Israel: an academic appraisal', *L'Eylah* (March 1988), pp. 11–15.
32 Charles S. Liebman and Eliezer Don-Yehiya, *Religion and Politics in Israel* (Bloomington, Indiana University Press, 1985), pp. 57–78; and Menachem Friedman, 'Israel as a theological dilemma', in Baruch Kimmerling (ed.), *The Israeli State and Society* (Albany, SUNY Press, 1989), pp. 165–215.
33 Cited in Eliezer Schweid, *The Land of Israel* (Rutherford, Associated University Presses, 1985), pp. 171–2.
34 Zvi Yehdah Kook, 'The sanctity of the Holy People in the Holy Land', in Yosef Tirosh (ed.), *Religious Zionism and the State* (Jerusalem, World Zionist Organization, 1978), p. 144 (Hebrew).
35 A good summary of the theological literature which proceeded from this school is found in Uriel Tal, 'Totalitarian democratic hermeneutics and policies in modern Jewish religious nationalism', The Israel Academy of Sciences and Humanities, *Totalitarian Democracy and After* (Jerusalem, The Magnes Press, 1984), pp. 137–57.
36 Cited in Charles S. Liebman, 'Jewish ultra-nationalism in Israel: converging strands', op. cit.
37 Rabbi Moshe Buchko, 'Treachery to the land of Israel', *Emdah*, no. 24 (March 1989), p. 9.
38 Zvi Yehuda Kook, op. cit.
39 The statement was issued on 4 November 1985, reprinted in *Davar* (22 November 1985) and translated in the International Center for Peace in the Middle East, *Israel Press Briefs*, no. 40 (December 1985), p. 17.
40 Michael Nehoria, 'Education outside the boundaries', *Emdah*, no. 18 (August 1987), p. 6.

14

CHANGE AND CONTINUITY IN AMERICAN JUDAISM
The case of Nathan Glazer

David Singer

I

Change and continuity proves extremely serviceable as a catch phrase in the context of discussions of the modern Jewish experience because its referents are clearly understood by all. Change points to the external forces – political, economic, social – shaping Jewish life in the modern period, while continuity alludes to the internal Jewish dimension, which has developed in response to these forces. As between the two, change is clearly the more dynamic element: the conditions of modernity serve as the stimulus; Jewish communal action comes as the response.

The debate that has raged of late between 'survivalists' and 'transformationists' over the present and future condition of American Jewry is most fundamentally a debate about change and continuity. While the names make for considerable confusion, survivalists stress the element of change, with transformationists giving the nod to continuity. My own intention is not to enter into this particular debate. Rather, I want to propose an alternative conceptualization, one that, I believe, better captures the essence of the modern Jewish experience. My thesis, in short, is that the greater the change, the greater the continuity; not continuity of Jewishness, however, but continuity of modernization. For Jews in the post-Emancipation situation, it is the process of modernization that is both normal and normative, constituting the element of continuity. Change, in so far as it enters the picture, takes the form of attempts at re-Judaization, seeking at a minimum to set a brake to the modernization process, and more ambitiously to make the Judaic element once again the central pivot of Jewish life. Successful re-Judaization, I would argue, has been extremely rare in the modern context.

To give specificity to my thesis, I want to apply it to an examination of developments in American Jewish religion since the Second World War. Fortunately, an excellent resource exists for this purpose, one that permits an ongoing monitoring of the Jewish religious situation. I refer to

Nathan Glazer's classic *American Judaism*[1] which, amazingly enough, has been continuously in print since 1957. The first edition went through eight impressions up to 1972. In that year a second edition appeared, containing a slightly revised text of the original, plus a new chapter updating developments between 1956 and 1972.[2] In 1987, Glazer found yet another opportunity to bring matters up to date by penning an essay, '*American Judaism* thirty years after',[3] this in response to a scholarly retrospective on his book that took up a whole issue of *American Jewish History*. (The retrospective carried the title 'Revisiting a classic' and included five separate essays.[4]) Finally, in 1989 Glazer added a substantial new introduction[5] to the second edition, including references to the most recent scholarly work in the field.

Even more impressive than Glazer's marathon achievement over time is the fact that the first edition was prepared when he was still in his early thirties and still without a PhD. It was as an up-and-coming 'New York intellectual' – writer, editor, part-time professor – that Glazer was invited by Daniel Boorstin to contribute the volume on Jewish life to the prestigious 'Chicago history of American civilization'. Glazer's book served as a companion to Winthrop Hudson's *American Protestantism* and John Tracy Ellis's *American Catholicism*. In the brief compass of a 149-page text, Glazer put forward a strikingly original interpretation of Jewish religious development in the United States. Virtually a third of the whole focused specifically on the period 1940–56.

Benny Kraut has aptly described *American Judaism* as a book that 'utilizes the methodologies of sociology and history and combines a posture of detached objectivity with an engaged personal vision, making the presentation all the more compelling'. Glazer was writing at a time – the mid-1950s – when religion was enjoying a remarkable revival of prestige among intellectuals, and he was clearly caught up in it. Looking back on that period from the vantage point of 1987, Glazer recalled:

> I was closer to something that I might call Judaist faith when I worked on *American Judaism* than ever since. . . . My only involvement with Jewish religion as anything more than unexplicated practice came in my early years at *Commentary*, when I participated for a while in a study group that read the *Mishneh Torah*, but not in any Orthodox or traditional manner, and more briefly met, at Irving Kristol's suggestion, with Seymour Siegel to read the Talmud. Clearly none of this took. But it left me with an appreciation of the Jewish heritage, a sympathy with the effort to maintain and continue it under the circumstances of modern life. But that is where it stayed. Thus I was writing the story of Jewish religion in America from the perspective of a non-believer, but one who acknowledged an identification with and membership in the Jewish people.

Daniel Boorstin was correct in observing in the editor's preface to *American Judaism* that Glazer 'writes from within the Jewish tradition'. For that very reason, however, the book had a strong elegiac quality, giving voice to a clear sense of irretrievable loss. Glazer certainly wished Judaism well, but on the basis of the evidence at hand he was forced to conclude that the prospects for the Jewish religion in the modern world were bleak indeed. Boorstin was being delicate in stating that Glazer 'does not always rejoice at this assimilation'. Glazer himself put the matter more bluntly in the penultimate paragraph of the volume:

> Once again, honesty requires one to say that it is likely that no satis-factory example [of Jewish religious life] can be given in the modern world, that those moments in Jewish history when the Jews were truly a people of priests and a holy nation required circumstances that never can be repeated.

What lay behind this bleak assessment? Quite simply, the process of modernization, which Glazer saw as undermining religion generally and Judaic life and faith most particularly. Religion, he averred, has 'suffered crushing blows and plays a completely different role in the world today from that which it played only a hundred years ago'. One key element in this situation was the impact of secularization. 'It seems to me,' Glazer observed,

> that science has had a devastating effect on religion. . . . For science, whatever the disclaimers of distinguished scientists, explains the world, which is what religion once did, and its explanation does not have any place for the notion of a non-earthly reality guiding man's course on earth. Hardly any significant number of people now interpret life in terms proposed by the major religions. They no longer live for salvation, no matter how defined, but for life on this earth, in this world, interpreted in purely non-religious terms.

Moreover, Glazer noted,

> science also changes the world and this makes the aim of a pleasurable life in this world, once a purely utopian idea for the masses of people, a real possibility. . . . When the fulfillment of life is seen by individuals and nations as the acquisition of possessions, they have abandoned their traditional religions – regardless of what they do on Sunday or how many churches they build.

The impact of secularization, Glazer argued, was especially pronounced in the case of Judaism for two reasons. First, modern Jews were positively enthralled with science and reason, values associated with the Enlightenment, which had brought Jewish political emancipation in its wake. This was epitomized in the Reform movement, the 'most consciously rational and universalizing Jewish religious tendency'. Second, traditional Judaism's emphasis on deed over doctrine left it bereft of intellectual resources in coping with a changed social reality. Glazer explained:

> Judaism emphasizes acts, rituals, habits, a way of life. Christianity, in contrast, places more emphasis on beliefs and doctrines. Judaism in its popular form, in the version in which it was taught to the East European Jews who were the fathers and grandfathers of the great majority of American Jews, tended to obscure distinctions between greater and lesser observances, to ignore doctrine . . . and to obscure the meaning of ritual. In effect, it taught a rigid set of rituals to cover one's entire life. This rigidity permitted no defense in depth, so to speak. As I have said, once one had found – as so many immigrants did – that it was more convenient to work on Saturdays or to shave or to abandon traditional dress, one had no body of doctrine to fall back upon that could explain what remained *really* important in Judaism – indeed, the question was whether *anything* was really more important than the rituals established by God's word. Under these circumstances, an entire way of life disintegrated.

All this however, was preliminary to Glazer's main thesis with regard to the impact of modernization on Judaism. This thesis, argued and illustrated at length in the pages of *American Judaism*, is that the modernization process has led to a fundamental split between Judaic faith and Jewish ethnicity. Judaism, Glazer stressed, was unique in being a 'nation-religion'. Judaic faith was 'tied up organically with a specific people', a 'tie so intimate that the word "Jew" in common usage refers ambiguously both to an adherent of the religion of Judaism and to a member of the Jewish people'. Since the 'combination of ethnic elements with Judaism is essential,' Glazer emphasized, the 'assimilation of Jews – that is, the disappearance of Jews as an identifiable and distinct people – is a real threat to the Jewish religion'. What has happened in the evolution of American Jewish religion, however, he insisted, was something quite different. The pendulum, in fact, had swung sharply in the opposite direction, with the religious element – Judaism – becoming clearly subordinate to the ethnic component – 'Jewishness'. Glazer put the matter as follows:

> the emphasis on the national characteristics, on the Jewish people, has become so strong within parts of American Judaism that it has obscured what seems to a modern mind the properly religious elements in Judaism – the relation to God, the idea of salvation, and the like.

In tracing the Judaism–Jewishness split over time Glazer developed the basic periodization for the study of American Jewish religion. He began with the colonial period (1654–1825), focusing on the 'dignified Orthodoxy' of the Sephardic Jews. From there he moved to the era of German Jewish immigration, charting the growth of Reform Judaism in both its moderate and radical versions (1825–94), and the opposition to Reform by the traditionalists of the nascent Conservative movement (1880–1900). Radical Reform, Glazer stated bluntly led to 'serious weakening of Judaism as a religion', because the 'thoroughgoing rationalism of the Reform leaders put them in opposition to the complex structure of Jewish ritual practice which had maintained Jews as a people apart'. Next on the agenda was the great age of East European Jewish immigration (1880–1920), which witnessed the wholesale collapse of Orthodox Judaism. 'The rate of attrition was so rapid,' Glazer observed, 'that it seemed two generations would end East European Orthodoxy.' Glazer then turned to the period 1920–40, in which a 'floundering religious life' stood in bold contrast to the flourishing forms of Jewishness. Elements of the latter, he indicated, included the following:

> Socialists, Communists, anarchists, Zionists of all types, territorialists . . . and combinations of them all, in the dense areas of Jewish settlement in the big cities, had their groups, their centers, their social events, their newspapers and periodicals. Outside of politics there were the cultural Yiddishists and Hebraists with their circles and centers, their publishing organizations, and newspapers and magazines.

> On a somewhat higher social level, there were other forms of Jewish life which had little or nothing to do with the Jewish religion. These were the philanthropic, defense, and benevolent societies.

In focusing on the period of immediate concern to us – 1940–56 – Glazer was confronted with a mass of evidence that appeared to directly contradict his thesis about increased Jewish ethnicity and decreased Judaism. These years saw the great push of second-generation American Jews into suburbia, a push that was accompanied by the phenomenal growth of Conservative and Reform synagogues, by a sharp rise in the number of children receiving some form of Jewish religious education, and even by a modest strengthening of what Glazer called the 'modified American standard of piety by which one attends services, lights candles on Friday night, and observes the major holidays . . . '. Did not all this indicate that a major religious revival was in the making, a revival of Judaism as against Jewishness? Glazer was openly sceptical:

> It is the social needs of the individual Jew, and the communal needs of the entire community, that the synagogue has met, and as an institution it is flourishing. During the past fifteen years, people have often asked whether the synagogue was meeting the religious needs of Jews. But the Jews themselves do not demonstrate any strong religious drive. They throng the Jewish centers and the center-synagogues but do not participate in any large numbers in the

services of the synagogue. The more sensitive rabbis, regardless of what the statistics show, still find themselves among a people remarkably resistant to religious feeling. Even the rabbinate is not very different in this respect from the people. . . .

The rabbi may wonder just what his function is. The Jewish law is now (except in Orthodox congregations) generally neglected, and the rabbi is no longer called upon to act as judge and interpreter. He can keep himself busy running his expanded synagogue and school and going to interfaith meetings, but does he have any role as a religious guide?

. . . [C]ommon is the feeling among large numbers of Jews that the institutions of Jewish religion are useful because they contribute to the continued existence of the Jewish people. The ancient notion that Israel exists to serve the law is here reversed: it is argued that the law exists to serve Israel.

In accounting for the growth of institutional Judaism in the 1940s and 1950s, Glazer fashioned an argument strikingly similar to that of Will Herberg in *Protestant, Catholic, Jew* and Marshall Sklare in *Conservative Judaism*, two books that appeared in 1955. Glazer's basic contention was that in 'moving from the city to the suburbs, the second generation has become self-conscious about religion', and that 'for the sake of the children, many adults become members of synagogues'. All this, of course, was in conformity with middle-class, gentile expectations in suburbia, a point that Glazer underscored:

In the new suburban communities to which hundreds of thousands of Jews have moved, it has been discovered that, subtly but certainly, American social life, at least in the respectable middle-class suburbs, moves to a large extent within denominational lines. Non-Jews expected that the Jew would have his own social community marked off from Catholic and Protestant communities. Now this enforced social community had the effect of making the secular Jew a 'captive audience' for the religious or at least institutional Jew.

Here then was a new wrinkle in the Judaism–Jewishness split: Jewishness is the form of Judaism, Jewish ethnicity parading as Jewish religiosity.

In summing up things in his concluding chapter, Glazer substituted pathos for hard-headed analysis as he openly lamented the sorry fate of the Jewish religion in the modern world. What, he asked plaintively, had become of Judaism's capacity to produce models of authentic religious life – the 'holy community'? With the single exception of the Brooklyn-based Hasidim, Glazer averred, such models simply did not exist on the American Jewish scene. Nor could they, he argued, since Jews had embraced an instrumentalist approach to religion. Glazer observed:

If we were to ask American Jews about their religious beliefs, we would find prominent the feeling that religion should keep in step with science, psychotherapy, and liberal politics, and that as long as it does so it is doing its job; the notion that religion is important for Jewish self-respect – a kind of adjunct to the defense agencies engaged in fighting anti-Semitism; the idea that Judaism is important in keeping the Jewish people alive and together – a kind of adjunct to the work of the Zionist groups. . . .

Genuine 'spiritual experience', Glazer maintained, was a rarity among Jews, so much so that 'any strong religious feeling is looked upon with suspicion in the Jewish community'. Given these circumstances, given the 'minimal relation to Judaism' that prevailed in American Jewish life, Glazer could see little hope at all for authentic religious renewal. The closing sentence of *American Judaism* reads: 'What can still come of it I do not know.'

II

In an interview in 1972[6] conducted with Glazer at the University of Arizona just prior to the release of the revised version of his book, Leonard Dinnerstein and Gene Koppel posed the question: 'What significant differences did you find in preparing the second edition of *American Judaism* as compared to the preparation of the first?' To which Glazer replied: 'That is a pleasant question because I think I can report positive differences. . . .' These positive differences had everything to do with Israel's Six Day War, which galvanized American Jews and introduced a new dynamism into various facets of American Jewish life. Glazer pointed to this in the title of the new chapter that he appended to the second edition: 'Epilogue: the year 1967 and its meaning, 1956–72'. In the period under review, he asserted, 'one overwhelming event, the Israeli war of 1967 and its consequences, transformed the scene, leading Jews to a new intensity of self-consciousness and a new level of concern for Jewish issues, among them religious issues'.

Glazer's discussion in the 1972 epilogue focused on the emergence of 'survivalism' as the regnant ideology of American Jews. By survivalism he meant 'the interest of Jews in surviving as Jews, with no additional interest in what the *content* of Jewish life and religion should be.' Glazer stated:

'Survival,' which had for so long been criticized by Jewish religious thinkers and theologians as quite inadequate as a basis for Judaism and which had been regularly denounced as '*mere survival*,' began to seem quite enough after 1967. Not perhaps enough for Judaism forever, but certainly enough for the moment. For without Jews, no further development of Judaism was possible, in any direction, whether that be simply the maintenance of the religious tradition, its adaptation to contemporary life, something in between, or something quite different. Survival was all-essential and thus survival became a theological category.

The survivalist outlook, Glazer argued, was reinforced by a rising tide of black militancy, by New Left hostility to Israel, by the emergence of the Soviet Union as the world centre of anti-Semitism, and by the growth of Holocaust consciousness, but it was shaped first and foremost by the 'extraordinary days of June 1967' in which the 'overwhelming *aloneness* of the Jews was made readily apparent'. In the wake of the Six Day War, Glazer indicated, Jews came to see themselves as 'specially threatened and specially worthy of whatever efforts were necessary for survival'.

Glazer was genuinely impressed with survivalism's energizing impact on American Jews, taking particular note of the rise of the Jewish student movement and the development of a serious current of theological reflection. Certainly this was a significant improvement over the situation in the early 1960s when 'interest in Jewish religion and Jewish issues . . . reached a nadir . . .'. At the same time, however, Glazer could not help but wonder about survivalism's ultimate import for Jewish religious life. While he did not state the matter directly in the 1972 epilogue – wishing, perhaps, not to strike a sour note there – the source of his concern was clear: the survivalism of the 1960s and 1970s looked suspiciously like the institutional Judaism of the late 1940s and 1950s, both being forms of ethnicity in the guise of religiosity. Glazer at least hinted at this in the epilogue when he noted that a concern with survivalism 'had existed since a substantial part of the Jewish people had turned from the traditional law'. He then went on to say:

> Was not the Jewish religion itself pressed into the service of mere survival, since so many Jews identified with synagogues and temples not because of concern for religion but because they wanted to stay with Jews, to strengthen the Jewish causes and communal life, and to ensure that their children married Jews – all pure 'survivalist' aims?

Outside the framework of the second edition, Glazer was much more open in questioning survivalism's adequacy as a foundation for Jewish religious life. Dinnerstein and Koppel, for example, inform us that when Glazer spoke at the University of Arizona in 1972 his

> main topic was survivalism: the tendency of American Jews – especially noticeable since the 1967 Arab–Israel war – to view the survival of the Jewish people as their most important goal. This priority has resulted in American Jews considering their religion as a tool to serve the needs of the Jewish people, thus reversing the traditional view that the Jewish people exist to serve God through their religion.

The language here is virtually identical to that in a passage cited above from the first edition of *American Judaism* in which Glazer disparaged the institutional religion of Jewish suburbia. Even more revealing is Glazer's closing comment in his 1987 *American Jewish History* essay:

> [After 1967] survivalism had become the central theme of Jewish life. Was it enough? As we know, this centrality is challenged by some leading Jewish thinkers . . . as creating an inauthentic and unbalanced Judaism. They seem to be making an important point consistent with my argument that Jewishness was overbalancing Judaism.
>
> Certainly survivalism was enough as an ideology for the Jewish *people*; what other claim on any people can be greater? Perhaps it was enough as a theology for the Jewish *religion*. But it did seem to me to restrict the scope of Judaism, and to reflect a weakening of its historic strength and claims.

Here the Jewishness/survivalism parallel is made explicit, and both are found wanting as underpinnings of a vital religious life.

Mention of Glazer's *American Jewish History* essay brings into focus the one major weak spot in his analysis of American Jewish religion and the one clear example that we have of successful re-Judaization in the face of modernization. I refer to Glazer's discussion of Orthodoxy, which was found wanting by a number of contributors to the 1987 retrospective on *American Judaism*. Benny Kraut argued that 'Orthodox Judaism in this book is conspicuous by its virtual absence', thus leading to a distortion of the historical record and leaving the 'dramatic upsurge in Orthodoxy from the 1960s on' without explanation. Jeffrey Gurock maintained that 'a generation of [Orthodox] activism, innovation and experimentation is unaccounted for', this 'lost generation' being the 'minority of committed young people of East European heritage who reached their majority between 1900 and 1920'. Edward Shapiro stated baldly that Glazer viewed Orthodox Judaism as an 'anachronism' and was thus 'nonplussed' by its vitality. In response to all this, Glazer conceded that nothing in *American Judaism* suggested the recent strength of American Orthodoxy . . .'.[7] Orthodox Judaism, which Glazer had taken to be, at best, a residual phenomenon – a '"saving remnant" that supplies the fund of Jewish knowledge on which all the rest draw', as he put it the first edition of his book – was back with a vengeance.

But which type of Orthodoxy are we talking about? The scholarly exchange in the pages of *American Jewish History* zeroed in on the modern Orthodox element – those Orthodox Jews who seek some form of engagement with modern society and culture – but this focus seems to me somewhat misdirected. To be sure, modern Orthodoxy has made significant strides since the Second World War, but this pales by comparison with the achievements of the traditionalist Orthodox sector – the 'black hat' yeshiva world and the Hasidic communities. Here is an Orthodox element that openly rejects modernity – limiting secular education, spurning modern cultural life; opposing contacts with both gentiles and non-Orthodox Jews; etc. – but is none the less thriving. All observers of the Orthodox scene agree that the traditionalists are by now the dominant group within Orthodoxy. Not only have they succeeded in moving the whole of the Orthodox community in a more traditional direction, they have managed to attract a substantial number of recruits – *ba'alei t'shuva* – from the most modernized sectors of American Jewry. This is re-Judaization on a significant scale.

When Glazer, in the concluding chapter of *American Judaism*, invoked the Brooklyn-based Hasidim as the model of the holy community, he was indulging in mere sentimentalism, as he himself acknowledged in his *American Jewish History* essay. Strangely enough, though, the sentimentalism of 1957 turned out to be the plain realism of 1987 and today. Orthodoxy and, again most especially, traditionalist Orthodoxy, has, as Marshall Sklare so nicely put it, defied 'the laws of religious gravity' in the modern context. Still, Glazer's critics did not claim that his misreading of the situation with regard to Orthodox Judaism was indicative of a larger pattern of misreading, and that other examples of successful re-Judaization could be readily cited. The revitalization of Orthodoxy stood as an important example of what was possible for Judaism in the modern world, but it was seemingly an isolated example.

III

Glazer's most recent assessment of American Jewish religion is to be found in 'Introduction, 1989', newly added to the second edition of *American Judaism*. Here Glazer comes full circle in reverting to the bleak outlook of the 1956 edition, and in underscoring the severity and seeming permanence of the Judaism/Jewishness split. What prompted this darkening of the analytical horizon, interestingly enough, was the emergence of the transformationist school (Glazer makes specific mention of the scholarship of Calvin Goldscheider and Steven Cohen and the popular writing of Charles Silberman) which sought, in no uncertain terms, to put forward a strikingly upbeat reading of the American Jewish situation. Glazer himself, as we have seen, had attempted to find grounds for optimism in the post-1967 Jewish condition, but he none the less felt compelled to demur strongly from the position that the transformationists now advanced. Their key claim, that survivalist-oriented scholars were confusing change with decline and dissolution, appeared to Glazer as an evasive tactic. Indeed, what the transformationists labelled as change – transformation – Glazer saw as radical discontinuity, the emergence of something 'very far from traditional Judaism, too far to maintain . . . Jewish commitment and identity at its present level'.

Glazer's key insight in 'Introduction, 1989' is to present transformationism as yet another link in the Jewishness/survivalism chain, to depict it as another attempt to substitute ethnicity for religion. The transformationists, he argues, are able to cling to an optimistic outlook because they 'accept whatever Jews do ("Jewishness") as Judaism'. Their sole concern is that a 'distinctive identity for Jews' be maintained; for them the fact that the 'traditional content of [Judaism] has been quite reduced' is not a problem. In the transformationist scheme 'Judaism survives [even if] it survives transformed'.

Glazer, however, rejects this as 'too easy' in that it ignores a basic question: 'What role can Judaism play for Jews and Jewish life when its content as religion, a religion of faith and belief, is radically reduced?' At present, Glazer argues, 'Judaism . . . deals with only one overwhelming concern, the physical survival of the Jews'. The Jewish religion has become the 'chief workhorse and ally of national survival'; it has 'quite lost touch with other values, other spiritual concerns'. To the transformationists such an instrumentalist approach to religion might not be worrisome, but Glazer sees it as ultimately self-defeating. Religion, he insists, 'does not survive on instrumental value alone'. Glazer continues:

> There is a paradox about religion's instrumental value: Religion has to be believed in for its own sake for it to serve instrumentally. If it is not believed in it loses even that value. Yet the element of noninstrumental faith in American Judaism is now radically reduced.

Glazer concludes 'Introduction, 1989' – the very last sentence – with an unqualified reaffirmation of the position that he first put forward thirty-three years ago: 'For the great majority of American Jews, Judaism remains an ethnic commitment more than a transcendent faith.' The consistency of Glazer's view over time, it should be evident, speaks not to any interpretive rigidity on his part, but rather to the essentially uniform character of Jewish religious life in the modern context. In describing the shift from Judaism to Jewishness, Glazer poses the question whether the 'change is of sufficient gravity for the question of continuity to be raised'. I would formulate the matter somewhat differently. I would ask whether there are any significant signs of change – of re-Judaization – amid the steady continuity of Jewish religious modernization. And my answer would be, with the single exception of Orthodoxy, no.

NOTES

1 Nathan Glazer, *American Judaism* (Chicago, 1957).
2 *American Judaism*, 2nd edn (Chicago, 1972). The new chapter is entitled 'Epilogue: the year 1967 and its meaning, 1956–72', pp. 151–86.
3 Nathan Glazer, '*American Judaism* thirty years after', *American Jewish History* (December 1987), pp. 277–84.
4 Edwin Gaustad, 'In the Classroom', pp. 208–10; Benny Kraut, '*American Judaism*: an appreciative critical appraisal', pp. 211–31; Norman Mirsky, 'Nathan Glazer's *American Judaism* after 30 years: a reform opinion',

pp. 232–46; Jeffrey Gurock, 'A generation unaccounted for in *American Judaism*', pp. 247–59; Edward Shapiro, 'The missing element: Nathan Glazer and modern Orthodoxy', pp. 260–76.

5 'Introduction, 1989', in *American Judaism* (Chicago, 1989), pp. xiii–xxix .

6 Leonard Dinnerstein and Gene Koppel, *Nathan Glazer, A Different Kind of Liberal* (Tucson, 1973).

7 This concession was qualified in part by Glazer's claim that the revival of Orthodoxy had more to do with 'institutional' factors than with 'faith and belief *per se*. Specifically, Glazer pointed to 'turmoil in the public schools, the growing strength of Orthodoxy in Israel . . frightened responses to the revolution in values [and] growing interest-group effectiveness in getting market response' – the last a reference to the easy availability of kosher food products.

15

PROTESTANT ATTITUDES TO JEWS AND JUDAISM DURING THE LAST FIFTY YEARS

Yaakov Ariel

The attitude of Protestantism to the Jewish people has undergone a momentous transition since the Second World War. New concepts have evolved within the major Protestant denominations concerning the Jewish nation, its role in history and its right to an independent existence in its ancestral homeland, the Land of Israel.

Any discussion of developments in Protestant attitudes towards Jews and Judaism during the past half-century must take into account that Protestantism is not a unified, monolithic religious entity. Unlike Catholicism, there is no single Protestant church but rather thousands of independent denominations, each differing from the others not only in theology and liturgy but also in their outlook on moral, social, political and other issues. We must, therefore, examine and analyse the attitudes of different trends and groups within Protestantism and try to fathom the roots of different, and sometimes greatly conflicting, attitudes and trends.

One can discern three major distinctive trends in the Protestant relationship to the Jewish people, Judaism and the State of Israel: that of liberal Protestantism, of conservative-evangelical Protestantism and of the dissenting denominations who are considered by mainstream Protestants to have deviated so far from the principles of Christianity as to lack any legitimacy.

LIBERAL PROTESTANTISM

The most profound transition in attitudes towards the Jews and Judaism since the Second World War took place among liberal Protestants. It should be borne in mind that liberal Protestantism is made up of numerous denominations, some of which also contain a conservative-evangelical wing. Despite this proliferation, they belong to interdenominational church organizations, maintain interdenominational theological seminaries and function within other joint frameworks. Notwithstanding certain liturgical and other differences which stem from different historical backgrounds, theologically and ideologically the liberal denominations have very much in common – so much so, in fact, that the influence of liberal thinkers is not limited to their own denomination.

Though early manifestations of the change which liberal Protestantism underwent in its attitude towards the Jews and Judaism could be discerned even before mid-century, it is during the last few decades that an almost revolutionary transition took place. The character, implications and context of these changes will be better understood after a short survey of the characteristics of liberal Protestantism and the developments that occurred within it during the past half-century.

What characterizes the liberal trend in Protestantism, which evolved and took shape during the last decades of the nineteenth century, is its acceptance of the spirit of the Enlightenment together with a willingness to adapt Christianity to the mood of the times. Only thus, believed liberal theologians, could Christianity continue to be a dynamic, influential force in a developing and changing society and culture. They were prepared to accept the legitimacy of new theories produced by various academic disciplines.[1] A case in point is the adherence of liberal Protestants to the higher criticism of the Bible, which gained a firm foothold in liberal seminaries. Many liberal religious thinkers became increasingly conscious of the issues of social justice and advocated social reform as fulfilment of the basic tenets of Christianity.[2] Some twentieth-century liberal churchmen were even influenced by elements of Marxist theory, incorporating them into their own brand of Christian thought. The most extreme expression of this trend has been the 'liberation theology' that became especially popular in the Third World during the 1970s and 1980s.

What is important for our discussion is the evolvement of a movement for international Christian unity and interfaith dialogue inspired and conducted by liberal Protestants. Its first manifestations can be traced to the World Parliament of Religion which convened in Chicago in 1893 and brought together liberal Protestants, Catholics, Jews, Buddhists, Hindus, members of the Bahai faith, Muslims, Greek Orthodox, members of the Eastern Christian churches and others. The Federal Council of Churches of Christ in America was established in 1906 as a federation of liberal Protestant denominations in the United States. American churchmen, influenced by the atmosphere of pluralism and interfaith unity in their own country, played a prominent role in the development of an international ecumenical movement. John Mott was awarded the Nobel Prize for Peace in 1946 for his half-century of unflagging efforts to achieve unity among Christians throughout the world. An additional impetus towards ecumenicalism came from the International Conference on Missions which convened in Edinburgh in 1910. Fearing that the proliferation of Protestant denominations undermined their work, especially in Asia and Africa, the missionaries called for efforts to achieve Christian unity. An important milestone on the way to international Christian unity was the establishment of the World Council of Churches in Amsterdam, in 1948. At its inception, the World Council included mainly liberal Protestant denominations, but over the years it has been joined by Orthodox and Eastern Christian churches. The Roman Catholic Church, which considers itself to be the universal church in which all of Christianity should unite under the authority of the Pope, did not join. The Pope, however, recognizes the World Council and is cognizant of the role it plays in Christendom, and even paid a visit to the Council's central headquarters.

This climate of interfaith dialogue, in which – as we have seen – liberal Protestants played a pioneering role, was expressed in Protestant–Jewish relations as early as the 1920s, when national councils of Christians and Jews were formed in England (1924) and the United States (1928), and somewhat later in South Africa. The immediate impetus in the United States was the need felt by liberal Protestants, Catholics and Jews for a united campaign against the racist principles propagated by such groups as the Ku-Klux-Klan.[3] Voices that called for legitimization of Judaism and the Jewish people while denouncing attacks against them, and that expressed support of the Zionist movement and the establishment of a Jewish commonwealth were heard in the Protestant camp as early as the 1930s and 1940s – long before the climate of interfaith dialogue became prevalent in the 1960s. The outstanding protagonists of this new attitude were the two leading American liberal Protestant theologians of the time, Reinhold Niebuhr and Paul Tillich.[4] In England, Anglican Canon James Parkes was a pioneering spokesman of this trend.[5] In 1932, the Pro-Palestine Federation was founded in the United States as a liberal Protestant organization supporting Zionism. It was followed ten years later by the Christian Council on Palestine with Niebuhr as one of its leaders, Carl Herman Voss as its secretary and thousands of Protestant churchmen among its membership. These organizations spoke out in the deliberations, public debate and struggles that preceded the establishment of the State of Israel.

Liberal Protestant support of Zionist and Jewish issues did not stem from messianic expectations or from a belief in the role of the Jews in the fulfilment of biblical prophecy. Rather, it flowed from moral and political principles, and from sympathy for a weak nation, which, they believed, embodies a just cause.[6]

All this notwithstanding, the mass of Protestantism did not, as yet, accept the progressive stance adopted by these leaders and groups. The attitude of numerous liberal Protestants towards the Zionist movement and the establishment of a Jewish commonwealth in Palestine was often far from positive.[7] Many Protestant churches continued their missionary activity among the Jews until the 1960s. Among the resolutions adopted by the World Council of Churches in 1948, alongside expressions of good will towards the Jews and recognition of their great suffering during the Holocaust, was a call for enhancement of the mission among the Jews and an outline programme to train missionaries to that end.[8] As the ecumenical spirit gained strength after the Second World War, a World Council of Christians and Jews was formed towards the end of the decade. The Council, to which today are affiliated about twenty national councils throughout the world, holds international conferences for Christian–Jewish dialogue.[9] The Nazi destruction of European Jewry already had a notable effect upon liberal Protestants immediately after the war, for example in the statements issued by the Assembly of the World Council of Churches at its first meeting in Amsterdam in September 1948: 'We cannot forget that we meet in a land [Holland] from which 110,000 Jews were taken to be murdered. Nor can we forget that we meet only five years after the extermination of six million Jews.'[10]

Whereas one can already discern the beginnings of a new attitude towards the Jews and their role in history among liberal Protestants in the 1920s–1930s, the real breakthrough occurred in the 1960s, both contemporaneously with and in the wake of Vatican II. The ecumenical spirit and the climate of interfaith dialogue were greatly reinforced by this Council and its resolutions. Protestant and Orthodox observers were invited to be present at its deliberations, and Pope John XXIII opened Vatican II by begging the forgiveness of non-Catholic Christians for the injustice they had suffered at the hands of the Church throughout the ages. Following Vatican II, which convened intermittently between 1962 and 1965, new frameworks for interchurch and interfaith dialogue were established, giving impetus to the ecumenical movement.[11] The *volte-face* of the Catholic Church in its traditional attitude to non-Catholic churches and to members of non-Christian faiths was positively received by liberal Protestant bodies, which in turn issued a series of statements similar in vein to those of Vatican II, including those which touched upon the relations of Christian churches with the Jews. Some of these statements went much further than Vatican II in their willingness for conciliation and dialogue with the Jewish people.

Such a climate of interfaith conciliation and dialogue implies a greater degree of mutual recognition and legitimacy. Liberal Protestants do not claim to be the sole true interpreters of God's commandments to the human race, nor do they claim that none but their co-religionists will achieve salvation. They are willing to admit that to some extent these are possible in other churches and even in other religions. This new stance was also expressed in an innovative change in the liberal Protestant understanding of the historical role of the Jews and Judaism. Only those familiar with the traditional anti-Judaic attitude of Christianity which styled itself as *verus Israel*, can grasp the revolutionary step involved in admittance of the legitimacy of Judaism as a religion which is able to grant its adherents spiritual succor and salvation.

One illustration of how the ecumenical spirit of Vatican II influenced Protestant denominations and church organizations is the manner in which they dealt with the charge of deicide. In this matter Protestants, like their Catholic counterparts, were motivated by a sense of guilt at the mass murder of Jews during the Second World War and by the realization that Nazi hatred of Jews had been fed by ages of anti-Semitic incitement which stemmed, in part, from Christianity's adverse and hostile attitude to Jews. During and after Vatican II, liberal Protestants proclaimed on several occasions – sometimes even more emphatically than Vatican II – that the Jews are not guilty of deicide. Among the first Protestant groups to issue such statements was the Synod of Bishops of the Episcopalian Church in the United States:

> The charge of deicide against the Jews is a tragic misunderstanding of the inner significance of the crucifixion. To be sure, Jesus was crucified by *some* soldiers at the instigation of *some* Jews. But, this cannot be construed as imputing corporate guilt to every Jew in Jesus' day, much less the Jewish people in subsequent generations. Simple justice alone proclaims the charge of a corporate or inherited curse on the Jewish people to be false.[12]

The National Council of Churches in the United States, an ecumenical, largely liberal, Protestant organization to which Protestant conservative and dissenting denominations take exception, issued the following statement: 'Especially reprehensible are the notions that the Jews, rather than all mankind, are responsible for the death of Jesus Christ, and God has for this reason rejected his covenant people.'[13]

Having acquitted the Jews of deicide, liberal Protestants now went one step further in order to clear the atmosphere of hatred which this and similar charges had created. An important undertaking in the late 1960s was a check of Protestant textbooks in use in Sunday school classes and elsewhere. Passages having anti-Semitic overtones or which drew an anti-Semitic portrait of the Jews were removed. A survey undertaken in 1972 found that the charge of deicide had almost completely disappeared from Protestant textbooks.[14] This in no way means that the Jews are no longer portrayed as the slayers of Jesus or as the moving cause behind his death in popular images of speech or in musical and theatrical works such as passion plays. In *Jesus Christ Superstar*, a stage production of the 1970s, the Jews cry out: 'Crucify him, crucify him.'

As part of the overall revision of Christian attitudes towards the Jews and Judaism, liberal Protestant theologians, and Catholics too, undertook to examine the corpus of Christian theological writing in order to acquire a more profound understanding of the ideas and claims that produced such a negative image of the Jews. A number of very impressive studies traced, among other subjects, the attitudes adopted by the Church fathers and leading theologians in the Middle Ages and the Reformation towards the Jews. Such studies often defended the New Testament against the charge of anti-Semitism, the claim being made that negative attitudes towards Jews do not appear in the Holy Scriptures but rather in later Church commentaries on the New Testament.[15]

Despite the proportionally great amount of attention devoted to the charge of deicide, it should be noted that notwithstanding the importance of this specific issue, it alone did not create the abyss which for years separated Jew from Christian. A major touchstone in an era of interfaith dialogue is the degree to which Protestant churches are prepared to recognize Judaism and the Jews as a legitimate religion and nation outside Christianity whose members do not accept Christian Gospel or Christ as the Messiah. And, indeed, a growing number of Protestant and Catholic theologians, in recent studies, do characterize Judaism as a religious community in covenant with God. This line of argument, which grants recognition and legitimacy to Judaism, appears in the works of Christian thinkers beginning with Reinhold Niebuhr and Paul Tillich from the 1930s onwards until those of Paul Ricoeur and David Tracy in the 1960s and 1970s.

In their conception of 'covenant theology', these theologians may be divided into two groups: those who believe that Judaism and Christianity are two legitimate interpretations of the same covenant and those who point to two separate covenants with God.[16] This outlook which places Judaism on an equal spiritual and moral footing with Christianity is more the province of English-speaking Protestants, especially in the United States. Within German Protestantism, this interpretation of covenant theology developed in a slower and more limited fashion.[17] The stance of some German thinkers underwent a more progressive transition when they felt the need to face up to the influence of English-speaking Protestants and to promote their own theological thinking among them. A case in hand is the attitude of Wolfhart Pannenberg towards Judaism and the Jewish people. In an important volume published in 1968, he claimed that the foundations of Judaism collapsed with the appearance of Jesus and that it was his rejection of Jewish religious law which led him to clash with the Jewish establishment of his day.[18] In a later book, published after his visit to the United States, he expressed regret for what he had previously written, now claiming that the historical God of Israel stands above that corpus of religious law to which Jesus dissented. He indicated that the two religions had much in common, thus – he believed – making dialogue and mutual understanding possible.[19]

A similar transformation can be discerned in Jürgen Moltmann. In *The Crucified God* (1974), Moltmann presented the execution of Jesus as a direct result of his campaign against Jewish religious law.[20] He also claimed that only Christ could bring salvation to mankind – to Jews as well as to Christians. However, he believed the Jews to be the true Israel, rejecting the traditional Christian interpretation by which Christianity replaced Judaism. Three years later, in *The Church in the Power of the Spirit*, a certain change is evident. Christianity, he now claimed, must adopt a positive attitude towards the Jews; in fact its relationship with the Jews is more important than that with any other element outside the fold. He called for an end to Christianity's overbearing attitude towards Judaism, claiming that the Jewish people will retain its unique mission side-by-side with the Christian church until the End of Days. Moltmann also expressed amity towards the State of Israel. Upon his Second Coming, Jesus will be revealed as the Messiah of Christians and Jews alike.[21]

Many Protestant theologians, like their Catholic counterparts, made an effort to contend with the significance of the Holocaust for Christianity.[22] In many cases, though obviously sensitive to the suffering which had been the lot of the Jews, they tried to ascribe a universal significance – over and above nationality or religion – to the murder of millions of innocent people.[23] Jewish spokesmen often denounced such an outlook.

Perhaps the most impressive and significant development in the attitude of liberal Protestants to Jews and Judaism during the past three decades is in the field of academic and intellectual interest in Judaism. This, too, is closely akin to developments among Catholics. There has been a growing interest in systematic study of Jewish history, thought, mysticism and religious law from the biblical period to the present. Jewish Studies have increasingly become part of the curriculum at Protestant theological seminaries, often taught by Jewish scholars who received their own training at rabbinical seminaries or Jewish and Israeli universities, and who follow the scholarly approaches which are used in the Jewish academic world. One example is Bible studies, which is no longer called 'Old Testament Theology' but rather 'The Hebrew Bible' and whose students today read biblical Hebrew in the Sephardic pronunciation prevalent in modern-day Israel. This is a development of prime importance, for it enables the uprooting of misinformed stereotypes and images which sprouted out of ignorance of the essence and values of Judaism. Any comparison of the works of contemporary liberal Christian writers with their predecessors just one generation ago points to a veritable revolutionary change in their apprehension of Judaism and growing use of this knowledge in the writings of Christian theologians, biblical scholars and church historians.

One instance of this change is in the presentation of the Pharisees in contemporary research produced by Christians. Influenced by works such as that of E. P. Sanders[24] and of Jewish scholars such as Jacob Neusner, Geza Vermes, David Flusser and others, there is growing awareness among Christian historians of the great extent to which the Pharisees influenced early Christianity.[25]

A no less impressive development is the fact that liberal Protestants (again, like the Catholics) have in effect put a halt to their missionary endeavours among Jews, which are now the sole province of conservative-evangelical Protestants or of dissenting denominations. This is a direct outcome of the new conception of the Jews as a nation with its own unique mission in history and of Judaism as a religion capable of granting salvation to its believers.[26]

Even though most liberal Protestants recognize that Judaism has a legitimate, separate existence side-by-side with Christianity; despite the fact that most of them expressed their shock at the destruction of European Jewry and took steps to uproot anti-Semitic stereotypes and images of the Jews and Judaism; and though it is a matter of fact that the majority of them do recognize Israel's right to existence within recognized and secure borders, it would be mistaken to assume that the attitude of liberal Protestantism towards the Jewish people and the State of Israel is only one of amity and friendship.

Certain liberal Protestant circles have given expression to their growing sympathy for the Palestinians – especially since the Six Day War – while strongly criticizing Israeli policy. Many of those active in the World Council of Churches have developed a strong commitment to national liberation movements, thus identifying the Israelis as oppressors.[27] Like the Catholics, many Protestant denominations have come to realize that their Middle Eastern co-religionists are mostly Arabs. Furthermore, one should bear in mind that in the past few decades Protestant churches in the developing countries have gained greater influence in international church councils and that these, like their mother countries, generally support the Arabs in the Middle East conflict.[28]

Spokesmen for Jewish organizations have characterized the anti-Israeli criticism and involvement of liberal Protestants as part of the process – at times unconscious – by which traditional anti-Semitism has been transformed into anti-Israel sentiment.[29] On the fringe of liberal Protestantism's attitude towards Israel one finds some who even deny the legitimacy of Judaism. In their conception, it would be best should all Jews convert to Christianity. This would lead to the end of the Jews as a nation and, *ipso facto*, of the Arab–Israeli conflict.[30] Jewish participants in Christian–Jewish dialogues on several occasions criticized what to them seemed to be great insensibility and a complete lack of understanding on the part of Protestants of the centrality of the State of Israel for the Jewish people.

CONSERVATIVE-EVANGELICAL PROTESTANTISM

The roots of the conservative-evangelical wing of Protestantism can be found in seventeenth- and eighteenth-century European Pietism which was a reaction to the official, established and formalistic church; in the nineteenth-century evangelical movement in Great Britain that developed against a background of reaction to the Enlightenment and in opposition to the established Church of England; and in the American revivalist movement which took shape during the early nineteenth century in reaction

to the spirit of the Enlightenment that held sway in America at the birth of
the Republic. The evangelicals believe that only individuals who underwent
a personal religious experience, in which they had been 'born again' and
accepted Jesus as their personal saviour, would be saved and granted eternal
life.

Evangelical Protestants are deeply committed to spreading the Christian
Gospel and oppose any legitimization of non-evangelical, non-Christian
religions, for only those 'born again' will be saved. Therefore, granting
legitimacy to the religious beliefs of others would be an act of injustice
towards them. They also emphasize the truth of the Scriptures as the
message of God to humanity and as the highest authority on how to live a
truly Christian life. They stand for a literal interpretation of the Bible,
strongly opposing both the higher criticism of the Bible and the lengthy
tradition of commentary beginning with the Church Fathers that at times
interprets passages in the Holy Scriptures as symbolism and allegory. For
many evangelical Christians, biblical prophecy concerning the restoration
of the House of David at the coming of the Messiah refers to the people of
Israel, not to the Christian church.

Messianic expectations of the imminent Second Advent of Christ and
the Millennium – the thousand-year Kingdom of God on earth – are
characteristic of the evangelical wing of Protestantism. They believe that
the Jewish people is destined to return to its ancestral homeland and, after
the apocalyptic events that are to precede the establishment of the Kingdom,
will take up its just place as the Nation of the Lord in the Holy Land, in
the Kingdom of the Messiah. This conception of the Jews as the historical
people of Israel and the belief in the important role they were to play both
in the events that would precede the coming of the Messiah and during
the Kingdom that would then be established were already evident in certain
segments of Puritanism and Pietism, as early as the seventeenth and
eighteenth centuries.[31] In the nineteenth century, these beliefs were widely
held by English, American, German and other evangelical Protestants.
'Christian Restorationists', and 'Christian Zionists' during the early stages
of that movement, came from these circles, their support for the restoration
of Israel to its land flowing from their eschatology.[32]

Contemporary evangelical Protestantism was largely shaped in the
'modernism versus fundamentalism' controversy that split the ranks of
Protestantism in the early twentieth century.[33] The fundamentalism that
had become equated with evangelical Protestantism in the United States
grew out of opposition to the liberal, 'modernist' trends which we have
described above. Fundamentalists opposed the acceptance of academic
theories which seemingly contradicted Christian beliefs, and especially
what was written in Holy Scripture; they refused to accept disciplines such as
biblical criticism and comparative religion, and rejected the trend towards
ecumenism and interfaith dialogue.

In the wider public arena, the 'modernism versus fundamentalism' controversy ended in defeat for the conservative ranks. They suffered the hardest blow in the wake of the 'Scopes Trial', conducted in Tennessee in 1925, when it became evident that American public opinion in general did not accept their interpretation. The fundamentalists, to a great extent, disappeared from the American public scene for many years, their voice rarely being heard in matters on the agenda of the nation. Between 1925 and 1967 the Zionist movement and the State of Israel received little actual support from evangelical Protestants. They expressed joy and satisfaction at developments in the Middle East, events which they interpreted as evidence that the present stage in history was coming to an end and the Second Coming of the Messiah was drawing near, but except for missionary activity their actual involvement and support was almost non-existent. This changed dramatically after the Six Day War.

A great transformation occurred in the status of evangelical Protestantism in the late 1960s and the 1970s. A subject of derision since the 'Scopes Trial', they now became a growing and dynamic power in public life, presenting themselves as an alternative to the open, pluralistic American culture and as willing to become involved again in an effort to shape American society and the republic in conformity with their own beliefs. 'Fundamentalist', which American public opinion equated with narrow-mindedness and reactionary ideas, was replaced by the neutral adjective 'evangelical'.

Within this resurgence of the conservative wing, that of the charismatic Pentecostalists, who believe that the individual could become directly exposed to the Holy Spirit, was most impressive. The number of their congregations increased greatly, but the change was not only quantitative. Evangelicalism, especially in its charismatic form, became ever more popular among urban college graduates and members of academic professions. Many young people who had joined the protest movements of the 1960s now found themselves being 'born again' within evangelical congregations where they discovered a sense of belonging, existential and emotional security, and clear-cut answers to their dilemmas and doubts.[34] For evangelical Christians, their messianic belief both justified the course of human history and served as a divine promise for individual and collective salvation. The number of those who supported the State of Israel as a result of their messianic religious beliefs greatly increased, as did their influence within American society. Precisely at the time when many liberal Protestants turned their back on Israel, evangelical Protestants emerged as a major source of active support of the Jewish State, becoming, in effect, part of the pro-Israel lobby on the American political scene. Their voice was heard in Washington when economic aid and political support for Israel were discussed in Congress.[35] Moreover, American evangelical Christians even developed the concept that the United States was divinely destined to play the role of a modern Cyrus:

341

to aid in the restoration of the Jews to their land, where they would once again establish a Jewish republic, and to guarantee the security and welfare of that state.[36]

One tangible example of the warm affection of evangelical Protestants for Israel and their willingness to support it even in the face of international antagonism and criticism was the establishment of the 'International Christian Embassy' in Jerusalem in 1980. This was a demonstration of overt support for Israel after most consulates and embassies had abandoned Jerusalem. The International Christian Embassy maintains branches throughout the world and distributes pro-Israel information.

The essence of contemporary support for Israel by conservative Protestants is similar to that which motivated nineteenth-century Christian Restorationists and Christian supporters of the Zionist movement in its early stages. Despite their enthusiasm for the State of Israel, their conception of the Jewish people, though not lacking in warmth and goodwill, is not free of prejudice and negative stereotypes. Though they recognize the Jews to be *verus Israel*, God's Chosen People which is to play a central role in the divine plan of salvation, they believe that until the Jews accept Jesus as their personal Messiah they will continue to be in a state of spiritual and moral degeneration. In conservative Protestant writings, for example, the Jews have often been portrayed as the vanguard of secular ideological and political movements such as communism, socialism, secular humanism, and others, which aim to destroy Christian civilization. Evangelical Protestants are sometimes also socially and economically prejudiced against the Jews. A study conducted in the early 1960s by two California sociologists, commissioned by the Bnai Brith Anti-Defamation League, pointed to more anti-Jewish prejudice among conservative than among liberal Protestants.[37] A similar study conducted in the mid-1980s among conservative Protestants, also commissioned by the Anti-Defamation League, showed a drastic decline in the extent of such prejudice among them.[38] This change may perhaps be accounted to the increased interest and involvement in Jewish and Israeli affairs on the part of evangelical Christians since the Six Day War and the subsequent augmented quantity of information on these topics available to them.

According to the evangelical Protestant conception, Judaism cannot grant salvation to its believers, nor can observance of its precepts have any value or serve any purpose since Christ's expiatory death on the Cross. Evangelical authors even expressed their bitter disappointment at the fact that in their obstinacy and blindness to the truth, the Jews did not accept Christ when he first appeared. Had they done so, the Kingdom of God upon Earth would then have come into being. The ambivalent attitude of conservative Protestants towards Jews finds expression time and again in the lectures and sermons of their leaders and prominent clergymen as, for example, in the slip of the tongue of Bailey Smith, then President of the Southern Baptist

Convention, who declared that God does not heed the prayer of a Jew.[39] In his portrayal of the glorious future awaiting the Jews, Jerry Falwell – intent upon praising them – said the following: 'A few of you today don't like the Jews. And I know why. They can make more money accidentally than you can on purpose.'[40]

The attitude of evangelical Christians to the State of Israel is largely instrumental. They regret its secular character (though they are apprehensive of the growing influence of Orthodox Jewry) and are critical of the fact that Israel is unaware of its historical, messianic role. The present state, according to conservative Protestants, is but a station on the way to the Kingdom of God on Earth which will be established with the Second Advent of the Messiah. In the apocalyptic events preceding that final stage, Israel is destined to become the kingdom of the Anti-Christ who, many of them believe, will be Jewish.[41]

Evangelical Christians are engaged in aggressive and extensive missionary activity among Jews. Among other results, this has given rise to groups of 'messianic Jews', of which 'Jews for Jesus' is the most outstanding example. These are actually Jews who have adopted the evangelical Protestant faith and its precepts.[42] Though conservative Protestants in principle oppose interfaith dialogue and do not recognize the legitimacy of a religious faith that is not founded upon acceptance of Jesus as a personal saviour, in the last decade we have been witness to some budding signs of an evangelical–Jewish dialogue. Such a dialogue is *a priori* problematical, for evangelical Christians are committed to propagating their faith while Jews are committed to safeguarding their continued existence as a unique entity.[43] Among the organizations established to further understanding between conservative Christians and Jews is the Holy Land Fellowship of Christians and Jews founded by Rabbi Yehiel Eckstein, with headquarters in Chicago. Eckstein emphasizes the importance of the Holy Land and the State of Israel to Jews and to evangelical Christians alike as the common basis for cooperation and understanding between the two groups.

DISSENTING PROTESTANT DENOMINATIONS

The attitude of the dissenting, marginal Protestant denominations towards the Jewish people and the State of Israel differs completely from that of liberal and evangelical Protestants. These denominations, of which the major ones are Jehovah's Witnesses, the Seventh-day Adventists and the Christian Scientists – and, in a somewhat different manner, the Mormon churches – are not recognized by mainstream Protestant denominations, whether liberal or conservative, as legitimate Protestant churches. In fact, the latter even unqualifiedly reject them as being 'non-Christian'.

By way of generalization, one may say that the marginal Protestant denominations adhere to the traditional conception of Christianity as the true successor to the people of Israel. Post-Christian Judaism, they believe, cannot bring salvation to its believers; the Jews, therefore, are in a state of 'spiritual darkness'. The other side of the coin is a claim to absolute exclusiveness: each of these churches claims that its members alone will be granted salvation and that the rest of humanity is doomed to perdition. Jehovah's Witnesses is the modern name of the group founded by Charles Taze Russell (1852–1916) as the 'Bible Students'. Russell believed in the central role assigned to the Jews in the heavenly plan of redemption and often preached on Jewish restoration to Zion and in support of Zionism.[44] However, his successor, Joseph Franklin Rutherford (1869–1942), instigated a theological turnabout expressed, *inter alia*, in a change of attitude towards the Jewish people and its return to Zion.[45]

The change in name, in 1931, to Jehovah's Witnesses expressed the sect's exclusiveness: they now believe that they alone fulfil God's will. All nations, they hold, are but kingdoms of Satan; the Witnesses, therefore, should not participate in public life, vote in elections, serve in the armed forces or pay taxes to a government. Their conception of the State of Israel is no different from their attitude to all states and they consider the Jews to be a legitimate object of missionary activity, just like the citizens of any other nation.

Despite their messianic beliefs, and though they keep the Sabbath on Saturday, the attitude of the Seventh-day Adventists towards Jews and Judaism is one of much reserve. The roots of this denomination go back to the Adventist movement led by William Miller in the 1830s and 1840s. Miller not attribute to the Jews any special role in his eschatological vision, and his attitude towards them to a great extent followed the traditional Christian one. When his prediction as to the date of Jesus's Second Coming proved to be mistaken, his movement collapsed, with only a small group of believers remaining faithful to his teachings, which had meanwhile undergone several changes.[46] The messianic event which they had awaited on earth had in fact occurred in heaven, claimed those who still adhered to the Adventist belief, and it was there that the Kingdom of the Millennium would be established. Palestine, therefore, had no special importance in the eschatological beliefs of the Adventists. The Seventh-day Adventists in their present form emerged in the 1870s and 1880s under the leadership of Ellen White. Despite its title, this movement places more emphasis on living a wholesome life, consumption of healthy foods and keeping physically fit than on Adventism and consecration of Saturday as the Sabbath. They see no reason for the existence of a separate Jewish nation and consider the Jews to be a legitimate object of missionary activity.[47] Though Israel is the only Middle Eastern state which permits the Seventh-day Adventists to operate freely within its borders, their attitude towards Israel is one of cold reserve.

This is not the case with the Church of Jesus Christ of Latter-day Saints, the official title of the central Mormon denomination, founded late in the third decade of the nineteenth century by Joseph Smith, a native of western New York who claimed to be the Prophet of the Lord. Smith added *The Book of Mormon* to the canon of Holy Scripture. In it America became the Promised Land and its residents were the Chosen People. However, in Smith's divinely revealed plan, Palestine remained the Promised Land of the Tribe of Judah which is destined to return to Zion when the messianic vision is fulfilled.[48] Smith, who was murdered at the beginning of the 1840s, took a great interest in the Jews and in the possibility of their restoration to their homeland. In 1840 he sent an elder of the church, Orson Hyde, as a messenger to Palestine via England, where he tried to persuade British Jews to return to the Holy Land. In October 1841 the Mormon messenger offered up a prayer on the Mount of Olives for the return of the Jews to their land.[49]

The Mormons were ostracized by members of the Protestant denominations. They had placed themselves outside the limits of Protestant consensus by claiming continuing prophecy and by adding to the corpus of Holy Scriptures. Moreover, Protestants were greatly vexed by Mormon attempts – albeit shortlived – to establish a biblical commonwealth which, among other attributes, sanctioned polygamy. Smith's followers, who rallied round Brigham Young in the central Mormon church (one of several Mormon denominations), concentrated their efforts on the establishment of the Kingdom of Heaven on Earth in Utah. The Jews and their possible return to the Holy Land were not uppermost in their minds for many years to come.

Late in the nineteenth and during the first decades of the twentieth centuries official Mormon representatives were sent to Palestine from time to time. They enthusiastically reported back to their co-religionists in the United States about developments of the renewed Jewish colonization of the Holy Land. The Mormon press devoted some space to different events concerning Jews, the Zionist movement and the challenges faced by the Jews in Palestine. These reports were generally of a favorable nature and expressed genuine concern for the Jews. In the years preceding and following the establishment of the State of Israel, the Mormons could be counted among its political supporters in the United States, though this was done passively, without substantial intervention in political affairs. This situation changed somewhat after the Six Day War. They established a branch of Brigham Young University in Jerusalem to enable groups of American students to spend a semester on the scene studying subjects related to Israel and the Middle East. When construction of the campus began on the Mount of Olives in the 1980s it aroused much public controversy and opposition on the part of Orthodox Jewish circles in Israel.

Contemporary attitudes of the Mormons to the Jews and the State of Israel are similar to those of evangelical Protestants. They support Israel even though they do not believe that Judaism can grant salvation to its adherents, and expect the Jews to convert to Christianity and join the Mormon church as the new millennium draws near.

We find similar attitudes in the second largest Mormon denomination, the Reorganized Church of Jesus Christ of Latter-day Saints, established in 1860 by those who remained faithful to the early theology of Joseph Smith and the Book of Mormon but who did not accept the leadership of Brigham Young. The organizational structure and liturgy of the Reorganized Church is more similar to that of a mainstream evangelical-conservative Protestant denomination. It adopted the remnants of the Adams Colony, founded by a Mormon who had left the mother church and organized a group of believers in the 1860s to settle in Jaffa, and has recently undertaken to restore the colony's few buildings still standing there and to establish a community centre.[50]

We have seen that developments in the attitude of Protestants towards the Jews during the past few decades seem to leave room for considerable optimism as to the future of the Christian–Jewish dialogue. The fundamental attitude of the liberal wing has become one of recognition and dialogue. As for the evangelical-conservative Protestants, their conception of the Jews as those who are destined to fulfil the vision of the Prophets has turned them into enthusiastic supporters of the State of Israel. The canvas of the Protestant–Jewish relationship, however, is not painted in bright colours alone. Though relations between liberal Protestant denominations and the Jewish people have improved, they are by no means perfect, nor do all liberal Protestants unqualifiedly accept the latter-day concept which grants legitimacy to the separate existence of the Jews as a religious entity enjoying Heavenly Grace. Furthermore, the fervent support of evangelical-conservative Protestants for Israel does not of necessity point to a change of heart which affords the Jews and Judaism a greater degree of recognition or positive evaluation. As for the more marginal Protestant churches, their reserved attitude towards Judaism and the State of Israel remains largely unchanged.

NOTES

1 For developments in Protestant thought during the final decades of the nineteenth and the early decades of the twentieth centuries, see Claude Welch, *Protestant Thought in the Nineteenth Century, 2: 1870–1914* (New Haven and London Yale University Press, 1985).

2 See, for example, Walter Rauschenbusch, *A Theology for the Social Gospel* (Nashville, Abingdon, 1981).

3 The establishment of these councils is described in William W. Simpson and Ruth Weyl, *The International Council of Christians and Jews* (Heppenheim, Martin Buber House, 1988), pp. 11–19.

4 See, for example, Reinhold Niebuhr, 'Jews after the war', *The Nation*, 21 (1942), pp. 214–16.

5 On Parkes and his contribution see Robert A. Everett, 'James Parkes: historian and theologian of Jewish–Christian relations' (PhD dissertation, Columbia University, 1982).

6 See Ronald Stone, 'The Zionism of Paul Tillich and Reinhold Niebuhr', *Christian–Jewish Relations*, 15, 3 (1982), pp. 31–43.

7 See Hertzel Fishman, *American Protestantism and a Jewish State* (Detroit, Wayne State University Press, 1973).

8 *The Theology of the Churches and the Jewish People: Statements by the World Council of Churches and its Member Churches* (Geneva, WCC Publications, 1988), pp. 5–9.

9 See Simpson and Weyl, *The International Council of Christians and Jews.*

10 *The Theology of the Churches*, p. 5.

11 Marcus Braybrooke, *Inter Faith Organizations, 1893–1979* (New York, Edwin Mellen Press, 1980); R. M. Brown, *The Ecumenical Revolution* (London, Burns Oates, 1967); L. E. Dirk, *The Ecumenical Movement* (New York, World Council of Churches, 1969).

12 Helga Croner (ed.), *Stepping Stones to Further Jewish–Christian Relations* (New York, Stimulus Books, 1977), p. 87. For similar statements in the 1970s and 1980s see Helga Croner (ed.), *More Stepping Stones to Jewish–Christian Relations* (New York, Stimulus, 1985).

13 Croner, *Stepping Stones*, p. 86.

14 Gerald Strober, *Portrait of the Elder Brother* (New York, American Jewish Committee and the National Conference of Christians and Jews, 1972).

15 See David Flusser, 'Jewish–Christian relations in the past and present', *Judaism and Early Christianity* (Tel Aviv, Sifriat Hapo'alim, 1979), p. 454 (Hebrew).

16 See John T. Pawlikowski, *What Are They Saying About Christian–Jewish Relations?* (New York, Paulist Press, 1980), pp. 33–67.

17 See Eva Fleischner, *Judaism in German Christian Theology since 1945* (Metuchen, NJ, Scarecrow Press, 1975); Charlotte Klein, *Anti-Judaism in Christian Theology* (Philadelphia, Fortress Press, 1978).

18 Wolfhart Pannenberg, *Jesus. Christ and Man* (Philadelphia, Westminster Press, 1968).

19 Wolfhart Pannenberg, *The Apostles' Creed in Light of Today's Questions* (Philadelphia, Westminster Press, 1972), foreword.

20 Jurgen Moltmann, *The Crucified God* (New York, Harper & Row, 1974).

21 Jurgen Moltmann, *The Church in the Power of the Spirit* (New York, Harper & Row, 1977).

22 For one of many examples, see Alice L. Eckardt and A. Roy Eckardt, *Long Night's Journey into Day* (Detroit, Wayne State University Press, 1988).

23 Eva Fleischner, *Auschwitz – Beginning of a New Era: Reflections on the Holocaust* (New York, Ktav, 1977); Abraham J. Peck (ed.), *Jews and Christians after the Holocaust* (Philadelphia, Fortress Press, 1982).

24 E. P. Sanders, *Jesus and Judaism* (Philadelphia, Fortress Press, 1985).

25 John T. Pawlikowski, *Christ in the Light of the Christian–Jewish Dialogue* (New York, Paulist Press, 1982).

26 See John S. Conway, 'Protestant missions to the Jews 1810–1980: ecclesiastical imperialism or theological aberration?', *Holocaust and Genocide Studies*, 1 (1986), pp. 127–46.

27 C. M. King, *The Palestinians and the Church, 1: 1948–1956* (Geneva, World Council of Churches, 1981); Larry Ekin, *Enduring Witness: The Churches and the Palestinians* (Geneva, World Council of Churches, 1985).

28 See R. J. Zwi Werblowsky, 'Jewish–Christian relations: new territories, new maps, new realities', in Otto D. Kulka and Paul R. Mendes-Flohr (eds), *Judaism and Christianity under the Impact of National Socialism*, (Jerusalem, Zalman Shazar Center for Jewish History, 1987), pp. 531–6.

29 Ruth Perlmutter and Nathan Perlmutter, *The Real Antisemitism in America* (New York, Arbor House, 1982).
30 Colin Chapman, *Whose Promised Land?* (Tring, Herts., Lion Publishing, 1983).
31 George M. Marsden, *Fundamentalism and American Culture: The Shaping of Twentieth-century Evangelicalism, 1870–1925* (New York, Oxford University Press, 1980).
32 See, for example, David Katz, *Philo Semitism and the Readmission of the Jews to England 1603–1655* (Oxford, Oxford University Press, 1982).
33 See, for example, David Rausch, *Zionism within Early American Fundamentalism* (New York, Edwin Mellen Press, 1978).
34 George M. Marsden, 'Unity and diversity in the evangelical resurgence', *Altered Landscapes: Christianity in America 1935–1985* (Grand Rapids, Mich., William B. Eerdmans, 1989), pp. 61–76.
35 Mark Silk, *Spiritual Politics* (New York, Touchstone, 1988).
36 See Yaakov Ariel, 'American fundamentalists and Israel', *Virtue and Necessity: Fundamentalist Trends vs. the Contemporary Middle East* (Jerusalem, Leonard Davis Institute, Hebrew University of Jerusalem, Policy Papers no. 32, 1989), pp. 1–26 (Hebrew).
37 Charles Y. Glock and Rodney Stark, *Christian Beliefs and Anti Semitism* (New York, Harper Torchbooks, 1966).
38 Lynne Lanniello, 'Release for press', Anti-Defamation League, New York (8 January 1986).
39 Flo Conway and Jim Siegelman, *Holy Terror: The Fundamentalists' War on America's Freedoms in Religion, Politics and our Private Lives* (Garden City, NY, Doubleday, 1982), p. 167.
40 Ibid., p. 168.
41 See Ariel, 'American fundamentalists and Israel', pp. 6–8 (Hebrew).
42 Arnold G. Fruchtenbaum, *Hebrew Christianity: Its Theology, History and Philosophy* (Grand Rapids, Mich., Baker Book House, 1974); David A. Rausch, *Messianic Judaism: Its History, Theology and Polity* (New York, Edwin Mellen Press, 1982).
43 A. James Rudin and Marvin R. Wilson (eds), *A Time to Speak: The Evangelical Jewish Encounter* (Grand Rapids, Mich., Eerdmans, 1987).
44 For Russell and his attitude towards Zionsim, see Yona Malachy, *American Fundamentalism and Israel* (Jerusalem, Institute of Contemporary Jewry, Hebrew University of Jerusalem, 1978), pp. 59–68.
45 Ibid., pp. 68–83.
46 For William Miller, the millennarian movement that he awakened, and its decline, see Leon Festinger, *When Prophecy Fails* (Minneapolis, University of Minnesota Press, 1956); Ronald L. Numbers and Jonathan M. Butler (eds), *The Disappointed* (Bloomington and Indianapolis, Indiana University Press, 1987).
47 Malachy, *American Fundamentalism and Israel*, pp. 21–40.
48 *The Book of Mormon*, 3 Nephi 20, pp. 20–30; 3 Nephi 29, pp. 1–4, 8–9.
49 Eldin Ricks, 'Zionism and the Mormon Church', *Herzl Year Book*, 5 (1963), pp. 147–74.
50 Reed M. Holmes, *The Forerunners* (Independence, Miss., Herald Publishing House, 1981); *idem, The Church in Israel* (Independence, Miss., Herald Publishing House, 1981).

16

CATHOLIC PERCEPTIONS OF THE JEWISH PEOPLE SINCE THE SECOND WORLD WAR

Benedict T. Viviano

Since 1945 there has been a radical shift in the relationship to Judaism of educated Catholic people as well as of the Roman Catholic Church in its official public teachings and policies. This is true both on the level of national bishops' conferences, and on the level of an ecumenical council, that is, the highest authority in the church. This policy shift is furthered by the regular work of the Vatican Secretariat for Christian Unity, with its department for Jewish–Christian relations, not to mention the work of individual theologians like Gregory Baum, Franz Mussner, Rosemary Reuther, John T. Pawlikowski, Charlotte Klein, Edward H. Flannery, Edward A. Synan, Friedrich Heer, Clemens Thoma, Eugene J. Fisher, Kurt Schubert, Gunther Stemberger, and the forerunner John Oesterreicher. On the institutional level this shift can be strikingly illustrated by the case of the Fathers and Sisters of Sion, a religious congregation founded in the last century to pray and to work for the conversion of the Jews. Since the Second Vatican Council at least, they have reoriented themselves to improve Jewish–Christian understanding.

The extent of this shift cannot be realized adequately without some awareness of the *status quo ante*. We can mention polemical passages in the New Testament and in some of the fathers of the church.[1] Then there is the tradition of preaching in which the Pharisees are representatives of everything wrong in religion and the Jews are held collectively, principally and permanently responsible for the death of Jesus.[2] With the expansion of the Christian empire came legislation restrictive of Jewish life. At times kings eager for cash expelled Jews from their kingdoms and seized their property and wealth. At times like the Crusades there were pogroms. There was a teaching of contempt.[3]

With nineteenth-century biological science there arose not only theories of evolution of species but also theories of racial superiority and inferiority, notably those of Count Gobineau, a Catholic.[4] The century culminated in the Dreyfus Affair, a prolonged trial with anti-Jewish implications.[5] (Pope Leo XIII compared Dreyfus to Christ in *Figaro*, March 1899.) Thus in the twentieth century, on top of theological and economic anti-Judaism, there was added the most dangerous form of all, pseudo-scientific racialist anti-Judaism. This biological racialist anti-Judaism is what, above all, led to the ovens of Auschwitz, rather than Christian religious teaching, or so, at least, I understand the causality of the Holocaust. Christian anti-Judaism on this view was a background factor which contributed to the overall anti-Jewish climate but was not the primary, immediate or direct cause of the Holocaust. The difference is obviously important. Christian anti-Semitism differed from biological anti-Semitism in that it aimed at the conversion of the Jew to Christianity, not at physical annihilation. It had been guilty of some violence, at times imposing exile or humiliation on Jews, often of contempt and fear, but this is different from extermination. The key point is that once Jews were converted, Christian anti-Semitism ceased. By contrast, the Nazis exterminated even baptized Jews, on racial grounds.

To be sure the picture before 1945 was not all negative. In addition to the civil emancipation of the Jews throughout most of Europe and the Americas in the nineteenth century, there were isolated efforts by Catholic scholars to undertake a positive approach to the Jewish religious heritage. I think especially of the major works by M.-J. Lagrange (*Le messianisme chez les Juifs*, 1909; *Le judaisme avant Jesus-Christ*, 1931) and by Joseph Bonsirven (*Le judaisme palestinien au temps de Jesus-Christ*, 1935),[6] as well as by J.-B. Frey,[7] Paul Riessler,[8] J. J. Brierre-Narbonne,[9] Jean de Menasce[10] and Renée Bloch.[11] Among Catholic philosophers, Jacques Maritain had a good influence, thanks to his wife Raïssa, a convert from Judaism.[12] On the popular level, the novels of Jerome and Jean Tharaud, brothers and members of the French Academy, portrayed hassidism sympathetically. (The brothers ended as Petainist anti-Semites.) French Christians in 1937 published a collective volume *Les Juifs* (Paris, Plon) to improve the atmosphere poisoned by the rise of Hitler. The major Catholic writer, Paul Claudel, took the lead in it. These authors worked under a cloud of suspicion and were voices crying in the wilderness. But their pioneering efforts bore fruit after 1945. Why?

There were three main reasons for the shift. The first of these was the biblical theology movement. Begun among Protestants in about 1935, this movement in its official form can be dated in the Catholic Church from the papal encyclical *Divino Afflante Spiritu* (1943). This encyclical letter had the effect of encouraging biblical studies on the basis of the original texts and languages, taking into account the implications of literary genres other than history. It explicitly approved the work of Lagrange and his school. It enabled theologians to break out of the prison of ahistorical scholasticism and to apprehend anew the teaching of Jesus, especially his message of the near approach of the kingdom of God to earth, against the background of apocalyptic inter-testamental Judaism, a background which had remained practically completely unknown to mainstream theologians for over a thousand years. The result can be spoken of as the re-Judaization of the Catholic imaging of Jesus.[13]

The popular as well as scholarly interest in biblical studies was furthered by two post-war discoveries: the Qumran manuscripts from near the Dead Sea on the one hand, and on the other the Palestinian targum Neofiti I, found miscatalogued in the Vatican library by Alejandro Diez Macho. These two discoveries presented early Judaism in forms calculated to appeal to Catholics. The Qumran scrolls contained several community rules that strongly resembled Catholic monastic rules. Thus Catholic religious orders throughout the world took an immediate interest in them. Codex Neofiti I included, among many other treasures, an expansion of Exodus 12:42 containing a four-stanza liturgical poem about the messianic meaning of Passover night. This text was brilliantly exploited by Roger LeDeaut to renew the theology of the Eucharist and the liturgy of Holy Saturday night.[14] It thus made a contribution to the liturgical renewal in the church. The practical results of these biblical studies were precisely the introduction in 1970 of regular readings from the Old Testament into the Sunday and weekday liturgies, and the transformation of the teaching of theology in seminaries and universities (see below).

The second reason for the positive shift of Catholic attitudes towards Judaism was the Holocaust, the Nazi genocide of Jews on the basis of a social Darwinist racial theory. The magnitude of this crime, the mass murder of innocent people, horrified Catholics and aroused their sympathy for the Jewish people, as it aroused the sympathy of all people. Pope Pius XI had denounced totalitarian and racist ideologies before the war. He had also uttered the classic sentence, 'We are all spiritually Semites.' Under Pius XII, however great his diplomatic verbal restraint, it has been estimated that half a million Jews were saved from extermination by European Catholics, notably by the future pope John XXIII.[15] As the full extent of the horror became known through films, books and penetrating analyses of thinkers like Hannah Arendt, Catholics undertook an agonizing examination of conscience. This too led to personal stories like the young pious Irish Catholic woman who having heard of the crime felt she must convert to Judaism to replace at least one of the victims of Auschwitz.[16] Auschwitz has become the central moral fact of the twentieth century, challenging any easy abandonment of ethics based on law, such as threatened Western civilization in the late 1960s.

The third reason for the shift in attitudes was the founding of the State of Israel in 1948. The amazing story of the birth of this state out of the ashes of the Holocaust and in the midst of war, plus the subsequent military victories, earned the respectful admiration of Catholics as of others.[17] The 1947 UN resolution to partition Palestine and thus to permit the creation of a Jewish state was in fact made possible by the votes of Catholic states who at that time constituted a majority of the United Nations General Assembly. The decisive vote was cast by Guatamala. This vote, favourable to partition, was achieved through careful long-term preparation by Zionists with links to Catholic opinion-makers, particularly in France. Thanks to the researches of Professor Ronald Brown of Harvard we can tell this story in some detail.[18]

So sensitive was the Jewish question on the eve of the Second World War in the eyes of the Vatican that it forbade Jesuit journals to discuss it in their publications from 1938 to 1948. Before the war Catholic periodicals largely ignored Zionism or treated it only episodically. The French Catholic daily *La Croix* was rather anti-Jewish and the Italian fortnightly journal *Civilta Cattolica* in 1897 said that the dispersion of Israel must continue, basing their view on the biblical texts Zechariah 12:3 and Luke 21:24. Only in 1946 did Catholics begin to consider the question in depth, and then under altered circumstances.

Up until 1945 right-wing opinion was the dominant voice in the Catholic world, both lay and clerical. Leftists had to struggle to be heard, whether in politics (*les abbés républicains*) or in theology (Lagrange, Chenu, Teilhard).[19] In the brief period 1945–50 the right temporarily lost its hold on power. This power vacuum allowed the rise of alternative elites in the French Catholic church. Emmanuel Mounier's journal *Esprit* advocated personalism, a code for Christian social democracy as opposed to monarchy or fascism or unrestricted capitalism. Henri Mandouze and Gaston Fessard were critical of racism in the pages of *Témoignages Chrétiennes*. Henri Colson, superior-general of the Sion fathers, founded *Cahiers sioniens* in 1947, with Paul Demann as editor.

In these journals Jewish converts to the Catholic Church advocated a Zionist solution to the Jewish problem in Europe. Members of the Jewish Agency like Wilensky, Glassberg and Rabinowitz convinced them that the planned Jewish state would be a secular one, without messianic pretensions to restore biblical Israel. This argument also rallied secular socialists to the cause. The support of the converts was thought to be further proof of Zionism's secular character. The result of these efforts at persuasion was the UN vote in favour of partition. At this time the UN was a 'Catholic club'. A Catholic veto was possible. But in fact almost all Catholic states voted in the UN for the creation of a Jewish state in 1947/8, so great was the prestige and influence of French Catholic opinion on them.

But a change in Catholic attitudes came quickly again. After 1949 it became clear that the new Jewish state was going to be in many ways religiously, messianically Jewish. First, the name chosen for the state was a shock. Herzl had wanted it to be called Judaea. (Wellhausen had distinguished sharply between ancient Israel as something good because law-free and Judaism as something bad because law-bound.[20] The secular Zionists bought his prejudiced theory in one of the ironies of history.) The use of a religious symbol, the Star of David, on the flag was another shock, and remains a stumbling-block to young Israeli Muslims. The legal enforcement of Kosher food rules in the army and elsewhere, as well as of the sabbath, was a further indication of this direction. Catholic opinion-makers awoke to the new situation as the international status of Jerusalem became a key question in the UN. The Zionists had first agreed to its internationalization, but the 1948 war changed their mind. Zionism's target audience shifted from the world powers to world Jewry and for that they needed to claim Jerusalem. The result was the 1949 UN resolution 303 which claimed that *all* of Jerusalem, east and west, should have an international status separate from both Israel and Jordan. A diplomatic innovation, the term 'collective non-recognition', was used to express that the member states, including the so-called Catholic ones, do not recognize Jerusalem as the capital of Israel. To this day most of their embassies are in Tel Aviv. Cardinals Spellman and Cushing and the American bishops' conference (then called the NCWC) took an active part in attaining this result, which went beyond the Vatican's own more moderate position.

But in the 1950s other Catholic elites felt it important to have a Catholic presence to the new state, e.g. the Dominicans of St Isaiah house (whose superior, Marcel Dubois, was in 1989 made a worthy of Jerusalem), the order of Notre Dame de Sion and the Carmelites of Haifa. Their work continues. Roman Catholic priests and sisters began to study at Jewish universities in Israel and America, as once Gershom Scholem had received his doctorate in a Catholic philosophy programme in Munich.

Moving on to the 1960s, we come to the Second Vatican Council (1962–5). This council marked an important step in the theological *rapprochement* between the church and the Jewish people. The conciliar Declaration *Nostra Aetate* (1965), on the relationship of the church to non-Christian religions, devoted its fourth paragraph to the church and the Jewish people. Besides giving official approval at the highest level to the friendly dialogue and sympathetic study which had already developed, it went further by eliminating any theological legitimacy to free-floating anti-Judaism, especially the charge of deicide and the various blood libels. Moreover, one of the unsung results of the council was the promulgation in 1970 of a new set of lectionaries for use in the daily and Sunday liturgies. In general, these lectionaries presented a much broader range of biblical texts to the worshipping faithful than was hitherto the case. But in particular it introduced a reading from the Old Testament at every Sunday mass. This has already had a major effect on the awareness by the faithful of their roots in the Hebrew scriptures. Subsequent papal and episcopal documents have only increased the degrees of reconciliation.[21] And one concrete embodiment of this new mood is the agreement between the Pontifical Biblical Institute in Rome and the Hebrew University of Jerusalem.

According to this agreement, students from the Biblical Institute, who are for the most part the future seminary professors of the Catholic world, spend a semester at Hebrew University, at reduced rates. This arrangement too cannot fail to have its effect.

The Vatican document 'Notes on the correct way to present the Jews and Judaism in preaching and catechesis in the Roman Catholic Church' of 24 June 1985 contains some advances on previous documents. It contains a more nuanced statement of the relationship both positive and negative of Jesus to the Pharisees. It puts a question mark beside the typological way of reading the Old Testament which too easily avoids its concrete reality. It also touches on a theology of two ways to salvation, one for Jews and one for Christians, sometimes called a theory of two covenants. If accepted, such a theory makes it unnecessary for either side to try to convert the other. But the document is almost silent about the Holocaust (it is the first to mention it) and is not especially coherent on Israel.

There remain some stumbling-blocks or difficulties in the way of full mutual reconciliation or trust. From the Catholic side we can mention three. The first is the failure of the Israeli government until very recently to resolve the Palestinian question. To be sure, the Palestinian leaders themselves were not ready until recently to negotiate a realistic partition and final political settlement. Western nations must realize that they have been requesting from the Israelis a generosity which would surpass that of the previous powers in the land, the Turks, the British and the Jordanians – none of whom gave political control over their lives to the Palestinians. Nevertheless, the continued military occupation of the West Bank and Gaza remained a moral blot on Israel's escutcheon and has led to the second, related, problem of Israel's long-range territorial ambitions. Certain maximalist claims caused Vatican diplomats in the past to be uncertain about the stability of Israel's frontiers. The Vatican was therefore reluctant to establish full diplomatic relations at the ambassadorial level with Israel. This has happily changed, following the end of the Cold War, the new attitudes in the Arab world, among Palestinians and in Israel itself.

The third obstacle on the Catholic side came not from the State of Israel nor from religiously serious Jews but rather from Jewish secularists. There are some Jews, especially in the USA, who are alienated from religious Judaism, yet identify themselves ethnically as Jewish, and who are persuaded that Jews of any sort are safest when Christians are weak, divided and lax in their faith.[22] They thus glorify the Enlightenment in its most pagan forms,[23] encourage sexual promiscuity, produce films and television programmes which ridicule Christian (and sometimes Jewish) symbols, values and customs (e.g., Norman Lear, Woody Allen), or foster publications which blame the church for all the sufferings of the Jews throughout history in an undifferentiated fashion.

On the Jewish side some recent stumbling-blocks to reconciliation included the papal beatification of Edith Stein, philosopher in the phenomenological movement and Carmelite nun, who was murdered as a Jew at Auschwitz. To Jews this beatification can seem an effort to appropriate the sympathies aroused by horror at the Holocaust for Catholics rather than for Jews. It is part of the debate over the uniqueness or non-uniqueness of the Holocaust, its 'ownership', its beneficiaries.

A second obstacle to dialogue was the willingness of the present pope to receive in official audience the chancellor of Austria, Kurt Waldheim, who was, as a young officer, allegedly involved in war crimes such as the massacre of Bosnian Serbs by Croatian separatists, though no evidence has been found that he acted against Jews. To Catholics the Pope's reception of Waldheim could appear both as an expression of Christ's mercy to sinners and as diplomatic pragmatism. To Jews it appeared as insensitive to their concerns, just as they so judged President Reagan's visit to the Bitburg military cemetery; in the case of Waldheim, it looked like a sordid example of support for the right-wing parties in Austria.

A third obstacle to dialogue was the presence of a Carmelite convent of sisters on the outer grounds of the death camp at Auschwitz. Jews have found this an offensive intrusion on a site of great significance to them and which, they feel, should be left intact, without palliatives. An international committee agreed to the removal of the convent. Then the Poles stalled, and Cardinal Glemp defended the delay and criticized the aggressive way in which Jewish pressure was being exercised. Finally the Pope intervened and the matter is more or less settled. The controversy is a good example of the meaning of the ongoing official dialogue. Even though there may be pockets of resistance, the momentum of the developing tradition, backed by the official bureaucracy, is practically irresistible.

We may close with the Pope's visit to the Rome synagogue on 1 April 1986. This unprecedented event was the culmination of twenty years of improved relations since the Council was formed. In his address the Pope said that the Jews were the elder brothers of the Christians, and he reaffirmed *Nostra Aetate* and subsequent documents. This visit must be seen in the context of the Pope's meeting with leaders of all world religions at Assisi that same year to pray for peace. From a Catholic perspective, the situation of Jews since the Second World War is indeed a new world.

(This essay is limited by several factors. First, it adheres strictly to its assignment, the *Catholic*, aspect. This means that it passes over in total silence the considerable work of Protestant, Anglican and Eastern Orthodox scholars and church bodies. The author is aware of some of this work and gratefully acknowledges his debt to it. No slight is intended by this silence, only adherence to an assignment. Second, this essay is not written by a professional specialist in modern Jewish–Christian relations, but, upon request, by a professor of New Testament studies who wrote his dissertation on the relation between an early rabbinic text and the New Testament, and who lives as a Christian in Israel. Finally, it was written before the Vatican recognition of the State of Israel, which underlines the extent of the radical change in Catholic attitudes towards the Jewish world.)

NOTES

1 Gregory Baum, *The Jews and the Gospel* (Westminster, Md., Newman, 1961); Franz Mussner, *Tractate on the Jews* (Philadelphia, Fortress, 1984); Norman A. Beck, *Mature Christianity* (Selinsgrove, Pa., Susquehanna University Press, 1985); A. Lukyn-Williams, *Adversus Judaeos* (Cambridge, Cambridge University Press, 1935).

2 R. L. Wilkins, *John Chrysostom and the Jews* (Berkeley, University of California, 1983); idem, *Judaism and the Early Christian Mind* (New Haven, Yale University Press, 1971); David P. Efroymson, 'Tertullian's anti-Jewish rhetoric', *Union Seminary Quarterly Review*, 36 (1980), pp. 25–37.

3 Jules Isaac, *Jésus et Israel* (Paris, Albin Michel, 1948). Cf. the review article by Pierre Benoit, *Revue Biblique* (1949), pp. 610–13, collected in his *Exégèse et théologie*, vol. 2 (Paris, Cerf, 1961), pp. 321–7.

4 Joseph Arthur, Comte de Gobineau (1816–82), author of the *Essai sur l'inégalité des races humaines* (1853–1855), which influenced theoreticians of Germanic racialism. Cf. Richard Hofstadter, *Social Darwinism in American Thought* (Boston, Beacon, 1955).

5 Cf. J.-D. Bredin, *L'Affaire* (Paris, Julliard, 1983), for example.

6 On Bonsirven's difficulties in getting his work published see Marcel Becamel, 'Le P. Joseph Bonsirven, S.J., et Monseigneur Mignot', *Bulletin de Littérature Ecclésiastique* (Toulouse) 71 (1970), pp. 262–73.

7 J.-B. Frey, *La théologie juive au temps de Jésus-Christ* (Rome, Biblical Commission, 1910); idem, *Corpus Inscriptionum Iudaicarum*, 2 vols (Rome, Pontificio Istituto di Archeologia Cristiana, 1936, 1952).

8 Paul Riessler, *Altjüdisches Schrifttum ausserhalb der Bibel* (Heidelberg, Kerle; 1966; first edn 1928).

9 J. J. Brierre-Narbonne, *Les prophéties messianiques de l'Ancien Testament dans la littérature juive* (Paris, Guethner, 1933), and many other works.

10 Jean de Menasce, *Quand Israel Aime Dieu* (Paris, Plon, 1931).

11 For English translations of two of Renée Bloch's principle essays on midrash, see *Approaches to Ancient Judaism* (Brown Judaica Studies l; Atlanta, Scholars Press, 1978), pp. 29–75.

12 Jacques Maritain, *Les Juifs parmi les nations* (Paris, Cerf, 1938); *Le mystère d'Israël et autres essais* (Paris, Desclée de Brouwer, 1965); etc.

13 John T. Pawlikowski, 'The Re-Judaization of Christianity – its impact on the church and its implications for the Jewish people', *Immanuel*, 22/23 (1989), pp. 60–74.

14 R. LeDéaut, *La Nuit Pascal* (Analecta Biblica 22; Rome, Biblical Institute, 1963).

15 Pinchas Lapide, *Three Popes and the Jews* (1967); Owen Chadwick, *Britain and the Vatican during the Second World War* (Cambridge, Cambridge University Press, 1986).

16 Devorah Wigoder, *Hope is My House* (Englewood Cliffs, NJ, Prentice-Hall, 1966).

17 Netanael Lorch, *The Edge of the Sword: Israel's War of Independence, 1947–49* (New York, G. P. Putnam, 1961); Dominique Lapierre and Larry Collins, *O Jerusalem* (London, Weidenfeld & Nicolson, 1972).

18 Ronald Brown, *The Catholic Press, the Birth of Israel, and the Problem of Jerusalem, 1947–1950* (Geneva, University of Geneva, 1988).

19 M.-J. Lagrange, *Personal Reflections and Memoirs* (New York, Paulist, 1985); F.-M. Braun, *The Work of Père Lagrange* (Milwaukee, Bruce, 1963); M.-D. Chenu, *Une école de theologie: le saulchoir* (Paris, Cerf, 1985); F. Leprieur, *Quand Rome Condamne* (Paris, Plon-Cerf, 1989).

20 John Rogerson, *Old Testament Criticism in the Nineteenth Century: England and Germany* (Philadelphia, Fortress, 1985).

21 E. J. Fisher, A. J. Rudin and M. H. Tanenbaum, *Twenty Years of Jewish–Catholic Relations* (New York, Paulist, 1986); G. Wigoder, *Jewish–Christian Relations since the Second World War* (Manchester, Manchester University Press, 1988); *Fifteen Years of Catholic–Jewish Dialogue 1970–1985, Selected Papers* (Vatican City, Vaticana, 1988); M.-T. Hoch and Bernard Dupuy, *Les Eglises devant le Judaisme, documents officiels 1918–1978* (Paris, Cerf, 1980); Michel Remaud, *Catholiques et Juifs: un nouveau regard* (Paris, Cooperative de l'Enseignement Religieux, 1985).

22 The above is my interpretation or extrapolation. What he actually says is, 'It is where liberalism is strong that Jews are safe', Peter Gay, *Freud, Jews and Other Germans* (Oxford, Oxford University Press, 1987), p. 166.

23 Peter Gay, *The Enlightenment*, 2 vols (New York, Viking, 1966, 1970).

17

THE SPANISH-SPEAKING
WORLD AND THE JEWS
The last half-century

Haim Avni

The past fifty years have been especially significant for the historical relationship between the Jewish people and the Spanish-speaking nations. The
year 1992, which marks the fifth centennial of both the expulsion of
the Jews from Spain and the discovery of America, presents us with a most
fitting opportunity to survey developments in contemporary times. In this
article we shall first describe the situation at the height of the Holocaust and
in the years immediately following the Second World War. We shall then
outline the form taken by these relations in recent years as reflected in
certain basic issues which influence the reality of Jewish life in the Spanish-
speaking countries, noting those which are deserving of further study.

1942 – JEWS IN THE SPANISH-SPEAKING WORLD

Spain

There were very few Jews in Spain on 1 April 1939, the day on which
General Francisco Franco Bahamonde declared victory of the forces under
his command and the end of the civil war. Only a few individual Jews
remained in Madrid, which in 1936 had a Jewish community of about 150
families. The community of Barcelona, which had counted some 5,000
persons at the outbreak of hostilities, no longer existed. The victorious
nationalist government rescinded the republican constitution of 1931 that
had guaranteed equal rights to all religious persuasions; it also refrained
from reinstating the monarchical constitution of 1876 which extended
tolerance to non-Catholics, allowing them to pursue their religious practices
– provided that they did so discreetly in seclusion and did nothing to prejudice 'Christian morality'. In effect, Franco's regime rescinded the legal
status of non-Catholics – including Jews – bringing them back to their
condition previous to 1855, the year in which they were granted, for the
first time, some implicit tolerance of their very existence. By the outbreak

of the Second World War there was no longer any public form of Jewish communal life in Spain. Though the government took no action against the remaining Jews and did not persecute them, to all intents and purposes it had restored the delegitimization that had characterized Jewish existence in Spain for hundreds of years.[1]

After the fall of France in the summer of 1940, thousands of Jewish refugees sought to enter Spain. They arrived among the tens of thousands who fled France, and continued to reach Spain throughout 1941. Though we do not know the exact number of those who were permitted to pass through Spain, we know that only some 500 remained there, most of them because they had no other choice. A country ruled by a regime that had won the civil war with the assistance of Nazi Germany and which since June 1941 was actively engaged in hostilities against the USSR, was no secure haven for Jews.[2]

The implementation of the 'final solution' in France during the summer of 1942 brought in its wake a new wave of some hundreds of Jewish refugees to Spain. This time all of them entered the country illegally through the Pyrenees and the prospects that they would be able to cross the border into Portugal – or to sail from a Spanish port – were next to nil. Once the Spanish authorities realized that in this case all the refugees were Jews, they intended, in October 1942, to expel them back to France. However, before they could carry out this intention, the Allies successfully landed on North Africa's shores on the night of 9 November and once more – just as in 1940 – the plight of the Jewish refugees became part of a more general issue. Since 'Free French' units participated in the Allied occupation forces in North Africa, thousands of young Frenchmen streamed to Spain in order to make their way to Morocco and Algeria. After protests from Nazi Germany and Vichy France, Spain decided to close its borders and deport any refugees who could be apprehended, but Allied pressure and the personal intervention of Winston Churchill once more caused a reversal of Spanish policy. As of March 1943, refugees – including Jews – were again allowed to enter the country, on the explicit condition that the Allies would provide for their needs throughout their stay on Spanish soil and that they would be evacuated as speedily as possible. In order to facilitate the extension of aid to stateless refugees and their transfer to other countries, the Spanish authorities permitted the Allies to open a special agency – as a branch office of the US Embassy – financed by several American welfare agencies, the major one among them being the American Jewish Joint Distribution Committee (JDC). Furthermore, they tolerated the activity of an unofficial representative of the JDC, ostensibly representing the Portuguese Red Cross but whose real affiliation was common knowledge, who operated a liaison office and welfare agency for Jewish refugees in one of Barcelona's hotels. Jewish organizations were forbidden to work openly and with official status in Spain.

Entrance into Spain with the object of permanent residence was forbidden even to a small number of Sephardi Jews who were Spanish nationals and were therefore allowed by the Nazis to escape the 'final solution'. They numbered at most 4,000 individuals, some 3,000 in France and the rest in the Balkans, especially in the Greek city of Salonika. During the two years that preceded the extermination of European Jewry, when the property of these Jews – many of them well off – was about to be confiscated, Spain directed its diplomatic representatives to register them as Spanish nationals while at the same time refraining from taking any action to forestall the application to them of any other measures applying to all Jews. Thus, these Spanish nationals were dependent upon the good-will of Spain's diplomatic representatives and their ability to manoeuvre between the limiting directives from Madrid and the ever-increasing persecution inflicted upon the Jews by the Germans. There were among these officials some who granted them effective protection; the test came, however, early in 1943 when the Germans demanded that Spain either remove its nationals from Nazi-occupied territories or leave them to share the fate of all other Jews. At first, the Spanish government was loath to comply with the demand to repatriate them, but from March 1943 it agreed to receive those whose papers had not lapsed and were completely in order, a condition which drastically reduced their number. Even these were only allowed to enter Spain in accordance with an arrangement decided upon by the authorities – that no group of such nationals could cross into Spain before every member of the previous one had left the country. Spain strictly maintained this procedure, which flowed from its stubborn opposition to the possible creation of a Jewish community on Spanish soil, even though it involved only small groups numbering 365, 155 or even no more than seventy-nine individuals, and despite the fact that the Foreign Ministry was well aware of the danger threatening the persons under its protection. At most, only 800 Jews of Spanish nationality were rescued through 'repatriation'.[3]

The legend that during the Holocaust Spain rescued many thousands of the descendants of those who were expelled in 1492 simply because they were part of the sphere of Spanish culture was effectively propagated after the war by the Franco regime and is widely accepted even today. It obscures the clear fact that just fifty years ago there was no room in Franco's Spain for an open, legitimate existence of any Jews, even for those few who carried the torch of Spanish culture in their countries of residence and held official papers providing Spanish nationality and protection.

Latin America – Jewish presence on the Continent

In contrast to Spain, there was not one country in Latin America which in 1942 prohibited or limited Jewish communal activities by law or any form of administrative decree. Once these nations had gained their freedom from Spanish domination early in the nineteenth century, all such restrictions were gradually abolished and conditions developed which enabled a renewed encounter between Jews and people bearing Spanish culture. This was especially true in the southern part of the continent, in what are termed the 'southern conus' (*cono sur*) countries – Argentina, Uruguay and Chile. From the late decades of the nineteenth century until the economic depression of the 1930s, these countries attracted millions of immigrants from Europe who gave to the nations of this region a clearly European character that may be termed 'Euro-America'. Among them were many Jews.

In 1939 Argentine Jewry marked the fiftieth anniversary of the beginning of Jewish immigration and agricultural settlement. The 820 immigrants who arrived on 14 August 1889 aboard a single ship – the *Weser* – founded the first colony. It was they, too, who induced Baron Maurice de Hirsch to make Argentina the scene of his scheme for massive colonization by Jews. His extensive financial investments and the activity of the Jewish Colonization Association (JCA) after his death were the impetus which placed Argentina on the map of Jewish immigration as a well-known destination, where agriculture was an important branch of the economy through which one could strike roots. One of the peak years of Jewish agricultural settlement was 1940: according to JCA statistics, its colonies included 3,454 farm units which supported 17,592 persons, while another 9,856 worked in the colonies as hired agricultural labourers or were employed in various trades and services. The total Jewish population of Argentina in 1940 was 254,000 of which the 27,448 farmers and others who lived in the colonies comprised about 10.8 per cent. Such a concentration of farmers made Argentinian Jewry unique among all the new communities in the Jewish dispersion.[4] At the same time, most of Argentina's Jews were concentrated in urban communities in many of the inland cities, but first and foremost in the capital, Buenos Aires. Their economic activity was based on all types of trading, on manufacturing – especially of items for popular consumption – and on craftsmanship. Cooperatives and mutual benefit societies played a dominant role in all of these economic fields, as they did in the Jewish colonies.[5]

In 1942 Argentinian Jewry was a highly pluralistic community. While the majority was of East European origin, there were also those who had come from North Africa, two separate communities of Syrian Jews – one from Aleppo and the other from Damascus – and Sephardic Jews from the Balkans and Turkey who spoke Judaeo-Spanish. To all of these were added, in the half-decade that preceded the outbreak of the Second World War, German-speaking refugees fleeing from the Nazi terror. Each of these immigrant groups developed its own communal institutions in accordance with the linguistic and cultural heritage that it brought from its country of origin. Only the East European Ashkenazic community split along political and ideological lines rather than in accordance with country of origin. The German-speaking Jews of Central Europe brought with them religious pluralism – Orthodox, Conservative and Reform. Religious practice and institutions were also the core of communal life for Jews of North African, Balkan or oriental origin. Though they all adhered to Orthodox Judaism, each community had its own forms of prayer, traditions and customs. They also maintained separate welfare and educational institutions, but all – except for the Jewish Communists – were members of DAIA, Delegación de Asociaciones Israelitas Argentinas, a political confederative body representing the Jewish community in its relations with Argentinian society, with the prime objective of combating anti-Semitism.[6]

Communal pluralism together with organizational centralism was also characteristic of the other two small Jewish communities in the southern part of the continent in 1942, those of Uruguay and Chile. The Jewish presence in these two countries was the by-product of the wave of immigration to Argentina: Uruguay as an interim station on the way to Argentina and Chile as a destination in its own right, to which Jews – especially of Ashkenazic origin – moved on after a short or lengthy sojourn in Argentina. Both these communities absorbed large numbers of German Jews during the Nazi era, increasing the Jewish populations of the two countries in 1942 to an estimated 37,000 in Uruguay and 25,000 in Chile.[7] In both countries, the majority of Jews concentrated in the capital cities. In addition to institutions established to meet their religious needs, these communities were marked by intensive political, Zionist and leftist activities. They also established Yiddish newspapers and unpretentious educational systems, as well as welfare agencies, cooperatives and mutual loan associations. However, in 1942 even the oldest of these institutions had existed for no more than thirty years, while those established by the German-speaking emigrants from Central Europe had been active for only a few years.[8]

Those parts of the former Spanish empire which lay north of Argentina, Uruguay and Chile were in no way influenced by the waves of European immigration of the late nineteenth and early twentieth centuries. Many of these countries did not try to attract immigrants while others, such as Mexico and Peru, were unsuccessful in their efforts to do so. The populations of most of these countries maintained the structure of the colonial period: an overwhelming majority were direct descendants of the native pre-Colombian population, intermingled, in varying degrees, with the heirs of the conquistadors and of colonists who had come from the Iberian Peninsula. Ethnically, therefore, these countries can be termed 'Indo-American'. In a few of them, such as Cuba, parts of Colombia, Panama and others, the local populations were greatly changed by the descendants of the slaves imported from Africa to labour in the plantation colonies of the Caribbean basin during the two centuries that preceded independence.

Those immigrants from Europe and the Middle East who did settle in these countries in various circumstances did not leave their mark on general society, remaining as national enclaves – 'colonies' – of foreigners. This was also true of the Jewish communities, which reached appreciable numbers in only two of these countries – Cuba and Mexico – because of their proximity to the greatest and most preferred destination: the United States.[9]

Cuba, since gaining its independence from Spain in 1898 with the active intervention of the USA, had in effect been a dependency of the latter. In addition to a small number of Jews holding American citizenship who settled in Cuba immediately after independence, many Sephardic Jews from Turkey arrived in the country before the First World War, and this wave increased in the first post-war decade, until the Great Depression. Many East European Jews hoped that the close relationship between the USA and Cuba and their geographic proximity would enable them to overcome the American immigration restriction laws which had been enacted in the interim, whether in a legal manner by waiting for immigration permits in Havana or by illegal entry in smugglers' boats. The distress of these immigrants in a country plagued by a deep economic recession and by a tropical climate to which they could not adjust prompted Jewish organizations in the USA to lend them material support and financial credit, and thus to encourage their absorption in Cuba. These efforts were partially successful, contributing to the establishment of an Ashkenazic community in Cuba alongside the older Sephardic one. After a short or lengthy stay in Cuba, some of these emigrants continued to the next stop of the passenger ships that docked in Cuban ports or in Vera Cruz in Mexico.

Here, too, Jews from the Middle East – predominantly from Syria – had preceded the establishment of an Ashkenazic community; as in Cuba, East European Jews were attracted to Mexico during the 1920s by its lengthy border with the United States. American Jewish welfare agencies, in their attempts to stop the flow of illegal crossings into the USA, extended aid to the immigrants in Mexico to encourage them to stay there. Better conditions of livelihood existed in Mexico than in Cuba. Gradually – despite the xenophobia that characterized Mexican society – a well-organized, ramified Jewish community developed there during the 1920s and 1930s. It was sub-divided into communities of Syrian Jews (even here there were separate communities of those who originated from Aleppo and from Damascus), of those who had come from the Balkans and Turkey, and of the majority group – East European Ashkenazim.

Just as in Argentina, the Ashkenazi communities in Cuba and Mexico were characterized by turbulent political activity. Each of the communities established its own religious institutions and educational system as well as benefit societies. All these were already in existence when refugees from the Nazi regime began to reach these two countries in the second half of the 1930s. It is estimated that, despite the difficulties that they had to face, some 12,000 refugees managed to enter Cuba, though most of them were able to continue their journey to other destinations during the Second World War, especially to the USA. Thus, the German Jewish refugees contributed very little to the development of the Cuban Jewish community which, according to one estimate, numbered 11,450 in 1942.[10] The number of such refugees that entered Mexico was considerably smaller, no more than an estimated 1,850 Jews, but these became part of the local Jewish community, creating another organizational framework in addition to those already in existence. A census conducted by the Mexican Jewish community in 1942 counted a population of 18,299, two-thirds of them in the capital city.[11]

Small Jewish communities had been established in other 'Indo-American' countries in the 1920s, but their expansion was either halted or appreciably slowed down in the 1930s so that in 1942 the influence of refugees from the Third Reich was hardly felt. This was the situation in Venezuela, where a small community of North African Jews had existed since the beginning of the twentieth century, to which was added a small community of East European Jews in the 1920s. Only one group of refugees was allowed admittance to Venezuela during the entire period of the Holocaust. Those who managed to enter the country despite restrictive measures had to present evidence that they had converted to Catholicism. Small Costa Rica, the most democratic country in Central America, with a population of clearly Iberian extraction, stubbornly prevented any growth of its small Jewish community which had developed since the 1920s, and in 1942 included about 600 persons. In that year, Peru was home to some 2,500 Jews, most of whom lived in the capital city of Lima and were organized in three separate communities. Only about 500 of them had arrived after the rise of Nazism. Somewhat less restrictive was Colombia which in 1942 had a Jewish community of about 5,800 persons in Bogotá and three other important regional cities. German-speaking Jews of Central European origin formed an important element in the local Jewish community. What the communities in all of these countries had in common was that by the middle of the Second World War they were firmly based and ramified, and their composition, on the basis of country of origin, was diversified.[12]

This was not the case in Bolivia, Ecuador, Paraguay and Guatemala, all 'Indo-American' states *par excellence*. True, there was some minor Jewish presence in each of these countries prior to the wave of refugees from Nazi oppression, but during the period 1938–42 in all of them there developed a concentrated Jewish community notable for its dissimilarity, in all aspects, from local society. The sudden, frantic influx of thousands of Jews coming from the centres of Central European urban culture, most of them German-speaking and rooted in Germanic culture, to backward colonial cities such as were at this time Asunción, Quito, La Paz and Guatemala City, was a cultural shock not only to the immigrants themselves but to local society as well. The legal and administrative conditions under which the newcomers were granted visas and the employment and housing problems which emerged wherever they tried to settle down were fertile ground for tensions between them and the local populations. Their contribution to the modernization of services, from which the host society benefited, and to the manufacture and introduction of new products was felt only at a later stage. However, in the meantime, by 1942 some 5,000 Jews in Bolivia, 3,200 in Ecuador, 3,000 in Paraguay and about 900 in Guatemala had managed to establish for themselves intensive communal and cultural frameworks. To this end they to a great degree utilized the financial means placed at their disposal by the American JDC.[13]

Conditions of Jewish life in Spanish America

In 1942 there were Jews in each of the eighteen countries that until the beginning of the nineteenth century had comprised the Spanish empire in America. By country of origin, Spanish American Jews spoke Yiddish, Judaeo-Spanish and the various dialects of Judaeo-Arabic: to all of these was added German. Thus, one can say that all branches of the Jewish people were represented among the Hispano-American nations. In a few states – such as Honduras, Nicaragua and El Salvador – the number of Jews did not exceed a few tens or hundreds. In one of them – the Dominican Republic on the island of Hispaniola – Jewish settlement attracted financial investment and world-wide attention incommensurate with the size of the community.[14] Despite the differences between the extent and character of Jewish presence in the various states of Spanish America, there are some elements common to all that influenced the conditions of Jewish life.

The first is the fact that the Jewish communities of Spanish America were the only ones throughout the world whose countries were not belligerents in the Second World War. After Pearl Harbor, most Spanish American countries and Brazil broke off relations with the Axis nations and many even declared war upon them. However, except for a unit of the Mexican Air Force (and a Brazilian contingent that fought on the Italian front), a state of war was not sensed throughout Latin America. Chile and Argentina even delayed breaking off relations with Germany; Chile did so in January 1943 while Argentina waited another year. They declared war on Germany only in the spring of 1945, perfect timing to enable them to join the Allies as members of the United Nations.[15] The war, then, was an economic blessing for the Spanish American nations, especially for the urban classes that produced for the local markets those goods which in normal times had been imported from Europe and the USA. Increased world consumption of the region's traditional exports were also an economic boon to those same economic elements and social classes, to which many Jews belonged or which they joined as the war dragged on. At war's end, the economic standing of any individual Jews, and of the communities in general, was much improved over conditions at the outbreak of hostilities.

At this time, and for the same reason, international Jewish organizations 'discovered' the Jewish communities of Spanish America. The World Zionist Organization, which had been active in Jewish communities throughout the world since the turn of the century, and especially since the First World War, by means of the Jewish National Fund and Keren Hayessod, now augmented its activity in the region. The World Jewish Congress (WJC), which had transferred its headquarters from Geneva to the USA due to the war, found that Central and South America were the only regions in which it could act directly. The JDC, followed by the American Jewish Committee, also despatched their representatives to the area in which HICEM (HIAS-JCA Emigdirekt) was already active. The competition among these organizations and, above all, the tense relations between the JDC and the WJC which had already affected activities in the USA and Europe, were now transferred to the Spanish American arena.[16]

Another fundamental issue which influenced the conditions of Jewish life was anti-Semitism. The universal campaign against the Jewish people launched by Nazi Germany had its local supporters in each of the Latin American states. Xenophobia, economic competition and fundamental Catholic beliefs provided fertile ground in which to plant the seeds of Nazi racism and the model presented by Germany; these were disseminated in Spanish America by Nazis among the immigrants from Germany and their supporters within Spanish-American society. The need to face up to violent incitement led to the establishment of representative federations of a political character in each of the Jewish communities. Jew-hatred influenced the authorities and had widespread repercussions on one central issue: immigration. In secret despatches, governments directed their representatives abroad not to grant entry permits to members of the Jewish religion, or even to those of the Semitic race, all this on various pretexts. Even in countries which did accept thousands of Jewish refugees within a short period of time – such as Chile and Bolivia – such restrictions were enforced after the period of grace, which in itself was generally marked by bribes. Representatives of the American Jewish Committee personally learned of the seriousness of these restrictions when their requests for entry permits in order to visit the Jewish communities met with inexplicable difficulties.[17]

Animosity, however, was not the only attitude adopted towards Jews in Spanish America. This became evident first to Rachelle Sefardi Yarden, and then to Moshe Tov and his colleagues in the Latin American Department of the Jewish Agency in New York who endeavoured, since 1943, to mobilize public support for the achievement of Zionist objectives. From 1944, and to an even greater extent from late in 1945, many 'committees for a Hebrew

Palestine' (Comité Pro-Palestina Hebrea) existed throughout Latin America. When a world conference of Christian pro-Palestine committees was convened in Washington in November 1945 with representatives from fourteen countries, the Mexican committee, established in 1944, was at least formally among the sponsors. Present at the conference were leading personalities from Venezuela, Paraguay, Cuba and other Spanish-American states who were already, or soon to become, active in the pro-Palestine committees of their own countries. Members or supporters of the Mexican committee included important personalities such as Lázaro Cardenas, Mexico's revered populist president from 1934 to 1940, and Vicente Lombardo Toledano, president of the Confederation of Latin American Workers (Confederacion de Trabajadores de América Latina) which had a membership of about five million. In addition to these adherents to revolutionary ideology, both renowned for their struggle against fascism, Franco and Nazism, the Mexican pro-Hebrew Palestine Committee included others known to be supporters of the Catholic Church – which was persecuted in revolutionary Mexico – as well as leading liberals.[18]

As UN involvement in the Palestine issue increased, so did the number of persons who joined the various pro-Palestine committees. Authors, poets, statesmen and other public figures became actively involved or came forward with statements of support. Spanish America was well represented on UNSCOP (United Nations Special Committee on Palestine) and the representatives of Uruguay and Guatemala, Rodríguez Fabregat and Jorge García Granados, played a central role in shaping its proposals. When on 29 November 1947 the time came for the UN General Assembly to vote on the Palestine issue, the Latin American states were a weighty factor in the passing of UN Resolution 188 which called for the partition of Palestine into Arab and Jewish states with economic union between them: thirteen Latin American states were among the thirty-three that voted for the resolution, providing the necessary two-thirds majority, while only one – Cuba – was among the thirteen that voted against. Under the circumstances that prevailed at the time, with the USA refraining from pressuring its neighbours to vote with it in the General Assembly in favour of the resolution, had the six Latin American countries which abstained – including Mexico, Argentina, Chile and Colombia – voted negatively, the scales would have tipped against the decision which provided international recognition for the establishment of the State of Israel.[19]

The reasons that motivated each country to vote in favour of the resolution are many and intricate; authoritative research has been conducted only in relation to a few of the states. The influence of the pro-Hebrew Palestine committees and the local Jewish communities are but two elements in the total picture, and probably not the most important of them. Global interests, special political precedents, internal issues and – last, but not least – personal relationships, form part of this composite tableau from which, of course, pressure by the Arab states is not lacking. Yet, all these do not detract from the basic fact that a region having a Catholic population, an area not directly involved in the Second World War and, in any case, further removed geographically than other regions of the world from the horrors of the Holocaust, and in which many elements did not hold a favourable attitude towards Jews, made such an overwhelming contribution to the renewal of Jewish national existence.[20]

This fact had its effect upon the identity of many Jews. Living in a region in which religious pluralism was not part of its social reality or ideology, Jews did not feel any external incentive to emphasize their religious identity. Consequently, formulations such as Chileans, Argentinians, Uruguayans or Peruvians 'of the Mosaic persuasion' would not have made the integration of Jewish immigrants into general society any easier. On the contrary, these newcomers were labelled according to their countries of origin as 'Russians', 'Turks', 'Germans' and so forth, and their ethnic affiliation with their former homelands was an accepted fact even if all of their children who were born in Latin America were, by law, citizens of the country of their birth. The natural identity with the Jewish people which all the Sephardic, North African and Syrian Jews brought with them to Spanish America was just as prevalent among the Ashkenazic communities. The ideological controversies within the latter groups between Bundists and Communists on the one hand, and the adherents of the various streams of Zionism on the other, were all conducted as 'an internal Jewish affair' and were echoed in the pages of the Jewish daily and periodical press that flourished in all the larger communities. After the Second World War, as awareness increased of the horrendous extent of the Holocaust, these internecine struggles were temporarily mitigated and communal life was marked by a growing identification with Jewish nationalist aspirations and the Zionist movement. This is the impression that even representatives of the non-Zionist American Jewish Committee, sometimes rather unwillingly, reported to their central offices in the USA. The criticism levelled by Zionist emissaries against the atmosphere of the *nouveaux riches* which prevailed in the Spanish-American Jewish communities, to which they appended demands for more intensive Zionist educational activities, did not contradict the basic fact that the majority of these Jews naturally and fully identified with the Jewish people. That the host countries did not view this identification as a case of 'dual loyalty' undoubtedly eased the adoption of such a stance.[21]

All these tendencies shaped the character of the renewed physical encounter of masses of Jews with Spanish culture some fifty years ago. With Spain at that time legally and mentally – although not physically – *judenrein*, it was Spanish America that provided the arena for the historic renewed contact between the Jewish people and the Spanish world.

What has changed since then?

1992 – JEWS AND THE SPANISH-SPEAKING NATIONS

Jews in Spain

In 1992, as Spain celebrated the 500-year anniversary of the discovery of America, it was estimated that about 12,000 Jews lived within her borders. Over half of them were concentrated in Madrid and Barcelona, with the rest in nine other cities, the major among them being Malaga, Seville and Valencia on the Iberian Peninsula, the island city of Palma de Mallorca and the two fortified port cities of Ceuta and Melilla on the North African coast across the Straits of Gibraltar, in which a stable Jewish community has existed uninterrupted for hundreds of years.[22]

A small number of Spain's Jewish residents in 1992 were Ashkenazim, either the remnants of the waves of the Second World War refugees or of those who reached Spain under various circumstances after the war. There were also a few Sephardic Jews from the Balkans who have survived – in Barcelona – from before the Spanish Civil War. The majority, however, were Moroccan Jews who settled in Spain after Morocco achieved full independence in the territories formerly dominated by France and Spain. With the exception of those who live in Ceuta and Melilla, therefore, what characterizes Spain's Jewish community today is that most of its members have but a short history on Spanish soil. This is especially true of the most recent group of immigrants, those who came in the late 1970s and early 1980s from Latin America, especially from Argentina. This latter group, prominently represented in certain professions, does not, as a rule, participate in Jewish communal life; their secular inclinations and Ashkenazic origins have caused them to stay away from the religious institutional frameworks which are predominated by the traditions of North African Jewry. It is this fact which undoubtedly led to the exaggerated and basically incorrect estimate of their numbers which has been widely accepted and even crept into print.[23]

The small size of Spain's renewed Jewish community in 1992 is in no way an indication of the current status of Jews in Spain; it especially does not reflect the revolutionary change in the attitude of official Spain towards the Jewish people. These changes are inextricably connected to the fact that the Spain of 1992 in no way resembles that of 1942. In contrast to an authoritarian regime, supported by several political and ideological elements which competed one with the other but were controlled high-handedly and with great cunning by the 'Caudillo', Franco, contemporary Spain is a pluralistic democracy, even though its symbol of sovereignty is the king, Juan Carlos, a direct descendant of the Bourbon dynasty. The Cortes – the parliament and senate – which in 1942 had been granted, by an edict of the 'Head of State' the status of an advisory body where representatives appointed by the regime could air their opinions, was in 1992 the real basis from which the government drew its legitimacy, a body in which decisions were taken by a majority vote of its members, representing various political parties, who had been elected by the people of Spain.[24] Contrary to the claim that Spain is one nation with one culture and one language – Spanish – a claim which completely overlooks the historical fact that modern Spain was formed out of regional ethnic groups whose cultures and languages have been brutally suppressed by the Franco regime, Spain's democratic constitution, ratified by referendum in 1978, declares one of its objectives to be 'to defend all Spaniards and peoples of Spain in the exercise of their human rights, their cultures and traditions, languages and institutions'. A lengthy section of the constitution is devoted to the right of self-determination and regional autonomy of the historical ethnic units which are part of Spain.[25]

In 1992, thirteen years after ratification of the constitution, Spain was in effect a federative state composed of autonomous regions, each of which fostered its local culture, language and historical heritage, sometimes in open animosity against and competition with the Spanish language. In the past, Barcelona's Catalonian citizens, who were forbidden by the Franco regime to make any public use of their own language, silently protested this repressive measure by performing their national dance, the Sardana, in front of the city's cathedral. Today it is official policy to enforce the public use of Catalonian as the primary language throughout Catalonia. Attempts by the Basques to revive their ancient language, which does not resemble Latin, have been far less successful than those of the Gallegos, the natives of Galicia, to return to their unique dialect, which is closely related to Portuguese.[26]

To the political and ethno-cultural diversity of contemporary Spain we may add religious pluralism. Paragraph 16 of the 1978 constitution decreed freedom of religion to be one of the human and civil rights of the people of Spain, that no religion would be afforded official status, and that 'the authorities will take into account the religious beliefs of the Spanish society and will maintain fitting relations of cooperation with the Catholic Church and the other denominations'. Outwardly, at least, this placed Judaism, as well as Protestantism and Islam, on the same footing as Catholicism, which had been the sole, official religion of Spain during the Franco regime.[27] Laws having bearing on religious practices which were passed later, such as the Law of Divorce, met with but little opposition from the populace, though similar legislation passed during the period of the Second Republic had led to widespread popular uprisings. The comprehensive law guaranteeing freedom of religion, enacted in order to give clear and detailed legal sanction to the principle expressed in the constitution, was also received with wide agreement. This is evidence of the revolutionary change in Spanish society in relation to a basic condition necessary for Jewish existence on Spanish soil.

In 1992, the process which assured full equality before the law to Spanish Jewry was completed when an official compact was signed between the

Ministry of Justice, representing the government, and the Federation of Jewish Communities in Spain. The compact covers all aspects of religious life. Synagogues would be immune from any government action that might prejudice their sanctity and, as all other Jewish religious institutions, would be exempt from taxation. The communities are entitled to receive their own sections in municipal cemeteries – this in addition to the right to establish private cemeteries, should they so wish – and will be permitted to transfer to them the remains of Jews who were interred in non-Jewish graveyards. Another section of the compact provides for the manner in which religious instruction will be given to Jewish pupils and students in government schools and universities. Rabbis will be authorized to perform weddings and to confirm the nuptials on marriage permits which will be issued in these cases by the civil marriage registries. Sabbaths and Jewish festivals are recognized as days of rest for Jewish employees and Jewish pupils who will so request; moreover, should entrance exams for posts in public agencies be set on the Jewish Sabbath or festivals, Jewish candidates will be given an alternative date. One provision of the compact obliges the government to consult with the Federation of Jewish Communities in Spain before enacting any legislation which may have a bearing upon any of the rights guaranteed in this very detailed document.[28]

There is no doubt that a compact signed as equals by the government of Spain and the Federation of Jewish Communities in Spain provided Spanish Jewry with a formal, detailed legal foundation for its existence as a community, the likes of which is not found in any state of Latin America. Obviously, the government was not unaware of the size of this small community. It is therefore logical to assume that this was a gesture of goodwill not to the Jews of Spain alone but towards the entire Jewish nation.

A more explicit gesture was the decision of the Spanish government to commemorate the expulsion of the Jews from Spain in 1492 within the framework of the events planned to celebrate 1992, the 500th anniversary of the discovery of America. In a series of impressive academic symposia, with the financial support and sponsorship of the authorities, scholars presented the results of the ramified research carried out in Spain for many years – which had intensified as 1992 drew near – of the history of the Spanish Jews and their culture. Public admittance of Spain's iniquitous act 500 years ago when it expelled the Jews – and its historic repercussions on Spain itself – received much attention during 1992. The high point came on 31 March when the monarch, Juan Carlos, and Queen Sophia joined Israeli President Chaim Herzog in a ceremonial service in the synagogue of Madrid. This historic meeting, precisely 500 years to the day after the 'Catholic Monarchs' Ferdinand and Isabel signed the expulsion decree, was meant to mark the end of one historic era and the beginning of a new one in the relations between Spain and the Jewish people.

This gesture of conciliation, of course, was directed at the Jewish people as a whole; it was meant to impress the Jews of the USA and the other Diasporas no less than those residing in Israel. Naturally, it also had special implications for Spanish Jewry. Despite full recognition of their rights as a religious community, the attitude that would be adopted towards them as part of the Jewish nation, whose centre of sovereignty lay in the State of Israel, left room for apprehension. The willingness of the Spanish monarchs to include in the agenda of President Herzog's state visit, a joint ceremony in the Madrid synagogue, undoubtedly allayed the apprehensions of those Spanish Jews who feared the charge of 'dual loyalty'. The full diplomatic relations between Spain and Israel, which had been established only six years earlier on 17 January 1986, after lengthy years of waiting, reached a new height in 1992.

The small number of Jews residing in Spain and the relatively short history of the present Jewish community, then, were not the real measure of the positive relationship which existed in 1992 between Spain and the Jewish people.

Changes in the Jewish presence in Latin America

The diffusion of Jewish communities in countries south of the USA was far different in 1992 than the map of Jewish presence in Spanish America in 1942. Many communities in the 'Indo-American' states have become drastically reduced in size, having almost disappeared. The Cuban revolution and Fidel Castro's rise to power in January 1959 caused most Jews to leave the country within a few years. In 1992, fewer than 700 Jews remained in Cuba.[29] The revolutions and civil wars that plagued Nicaragua and El Salvador in the 1970s and 1980s put an end to their small Jewish communities. Earlier, in less dramatic circumstances, the number of Jews living in Bolivia, Paraguay and Ecuador continually dwindled. Journalist Benno Weiser, later to become an Israeli diplomat, defined the years he spent in Ecuador as 'Eight years on Ararat'. Indeed, for most of the Jews who entered these countries during the Holocaust period, they were but a 'night asylum'. It is estimated that in 1992 no more than 600 Jews remained in Bolivia and 900 in Paraguay and in Ecuador. The terror rampant in Colombia's cities in the 1970s and 1980s and the lengthy economic slump suffered by Peru, ruled by a leftist military junta between 1968 and 1974, prevented any increase in their Jewish populations which in 1992 stood at an estimated 6,500 and 3,500, respectively. Extreme political upheavals and severe economic crises that brought in their wake military dictatorships characterized by government error and violation of human rights were the lot of the 'Euro-American' states of the southern triangle of South America the 1970s and early 1980s.. Here, too, there was a noticeable decline in Jewish population figures. In 1992 these were estimated to be 218,000 for Argentina, 24,000 for Uruguay and 15,000 in Chile.[30]

Demographic deterioration – the low fertility rate of Jewish families as well as processes connected with social disintegration and intermarriage – were among those causes which accounted for dwindling Jewish communities. However, a more important influence – in many cases the decisive one – was the fact that for several decades preceding 1992 Spanish-speaking America had become a region from which Jews emigrated, rather than one to which they immigrated. Both the great number of South American immigrants to Israel as well as the many who moved to the USA, the preferred destination for members of the Jewish communities of Cuba, Colombia and Central America, are evidence of this trend. During these decades, organizations and even independent communities of Spanish-speaking Jews have been established in Miami, San Diego, Dallas and other American cities. The growth of Jewish communities in certain Latin American countries which enjoyed political and economic stability – Panama (5,000 persons in 1992), Venezuela (20,000) and Mexico (35,000) – is also to a certain extent the result of emigration from other states in Central and South America.[31]

The pattern of Jewish dispersion within each country was also much different in 1992 compared to that of 1942. The Jews were almost totally concentrated in the major cities, especially in the capitals. Very few Uruguayan Jews lived outside of Montevideo. The overwhelming majority of Chilean Jewry lived in Santiago, though small communities continued to exist in Viña del Mar and Valparaiso. This was the case with Guadalajara as compared with Mexico City, of Maracay, Maracaibo and Valencia in Venezuela as compared with Caracas, while a similar situation obtained in the other countries. In Argentina, which had the biggest Jewish population in 1992, some small or medium-sized communities continued to exist in provincial capitals and a few other cities, but the former pattern of Jews living in smaller towns, villages and on homesteads that had been characteristic of Argentinian Jewry fifty years ago, had disappeared. A few small Jewish communal organizations did emerge in Argentina's development areas, especially in the south as a result of the economic opportunities they offered at a time when the metropolitan areas were in difficulty, but this did not change the overall picture. The high concentration in the cities, and within them in central neighbourhoods, created a situation in which, despite the reduction in their numbers, the prominence and influence of Jews was not reduced. On the contrary, due to their improved economic condition, it may even have increased.

Indeed, Spanish-American Jewry did undergo very striking economic changes. First of all, only a few traces remained in 1992 of the widespread Jewish agricultural sector of fifty years ago. In 1960, 2.3 per cent of Argentina's Jewish population engaged in economic activities relating to agriculture; in the provinces – i.e. excluding the greater Buenos Aires area – this figure reached 10.9 per cent of economically active Jewish males, a figure no doubt unique among all Jewish communities in the Diaspora.[32] However, when in 1989 Argentinian Jewry marked the centennial of agricultural settlement, the tone of the speeches was one of nostalgic reminiscences about a phenomenon of the past, in striking contrast to those of the fiftieth anniversary in 1939 or even to the celebration of the seventy-fifth anniversary in 1964. Had the organizers of the centennial celebrations made a systematic survey, they might have learned that even in 1989 extensive tracts of land in the Jewish colonies, which had disappeared by now, were still owned and farmed by Jews using methods befitting the mechanized, extensive capitalist economy now characteristic of Argentinian agriculture. Such a survey might still have found Jews in key positions in the agricultural cooperatives and industries which had been established many decades earlier by the Jewish colonists and that continue to exist after the rural population changed. However, all these were not then – and even less in 1992 – but an infinitesimal part of the total of economically employed Jews in Argentina. In other Spanish-American countries, no traces are left of the limited agricultural efforts made by their Jewish residents.[33]

Many of the economic institutions that existed fifty years ago – mutual benefit associations and trade cooperatives – have also disappeared. They were established to fill the need for capital by small workshops and tradesmen, but as Jewish industrialists and merchants climbed the economic ladder these institutions became redundant. In their final stages, they were in effect pseudo-banks which benefited from their special status as cooperatives. When this status was undermined – especially after 1969 in Argentina – they became small banks which merged with larger financial institutions or themselves turned into medium-sized banks. This was the fate of Jewish banks in Chile, Uruguay and Mexico. The developments which brought about these changes were, of course, first and foremost connected with trends under way in general society and in the economic classes to which the Jews belonged. However, this transformation was also influenced by processes within the communities and by an order of priorities which was unique among the Jews. The manner in which these internal and external factors influenced the economic basis for Jewish existence in the Spanish-American states remains, unfortunately, still to be studied.[34] However, even casual observation of Jewish life in these countries will bring to light clear signs of the results wrought by these processes.

The high standards of the neighbourhoods in which Jews tended to concentrate in 1992 – and the inferior quality of those which they had vacated – are indicative of the appreciable rise in the income level of many Jews. The economic gap between the immigrant generation fifty years ago and their children today is clearly discernible when one compares the level of formal education. The massive breakthrough of the second generation into the medical, technical and legal professions was a direct result of the academic education which their parents afforded them. Even when the sons were marked to continue the family profession or business, many of them, in 1992, have the benefit of a university education which enables them to develop the family establishment along more modern lines. These changes have made many of the Jewish welfare agencies redundant. Jewish medical organizations and agencies established to combat certain diseases – such as tuberculosis – have either disappeared or become philanthropic agencies engaged in welfare activities among the general public. For several decades, the Ezra Jewish hospital in Buenos Aires has served more as a framework for the training of Jewish doctors rather than as a treatment centre for the Jewish population, the objective for which it was originally established.

The Jewish condition, however, is not only one of increased wealth. During the past decade, recurring economic crises and galloping inflation have led to a deterioration in the economic status of the lower and medium levels of the middle classes, especially in the Euro-American states. The Jewish community, of course, has also been affected by these developments. Thus, alongside the Jewish *nouveaux riches* in 1992 there were also many who had recently entered the ranks of the poor. The president of the Ashkenazic community in Buenos Aires announced that, in 1992, 6,500 of its members received some welfare support from the community – 5,000 of them on a regular basis. This was a substantial percentage when one considers that the entire community, according to its president, numbered 18,500 families.[35] What was the exact nature of poverty in this and other Jewish communities? What percentage of the poor were younger families, as compared to the elderly and disabled? These are questions which still await research and study. However, even if the economic crisis did momentarily retard the atmosphere of prosperity, it obviously did not prevent – even in the countries hardest hit – the trend that characterized the Jewish community in general as it increasingly availed itself of Jewish leisure time and educational services.

Jewish identification and relationship with the host society

The spartan community centres that catered to the needs of the former generation had, by 1992, given way in many places to Jewish sport facilities and recreation camps. This was an obvious attempt to provide the newly affluent and well-to-do with the opportunity to follow the weekend leisure-time patterns of the upper middle classes in a Jewish atmosphere. More widespread and no less impressive evidence of both the improved economic status and of the Jewish identification of Latin American Jews is provided by the Jewish educational systems that exist in all of the states. The majority of school-age children studied in spacious facilities, most of them fairly new and furnished with modern equipment. A world-wide survey conducted in 1981–3 showed that in Argentina 53 to 55 per cent of the Jewish children aged 3–17 attended Jewish *day* schools while an additional 9 to 11 per cent participated in afternoon classes, supplementing the education they received in the public schools. All in all, this meant that 62 to 66 per cent of Jewish school-age children received a formal Jewish education. In the other Latin American states, taken together, the percentages were even higher: 68 to 72 per cent attended Jewish day schools and an additional 1 per cent received supplementary Jewish education. At the time the survey was conducted, Argentina's Jewish educational system was on the same level as those of South Africa and Australia in relation to the percentage of children attending the schools (62 to 66 per cent in each country), but ranked higher in the percentage of those attending day schools. No other Jewish community throughout the world could compare with Spanish America (excluding Argentina), which had the highest percentage of children who received a formal Jewish education.[36]

This situation was in striking contrast to the meagre Jewish education provided in Spanish America fifty years ago. Then, most Jewish schooling was supplementary to that of the public educational system and was provided only to kindergarten and elementary school-age children. The first Jewish high school was established in Argentina only in 1940, and by 1945 there were only three such schools. The percentage of children attending Jewish schools at that time was very low.[37] The Jewish educational system has since then undergone an indisputable revolutionary change. There is no doubt that in 1992 Jewish parents – the great majority of whom were native-born – provided their children with a Jewish education, from kindergarten to high school, of a higher quality than that which the immigrant generation gave to its offspring. In the 'Indo-American' countries, the most obvious reason for this extreme turnabout is the relatively poor level of the public educational systems; in the Euro-American countries the reason might be the deterioration of public schools as a result of politicization and the crime rate, which have penetrated them in the last few decades. These conditions led to a situation in which the social classes to which most of the Jews belong tended to provide their educational needs by means of private school systems. The fact that Jews have fostered their own schools is both a clear sign of their affluence as well as an indication of their preference for Jewish education over other private schooling.

The very existence of separate Jewish education raises the question of the reaction of general, non-Jewish society to the efforts to perpetuate Jewish uniqueness. For anti-Semites, Jewish 'separatism' is one of many pretexts for their animosity; other segments in the host society judge the Jewish – or any other minority – educational system according to their perceptions of their own national society. For those who consider their societies to be religiously, culturally and ethnically pluralistic, Jewish education might be considered perfectly legitimate; those who maintain monolithic tendencies surely look upon Jewish uniqueness as a foreign phenomenon, to be tolerated to one extent or another. Their level of tolerance might tend to fluctuate in accordance with changing conditions of place and time.

In 1992, Spanish-speaking America did present a wide spectrum of such attitudes. In Mexico, Venezuela, Panama, Peru and other Indo-American countries, the existence of the Jewish community is grounded to a great degree in the tolerance extended towards other ethnic immigrant communities, all of them considered to be essentially foreigners. The wide social gaps which characterize these countries give the economic class to which the majority of Jews belong a legitimate right to uniqueness. In Argentina, on the contrary, conditions were transformed in accordance with political changes. During Perón's first presidency (1946–55) and again throughout the military regimes of 1966–73 and 1976–83, the concept that Argentinian society is a monolithic entity, whose history and religious identity are Catholic, gained the upper hand. The corollary of this assumption was that the Jewish community is a foreign element, which is entitled *as such* both to preserve its uniqueness and to be tolerated. During the decade after democratic rule was reinstated in 1983 the government – whether for reasons of ideology or in order to further the country's interests in the international sphere – has stressed the pluralistic character of Argentinian society, both as a realistic description of the status quo and as a desirable social condition. This has granted the Jewish community a high degree of acceptance as equals as well as of legitimization of the perpetuation of its unique character as suggested by the provision of Jewish education.

The solidarity evinced by the Jewish communities with the State of Israel has been another major issue of the legitimacy of Jewish identification. The fact that all South American societies tend to identify immigrant communities with their countries of origin made that solidarity acceptable. Israeli ambassadors were very frequently referred to – even by the highest government officials – as representing 'their colony' (*su colonia*), the Jewish community. On the other hand, Jews who openly avowed Zionism, or at least did not deny having Zionist inclinations, filled senior governmental positions, even serving as ministers in the cabinet of Argentinian President Alfonsin (1983–8). Other Spanish-speaking American states – Chile, Guatemala, Honduras and Panama – appointed Jews as ambassadors to Israel.[38]

What lay behind this situation were the good – often very close – bilateral relations between the Latin American states and Israel. With the exception of Cuba, which severed diplomatic ties in 1973, these relations stood up to the test of the difficult period following the Yom Kippur War, when the world petroleum crisis enhanced the economic status of the Arab states, in addition to their importance as a large bloc of representatives and votes in the UN and its agencies. Solidarity and close relations with Israel under such circumstances could possibly have been detrimental to the vital interests of these countries. The mobilization of Arab immigrant communities in Latin American countries – Palestinians, Lebanese and Syrians – in active support of the Arab cause after the Six Day War (some of these groups being larger than the local Jewish community), was a new internal element that could have had a disrupting effect upon relations of these countries with Israel. Yet, in the UN vote in 1975 on the resolution equating Zionism with racism, though Mexico did vote in favour, the other Latin American states either opposed the resolution or abstained; thus the bloc of Latin American members on the whole adopted an attitude more favourable to Israel than any other bloc in the UN. Though the field of Israeli–Hispano–American relations still awaits research, it can be safely affirmed that they had no adverse effect on the recognized legitimacy of support for Israel by the Jewish communities of these countries.[39]

From the demographic, economic and political viewpoints, then, the relations created between the Spanish-speaking American nations and the Jewish people, through the agency of the Jewish communities in these countries, are of a deep and lasting nature. This also seems to hold true in the case of cultural relationships.

The Jewish schoolchildren of 1992 – and their parents, too – were no longer consumers of Jewish culture in Yiddish and Hebrew. The Yiddish atmosphere that as late as thirty years ago permeated the streets of central Buenos Aires disappeared with the closing down of the two Yiddish daily newspapers and the numerous literary and other periodicals formerly published in that language. A similar fate was suffered by the flourishing Yiddish press in Uruguay, Mexico and Chile. The schools established by the founding generation of Jewish immigrants in order to perpetuate the use of these two Jewish languages failed produce a new generation that 'consumed' Yiddish and Hebrew culture in any form – including the theatre. By 1992, publications in these two languages had been replaced by weeklies, monthlies and other periodicals in Spanish, some of them partly or wholly devoted to Jewish topics. The economic stability and circulation figures of these publications seem, for the moment, to be less than of those which served the preceding generation. On the other hand, Jews were fairly prominent in all spheres of Spanish-language culture in most Latin American countries in 1992. These authors, dramatists, stage and film directors, journalists and members of the media are well steeped in Spanish culture, contributing to its innovations and helping to shape contemporary trends. This contribution – especially in the field of literature – has received much scholarly attention during the past decade. Scores of papers dealing with the works of Jewish Spanish-American authors have been presented at academic colloquia and published. What remains to be ascertained is the degree to which these authors have already been able to make the non-Jewish, Spanish-speaking world aware of general Jewish themes, and especially of the unique life style of those Jews who have settled among them.[40]

The renewed encounter between the Jewish people and Spain goes back only a few decades. By that time, in Spanish-speaking America, the renewed encounter between Jews and Spanish culture had already been well under way. We have outlined the major contours of that renewed meeting of the two ancient heritages, which co-existed on Spanish soil during a millennium until 500 years ago. Detailed study of the problems surveyed here still lies ahead of us. Above all, there remain questions: What will be the outcome as Jews take root in Spanish culture? To what extent will Jewish creative works in Spanish serve as a bridge between the two worlds? To what extent will they – and the Jewish communities in general in all Spanish-speaking countries – be instrumental in bringing to a close the historical rift whose beginning, 500 years ago, was given so much public attention in 1992?

NOTES

1 Haim Avni, *Spain, the Jews and Franco* (Philadelphia, Jewish Publication Society of America, 1982), pp. 8–12, 34–5, 68–9.
2 Ibid., pp. 91–2. The estimate of the number of Jews who have passed through Spain (30,000) is apparently too high and requires further research. See Antonio Marquina y Gloria Ines Ospina, *España y los Judios en el Siolo XX* (Madrid, Espasa Calpe, 1987), pp. 164, 166–8.
3 Haim Avni, *Spain, The Jews*, op. cit., pp. 179–99; Antonio Marquina, *op. cit.*, pp. 222–5.
4 Haim Avni, 'Argentine Jewry: its socio-political status and organizational patterns', *Dispersion and Unity* (Jerusalem), no. 12, (1971) 137; Sergio DellaPergola, 'Demographic trends of Latin American Jewry', in Judith Laikin Elkin and Gilbert W. Merkx (eds), *The Jewish Experience in Latin America* (Boston, Allen & Unwin, 1987), p. 92.
5 Victor A. Mirelman, *Jewish Buenos Aires, 1890–1930. In Search of an Identity* (Detroit, Wayne State University Press, 1990), pp. 39–45.
6 Haim Avni, 'Argentine Jewry', op. cit. (1972), nos. 13–14, pp. 161–9.
7 Estimates according to Louis Sobel, 'Jewish community life and organizations in Latin America', *The Jewish Social Service Quarterly* (June 1944), vol. 20, no. 4, p. 180, repeated in *American Jewish Year Book* (*AJYB*) (1944/5), no. 46, p. 500.
8 Filantropia, *Zehn Jahre Aufbauerbeit in Südamerika* (Buenos Aires, 1943), pp. 230, 240.
9 Two recent PhD dissertations deal with the history of these two communities. See Margalith Bejarano, *The Jewish Community of Cuba 1898–1939: Communal Consolidation and Trends of Integration under the Impact of Changes in World Jewry and Cuban Society* (The Abraham Harman Institute of Contemporary Jewry, The Hebrew University of Jerusalem, 1992); Judith Bokser Misses (de Liwerant), *El Movimiento Nacional Judio, El Sionismo en Mexico, 1922–1947* (Mexico D.F., Facultad de Ciencias Politicas y Sociales, Universidad Nacional Autonoma de Mexico, 1991).
10 Margalith Bejarano, op. cit., p. 57; S. Kaplan, R. Moncarz and J. Steinberg, 'Jewish emigrants to Cuba 1898–1960', *International Migration Quarterly*, Review of the International Organization for Migration, XXVIII, no. 3, (September 1990), p. 309.

11 Haim Avni, *Mexico – Immigration and Refuge*, Working Paper no. 177, (Washington, DC, Latin American Program, The Wilson Center, 1989), p. 62; Tobias Maizel, 'Judios en Mexico', in Leon Sourasky (ed.), *Historia de la Comunidad Israelita de Mexico 1917–1942* (Mexico City, 1965), pp. 273–4.

12 Louis Sobel, op. cit., p. 180.

13 Ibid.

14 Brookings Institution, *Refugee Settlement in the Dominican Republic, A Survey Conducted under the Brookings Institution* (Washington, D.C., 1942). See also *Capacity of the Dominican Republic to Absorb Refugees, Findings of the Commission appointed by the Executive Power of the Dominican Republic to appraise the Report of the Brookings Institution Concerning the Colonization of Refugees in Santo Domingo* (Trujillo City, 1945).

15 The Central American and Caribbean nations followed the United States in December 1941 and declared war on Germany and Italy. Mexico then broke its relations with the 'Axis' powers and declared war on 22 May 1942. Bolivia, Ecuador, Paraguay, Peru and Uruguay broke relations in January 1942 and Colombia and Venezuela even earlier, in December 1941, but declared war only late in 1943 or 1944 or even at the beginning of 1945. 'The Americas and World War II' (Washington DC, Judicial Division of the Pan American Union, 1 April 1944).

16 Haim Avni, 'Patterns of Jewish leadership in Latin America during the Holocaust', in Randolph L. Braham (ed.), *Jewish Leadership during the Nazi Era* (New York, Columbia University Press, 1985), pp. 87–94, 106–14.

17 AJDC (Archives of the American Joint Distribution Committee), South America General 1943–1944, Jacob Landau to Joseph C. Hyman (13 February 1945), pp. 1, 4, 5 and *passim*.

18 Judith Bokser Misses, op. cit., pp. 246–60.

19 United Nations, Official Records of the Second Session of the General Assembly, Resolutions, 16 September to 29 November 1947, Lake Success, New York.

20 Ignacio Klich, 'A background to Perón's discovery of Jewish national aspirations', AMILAT, *Judaica Latinoamericana, Estudios Historico-Sociales* (Jerusalem, Magnes Press, 1988), pp. 192–223; Benno Weiser, 'The history of one "yes"', *Midstream* (November 1977), pp. 62–70.

21 AJA (American Jewish Archives), Morris D. Waldman Papers, Report on visit to Latin America by Morris D. Waldman (November 1944), pp. 12–13; Sylvia Schenkolewski, 'Zionists versus the Left in Argentina', and Judith Liwerant, 'The dispute between Zionists and their leftist opponents in Mexico', Haim Avni, Gideon Shimoni (eds), *Zionism and its Jewish Opponents* (Jerusalem, Hassifriya Hazionit, 1990), pp. 181–90, 191–204 (Hebrew).

22 Tourespana, *A Journey through Jewish Spain* (Madrid, 1992), p. 32; AJYB (1991), vol. 91, pp. 456, 458.

23 Joseph Bengio, 'Les juif Marocains en Espagne', *Juifs du Maroc. Identité et Dialogue* (Paris, 1980), pp. 354–7. This author claimed that some 300,000 Argentinians, among them 15,000–20,000 Jews, settled in Spain during the military regime in Argentina. The national census of 1980 in Spain found only 13,077 Argentinians; the 1970 census reported 7,784. See Susana Schkolnik, 'Volumen y caracteristicas de la emigracion de Argentinos a través de los censos extranjeros', in Alfredo E. Lattes *et al.* (eds) *Dinamica Migratoria Argentina 1955–1984 – Democratizacion y Retorno de Expatriados* (Buenos Aires, 1987), vol. I, p. 99.

24 'Constitutive Law of the Cortes of 17th July 1942', Spanish Information Service, *Fundamental Laws of the State, The Spanish Constitution* (Madrid,

1967), pp. 93–107, 174. See also *Costitución Española* (Madrid, Boletin Oficial del Estado, 1983), articles 66–80, pp. 53–62, and there 'Titulo III. De las cortes generales, capitulo primero.

25 Ibid., preface, p. 19, and articles 137–58, pp. 91–113.

26 Andres F. Rubio, 'Aumenta el "Zapping" linguistico en España', *El Pais* (28 August 1992), p. 18. According to the 1991 national census, 92.5 per cent of the inhabitants of Catolonia understood Catalan, 67 per cent spoke it and 36.4 per cent wrote the language. In 1986, 25 per cent of the 2,100,000 inhabitants of the Basque province spoke the local language and another 18 per cent claimed to understand it.

27 *Constitución Española*, op. cit., article 16, p. 17.

28 Ministerio de Justicia, Acuerdo de Cooperación del Estado Español con la Federación de Comunidades Israelitas de España. I thank Professor Luis Giron from the Universidad Complutense, Madrid, for having provided me with a copy of this document.

29 Moshe Asssis, 'Cuban Jewry during thirty years of revolution (1959–1989), *Yahadut Zemanenu, Contemporary Jewry, A Research Annual* (Jerusalem, 1990), no. 6, pp. 328–9 (Hebrew).

30 Benno Weiser, 'Ecuador: eight years on Ararat', *Commentary* (June 1947), no. 3, pp. 531–6; *AJYB* (1991), no. 91, p. 452.

31 Ibid.

32 Haim Avni, *Argentina and the Jews, A History of Jewish Immigration* (Tuscaloosa, University of Alabama Press, 1991), p. 205.

33 'Actos conmemorativos del centenario de la colonización agricola judía en la Argentina', Centro de Estudios Sociales – DAIA, *A Cien Anos de la Llegada del 'Weser' – Indice Segunda Epoca* (July 1990), no. 3, pp. 197–207. In 1988 Jews were still at the helm of the La Mutua Agricola (the agricultural marketing cooperative) and of SANCOR (the big dairy products industry), in Mosesville and in the nearby Sunchales, both founded by the Jewish colonists and the JCA. In that year almost all the land of the ex-colony Montifiore in the north of the Santa Fe province belonged to and was cultivated by a few Jewish farmers who lived in Ceres, a nearby town.

34 Moshe Sirkin, 'The economic structure of Jews in Argentina and other Latin American countries', *Jewish Social Studies*, (Spring 1985), vol. 47, no. 2, pp. 115–34, is one of the few contributions to this important field. It is essentially based on data from 1960. See also Lowell Gudmundson, 'Costa Rican Jewry: an economic and political outline', in Judith Laikin Elkin and Gilbert Merkx (eds), *The Jewish Presence in Latin America* (Boston, Allen & Unwin, 1987), pp. 219–31.

35 *Boletin Informativo OJI* (Buenos Aires) (August 1992), no. 597, p. 10.

36 Sergio DellaPergola and Uziel O. Schmelz, 'Demography and Jewish Education in the Diaspora: trends in Jewish school age population and school enrollment', in H. B. Himmelfarb and S. DellaPergola (eds), *Jewish Education Worldwide. Cross Cultural Perspectives* (Lanham, MD and Jerusalem, Institute of Contemporary Jewry and University Press of America, 1989), pp. 55–6.

37 Efraim Zadoff, 'Un analisis comparativo de las redes educativas judícas de Mexico y Argentina 1935–1955', AMILAT, *Judacíca Lationoamericana, Estudios Historico-Sociales* (Jerusalem, Magnes Press, 1988), pp. 129–48. In Argentina, in 1940 and in 1950, only some 14 and 27 per cent, respectively, of Jewish children of elementary school age attended Jewish schools; in Mexico, in 1943, Jewish education reached 43 per cent of the school-age children.

38 Edy Kaufman, Yoram Shapira and Joel Barromi, *Israel–Latin American Relations*

(New Brunswick, NJ, Transaction Books, 1979), pp. 33–42. President Juan Domingo Perón was the first to nominate a Jew – Dr Pablo Manguel – as the first ambassador of Argentina in Israel. The Jewish writer Marcos Aguinis served as Minister of Culture in President Raul Alfonsin's cabinet.

39 The first major contribution to this field is the volume by Kaufman, Shapira and Barromi. See United Nations General Assembly, Thirtieth Session, Agenda item 68, 'Resolution adopted by the General Assembly, 3379 (XXX). Elimination of all forms of racial discrimination', 2400th plenary meeting, 10 November 1975. The resolution was adopted by plenary by seventy-two in favour, thirty-five against, thirty-two abstained.

40 Saul Sosnowski, 'Los escritores Judíos de America Latina: un puente hacia la historia', *Cloquio* (Buenos Aires, 1984), vol. 6, no. 12, pp. 7–31; Kessel Schwartz, 'Israel as fact and fiction in contemporary Spanish American prose', *Jewish Social Studies* (Winter 1987), vol. 49, no. 1, pp. 61–8; Leonardo Senkman, *La Identidad en la Literatura Argentina* (Buenos Aires, Pardes, 1983).

Part IV

18

BREAKING THE MOULD
The maturing of Hebrew literature
Gershon Shaked

In its initial stages Israeli society attempted to consolidate a cultural reality which contained its own distinctive behavioural modes and concordant language of signs. Immigrants who came from the Diaspora to Israel brought with them a wide diversity of behavioural conventions and in order to create a model acceptable to the majority of the population it was essential for both society and literature to consolidate a common language (in the widest sense of the term).[1] Anyone who then attempted to come to grips with existing reality and to deform it in order to demonstrate both its lack of worth and the desirability of creating an alternative, had first to relate to the presumed reality prevalent among the expected readers.[2] The attempt to deconstruct a model is based upon the assumption that in the reader's world there is always an image that can be referred to – the best example is perhaps Mendele Mokher Seforim (1835–1917).[3]

At the beginning of the twentieth century, society in Eretz Israel was highly fragmented; there were as yet neither integrated semiotic standards (that is, standards for a system of clear signs which identified modes of behaviour or social belonging and were understood by the majority of 'speakers') nor generally recognized social values. Nevertheless, certain dominant norms rapidly crystallized since the society was essentially Zionist, most of the immigrants having come to the country for ideological reasons. Its leaders emanated from the Second Aliyah (1904–14) and later from among the pioneers of the Third Aliyah (1919–23) who learned Hebrew in the Diaspora and prepared themselves culturally and socially prior to their emigration, developing norms even before their arrival in Eretz Israel. After their arrival, some of the envisaged norms were realized but others vanished.[4] Writers felt bound to embody these norms and even to create them. Actually, these immigrants did not as yet have an agreed language of signs. The literature produced an apparent language of signs so that at times it is difficult to determine whether literature created an apparent reality which then became actuality because people imitated the language of signs which literature offered; or whether the potential language of signs (which was as yet only a dream and not a reality) created literature. The process was entirely complementary: the ideology both preceded the language of signs and made its mark on it.

Writers like Ever Hadani (pseudonym of Aharon Feldman, 1899–1972), Alexander Karmon (born 1886), David Maletz (1899–1981) and Nathan Bistritski (later Agmon, 1896–1980); and even more complex writers like Hayyim Hazaz (1898–1973) and Shmuel Yosef Agnon (1888–1970) were faithful to the ideology of the Second Aliyah. In this case, the ideology created society's language of signs, which were based on the polarity between those who fulfil the ideology of pioneering Zionism and those who, in the eyes of the Zionist pioneer, do not. A photograph of a Jew ploughing and sowing was contrasted as a positive ideological icon with the negative one of a photograph of a Jew dressed in the clothes of the 'Baron's culture' of Edmond de Rothschild or members of the old *yishuv*.

Some writers attempted to present the terrible confusion as the actual behaviour of their protagonists in contrast to their ideological vision, that is to create a fiction about what seemed to be real for those writers. And there were those who in their fiction described the reality according to the desired ideological norms which the literature as a branch of that ideology wished to project upon society. In other words there were those who tried to describe how the ideologies of Theodor Herzl (1881–1904), Aharon David Gordon (1856–1922), Ber Borochov (1881–1917) and the leaders of the labour movement were being fulfilled and others who described the deviations from these ideologies.

The social anti-norm was embodied in literary characters who did not fulfil the normative criteria. They would appear to be characters who offer another option (an alternative system in the hierarchy of systems) or figures through whom the author strengthens the dominant norm by demonstrating that the alternative option leads to a dead end.[5]

Yizḥak Kumer in Agnon's *Temol Shilshom* ('Bygone Days', 1945) does not fulfil the norm set by the immigrants of the Second Aliyah who came to the country in order to 'build and be rebuilt'. He does not realize the dream of the Lemberg Zionists who asked to be photographed with him while he is ploughing and sowing, a dream which he himself envisioned as the consummation of that ideology to which he had pledged allegiance.

At the beginning of the novel Kumer tries to be like those pioneers who fulfilled the values of his dreams; at the end of the novel he resembles those members of the old *yishuv* from whom he wanted to escape when he abandoned his country in order to come to the Promised Land, and he finally dies as one of them. He represents the inability of young people to cope with the harsh ideological demands which the new Zionist faith required of its believers, who were tossed between these claims and the faith of their fathers which they bore with them from their homes.

Yizḥak Kumer did not choose the language of signs of his Zionist friends but rather sought refuge in the safe and certain world of his ancestors. The protagonist fails to achieve the Zionist ideal, but in the background and in the reader's consciousness are those characters who succeeded; those who, unlike the protagonist were able to become part of the country, to 'build and be rebuilt'. One must bear in mind that *Temol Shilshom* was published in 1945, at a time when the Zionist settlement had already stabilized and accomplished perhaps more than it had promised. Agnon presented a secondary system which is about to be overthrown (the religious community of the East European town) in contrast to the burgeoning system (Zionism) which was overpowering society, and he exposed the weaknesses of both. The intended recipient identified with the system the novel had pushed into the background (the ideal of *Helkat ha-Sadeh* ('The Plot of Land')) and rejected the system which was pushed to the fore (the small town of Jerusalem). Agnon succeeded in creating for his readers an ambiguous organization of affinities for the primary systems which were available (religion and Zionism), despite the fact that in reality he knew that the system in which Kumer had failed was the one which would triumph in the historical perspective (at any rate from the standpoint of when the novel was written). However, Agnon was still able to hint at the fact that even the triumphant system might contain contradictions within itself.

In *Ha-Yoshevet ba-Gannim* ('O You Who Linger in the Garden', 1944) the Yemenite protagonist, Meri Alsaid, is convinced that the Messiah will bring redemption. His son – whose name, ironically, is Zion – relates with materialistic scepticism to the messianic idea and to its Zionist trans-formation. For Zion, the so-called Zionist, son of the messianic father Meri Alsaid, Zionism is simply one of the ways to improve his social and economic position. Only the granddaughter, Rahmiyya, finds her way to utopia, which in this case is the kibbutz. To the readers of the 1940s the failures of Kumer and Zion are the exceptions to the rule. The blossoming of the ideal in the utopian kibbutz as an option which is contrasted with the failures of the protagonists (implied in Agnon and explicit in Hazaz) was accepted as self-evident by the readers of the 1940s, in whose consciousness the ideological system governing the solutions to these problems prevailed. Agnon and Hazaz did not describe a clear-cut movement of penitents or materialists, but rather exceptions who attested to the partial success of the general rule. Reading these novels today we may derive a different meaning, since deviation from the Zionist model is no longer exceptional but rather a prevalent phenomenon.

Today, these two writers appear as prophets of what was to come in the 1970s and 1980s. But in the 1940s they portrayed in their protagonists' deviations, the victims of the bewilderment and contention which their sons or their friends were destined to overcome.

It is important to note that these writers implemented what the ideology rejected. The ideology praised the image of the secular pioneer or one who combines Torah with labour. Agnon created a major character who presents the other side of the coin – someone who represents the hidden longings of that generation for whom, despite their acceptance of the prevalent ideology, the sublimated yearnings were nevertheless part of their lives. Here literature fulfilled an important function: it did not permit readers to live only a rational ideological life but drew their attention to their sublimated passions and desires. Yizḥak Kumer's return to Me'ah She'arim (an orthodox religious quarter in Jerusalem; *Temol Shilshom*) or the conversion of the messianic dreams of the father Meri Alsaid into cash by his son Zion (*Ha-Yoshevet ba-Gannim*) were not simply deviations from the ideology but were a very deep expression of flesh-and-blood creatures who, rejecting the ideological pressures, were moved by more powerful subconscious forces which not only caused changes in their lives but even brought about their deaths.

It is important to point out that literature determined criteria for society. The uniformity of the ideological society to a large extent exists also in literature; despite the fact that the best writers frequently deal with the exceptions to the rule, they also have a clear awareness of the rule. The characters of this literature are sociological types, stereotypes who embody the attempt of an entire society to grasp at some sort of permanent reality with which one can live and contend. When Yosef Luidor (died 1921) or Meir Wilkanski (1882–1949) or Shlomo Zemach (1886–1974) describe their pioneers and their fighters they do not bother with a one-time fashioning of their characters but rather emphasize the roles that these characters play or should play in a specific society according to a predetermined and fixed ideology. There is no literature without a reservoir of such stereotypes and even with the more individual achievements one can still recognize the sociological stereotype which the complex character represents.

One can arrive at an individualization of a stereotype by presenting it in a complex situation or by presenting an anti-stereotype which is perceived as such in a given context, because its world of values is within one of the sub-systems which contend with the dominant system, Joseph Hayyim Brenner's (1881–1921) characters in *Ba-Ḥoref* ('In Winter', 1902) are *not* anti-stereotypes but are rather typical of a social group of detached Jewish intellectuals in Eastern Europe. Brenner's protagonists in Eretz Israel as presented in *Mi-Kan u-mi-Kan* ('From Here and There', 1911) and in *Shekhol ve-Kishalon* (1920; *Breakdown and Bereavement*, 1971) are very similar in nature to those whom he presented in his East European works; but their significance has changed in the context of their new social framework, because the stereotypical image of the pioneer had already been created in Eretz Israel at the time of the Second Aliyah. Brenner's Eretz Israel novels stand in contrast to this stereotype. They are a challenge to it – an expression of the assumption that, despite the aspirations of the ideologists to create the 'new Hebrew', the old type of detached Jew still exists and operates in Eretz Israel. A few minor characters (like Ḥanoch Ḥefetz in

Shekhol ve-Kishalon and Amram in *Mi-Kan u-mi-Kan*) point to another possible sub-system which in the works of other writers already represent the dominant system.

In the Diaspora stories, someone who is not detached, bewildered or erotically sick is an exception. In contrast, the new Eretz Israel society wished to create a new stereotype and the old one became an antithesis to the thesis which was already in the social background knowledge of the assumed readers. Brenner did not allow his generation to repress the fact that changing one's homeland does not change a person and that the shadow of the past accompanies one even to the Promised Land.

As literary works were written in a later period and the new Eretz Israel social reality became more established, the old stereotypes in their new context became less stereotypical, appearing more frequently as unique and incongruous individualistic characters. Such is the case with Agnon, who created characters from the Second Aliyah in *Shvu'at Emunim* (1943; *Betrothed*, 1966) or in *Temol Shilshom*. In the 1930s and 1940s Yizhak Kumer and Yaakov Rechnitz are not seen as ordinary characters typical of the new society, but rather as out of place according to the assumed image of readers raised on the grandeur of heroes of the Second Aliyah who built the country. Kumer and Rechnitz are perceived in the 1930s and 1940s as incongruous characters, as victims in the struggle to build a new society. Those who saw the successes of the Second and Third Aliyah in settling the country could not accept the botanist, who worked as a Latin teacher and planned to leave the country, as typifying that particular social reality which they created for themselves on the basis of extra-literary sources of information.

If the text is powerfully convincing it can lead readers to reconsider their perception of society and if the readers re-examine the historical sources unswayed by mythological assumptions which created the portrait of the members of the Second Aliyah as giants, they may find that Agnon's literary model is much closer to historical truth than the mythological model which accompanied them from their youth. In any case it appears that Agnon did not allow his recipients to immerse themselves in mythological fantasies but rather showed them that other forces were at work beneath the ideological surface: figures of detached immigrants who yearned to return to their mother's bosom and were unable to sever the umbilical cord which bound them to another culture.[6]

When the generation of writers who were born in Eretz Israel reached literary maturity the ideology of the Second Aliyah (labour, defence, kibbutz, training for *aliyah*, 'in this precious land of our forefathers all the hopes will be fulfilled', 'we came to this land to build and be rebuilt', etc.) took on an *entirely different meaning*. It was no longer the abstract ideology of people who had lost their traditional religious language of signs and tried to find new forms of expression for their ideology, but rather an ideology that found its language: in education, in social ceremonies (like the 15th of Shevat, the bringing of *Bikkurim* (first fruits), the Passover Seder, planting of trees to commemorate someone's death, the Jewish National Fund's Golden Book) and in other social components (song, dance and literature).

These writers and their protagonists were educated on the new language of signs which their parents created through much effort in order to provide their children with what they themselves had lost – a language. Just as a large number of the children were born into the Hebrew language which their parents had had to acquire with so much effort, so they were also born into the language of signs which their parents created in a long and complex process of secularization of the traditional language, its adaptation to the new world of the Middle East and the blending of that world with the East European culture they had brought with them.

The children are already 'new Hebrews', the products of these ceremonies, born into the Hebrew kindergarten, the *Bet Hinnukh* for the workers' children, the general elementary school and the agricultural schools, the gymnasiums and particularly the youth movements. The language of signs which became the dominant language of the new establishment was consolidated in the youth movements.[7]

One cannot understand Hebrew literature without the values of the youth movement and its language of signs. The language of the under-ground movements and the army in its early stages in one way or another evolved from the language that was consolidated in these movements. In the youth movements the pseudo-Russian or pseudo-Eastern songs and the pseudo-Romanian, Polish, Russian and Yemenite dances were transformed from artificial forms of expression of a society trying to create a new language of signs for itself, into the reliable expression of a society which accepted this artificial legacy as wholly *natural*. The children of the youth movements did not think of Smetana when they sang *Ha-Tikvah*, nor recall a Polish dance when they danced the Karkoviac or the polka, or the Circassians when they danced the Cherkassia; in all these they perceived the independent legacy of a new culture which was their own.[8]

For example, all the protagonists of S. Yizhar (born 1916), however intro-vert they may be and much as they may oppose their time and place, none the less accept the authority of youth movement values and speak in its language of signs. Even when they distance themselves from these values or betray and revolt against them, they are ever present. Such was also the case with Uri, Ami and Elik, the protagonists of Moshe Shamir (born 1921), Shlomik in *Hedva va-Ani* ('Hedva and I', 1964) by Aharon Meged (born 1920), the protagonists of Nathan Shaham (born 1925) in *Tamid Anahnu* ('Always Us', 1952), of Yigal Mossinsohn (born 1917) in *Aforim Ka-Sak* ('Grey as a Sack', 1946) and even the exceptional protagonists in Mossinsohn's *Derekh Gever* ('A Man's Way', 1953), Shamir's *Tahat ha-Shemesh* ('Under the Sun', 1950) and *Ki Eirom Attah* ('You Are Naked',

1959), Shlomo Nitzan's (born 1922) *Beno le-Benum* ('Between Him and Them', 1953), *Zevat be-Zevat* ('Togetherness', 1956) and *Yated la-Ohel* ('Peg for the Tent', 1960). Despite the existence and presentation of various sub-systems (like Revisionist Zionism in Mossinsohn's work), the main system of the labour youth movement of Eretz Israel predominated.

It is not by chance that realism was the prevailing tradition, despite various writers who were exceptions to the rule. In order to place on a firm foundation an entire cultural condition, the writers assumed (consciously or sub-consciously) that they must create some sort of link between the system of signs expressed in language and any other system of signs which the writers felt should be emphasized as existing and functioning. The reading and viewing public first wished to see a literary or theatrical consolidation of the social reality which they had created but as yet did not perceive in its full potency or implications. Each additional presentation of the youthful sabra charm (such as *Hu Halakh ba-Sadot* ('He Walked in the Fields', Shamir, 1947) and *Be-'Arvot ha-Negev* ['In the Negev Prairie', 1949)) at the Cameri or Habimah theatres confirmed for the audience, which was still mainly composed of immigrants, that they had indeed succeeded in creating a new society and that the language of signs did function.[9]

Art fulfilled society's expectations and its positive acceptance in turn strengthened it to continue to create according to the criteria that society established for it. Clearly, this type of fiction became impoverished both from a literary point of view and in terms of its values because, unlike its predecessor, it neglected the dark side of social reality.

Agnon and Brenner – and to a certain extent Hazaz and Bistritski – wrote about this dark side and also illuminated the bright side. They presented the people of the Second Aliyah from the standpoint of Kumer and Rabinovitz and the characters from the Yemenite *aliyah* from the point of view of Zion, the materialistic son of Meri Alsaid. What was pushed aside by the ideology – the bereavement and the failure of 'the founders as human beings' – was exposed by the literature, which did not allow the sublimation of yearnings and doubts to operate in a closet. The writers of the 1940s and 1950s, from Yizhar onwards, were ambushed unawares by the dark side which peered from the sub-conscious, but in the text did not always come out in the open: the strange family life of Uri's family in *Hu Halakh ba-Sadot*, a few erotic infidelities which undermined the establishment in the works of Mossinsohn (in the novel *Derekh Gever*) or some exaggeration of the norm in Shamir's *Melekh Basar va-Dam*, 1954 (*The King of Flesh and Blood*, 1958) in the character of Alexander Yannai (King of Judaea, born *c.* 126, died 76 BCE) an exaggeration which would seem to have created its own normative antithesis in the character of the brother Avshalom. However, these factors were sublimated because reality demanded – and literature responded to – an internal and external need to approve of *what was achieved by toil*, so that even works which contained a degree of rebellion were interpreted as works affirming the establishment, in accord with the readers' expectations.

The dark side of Israeli society first emerged because of the social changes that resulted from the establishment of the state, which transformed a *yishuv* of volunteers into one of reluctant immigrants or immigrants who had not undergone ideological preparation for their *aliyah*. The disproportion between amorphous immigrant groups and the veteran 'leadership' group was so great as to swamp the latter, who consequently changed their objectives from personal and physical self-fulfilment to the instruction of others. The bureaucratic responsibility of social administration to a large extent impaired the existential fulfilment of the very values which the leadership group had created;[10] the mass immigration also undermined the cultural codes which the leadership group had created, since the youth movement had to contend with the language of signs imported by the *She'erit ha-Pletah* ('the surviving remnant', i.e. Jewish displaced persons after the Second World War) and the Middle Eastern immigrants.

While earlier waves of immigration generally adapted and assimilated the language of signs prevalent in the *yishuv* which had crystallized from the time of the Second Aliyah, the mass post-Second World War and especially post-1948 immigration rejected it as a culture of masters forced upon them against their will. Thus the language of signs changed from an elitist one broadly accepted by the majority (even when they did not accept some of the details) into the language of nostalgic fringe-groups. The political expression of these cultural changes revealed itself only much later, from the mid-1970s onwards.

In the 1950s, coming to grips with the novel language of signs of new immigrants was still rare. Writers who described the new *aliyot* did so from the patronizing viewpoint of observing a primitive society that needed to be educated to receive the values and codes of the patron society.

In her book *1948 – Ben ha-Sefirot* ('1948 – Between the Calendars', 1981), written many years after the event, Netiva Ben-Yehuda (born 1928) describes the contemptuous attitude of the 'pure' *sabras* (native-born Jews of Eretz Israel) towards the new immigrants (chiefly the Holocaust survivors). According to Ben-Yehuda the native-born *sabras* unequivocally demanded that the immigrants instantly and without any argument discard the culture they had brought with them and adjust to the language of signs and the life style of the 'young Hebrew'.

> This view was most emphatically expressed by the members of the left wing youth movement. Chiefly by *Ha-Maḥanot ha-Olim* ['the Ascending Hosts', a pioneering Jewish Scout movement]. *They were the most authentic models of the sabra, the Palmaḥnik, the new young Hebrew* [author's italics]. We of the Scout movement who were by nature more liberal, did not fully succeed in achieving this ideal

model. We also suffered a lot because we were not exactly like them, like the youth of *Aḥdut ha-Avodah* [Zionist Socialist Labor Party]. At least they still gave us a chance. They allowed us to forget our defect – on condition that we change quickly, that we declare, as they did, that we were going to fulfil the ideals, to join the party etc. But as for the new immigrants, they were not even given a chance. 'First we'll see what becomes of him; then we'll see.' And 'what becomes of him' meant how quickly he divests himself of all the Diaspora features and adopts the image of the real sabra. Those of the new immigrants who knew Hebrew in the Diaspora and were members of a corresponding youth movement readjusted most easily. It wasn't only that we couldn't stand their *galut* mannerisms or their clothes; we didn't even let them speak if they had the slightest *accent*. You can't talk like us – so shut up.

(1948 – Ben ha-Sefirot, p. 71))

The dominant system tried to impose itself on the sub-systems which the various groups brought with them from the Diaspora. This is probably how one should interpret the books of Shlomo Schwartz-Shva (born 1929) on the Yemenite settlements in the Judaean Hills, *Anashim Ḥadashim ba-Harim ha-Gvohim* ('New People in the High Mountains', 1953) and about life in the Israeli transit camps of the 1950s, *Makom She'eyn lo Shem* ('A Place Without a Name', 1957). In both these books the patronizing element outweighs that of empathy and compassion.

But the consummated hopes of a revolutionary society based on ascetic values stood in almost total contradiction to the reality of the present, which functioned with an eye only for the future. When the hopes became reality, it transpired that the heroes were tired and they expected, even demanded, that *never again* would they be asked to sacrifice self-fulfilment, present joys or pleasures, on the altar of the future.[11] Henceforth, the life of the flesh was more important than that of the spirit and the garden of earthly delights more precious and wonderful than the Garden of Eden. Ascetics turned into materialists and hedonists, changing the basic norms of the *yishuv* when it became a sovereign state.

Many Hebrew writers refused to accept the change in the *yishuv*. A large number of native first-generation authors have written nostalgic novels which express yearnings for the 'good old days' or novels of social protest criticizing the materialistic revolution which took place in the *yishuv*. The list is a long one: from Meged's *Ḥedva va-Ani* and *Ha-Ḥeshbon ve-ha-Nefesh* ('The Reckoning and the Soul', 1953) by Hanoch Bartov (born 1926), through *Ḥayye Elyakum* ('The Life of Elyakum', Trilogy, 1953–69) by Benjamin Tammuz (1919–89), and *Ereẓ R'hokah* ('A Distant Land', 1981) by Yizhak Ben-Ner (born 1937), including works such as Mossinsohn's *Yehuda Ish Keriyyot* ('Judas', 1963), *Guf Rishon, Rabbim* ('First Person

393

Plural', 1968) by Shaham, Bartov's *B'emẓah ha-Roman* ('In the Middle of it All', 1984), Shlomo Nitzan's *Sha'ah G'nuvah* ('Stolen Time', 1972) and *Tofkosch* (1976), Shamir's *Hinomat Kalah* ('The Bridal Veil', 1985).

The nostalgia of writers who are not prepared to change the old for the new is particularly present in the work of David Shahar, a writer of the same generation as the native-born authors, who emerged in the 1950s. The major theme of his multi-volume work *Hekhal ha-Kelim ha-Shevurim* ('The Palace of Shattered Vessels', 1969–89) is nostalgia for the pre-state period – the time of Ottoman rule and the British Mandate. Shahar compares the young woman of the present, who resembles Yaeli the daughter of Judge Gotkin, with the original Yael of the Mandatory period.

> Just as Yael Gotkin who suffered from exposure to the sun, detested working in the kitchen and didn't know how to cook, decided to go out into the blazing sun of the Judaean desert as a cook for members of the *Gedud ha-Avodah* ['Labor Legion', first country-wide commune of Jewish works in Palestine, founded in 1920], so too the pupil of Yehuda Sasson comes out naked onto the theatre stage – out of conviction and a sense of pioneering feeling – in order to present a woman urinating, in the name of the sacred art of theatre.
> (David Shahar, *Yom ha-Rozenet* ('Day of the Countess', 1976), p. 63)

The polarity between the two women highlights the revolutionary nature of the 'progressive' norms which the 'regressive' author detests.

The new literary figures who appeared after the social revolution were no longer nostalgic or regressive. They started posing weightier questions, prompted by their disappointment with the Zionist revolution. Though they did not cling to the past, they sometimes negated the entire structure and cast doubts on its continuity. While the previous generation of writers saw a supreme ideal in the existential struggle of the Jews in Eretz Israel, writers like Avraham B. Yehoshua (born 1936), Yizhak Orpaz (born 1923), Yoram Kaniuk (born 1930), Yaakov Shabtai (1934–82), Amos Oz (born 1939) and many others have questioned whether the struggle for survival was worthwhile. Was it really worth the effort spent to forgo the comforts of life and engage in a physical struggle which took such a great human toll in order to achieve a future so little better than the present?

In grappling with the darker side of Israeli reality some writers also sought to create eccentric characters, exceptions to the rule. The exaggerated eccentricity of the characters was intended to surprise and shock the bourgeois Israeli reader, who was accustomed to stereotypical characters. An outstanding example of this style is the novel *Ha-Ḥayyim ke-Mashal* ('Life as a Parable', 1958) by Pinhas Sadeh (born 1929). The power of the novel derives more from its place within the semiotic system of the 1950s than from its inner literary essence. The confession is highly exaggerated, requiring stratagems of design that are erotic and perverted according to

Israeli standards at the time of writing in 1958. I stress the date because what was perverse for Israelis at that time was not so for Americans and Europeans who had already read Henry Miller and D. H. Lawrence on the one hand or Mikhail Petrovich Artsybashev (1878–1927, Russian prose writer) on the other. In the Israeli context, a novel with Christian connotations, attempting to revive Frankist myths by declaring (as the Frankists did) that in order to achieve grace one must first transgress, is a modern work which presents the sublimated dark side of Israeli society (passions, Christianity, primacy of the principle of the individual as opposed to the general welfare) as the positive reverse side of the light.[12] Furthermore, Sadeh tried to dissociate himself from the youth movement's values and create a kind of private myth rooted in a Christian language of signs, which the reader perceives as esoteric and eccentric, even though it is written in Hebrew. Some readers loved the book because it released them from the coercive burden of the Israeli language of signs forced upon them by the supreme collective 'I' (the forefathers whom they had internalized). It was as if a leash had been removed and an Israeli was allowed to behave according to his hitherto most hidden lusts in matters concerning relations between the sexes.

This is also true of the novel by Yehuda Amichai (born 1924) *Lo me-'Achshav lo me-Kan* ('Not of This Time, Not of This Place', 1963) in which the dark side is depicted in contrast to the extant dominant system. Amichai's protagonist is a kind of schizophrenic – abandoning his wife (who is the daughter of his commander in the Palmaḥ) for a non-Jewish woman living in the country and also betraying his country by returning to Germany and relating to it as the land of his childhood rather then as a historical monstrosity. Both of these elements constitute a total undermining of the accepted value system of the Hebrew *yishuv*. The thematic innovation in these works is based on a clash with the reader's expectations. One can only shake up the bourgeois if they are affected by the world of values or by the artistic and revolutionary norms which set out to shock them. During the late 1950s and the beginning of the 1960s these books did have a shocking effect. Today a Jew who has an affair with a non-Jewess or who takes a trip to Germany no longer makes an impression on anybody.

The appearance of such deviations in literature accustomed the recipients to the fact that such options were legitimate, that they are part of life even though they might not yet be ideologically accepted. They suggested that the dark, repressed part of Israeli existence, was no less worthy of expression than the rational and ideological part which had become exhausted by overuse, losing its vitality in the new social conditions.

These anti-norms became more significant in the works of David Shahar, Aharon Appelfeld (born 1932), A. B. Yehoshua, Amalia Kahana-Carmon (born 1926), Amos Oz, Yehoshua Kenaz (born 1937), Yaakov Shabtai,

Yizhak Orpaz, Yoram Kaniuk and others. These writers created new characters and new events which were, by and large, an expressionistic or symbolic representation of those dark hidden forces in the soul of the nation that had hitherto been repressed. This process of change also revealed a change in the position of the major writers in the literary republic. Though Dan Miron, a major literary critic, acclaimed Yizhar and Shamir,[13] two of the generation's outstanding writers, who had been the exponents of the system dominant in the 1940s and 1950s, a slow process of change ensued within the literary republic which pushed these two and their colleagues into the background, while writers of the 'new wave' came to the fore.[14]

Doubts regarding the legitimacy of Zionist existence are already conspicuous in the works of Shamir and Yizhar. In two of Yizhar's stories about the War of Independence – *Sippur Ḥirbet Ḥizah* ('The Story of Ḥirbet Ḥizah', 1949) and *Ha-Shavui* ('The Prisoner of War', 1949) – he openly challenges the moral justification for the Israeli conquest resulting from the War of Independence. Moshe Shamir, in his novel *Melekh Basar va-Dam* (1954; *The King of Flesh and Blood*, 1958), presents the antithesis of the protagonist Yannai, a 'king of flesh and blood', in the character of Avshalom, his brother and shadow.

Doubts from within about the legitimacy of Zionism went back to the 1920s when *Berit Shalom* ('The Peace Association') was ready to make extraordinary concessions to reach a peaceful settlement with the Arabs of Palestine.[15] The poems of Uri Zevi Greenberg (1894–1981) *Kelev Bayit* ('House Dog', 1919), *Ezor Magen* and *Ne'um Ben Ha-Dam* ('A Zone of Defence', and 'Address of the Son-of-Blood', both 1930) were outstanding examples of the opposite view.[16] The social and literary promotion of the fighter in Hebrew literature, from Moshe Smilansky (1874–1953) in heroic stories like *Ḥawaja Nazar* ('Mr Nazar', c. 1900) and *Avner* (c. 1900) through his nephew Yizhar Smilansky (S. Yizhar) in his novella *Ha-Ḥorsha Asher ba-Givah* ('The Grove on the Hill', 1947) up until Shamir and Mossinsohn (and in a variety of writers who preceded the native-born Israeli authors) was a more moderate expression of the 'violent struggle' trend. The 'guilt feeling' underlies and is to some extent explicit in the war stories of the two major writers of that generation – Shamir and Yizhar. Aharon Meged later continued this trend in the *Ir Levanah* ('White City') chapter of his book *Mikreh ha-Kesil* (1960; *Fortunes of a Fool*, 1962).

In a minor novel by Medad Schiff (born 1925) *Shim'on Zahamara* (1951) there is already a hint of the colonization process which is morally complex and ambiguous. Thematically, this novel is unusual despite its being structurally conventional. Structurally the novel is naturalistic, based upon a melodramatic plot. Its naturalism is expressed in a technique also used by John Dos Passos, called the 'newsreels', in which the author interpolates actual international political events as well as Jewish ones (these interpolations are printed in small type) alongside the fictional narrative, which relates the strange life of the half-breed son of a Syrian Jewish father and a Lebanese Christian–Arab mother, who wavers between the nationalistic Zionism of his father's family and the Arab nationalism of his mother's.

Initially he participates in the War of Independence and identifies with the Jewish part of his personality, but later unable to bear the dichotomy in his heart, he flees across the border. Generally the novel tends to deal ironically with Zionist values. The author identifies with the protagonist and protests against the persecution of the half-breed. This is a work which rebels against the Zionist establishment, stresses the discrimination against Israeli Arabs and describes the tragedy of two peoples fighting over the same piece of land, each in their own way espousing a just cause:

> Did there awaken within him an atavism, a legacy from father and mother, both scions of stiff-necked races – one obstinately proclaiming its uniqueness in the Diaspora and the other stubbornly maintaining its uniqueness in the heights of its mountains? Did he see himself as a traitor to his mother when he assimilated himself with this wave of conquerors, builders of blocks of houses and strips of asphalt, this rabble who descended upon his country, clinging to its southwest corner and refusing to let go . . .?
>
> (*Shim'on Zahamara*, p. 87)

Through a minor character call Jamjun, the author hints at a possible solution to the conflict, based upon the *Weltanschauung* of the Canaanite movement (which began its activities as a group in 1942) who preferred indigenous Hebrews to any link with Diaspora Jewry. This is a novel which presents and brings to the foreground one of the thought-systems which existed in the *yishuv* (Canaanism) and its struggle with the dominant ideological system of Zionism.[17] This original work may be seen as a precursor of later works that reshape values to create an apparent antithesis to the accepted Zionist norms at the heart of the system, such as the later works of Benjamin Tammuz, A. B. Yehoshua and others.[18] Here too one can describe the situation in terms of values which have been moved to the foreground and others which have been marginalized or pushed into the background.

Up until the War of Independence, the war of survival and the war of 'liberation' were in the forefront of society's values while the feeling of guilt regarding the so-called victims of colonization and conquest was repressed. The Zionist enterprise was justified without stressing the guilt feelings which lay in wait for the appropriate moment to reveal themselves.

A strange revolution took place in the mid-1950s. One could almost say that nothing succeeds like success. The two Israeli victories – the War of Independence and the Sinai Campaign – paradoxically strengthened the trend that stressed the Jewish guilt feeling. The point of departure – that the Jews in Eretz Israel, with their backs to the wall, were fighting a battle of the few against the multitude, which was so typical of Nathan Alterman (1910–70) in his poems *Magash ha-Kesef* ('The Silver Platter') and *Ir ha-Yonah* ('Wailing City') (both 1957) – was pushed back in favour of an awareness that the Jews had defeated the Arabs, the latter becoming transformed into a persecuted minority within Israeli society.[19]

Furthermore, because of this development and other changes in Israeli society, the 'new Hebrew' lost his central position in both reality and in literature. Even in literature as an art form, the realistic tradition and its values had become obsolete through over-use. Social developments reinforced internal literary ones as the old stereotypes lost their central function. There was a tendency among many writers to demythicize the 'new Hebrew' as the hero of the generation. The appearance of the Holocaust survivor as a legitimate character in society created a spiritual platform which now allowed the presentation of the Israeli hero as the anti-hero. This reversal takes place mainly in the works of Amos Oz and A. B. Yehoshua. The bewildered, wretched and unredeemed Israeli intellectuals in A. B. Yehoshua's *Mul ha-Ye'arot* ('Opposite the Forest', 1968) and Amos Oz's *Minzar ha-Shatkanim* ('The Trappist Monastery') and *Derech ha-Ruah* ('The Way of the Wind') from the collection of stories *Arzot ha-Tan* ('Where the Jackals Howl', 1965) replaced the fighters and pioneers.

In A. B. Yehoshua's novel *Ha-Me'ahev* ('The Lover', 1976) Arditi, the *yored* (*émigré*) who, disguised as an ultra-Orthodox religious Jew, is a deserter from both the frontline and the homefront during the months of the Yom Kippur War, is the complete antithesis of what was the accepted image of the Israeli 'hero'. The deserter, *yored* and ultra-Orthodox Jew, were loathsome types in the Zionist society of the 1940s and 1950s. However, in Yehoshua's novel the figure that combines all these despicable characteristics is the potent protagonist. He is one of the two lovers who replace the father and legal husband who represents the 'normal' Israel. Na'im, the Israeli Arab, as a member of a persecuted minority, is much closer to the Jewish image of bygone days than to the image of the present-day Arab. Even this character has been brought to the foreground and is perceived as virile in contrast with his master, who has lost his strength and authority. The *yored* steals the wife from the typical Israeli male while the Arab takes his daughter. The Israeli who represents the social elite of the 1940s and early 1950s is no longer a master in his own home. His language of signs and world of values have lost their meaning because they have outlived their time and their internal strength.

In 1987 Amos Oz, in his novel *Kufsah Shehorah* ('Black Box') writes an allegory about the decline and fall of Gideon Alexander, a native-born Ashkenazi who is being destroyed by a psychosomatic cancer while his place and home are being taken over by Michael Somo, an oriental Jew who tends to favour the Greater Israel ideal. Between them there is a cultural abyss, a different language of signs.

398

The *yored* as a new kind of antithesis to the *oleh* and pioneer begins to take a more central position in Hebrew literature, in the guise of either a traitor, an apostate or simply a person who attempts but fails to escape the clutches of the dominant Israeli mother. This theme plays a central role in Benjamin Tammuz's novel *Minotaur* (1980), *Gerushim Me'uḥarim* ('Late Divorce', 1982) by A. B. Yehoshua and *Sus Eẓ* ('Rockinghorse', 1973) by Yoram Kaniuk. The norm was now replaced by the anti-norm, just as the comic or pathetic and positive realism was replaced by expressionistic works which reveal the grotesque absurdities underlying Israeli life. The idea of emigration from Israel, which was repressed in the social consciousness or swept under the cultural carpet since the time of Brenner's character, Diasporin, now recurs as a critical factor in literature. Emigration as an act of flight from the mother's bosom, as an act of self-fulfilment or as a revolt against Zionist–Jewish coercion, is a significant anti-Zionist theme. What was once in the background has moved into the foreground, but one must remember that these authors rely on the fact that in the reader's consciousness the old Zionist norms were still operative, even if weakened. Without them, such literary works would not be effective.[20]

The examples given are only a few from among the many that exist. For example, the first novel by Meir Shalev (born 1948) *Roman Rusi* ('A Russian Novel', 1988) is not innovative; he simply takes the anti-myth to a grotesque extreme. The plot is about Second Aliyah pioneers who left Eretz Israel but return in their coffins, to be buried on the moshav against full payment, for the financial benefit of the wretched protagonist heir.[21] The protagonist is a naive reincarnation of Zion, the son of Hazaz's Meri Alsaid.

Nathan Alterman[22] maintained that there were two ways of perceiving the Holocaust: through resistance and revolt or through the *Judenrat* as another kind of strategy of survival. Israeli society and Hebrew literature preferred the resistance and repressed the fact that the majority of European Jewry went to their deaths like sheep led to slaughter. It was only as a result of the Eichmann trial (April to December 1961) that full awareness of the latter option penetrated the consciousness both of the young writers and of the general public. Haim Gouri (born 1923), the living symbol of the 'new Hebrew', published a chronicle of the Eichmann trial called *Mul Ta ha-Zekhukhit* ('Facing the Glass Booth', 1962) and a non-heroic novel *Iskat ha-Shokolad* (1965; *The Chocolate Deal*, 1968).

The heroic conception of the Holocaust concurred with the thought-system and the dominant language of signs. The writers imposed the heroic fighting Zionist *Weltanschauung* on the world of the oppressed, imprisoned and massacred concentration and extermination camp Jews.

The trilogy *Sha'ul ve-Yohannah* ('Saul and Joanna', 1956–67) by Naomi Frenkel (born 1920) about the decline and fall of an assimilated German Jewish family, is a belated response to the Holocaust experience, as is the saga by Alexander (born 1921) and Yonat (born 1926) Sened, *Bein ha-Metim u-vein ha-Hayyim* ('Between the Dead and the Living', 1955–64) which relates the decline, fall and end of Polish Jewry.

From the mid-1950s the reactions to the Holocaust often included glorified descriptions of the besieged Jewish fighters. The Seneds end their saga in the Warsaw ghetto; Naomi Frenkel ends her trilogy with a part of the assimilated family deciding to emigrate to Eretz Israel. The Seneds' work, like Frenkel's, is to a large extent an apotheosis for the choice of revolt and strives to present Zionism as the lesson to be learned from this historical catastrophe.

Aharon Appelfeld (born 1932) changed the heroic concept of the Holocaust, refusing to fling a cloak of simplistic local Zionist values over the history of European Jewry prior to and during the Holocaust. He sought to describe the Jewish catastrophe from the survivors' point of view. His works were calculated to induce a renewed introspection in Israeli society since his literary model forced it to alter the self-image of the Holocaust period which it had tried to create for itself. Appelfeld revised the balance between martyrdom and heroism in his literary model, revealing what has since been historically confirmed, namely, that the heroism was a mere drop in the ocean of the Holocaust.

Since his first book of stories *Ashan* ('Smoke', 1962) right up until his most recent works, Appelfeld has elevated the survivor into a hero. He also extended the circle of Israeli characters and incorporated the survivors and refugees, who hitherto had been minor, marginal characters in the works of the native writers, into the mainstream of the literary model. Together with several other writers such as Shammai Golan (born 1933) and Itamar Ya'oz-Kest (born 1934), Appelfeld spoke out on behalf of those who had been repressed in the Israeli consciousness and demonstrated that these characters were a legitimate part of the society and of its literature. Survival was to be perceived as no less 'heroic' than a military struggle against one's enemies.

Appelfeld's protagonists are not fighters and partisans but survivors who escaped by the skin of their teeth. Victims such as Katy, Bertha and Cilly or characters who continue to fight the battle of survival even after they have been saved, are the true heroes, as in the story *Be-Iy'ye Saint George* ('The Islands of Saint George', 1965). They did not participate in the uprising or join the partisans but simply succeeded in surviving or were killed in a merciless world.

Even when these protagonists reach Eretz Israel they do not undergo a metamorphosis, then and there becoming 'new Hebrews', but rather, like Brenner's protagonists, they are miserable and detached in the very place which was meant to be a shelter, refuge and homeland. As before in Brenner's work, so now in Appelfeld's, a change of place does not change the person:

and only now after a long dream, a person understands that he is a stranger in this hot climate. Like stray birds carried by winds far away from themselves. They lost their land, yearnings madden them and that's why they turn their necks strangely, as if perpetually pursued.

(*Ha-'Or ve-ha-Kutonet* ('The Skin and the Cloak', 1971), p. 39)

The novella *Mikhvat ha-'Or* ('Searing Light', 1980) is a painful story about the alienation of survivors in Eretz Israel. The educational institution to which they have been sent, where they are to be re-educated in Zionism, appears to them like a concentration camp.

Appelfeld gave a new and brutal interpretation to the period preceding the Holocaust as he did for the period succeeding it. In *Tor ha-Pelaot* ('The Age of Wonders', 1978) and *Badenheim 1939* (Hebrew 1975, English 1981) he describes a confused, deaf and dumb, assimilated Jewry which does not want to grapple with impending disaster, preferring to ignore it until the last minute, and running headlong towards its own destruction like a community accepting the judgement it deserves. Appelfeld stresses not so much the German responsibility in the extermination process but rather the role of the Jews who did not foresee its approach, and therefore must also bear some responsibility for it, since – ignoring the warnings and dangers – they were, in a way, drawn to their own destruction. Although Appelfeld does not write about fighters and revolutionaries, his model hints at the Zionist prognosis which blames Diaspora Jewry for enjoying its loss of identity, its dreams of assimilation, for providing the conditions which brought about its own destruction. '... Another thirty years, another fifty years and we would have assimilated without recognition, but the demons wanted the game to continue and so it did' (*Shanim ve-Sha'ot* ('Years and Hours', 1975), p. 133). His view of the Holocaust survivors is both original and extremely dismal. Pursued for life, they never recover; some of them believe the Holocaust years were the best period of their lives because they fled into the forests where they were able to live like free birds, without any responsibility.

In their novels *Yemei Ziklag* ('The Days of Ziklag', 1958) and *Shanim ve-Sha'ot*, two of the most important Hebrew writers, S. Yizhar and Aharon Appelfeld, respectively, deal with two of the most central existential questions for the Jewish people in the twentieth century, putting words into the mouths of their protagonists.

Yizhar's protagonists, who fought at ancient Ziklag (a strategic hill in the Negev which defends the area against the attacking Arab armies) feel that the 'Days of Ziklag', a period of seven days, when they fought for their own lives and for the life of the nation, represented perhaps the most wonderful period in their lives:

Oh, yes. Suddenly you will realize that the most wonderful days you had in your lousy life were precisely the days of Ziklag. And the war.

One morning you'll get up and discover that all the world around you is grey and boring and sad and small. And every morning you have to run to work, and you have nothing except all those trivialites and unimportant jobs, in order somehow to go on living, somehow to go on, once again you aren't just another face amongst one hundred thousand other similar faces, and you'll start singing nostalgic songs, not only about that night – the devil take it, and about yesterday and the day before and you'll drag your kids to show them: 'Here is Ziklag, this is where your daddy was when he was in his prime, when he wasn't bald and didn't have worries.'

(Yemei Ziklag, p. 733)

In both Yizhar and Appelfeld's anti-heroes, one can find a demystification and remystification of the central existential experiences of the Jewish people in the twentieth century. Far from causing only suffering, depression and death, the War of Independence and the Holocaust – the decisive experiences of a whole generation – were, for the survivors, the best years of their lives.

While in retrospect such a view of the War of Independence period is not altogether surprising, the remythicizing by the survivors (and not necessarily the fighters and resistance members) of the Holocaust period most certainly is. The new self-consciousness enabled a revised appraisal of the survivors, who were depicted not as the native Israeli wished to see them but rather as the survivors saw themselves: neither as the dust of the earth, nor as heroic partisans fighting for their lives, cast in the image of the resistance fighter and poet Abba Kovner (1918–87), but rather as characters who survived through some terrifying collective error on the part of their society, who do not accept the new world-order but have a strange nostalgic yearning for the horrible hole breached in their lives, which became the one and only period in which they experienced genuine living.[23]

A *Weltanschauung* which had been largely subordinate in the latter part of the Holocaust period overpowered the Zionist viewpoint, which had coerced the spectators into a vision that accorded with the heroic expectations of Eretz Israel fiction in the 1940s. Aharon Appelfeld and Uri Orlev (born 1922) plainly rejected the dominant ideology which insisted upon branding the Holocaust of European Jewry with a heroic stamp that resulted from the demands and expectations of the Israeli *yishuv*.[24] Similarly, Netiva Ben-Yehuda, in her book *1948 – Ben ha-Sefirot*, attempted to remove the cloak of myth surrounding the Palmah and to construct a model which would present the 'facts'.

The most important development in Israeli fiction since the latter part of the 1950s is the rejection of the assumption that Eretz Israel is a melting-pot for the Jewish people. The young elite of the *yishuv* (in the youth movements, settlements and army) were convinced that the language of signs which their parents had attempted to consummate, was the one and only language worthy of prevailing in Eretz Israel. The Canaanite movement was an extreme expression of this demand but its world-view was destroyed by the new waves of immigration and the crises which racked the elite group after the establishment of the state. The forced surrender of 'one tongue, one language' brought about an ever-increasing differentiation of protagonists and their exploits in the land, with which modern Israeli literature has had to grapple. Attempts to dehistoricize this literature result in there being no central figure or dominant plot, rather the fringe becomes central to literature. A. B. Yehoshua's protagonists in his most recent novels *Molcho*, 1987 (*Five Seasons*, 1989) and *Adon Mani* ('Mr Mani', 1990) are still very much connected to history but they try to live on its fringe. Amos Oz tried for his part to save the protagonist of his novella *La-Da'at Isha* ('To Know a Woman', 1989) from the clutches of history. By creating antithetical characters (or characters who declare their opposition to the thesis), Oz and A. B. Yehoshua are still grappling with the theses and norms of their society. Their works represent in some respect an antithesis which assumes the strong and vital existence of the thesis. Though this diversion to the fringe had already appeared parenthetically in the works of the previous generation, as can be seen in the Petah Tikvah stories by Hanoch Bartov (born 1926) and stories about little Eretz Israel by Benjamin Tammuz, the phenomenon first takes on major proportion in the 1960s.

Examples of the differentiation process can also be found in the works of Nissim Aloni (born 1926), Yossl Birstein (born 1920), David Shahar, Yehoshua Kenaz (born 1937), Yeshayahu Koren (born 1940), Hanoch Levin (born 1943), Amalia Kahana-Carmon, Ruth Almog (born 1936) and Yaakov Shabtai (1943–82) and later in the works of Dan-Benaya Seri (born 1935), Hannah Bat Shahar (born 1944), Yehudit Katzir (born 1963), Orly Castel-Bloom (born 1960) and others.

The phenomenon found its perhaps most extreme and comprehensive treatment in the non-Israeli book *Ma'of ha-Yona* ('The Flight of the Dove', 1990) by Yuval Shimoni (born 1955) the grandson of David Shimoni (1886–1956), the most Israeli and Zionist of the poets of Bialik's generation. The protagonists of the book are neither Jews nor Israelis but Americans and French; moreover, Shimoni writes European literature in the Hebrew language, like David Vogel (1891–1944) in *Nokhah ha-Yam* ('Facing the Sea', 1932) and in *Hayyei Nesuim* ('Married Life', 1929–30), two works which were outside the accepted literary tradition of their generation.

There are many other examples of the differentiation process. David Shahar portrayed impressive, varied and unconventional Jews in the Street of the Prophets in west Jerusalem during the Ottoman and British Mandate periods (pre-1917 and 1917–48). Nissim Aloni depicted the blue-blooded Sephardim of south Tel Aviv. Haim Be'er (born 1945) in his book *Nozot*

('Feathers', 1979), following David Shahar, portrayed the fringe Jews among the secular and ultra-Orthodox population in Geula Street in Jerusalem. Dan-Benaya Seri in his book *Zipporei Zel* ('Birds of Shade', 1987) depicted the grotesque, perverse existence of Bukharan and Yemenite Jews on the fringes of Jerusalem life. Amalia Kahana-Carmon and Ruth Almog delineated the world of frustrated, solitary women fighting their own personal battles which sometimes turn into a general social struggle: the student revolt in France as presented in Ruth Almog's book *Shorshei Avir* ('Dangling Roots', 1987) or the historical outcry which fuses the oppression of the Diaspora with the oppression of the woman in Amalia Kahana-Carmon's book *Le-Ma'alah be-Montifer* ('Up in the Montifer', 1984). These writers deal with the remote corners of Israeli existence: remote neighbourhoods, remote communities and remote inner corners of the epicentre. Aharon Meged's *Foiglman*, 1988 and Yossl Birstein's *A Face in the Clouds* (1991), describe the life of the Yiddish survivors of the East European *shtetl*. Yaakov Shabtai depicted the remote corners of the private lives of minor leaders of the labour movement. He described the hidden life of the leadership group in his novel *Zikhron Devarim* ('Memorandum', 1977) but also uncovered the fringe lives of shopkeepers and little people, in his collection of stories *Ha-Dod Perez Mamri* ('Uncle Perez Takes Off', 1972).

In his novel *Aharei ha-Haggim*, 1964 (*After the Holidays*, 1987) Yehoshua Kenaz began by describing a perverted world in some god-forsaken settlement and continued by describing the strange life in a Tel Aviv neighbourhood in his book *Ha-Isha ha-Gedolah min ha-Halomot* ('The Great Woman of the Dreams', 1973) and later created a story about the development of neurotic children during their adolescence in his book *Moment Musikali* ('Musical Moment', 1980). In his brilliant last novel *Hitganvut Yehidim* ('Heart Murmur', 1986) he created a world which relates to various social problems in Eretz Israel by concentrating them in a military training-camp full of anti-heroes, which contains within it a variety of ethnic and social contrasts and a conflict with the norms of the 'heroic' society. However, in this training camp for second-class (non-combatant) soldiers, all the problems take on a different meaning. Here one does not solve the basic existential problem of Jewish life in Eretz Israel but rather the petty problems of petty people thrown together in a particular place at a particular time. Someone called this novel the *Yemei Ziklag* of the 1950s – *Kaf Lamedim* (soldiers with a low physical profile who are classified for non-combat duty). These unfortunate recruits fight their major battles against their commanders, rather than against the Arabs. Yehoshua Kenaz succeeded in creating a single framework for characters who have many different voices unlike in S. Yizhar's *Yemei Ziklag* where all the protagonists speak the same language. The recent immigration has not as yet jumbled the languages nor created a clash of cultures. Yizhar's novel contains characters who all come from a more or less similar if not identical social background and who, each in his own way, comply with the world-view of the Eretz Israel labour movement and speak the same language of signs.

In *Hitganvut Yeḥidim* there is one recruit, an immigrant from Romania known as Efes Efes (meaning zero-zero), who hopes that his son will be a native among natives. But the recruits from the oriental communities continue to speak their own language and reject an immigrant who speaks the youth movement language. Avner finds himself in a dilemma as a Sephardi who desires to become an Ashkenazi. He is a problematic character because he wants to change languages and, like the assimilated Jew who leaves one culture without as yet having been accepted into another, he remains neither here nor there. The struggle between the fringe and the centre has become the subject of the novel. Kenaz tries to mediate between the 'warring' languages by stating that people can live together in the same social pressure-cooker provided that society accepts the facts of life and understands itself as a group of people fated to live together despite its members speaking different languages. Alon, the kibbutznik, commits suicide because he still lives with the norms of *Yemei Ẓiklag* in a society of *Kaf Lameds* whose norms are different from his own.

This contrast between the resurrected fringe and the centre finds its powerful expression in the following extract from the strange and interesting novel *Bernhard* (1988) by Yoel Hoffman:

> In his childhood Bernhard flew through the skies of Lapland on the back of a wild duck. Many strange things happened to him and to Sigmund and Clara. Sigmund and Clara died and Bernhard came to Palestine alone and married Paula and Paula died too and all those years Bernhard didn't say '*ahalan!*' ['hello' in Arabic, adopted also in Sabra Hebrew slang] even once ... and those paunchy types who wander around Palestine saying '*ahalan!*' disgust him. He wants to ask: 'Isn't Bernhard the son of Sigmund a human being too?' Sometimes those of little faith and slight flesh say '*ahalan!*' (in an unnatural way) and when Bernhard sees them he feels ashamed as if they had exposed their genitals [p. 38].

In this book the '*ahalan!*' types are the self-satisfied ones with whom Bernhard refuses to assimilate and he consciously rebels against their language of signs, of which '*ahalan!*' is the most distinct symptom. Hoffman stresses both the stereotypical character of the 'new Hebrew' who in a certain period was held up by literature as an ideal worthy of admiration and that of the other stereotype who exists in the country to no less an extent.[25]

Over a period of years Israeli literature was uncovering many groups with their own thought-systems, extending its models of observation and slowly but surely overcoming the exclusivity of the dominant model.[26] What was previously repressed or exhibited only as a stereotype (like the minor character of the shrewd and agile Yemenite) was now brought to the centre of consciousness. In this way, literature contributes to an ever-increasing pluralistic illumination of the society to which it relates. Mordechai Tabib (born 1910) is a Yemenite author who writes about Yemenites who try to break out of their ethnic mould and join the youth movement group. *Kinoro Shel Yossi* ('Yossi's Violin', 1959) tells the story of the life and death of a Yemenite youth who, like his Ashkenazi friends, died in the War of Independence. Tabib, like Burla, perceives the language of his society not as something which commits him but rather as something from which he must free himself. A large part of Burla's works such as *Bat Ziyyon* ('Daughter of Zion', 1930–1), *Ba'al be-Amav* ('The Husband with His People', 1962) and *Senunit Rishonah* ('The First Swallow', 1954) reach the conclusion that the kibbutz is the common social ideal which Ashkenazi society set up as a model for the old Sephardi *yishuv* and only those who join the kibbutz will become part of the main Zionist meta-plot. Even Yehudit Hendel's Sephardic protagonist in *Rehov ha-Madregot*, 1956 (*The Street of the Steps*, 1963) is one of those who is disappointed that the *yishuv* after the War of Independence does not fulfil the precepts of the Zionist meta-plot. It was only much later that a few writers from the oriental communities found their language and their world to be something positive which one must come to grips with from the inside.

The '*ahalan!*' character has become almost marginal. The uniformity of the melting-pot has failed. Israeli writers, like their fellow writers in the United States, have begun to recognize the uniqueness of the tribes and of various other social groups in this varied, strange and pressured Eretz Israel. The hierarchy of older thought-systems and the dominance of the conventional language of signs have become confused. The pressure-cooker did not succeed in blending the wide range of characters into one soup. They live together because of the lid that covers them and because there *still* exists some sort of commitment to the larger Israeli society, despite the extensive process of differentiation.

The old semiotic uniformity and social norms have broken down to be replaced by a new pluralism which accentuates the disparate, despite the pressure-cooker effect which imposes a common destiny on everyone. There is perhaps a certain grandeur in this experiment to secure a Hebrew culture whose language of signs is in the process of disintegration, yet which continues to manifest a complex, strange and dramatic life that has undoubtedly enriched contemporary Israeli literature.

NOTES

1 Wolfgang Iser, *The Act of Reading, A Theory of Aesthetic Response*, (Baltimore and London, Johns Hopkins University Press, 1978), for some of the basic principles from which my analytical assumptions derive. See also Itamar Even Zohar, 'The growth and consolidation of a local indigenous Hebrew culture

in Eretz Israel, 1882–1948', *Catedra* (Tammuz, 1979) vol. 16, pp. 165–89 (Hebrew).

2 This is what Joseph Hayyim Brenner meant in his article, 'The Eretz Israel genre and its accessories' (1911), in *The Complete Writings of Brenner* (1961), pp. 268–70, particularly p. 269 (Hebrew).

3 Gershon Shaked, *Between Laughter and Tears, Studies of the Works of Mendele Mokher Seforim* (Tel Aviv, 1965), pp. 13–35 (Hebrew).

4 Gershon Shaked, *The Changing Centres of Contemporary Hebrew Literature – Codes and Models, Works and their Recipients, Four Chapters in Reception Theory* (Tel Aviv, 1987), pp. 12–36 (Hebrew).

5 Gershon Shaked, *The Dream and the Boulder: Different Aspects in Agnon's Writings* (Tel Aviv, 1989), pp. 72–6; 84–90 (Hebrew).

6 Gershon Shaked, 'Portrait of the immigrant as a young neurotic' (Agnon's *Shevuat Emunim*), 'Prooftexts' (1987), vol. 7, pp. 41–52.

7 'It wasn't just an army – a people that crystallized in our camps. It was a youth movement in the full sense of the word. A real revolutionary movement. Within a few days we developed new forms of life. A new style of behaviour, in speech and dress. It emerged from within ourselves without our having to imitate anyone or anything, with elemental simplicity, from the character of the generation. It is possible that even if the war had not broken out this youth movement would have developed, and it would have directed history with great creative deeds, because in fact this was really a ripening of a new generation – the first to develop in the country's climate of freedom. This large movement needed a symbol, a trademark that would represent its character as a people's army exalted by the spirit of the individual rather than blurring it. We didn't have uniforms. We wore the clothes which we brought from home. And suddenly thousands of soldiers started wearing the same sort of hat, without being ordered to do so – the stocking cap.

The *"Kovah Tembel"* [lit. "dunce cap"] or the "Mikveh cap" [named after the cap worn in the Mikveh Yisrael agricultural school founded in 1870] symbolized the pioneering period; but this war produced its own hat – that funny stocking that took on many, many shapes.' (Uri Avneri (born 1922), *Besdot Pleshet 1948, Yoman Keravi* ('In Philistine Fields 1948, A War Diary', 1949), p. 18.)

8 Gershon Shaked, 'Will we find enough new blood?', *There is No Other Place* (Tel Aviv, 1989), pp. 13–29 (Hebrew).

9 There is no rule without its exception. Not all the writers of the 1950s onwards were dependent on the language of signs created in the youth movements. There were other writers who depicted the *yishuv* during the Ottoman and British Mandate periods who did not need a new language of signs. Among them were: Yehude Burla (1886–1969), Yizhak Shami (1888–1949), Ya'akov Yehoshua Churgin (1898–1990), Aharon Reuveni (1886–1971), Dov Kimhi (1889–1961) in his novel *Bet Hefez* ('In the House of Hefez', 1951), Yehoshua Bar Yosef (born 1912) in his stories *Ha-Bayit ha-Hadash* ('The New House', 1946) and *Ir Kesumah* ('Magic City', 1950). All of them drew their material from a world that was different from the pioneering circle.

David Shahar is the heir to this tradition in his multi-volumed work *Hekhal ha-Kelim ha-Shevurim* (1969–89). The novels contain a large number of Canaanite motifs; e.g. in *Ha-Masa'le-Ur Kasdim* ('A Voyage to Ur of the Chaldees', 1976) or in the poems to Tammuz by Ashba'al Astarte (Berl Rabban) in his novel *Yom ha-Rozenet*.

To a certain extent these Canaanite elements in Shahar's work are justified because he is writing about an indigenous population rather than about immigrants or pioneers. The semiotics of the indigenous protagonists were different from that which appears in the writings of the generation nurtured on accepted youth movement symbols. Theirs was a complete world (which Shahar constructed) revealing on the fringe of the *yishuv*, a group whose roots were in the Levant (perhaps even extending back to ancient Canaan). A. B. Yehoshua's *Mar Mani* is also close to this tradition.

10 Dan Horowitz and Moshe Lissak, *From Yishuv to a State, The Jews of Eretz Israel during the British Mandate as a Political Community* (Tel Aviv, 1979), pp. 293–9.

11 An ascetic puritanism also expressed itself in the society's attitude to sex, which was forcefully presented by Netiva Ben-Yehuda in her book *Ben ha-Sefirot – 1948*, a critical attempt at demythicizing the period by 'reconstructing the experience from a state of tranquillity'.

> So in these things he was a real rookie, he simply didn't know how to start. In general it was a laugh how Victorian puritanism dominated the Palmaḥ. I don't know what it was like in the early years of the Palmaḥ, with all the cock-and-bull stories, but during the War of Independence I think one could enter the Palmaḥ in the Guinness Book of World Records as the purest army in the world. At least with regard to sexual matters. The number of couples who had sexual relations can be counted on the fingers of two hands. Ninety-nine per cent of all the guys killed in this war died as virgins [p. 266].

Netiva Ben-Yehuda expresses disapproval of this puritanism just as she holds no brief for other aspects of the national myth. Her book is an expression of the native Israeli's revolt against the normative restrictions which they themselves accepted as a result of internalizing the values they were taught.

12 Yehoshua Kenaz created a number of eccentric characters in his two novels: *Aharei ha-Haggim*, 1964 (*After the Holidays*, 1987) – Ḥayyim Weiss, his wife Bracha, his second wife Ḥasida and his two daughters Riva and Batsheva; and *Ha-Isha ha-Gedolah min ha-Ḥalomot* – Aliza, Alfred, Levana and Ẓiyyon, Malka and Shmulik, and the blind Rosa.

David Shahar's *Hekhal ha-Kelim ha-Shevurim* contains many interesting eccentric characters, more plausible than the protagonist of Pinhas Sadeh's novel *Ha-Ḥayyim ke-Mashal*. Shahar presents a supra-national relationship between his eccentric characters who consist of a strange mixture of Jews, Arabs and Britons. For example: a group of unconventional people are gathered in Café Gat in the Street of the Prophets in Jerusalem. The narrator–protagonist–observer dotes on the past, on the atmosphere of the Ottoman–Mandatory period which was conducive to creating a bond between these characters. Gavriel Luria plays a violin which a solitary German Jew sold to Bulos the Arab. Oritah at first dances with the Englishman Gordon and then with the Arab Bulos to the great sorrow of Daud, her father's chauffeur. A brilliant description of the pre-Zionist experience created by eccentric characters outside the circle of conventionally accepted characters (*Yom ha-Rozenet*, pp. 38ff).

13 Dan Miron, *Four Aspects of Hebrew Literature* (Tel Aviv, 1962), pp. 173–275 (Hebrew).

14 Gershon Shaked, *A New Wave in Hebrew Literature* (Tel Aviv, 1970) (Hebrew). The book contains articles written in the 1960s on Yehuda Amichai, Aharon Appelfeld, A. B. Yehoshua, Amos Oz and Amalia Kahana-Carmon. During this period the critics who most advanced the New Wave writers were Nathan Zach, Dan Miron, Gabriel Moked and the present writer.

15 Ibid., note 12, pp. 200–1.

16 *Idem*, pp. 201–2.

17 Baruch Kurzweil, 'The nature and sources of the "Young Hebrews" Movement ("Canaanites")', *Our New Literature – Continuity or Revolution?* (Tel Aviv, 1959), pp. 270–300 (Hebrew). Kurzweil pointed out the centrality of the subsidiary Canaanite 'thought system' within Israeli society. He rightly maintained that its covert influence amongst the young was much greater than the number of registered members of the movement. 'For instance, it seems to me that *Yemei Ziklag* by S. Yizhar is a clear example of a Canaanite literary document.' Ibid., p. 274.

18 Two decades after Medad Schiff's novel was published Miriam Schwartz published her novel *Korot Havah Gottlieb* ('The Life of Ḥavah Gottlieb', 1968) which deals with the relations between a Jewish woman and an Arab man and society's reactions to them. This is the story of Ḥavah Gottlieb, a young woman from an ultra-Orthodox family who falls in love with an Arab (Maḥmud), lives with him (despite the fact that her brother and father were murdered by Arabs) and becomes pregnant. She moves to Tel Aviv where many men fall in love with her and shortly before she is due to give birth, moves to a kibbutz where the men also fall in love with her. Her request to be accepted as a member of the kibbutz is rejected when it is revealed that the father of her child is an Arab communist. In what appears to be an act of suicide, Ḥavah Gottlieb is run over by Gidi (a Tel Avivian who wanted to marry her) and is buried at the kibbutz.

The novel attempts to show that the kibbutz and Mea She'arim are very similar – closed, puritanical societies, which do not permit non-conformity.

Various other writers presented the point of view of their non-Jewish or so-called Jewish characters: Benjamin Tammuz to a large extent followed in the footsteps of Schiff with his novel *Ha-Pardes*, 1976 (*The Orchard*, 1982). The two protagonists of the novel are the brothers Daniel and Ovadiah – one took on an Arab identity and the other took on a Jewish identity. In David Shahar's *Yom ha-Rozenet* (pp. 93–6) there is an interesting character called Lewidor, the silent Jew who converted to Islam in order to persuade the Arabs to return to the Arabian peninsula. He is presented as Willy the Jew (a holy madman).

There are two characters in A. B. Yehoshua's *Mar Mani* – one who proclaims that all the Arabs are really Jews and therefore one must strive to return them to Judaism and the other who tries to convince the Arabs after the Balfour Declaration that they should establish their own state in one half of Palestine.

The preference for Arabs over Jews by the native Jews of the 1940s generation with their 'Canaanite' character is expressed by Netiva Ben-Yehuda in her book *Ben ha-Sefirot – 1948* (p. 50).

> It's a fact that we not only don't hate the Arabs; quite the opposite. They are the models for the sabras in the country. It's the Jews we hate. The Diaspora Jews. But the Arabs? Just see how we imitate them. How we're dying to be like them. From the time of *Ha-Shomer*. We dress like them. We adopted lots of Arab words. Lots of customs – coffee, horses, bonfires. They are definitely our model.

19 Gershon Shaked, 'Pursuers? Pursued?', *There is No Other Place* (Tel Aviv, 1988), particularly pp. 75–7 (Hebrew).

20 Ibid., 'Between apostasy and emigration', pp. 114–37 (Hebrew).

21 The works of David Grossman *Ḥiyyukh ha-Gedi*, 1983 (Smile of the Lamb, no date) and *Ayyen Erekh: Ahavah*, 1986 (*See Under: Love*, 1990) continue the tradition of coming to grips with the Zionist meta-plot. In both these novels Grossman deals with the central symbols and events, attempting with great skill

to imbue them with a new meaning. Though he creates new technical para-
digms, he does not alter the tradition established primarily by Pinhas Sadeh,
Yehuda Amichai, Amos Oz, A. B. Yehoshua and, more specifically, by Aharon
Appelfeld.

22 Nathan Alterman, *On Two Paths*, Pages from a Notebook (with a postscript by
D. Laor) 1958 (Hebrew).

23 Netiva Ben-Yehuda says similar things twenty years later in *Ben ha-Sefirot –
1948*, pp. 69–70. The sensation of clinging to the experience of youth and
friendship is still valid for the native-born writers of the 1940s generation.

> What is important is the ethos of friendship and society. In general – we
> all helped each other a lot. Everyone had a thousand-and-one tricks. And
> when none of them worked we weren't ashamed to ask a friend for help.
> Where do you take the strength to help, and the will, and how come you
> don't get annoyed with him – who knows? You run and hop to it to help,
> knock yourself out, and not only don't you curse, but you love this
> moment and you'll remember it forever and hanker for it and cling to it,
> and in all the rough moments in the future, you'll recall it and try to suck
> more 'help' from it. And we're also speaking about the moments when you
> helped and those moments when they helped you. You preserve it, lock it
> in your heart, in the place where you keep your most precious treasures,
> also how you'd kill yourself for a friend and how the friend would kill
> himself for you. These are the best things that you take with you from the
> war. That's your loot. Your inalienable assets. Which will be with you for
> the rest of your life. . . .

Compare also Yizhak Tischler: 'The period of my agricultural training was the
most beautiful in my life because I was lucky to be born in 1929. The struggle
and the War of Independence were for me, as for all my friends, the years of
maturing and could there be any more beautiful years to grow up in? Maturity.
A process that was sealed on this ridge. Malkiyya. [Site of the former Arab village
near the Lebanese border where Lebanese troops invaded Palestine and
were repulsed by Palmah units in May 1948.]' (Yizhak Tischler (born 1929),
Aharonim al ha-Rekhes ('The Last on the Ridge', 1970), p. 71. See also note 10.

24 Uri Orlev (born 1931) in his book *Hayyalei ha-Oferet* ('The Lead Soldiers', no
date) preceded Appelfeld in presenting the persecuted and survivors of the
Holocaust from the perspective of an innocent child who does not understand
the enormity of the horror. Appelfeld, however, opened a new vista for native
Israeli writers to present a different view of the Holocaust and its survivors. See,
for example, Haim Gouri's *Iskat ha-Shokolad*, Yoram Kaniuk's *Adam Ben Kelev*,
1968 (*Adam Resurrected*, 1971), David Schutz's *Ha-'Esev ve-ha-Hol*, 1978 ('The
Grass and the Sand', French edition 1981) and, finally, David Grossman's
Ayyen Erekh: Ahavah. For a discussion of the attitudes of various groups in Israel
to the Holocaust see Gershon Shaked, 'Facing the nightmare, Israeli literature
on the Holocaust', *The Nazi Concentration Camps* (Jerusalem, Yad Vashem,
1984), pp. 683–96.

25 See Meshulam Tochner, 'A change of the cultural guard', *Behinot be-Bikoret ha-
Sifrut* (1952), vol. 3, pp. 30–4. This is a very important article because it
expresses the concealed yearnings of Tochner's generation (Third and Fourth
Aliyah [1924–8]) for the 'new Hebrew' who will replace Brenner's detached
protagonists with whom Tochner's generation secretly identified while apparently revolting against them.

26 We have already cited some examples: from the exotic characters of Nissim
Aloni to the perverted ones of Dan-Benaya Seri. The mentality of the Jews of

Germany interested Nathan Shaham both in *Guf Rishon Rabbim* and in *Revi'iyat Rosendorf* ('Rosendorf Quartet', 1987) and Aharon Megged in his novella *Heinz, Beno ve-ha-Ruakh ha-Ra'ah* ('Heinz, Son, The Evil Spirit', 1975). One could cite a long list of additional examples.

19

THE JEWISH WRITER AND
THE PROBLEM OF EVIL

Ruth Wisse

In the United States at this time liberalism is not only the dominant but even the sole intellectual tradition. For it is the plain fact that nowadays there are no conservative or reactionary ideas in general circulation. This does not mean, of course, that there is no impulse to conservatism or to reaction. Such impulses are certainly very strong, perhaps even stronger than most of us know. But the conservative impulse and the reactionary impulse do not, with some isolated and some ecclesiastical exceptions, express themselves in ideas but only in action or in irritable mental gestures which seek to resemble ideas.[1]

Lionel Trilling's prefatory remarks to the very influential collection of essays on literature, *The Liberal Imagination* (1950), is an excellent starting-point for an examination of continuity in Jewish literature of the post-war period, since liberalism had become by the time of its publication the sole intellectual tradition of America, and even more so of the modern Jewish intellectual tradition. From the dawn of emancipation, the cast of modern literacy culture in Yiddish, the European Jewish vernacular, moved away from what were perceived to be the conservative and reactionary impulses of European politics and the imposed discipline of the Halakhic way of life – towards liberalism, an atmospheric term that signified the emancipation of the individual from the collectivity: the substitution of empirical investigation for faith as the province of mind, of Man for God as the determinant of history; a belief in progressive brotherliness and equalization of society, in a future infinitely better than the past and appreciably better than the present. Politically, Jews who wished to advance in post-feudal societies had to align themselves with liberal and left-of-liberal parties since the conservative and nationalist actions frequently promoted their cause by trying to limit Jewish advancement. If liberalism gradually overtook parts of Western society, it virtually captured modern Jews.

Consider Tevye the Dairyman, the most popular character in Jewish fiction, Sholem Aleichem's representation of the conservative Jew who bends to the pressure of liberalizing ideas. The most powerful of these ideas and chief warrant of the emancipation of the individual from society is love, and the monologues of this rural Ukrainian Jew, written over a period of twenty years, trace the impact of romantic love on two generations in tandem. Tevye's daughters argue that a father's child may marry according to the dictates of her heart rather than the dictates of her father because the heart is a truer moral guide. If acted upon, this idea is sufficient in itself to destroy any traditional society. 'It's beyond belief,' says Chava to her father, 'how you have a verse from the Bible for everything! Maybe you also have one that explains why human beings have to be divided into Jews and Christians, masters and slaves, beggars and millionaires . . .'.[2] A liberal egalitarian universalist, she knows that the artificial boundaries established by her father's tradition cannot be serviceable for children of the heart who recognize only the spontaneous brotherhood of humankind.

The religious way of life that Tevye observes distinguished itself by its ability to confront evil in the unredeemed world. Jews were the people who resisted all premature claims of Messianic redemption, insisting that observance of the Law was the only way to discipline the wayward human spirit. But by the time Tevye is forced to choose between the Jewish God who granted the Torah and the benevolent universalism of his daughter, he is already enough of a liberal himself to wonder whether Jewish particularism is altogether just. True, when Chava runs off to marry a Gentile he sits *shiva* for his daughter and refuses to let her name be spoken again. He does what every Jew must do who values Jewish continuity. Yet he tells us how close he comes to succumbing to Chava – this temptress of a daughter – over his nay-saying God. Had Chava's marriage to the Ukrainian Chvedko not required her conversion to another religion, and had there been no anti-Semitic priest to taunt Tevye with the loss of his daughter, we are provoked to wonder whether he might not have adjusted to the mixed marriage. In fact, in the episode that was written several years thereafter, involving Beylke the youngest daughter, Tevye the traditional father turns into the spokesman for romantic love, and protests Beylke's mercenary marriage because it was calculated on material rather than emotional considerations. He holds up to her as a model the older sister Hodel who ran off to Siberia with her revolutionary husband. (Here, as in Trilling's definition, the sincere liberal may not be a revolutionary, but he admires the 'idealism' of the revolutionary.) By the later chapters of this family saga Tevye himself distinguishes between, on the one hand, the spirit of loving-kindness that does not need to be buttressed by traditional forms of Jewish observance and, on the other, the materialist spirit that practises vulgarity and greed behind a mask of social conformism. Sholem Aleichem implicitly approves the substitution of liberal values for the Halakhic way of life as long as it does not require conversion, that is, a direct assault on the Jews in favour of another religion.

Thus, through the figure of Tevye, Sholem Aleichem suggested that Judaism could thoroughly accommodate itself to liberalism by recognizing in the Jewish religious tradition its essential spirit affinity with the new secular political movement. This was the minimal position of almost all the Yiddish writers between the two world wars, as well as of their American Jewish counterparts. Apart from Hillel Zeitlin in Warsaw, I know of no major modern Yiddish writer or intellectual of the inter-war period who upheld traditional values. Sholem Asch, the most famous Yiddish writer of the inter-war period, spent the late 1930s writing a trilogy on the life of Jesus to demonstrate the common origins of both Christianity and Judaism in a theology of love.[3] On the other side of the spectrum, David Bergelson's Yiddish novel *Midas Hadin* (1926) promoted the self-discipline demanded by communist totalitarianism, not Jewish Law.[4] Yiddish culture pronounced itself ready to offer sacrifice for the good of mankind but not for the Jewish idea of the good which appeared mean and exclusive.

During the 1920s and 1930s, Yiddish culture drifted decisively leftward, and communism, which presented itself as the ultimate incarnation of what liberalism was too cowardly to attain, loomed as the chief moral authority. Obviously, the majority of Yiddish writers and intellectuals were not communists, far from it. But in the shrinking world of Yiddish letters, communism exerted an increasingly powerful influence. The contrast between state support for Yiddish culture in the Soviet Union and its neglect elsewhere – the abandonment of Yiddish in America on the part of acculturating immigrants, the hostility to Yiddish in Palestine on the part of militant Hebraists, and the impoverished milleu within which Yiddish struggled to maintain itself in Poland – had to affect the political judgement and cultural taste of Yiddish writers.

The explosion of hope, of reckless self-consecration to the future, was part of the general *Zeitgeist*, for those young people who had survived the war must have been desperate to believe in its cleansing, redemptive powers. There were those like the youthful Peretz Markish who said that modern Yiddish literature was now reborn with the Revolution, and who, without ever joining the Bolsheviks or consigning any real political credit to the process of Bolshevization, seemed to hail the revolutionary spirit through the explosion of their metaphors and poetic diction. Whereas reliable political studies will draw a discrimination picture of the actual process of Sovietization through bureaucratic institutions and ac-cession to power, cultural struggles are often lost or won by the confident voice of a poet who declares himself the unacknowledged legislator of the world. The romantic energy of Yiddish culture between the wars was to be found in the revolutionary camp.

The communists put the rest of the Jewish cultural world so thoroughly on the defensive that they assumed a kind of rabbinic authority even for many of those who disagreed with their rulings. An example from the American scene dramatizes this influence: after the Arab riots in Palestine in August 1929, when the American Communist Yiddish newspaper *Freiheit*, following the Soviet Party line, condoned the slaughter of Jews in Hebron and Safed as the first welcome spark of an anti-imperialist revolution, many Yiddish writers who had written for the newspaper disocciated themselves publicly from its policy. Yet several months later, in the pages of the alternative newspaper the had established to affirm their political independence, the Yiddish poets Menaham Boreisho and H. Leivick wrote to a Zionist editorialist:

> If with a knife at our throat we would have to choose: You [the Zionists] or the Yevsektn [the Jewish communists], we will choose the Yevsektn. Not because they please us, they don't. But they are young, and behind them stands a great and fruitful idea. If they are blind in certain things, they may in time begin to see . . . they have the potential. YOUR camp is the generation of the desert, in every respect. It is perhaps brutal to say so but – your time has passed, in truth, forever.[5]

This was the voice of writers who had broken away from the communist camp. Nevertheless, they continued to accord value to communism and to invest it with hope, because within the literary intellectual community it was a matter of faith that progress from Jewish particularism to international socialism was inevitable, and they did not wish to be left behind on the road of progress. The synthesis which some of the writers and intellectuals claimed to be seeking between liberal and Jewish values was real enough, but it meant that the Jewish religion and nation would be subordinated to the liberal left, not leftism to the requirements of Jewish religion or nationhood.

So the question of continuity in Jewish intellectual and the literary life since the Second World War should be phrased as follows: Does liberalism as Trilling denied it and as Yiddish culture so enthusiastically embraced it remain the sole intellectual tradition of the Jews of our time?

In approaching this question, let us note at least a few qualifications to the general consensus on liberalism in Jewish *belles-lettres* prior to the Second World War. The most obvious of these is to be found in Hebrew literature. The Hebrew writers, Zionists by implication, were embarked on a much lonelier cultural endeavour, one rooted in the national experience of a particular people, and declared reactionary according to Communist fiat. The Hebrew writers were not, as were the Yiddish and English-speaking Jews, implicitly pinning their hopes on the anticipated tolerance of welcoming societies, but they were going it alone as a small people. Hebrew was a tribal language tied to a long and sorrowful literary heritage. Obviously, the revival of Hebrew as a spoken language, and the national impulse of political Zionism of which it formed a part, were also radical, secular and modern assaults on traditional Judaism; liberal ideas fed the Zionist movement no less than it did the Jewish Labor Bund. But the choice of Hebrew (at a time when it was only written by choice) implied qualification of the liberal outlook through association with a specific and unpopular people. It is no accident that Hebrew literature should have been so much grimmer, more pessimistic than its Yiddish counterpart.[6]

By the mid-1930s a number of Yiddish writers had also begun to demur from the dominant liberal-left. Isaac Bashevis Singer's astonishing novel *Satan in Goray*, called anachronistic when it was published in 1935, was the first salvo of Bashevis's lifelong war against the tidal wave of liberal optimism that swept away his generation before it was swept away by the Nazis.[7] Two American Yiddish writers who returned to Poland in the 1930s – Jacob Glatstein and Judd Teller – were sufficiently affected by their encounter with Polish Jewry to close the door, however reluctantly, on Western civilization. Sobered by their awareness of the looming threat of anti-Semitism on the left and the right, they quit the cosmopolitan camp to return to the 'dust' of the Jewish street.[8] For Teller, this meant the temporary abandonment of poetry as a craft. In general, the minority of Yiddish writers who demurred from the liberal consensus wrote as grimly as Agnon, but they remained a minority.

The Liberal optimism of Yiddish culture did not survive the Second World War. Its future tense evaporated, and the present tense was not too strong either. Memorialization became the overriding preoccupation of the Yiddish remnant, of ordinary Jews who felt compelled to record their wartime or pre-war experiences in personal or communal *yizkor* books, as well as of the most sophisticated writers. Actually, the commemorative or anthropological impulse had been part of Yiddish literature right from its emergence in the modern period. Even such pioneering Yiddish writers of the nineteenth century as Yisroel Axenfeld, Ayzik Meir Dik and Yitskhok Yoel Linetski knew that as the critics of a rapidly evolving society, they had to try to preserve in literature what they were trying to alter in life. Nostalgia played an especially prominent role in Yiddish drama, and there is hardly a play in the modern Yiddish repertoire, from Abraham Goldfaden and Jacob Gordin onwards, that does not contain at least one or two traditional scenes of a wedding, a circumcision, a Sabbath ceremony, or some other ritual. The masterpiece of the Yiddish state and film, S. Ansky's *The Dybbuk*, is a virtual tapestry of folk elements woven into a tight dramatic whole.[9]

After the destruction of the Jewish communities of Europe the task of commemoration assumed an unparalleled urgency, not simply for the sake of record, but as part of an altered philosophic position that now looked to the past for transcendent value. At the dramatic centre of a number of Abraham Sutzkever's prose, poems and poetic tales are endangered Yiddish words, quirks of speech of a former relative or neighbour or expressions common to his Vilna street or region that had now to be fixed to prevent their disappearance forever. Before the war, Sutzkever had been part of the dynamic literary group Yung Vilna that joked about '*die laydn fun yunge verter*' (the sorrows of young words), punning on Goethe's *The Sorrows of*

Young Werther. Overnight, surviving Yiddish writers had been turned into custodians of the once-young words of a flourishing language, now pushed to the brink of extinction.[10]

After the war, Yiddish culture could no longer deny the ubiquity of evil. It had to admit the insufficiency of liberalism as an explanation of events, and as a means of influencing them. One could argue that nothing the Jews might have done in Europe could have affected their fate at the hands of so determined an enemy, but conceptually, as a view of the world, liberalism had been exposed as the falsest messiah of them all. The child held up on its mother's shoulders for its last gasp of air in the gas chamber could hardly be impressed with the certainty that the emancipation of reason would result in the emancipation of mankind, or in the probability of human progress, or in the kindly dictates of the heart. Because that child of Yiddish culture also represented the future of Yiddish culture, writers in the language had to credit its experience (as the English and Hebrew literary communities did not).

The enormity of the evil that selected the Jews as its target seemed to recall something weirdly familiar. The Jews were once again the chosen people. As Hannah Arendt argued in *The Origins of Totalitarianism*, anti-Semitism served as the negative organizing principle of both the anti-democratic left and right, and (as in enthusiasm for her theory she also overlooked) it still remained the organizing ideology of powerful nationalist, anti-totalitarian movements.[11] Totalitarian ideologies and nationalist passions swept liberalism away as one might swat a fly, and used the Jew – alternately the Jew as capitalist conservative and the Jew as radical reformer – to explain what was most corrupt or terrifying in the process of modernization. The Jew was 'at the bottom of the pile' of Europe's collapse because he was accused of having eaten away at its solid foundations. Any lingering temptation to seek refuge in the left was scuttled by Stalin's round-up and murder of Yiddish writers, a mass execution that once again struck at the Yiddish sector of Jewry in particular.[12]

The Yiddish writers were forced to see what others could ignore, that modernity had appointed the Jews as the proof of liberalism's failure as an interpretive view of the world. Jews might have abandoned their divine mission for the human scale of life on earth, but they had been rendered mythic in the imagination of enemies. Whether or not they had ever been an idea in the mind of God, the Jews were now an *idée-fixe* in the mind of the world: as the projection of evil, they were its designated target. The extremity of the idea of Jew-hatred forced the return of the idea of God.

God, a very Jewish God, makes a strong comeback in post-war Yiddish literature. For some writers *He* is the only addressee there is left to talk to in Yiddish, for others the only sufficiently worthy antagonist. Kadya Molodovsky writes: '*El khonen* God of Mercy/ choose/ another people./ We are tired of death, tired of corpses. Choose/ another people.'[13]

Aaron Zeitlin explores his God in dozens of poems:

> Being a Jew means running forever to God
> even if you are His betrayer . . .[14]

But elsewhere Zeitlin insists on just the opposite: 'As it is written: *mekheyni-no*/ erase me/ *misifrekho* – from your book/ *asher kotavto* – that you have written/ and in which you inscribed me./ Pretend/ that I was never a letter in your book.'[15]

Jacob Glatstein breathes paradox as he taunts God for His vanishing act: '*On yidn vet nisht zayn kayn yidisher got*. Without Jews, no Jewish God./ If, God forbid, we should quit/ this world, Your poor tent's light would out.'[16]

God is the vehicle of rage. Chaim Grade instructs the corpse of a Jew who was killed in the Kielce pogrom: 'Don't forgive if even God Himself should come to you in the grave/ And on his knees ask your forgiveness for the world.'[17]

The God of *shfoykh khamoskho* who had symbolized for the liberal Jew everything most narrow and chauvinistic in the Jewish psyche is the God to whom Yiddish writers returned, the very God who made divinity necessary. Here is Judd Teller's *tfile fun a yid in di hayntike teg*:

> O God of holy rage!
> Take revenge on the uncircumcised of Germany.
> Gird yourself in the great deeds of our legend.
> Contaminate them with the illness that rusts the marrow of the
>   bones.
> That cracks the joints and corrodes the knuckles
> And causes the penis to bleed as is not in the nature of a man.
> As you would flatten tin, hammer their bodies
> so that nothing survives
> their lust for our daughters and wives.[18]

The sound of the Yiddish original is as harsh as the meaning: *farkrenk zey mit der krenk vos makht rost funem markh in di beyner/ zhavert di knokhn un brekht di gelenken/ un makht dem zeykher blutikn vi s'iz gornit di teve fun a man*. Teller offers up this prayer in the name of the saintly Hasidic Rabbi Levi Yitzkhok of Berdichev, famed for his heart-rending petitions to God. The sweet and gentle Jewish *zaddik* had belatedly discovered that all men did not try to perfect themselves by reining in their aggression. Because the Jewish God had been aware of this all along, He was ultimately trust-worthy, and called back by the Yiddish remnant into service.

In a similar vein, *The Magician of Lublin* is Bashevis Singer's parable of the modern Jew.[19] The magician Yasha in this post-war novel about pre-war Poland is the secular Yeshu, a god-like artist who can charm the natural world. He can break free of any man-made lock. He can speak to animals and enthral women. Through his mastery he has found a way of spanning the Jewish and Gentile worlds, and when the book takes him up, at the height of his powers, he has found a way of satisfactorily juggling his traditional Jewish wife, his peasant Polish mistress, the coarse widow of a thief, and a very aristocratic Christian lady who seems to want him as badly as he wants her. But there is something that trips him up – something in himself more than in the surroundings, though it is clear that even had he retained his powers, the Poles would not have allowed him to walk his tightrope indefinitely. While attempting a robbery, to get enough money to run away with his Christian beloved, he falls and sprains his ankle. What is revealed to Yasha through his fall is that he cannot be trusted: once the Jew becomes a little bit secular and makes himself rather than the Torah the arbiter of his life, he becomes part of the evil that the Law was designed to curb. Yasha's liberal instincts lead him inexorably towards sin, and he cannot rely on them to keep him good. So he immures himself, literally, in a self-made cell, just as another Penitent in a later Bashevis Singer novel will immure himself behind the symbolic gates of Mea Shearim.[20] While the protagonists of Bashevis Singer either recognize the human potential for evil as the Torah does and live by its laws, or follow the ways of the gentiles and become indistinguishable from them, their author worked both sides of the street; preaching sanctity, he wrote about sin. In full awareness of his own performance on the moral tightrope, Bashevis Singer adopted and felt most comfortable in the literary voice of the demon. In his imagination the modern writer is the demon who exploits liberalism and licence as the most effective tools of his trade.

Singer's submersion in evil puzzled many readers. He was accused of misrepresenting his Jewish ancestors who had developed a civilization of remarkable containment, self-discipline and decency. The protest is morally valid, for Singer did distort and exaggerate the world of his ancestors, but it is artistically irrelevant. Limited as Singer was in his knowledge of the Yiddish-speaking world of Polish Jews, he was forced to express whatever view he held of life within its confines. As the son of a rabbi and a rabbi's daughter, he appears to have ascribed to the strictures of his parents the powers of the super-ego, punishing those of his heroes and heroines who succumbed, as he did, to the *id*. Missing is the middle ground of the resilient ego that insists on becoming itself. One could argue that the Manichean spirit of much of Bashevis Singer's fiction is itself alien to 'rabbinic Judaism' and a product of the same gentile influence he was decrying. But our subject here is the fate of the liberal consciousness in post-war Yiddish culture, and that consciousness Bashevis discredited in text after text.

A man admires his own wisdom and is proud of his knowledge, but as soon as a little desire begins to stir in him he forgets everything else. Reason is like a dog on a leash who follows sedately in his master's footsteps – until he sees a bitch. . . . Any man can rationalize whatever he wants to do. Is it true that only a little while ago he was saying the opposite of what he is now saying? He'll tell you he was wrong then. And if he lets you prove to him that he wasn't wrong then, he'll shrug and say, 'When I want to do something, I can't be an Aristotle.' . . . The one way out is this. A man should choose between good and evil only as the Law chooses for him. The Law wants him to be happy. . . . Even when a man understands rationally what he should do, he must never forget that before all else he should do it because the Law tells him to do it. That is how he can guard against the time when his reason will have no power to command him.[21]

This quotation is not from the fiction of Bashevis Singer, but from the work of his major rival Chaim Grade. It is the voice of the antagonist in 'My quarrel with Hersh Rasseyner', an essay in fictional form, written in 1951, that might have served as the prooftext for the topic 'Continuity and change in Jewish life after World War II.' Rasseyner and Chaim Vilner, Grade's fictional representation of himself, had been students in the Mussarist yeshiva before Vilner quit the movement in 1930 to become a secular Yiddish writer. The story chronicles three accidental meetings between them, two before the war in Poland, and a third chance encounter in Paris after the war.

Their meeting on the far side of the chasm of the Holocaust confirms Jewish continuity, since they take up their pre-war argument as if nothing had changed. Rasseyner is more firmly convinced than ever before of the need for Halakhah, while Vilner argues as strongly as he did before the war for the greatness of the artistic spirit that breathes life into stone. Grade ascribes to Vilner the humanist spirit of *Yo* – [Yes!] – the book of poems of forced affirmation that he had published in the 1930s, and of his long narrative poem about the Mussarists that repudiates their stifling ethicism.[22] But whereas Grade had once taken absolutely for granted the ethical and philosophic superiority of Western liberalism over the harshly ascetic brand of Judaism in which he had been educated, he now ascribes to Hersh Rasseyner his antagonist a powerful counter-argument against European humanism. After Hitler, the tables are turned. As Chava once got the better of Tevye in her 1906 argument with him, so in a literary reversal, Hersh Rasseyner scores over Chaim Vilner in their sustained Parisian debate of the late 1940s. Whereas Grade's post-war fiction still accords the spirit of liberalism a much more robust position than it is allowed in Bashevis Singer's work, all his most convincing creations – Hersh Rasseyner, the Rebetsin in the story of that title, and Tsamakh Atlas in the novel *The Yeshiva* – are temperamentally vicious, irascible old-fashioned moralists; it is their spirit that prevails in the best of his work.

We attempt to speak of the Jewish people as though it were an indivisible entity, yet an inquiry into the continuity of Jewish culture in the post-war period offers a serious challenge to this assumption, at least as regards Jewish writers and intellectuals. Judging from literature, the experience of secular Jews is determined by their political environment, and almost entirely dictated by linguistic circumstance. While the Yiddish writers were bound to the European fate by their European language, American Jews writing in English were imaginatively detached from the fate of the Jews of Europe, both during and after the war. By now historians have tried to spread the responsibility for the destruction of European Jewry to almost everybody in America, from the Roosevelt administration to the Zionist Organization. But the most striking of omissions (if one is going to talk in these terms) is the attitude of American Jewish intellectuals both during and after the war, to the fate of the Jews. I intend to address this question in detail elsewhere,[23] but here let me put the matter very crudely. The worst of times for European Jewry was the beginning of the best of times for American Jewry, and especially for the Jewish intellectuals. The unqualified triumph of liberalism as Trilling describes it reflects the buoyant post-war spirit of America, of which the Jewish writers and intellectuals were among the chief beneficiaries. The erasure of the Yiddish Jews in Europe and the national resurgence of the Hebrew Jews in Israel benefited to an equal degree the English Jews of America and allowed them to nourish their optimistic and rational view of the human species without unseemingly historical distraction. Graced with the mystique of victims on the one hand, and with the phoenix-image of reinvigoration on the other, American Jews including writers and intellectuals found their status transformed without any cost to themselves at the hands of either European or Arab enemies.

Some of this Trilling may have realized himself, though he makes no direct reference to it in his critique of the liberal imagination. Because, of course, the passage with which I began the paper was part of Trilling's subtle but most penetrating re-examination of liberalism in the spirit of *khatat neurim*, the sins of youth. By the time he published *The Liberal Imagination* in 1950, Trilling had come to realize some of the serious limitations of the predominant views of his culture, and it was these he subjected to scrutiny in this series of critical essays. Psychoanalysis, in particular, had made Trilling realize the failure of what he called the liberal imagination to credit some of the most important parts of human experience:

> So far as liberalism is active and positive, so far, that is, as it moves toward organization, it tends to select the emotions and qualities that are most susceptible of organization. As it carries out its active and positive ends it unconsciously limits its view of the world to what it can deal with, and it unconsciously tends to develop theories and principles, particularly in relation to the human mind, that justify its limitation.[24]

Trilling worried that in its dedication to progress and reason, liberalism drifts towards a denial of the emotions and imagination. He dramatized some of the connections between liberalism's failure of imagination and the dangerous consequences of that failure in his novel *Middle of the Journey* (1947), without once, however, referring to its effect on the fate of the Jews.

Middle of the Journey is a novel of ideas that marks a significant turning-point in American intellectual history.[25] It sets out three major positions through a trio of characters: Gifford Maxim, modelled on Whittaker Chambers, is a communist spy who has just broken with the party because of a powerful religious impulse, and is trying to resume a visible American identity to prevent being killed by Moscow's agents; the 'sincere liberal' Nancy Croom and her husband Arthur are fellow travellers who do everything to help the party, short of joining its ranks; John Laskell is a New York intellectual, a friend of both Maxim and the Crooms.

Laskell, who comes closest to representing the book's point of view, finds fault with the Crooms in three interrelated ways: first, he is angry that they are unable to deal with death. The book opens when Laskell is recovering from a near-fatal illness, but cannot talk to them about his experience because there is no room in their positive view of life for the things that lie beyond their control. A liberalism that cannot respond to and live readily with death is destructive to the life it pretends to enhance.

This denial of death is closely linked to the denial of evil. A sub-plot in the novel involves a suburban version of natural man, a local drunk whom the Crooms employ. The Crooms refuse to recognize the irresponsible, anti-social and exceedingly dangerous qualities of this man, and their indulgence of him encourages his wickedness and contempt. A liberalism that ignores and misrepresents the destructive impulses of human nature promotes the barbarian.

The programmatic optimism of the Crooms is closely linked to their embrace of communism. The Crooms are such committed ideological liberals that they cannot believe in the murderous deeds of the Soviets, even when the evidence is placed squarely before them. Had it been up to them, they would have let Gifford Maxim be shot many times over rather than re-examine the basis of their credulity. When the communist rejects the evil of his past association, they cannot forgive him for shattering their ideal. The book reveals that liberal morality, which prides itself on its benevolence and charity, is actually the enabling partner of evil in both its personal and political manifestations.

We might think of this novel as a kind of 'My quarrel with the Crooms', in which Trilling confronts the liberal orthodoxy that had replaced Jewish orthodoxy. Like Chaim Grade, Lionel Trilling remains dialectically yoked to the faith in which he had been raised, but being, as it were, a further generation removed from Halakhic Judaism, Trilling is already a liberal by faith, not a Jew by faith. In recognition of this fact, the character who bears his ideas in the book is not a Jew, and when Trilling speaks in his writings as 'we', he means we of the English literary-intellectual liberal tradition.

This de-judaization, by denuding the central character John Laskell of any social substance, may have cost Trilling a great deal artistically, but it speaks most powerfully to the state of the American Jewish literary tradition of his time. Trilling was certain that the guiding principles and shaping ideas as well as the ideals of his generation had been formulated by such 'secular rabbis' as Hegel and Marx, John Stuart Mill and Matthew Arnold, and that the bit of ethnic coloration his parents had contributed to his identity was irrelevant to his artistic-intellectual life. He did not consider this a 'denial' of Jewishness, but an acknowledgement of cultural realities. The American Jewish writers and intellectuals, raised in the American public school system, in a splendid culture of democratic impulse, and in left-wing finishing schools, were confirmed liberals not confirmed Jews. If *Middle of the Journey* is a landmark in American cultural history – and I believe it is – then the eclipse of the Jews is as important as all else that figures within the novel.

All the same, though John Laskell is not a Jew, and although the fate of European Jewry is nowhere mentioned, Lionel Trilling's exposure of liberalism to moral scrutiny admitted the possible legitimacy of the Jewish experience, at least by implication. The issues that separate Laskell from the Crooms were the very same issues that had alienated American Jewish intellectuals from their threatened co-religionists (if the term be allowed). The Jews (like Laskell) had been singled out for death; they had been betrayed by communism in obverse proportion to their hopes for its protection, and they were irrefutable proof that the malice of the underclass, if condoned by theories of natural goodness, will be provoked to ever-greater acts of violence. Sincere liberals like the Crooms would have had to choose between Jews and their liberal faith, because they could not rescue the first without defying the second. John Laskell marks the dividing line between the liberal left that turns against the Jews, and the liberal right, or what later came to be called neo-conservativism that fights communism and otherwise engages in political self-defence. He represents the earliest example of the post-war reckoning among American Jewish intellectuals, who had either to rethink their sincere liberalism in these very same terms or to keep distancing themselves from questions of Jewish survival as incompatible with their beliefs.

American Jewish culture has since then split along these lines: writers and intellectuals like Saul Bellow and Norman Podhoretz and Cynthia Ozick who ask liberalism for an accounting are free to defend the Jews outright. They are not subject to divided loyalties. Those who remain true to the optimistic spirit of liberalism and political leftism like Grace Paley and Irving Howe and E. L. Doctorow must keep the Jews on trial because Jewish national and religious experience contradicts the canons of their faith.

For writers of the second kind, suffering is the only safe ground where the Jewish experience does not conflict with liberal assumptions. Bernard

Malamud's Jewish sufferers are prophets of liberalism. The shopkeeper in
The Assistant, Morris Bober, explains to his Christian apostle Frank Alpine
that to be truly Jewish does not require adherence to a formal tradition,
but rather to the spirit of goodness that lies behind the tradition. This is
subsequently confirmed in the novel by the rabbi who in delivering Morris
Bober's eulogy agrees that 'he was true to the spirit of our life – to want for
others that which he wants also for himself . . . he suffered . . . he endured,
with hope'.[26] The idea of Jewishness that is espoused by Malamud is actually
a Christian idea of suffering, so that when Frank Alpine converts to Judaism
one Passover through circumcision, both the symbolism of resurrection and
the value system of pain derive more from the Christian idea of the Jew than
from any idea of Jewish nationhood, religion or civilization. Malamud
forged a literary style in English that is highly evocative of Yiddish, so that
his writing appears to be steeped in the culture of traditional Jewishness.
Yet, thematically, the Jewishness of the Jews was as alien to Malamud as it
was to Arthur Miller, Lillian Hellman, Clifford Odets and a host of others.
Arthur Miller's protest novel against anti-Semitism, *Focus*, and Laura
Hobson's similarly pitched novel *Gentleman's Agreement* include, as part of
their defence of the Jews, an explicit repudiation of the idea of Jewish
peoplehood.

Obviously, individual works of literature are not reducible to the categories that one may use to describe them, and any such broad cultural
overview as I am attempting can be refined by any number of exceptions
and qualifications. But certain trends do emerge from this general analysis.
The appointment of the Jews – by various European political movements in
the first part of the century, by various Arab movements in the second
part of the century – as targets of genocide – has made Jews the testing
ground of liberalism very much against their will. The liberal faith that most
Jewish writers and intellectuals embraced in the modern period in the hope
that it would prove their salvation was quite simply contradicted by the
experience of the Jewish people as a whole. Even if one could have arranged
a convenient marriage between liberalism and Judaism as the Reform
movement tried to do within the Jewish family, that still left the powerful
reality of anti-Jews who could not be reshaped by the creative imagination
alone.

What we call the Jewish reality did not involve all sectors of the Jewish
people to the same degree. The destruction of Yiddish culture imposed on
Yiddish writers a knowledge that their American Jewish counterparts were
freer to ignore. Thus the tradition of liberalism could persist in English, and
in some sectors of American Jewish culture enjoy a post-war revival, even as
Yiddish culture was pricked into terrible sobriety.

One final note: in a curious reversal, Hebrew literature, which was
formerly the outstanding exception to the pervasive liberalism of Yiddish
and American Jewish literature, has now become its home. There are Israeli

writers and intellectuals who claim, not with Trilling's uneasiness but with considerable pride, that the liberalism of the left is 'not only the dominant but even the sole intellectual tradition' of Israel today.[27] When the State of Israel took its place in the community of nations with a socialist government to boot, it became the new repository of Jewish liberal hopes, and the young Israeli writers who grew up in what their ideology had promised would be a normal country, have been intent on joining the international brotherhood of writers, which is a liberal union. The Hebrew experience had once seemed antithetical to universalist egalitarian humanist ideals because it had to protect – through arms and through national allegiance – a particular people with an ancient pedigree. Once the second generation of Israeli writers became intent on proving themselves part of the great brotherhood of poets, they became arch-liberals, repeating exactly the pattern of the Yiddish writers in their first courtship of the great wide world a century earlier.

In that kind of spontaneous creative impulse that tells us so much more than the author thought he was revealing, David Grossman placed at the centre of his novel *See: Under Love* a series of stories of radical innocence about the 'children of the heart'. The hero of the novel, himself a writer, adopts as his inspiration these Yiddish stories that were composed by his uncle between the world wars in Poland, and he wants to wrap himself in the mantle of what he believes to be their profound moral truth. It is clear that Grossman is not only in love with these children of the heart, but believes that this model of innocence survived the destruction of all the innocent children as Auschwitz. For all his creative brilliance and keen intelligence, the author does not see the irony of his attraction to that part of the Jewish moral impulse that was the most profoundly discredited by history and cultural history.

Liberal orthodoxy in post-war Jewish culture has shifted from the once-most-threatened Jewish sphere in Europe to the currently-most-threatened Jewish sphere in Israel. In American Jewish culture it is a matter of debate.

NOTES

1 Lionel Trilling, *The Liberal Imagination: Essays on Literature and Society* (New York, Viking, 1950). The preface from which this passage is taken is dated New York, December 1949.

2 Sholem Aleichem, 'Chava', in *Tevye the Dairyman and the Railroad Stories*, trans. Hillel Halkin (New York, Schocken Books, 1987), p. 72.

3 Sholem Asch, *The Nazarene*, trans. Maurice Samuel (New York, Putnam, 1939); *The Apostle*, trans. Maurice Samuel (New York, Putnam, 1943); *Mary*, trans. Leo Steinberg (London, Macdonald, 1950).

4 David Bergelson, *Midas Hadin*, parallel editions in Kiev and Vilna, 1929.

5 Editorial, *Vokh*, issue 3, 18 October 1929. I presented an unpublished paper of this publication at the Harvard Symposium on History and Literature, April 1982. In the lengthy statement of purpose of the first issue (4 October 1929)

point 5 reads: 'We consider the October Revolution the greatest event in the life of past generations. By transferring power to the hands of workers, the Revolution simultaneously liberated nations, ensured their independence, and undertook the development of their cultures.'

6 The philosophic and temperamental pessimism of Joseph Chaim Brenner, Micah Joseph Berdichewski, Chaim Nahman Bialik and others associated with the modern Hebrew renaissance is heavier than the mood of most of their Yiddish literary contemporaries; the subject awaits a full comparative study.

7 Isaac Bashevis Singer, *Der sotn in goray* (1935) trans. *Satan in Goray*, by Jacob Sloan (New York, Noonday Press, 1955).

8 The phrase appears in Jacob Glatstein's famous poem 'A gute nakht, velt' dated April 1938, trans. 'Good Night, World', by Benjamin and Barbara Harshav (eds), *American Yiddish Poetry* (Berkeley, Los Angeles and London, University of California Press, 1986), pp. 305–7. Analysis of J. L. Teller's philosophic reorientation in Dan Miron, 'J. L. Teller: upsurge and collapse of American Yiddish modernism', in *Ha-sifrut*, New Series 3–4 (Summer 1986), pp. 55–90 (Hebrew).

9 S. Ansky, 'The Dybbuk', trans. Golda Werman in David G. Roohies (ed.), *The Dybbuk and Other Writings*, (New York, Schocken, 1992), pp. 1–49.

10 This idea is developed somewhat more fully in my introduction to Abraham Sutzkever, *Di nevue fun shvartsaplen* (Prophecy of the Inner Eye) (Jerusalem, Magnes Press, 1989), pp. v–xix.

11 Hannah Arendt, *The Origins of Totalitarianism*, 2nd edn (Cleveland and New York, Meridian Books, 1958).

12 The actual quotation from T. S. Eliot's 'Burbank with a Baedeker: Bleistein with a cigar', reads: 'The rats are underneath the piles./ The Jew is underneath the lot'. *The Complete Poems and Plays 1909–1950* (New York, Harcourt, Brace & Co., 1952), p. 24.

13 Kadya Molodovsky, '*El Khonan*', trans. 'God of Mercy' by Irving Howe in *The Penguin Book of Modern Yiddish Verse*, Irving Howe, Ruth R. Wisse and Khone Shmeruk (eds) (New York, Viking 1987), pp. 330–3.

14 Aaron Zeitlin, '*Zayn a Yid*', trans. 'To be a Jew' by Robert Friend in *The Penguin Book of Modern Yiddish Verse*, op. cit., pp. 538–9.

15 Aaron Zeitlin. Where no translator is cited, the translations are mine.

16 Jacob Glatstein, '*On Yidn*', trans. 'Without Jews' by Cynthia Ozick in *The Penguin Book of Modern Yiddish Verse*, op. cit., pp. 434–7.

17 '*Kelts*' (dated Lodz, 1946) in *Shayn fun farloshene shtern* (Light of Extinguished Stars) (Buenos Aires, Association of Polish Jews in Argentina, 1950), p. 74.

18 J. L. Teller, '*Di tfile fun a yid in di havntike teg* (Prayer of a Jew of Today), in *Durkh yidishn gemit* (Tel Aviv, Israelbukh, 1975), pp. 86–7.

19 Isaac Bashevis Singer, *The Magician of Lublin*, trans. Elaine Gottlieb and Joseph Singer (New York, Noonday Press, 1960). Only subsequently was the book published in its Yiddish original, *Der kuntsmmakher fun lublin* (Tel Aviv, Hamenora Publishing House, 1971).

20 Isaac Bashevis Singer, *Der bal-tshuva* (Tel Aviv, Peretz Farlag, 1974); *The Penitent* (New York, Farrar, Straus & Giroux, 1983).

21 Chaim Grade, '*Mayn Krig mit hersh rasseyner* (1951), trans. 'My Quarrel with Hersh Rasseyner' by Milton Himmelfarb in *A Treasury of Yiddish Stories*, 2nd edn, Irving Howe and Eliezer Greenberg (eds), (New York, Viking, 1981), pp. 624–51. The quotation is from p. 635.

22 Chaim Grade, *Yo* (Vilna, 1936); *Musarnikes* (Vilna, 1939).

23 Unpublished paper on the New York Intellectuals at the Annual Conference of

the Association for Jewish Studies, Boston, 1990. See also 'The New York (Jewish) intellectuals', in *Commentary* (November 1987), pp. 28–38.

24 Lionel Trilling, Preface, op. cit.

25 Lionel Trilling, *Middle of the Journey* (New York, Viking, 1947).

26 Bernard Malamud, *The Assistant* (New York, Farrar, Straus & Cudahy, 1957).

27 At the recorded proceedings of the conference on 'The writer in the Jewish community: an Israeli–North American dialogue', in Berkeley, 24 October 1988, Amos Elon claimed that Israel was the only country in which *all* the intellectuals were in political agreement. Among the Israeli participants who were present were Haim Beer, Meir Shalev, Meir Wieseitier, Dahlia Ravikovitch, Ruth Almog and others – only Hanoch Bartov protested against this characterization.

20

STATE AND REAL ESTATE
Territoriality and the modern Jewish imagination

Sidra DeKoven Ezrahi

> *I like a golem believed everyone. In the first place,*
> *everything is possible, as it is written in the Wisdom of*
> *the Fathers, I've forgotten just how. . . .*

Forgetting, like remembering, can be a collaborative effort, and may even be compounded rather than alleviated by the recuperative effort of translation. The above passage is from Saul Bellow's famous translation of Isaac Bashevis Singer's short story, 'Gimpel the Fool'.[1] It is in this text, which has become something of a classic in modern Jewish literature, that Gimpel and his bride, the 'virgin' Elka, stand under the canopy while the 'master of revels makes a "God 'a mercy" in memory of the bride's parents'.[2] The distance between 'God 'a mercy' and *El maleh rahamim* is, it seems, the terrain that Gimpel *tam* must cross in order to enter the pages of *Partisan Review* and become naturalized on American soil. The year is 1953. Can it be said now, over forty years later, that the deterritorialized 'God 'a mercy' – Gimpel in a Baptist church, as it were – served as a marker or way-station until readers would be ready once again to hear *El maleh rahamim* under the *huppah*? Or is this displacement, like Gimpel's forgetting the prooftext from Pirkei Avot, symptomatic of a more endemic condition – a kind of collective Alzheimer's – in relation to which there could be dramatic acts of compensation but no recovery?

There was, in any case, as much cover-up as exposure in Bellow's 'Gimpel'. The translation that launched Bashevis Singer's American career made the text available without making it transparent, so obscuring many of the original signs as to render them all but irretrievable.[3] The mass migration of Jews from Eastern Europe to the United States had been followed, within one generation, by a cultural amnesia that is manifested in the displacement of Jewish territories and texts.

There are in effect two levels of effacement here. When Gimpel forgets the passage from Scriptures, the presumption is that his primary, intra-textual, audience will 'remember'; but Bashevis Singer, writing the original Yiddish story in America in 1945, when already faded memories of canonic Jewish texts are being undermined altogether by the annihilation of the world that housed those texts, could be invoking the signs of a more radical loss.[4] Every act of literary appropriation becomes from now on an act of rescue, measured not within the normal parameters of inter-linguistic discourse but as one more outpost against oblivion. With the appearance of Bellow's Gimpel and Irving Howe and Eliezer Greenberg's 'treasury' of Yiddish stories, 1953 becomes the year that inaugurates the American attempt to reclaim a lost Jewish place and a severed Jewish story.

'I am Gimpel the fool. I don't think myself a fool . . .' the American Gimpel announces. Eleven years later, in 1964, Gimpel's translator published a novel that begins, 'If I'm out of my mind, it's all right with me, thought Moses Herzog.'[5] As privileged readers we come to the text expecting that Herzog is no more out of his mind than Gimpel is a fool.[6] Bellow in his translation has provided not only cultural mediation but also the sub-text for his own writing; I. B. Singer becomes, perhaps more than any other East European Jewish writer in America, the most authentic and authenticating Jewish reference, as his shtetl becomes authentic Jewish geography.[7] We can also recognize in this little inter-textual transaction a cultural type who managed to survive the war and the rocky voyage between Jewish spaces and languages. Ruth Wisse defined the type in her illuminating book on the shlemiel as modern hero.[8] The transmigration of the fool, with his clearly defined social role in the European imagination, into the neurotic academic in his American isolation suggests something about the cultural contexts and their respective definition of the critical outsider.

Moving east and translated into Hebrew, the shlemiel never made it past the port authorities in Israel. Natan Alterman even wrote his epitaph in the wartime poem, *Mikhtav shel Menahem Mendel* ('Menahem Mendel's Letter'). Published in *Hatur hashevi'i* on 9 March 1945, Menahem Mendel's 'letter' to his wife Shaineh Shendel contains a graphic report on the deaths of the characters in Sholem Aleichem's house of fiction. But these lines are more than a memorial to the Yiddish spirit; they also serve as a compassionate barrier of exclusion of certain non-viable figures from Eretz Israel:

> . . . *'ad nizavnu betokh hagolah,*
> *abirei hehalom,*
> *geonei ha'oni,*
> *giborei hasifrut hayehudit hagedolah,*
> *hanofelet basheleg kamoni . . .*[9]

Tevye, Mottl, Pinyi, Stempenyu and Menahem Mendel himself – the quixotic 'knights of the dream', 'geniuses of penury', 'heroes of the great Jewish literature that falls in the snow' in the very midst of (*betokh*) a place called *golah* – are by definition unsuited for the topography and climate of Palestine. The viability of the shlemiel in America and his near-extinction in Israel may be a function of such atmospheric forces exercised on Jewish characters in different spaces. Following Dov Sadan, Ruth Wisse suggests an affinity, at least in popular European culture, between the Wandering Jew and the shlemiel; Peter Schlemihl's 'lack of a shadow . . . is the closest metaphorical equivalent for the lack of a homeland'.[10] And Paul Celan, survivor of labour camps in Transnistria, living in France and writing in German – perhaps the most unmoored Jewish poet in the post-Holocaust world – wrote, in his prose-parable, *Gespräch im Gebirg*, of the Jew who left his house and set out through the mountains, 'went under clouds, went in the shadow, his own and not his own – because the Jew, you know, what does he have that is really his own, that is not borrowed, taken and not returned . . .'.[11]

It goes without saying that even if they make it to the 'homeland', not all of the ingathered are content to stay put. The dialectics of a culture predicated on the teleology of territory as *homeland* and travel as *homecoming* almost requires the adversarial presence of dislocated and unpatriated souls. In no smaller measure after the Second World War than in the early decades of the century, what seems to distinguish the Hebrew *helekh* or *talush* or *mehager* (the wanderer, the misfit)[12] from his American Jewish counterpart is precisely the dark and heavy shadow he must drag with him over consecrated ground, the burden of territoriality and the elusiveness of homecoming. His subversive presence within Hebrew culture reflects a normative intolerance for the gap in which the shlemiel thrives elsewhere – the gap between inner and outer reality or between ideal and real worlds. Gimpel is, ultimately, the shlemiel as storyteller, the wandering bard whose gullibility is a kind of negative capability generative of an infinity of possible worlds: 'There were really no lies. Whatever doesn't really happen is dreamed at night. It happens to one if it doesn't happen to another, tomorrow if not today, or a century hence if not next year.'[13] The Israeli struggle with reality as an unrealized utopia may encourage the imagination to remain confined within more rigid binary structures.[14]

Tested by such liminal figures as the shlemiel, the wanderer and the storyteller, the Zionist cultural alternatives are meant to reify and stabilize collective visions of redeemed spaces and stories; not only grounded in this soil, but coterminous with it, the sacred texts and language are repatriated and once again become autochthonous. Territory and text are as public and overdetermined in Israel as they are private and underdetermined in America; the borders become, over time, as confining and claustrophobic, as defining of the non-negotiable line between self and not-self in the Holy Land as the American frontiers are the elastic signposts of the infinitely expandable self.[15]

If until the middle of this century the most widespread orientation towards Jewish space was as protean and permeable, bounded at its outer limits only by the extremes of exilic time – as, above all, non-territorial – the Second World War foreclosed this option. 'Kasrilevke on wheels'[16] becomes an anachronism beside the redrawn Jewish map with its specific physical coordinates: New York, Montreal, Chicago, Buenos Aires, Tel Aviv, Jerusalem. America in the twentieth century afforded the Jew a unique opportunity to begin over – while marking the place of the discarded culture through reference, through *partial* translation and through transmutation of an inherited vocabulary into indigenous terms. There develops, then, a strange dialectic of simultaneous reference to and effacement of the Jewish literary and linguistic canons. Coded in modern Jewish literature as either an exercise in immobility – S. Y. Abramovitch's (Mendele's) *Travels of Benjamin III* – or as a voyage of redemption – S. Y. Agnon's *In the Heart of the Seas* – the journey motif was redefined almost from the moment Jewish writers found their voice in the American chorus; the sortie into American spaces was a voyage of discovery and of naturalization, an adaptive strategy that took the lay of the land and then staked out a personal claim.

Once the children of the immigrant Jews had left the urban ghetto with its intermediate linguistic and geographical spaces, the search for constitutive texts would take on greater urgency as part of the larger search for cultural territory. These native Americans were in fact engaged in aggressive and dazzling acts of appropriation that parallel and, in certain respects, faintly echo the monumental dramas of repatriation being enacted in the Holy Land.

The repression of or very selective access to Jewish memory is supported, on the one hand, by the image of the American Adam who embodies new beginnings in life and language ('. . . the origin of words is lost like the origin of individuals', comments Alexis de Tocqueville on nineteenth-century America[17]) and, on the other, by the association with vestiges of Puritan rhetoric that link the early American conquests with the reclamation of sacred territory by the ancient Hebrews.[18] Both images were so empowering that even immigrants writing in Yiddish believed, for a moment anyway, that they might succeed in inscribing their lives on the American landscape. H. Leyvick envisioned the words 'Here lives the Jewish people' emblazoned on the New York skyline.[19] (That these writers remained, ultimately, alien on such hospitable soil – and that their chapter in American letters proved to be written in invisible ink that would become partially legible only through the recuperative efforts of translators and scholars some sixty years later – is one of the profound ironies of this enterprise; it is, nevertheless, consistent with the larger cultural patterns of repression, substitution and partial recovery that we are exploring.[20])

The poetry and prose of the immigrant generation were largely an exercise in spatial reorientation and a search for literary correlatives of the drama of acculturation. The iconography of the *goldene medina* embraced, in the first instance, the Statue of Liberty and the vertical architecture of the urban landscape.[21] The democratic tropes of mobility were captured in the infinitely expanding frontiers of Whitman's verse and in the city cadences and cacaphonies available in contemporary modernist forms. But the mimetic impulse is present even among the most avant-garde of the Yiddish poets; and it is the predominant force among the immigrant writers who venture into English prose. The evolution of Jewish approaches to inner and outer spaces can be measured in the changing state of the *real* in the literary imagination. The realism in the fiction of the first generation was a mapping-out, the realism of the second an appropriation and a realignment. The precise naturalism of writers such as Abraham Cahan, Anzia Yezierska, Mary Antin, Daniel Fuchs and later, in modified form, the realism of Alfred Kazin, mirror the keen, object-focused eye of the surveyor and the language of democracy.[22] Henry Roth's *Call it Sleep* (1934), in which the myriad forces of the immigrant experience and forms of expression culminate and are refashioned, is the full realization of the shift from the language of the naturalist or observer to that of the actor who participates in the very definition of the environment. The odyssey of David Shearl proceeds by carefully constructed, concentric geographic circles, from the inner sanctum of the home through the circumscribed arena of the neighbourhood into the vast undefined regions beyond. The claustrophobia and semiotic boundaries of the known world vie with the dangers and seductions of unexplored space. The linguistic correlative of this dynamic diminishes the strict ontological status and confinement of the palpable, mundane world, introducing new possibilities for mobility; the lyrical prose of the narrating self[23] is a redemptive poetic repatriation of the displaced syntax of the child locked in a universe of misunderstanding and incomprehension.

One cannot overstate the centrality of *Call it Sleep* as a site of magical transformation in the process of displacement and relocation in the modern Jewish imagination. That it represents or anticipates in certain key respects a post-war consciousness may be supported by the fact that although it first appeared in 1934, it gained a significant audience only thirty years later. When Irving Howe or Murray Baumgarten argues that Yiddish is the sub-text of much of the fiction of the post-war decades,[24] he refers to a gesture or an inflection, but rarely to the practice of literary allusion that would indicate that a culture is engaged in an ongoing renegotiation of its past. Such continuity would be measured of course as much in the discontinuities, the misreadings, as in the innocent allusions. But the second generation of American Jewish writers had so succeeded in suppressing or camouflaging the culture of origin that *Call it Sleep* appears to be nearly the only text demonstrating a true inter-linguistic dialogue. Yet even here, despite explicit allusions to the Hebrew scriptures as repository of the language of revelation and the presumption of Yiddish as the normative language, the Jewish languages and texts are in fact salient by their *absence*. The warm dyadic speech that flows between Genya Shearl and her son David is a 'Yiddish' translated for purposes of the narrative into a lyrical English. That is, the Yiddish is presumed but not really enacted as a linguistic layer, except for occasional aphoristic or inflected phrases. And that is the true achievement of Henry Roth: rather than being content as some of his predecessors were with transcribing Yiddish into a limping English dialect – the street language of the immigrant – he transposes it in the mother's discourse so that it receives a poetic cadence of its own. The culture or language of origin is thus marked-off and engaged through the most radical act of translation, of carrying over, into the highest register of the host language.[25] The Hebrew, on the other hand, is present as an untranslated, indecipherable medium: Hebrew is a

> strange and secret tongue. . . . If you knew it, then you could talk to God. (Furtively [in *heder*], while the rabbi still spoke David leaned over and stole a glance at the number of the page.) On sixty-eight. After, maybe, can ask. On page sixty-eight. That blue book – Gee! it's God.[26]

Here place, in the sense of *makom* and *ha-makom*, human and divine, is not only marked or embedded in the text; it *is* the text. But it is the text as seen through a glass darkly, the text as effaced, as absence, as loss. For the moment, both the Hebrew and the Yiddish as canonic languages and texts are as present as those dark squares in the family photo album where the pictures of the patriarchs are missing.[27]

The Hebrew literature of these same years reveals an (at times oppressive) sense of presence that parallels the absences salient in immigrant cultures elsewhere. S. Y. Agnon, a writer who straddles several cultural universes, dramatizes the intricacies of placement and displacement, the role of meta-physical yearnings in the reclamation of physical places in the Holy Land, in his story 'Tehila', set in the Mandate period: 'misha 'ar yaffo ulema 'alah 'ad lakotel hama 'aravi nimshakhim veholkhim anashim venashim mikol ha'edot shebirushalayim 'im 'olim hadashim sheheviam haMakom lime-komam va 'adayin lo matzu et mekomam.' ('From Jaffa Gate as far as the Western Wall, men and women from all the communities of Jerusalem moved in a steady stream, together with those newcomers whom The Place had restored to their place, albeit their place had not yet been found.'[28]) While the English concept of 'home' as a private, inviolable yet widely encompassing arena[29] hardly finds its correlative in the Hebrew lexicon, the correspondence (and distance) between the human plane and the divine, inadequately translated here as 'place' and 'Place', are embedded in the renewed contact between the Jews and their sacred centre.

Such a centre is inaccessible to nine-year-old David Shearl on two counts: it has been de-territorialized and it has become indecipherable. If we can project him into an extra-textual future, we can envision him as a young adult rediscovering the Bible in all its majesty – through the King James Version. The loss of what Harold Bloom calls an 'ancestry of voice'[30] will find compensation in monumental cultural acts of appropriation that again involve the mediation of translated texts.[31] Simultaneously, however, a direct and unmediated relationship is being established with the American physical and literary terrain. It has been argued that, in the competition over the 'usable past' between the native-born and the 'barbarians' that filled many of the literary pages in the early and middle decades of this century, the immigrants or their children, 'having no culture in which to be home', fabricated one. 'The children of the Mayflower tended to invent Western culture', claims Marcus Klein, and 'children of the immigrants ... tended to invent America'.[32] In 1942 – the ironies of synchronic Jewish–American time are as old as 1492 – Alfred Kazin published a book enunciating a critical vocabulary that might be seen as the hallmark of the post-war group broadly associated with *Partisan Review*.[33] Kazin demonstrates the connection between territory and text in the very title of this book, *On Native Grounds*; in the five-page introduction to his study of modern American writers, Kazin uses the possessive pronoun 'our' twenty-seven times; the repeated invocation of 'our national civilization', 'our modern American literature', 'our society', 'our culture',[34] is a catechism by which the son of immigrants appropriates the American canon as surely as he appropriates the American landscape by walking the length and breadth of Brownsville in his autobiographical *A Walker in the City*. As Mark Shechner observes, the library has replaced the synagogue as sacred centre;[35] it is, however, differentiated from religious space by the sense that, as reader, 'Alfred' both receives and constructs a tradition out of the plurality of texts on its 'public' shelves.[36] Reflecting but also fixing the terms of the enterprise, Kazin in 1942 invokes a vocabulary of alienation or marginality meant to signal both a Jewish and an American sensibility. 'The greatest single fact about our modern American writing', he writes in that same preface, is

> our writers' absorption in every last detail of their American world together with their deep and subtle alienation from it. There is a terrible estrangement in this writing, a nameless yearning for a world no one ever really possessed. ... What interested me here was our alienation *on* native grounds – the interwoven story of our need to take up our life on our own grounds and the irony of our possession.[37]

The endemic American quest for a lost – and irrecoverable – community will dovetail eventually, as I have suggested, with a nostalgia for Jewish spaces in the poetry and prose of some of these writers and their successors. Whether through acts of translation or imaginative appropriation, both the shtetl and the Lower East Side will become mythic Jewish fields of reference.[38] Delmore Schwartz's story 'America, America' becomes the *locus classicus* of this complex pilgrimage for writers who, as Irving Howe put it, may have

> left behind the immigrant world but [still carried] its stigmata . . .
> stamped on their souls. . . . If they were uncertain . . . as to who they
> were, they knew what they had been. . . . The immigrant world gave
> its literary offspring . . . memories, it gave them evocative place names
> and dubious relatives, it gave them thickness of milieu.

It gave them 'just enough material to see them through a handful of novels and stories.'[39]

For some time, though, the 'usable past' will continue to consist primarily in a posture and the fragments of a language. What a number of critics and writers, including Kazin, Schwartz and Isaac Rosenfeld, were offering as cultural currency was the critical function of alienation or estrangement in American democratic tradition. Although already articulated as a theme of modernist literature, the alienated sensibility became so fully identified with a specific circle of New York Jewish intellectuals in the 1940s that *The New Yorker* is reported as inquiring whether there were 'special typewriters in the *Partisan Review* office with entire words like "alienation" stamped on each key'.[40]

In symposia held in 1944 and 1946 and in subsequent essays, poetry and fiction, the theme of Jewish marginality is explored from every possible angle but one. During the very years that Europe has turned all its Jews into aliens and is proceeding to exterminate them, second-generation Jewish writers in America are adopting alienation as a voluntary moral stance – a perception anchored neither in the current events in Europe nor in the theodicy of exile and redemption that had structured Jewish itinerancy for two millennia and the Jewish homecoming of the twentieth century.[41] The rhetoric of displacement is the same but the tenor is entirely different, suggesting the longevity of rhetoric beyond the viability of other forces of cultural consciousness. When these writers affirm, paradoxically, both the marginality and the centrality of the Jews in America (or of what is defined as 'Jewish' in America), alienation represents not only or primarily a historical or a collective condition but an existential and a moral choice. It may also have provided, for a time, a conceptual bridge facilitating and to some extent camouflaging the shift in intellectual loyalties from Marx to Freud, from communal or social reform to self-absorption, or from what Mark Shechner calls the politics of 'social redemption' to the 'politics of self-renewal . . . from Socialism to Therapy'.[42] The spirit of the 1940s is manifest in dramatic reinterpretations or 'revisions' of such patently proletarian texts from the previous decade as Clifford Odets's *Awake and Sing*. In 1946, Daniel Bell explored the sociology of alienation in an article in the *Jewish Frontier*, claiming that 'the quality of being lost' was the 'most pervasive symptom of the alienation of our times', he assigned to the 'footsore' Jew a synecdochal function as the 'image of the world's destiny'.

'As long as moral corruption exists, alienation is the only possible response', he continued, and went on to indict Odets for 'delineating the frustration of Jewish life, not its alienation, the effect, not the source'. Bell would turn Odets's social reformer, Ralph Berger, into an *alienated intellectual*, and substitute contemplation ('understanding') for action ('muddled aggression') as the truly Jewish moral imperative.[43]

In the quarter-century beginning in the mid-1940s, Saul Bellow's fiction becomes a crossroads of these themes. His territorialism originates, like that of his predecessors, in the realism of the immigrant son's primary bid for a foothold: 'I am an American, Chicago-born', proclaims Augie March in the 1953 novel that bears his name[44] – and if his claims to localism appear to be at war with his dazzling antics as a picaro, as a kind of secularized, camouflaged wandering Jew, it may be because we have not yet taken the full, continental, measure of acculturation in the American landscape.[45] Augie's preoccupation with the minutest details of his environment is an urban recapitulation of the voyages of discovery that are also self-conscious acts of possession:

> Look at me going everywhere. . . . Why, I am a sort of Columbus of those near-at-hand and believe you can come to them in this immediate *terra incognita* that spreads out in every gaze. I may well be a flop at this line of endeavor. Columbus too thought he was a flop, probably, when they sent him back in chains. Which didn't prove there was no America.[46]

By the time Moses Elkana Herzog appears on the horizon of Bellow's fictional landscape (1964), a process has been completed whereby *wandering* as a Jewish condition and curse has been largely supplanted by *mobility* as an American opportunity. As Herzog rides through the city's bowels by subway, drives along its main arteries by car, races along the surrounding countryside and waterways by train and ferry – and hovers, finally airborne in a westbound jet, over the entire continent – his reach expands infinitely ('as heaven is my witness'[47]). He has scattered his life over the entire continent, carrying keys to his home in Ludeyville, to his mistress's and his own New York apartments, to the Faculty Lounge at the University of Chicago and sundry other places. (The key as metonymy of the real estate of the American Jew invites comparison with the key as metonymy of sacred – and collective – space in Agnon's interbellum novel, *A Guest for the Night*.[48]) Herzog in the city, Herzog as a walker in the city – Montreal, New York or Chicago – like Kazin's 'Alfred' before him, is alternately assaulted and caressed by its sights, sounds and smells and embraced in powerful rituals of consecration; he is as organically connected to it as he professes to be estranged from it.[49] 'He was perhaps as mid-western and unfocused as these same streets. . . . Out of [the city's] elements, by this peculiar art of his own organs, he created his version of it.'[50]

The urban setting that challenges the imagination to transform Jewish into American tropes of itinerancy and community yields ultimately to a powerful myth of homecoming. The vacation house in the Berkshires, which Herzog himself defines as a 'symbol of this Jewish struggle for a solid footing in White Anglo-Saxon Protestant America'[51] – a clear claim for private property as the *real estate* of the Jew – reflects a profound form of patriation.[52] As the final station in Herzog's frenetic wandering over the North American continent, it represents both the urban American sanctification of the pastoral realm and a re-mythification of the Jewish fantasy of return to a pre-lapsarian, pre- (or post-) exilic state. The home in the Berkshires comes close enough to being reclaimed as wilderness to qualify as primary American space. Sitting or lying in the disrepair of his home or in the overgrown tangle of his garden, Herzog suspends the search for a historical or interpersonal resolution of his urban estrangement and supplants it with a biblical acquiescence that suggests an entirely different order of being-at-home: 'Here I am. *Hineni*,' he says, echoing what is a profoundly *spatial* response to the divine summons. 'I am pretty well satisfied to be, to be just as it is willed, for as long as I may remain in occupancy.'[53] The presence of the original Hebrew text – with its translation – reinstates an explicit intertextuality into this discourse. Herzog has repossessed both text and territory *and* the matrix that unifies them. (Perhaps now '*El maleh rahamim*' can again be heard under the *huppah*?)

If Gimpel and Herzog begin their 'autobiographical' tales with a very similar presentation of self *vis-à-vis* society ('I am Gimpel the fool. I don't think myself a fool' . . . 'If I'm out of my mind, it's all right with me, thought Moses Herzog'), it is in the closure of each narrative that we can measure the real distance between them. Gimpel takes up his staff and goes out into the world, invoking in his wandering both the theodicy of exile and his designated cultural role as storyteller. Herzog at the end of his narrative is lying perfectly still. Having recapitulated inherited categories of exile within the expanse of a long interior monologue, he now realizes the profound possibilities for their resolution within the confines of his own – private – property as mythic American space and the recaptured rhetoric of the Hebrew scriptures.

When the cultural boundaries of the group have become so permeable that migrant types find their way easily into the surrounding culture, when fragments of historical and textual memory have been recalled and subjected to a new syntax, the parameters and the nature of the literary discourse have undergone radical revision. It is precisely here, in this intersection of cultural exchange, that we may begin to discern a new paradigm informing the literature of American Jews. There has been much critical discussion about whether the Jews over the last century, and especially since the Second World War, have developed a 'regional' literature in America comparable to southern literature or black literature, and, if so what is the longevity

– or 'shelf-life', as it were – of such a phenomenon.[54] Since whatever else that literature may be, it has only partially recaptured the bilingual or polylingual quality that characterized all the Jewish literatures of the Diaspora, it is tempting to look for analogues in the German Jewish litera-ture in the first half of this century. The German literature of the Jews of Prague, particularly that of Kafka, is defined by Gilles Deleue and Felix Guattari as a '*littérature mineure*' constructed by a minority within a major language. The 'first characteristic of minor literature … is that in it language is affected with a high coefficient of deterritorialization'. And if the 'writer is located in the margins or completely outside his or her fragile community, this situation allows the writer all the more possibility to express another possible community'. 'Minor' literature manifests the profound restlessness of 'living in a language not one's own'. What is a problem for immigrants becomes, in this view, an *opportunity* for their children: 'how to become a nomad and an immigrant and a gypsy in relation to one's own language?'[55]

What appears to be a tailor-made definition of the Jewish presence in American letters is reinforced, of course, by the growing influence in post-war America of Kafka and the existentialist philosophers, mediated and authenticated by the presence of such Jewish refugees as T. W. Adorno and Hannah Arendt. For the New York intellectuals loosely identified with *Partisan Review*, Arendt herself becomes a figure of the compounded exile of the Jewish 'pariah' and the European *émigré*;[56] yet it is precisely in the ensuing discourse on exile that one can measure the real distance between the identity of German Jewish writers in America and the reflected rhetoric of their American-born colleagues.[57]

The unharnessed generation that came of age in the late 1930s and 1940s, that inherited a repressed tradition, a cultural amnesia, succeeded in encoding in the language of alienation what had already become in fact a profound claim to being-at-home. These writers do not so much articulate a subversive or revolutionary alternative to the major or dominant culture as seek a place in it; it is in this sense that they fail ultimately to inscribe on the American landscape a truly de-territorialized, 'minor' literature.

All newcomers have to forget in order to become Americans, and acts of partial retrieval by successive generations may involve only so much memory as is needed to retain the licence to hold American society at some distance. The alienation of the immigrants and their descendants becomes in America a means for the democratization of individualism, a part of the larger American epic of the negotiations between self and society; alienation and marginality are subsumed, then, under the very American concept of community as a structure that rests on individual autonomy, dissent and the radical option. Although for the Jewish children of immigrants the act of self-alienation is dialectically related to the Jewish theme of wandering, it only highlights the enormous distance between the condition and the gestures of exile. While writers such as Isaac Bashevis Singer and philosophers such as Hannah Arendt provided a vocabulary, a reference, and an authenticating presence, it was precisely by adopting or co-opting 'alienation' as a voluntary condition and a central moral position – by becoming the outsider as insider – that the first generation of native American Jews superseded their inherited status as strangers, as 'aliens', as the unshadowed other. Irving Howe locates the crisis in late twentieth-century American Jewish fiction in the loss of the immigrant milieu, that is, as a 'crisis of subject matter';[58] Shechner locates it in the loss of a critical stance.[59] Whether it is to be celebrated or lamented, the extent to which the writers who came of age in the 1940s managed to exchange mobility for wandering, Herzog for Gimpel, is the extent of their re-territorialization on American soil.

NOTES

1 Isaac Bashevis Singer, 'Gimpel the Fool', trans. Saul Bellow, *Partisan Review*, 20 (May 1953), reprinted in Bashevis Singer, *Gimpel the Fool and Other Stories* (New York, 1957), p. 10 (emphasis added). 'Gimpl tam' was published in *Yidisher Kemfer* (30 March 1945).

2 Ibid., p. 12.

3 There are a few words from the original text that are left untranslated in Bellow's 'Gimpel' – words from the culinary lexicon ('kreplach'), the sacramental lexicon ('mezzuzah') and the rogues' gallery ('golem', 'schnorrer') that had already established their own place in the American conversation.

4 That the relations between Gimpel's 'amnesia' and the vagaries of the English text go deeper than the changing decorums of translation can be seen in the relative function of internal knowledge. The correctives for 'amnesia' embedded in the internal knowledge shared by a storytelling circle are a locus of much of the humour in Yiddish fiction; the malapropisms and misquotes of Sholem Aleichem's semi-literature characters, for example, are a function of group memory and can help us delineate the boundary between collective knowing and collective forgetting: 'When the wise men of Kasrilevke quote the passage from the Holy Book, "Tov shem meshemen tov", they know what they're doing. I'll translate it for you: We were better off without the train.' Sholem Aleichem, 'On account of a hat', trans. Isaac Rosenfeld, in *A Treasury of Yiddish Stories*, Irving Howe and Eliezer Greenberg (eds) (New York, 1954), p. 113. In this case, in which translation is of the essence, the English version is a fair equivalent of the original ('Iber a hitel', in *Fun Pesah biz Pesah: Ale verk fun Sholem Aleichem* (New York, 1927), p. 246).

5 Bashevis Singer, 'Gimpel the Fool', p. 9; Saul Bellow, *Herzog* (Harmondsworth, 1964), p. 7.

6 There is, however, a great distance between Gimpel as 'tam' – a spiritual category that connotes integrity and fullness as well as gullibility and receptivity – and Herzog's psychic imbalance as possible moral response to the world's inadequacies. Of the many discussions of insanity or madness as a mid-twentieth-century cultural stance, the conclusion to Lionel Trilling's *Sincerity and Authenticity* (Cambridge, Mass., 1972) is still one of the most provocative. See also Janet Hadda, 'Gimpel the Full', *Prooftexts*, 10, no. 2 (May 1990).

7 Compare, in this regard, the trajectory of Bashevis Singer's career with that of his brother, I. J. Singer. See Anita Norich, *The Homeless Imagination in the Fiction of Israel Joshua Singer* (Bloomington, 1991). Most of Bashevis Singer's critics, like most of his readers, are familiar only with the translated texts; the mediating function of the translator in recovering a lost cultural memory is explored in Cynthia Ozick's programmatic story 'Envy: or Yiddish in America' in her *The Pagan Rabbi and Other Stories* (New York, 1971). The main character, patterned after the Yiddish poet Jacob Glatstein, writes to his would-be translator:

> . . . whoever forgets Yiddish courts amnesia of history. Mourn – the forgetting has already happened. A thousand years of our travail forgotten. Here and there a word left for vaudeville jokes. Yiddish, I call on you to choose! Yiddish! Choose death or death. Which is to say death through forgetting or death through translation. Who will redeem you? . . . All you can hope for, you tattered, you withered, is translation in America! [pp. 74–5]

8 Ruth R. Wisse, *The Schlemiel as Modern Hero* (Chicago, 1971).

9 Natan Alterman, 'Mikhtav shel Menahem-Mendel', from 'Mikol ha'amim', in *Hatur hashevi'i*, 1 (Tel Aviv, 1977), pp. 12–14.

10 Wisse, *Schlemiel as Modern Hero*, pp. 125–6.

11 Paul Celan, 'Conversation in the mountains', trans. Rosmarie Waldrop in *Paul Celan: Collected Prose*, Rosmarie Waldrop (ed.) (New York, 1986), p. 17.

12 In an interview, Aharon Appelfeld referred to his own characters, Holocaust survivors in Israel, as '*mehagrim*' (emigrants). See Shulamith Gingold-Gilboa, 'Aharon Appelfeld: Kol hasetarim geluyim', *Iton 77*, 46 (October 1983). Much has been written on the figure of the 'misfit' in Hebrew literature; most recently, a renewed interest in the work of Y. H. Brenner and his displaced characters may reflect the general malaise in Israeli culture and the renegotiation of certain fundamental assumptions. See Menahem Brinker, '*Ad hasimta hateverianit* (Tel Aviv, 1990).

13 Bashevis Singer, 'Gimpel the Fool', pp. 22–3.

14 An alternative to the utopia/dystopia dichotomy is offered in Ernst Bloch's Marxist theory of the utopian function of art as a theory of desire and 'anticipatory illumination' that does not deny the connection between landscapes and 'wish-landscapes'. 'The concrete utopia stands at the horizon of every reality; the real possibility encloses the open dialectical tendency-latency until the very last moment', he writes in his essay on 'The artistic illusion as the visible anticipatory illumination' (in Ernst Bloch, *The Utopian Function of Art and Literature: Selected Essays*, trans. Jack Zipes and Frank Mecklenburg (Cambridge, Mass., 1988), p. 155). 'The unconcluded movement of the unconcluded matter', a gloss on Aristotle's 'unfinished entelechy' (ibid.) allows one to translate despair over the absence of utopian fulfilment, which can generate binary artistic structures, into the hope of the not-yet-realized that can generate an infinitude of fictive possibilities.

15 The phenomenon of Harold Bloom's *Book of J* (1990) and the controversy it has stirred are an extreme example of the aimless, open-ended nature of American Jewish approaches to sacred texts. For a discussion of the ideological implications of myths of the American frontier, see Sacvan Bercovitch and Myra Jehlen (eds), *Ideology and Classic American Literature* (Cambridge, 1986).

16 Quoted from I. I. Trunk's 1937 essay on Sholem Aleichem in Dan Miron, 'Masa be-eizor hadimdumim' (afterword to *Sippurei rakevet*, trans. Dan Miron

(Tel Aviv, 1989), p. 243. A comparative overview of changing Jewish concepts of exile and territoriality from the perspective of the end of our millennium might begin by acknowledging that monotheism as it developed in rabbinic and post-rabbinic Judaism actually allowed the Jews to be in 'God's country' anywhere in the pre-messianic world, providing a normative framework for being (provisionally) at home in the remotest corners of '*golus*'. As such, the territorial embrace of the religious Jewish imagination is far broader than the confines of a nationalism conceived within specific boundaries. This broad sense of entitlement, underscored by Enlightenment ideas, facilitates early Jewish mobility and acculturation in America. The impact of Israel as a territorial option on the imagination of American Jews in the latter half of the century is a subject unto itself. For a wide-ranging analysis of 'exile' in ancient and modern Jewish thought, see Arnold Eisen, *Galut: Modern Jewish Reflection on Homelessness and Homecoming* (Bloomington, 1986).

17 Alexis de Tocqueville, *Democracy in America*, vol. 2 (New York, 1945 (Paris, 1835)), p. 72. See also R. W. B. Lewis, *The American Adam: Innocence, Tragedy and Tradition in the Nineteenth Century* (Chicago, 1955).

18 See Sacvan Bercovitch, quoting Melville on the rejection of the past and the Americans as the new Hebrews conquering sacred land, in *The American Jeremiad* (Madison, 1978), p. 177.

19 H. Leyvick, 'Here lives the Jewish people', in *Yiddish Poetry in America*, trans. and ed. Benjamin and Barbara Harshav (Berkeley, 1986), p. 697.

20 See Ruth Wisse, '*Di Yunge*: immigrants or exiles?', *Prooftexts*, 1, no. 1 (January 1981); and *idem*, *A Little Love in Big Manhattan* (Cambridge, Mass., 1988). It would take a few more decades and the mediating presence of such diverse critics, translators and anthologizers as Irving Howe and Ruth Wisse and a host of scholars demonstrating new hermeneutic approaches to Jewish texts before the vast realms of Yiddish and Hebrew literature, Jewish mysticism and Hassidism as well as biblical, midrashic and medieval texts would become available to the fully acculturated children and grandchildren of the immigrants. 'How can we sing our songs in a foreign land?' asks Geoffrey Hartman in 1986; 'The Jewish imagination, like any other, must exert itself and risk profanation, or fall silent and risk atrophy' ('On the Jewish imagination', *Prooftexts*, 5, no. 3, p. 205). His own later work is a mighty attempt to recapture the text as a scholarly and personal resource from the silence that was also the deafness of his generation.

21 'When the New York skyline burst upon him, the Jewish immigrant immediately perceived of America's greatness in vertical terms', writes Judd Teller, who, as Y. Y. Teller, was an important voice in Yiddish poetry before the Second World War (Judd Teller, *Strangers and Natives: The Evolution of the American Jew from 1921 to the Present* (New York, 1968), p. 38). For a fascinating exploration of the presence of Miss Liberty in the immigrant imagination, as well as a comparative analysis of immigrant cultures and their place in the American mind, see John Higham, *Send These to Me: Jews and Other Immigrants in Urban America* (New York, 1975).

22 This process is in no small measure shaped by the realism and spirit of social reform that characterized those American writers such as William Dean Howells and Hutchins Hapgood who first discovered the New York ghetto, its artists and writers. In tracing lines of influence, one might consider Alfred Kazin's analysis of the

> early realists, with their baffled careers and their significant interest in 'local color,' cultivating their own gardens, who encouraged in America

that elementary nationalism, that sense of belonging to a particular time and a native way of life, which is the indispensable condition of spiritual maturity and a healthy literature.

See also his discussion of the evolution of the documentary mode in imaginative literature and the centrality of the camera as instruments of a new social consciousness (Alfred Kazin, *On Native Grounds: An Interpretation of Modern American Prose Literature* (New York, 1942), p. 17 and *passim*).

23 For a very enlightening discussion of the bifurcation of the narrative voice in *Call it Sleep* into the 'experiencing self' and the 'narrating self', see Naomi Diamant, 'Linguistic universes in Henry Roth's *Call it Sleep*', *Contemporary Literature*, 27 (1986), pp. 336–55.

24 Irving Howe defines and qualifies what replaced the traditional Jewish 'internal bilingualism of Hebrew and Yiddish' in American Jewish fiction as 'a precarious substitute, a half-internal and half-external bilingualism of Englished Yiddish and Yiddished English, from which there sometimes arises a new and astonishing American prose style . . .' (*World of Our Fathers* (New York, 1976), p. 588). Murray Baumgarten makes bolder claims for

> modern Jewish writing [as] a chapter in what Max and Uriel Weinreich called the history of Jewish interlinguistics. . . . If these works [from Henry to Philip Roth, from Malamud to Kazin] are written in English, it is a language with Yiddish lurking behind every Anglo-Saxon character. . . . Yiddish transforms the modern language in which the Jewish writer functions.
>
> (Murray Baumgarten, *City Scriptures: Modern Jewish Writings* (Cambridge, Mass., 1982), p. 10, 28)

25 There is a two-line untranslated Yiddish dialogue at the end of the Prologue between Genya Shearl, who has just disembarked at Ellis Island with her young son, and her husband Albert, who has been living in America for some months ("'*Gehen vir voinen du? In Nev York?' 'Nein. Bronzeville. Ich hud dir schoin geschriben'*"). Its lonely status only underscores its absence in the rest of the narrative and the radical nature of the 'translation' that is being enacted throughout (Henry Roth, *Call it Sleep* (New York, 1962), p. 16).

26 Ibid., pp. 213, 227.

27 Following Mihail Bakhtin's model, much work has been done on heteroglossia and polyphony in American sub-cultures (black, Chinese, Hispanic). Its value for a new hermeneutics of American Jewish culture is demonstrated in Hana Wirth-Nesher's illuminating analysis of bi- or multi-lingualism and diglossia in Roth's novel ('Multilinguilism in *Call it Sleep*', *Prooftexts*, 10, no. 2 (May 1990)). She argues that throughout the narrative, though written in English, the American language and culture are present in their alterity (it is the English element which 'appears to be foreign, as "other" within the rest of the *English* text') and that only in the final scene, where David 'dies' and is 'reborn' through his self-induced electrocution at the train tracks, where the allusions to a presumed Hebrew/Yiddish culture recede and are replaced by an inter-textual dialogue with English and European literature, does he 'die out of his immigrant life and [become reborn] . . . into the world of English literacy and culture, the world of Henry Roth's literary identity, but at the cost of killing both the father and the mother' (pp. 305, 309). I would argue that, whereas such a reading may account for the dramatic nature of the transaction taking place between the experiencing self and its environment, and that it may indeed be a kind of recapitulation of the writer's own *rite de passage*, the presence from

the beginning of the narrating self with its fully articulated poetic voice enacts this process throughout the text, both in the Joycean flow of intra-psychic dialogue and in the luxuriating, almost overwritten, metaphoric passages interspersed throughout ('trinkets held in the mortar of desire, the fancy a trowel, the whim the builder. A wall, a tower, stout, secure, incredible, immuring the spirit from a flight of arrows, the mind, experience, shearing the flow of time as a rock shears water' (p. 35)). I would endorse Wirth-Nesher's conclusion that this book both represents the culmination of the immigrant narrative with its multi-linguistic resonances – and marks its demise. ('It is no wonder that Roth could write no second book' (p. 311).)

28 S. Y. Agnon, 'Tehila', in *'Ad hena* (Jerusalem, 1972), p. 183. Trans. by Walter Lever in *Firstfruits*, James A. Michener (ed.) (Greenwich, Conn., 1973), p. 62.

29 See David Sopher's discussion of the American and English resonances of 'home':

> The rich meaning of the English lexical symbol is virtually untranslatable into most other languages. The distinguishing characteristic of the English word, which it shares to a certain extent with its equivalent in other Germanic languages, is the enormous extension of scale that it incorporates. . . . It can refer with equal ease to house, land, village, city, district, country, or, indeed, the world. . . . The Romance word for 'house' . . . takes on some of the warmth associated with 'home' in English, but it remains a symbol for a firmly bounded and enclosed space, which 'home' is not.
>
> (David Sopher, 'The landscape of home', in *The Interpretation of Ordinary Landscapes: Geographical Essays*, D. W. Meinig (ed.) (New York, 1979), p. 130)

Gaston Bachelard's exploration of the *house* ('life begins well, it begins enclosed, protected, all warm, in the bosom of the house') confirms a French orientation towards physically defined space as primary and maternal; 'without it, man would be a "dispersed being"', he adds (Gaston Bachelard, *Poetics of Space*, trans. Maria Jolas (Boston, 1964), p. 7). The Hebrew *bayit* carries the same connotation of physical specificity – and within the Zionist vocabulary, a similar defence against dispersion – as the French *maison*.

30 Harold Bloom, *A Map of Misreading* (Oxford, 1975), p. 17.

31 See, for example, recent encounters with the Scriptures collected in David Rosenberg's anthology, *Congregation: Contemporary Writers Read the Jewish Bible* (San Diego, 1987).

32 Marcus Klein, *Foreigners: The Making of American Literature, 1900–1940* (Chicago, 1981), p. x. See also John Higham's discussion of the ongoing debate between those who, harking back to John Jay's argument in the second of the Federalist papers, claim that Americans are descended from a monolithic culture and population, and those who, following Tom Paine in *Common Sense*, argue that pluralism is endemic to the American definition of self. This struggle is, perhaps, embodied in the competition between the 'melting pot' and the 'social fabric' as icons of socialization (*Send These to Me*, pp. 3ff.).

33 Kazin himself, although a contributor to *Partisan Review*, is more closely affiliated during these years, as writer and editor, with *The New Republic*.

34 Kazin, *On Native Grounds*, pp. vii–xii.

35 Mark Shechner, *After the Revolution: Studies in the Contemporary Jewish-American Imagination* (Bloomington, 1987), p. 47.

36 'America' emerges in the work of Sacvan Bercovitch and others as a socio-cultural

reality created by primary texts such as the sermons of Jonathan Edwards, the Declaration of Independence, the Gettysburg Address, 'The American Scholar' (see his Afterword to *Ideology and Classic American Literature* and *American Jeremiad*). Jews born in America with dim memories of specific Jewish texts may nevertheless have retained enough *text-mindedness* to become engaged in the literature and the law of the land as conduits into the American spirit. Harold Bloom records the attenuation of that 'Jewish love for a text' in America of the late twentieth century and concludes his essay on 'Free and broken tablets: the cultural prospects of American Jewry' with the dim hope that 'an American Jewry that has lost its love for a text like the 102nd Psalm might recover, in time, such a love, if it were capable first of loving some text, any text' (Harold Bloom, *Agon: Towards a Theory of Revisionism* (New York, 1982) p. 329).

37 Kazin, *On Native Grounds*, p. ix. There is a delightful sense throughout this early work of the deliberate but somehow inevitable nature of the American literary enterprise of discovering a past, the 'unabashed recovery of an American mythology. . . . The past now lay everywhere ready to be reclaimed, waiting to be chanted and celebrated', he writes in the chapter 'America! America!' (ibid., pp. 508–9). The title of this chapter could be an ironic redefinition of the territory of Delmore Schwartz's story by the same name which, published two years earlier in *Partisan Review*, explores the life of the immigrant as subject of a more authentic, more usable, past. In an entry from his journal of 1942, published only some fifty years later, Kazin acknowledges the complex sources of his own passionate engagement with American literature:

> I have never been able to express the pleasure I derive from the conscious study of Americana . . . I love to think about America, to look at portraits, to remember the kind of adventurousness and purity, heroism and *salt*, that the best Americans have always had for me. Or is it – most obvious supposition – that I am an outsider; and that only for the first American born son of so many thousands of mud-flat Jewish-Polish-Russian generations is this need great, this enquiring so urgent? Yet the most extraordinary element in all this is something it is difficult, perhaps hazardous, to express; that is, the terrible and graphic loneliness of the great Americans. . . . Each one that is, began afresh – began on his own terms – began in a universe that remained, for all practical purposes, his own.

In his Journals written over the next few decades one detects the unravelling of that package: commenting, on 23 July 1957, on his *A Walker in the City*, published in 1951, he speculates: 'Can it be that *Walker* was written out of nostalgia for my poor old revolutionary home. . . . I feel more and more that what happened to me during the war years . . . came from the loneliness of having lost one's instinctive, true, spiritual home.' Finally, on 8 September 1963, the journal entry made after a visit to Edmund Wilson's 'wonderful "old" house" in Wellfleet' is a kind of melancholy return to the gabled houses he had appropriated in the 1930s and 1940s with the vigour of the young explorer:

> Everything in this house is passed down or acquired by someone who could recognize immediately its historical application to himself. By contrast everything I own I have bought for myself or have had to decide its merit in relation to an entirely new situation. . . . I have *never* felt like an American. But that's because I've given up trying to feel like an American. . . . The lack of tradition is the lack of familiarity in many basic associations, and I know that I am outside them, trying to figure

out what to do, what to think in relation to many basic American traditions.

('The Journals of Alfred Kazin' (excerpts), Richard M. Cook (ed.),
American Literary History, 2, no. 2, pp. 243, 245, 250)

See Bachelard's exploration of attics and cellars as enclosing and contextualizing different layers of consciousness (in his *Poetics of Space*, pp. 6ff). In a Yiddish poem entitled 'Cellars and attics', American Yiddish poet Malka Heifetz-Tussman invokes and explores the ancestral home, with its nooks and crannies, its treasures and mementoes – as an effaced presence ('Indeed, where is my grandfather's house?') [*Yiddish Poetry in America*, p. 611].

38 The distance between the shtetl and the American Jewish ghetto as 'mythic space' should not be minimized; it can be measured in terms of access. That Kazin can walk in the streets where 'Alfred' grew up and Bashevis Singer cannot, relegates the streets of Bilgoray or Frampol entirely to the status of memory, even, paradoxically, freeing it from certain historical constraints. Because, as Judd Teller writes, 'the bearded generations . . . decimated by German genocide . . . are remote and unreal, like the weightless, levitating figures of Chagall's canvases, one may vaguely relate to them, without the risk of being mistaken for them' (Teller, *Strangers and Natives*, p. 262). Recent Jewish 'pilgrimages' to the sites of former *shtetlach* in Poland only dramatize their obliterated presence in the physical landscape of post-war Europe.

That the process by which the Lower East Side was appropriated as mythic space was fairly self-conscious is attested to in Kazin's essay on *A Walker in the City*, written in 1986; seeking to write a very ambitious 'personal epic' about the city of New York, he recalls that he 'suddenly opted for a small country, my natal country' – Brownsville ('My New Yorks: writing *A Walker in the City*', *The New York Times Book Review* (24 August 1986), p. 29). The negotiation of place is one of the chief privileges and burdens of immigrant and first-generation native writers. 'For as a midwesterner, the child of immigrant parents, I recognized at an early age that I was called upon to decide for myself to what extent my Jewish origins, my surroundings (the accidental circumstances of Chicago) . . . were to be allowed to determine the course of my life', writes Saul Bellow in his foreword to Allan Bloom's *The Closing of the American Mind* (New York, 1987), p. 13. For a discussion of the 'place of place' in fiction generally and in 'regional literature' in particular, see Eudora Welty, 'Place in fiction', *The South Atlantic Quarterly* (January 1956). In his analysis of the fiction of Carson McCullers, Flannery O'Connor and other Southern writers, Richard Gray invokes the 'triangular relationship between personal feeling, regional landscape, and moral reference' (Richard Gray, *The Literature of Memory: Modern Writers of the American South* (Baltimore, 1977), p. 268).

39 Irving Howe, 'On Jewish-American Writing', *Tel Aviv Review*, 2 (Fall 1989/Winter 1990), p. 344; *idem*, 'Strangers', in *Celebrations and Attacks: Thirty Years of Literary and Cultural Commentary* (New York, 1979), p. 19.

In Delmore Schwartz's story 'America, America', a mother's memories of immigrant culture are captured, on the very edge of oblivion, to provide grounding for the restless imagination of her native-born son. But it is the double voice, predicated on the ironizing distance of the narrator from his subject, that rescues not only the writer from a paucity of cultural resources but also the immigrant story from its inherent banality.

40 Quoted from Norman Podhoretz's *Making It*, in Mark Shechner, *After the Revolution*, p. 18.

41 In February 1944, the editors of *The Contemporary Jewish Record* conducted a symposium of Jewish writers 'under forty' whom they placed in the 'front ranks of American literature'. Suggesting that 'American Jews have reached the stage of integration with the native environment . . . [no longer as] spectators . . . but [as full participants in the cultural life of the country', they may have touched on one of the central, spatial, metaphors of American Jewish culture in the second half of the twentieth century. In turn, rather than embracing such 'integration', several of those who participated in the symposium delineated a peripheral space for the Jewish writer that was to be understood as somehow central to the cultural enterprise. Isaac Rosenfeld stated that the Jew is a 'specialist in alienation, . . . the outsider [as] . . . perfect insider', and Delmore Schwartz affirmed that 'the fact of being a Jew became available to me as a central symbol of alienation ('Under forty: a symposium on American literature and the younger generation of American Jews', *Contemporary Jewish Record* (February 1944), pp. 3, 35 36, 14). See also Schwartz's essay on the 'Vocation of the poet', in which he writes that 'the Jew is at once *alienated* and *indestructible*; he is an exile from his own country and an exile even from himself, yet he survives [*sic*!] the annihilating fury of history. In the unpredictable and fearful future that awaits civilization, the poet must be prepared to be alienated . . .' ('The vocation of the poet' (1951), reprinted in *Selected Essays of Delmore Schwartz*, Donald A. Dike and David H. Zucker (eds) (Chicago, 1970), p. 23; emphasis added). It may be useful to recall that 'alienated' and 'indestructible' are the mythical attributes of the Wandering Jew. The place and function of Jew, exile and poet converge for Schwartz at the very centre of American civilization in the middle of the twentieth century. Isaac Rosenfeld was one of the only writers to begin in the late 1940s to come to terms explicitly with the devastation of Jewish civilization in Europe; see his essays on 'Terror beyond evil' published in the *New Leader* (February 1948) and 'The meaning of terror' published in *Partisan Review* (January 1949), both reprinted in *An Age of Enormity*, Theodore Solotaroff (ed.) (Cleveland, 1962), as well as his allegories of terror that were collected posthumously in *Alpha and Omega* (New York, 1966). In translating Isaac Bashevis Singer's 'The little shoemakers', he also helped to establish the modern Jewish narrative of exile (in *A Treasury of Yiddish Stories*, pp. 523–44).

42 Mark Shechner, *After the Revolution*, p. 7.

43 Daniel Bell, 'A parable of alienation', *The Jewish Frontier* (November 1946), p. 16.

44 Saul Bellow, *The Adventures of Augie March* (New York, 1953), p. 3.

45 On the imagination of America as an 'integrated whole', as a continental 'home' beyond regional loyalties, see Sopher, 'The landscape of home', pp. 144ff.

46 Bellow, *Augie March*, p. 536.

47 Bellow, *Herzog*, p. 248.

48 Sidra DeKoven Ezrahi, 'Agnon before and after', *Prooftexts*, 2, no. 1 (January 1982), pp. 78–94. The key as metonymy of access to sacred as to private space is as ancient in Jewish literature as the aggadah of the priests who, claiming they were no longer worthy custodians, threw the keys to the burning Temple heavenward (Pesikta Rabati: p. 131a). David Roskies recalls the legend of the keys to ancestral homes in fifteenth-century Spain and Portugal retained by Moroccan Jews into the twentieth century (*Against the Apocalypse: Responses to Catastrophe in Modern Jewish Literature* (Cambridge, Mass., 1984), p. 1). Herzog's multiple key-ring finds its counterpart in the 'broken key' as exemplum of the estrangement of the Jewish refugee in New York in I. B. Singer's story 'The key' (*idem, A Friend of Kafka* (Harmondsworth, 1972)).

49 For a fascinating study of the urban odyssey in American literature, of the 'compassionate walker ... [on the] sidewalk as a source of moral as well as aesthetic perspective' in contrast to the 'skyscraper [or airplane] experience' that helps to 'revivify an epic perspective on human possibilities in the modern world', see Michael Cowan, 'Walkers in the street: American writers and the modern city', *Prospects* (Fall 1981), pp. 288, 285, 291, and *passim*. It might be interesting to compare 'walking in the city' and 'lighting out' as tropes of American mobility.

50 Bellow; *Herzog*, pp. 266, 285.

51 Ibid., p. 316.

52 Tenancy, occupancy and ownership are more than signs of the upward mobility and the *embourgeoisement* of the Jew in America. Tenancy as an expression of a provisional foothold in America – haunted by the fear of eviction – is explored by nearly every immigrant and proletarian writer, from Yezierska to Fuchs and Odets. In Bernard Malamud's *The Tenants* (New York, 1971), a condemned tenement is the no-man's-land of an urban encounter between the footloose black and the footloose Jew. (Most of Malamud's characters are ungrounded, closer to the European than the American figure of the Jew as wanderer, as shlemiel. See his 'The Jewbird' in *Idiots First* (New York, 1964).) In his biography of Delmore Schwartz, James Atlas quotes from Schwartz's (endless) poem, 'Genesis', in which he writes of a character very much resembling his own father, who '"knew well that they had brought with them from Europe/ The peasant's sense that land was the most important thing and the owner of land/ A king!" Real Estate was a strategic line to be in,' Atlas continues, 'and Harry Schwartz [Delmore's father] had made himself a wealthy man by the time he met' Delmore's mother (James Atlas, *Delmore Schwartz: The Life of an American Poet* (New York, 1977), p. 6). Mordecai Richler's Duddy Kravitz is a Canadian caricature of the Jew as landlord (Mordecai Richler, *The Apprenticeship of Duddy Kravitz* (Boston, 1959)).

53 Bellow, *Herzog*, pp. 317, 347.

54 It was probably Irving Howe who first introduced the notion that the work of Jewish writers who came of age in the 1940s and 1950s may constitute a 'version of American regionalism' (*World of Our Fathers*, pp. 585ff). In subsequent articles he has redefined that phenomenon as more transitory: see Howe, 'Strangers', and *idem*, 'On Jewish-American writing'. See also Robert Alter on American Jewish writing as a transitional phenomenon in 'Sentimentalizing the Jews' (1965), reprinted in his *After the Tradition: Essays on Modern Jewish Writing* (New York, 1971) and 'The Jew who didn't get away: on the possibility of an American Jewish culture', in *The American Jewish Experience*, Jonathan D. Sarna (ed.) (New York, 1986); John Hollander, 'The question of American Jewish poetry', *Tikkun*, 3, no. 3 (May–June 1988).

55 Gilles Deleuze and Felix Guattari, *Kafka: Toward a Minor Literature*, trans. Dana Polan, in the *Theory and History of Literature* series (Minneapolis, 1986), pp. 16, 17, 19.

56 The term is Hannah Arendt's own; see her essays from the 1940s on the Jew as refugee and as pariah, reprinted in *Hannah Arendt, the Jew as Pariah: Jewish Identity and Politics in the Modern Age*, Ron H. Feldman (ed.) (New York, 1978).

57 'In the 'thirties and 'forties,' writes Henry Pachter,

> the exiles achieved their stature not in spite of their alienation but because of it. America, deeply shaken by the Great Depression, was passing through a moral and cultural crisis. With intellectuals now the 'in' thing is to be 'out,' and conformism now expresses itself in conforming with the non-conformists. In such a situation the ideal-type exile can be very

effective as a model; he represents alienation in his person and he describes it in his work. But a deep misunderstanding occurs here. To him, dissent from society is radical and total; to his audience, dissent is only partial . . . the meaning of alienation has become so fuzzy that the final effect of so much pseudo-alienation is no alienation at all.

Pachter goes on to say that 'Arendt had the unfortunate intuition that America needed Kafka, and people who lived quite comfortably in the world he had scorned, assured each other gleefully that they were living in a Kafkaesque world; . . . perhaps it was meant to épatez les bourgeois, but it only tickled them' (Henry Pachter, 'On being an exile', in *The Legacy of the German Refugee Intellectuals*, Robert Boyers (ed.) (New York; 1969), pp. 7, 43). In 1946 *Partisan Review* devoted an entire issue to the new French thinkers and William Barrett translated Arendt's essay entitled 'What is existenz philosophy?' Recounting his 'adventures among the intellectuals', Barrett locates Arendt in her 'chosen role as interpreter of European culture to Americans' (William Barrett, *The Truants: Adventures Among the Intellectuals* (New York, 1982), p. 100). For a somewhat dissenting view, see Walter Kaufmann, who claims that the impact in America of intellectuals who had emigrated or been expelled from Central Europe was less than one would expect:

The most important way in which the Nazi regime promoted existentialism and the literature associated with it was not by compelling many people to emigrate but rather by killing so many more. As fear and trembling, dread and despair, and the vivid anticipation of one's own death ceased to be primarily literary experiences and, like the absurd visions of Kafka, turned into the stuff of everyday life, the originally untimely Kafka and Kierkegaard became popular along with Jaspers and Heidegger, Sartre and Camus, who were fashionable from the first. . . .

(Walter Kaufmann, 'The reception of existentialism in the United States', in *The Legacy of German Refugee Intellectuals*, p. 85)

58 Howe, 'On Jewish American writing', p. 347. See also *idem*, 'Strangers', p. 19.
59 In his critique of the social and political implications of the transformation of the Jewish American intellectual from 'champion of maladjustment' with his contempt for all 'ideal constructions' to champion of the 'affirmative imagination' (a shift monitored over the years in the pages of *Commentary*), Shechner also offers a eulogy to the 'so-called Jewish novel': 'If it is true, as some believe . . . that the so-called Jewish novel is dead, that is partly so because [of the attenuation in America of] the tension between the self and the world, the knot of unregenerate trouble at the heart's core that once supplied the traction and drive of the imagination in *galut* . . .' (Shechner, *After the Revolution*, p. 22).

This chapter first appeared as an article in *Studies in Contemporary Jewry* (Oxford University Press, 1992) vol. 8, pp. 50–67.

INDEX

455

Nazis/Nazism 2, 51, 52, 150, 155, 179, 196, 251, 269, 272, 274, 286, 359, 361
neo-conservatism 107
neo-Nazis 8, 275, 283, 284
Neusner, Jacob 338
new Jewish politics, becoming professionals and insiders 95–101; broader agenda, coalitions and issue networks 104–5; creating community consensus 101–3; ideological differentiation 105–9; loyalties dual, divided and single 103–4; main features 93–5, 111–12; new threats, allies, split coalitions 109–11, *see also* politics (in America)
New Left 157
The New Republic 183, 184
The New Yorker 435
Niebuhr, Reinhold 334, 337
Niles, David 181
Nitzan, Shlomo 391
Nixon, Richard 156, 172, 173, 174, 175, 178, 179, 180, 182, 183, 184
NJCRAC *see* National Jewish Community Relations Advisory Council
Noah, Mordecai 147
North Africa 67–8, 70–1, 72, 74, 75, 234, 237, 361
Nostra Aetate (Vatican Council, 1965) 274, 353, 355
'Notes on the correct way to present Jews . . .' (Vatican, 1985) 354

October Revolution 426
Odets, Clifford 424, 435
Oesterreicher, John 349
On the Issues (AJC) 104
'one people' (Am Ehad) 142
'Operation Exodus' 190
Orbach, Maurice 255
'Organization for the Preservation of Historic Monuments and Places' 228
Oriental Jewry 7
Orlev, Uri 402, 410
Orpaz, Yizhak 394, 396
Orthodox Jews 107–8, 149, 152, 189, 303–4, 308–10, 324, 328, 330
Otechestvo 279
Oz, Amos 394, 395, 398, 403, 408
Ozick, Cynthia 423, 440

PAC *see* American Israel Public Affairs Committee (AIPAC)
Pachter, Henry 447–8

PACs *see* political action committees
Palestine 7, 178, 273, 274, 276, 351, 354, 377
Palestine Liberation Organization (PLO) 155, 158, 163, 176, 180, 186, 187, 188, 256, 260, 291
Palestine Mandate 252, 254–5
Paley, Grace 423
'Pamiat' (Pamyat) 209–10, 213, 214, 228–9, 277, 278, 279–80, 280
Panama 377
Panama Canal Treaty 184
Pannenberg, Wolfhart 337
Paraguay 365, 367, 372
Parkinson, Cecil 264
Partisan Review 435
Passfield White Paper 251
Pauker, Anna 283
Pawlikowski, John T. 349
Pentecostalists 341
Percy, Charles 180
perestroika 200, 280
Péron, Juan 377
Peru 362, 368, 372, 377
Pétain, Marshal 273
Petersen, W. 14
Pharisees, influence of 338, 349
'philo-Semitism' 275–6, 282
Pinter, Rabbi Avroham 261–2
Piratin, Phil 251
Pius XI, Pope 351
Plancey, Alan 265
Planned Parenthood 153
PLO *see* Palestine Liberation Organization
Poale Zion 254, 255
Podhoretz, Norman 423
pogroms 8, 229, 271; Kielce 45, 61, 418; *Kristallnacht* 2, 59
Poland 4, 49–50, 61, 62, 63, 67, 234, 270–1, 273, 414; anti-Semitism in 270–1, 277–8, 281–2, 289
Polish Jewry 275
political action committees (PACs) 98–9, 105, 180, 181, 189, 191
politics (in America), issue of survival 90–3; pattern of 86–8, 111–12; relations with Israel 89–90; social, economic and cultural status 88–9, *see also* new Jewish politics
politics (in England), and Anglo-Jewry **249–66**
Pollard affair 189
Prague Spring 277